THE
ABC-CLIO
COMPANION TO

The 1960s Counterculture in America

On 9 May 1970, thousands of America's youth gather in front of the White House to protest Nixon's involvement in Cambodia and the Kent State slayings. This is just one of the many protest demonstrations of the 1960s.

THE
ABC-CLIO
COMPANION TO

The 1960s Counterculture in America

Neil A. Hamilton

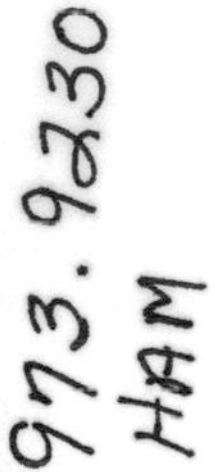

Library of Congress Cataloging-in-Publication Data

Hamilton, Neil A.
The ABC-CLIO companion to the 1960s counterculture in America / Neil A. Hamilton
p. cm. (ABC-CLIO companions to key issues in American history and life)
Includes bibliographical references (p.) and index.
1. Subculture—United States—History—20th century—Encyclopedias. 2. Social history—1960–1970—Encyclopedias. 3. United States—Social life and customs—1945–1970—Encyclopedias. I. Title. II. Series.
E169.02 .H3515 1997 973.923'03—dc21 97-36735

ISBN 0-87436-858-8 (alk. paper)

03 02 01 00 99 98 10 9 8 7 6 5 4 3 (cloth)

ABC-CLIO, Inc.
130 Cremona Drive, P.O. Box 1911
Santa Barbara, California 93116-1911

This book is printed on acid-free paper ∞.

For Voyagers Everywhere

ABC-CLIO Companions to Key Issues in American History and Life

The ABC-CLIO Companion to American Reconstruction, 1862–1877
William L. Richter

The ABC-CLIO Companion to the American Labor Movement
Paul F. Taylor

The ABC-CLIO Companion to the American Peace Movement
Christine A. Lunardini

The ABC-CLIO Companion to the Civil Rights Movement
Mark Grossman

The ABC-CLIO Companion to the Environmental Movement
Mark Grossman

The ABC-CLIO Companion to the Media in America
Daniel Webster Hollis III

The ABC-CLIO Companion to the Native American Rights Movement
Mark Grossman

The ABC-CLIO Companion to Transportation in America
William L. Richter

The ABC-CLIO Companion to Women in the Workplace
Dorothy Schneider and Carl J. Schneider

The ABC-CLIO Companion to Women's Progress in America
Elizabeth Frost-Knappman

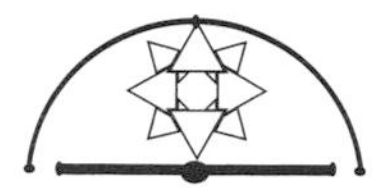

Contents

Preface

The *ABC-CLIO Companion to the 1960s Counterculture in America* presents an encyclopedic overview of the people, groups, and events that challenged mainstream society and made this period among the most tumultuous, and controversial, in U.S. history. Here for the first time is assembled in one A-to-Z volume information about the counterculture's cultural and political protests, the forces that produced them, and their impact on society at large.

The ABC-CLIO Companions series is designed to provide the nonspecialist with concise, encyclopedic guides to key movements, major issues, and revolutions in American history. The encyclopedia entries are arranged in alphabetical order. Cross-references connect related terms and entries. A chronology of key events provides a handy overview, and a bibliography is provided to facilitate further research.

I would like to thank Henry Rasof for originating the idea for this book and inspiring me to write it. I would also like to thank Bret Heim, Government Documents and Reference Librarian at Spring Hill College, for his invaluable help in uncovering sources, and the interlibrary loan staff for their prompt and courteous acquisition of materials. A sabbatical granted to me by Spring Hill College proved essential in completing this book. Martha Whitt, senior editor at ABC-CLIO, provided invaluable guidance, communicated graciously, in bringing this manuscript to its final form. Finally, I would like to thank my mother and brother for their moral support and encouragement.

Introduction

A writer for the *New York Times* surveyed parents, teachers, and school counselors in 1968 and discovered that, to a person, they believed America's youth disdained mainstream values. The writer rhetorically asked: "Were the worrisome qualities they saw in . . . young people—sexual libertarianism, angry politicism, vehement rejection of adult authority, and a widespread disposition to experiment with drugs—simply the sixties-style manifestation of the usual teenage rebellion against the adult world?"

As it turned out, youthful energy did propel the counterculture, but it went well beyond a teenage rebellion—the kaleidoscopic challenges involved both culture and politics, shaking them to their core.

The varying degrees to which people, young and old, accepted change makes it difficult to define the counterculture and assess its long-term results. Some historians distinguish between the *counterculture* and what they call the *movement*. The former, the counterculture, they define as those persons and groups who challenged prevailing cultural practices. Hippies fit this category, for they wanted to create an alternative society founded on psychedelic enlightenment and communal relations.

These historians define the movement as those persons and groups who sought to overthrow the existing political system and replace it with a populist one, perhaps rooted in socialism or, for extremists, Marxism or anarchy. The New Left fit this category, for it considered the national government and corporate capitalism oppressive and wanted to radically alter both.

Other historians, however, reject this delineation. They believe that if any separation existed between counterculture and movement, it did so for a brief, inconsequential time. Hippies who at first totally rejected politics soon involved themselves in it; New Leftists who espoused political ideologies soon adopted hippie ideals about love and community. In short, the cultural was political, and vice versa. This leads to a broader definition, one used as a criterion in deciding which entries to include in this encyclopedia, that the counterculture encompassed cultural *and* political challenges to mainstream values and practices. In short, the movement is subsumed under counterculture. (For analytical purposes, however, the narrative for many entries tries to distinguish between the cultural or political emphasis involved.)

The counterculture had its roots in the 1950s, a decade when the cold war gripped America and encouraged conformity. Suburbia displayed this sameness: look-alike houses, cars with big tail fins, television shows whiter than white. And it appeared in harsher form, too: racism, censorship, blacklists, lives forever ruined.

Yet beneath the conformity, discontent pulsed. Beat writers such as Jack Kerouac, William Burroughs, and Allen Ginsberg offered alternative subjects and styles. Beatniks appeared who admired the beats, and rejected eight-to-five jobs, monogamous relationships, and living in the suburbs. They experimented with sex, drugs, and attitudes as they tried to live for the moment.

At the same time, rock 'n' roll music provided a larger, mass challenge to conformity. Elvis Presley, Little Richard, Chuck Berry . . . they bopped and gyrated to a blues-infused music that worried older Americans who criticized rock, even labeled it dangerous, for bringing sensual black influences into white suburbia, the very influences young people liked. But, despite its challenge to conformity, rock did not promote a political message, nor did it offer a vision that society could be different; rather, it expressed an adolescent rebelliousness that both the music and its listeners expected to fade when youths became adults.

The beats, rock 'n' roll, and conformity produced a peculiar mix leading to the counterculture. For youngsters who would not reach their teens until the 1960s, the beat writings awaited them as a commentary on society's oppression—a commentary that corresponded with the civil rights movement and the Vietnam War. Fifties rock helped establish a youth culture, an us-versus-them setting that the counterculture later tapped. And while many youngsters enjoyed conformity and the material prosperity that accompanied it—fine clothes, shiny bicycles, and comfortable homes—it numbed them to conditions outside the white middle class and made them more susceptible to discontentment and rebellion when another world intruded, when the limits to prosperity and democracy ripped away their protective shroud.

In fact, the shroud lifted a bit ten years before the counterculture era, in the 1950s, when African Americans protested racism, and in their actions exposed society's injustice. The Montgomery, Alabama, bus boycott and other efforts by Martin Luther King, Jr. jarred white America into confronting Jim Crow segregation.

For the counterculture generation, though, a greater revelation came in 1960 when black college students in Greensboro, North Carolina, staged a sit-in at a segregated lunch counter. The television and newspaper coverage of the students' bravery and of the whites who assaulted them stirred black and white youths across America. Society appeared undemocratic. Society appeared cruel. Young reformers decided to take the lead in making America live up to its professed ideals. After Greensboro, black students and their white supporters rallied to fight racism.

With this upsurge, there emerged the Student Nonviolent Coordinating Committee (SNCC) under whose direction young people traveled to Mississippi, Alabama, and other southern states to work for black voting rights. These volunteers experienced oppression and violence firsthand. In doing so, they learned tactics and strategies for fighting injustice: marches, sit-ins, boycotts. In this more youthful, confrontational stage, the civil rights movement propelled America into the counterculture.

So, too, did the presidential administrations of John Kennedy and Lyndon Johnson. While Kennedy enthralled young people with his youthful vigor and idealistic image, by 1963 he had alienated an activist core impatient with his slow approach to civil rights legislation, his conservative appointments to the federal courts, and his reluctance to support SNCC. Then an assassin killed Kennedy, and those youths who still considered him the best hope for reform suspected society would never let change happen, not in any meaningful way.

Kennedy's successor, Lyndon Johnson, used the anguish over the assassination to push legislation through Congress that brought momentous strides in civil rights.

But young people did not trust him. They did not like his wheeling and dealing, his backcountry Texas character. And something else bothered them, barely visible early on and recognized among the young by only a few college students at that time: the Vietnam War.

Along with the civil rights movement and the sheer numbers of young people, evident in the "baby boom," the Vietnam War may have been the strongest element in creating the counterculture: the war's deaths and government lies prominently displayed mainstream society's oppression and corruption.

No coincidence, then, but a strong cause-and-effect relationship worked to produce a rebelliousness in San Francisco, the North Beach area of which had long been a beatnik enclave, while America's involvement in Vietnam deepened. In 1964 and 1965, the beatnik culture transformed into a hippie one. Where the beatniks had been pessimistic about alternatives, hippies exuded optimism. Lively, colorful, vibrant, hippies believed they could build an alternative society that rejected materialism and selfishness for mysticism and community—one based on LSD. This hallucinogenic (and at that time legal) drug fed their heads and created psychedelia, a form of expression related to distorted perceptions.

More than any other countercultural group, hippies reflected a deep discontent with technocracy—society's reliance on scientific experts who ruled coldly and dispassionately and who wielded enormous power. Hippies said good-bye to that and hello to the mystical spirit, oneness with the universe—life as passion, passion as life, harmony, and understanding. And the hippies believed they could develop their vision in San Francisco's Haight-Ashbury district, where they congregated.

Yet the emerging counterculture developed in many different directions, and for this San Francisco's Bay Area provided a microcosm: in addition to hippies in Haight-Ashbury, there were political activists in Berkeley. The civil rights movement encouraged the activists, as did the Port Huron Statement—issued in 1962 by Students for a Democratic Society (SDS)—that criticized mainstream America as undemocratic and uncaring. SDS emerged as a New Left organization and challenged conservatives and liberals alike while calling on college students to take an active role in creating a participatory democracy, run not by technocrats but by the people.

Amid this discontent, a student protest, the Free Speech Movement, erupted in 1964 at the University of California in Berkeley. Mario Savio, leader of the protest, said:

> There is a time when the operation of the machine becomes so odious, makes you so sick at heart, that you can't take part; and you've got to put your bodies upon the gears and upon the wheels, upon the levers, upon all the apparatus and you've got to make it stop. And you've got to indicate to the people who run it, to the people who own it, that unless you're free, the machine will be prevented from working at all. (Pace 1996, C21)

Machine, apparatus, odious—the words fell on receptive ears, young people who felt oppressed and ready for action.

So the counterculture emerged—hippies and college-based political activists tied to a New Left. And more, much more.

Music changed. At first, young people flocked to folk music with its social and political consciousness and to the early Beatles with their innocent lyrics and happy tone; then they listened to psychedelic rock with its distorted sounds and hallucinogenic imagery, then to a harsher, politicized rock as antiwar protests grew heated and the gulf between counterculture and straight society widened.

Artists experimented. They used happenings, performance art, fluxus, psychedelic images, posters. They produced experimental movies with no plot, with little plot, with amateur actors, with rock soundtracks, *Easy Rider*. Nudity appeared in Broadway shows; musicals declared the Age of Aquarius.

All tumbled together. All cascaded, a countercultural rush. The cultural and the political. Brown power. Gay rights. Black

Panthers—who declared black power, black pride, black is beautiful—who carried rifles, started schools in the ghettos, wore their hair Afro style.

After 1968, political activists hardened, hippies fled. That is, the counterculture took more twists and turns—everything from Weatherman, a group that advocated overthrowing the federal government through violence, to the back-to-the-earth movement, hippies who left Haight-Ashbury and the cities and sought solace in the countryside where they could farm the land.

These changes have led many historians to conclude that the counterculture went through stages: an early stage, prior to 1968, when the civil rights movement worked its greatest influence and young people expressed optimism about change; a middle stage, from 1968 to 1970, when polarization intensified and the core both within the counterculture and society at large no longer held; and a late stage, after 1970, when new activist groups came to the fore, stirred by the previous developments.

Thus, the 1960s counterculture did not end in 1969. Rather, it continued into the early 1970s, although in different form, with some elements in retreat and others strident. For example, at this time women's liberationists emanated from the counterculture and reflected its spirit and drive. The term "1960s counterculture," then, cannot be strictly tied to the numerical decade.

Not all historians agree on chronology, however, and so imprecision exists as to when the counterculture began and when it ended, much as it exists as to what can be accurately called countercultural and what cannot. This poses a difficulty in determining what should be included in this encyclopedia. (Keep in mind, however, that this is not an encyclopedia of the 1960s but of the *counterculture* in its broadest sense, and as it unfolded during that decade and continued into the early years of the following one.)

This work contains not only examples of the counterculture but also developments that propelled and shaped it. Hence, entries discuss the 1950s, primarily the beats and, to a lesser extent, civil rights. Overall, the entries emphasize the most important countercultural developments in their fullest diversity—cultural, social, and political. Although San Francisco and its environs appear prominently, the encyclopedia provides a scope that extends well beyond the Bay Area.

Most entries contain cross-references that allow the reader to pursue the many interconnected events. And they contain, as well, references for further reading. (In the case of prominent authors, the lists contain only those works that directly influenced the counterculture.)

As the counterculture expanded, the lines between it and mainstream society paradoxically widened and blurred as people chose sides or as institutions co-opted the rebellion. The latter included businesses or people who wanted to make money. Thus, should rock bands such as the Monkees be included as countercultural? Or the artist Peter Max? Or the miniskirt? They are presented here because, despite their commercial nature, they had substantial roots in the counterculture, confirmed the strength of countercultural influences through the co-opting that did take place, or challenged societal values so strongly they helped to revolutionize them (the miniskirt, for example, affecting sexual attitudes).

The counterculture's pervasive influence appeared in comments made in 1968 by a high school student. "The main thing that's taught us in school," said the student, "is how to obey the rules, dress in our uniforms, play the game and NO, DON'T BE UPPITY! Oh, we're trained for participating in the democratic process—we have our student governments—they can legislate about basketball games and other such meaningful topics. Don't mention the curriculum. THEY'LL tell us what to learn."

This student discussed uniting with students from other schools. As a union, they would make the following demands:

> An end to all military assemblies; abolition of dress codes and haircut regulations; hiring of

> more Negro and Puerto Rican teachers; placement of draft resistance guides in school libraries; student-run assemblies on political topics chosen by the students; free distribution of birth-control literature and devices; publication of all first names of all teachers so students will not have to address them as Mr. or Miss. (Stern 1968, 67)

Meaningful changes, yes. Symbolic, also yes. The student realized this:

> We expect that the principals will turn us down on a lot of these issues. When they do, this will prove to the students how oppressive the authorities are. (ibid.)

At which point the students would have to rebel—part of the kaleidoscopic challenges that created a counterculture whose changes remain imprinted on American society.

THE
ABC-CLIO
COMPANION TO

The 1960s Counterculture in America

Acid

Acid means LSD. The word originated in 1966 as slang for the drug whose formal name is lysergic acid diethylamide, a psychedelic prevalent among hippies. Ken Kesey, a writer and partaker, said about LSD's effect:

> We had built up this armor that would not let us look left or right to the gardens on both sides. The road that was straight in front of us led straight down to the Bank of America, and nothing could have changed it nearly so much as acid. Acid was a gift from the gods. (Joseph 1974, 381)

See also Acid Tests; LSD.

Acid Rock

Emanating from San Francisco in the mid 1960s, acid rock incorporated and tried to replicate the psychedelic drug experience. This music featured a simple beat, lyrics that either made direct references to drugs or communicated mystic messages, and electronic distortion—played loudly. Often, a light show accompanied the music. The Grateful Dead took acid rock to improvisational heights; other acid rock bands included Jefferson Airplane and Iron Butterfly.

See also Grateful Dead; Jefferson Airplane; Rock Music.

Acid Tests

When the author Ken Kesey and his Merry Pranksters began the Acid Tests in the mid-1960s, they intended them to be mass initiations into the psychedelic world of LSD.

The typical Acid Test consisted of Kesey and the Pranksters renting a hall, setting up strobe lights and psychedelic posters, providing a band to play rock music—often the Grateful Dead—and inviting those who came to take LSD, then a legal psychedelic, which they mixed with Kool-Aid, Pepsi, or coffee. In *Acid Dreams*, Martin A. Lee and Bruce Shlain describe Acid Tests as "weird carnivals with videotapes, flashing strobes, live improvised rock and roll . . . lots of bizarre costumes, and dancing." (125) A poster announcing one of these events read: "Can YOU Pass the Acid Test? Featuring—The Grateful Dead, The Merry Pranksters and Their Psychedelic Symphonette, The Stroboscopic Ballet Machine, Roy's Audioptoics, Del Close and His Phantasmagoria, Hugh Romney Might Hum and YOU."

The Acid Tests publicized LSD—in fact, in the March 1967 issue of *Ramparts* magazine, writer Warren Hinckle says that Kesey "did for acid roughly what Johnny Appleseed did for trees"—and although for the moment it remained primarily a drug consumed in San Francisco's hippie Haight-Ashbury district, a wider audience soon used it. Tom Wolfe, the leading writer on the Pranksters, claims in *The Electric Kool-Aid Acid Test* that the drug's popularization "came straight out of the Acid Tests—in a straight line leading to the Trips Festival of January 1966. That brought the whole thing out into the open." (Hodgson 1976, 329)

See also Drugs and the Drug Culture; *The Electric Kool-Aid Acid Test;* Kesey, Ken; Leary, Timothy; LSD.

References Lee, Martin A., and Bruce Shlain, *Acid Dreams: The CIA, LSD, and the Sixties Rebellion* (1985); Wolfe, Tom, *The Electric Kool-Aid Acid Test* (1968).

Afro

The trend toward long hair in the 1960s brought on the Afro, a hair texture that symbolized black pride (although the style did not come from Africa), and first appeared in 1967 as an assault on traditional hairstyles and sensibilities. In addition to growing hair long, creating an Afro required teasing it into tight curls massed atop the head, creating a rounded, bushy effect. Some whites adopted Afros, which for them usually required perming.

Age of Aquarius

A utopian vision saturated the counterculture: a belief that hate, war, and selfishness would soon be replaced by sincerity, community, and love. Astrology alluded to such a day, when the constellation Aquarius would be the primary influence. Most astrologers considered the 1960s to be in the Age of Pisces, which the world had been in for about 2,000 years. They believed also that humankind stood on the brink or dawning of the Age of Aquarius, a transcendent time when self-knowledge, intuition, and harmony would prevail.

To the counterculture, hippies who embraced love and mysticism represented this coming new age. This idea was expressed in "The Age of Aquarius," a song from the hit Broadway musical *Hair*, that declared an era devoid of "falsehoods" and filled with "mystic revelations."

Alcatraz

When American Indians occupied Alcatraz and raised their flag above this abandoned federal prison (a banner displaying a red teepee under a broken peace pipe on a field of blue), they announced their desire for liberation and an end to government treachery.

The occupation began in November 1969 when 80 protesters took over the island based on an old treaty that gave Sioux Indians the right to claim unused federal land. They wanted the U.S. government to surrender Alcatraz and provide money for an Indian cultural center.

Over the next few months, about 10,000 Indians visited their embattled kinsmen, and the activist American Indian Movement gave its support. Some protesters began broadcasting "Radio Free Alcatraz" to reveal the dreadful conditions facing most Indians throughout the nation. In response to the protest, newspapers and magazines ran stories detailing life on the reservations—where unemployment ran well over 50 percent, most people lacked running water, and disease and alcoholism existed in epidemic proportions.

The Indians who occupied Alcatraz drew the connection between their action and conditions elsewhere when, satirically, they said the island fortress resembled most reservations in its isolation, inadequate sanitation facilities, unemployment, nonproductive land, and lack of schools. Further, those who had once lived there had "always been held prisoners and kept dependent on others."(Hurtado and Iverson 1994, 523) The protesters vacated Alcatraz in 1971 without getting their cultural center.

See also American Indian Movement.

Alice's Restaurant

Released in 1969, this movie was based on the lyrics to Arlo Guthrie's popular folk song, "Alice's Restaurant." Arthur Penn, noted for another prominent sixties movie, *Bonnie and Clyde*, directed *Alice's Restaurant* and Guthrie starred in it, along with James Broderick and Tina Chen. Young people liked the movie for the same reason they liked the song: through humor and satire it revealed mainstream society's hypocrisies and glamorized countercultural beliefs.

See also Guthrie, Arlo.

Alpert, Richard (Ram Dass) (1931–)

Along with his friend Timothy Leary, Richard Alpert led a psychedelic revolution based on the drug LSD. In the late 1960s, he promoted spiritual rebirth through Eastern mysticism.

Alpert was born on 6 April 1931 in Boston, Massachusetts, to George Alpert, a wealthy lawyer, and Gertrude Levin Alpert. He attended Williston, a private school in Massachusetts, for his secondary education and obtained his bachelor's degree in 1952 from Tufts University, his master's in 1954 from Wesleyan University, and his doctorate in 1957 from Stanford University. The following year, he began teaching at Harvard as an assistant professor of psychology.

There, Alpert met Timothy Leary, a colleague in his department who directed a project to study the effects of hallucinogenic drugs. They established a solid friendship and co-taught courses. Alpert took psilocybin and reported: "I felt a new kind of calmness—one of a profundity never experienced before. I have just found that . . . scanning device—that point—that essence—that place beyond." (Stevens 1987, 155) Soon after, he took LSD, and his mystical journey convinced him that psychedelics could open the subconscious and bring a person into union with the universe.

In 1963, Harvard fired Alpert (shortly after it had fired Leary) for having dispensed drugs to a student, and the former professor concentrated on his writing and, with Leary, encouraged society to use LSD. Four years later, Alpert suffered from depression and decided to leave the LSD scene and seek a spiritual rebirth in India. He journeyed to the Himalayas, where he studied Hinduism under Neem Karoli Baba. The following year, he returned to the United States with a new name, Baba Ram Dass, and in 1969 gave a course on Raja Yoga at the Esalen Institute in San Francisco, California. His book *Be Here Now*, published in 1971, circulated widely among college students, and his religious philosophy earned him an enthusiastic following.

Yet in the 1970s, Alpert underwent more turbulence as he disputed with other spiritual leaders and questioned his own faith—whether he had really found an enlightened path or not. In the 1990s, he continued to lecture and offer spiritual advice.

See also Leary, Timothy.

References Alpert, Richard, and Sidney Cohen, *LSD* (1966), and as Ram Dass, *Be Here Now* (1971); Stevens, Jay, *Storming Heaven: LSD and the American Dream* (1987).

Altamont

The Rolling Stones rock band portrayed their forthcoming 1969 free concert at the Altamont Raceway near San Francisco as another Woodstock, but throughout that year, and especially in the weeks after Woodstock, a polarized atmosphere gripped America—one filled more with fear than with love, with Charles Manson's gruesome murders than with hippiedom's innocence. In short, all the vibes seemed wrong. Jerry Garcia, rock singer with the Grateful Dead, later said: "It was in the air that it was *not* a good time to do something. There were too many divisive elements." (Graham and Greenfield 1992, 294) As it turned out, Altamont deteriorated into a violent, blood-soaked horror.

The idea for a free rock concert originated with the Rolling Stones. During their 1969 tour of the United States, critics called their ticket prices exorbitant and complained about the band's egotistical behavior. Stung by this, Mick Jagger, the lead singer and leader of the Stones, announced at a press conference in November that the band would organize and headline a free concert in San Francisco.

The Stones, however, gave little thought to planning the event, and as its scheduled date, 6 December, approached, chaos took over. Initially, the promoters announced Golden Gate Park as the concert site, but after discovering that the city required a high bond to cover possible damage, they switched the venue to Sears Point Raceway and erected a stage there. Just 24 hours before the concert, however, Filmways, owner of Sears Point, demanded distribution rights to the movie the Stones planned to make of the event, a demand the band rejected. At the last minute, Dick Carter, who owned Altamont Raceway near San Francisco, agreed to hold the concert at his property—a gray, grubby, ill-kept facility, tottering near bankruptcy.

When the first spectators began arriving early in the evening of 5 December, they found technicians still setting up the stage and the speaker system. By the next morning, 100,000 had jammed Altamont raceway, many abandoning their cars, caught in heavy traffic, and walking eight miles or more to the site.

The crowd increased to 300,000 in the afternoon, already beset by understaffed facilities, bad drug trips, and unruly behavior when the Hell's Angels arrived. To this day, no one knows who originated the idea to use the Angels for security; some claim the Grateful Dead, others the Rolling Stones—most likely the idea came from both. In any event, the Angels brought with them a yellow school bus filled with beer, wine, and LSD tablets, and carried chains, knives, brass knuckles, and sawed-off pool cues weighted with lead.

As Santana, the first band, played, the Angels began attacking anyone who approached the stage, a low platform just four feet above the ground. With their pool cues, they beat one kid senseless and attacked a photographer, kicking and stomping him as he lay bleeding, then hitting him with his own camera.

The situation worsened when Jefferson Airplane began its set. Grace Slick, the band's lead singer, had to stop the music and plead: "Please people, please stop hurting each other." (Anderson 1995, 281) When Marty Balin, Airplane's lead guitarist, tried to protect a black youth whom the Angels had attacked, they knocked him unconscious. Later, Crosby, Stills, Nash, and Young took the stage and gave what observers called a nervous and perfunctory performance, leaving immediately after—and well understandable, for during the group's set the Angels charged unprovoked into the crowd, flailing away with their pool cues.

The Rolling Stones did not appear until nightfall, waiting for the sun to set so the stage lights would take effect, and in the process making a nervous crowd more nervous. By this time, the Angels had parked their motorcycles around the stage, huge bikes, and had clearly commandeered the scene. When the Stones appeared—fully aware of what had transpired—they did so surrounded by a phalanx of Angels. Then out of ignorance or ego, the band launched into "Sympathy for the Devil," a number that normally roused even placid crowds to a feverish pitch, let alone one beset by violence.

As the Stones played, the crowd surged forward, pushing against the Angels' bikes, knocking them over. According to Dennis McNally, a writer and publicist, a few "maniacs" in the crowd challenged the Angels. (Graham and Greenfield 1992, 297) Violence erupted as the Angels beat those situated near the stage. Jagger stopped the music. "All I can do is ask you—beg you to keep it together," he said, shaken. "It's within your power." (Norman 1984, 304)

Slowly, the Stones went into another song, "Under My Thumb." At that point, Meredith Hunter, an 18 year-old African-American, ran toward the stage, trying to flee six Angels who had been hitting him. He pulled a gun, and an Angel stabbed him in the back with a knife, bringing him to the ground. As he lay there, and said "I wasn't going to shoot you" (Booth 1984, 364), the Angels clubbed and kicked him, smashed his face with a garbage can, and stood on his head. The Stones, who could not see the attack, heard cries for help, stopped playing, and called for a doctor to come forward. Within a short time, Hunter died.

After Stones' guitarist Keith Richards pointed at the Angels and screamed into the microphone, "Hey, man, look, we're splitting, you know, if those cats—we're splitting, man, if those cats don't stop beating everybody up in sight—I want 'em *out of the way, man!*," the band resumed playing, perhaps fearing that without music the violence would get worse, or maybe acquiescing to demands by the Angels to keep playing, or else. When the Stones finished, they and their entourage quickly left—14 frightened people crammed into a helicopter meant to hold 8.

In the days immediately after the concert, mainstream newspapers portrayed the event as largely successful. But San Francisco's KSAN radio station and *Rolling Stone* magazine heard reports to the contrary from those at the concert and exposed what had happened. The magazine called the Rolling Stones "rock's ultimate narcissists, gaudy and uncouth practitioners of western materialism, [who] seemed to the Woodstock spirit what Hitler was to the 1936 Olympics." (Draper 1965,1)

Rolling Stone blamed Mick Jagger and company for the tragedy, noting the band had put on an ill-planned free concert, and then filmed it as a way to make money—ostensible selflessness wrapped in greed. (The entire concert, including the knifing, appears in the movie *Gimme Shelter*.) Another observer called Altamont the Woodstock Nation's Pearl Harbor. To many, it signified that the younger generation had become as violent as the older one, that the counterculture as a better alternative had collapsed.

See also The Rolling Stones; Woodstock.

References Anderson, Terry H., *The Movement and the Sixties* (1995); Booth, Stanley, *Dance with the Devil: The Rolling Stones and Their Times* (1984); Eisen, Jonathan, ed., *Altamont: The Death of Innocence in the Woodstock Nation* (1970); Norman, Philip, *Symphony for the Devil: The Rolling Stones Story* (1984).

American Indian Movement

Influences that interacted in the counterculture can be seen in the American Indian Movement (AIM). Although as a protest organization to help Indians AIM owed its formation largely to problems affecting that population, it modeled its initial tactics after the California-based Black Panthers. And similar to the Panthers, AIM encountered illegal efforts by the federal government to crush it.

Dennis Banks, George Mitchell, and Mary Jane Wilson—Anishinabes who lived in Minneapolis, Minnesota—founded AIM in 1968 as an organization to patrol the city's Indian ghetto and monitor police actions. They wanted to prevent false arrests, harassment, and brutality, much as the Black Panthers had in African American neighborhoods. Their efforts greatly reduced these incidents.

In 1969, AIM reached beyond Minneapolis, and began developing a national organization. The Indians of All Tribes (IAT) protest in California sparked this effort. That year, IAT, supported by AIM, occupied Alcatraz Island, recently abandoned as a prison, and demanded that under existing treaty provisions it be turned over to them. Although IAT did not accomplish its goal, the occupation called attention to Indian grievances and encouraged younger Indians, such as those in AIM.

By 1970, AIM chapters had formed in San Francisco, Los Angeles, Denver, Chicago, Cleveland, and Milwaukee. Their members came from many different tribes: Santee, Oglala Lakota, Ponca, Navajo, Oneida, Cherokee, Winnebago, and others. This represented AIM's desire to surmount tribal differences and unite all Indians. At this time, AIM established "survival schools" to help Indians function off the reservations.

AIM leader Russell Means organized demonstrations that attracted media attention. On 4 July 1971, he held what AIM called a "countercelebration" atop Mount Rushmore in South Dakota. The Oglala Lakota considered this popular tourist attraction sacred and improperly held by the government, since it had been taken from them forcibly and illegally in the nineteenth century. On Thanksgiving Day that year, AIM took over the *Mayflower* replica ship at Plymouth, Massachusetts, and painted Plymouth Rock red.

Then in February 1972, Means led 1,000 Indians into Gordon, Nebraska, where they protested the refusal of local authorities to file charges against two white men implicated in the murder of an Oglala Lakota. As typical in many states, white persons involved in crimes against Indians seldom faced prosecution. After the protest resulted in the two men being tried, found guilty, and sentenced to prison, AIM's prestige rose. AIM, however, gained the attention of the federal government, and within a short time the FBI secretly infiltrated the organization and began illegal acitvities to destroy it, thus following long-standing federal procedure to contain noncompliant Indians.

In the summer of 1972, about 2,000 Indians from more than 100 reservations traveled in a caravan to Washington, D.C. The AIM leaders who organized this protest called it the "Trail of Broken Treaties." They scheduled rallies and meetings with federal officials to discuss problems on the reservations. At first the officials agreed to speak with the Indians, but then they reneged. This caused 400 protesters to occupy the building housing the Bureau of Indian Affairs (BIA). They soon got the Nixon administration to listen to their demands, after which they evacuated the building, but not before taking with them confidential files that showed corrupt BIA activities regarding land and mineral rights on several reservations.

Yet another incident occurred the following year when a violent confrontation erupted between AIM and federal authorities at Wounded Knee on the Pine Ridge Reservation in South Dakota. For months prior to this, tension had been mounting on the reservation between traditionalists, who wanted more self-governance for reservation Indians, and a minority group led by Richard "Dickie" Wilson. The BIA and other federal agencies backed Wilson in his election to the Sioux tribal presidency. Federal officials believed Wilson would grant more favorable concessions to white ranchers on the reservation, would not protest plans to develop nearby uranium mines that would likely contaminate the area, and would allow the federal government to continue its secret plan to illegally take reservation land in order to get at rich uranium deposits near Sheep Mountain. In short, they considered Wilson a pliable agent.

Traditionalists who opposed Wilson experienced harassment and physical assaults. Wilson forbade his opponents from even meeting, and he used money from the BIA to finance a squad of special police that enforced his dictates. At a meeting that violated Wilson's ban, the traditionalists

Wrapped in an upside-down American flag, a woman and a surrounding group of about 400 American Indians occupy an auditorium at the Bureau of Indian Affairs on 2 November 1972. Protesters organized the demonstration after government officials refused to meet with American Indian Movement leaders during the Trail of Broken Treaties protest.

asked AIM to support them, and the organization agreed, deciding to converge on the reservation at Wounded Knee. This site had symbolic importance because there, nearly 100 years earlier, U.S. Army soldiers had massacred many Sioux—mainly elderly people, women, and children.

AIM planned to hold a press conference and then leave, but the protesters found their exit barred by Wilson's police and, later, U.S. marshals. As a result, about 200 AIM protesters confiscated weapons from a trading post and barricaded themselves there. The federal government reacted by calling in enormous firepower: 17 armored personnel carriers, 130,000 rounds of M-16 ammunition, 41,000 rounds of M-1 ammunition, 12 M-79 grenade launchers, 100 rounds of M-40 explosives, several helicopters, and Phantom jets. Federal officials claimed that AIM had taken hostages, but this turned out to be incorrect. Meanwhile, AIM supporters sneaked through the government's lines and provided the entrapped Indians with food, additional weapons, and ammunition. As the standoff continued, the FBI arrested people in various areas of the nation for gathering canned goods and clothing destined for AIM.

After shots rang out—no one knows who fired first—the government forces bombarded AIM, and over the next few weeks sporadic fighting killed two Indians in the AIM compound. On 11 March 1973, the government temporarily lifted its siege to allow the AIM Indians to leave. They expected a mass exodus, but instead hundreds of Indians from surrounding settlements came into Wounded Knee to support AIM. The Indians held out from 28 February to 7 May, at which time AIM reached an agreement with the federal authorities that ended the siege. The government subsequently abandoned nearly all of its promises.

After this "Second Battle of Wounded Knee," as it became known, Means announced he would seek the Sioux tribal presidency in 1974; he said that if elected, he would return power to the council of elders, the traditional ruling body that had been bypassed and weakened by Wilson because its members opposed his policies. Means lost the election in balloting widely believed to have been fixed.

In the meantime, the federal government prosecuted Means for what had happened at Wounded Knee. He was found not guilty on 37 felony counts—but only after extensive hearings and trials that lasted three years and required an enormous expenditure by him.

At the same time, the FBI investigated hundreds of Sioux connected to AIM, compiling 316,000 files, making 562 arrests, obtaining 185 indictments—leading to only 15 convictions, and those for minor offenses such as trespassing. As the FBI conducted its investigations, violence continued on the Pine Ridge Reservation and about 69 AIM supporters died there, in many cases likely murdered by persons affiliated with Wilson's police. Curiously, the FBI failed to solve the murders despite there being eyewitnesses to them.

In 1975, another violent showdown between AIM and federal agents at Pine Ridge shattered the Indian organization and left its leadership in disarray. Dennis Banks, convicted of riot charges, fled to California, where the governor granted him political asylum. A trial on similar charges resulted in the conviction of Russell Means.

Shortly after this, in 1977, a sensational case involved a young, charismatic Indian leader, Leonard Peltier. The federal government indicted him and two other Indians, Bob Robideau and Darrelle "Dino" Butler, for having killed two FBI agents in the 1975 showdown. The government failed to get Robideau and Butler convicted, but it succeeded with Peltier. This conviction came, however, only after the judge prohibited Peltier from pleading self-defense (a strategy employed successfully by Robideau and Butler) and the government used highly questionable procedures. (Peltier remains in jail, serving two consecutive life terms.) In the meantime, the federal government, working with Wilson, obtained the mineral rights at Pine Ridge it had coveted.

When the 1970s ended, AIM disbanded as a national organization, but continued to function in several localities. In the early 1980s, it won a court case declaring the entire Black Hills of South Dakota a site of spiritual importance to the Lakota Nation, and in 1990 it helped Indians in Wisconsin defend their traditional treaty rights. Emerging out of the 1960s counterculture, AIM had not surrendered. Russell means observed: "AIM never died. It only changed form."

See also Alcatraz; Black Panthers; Peltier, Leonard.

References Churchill, Ward, and Jim Vander Wall, *Agents of Repression: The FBI's Secret Wars against the Black Panther Party and the American Indian Movement* (1988); Deloria, Vine, Jr., *Custer Died for Your Sins: An Indian Manifesto* (1969); Hurtado, Albert L., and Peter Iverson, *Major Problems in American Indian History* (1994); Matthiessen, Peter, *In the Spirit of Crazy Horse* (1991).

American Indians, Counterculture's Admiration of

Hippies admired American Indians. They identified with the Indian alienation from mainstream society, desired the mysticism Indians embraced, and wanted to emulate the Indian attachment to nature. As a result, hippies formed what they called tribes and lived near Indians in the Southwest, especially New Mexico. In underground newspapers they extolled Indians: in 1967, the *San Francisco Oracle* devoted an entire issue to Indian life. Although most Indians generally accepted this homage, they sometimes considered hippie beliefs too shallow, too rooted in white values.

Hippies advocated treating nature with awareness and respect, as a living, harmonious organism, which they likened to Indian cultural practices. One hippie said: "The American Indian tribal life before the Europeans came to this continent appeared to be the ideal expression of that harmony." (Cohen 1991, xl) And the *Oracle* drew a mystical connection when it said:

> Do you not see that in mythic time a broken bargain with Hopi priests can be repaid by Vietcong warriors? . . . Myth kicks you in the ass, man; knocks you down from those high towers and missile sights. You think you can bury a tribe, reduce it to a rare language, quaint religion, a few dancing dolls, remove it thus from the earth? (xli)

Reference Cohen, Allen, *The San Francisco Oracle, Facsimile Edition: The Psychedelic Newspaper of the Haight Ashbury, 1966–1968* (1991).

Amerika

As the federal government reacted to antiwar demonstrations by at first increasing, rather than decreasing, the nation's involvement in Vietnam, and as authorities acted to crush student protests, many young people in the late 1960s began respelling America with a *k*—Amerika. To them, this Germanic lettering symbolized a Nazi-like nation—racist, fascist, oppressive, and out to destroy them and individual freedom. In a communiqué, the Weather Underground declared in 1970: "All over the world, people fighting Amerikan imperialism look to Amerika's youth to . . . join forces in the destruction of the empire." (Jacobs 1970, 509)

See also Weather Underground.

The Animals

Originally a British rhythm and blues group, the Animals brought an edge to rock music in the mid-sixties that offered an alternative to the more melodic songs then being played by the Beatles.

The Animals began in 1960 as the Alan Price Combo. Two years later, Eric Burdon joined the group as its lead singer and introduced a rougher, wilder, and more eclectic sound. In 1963, they adopted the name "Animals" from their fans, who referred to them as such. The band had its first big hit in 1964 with "The House of the Rising Sun," an old folk song recently revived by Bob Dylan. Burdon's tough-edged voice, his use of blues techniques, and the band's rock instrumentation impressed Dylan, and it may have encouraged him to infuse rock music into his own work.

A peace demonstrator confronts military police during an anti–Vietnam War protest in front of the Pentagon on 21 October 1967.

As "House of the Rising Sun" reached number one on both the American and British charts, the Animals toured the United States, where their unkempt appearance, at least in comparison to the Beatles, caused a stir. The band recorded another hit in 1965, "We've Got To Get Out of This Place," but friction within the group caused it to disband a year later. Burdon then organized a new band that he called Eric Burdon and the Animals and proceeded to record several highly acclaimed records, most notably "San Franciscan Nights" in 1967 and "Sky Pilot" in 1968, which reflected the California hippie scene.

See also Rock Music.

Antiwar Protests

Antiwar protesters never had an easy time of it. They went up against the experience of World War II that said Americans should stand solidly behind their nation's war effort—the standard by which the older generation measured young people who protested the conflict in Vietnam. In reality, antiwar protests have had a long tradition in America: in every war from the Revolution through World War I, substantial numbers of people opposed combat and made their opposition known through demonstrations and other tactics.

But World War II bred an assumption that the national government would never pick a wrong fight and would never lie to the people—an assumption made stronger by the cold war when it appeared that the showdown with the Soviet Union was a clear choice between Russian evil and American good. Thus, anyone who demonstrated against the war in Vietnam (or for that matter the earlier Korean War) stood a good chance of being labeled unpatriotic, even communistic.

Through the mid-1960s, few people protested the Vietnam War, and those who did—mainly a handful of students on college campuses—were derided. In 1965, *Life* magazine called the protesters "chronic showoffs" who had failed to realize the stakes: freedom protected should America win, tyranny triumphant should America lose. The *New York Daily News* labeled them "beatniks, pacifists, and damned idiots." (Anderson 1995, 144)

The national government weighed in, too, showing little toleration for demonstrators. The attorney general intimated that Communists directed the antiwar protesters, FBI director J. Edgar Hoover declared that the Communist Party supported the demonstrations, and the Senate Internal Security Subcommittee held hearings in search of subversives. These charges lacked validity. At the time, no Communists led antiwar efforts, and few participated in them. Later in the decade, as the antiwar movement intensified, extremists appeared and directed, or at least attempted to direct, some protests, but they never numbered more than a small minority.

As late as 1965, then, few young people participated in antiwar activities, and, in fact, many more supported the war and signed petitions to that effect: 16,000 students at Michigan State University, 9,000 at the University of Wisconsin, 4,000 at Rutgers University. Among those who did protest, a split occurred between liberals, who thought President Lyndon Johnson mistaken in his Vietnam policy, and radicals, who thought him guilty of a malevolent plot. As the war deepened, the radical view prevailed.

Not until 1967, as evident in the march on the Pentagon that October, did antiwar demonstrations attract large numbers. By that time, Johnson had committed several hundred thousand American troops to Vietnam, while increasing the bombing of that nation. Most protesters demanded that the United States "get out now," but this position still found few supporters among the general public. Not until 1971 did opinion polls show that Americans favored immediate withdrawal from Vietnam. (By this time, President Nixon had already begun to bring troops home.)

The protests, from the teach-ins held in the early 1960s to the "Moratorium" held as the decade ended, contributed greatly to Americans seeing the war as a mistake. But they exposed something else, deeper, with a longer-lasting effect on the American psyche: that the national government had lied; that as stories of its lies circulated, it lied again; and that, given the way power worked in Washington, it would likely continue to lie in the future (a fact most prominently revealed by Watergate in the 1970s and the Iran-Contra Scandal in the 1980s). What did this mean for democracy—had it died? Through their actions, antiwar protesters had raised the question.

See also March on the Pentagon, 1967; Moratorium; Students for a Democratic Society; Teach-In.

References Anderson, Terry H., *The Movement and the Sixties* (1995); DeBenedetti, Charles, *The Peace Reform in American History* (1980); Heineman, Kenneth J., *Campus Wars: The Peace Movement at American State Universities in the Vietnam Era* (1993); Small, Melvin, and William D. Hoover, eds., *Give Peace a Chance: Exploring the Vietnam Antiwar Movement* (1992).

Avalon Ballroom

Originally designed as a swing ballroom, the Avalon had a second life in the 1960s as the site for rock concerts staged by Chet Helms's concert-promoting business called "The Family Dog." The Avalon occupied the upstairs portion of a building constructed in 1911 on the border of San Francisco's Haight-Ashbury district, at the corner of Sutter and Van Ness.

Helms liked the Avalon for its roominess and capacity—it could hold over 1,000 people—which allowed substantial space for dancing, an integral part of concerts back then. He liked, too, its L-shaped balcony, the wooden floor that bounced, the small stage tucked into one corner, and the ornate pilasters and columns. Most recently, the Avalon had been used for Irish dances, but its owner agreed to lease it to Helms.

Whereas years earlier swing sounds had filled the Avalon, in the sixties, psychedelic rock pulsated, replete with light shows. The Avalon hosted the Blues Project (Helms' first concert there), Big Brother and the Holding Company, the Paul Butterfield Blues Band, the Doors, the

Grateful Dead, and many more. With its proximity to the burgeoning Haight-Ashbury hippie district, the Avalon attracted large crowds. Helms dominated the Avalon scene from 1966 until he lost his permit in 1968, at which time other promoters periodically offered shows. In the 1970s, the Avalon was remodeled into a theatre.
See also The Family Dog; Helms, Chet.

Awareness Festival

Psychedelic promoter Stewart Brand staged the Awareness Festival at San Francisco State College on 1 October 1966, an eclectic celebration in harmony with the hippie scene. The festival featured a light show in the women's gym while the Esalen Foundation, a psychiatric research group, led a "sensory awareness" seminar in the men's gym. Meanwhile, at a flea market outside, conga drummers played; the Grateful Dead played several sets; and at midnight, Brand enthralled a crowd in the college auditorium by setting off hundreds of flashbulbs to simulate a Russian nuclear attack.
See also Trips Festival.

B

Back-to-the-Earth Movement
In the late 1960s, many hippies settled in sparsely populated areas of northern California, Oregon, Colorado, New Mexico, Vermont, and other states. This back-to-the-earth movement came from a desire to escape crowded, impersonal, polluted cities and live close to nature, peacefully and harmoniously. In rejecting middle-class materialism and trying to live off the land, some back-to-earth hippies formed communes, others established family homesteads. In 1968, the *New York Times* reported that many of the city's hippies had moved to the country and set up communes in Vermont and Massachusetts. Some had even gone out west to "live among Indian tribes."

See also Commune.

Baez, Joan (1941–)
Shortly after completing a recording session in 1968, Joan Baez stated: "No matter how many good or bad records I make, the important thing is to get people to stop murdering each other." (Grissim 1968, 14) This folk musician, known for her extraordinary voice, did more than sing about social issues—she dedicated her life to participating in protests and movements that would fight injustice through nonviolent means. With this, she emerged as a leading figure in both the musical and political counterculture.

Baez was born on 9 January 1941 on Staten Island, New York, to Albert V. Baez, a physicist who had emigrated from Mexico, and Joan Bridge Baez, a Scottish immigrant. In the 1950s, her family moved to Palo Alto, California, where she went to school and, at age 13, developed an interest in music. She played the ukulele before getting her first guitar. Baez considered folk music more authentic than rock 'n' roll, and so gravitated toward it.

At the same time, her interest in social issues intensified, largely for two reasons: she felt discriminated against when her schoolmates shunned her because she looked Indian; and her father, a Quaker, instilled her with pacifist ideas. In high school, her rebelliousness appeared when she refused to participate in civil defense drills or wear skirts.

After graduating in 1958, Baez moved with her family to Boston, where her father taught at Harvard University and the Massachusetts Institute of Technology. She attended Boston University but soon withdrew because she disliked the rigidity of academics and, in any event, preferred to play her music.

Over the next few months Baez gained a substantial following in the coffeehouses that dotted Cambridge, Massachusetts, and in 1959 garnered national recognition, at only 18 years of age, when she played at the Newport Folk Festival. Within two years, she signed a contract with Vanguard Records, released her first album, *Joan Baez*, toured with Bob Dylan, and increased her major concert appearances to over 20 annually. She refused, however, to sing on *Hootenanny*, a folk music show on ABC television, after the network banned musician Pete Seeger from appearing because of his leftist beliefs.

Her melodic soprano voice and straightforward delivery attracted a wide audience, as did her delicate picking style on the guitar. In *When We Were Good*, music historian Robert Cantwell says that "Baez embodied, symbolized, and enacted . . . [a] powerful synthesis of sexual obsession, social prestige, erotic longing, and poetic representation." (340) Her music dovetailed with an emerging folk music revival with its themes concerning racial and economic oppression, society's downtrodden, war, and the longing for a simpler past.

By this time, the civil rights movement had unfolded, the counterculture was stirring, and Baez participated in her era's political protests with enthusiasm and commitment. In fact, while she lived in California and continued recording and developing her music, she spent most of the 1960s engaged in movements. She played benefits for civil rights and antiwar groups and appeared at rallies.

Beginning in 1964 and continuing for several years after, she withheld payment on a portion of her federal income tax as a way to protest financing the Vietnam War. In 1965, she founded the Institute for the Study of Non-Violence, starting it in a former schoolhouse near where she lived in the Carmel Valley. She believed firmly in nonviolent protest, a position that caused disagreement with some antiwar activists and with the Black Panthers, whom she once criticized for having called cops "pigs" and for carrying guns.

The following year, she joined a silent march in Grenada, Mississippi, to protest the beating of black elementary schoolchildren by the parents of white students, and performed at a benefit to help Chicano farmworkers then on strike in Santa Monica, California. In 1967, she was arrested twice, once in October and again in December, for protesting the draft by engaging in a sit-in outside the Oakland Induction Center. At the same time, she provided money to The Resistance, a prominent antidraft organization begun by David Harris, a student at Stanford University. She and Harris married in 1968, a union that lasted for three years before ending in divorce.

Her musical work continued, too, and she released two highly successful albums, *Baptism*, in 1968, and *Any Day Now*, in 1969, the year she appeared on stage at Woodstock. After the 1960s, her social commitment remained fused with her work as an artist, although she took a more commercial turn with her music after she signed a contract with A & M Records. For them, she recorded two hit singles, "The Night They Drove Old Dixie Down," and "Diamonds and Rust." In the late 1970s, she helped form an international human rights commission, Humanitas.

Baez claimed she never practiced singing, that it just came naturally, and she has never had professional guitar lessons—perhaps this has allowed her to wrap her ballads in unadorned beauty while her humanitarianism advanced social justice. "In the Sixties, we may have been working uphill in an avalanche," she said, "but enough of us didn't feel like that."(Sager 1987, 163)

See also Dylan, Bob; Harris, David; *Hootenanny;* Seeger, Pete.

References Baez, Joan, *And a Voice To Sing With: A Memoir* (1987); Cantwell, Robert, *When We Were Good: The Folk Revival* (1996); Grissim, John, Jr., "Joan Baez," *Rolling Stone*, 7 December 1968, 12–14; Sager, Mike, "Joan Baez," *Rolling Stone*, 5 November–10 December 1987, 163–164.

Bag

This word had two prominent meanings. For one, it referred to a quantity of drugs, usually marijuana, stored in a plastic bag or baggie. Thus the question "How much for a bag?" referred to whatever quantity of marijuana a seller packaged in that way, often an ounce or half-ounce.

Another meaning for the word emerged in 1960, referring to a person's occupation, livelihood, main activity, or style of doing things. Regarding a friend preoccupied with, say, doing homework, a person might comment to another, "That's his bag, man, leave him alone."

Baker, Ella (1903–1986)

Although an older veteran of the mainstream civil rights movement, in 1960 Ella Baker helped found the Student Nonviolent Coordinating Committee, an organization of young college students who developed radical confrontation to fight racial injustice.

Born in 1903 in Norfolk, Virginia, Ella Baker grew up on her family's small farm located near Littleton, North Carolina. Her maternal grandfather influenced her greatly. He had been a slave and worked hard to become a landowner while fighting to advance civil and voting rights for African Americans. Her grandmother also influenced her—a strong figure who never accepted white society's oppression. In all, young Ella learned pride, commitment to social reform, and resistance to white domination.

In 1918, Baker studied at a private high school in Raleigh, where she excelled as a debater. From there, she attended nearby Shaw University and in 1927 graduated as class valedictorian with a major in sociology. During the 1930s, as the Great Depression gripped America, she lived in Harlem, where her long involvement in politics and social reform began. In 1930, she joined the Young Negroes Cooperative League, which formed consumers' cooperatives to advance black economic power. The League coincided with her belief, one she adhered to throughout her career, that organizational power should flow from the masses up, not from the top down.

At this time, she worked also for the federal Workers' Education Project to help develop skills among the unemployed. In this activity, she came into greater contact with leftist reformers and adopted socialist ideas. She edited two newspapers, the *West Indian News* and the *National News*.

Baker's involvement in black civil rights intensified in 1940 when she started working as a field secretary for the National Association for the Advancement of Colored People (NAACP). As in her previous projects, she was an indefatigable worker, willing to knock on doors if necessary to motivate people and organize them. Furthermore, she refused to accept a second-class status for women in the male-dominated political culture.

In 1943, the NAACP appointed Baker director of branches. In this capacity she traveled widely in the South and organized local chapters, including one in Greensboro, North Carolina, that several years later helped stimulate black activism and a massive sit-in demonstration. In 1946, however, she quit her national position, although she continued to work for the NAACP in New York. She had grown discontent with the NAACP's emphasis on court remedies to end racial segregation, a strategy she considered too slow and too removed from the masses. She desired a militant approach, one that would activate large numbers of people, and she wanted an organizational structure that obtained its vibrancy from the grass roots.

After the famous Supreme Court decision in the case of *Brown v. Board of Education* (1954), Baker served on an advisory commission established by New York City to desegregate the schools there. In 1956, she helped found In Friendship, a short-lived group meant to raise money for civil rights efforts in the South. Then, the following year, she assisted in putting together an extremely influential organization, the Southern Christian Leadership Conference (SCLC). Martin Luther King, Jr. headed the SCLC, but as its executive director, Baker crafted its structure and expanded its membership.

She had a falling out with King, however, when she objected to the SCLC's overwhelming dependence on him. Charismatic leaders, she once observed, often turned out to have feet of clay. At this time, a new avenue appeared for her militancy when, in 1960, college students in Greensboro began a sit-in to desegregate the lunch counter at Woolworth's. The bold protest led to sit-ins in several other southern cities and displayed the young people's discontent with the prevalent NAACP and SCLC strategy.

Baker feared that if left unorganized, the student protests would dissipate; furthermore, she wanted to expand the youthful energy that could invigorate the civil rights effort. At her urging, the SCLC sponsored a meeting of student leaders at Shaw University in April 1960. These students came from black colleges in the South and North. King addressed the gathering, as did James Forman and Baker. In her speech, "More than Hamburgers," she urged the students to go beyond lunch counter sit-ins and use direct action to end racial segregation, educational deprivation, and poverty. In referring to the older civil rights leaders, she declared: "The younger generation is challenging you and me. They are asking us to forget our laziness and doubt and fear, and follow our dedication to truth to the bitter end." (Sitkoff 1981, 92)

Baker fully agreed with the students when they indicated their distrust of King and the other elders, whom they feared would co-opt the direct-action movement for their own purposes. As civil rights leader John Lewis observed about her: "She was much more radical than King . . . well to the movement's left. She was very creative. She did not want the students used by the SCLC or the NAACP. She left a deep imprint on us." (Viorst 1979, 120)

Baker's energy and advice helped convince the students to develop a mass organization emphasizing direct action, one that, although still in agreement with King's nonviolent philosophy, would exist independent from the SCLC. Before the end of the year, the young protesters established the Student Nonviolent Coordinating Committee (SNCC), and the SCLC fired Baker.

She continued her work, though, and four years later joined in organizing the Mississippi Freedom Democratic Party (MFDP) that challenged the seating of the all-white delegation at the Democratic National Convention. The MFDP failed in its mission, but the effort highlighted the deepening belief that the Democratic Party and other establishment institutions could not be trusted to advance substantial social change.

Indeed, her influence went well beyond African American society and affected many whites who concluded that the nation needed activism to fight racism, end the Vietnam War, advance women's rights, and undertake other reforms. The broadness of her influence and vision is reflected in her words that transcend both the 1960s and her death in December 1986: "Remember, we are not fighting for the freedom of the Negro alone," she said, "but for the freedom of the human spirit, a larger freedom that encompasses all mankind."

See also Greensboro; Student Nonviolent Coordinating Committee.

References Baker, Ella Jo, "Developing Community Leadership," in *Black Women in White America*, ed. Gerda Lerner (1972); Cantarow, Ellen, and Susan Gushee O'Malley, "Ella Baker: Organizing for Civil Rights," in *Moving the Mountain: Women Working for Social Change*, ed. Ellen Cantarow, et al. (1980); Dallard, Shyrlee, *Ella Baker: A Leader behind the Scenes* (1990); Grant, Joanne, *Fundi: The Story of Ella Baker*. New Day Films (1981); Sitkoff, Harvard, *The Struggle for Black Equality, 1954–1980* (1981); Viorst, Milton, *Fire in the Streets: America in the 1960s* (1979).

Baldwin, James (1924–1987)

An eminent African American essayist and novelist, James Baldwin illuminated the black person's oppression in America and raised the consciousness of young white radicals who joined the fight for civil rights and democracy in the 1960s.

Baldwin was born in New York's Harlem on 2 August 1924. His mother, Berdis Emma Jones, worked as a domestic servant. In 1927, she married a preacher, David Baldwin, from whom James took his last name. James grew up amid great economic and emotional deprivation. He lived in poverty, had to spend most of his time caring for the other children in his large family, and had to endure his stepfather's harshness and belittlement—David Baldwin frequently called James unimportant and ugly.

James turned to school and books as an escape. Encouraged by an elementary schoolteacher who saw great promise in him, he read voraciously: Harriet Beecher Stowe, Robert Louis Stevenson, Dickens, and Dostoyevsky, all before he reached his teens. He turned to religion as well, and in 1938, at age 14, began preaching at Mount Calvary of the Pentecostal Faith Church. His emotional sermons won great acclaim and gained him a considerable following, but they also won him the greater enmity of his father, jealous over James's success. Within three years, James discontinued his preaching and broke with Christianity. At a later date, he criticized his former religion for relying on ignorance and fear.

As a child, James desired to write, and he carried this with him to Dewitt Clinton High School in the Bronx, New York. Several teachers there encouraged him, and he edited the school's literary magazine, *Magpie*. When he graduated in 1942, he got a job working in a war industry plant in New Jersey, an experience that affected him deeply, for he encountered virulent racism unknown to him within heavily black Harlem.

In the mid-1940s, Baldwin moved to Greenwich Village, where he made contacts that boosted his literary career, especially his friendship with the author Richard Wright. Baldwin's biographer, James Campbell, refers to Wright in *Talking at the Gates* as the young man's surrogate father. The older author read Baldwin's early material and, impressed, helped him obtain a grant to continue his work.

Soon, Baldwin found acceptance for his essays when *The Nation*, *Partisan Review*, *Commentary*, and other magazines and journals published them. He remained, however, discontent with racism, his continuing poverty, and his seemingly futile struggle to produce a novel.

As a result, in the late 1940s, he moved to Paris and overcame his futility with *Go Tell It on the Mountain*, published in 1953 to critical acclaim. In fact, over the years it remained the most respected of his novels. Largely autobiographical, it describes his childhood in Harlem and the stepfather who hated him. Yet another novel, this one published in 1956, reflects his personal life: *Giovanni's Room*, which deals with homosexuality. Baldwin believed he should be open about his sexual orientation; he was determined "not to treat [it] like a skeleton in the cupboard." (Campbell 1991, 33)

Baldwin returned frequently to the United States, and in the 1950s, while he continued writing essays, novels, and some plays, he helped promote civil rights demonstrations. He said: "No society can smash the social contract and be exempt from the consequences, and the consequences are chaos." In 1963, Baldwin announced his opposition to the war in Vietnam and criticized discrimination against homosexuals.

During that same year, his *The Fire Next Time* was published. This short book, comprising two essays, earned him a considerable audience among white, intellectual college students attracted to its critique of racism. *Fire* expresses Baldwin's long-held belief that segregation victimizes whites as much as it does blacks, for it causes whites to ignore their own weaknesses. He expresses his discontent with white liberals—which also touched a nerve with college students who considered liberalism a sell-out to the status quo—and warns that change must come for disaster to be averted. In one passage he says:

> White Americans find it difficult as white people elsewhere do to divest themselves of the notion that they are in possession of some intrinsic value that black people need, or want. And this assumption—which, for example, makes the solution to the Negro problem depend on the speed with which Negroes accept and adopt white standards—is revealed in all kinds of striking ways, from Bobby Kennedy's assurance that a Negro can become president in forty years to the unfortunate tone of warm congratulation with which so many liberals address their Negro equals. (108)

In another passage he asserts:

> If we—and now I mean the relatively conscious whites and the relatively conscious blacks, who must, like lovers, insist on, or create, the consciousness of others—do not falter in our duty now, we may be able, handful that we are, to end the racial nightmare, and achieve our country, and change the history of the world. If we do not dare everything, the fulfillment of that prophecy, re-created from the Bible in song by a slave, is upon us: *God gave Noah the rainbow sign, No more water, the fire next time!* (119–120)

Baldwin died from cancer on 30 November 1987 in France. The *New York Times* hailed his intense essays that "helped break down the nation's color barrier."

See also Black Power; Civil Rights Movement.

References Baldwin, James, *Another Country* (1962), *The Fire Next Time* (1963), *Giovanni's Room* (1956), *Go Tell It on the Mountain* (1953), *Going To Meet the Man* (1965), *Nobody Knows My Name* (1961), and *Tell Me How Long the Train's Been Gone* (1968); Campbell, James, *Talking at the Gates: A Life of James Baldwin* (1991); Weatherby, James, *Artist on Fire: A Portrait* (1989).

Banana Peels

On 5 March 1967, every grocery store in San Francisco's Haight-Ashbury district sold out of bananas. The rush, or more accurately, ruse was on: two days earlier the *Berkeley Barb* had printed a story asserting a person could get high on bananas. The story had originated with the rock band Country Joe and the Fish, whose members reported they had smoked banana peels and gotten stoned. The *Barb* article included a recipe for toasting banana peel scrapings. At a concert after the story broke, Country Joe's guitarist lit up a banana joint on stage and then passed several around. After the mainstream *San Francisco Chronicle* repeated the banana peel story, banana sales across the nation surged. The banana peels, though, produced no effect other than nausea when consumed in large quantities.

Bank of America

To the counterculture, the Bank of America symbolized oppressive corporate capitalism—impersonal, greedy, tied to the war machine. When hippies looked at the Bank of America building in San Francisco, they saw a stark contrast to the alternative way of life they wanted to build; when New Leftists and other politicized radicals looked at it, they saw something to conquer. On 4 May 1970, after the bloody confrontation between National Guard troops and students at Kent State University in Ohio, a riot erupted in Isla Vista, outside Santa Barbara, California, in which the crowd attacked and burned the local branch of the Bank of America. As to why, one protester explained: "It was the biggest capitalist thing around." (Gitlin 1987, 401) Angry protesters targeted other branches, and by year's end officials with the bank reported two dozen fires or bombings against their buildings.

See also New Left.

Reference Gitlin, Todd, *The Sixties: Years of Hope, Days of Rage* (1987).

Banks, Dennis (1930?–)

Dennis Banks, an Anishinabe Indian, helped found the militant American Indian Movement (AIM) to protect tribal and civil rights.

Banks was born on 12 April 1930 (some reference sources give the date as 1937) on the Leech Lake Indian Reservation in northern Minnesota. In 1968, he, along with George Mitchell and Mary Jane Wilson, organized AIM in reaction to the mistreatment of Indians in Minneapolis. AIM soon expanded its concerns, and in 1969 supported the occupation of Alcatraz Island by protesters demanding its return to Indian control.

In 1973, Banks led an AIM demonstration in Custer, South Dakota, against biased court proceedings that had found a white man innocent of murdering an Indian. Later that year, he participated in the infamous showdown between AIM and federal forces at Wounded Knee on the Pine Ridge Reservation in South Dakota. After the conflict, the federal government prosecuted Banks, but a jury acquitted him. He was, however, convicted of riot and assault relating to the Custer protest. Rather than serve time, Banks fled to California, where the governor granted him asylum.

In the late 1970s and early 1980s, Banks held various teaching positions. He surrendered to federal authorities in 1985 and served 18 months in prison. After his release he worked as a drug and alcohol counselor on the Pine Ridge Reservation.

See also American Indian Movement; Means, Russell; Peltier, Leonard.

Reference Matthiessen, Peter, *In the Spirit of Crazy Horse* (1991).

The Beach Boys

The Beach Boys all hailed from Hawthorne, California, and although only one of them knew how to surf, their rock sound and image reflected surfer-oriented southern California—tanned, young, affluent—and made them the only American band able to consistently compete with the Beatles during the 1960s British music invasion.

Three brothers, Brian, Carl, and Dennis Wilson; their cousin, Michael Love; and Brian's friend, Alan Jardine, formed the Beach Boys in 1961, originally calling themselves Carl and the Passions, and later the Pendletons, before settling on their more famous name. In the summer of 1962, they capitalized on the craze for surfing records then sweeping California with *Surfin'*, a modest seller on the national charts. They then switched from a small recording label to Capitol Records, and had their first top-20 hit, "Surfin' Safari." Their fourth record, released in 1963 and titled *Surfin' USA*, became their first million-seller and made them internationally popular. That same year, they produced three top ten albums, and the following year three more, including their first number one LP, *Beach Boys Concert*. In all, between 1963 and 1965 they produced nine albums.

Up until 1966, their songs contained simple lyrics that accompanied an equally simple beat and harmonies—songs promising "two girls for every boy," and proclaiming "she'll have fun, fun, fun, 'til her daddy takes her T-Bird away." But that year, as surf music passed its peak, they recorded the LP *Pet Sounds* and took a new direction, using orchestration and a heavier sonance, in many ways more mature. This led to Brian Wilson working on "Good Vibrations," which had the Beach Boys using an organ, flutes, and enough overdubbing and harmonizing to produce a choirlike sound.

With "Good Vibrations," the Beach Boys complemented the musical experimentation then under way by bands in San Francisco and by the Beatles, and also presaged what the latter group would do in 1967 on *Sgt. Pepper's Lonely Hearts Club Band*.

Beset by Brian Wilson's depression, drug abuse, and nearly total seclusion, the Beach Boys almost fell apart after "Good Vibrations." They formed their own record label, though, and toured in the 1970s with limited success. On 28 December 1983, Dennis Wilson drowned. Despite this setback, the Beach Boys rebounded in 1988, with "Kokomo," their first hit record in 20 years.

See also Rock Music.

References Preiss, Byron, *The Beach Boys* (1983); Ward, Ed, Geoffrey Stokes, and Ken Tucker, *Rock of Ages: The Rolling Stone History of Rock & Roll* (1986); Wilson, Brian, *Wouldn't It Be Nice: My Own Story* (1991).

Beads

Many countercultural youngsters wore beads. For males in particular, beads displayed rebellion against the neckties mainstream society said they should wear, and they showed attachment to hippie values; thus, "love beads" announced the wearer's humanity in contrast to the older generation's materialism. As a result, beads symbolically separated one generation from another. In time, youngsters wore them merely to show they were cool.

Beat

The word *beat* refers to the writers of the 1950s—essayists, poets, and novelists—who challenged traditional society—its literature and its values. Author Jack Kerouac popularized the term in the early 1950s, one probably coined by his friend Herbert Huncke. In their writing, the beats emphasized a new consciousness to challenge conformity and its oppression. Eastern religion, nature, Walt Whitman, and Henry David Thoreau thus attracted them.

Zen Buddhism had a special appeal because it considered meditation, intuition, and mysticism more important than achievement, rationality, and materialism. The poet Allen Ginsberg, for one, embraced

Zen, and many beats were influenced by him. Jazz worked its influence, too, for its improvisational flow, or its blow, as Kerouac called it, sent the mind, and the beats' writing, in free fall—building, tumbling, scattering, and rebuilding intuitively.

The beats included other writers in addition to Ginsberg and Kerouac, most notably Gary Snyder, Lawrence Ferlinghetti, and William Burroughs. They wandered America and explored their minds through mysticism, drugs, and experimentation, searching for enlightenment, inveighing against civilization's hypocrisies and brutality. The mysticism they embraced and expressed did not entail asceticism; quite the reverse, it meant embracing the body and the holiness found in everything, including the sordid and the obscene.

Ginsberg said, "The point of Beat is that you get down to a certain nakedness where you are actually able to see the world in a visionary way." (Plummer 1981, 46) Kerouac likened the word to beatific, meaning a blessed people. Mainstream *Time* magazine, however, called them "the mendicants of marijuana and mad verse." (6)

See also Beatnik; Burroughs, William S.; Ginsberg, Allen; Kerouac, Jack; Mailer, Norman; Snyder, Gary.

Reference Plummer, William, *The Holy Goof: A Biography of Neal Cassady* (1981).

The Beatles

No other rock band so captivated the counterculture, reflected it, and shaped it than the Beatles. Yet the Beatles went beyond a countercultural influence: as the most important band in the history of rock 'n' roll, they reshaped the medium and left a broad imprint on Western culture.

The Beatles' roots extend back into the 1950s, when American rock 'n' roll music permeated England's youth culture. The state-run radio stations seldom carried the singers English teenagers wanted to hear, especially Elvis Presley, so they resorted to pulling in stations from Luxembourg and elsewhere, listening through the static to the music that enthralled them. Among those listeners was an iconoclastic, rebellious, and often surly young man, John Lennon.

In 1957, Lennon, who lived in Liverpool, put together a band called the Quarrymen. That July, when they played at a picnic, he met Paul McCartney, and although the two had greatly different personalities—with McCartney self-righteous, conscientious, and deferential to elders—they had a common interest in guitars and rock music. Lennon invited McCartney to join the Quarrymen, and they soon began writing songs together. In 1959, when the band had a brief existence under the name Johnny and the Moondogs, McCartney convinced Lennon to let George Harrison join them. Harrison had been hanging around the group, but Lennon had not been impressed with his guitar playing. Despite this, he agreed, and the band had another member. Soon after, Stu Sutcliffe, a fellow student of Lennon's at the local art college, joined them on bass guitar—not because he could play the instrument, which he could not, but because he had money the group needed. For the time being, the band used several different drummers to complete its makeup.

At this time, Liverpool teemed with rock bands. Nearly every neighborhood had one and there even appeared a newspaper that discussed the Liverpool rock scene. Later in 1959, Johnny and the Moondogs arranged to audition for an agent who liked them enough to send them on a tour through Scotland. Shortly before the audition, the band had again changed its name, this time to the Silver Beatles, meant to be a takeoff on Buddy Holly's group, the Crickets. Lennon suggested spelling "beetles" as "Beatles" to play on the phrase "beat music."

After the Scottish tour of decrepit venues, the Silver Beatles continued playing the Liverpool scene, making little money and suffering physical attacks from thugs. Before year's end, they added a handsome drummer, Pete Best, and performed in Hamburg, Germany. There they experienced yet another round of seedy bars and horrendous living conditions, such as the

The Beatles arrive at Kennedy Airport on 7 February 1964 and are greeted by thousands of screaming teenagers.

lodging provided them in a movie theatre where they lived for weeks: tiny spaces with bunks jammed behind a movie screen, roaches scrambling about. Nevertheless, the Hamburg trip benefited the band greatly, and they returned to Liverpool with a tighter sound. Lennon recalled: "It was Hamburg that had done it. . . . It was only back in Liverpool that we realized the difference and saw what was happening." (Brown 1983, 49)

In February 1961, the Beatles—they had recently dropped "silver" from their name—began playing at the popular Cavern Club, and soon became the house band. They made another trip to Hamburg in April, at which time Stu Sutcliffe's German girlfriend changed their appearance, introducing them to collarless sport jackets and another new style: combing their hair forward and cutting it in bowl-shaped bangs. During this trip, Sutcliffe decided to quit the band and remain in Germany to live with his girlfriend, whom he married, and concentrate on his art. (He died less than a year later from a brain hemorrhage suffered months earlier when thugs attacked him after he and the band had finished playing at a show in Liverpool.)

Near the end of the year, a young, wealthy record-store owner, Brian Epstein, watched the Beatles play at the Cavern Club and then proposed to them that he become their manager. The Beatles agreed, beginning a relationship that would take them to the top of rock.

Epstein plunged into the task, getting the Beatles to present a cleaner image, acceptable to a wider audience. Try as he did, though, he was unable to get any record companies interested in them—until in May 1962, they auditioned for George Martin, a producer at Parlophone Records, a division of a large company called EMI. Martin signed them to a contract, but only after they agreed to get rid of Pete Best, whose drumming he did not like. The Beatles replaced Best with Ringo Starr (born Richard Starkey), the drummer with a popular Liverpool group, Rorey Storme and the Hurricanes, but Martin considered Starr's talent so limited he used him only minimally in the Beatles' first recording sessions.

Much as Epstein proved crucial in the Beatles' success, so too did Martin. The producer brought with him an outstanding knowledge of musical instruments and composition based in the classical field, an ability to use the recording studio artistically, and a talent to pull from the Beatles their best work. On 11 September 1962, the Beatles recorded two Lennon-McCartney originals, "Love Me Do" and "P.S. I Love You." For the latter, Martin put together the group's trademark harmonies. The records sold well, but their first number one hit in Britain did not come until March 1963 when "Please Please Me" climbed the charts. Publicists labeled the Beatles' sound, and that of other groups from Liverpool, as the "Merseybeat," after the Mersey River that flowed through the city.

That same year, the Beatles released two records in the United States that went nowhere. The failure convinced Epstein that to be successful in America he would have to take the Beatles there. Fortunately, he had a receptive supporter in TV host and impresario Ed Sullivan, who knew about the massive crowds turning out in England to see the Beatles. At the same time, Capitol Records, the EMI division in the United States, decided to sink some money into promoting a new release by the band, "I Want To Hold Your Hand."

As the song moved up the American charts, the Beatles, scheduled to appear on the *Ed Sullivan Show*, arrived in New York City on 7 February 1964, greeted by thousands of screaming teenagers at Kennedy Airport. Sullivan had never seen anything like it: 50,000 ticket requests for his show held in a theatre that seated only a few hundred, and on the night of 9 February tremendous ratings as 53 million viewers tuned in for what he considered a novelty act. Sullivan introduced the Beatles by telling Americans to "judge for yourselves."

The Beatles appeared on Sullivan's show again the following week, and by the time they left the United States on 22 February, their fame had exceeded that of Elvis Presley. But would they last? Many critics thought not. Several factors, however, worked against this view: the hunger of American teenagers for rock 'n' roll different from the blandness that had overcome most acts, the talent of Lennon and McCartney as songwriters, Martin's acumen, and Epstein's shrewd show-business tactics.

These factors, among others, allowed the Beatles to develop and grow as the counterculture emerged and changed, and assured their staying power through the decade. In 1964, they filmed their first movie, *A Hard Day's Night*, which, after its release the following year, earned critical acclaim and tremendous commercial success. In August 1964, the Beatles began their first extensive tour of the United States, during which a momentous event occurred: they met Bob Dylan, who introduced them to marijuana.

The drug soon influenced their music, evident in songs from their second movie *Help!*, filmed in 1965, in which they moved away from simple boy-meets-girl themes and their earlier instrumentation to use ambiguous lyrics and diverse, complex arrangements, incorporating, for example, the Indian sitar. This change appeared more evident later that year with *Rubber Soul*, for the first time an album whose songs displayed a collective identity rather than a throw-together of singles, and as such a revolutionary development in rock.

The Beatles followed this with *Revolver*, an even more introspective LP. In England, the album included "Dr. Robert," a not-so-veiled reference to drugs. The Beatles had recently experimented with LSD, and it showed. On the record, Lennon used sounds from tapes played backwards, a technique he had discovered when one night, while under the drug, he accidentally loaded a song into a recorder the wrong way.

Then, in 1967 came their infamous album *Sgt. Pepper's Lonely Hearts Club Band*. Acclaimed by pop and classical music critics alike, it contained diverse compositions woven together to form a theme by which the Beatles created a mock band—Sgt. Pepper's—as their alter egos. The songs ranged from "When I'm Sixty-Four," a straight pop number, to the eerie "A Day in the Life," to the psychedelic "Lucy in the Sky with Diamonds." The Beatles had arrived as artists, and *Sgt. Pepper's* displayed not only their personal changes but also the counterculture's mysticism, drug experimentation, and challenge to traditional forms.

Although Brian Epstein died in August 1967, the Beatles continued their success. Their LP *The Beatles*, more popularly called the "White Album," released in 1968, contained 30 songs in a two-record set. Once again, critical acclaim and huge sales came their way. But an astute observer may have noticed that the songs had become more divergent and, in doing so, centered around each individual Beatle. In fact, the band did not work well together in the studio and McCartney even refused to use most of Starr's drumming, choosing, instead, to dub in his own. While divergent musical interests had overtaken them, other factors caused problems, notably the presence of Lennon's new girlfriend Yoko Ono—whom McCartney and Harrison disliked having in the studio—and squabbles involving finances. The latter erupted when McCartney maneuvered to gain an upper hand over Lennon by secretly acquiring additional stock in their music publishing company.

Tension grew worse in 1969 when the Beatles filmed *Let It Be*, a movie showing them at work recording their new album of the same title. Although edited before its release, the movie still showed the Beatles on edge (and in their last public performance together, an impromptu appearance playing the song "Get Back" on a rooftop in London at their Apple studios). By that time, Lennon had released his own recordings, done with Yoko Ono, and clearly wanted to leave the band. George Martin later evaluated the situation: "It was a tough time, really tough. They were so much at each other's throats. With John and Paul I think it was like two cocks fighting, in a way. They were jockeying for position, and John did want to be dominant. It wasn't the fault of George or Ringo at all. It was mainly John. And, of course, Paul being bossy and trying to get things together, trying to counter John, only put other people's backs up, too." (Smith 1995, 89)

Still, the Beatles went into the studio one last time in the summer of 1969, and *Abbey Road* resulted, which Martin today considers a reconciliation album. Yet the LP's lyrics reveal their troubles and impending breakup; for example, "You never give me your money, you only give me your funny paper," a reference to contractual hassles. By the fall, the Beatles had dissolved, although public announcement of the situation did not come until the following spring.

All of the former Beatles released their own albums in the 1970s, to mixed reviews but generally good sales. Lennon's albums often reflected substantial experimentation—and for that they received some stinging criticism, while McCartney's reflected nothing innovational, and for their blandness received sharp rebukes. (Lennon called them songs for Muzak.) As the decade ended, the four former Beatles reconciled and even assisted one another on their albums. Talk intensified about a possible reunification, but on 8 December 1980 an assailant shot and killed Lennon outside his home in New York City.

The remaining Beatles continued their musical careers in the 1980s and then, in 1995, returned to the studio to put together two unusual songs under George Martin's direction, both originally recorded by Lennon. McCartney, Harrison, and Starr added their vocals and instrumentation to his, creating a reunion of sorts.

With their accomplishments, frailties, overindulgences, talent, and insight, the Beatles remain indelibly tied to the sixties. "And in the end," sings Paul McCartney on *Abbey Road*,

> The love you take
> Is equal to the love
> You make.

See also Ono, Yoko; Rock Music.

References Brown, Peter, and Steven Gaines, *The Love You Make: An Insider's Story of the Beatles* (1983); Davies, Hunter, *The Beatles: The Only Authorized Biography* (1992); Norman, Philip, *Shout! The Beatles in Their Generation* (1981); Smith, Giles, "The Beatles' Straight Man," *New Yorker*, 20 November 1995: 84–90; http://kiwi.imgen.bcm.tmc.edu:8088/public/rmb.html.

Beatnik

The word *beatnik* is often used synonymously with *beat*, but more accurately a difference exists: *beat* refers to the writers who challenged middle-class conformity in the 1950s, people such as Allen Ginsberg and Jack Kerouac, whereas *beatnik* refers to those who followed these writers and emulated their way of life (mostly young, white dropouts from the middle class). Beatniks embraced intuition over rationality and mysticism over scientific thought; they lived for the moment and rejected traditional values, such as eight-to-five jobs and monogamous relationships; they used hip language, listened to jazz and blues, frequented coffee shops, and often indulged in drugs. Many beatniks held out little hope for a better future, and their sometimes somber attitude differentiated them from the later colorful hippies. Still, there existed much in the beatniks that carried into the 1960s counterculture, a fact noted by many observers who saw continuity across the two decades in the rebelliousness against middle-class conformity.

See also Beat.

Be-In

In January 1967, the *San Francisco Oracle* described the Human Be-In at Golden Gate Park as "a union of love and activism previously separated by categorical dogma and label mongering." The *Oracle*, a hippie newspaper that promoted the event, saw the be-in as exemplifying "a Renaissance of compassion, awareness, and love in the Revelation of the unity of all mankind. The Human Be-In is the joyful, face-to-face beginning of a new epoch." (Cohen 1991, 90) The event's promoters wanted to bring together hippies and political radicals and thus end the major division that existed within the counterculture.

Several thousand young people showed up at Golden Gate Park, where they heard speeches by antiwar activists, along with cultural revolutionaries such as Timothy Leary and Allen Ginsberg; listened to the Grateful Dead, Jefferson Airplane, and other bands; handed each other flowers, incense, poems, and drugs; and engaged in "om" chants and Hindu rituals to stave off evil spirits. But, as the name of the event suggests, the real heart of the gathering was the people themselves, coming together and grooving.

During the sixties, numerous other be-ins occurred across the nation, where young people celebrated life and displayed hippie trappings: Day-Glo vans, bell bottoms, colors, colors, and more colors. Sometimes be-ins incorporated political messages, as happened at Golden Gate Park, but usually they did not. Instead, young people listened to bands, danced, threw frisbees, and did drugs as the be-ins attempted to foster a psychedelic community.

See also *San Francisco Oracle*.

References Cohen, Allen, *The San Francisco Oracle, Facsimile Edition: The Psychedelic Newspaper of the Haight Ashbury, 1966*–1968 (1991); Perry, Charles, *The Haight-Ashbury: A History* (1984); Perry, Helen Swick, *The Human Be-In* (1970).

Bell Bottoms

Worn first among hippies, bell bottoms emerged in the mid-1960s as popular pants among young people. They evolved from sailors' pants, which were cut into a bell shape from knee to ankle. Bell bottoms in the sixties fit tight around the thigh and then flared out from the knee. In styles both for men and women, the bell shape at the lower leg varied in size from a modest width to a substantial one, or what were called elephant bells. Bell bottoms usually hugged the hips and were held in place by wide belts, sometimes embroidered with peace signs, mushrooms, or other emblems attractive to the counterculture.

Benny

Benny referred to Benzedrine or Benzedrine pills used as a stimulant or to obtain a mild high.

Berkeley

See University of California–Berkeley.

Berkeley Barb

On 13 August 1965, Max Scherr launched the *Berkeley Barb* as a radical left newspaper, an alternative to the conservative *Oakland Tribune* and other staid local publications. Scherr had worked as a lawyer and union organizer and owned a bar. As college students began protests at the University of California–Berkeley on behalf of free speech and against the Vietnam War, Scherr decided to begin a publication that, as he put it, would not seek the understanding of its readers but rather cause them to feel anger, guilt—whatever was necessary to raise their social consciousnesses.

The *Barb* focused on movements that challenged the mainstream and included stories supporting the free speech movement, a play by the controversial African American playwright LeRoi Jones, and substantial coverage of antiwar demonstrations. Scherr, known for his reclusion and commitment to his work, attracted writers and artists who appreciated his style of allowing them to handle controversial material as they saw fit. The newspaper earned a reputation as the voice of the Berkeley protest movement. As such, it was not adverse to criticizing countercultural developments that seemed to go astray. In November 1966, for example, the *Barb* had the following to say about a sell-out to mainstream society:

> The Charlatans recently filmed a hair tonic commercial. What is their excuse for contributing to an unlovely and crumbly state of mind, a lie (people will love you if your hair's combed/breath's bright). . . . Why is it necessary to pay two and a half dollars to go to a dance? What's revolutionary about that? . . . Why not pressure the city into putting on block dances, parking lot dances, FREE dances. Would Chet Helms and Bill Graham oppose that? That would be a revolution; something joyous and free in America. It seems curious that the first public manifestation of psychedelics was the dances at two and a half a shot. Liberation on weekends. Get rid of your filthy materialistic cash . . . give it to me.

Scherr's relations with the left grew strained in 1969 when some radicals at the *Barb* demanded he reject profit making and turn the publication into a worker-owned and operated "people's paper." Scherr offered to sell the newspaper to his staff, but no agreement emerged, and the more discontent broke away to form the *Berkeley Tribe*. Scherr finally sold the *Barb* in 1973 but continued as editor for another five years. The newspaper folded in 1980.

See also Free Speech Movement; Underground Newspapers; University of California–Berkeley.

Reference Peck, Abe, *Uncovering the Sixties: The Life and Times of the Underground Press* (1985).

Berrigan, Daniel (1921–)

Like many others in the counterculture, Daniel Berrigan, a Jesuit priest, sensed that technology had overrun America, making it inhuman, impersonal, and cruel. Nowhere was this more evident than in the Vietnam War. With this in mind, and deeply committed to Christian peace, Berrigan joined his brother Philip in protests against the war that raised tremendous controversy and resulted in both men spending time in prison.

Berrigan was born on 9 May 1921 in Virginia, Minnesota. During the Great

Depression, his father, a union activist and socialist, moved the family to Syracuse. At an early age, Daniel Berrigan had become obsessed with the suffering he saw in the world, and when he entered his senior year in high school, he decided to join the Jesuits (Society of Jesus). Consequently, after graduation in 1939, Berrigan began training for the priesthood. He was ordained on 21 June 1952, and followed this with a spiritual retreat.

In 1954, Berrigan began teaching French and theology at the Jesuit-run Brooklyn Preparatory School in New York. While there, he led students in a project to help impoverished Puerto Ricans and blacks in Brooklyn and the Lower East Side.

Along with his energy and commitment to humanitarian causes, Berrigan possessed a high degree of intelligence and a keen writing talent, and in 1957 won the Lamont Prize and nomination for a National Book Award for his collection of poems, *Time without Number*. That same year, he was appointed professor of New Testament Studies at La Moyne College, a Jesuit school, in Syracuse, New York. He created controversy when he led students in rent strikes and picketing to help ghetto residents, an action that often challenged those among the college's wealthy donors who owned ghetto property.

A critical turning point occurred for Berrigan in 1963 when he attended the Christian Peace Conference in Prague, Czechoslovakia, and from there journeyed to Russia and South Africa. At the conference he listened to complaints about the Vietnam War; in Russia he witnessed Catholics bravely maintaining their faith amid government persecution; and in South Africa he saw apartheid in its most brutal form. He later said his trip overseas helped him realize "what it might cost to be a Christian. What it might cost even at home, if things continued in the direction I felt events were taking." (Curtis 1974, 41)

Soon after his return to the United States in 1964, he plunged into the civil rights and antiwar movements. Along with his brother Philip and with Thomas Merton, a liberal Trappist monk and writer, he founded Catholic Peace Fellowship, the first Catholic antiwar organization in the nation. Near the same time, in the spring of 1965, he joined the civil rights march at Selma, Alabama, and with his brother Philip signed a Declaration of Conscience, sent to the White House, that declared their total opposition to the Vietnam War. Berrigan gained considerable attention when he defended the actions of David Miller, a Catholic who, in October 1965, burned his draft card in front of the armed forces induction center in Manhattan—the first burning since a new law had gone into effect imposing stiff penalties for the offense.

For its part, the Catholic Peace Fellowship ran advertisements in several publications, denouncing the war as immoral and calling for an end to violence by American troops and the Vietcong. Berrigan's antiwar actions raised enormous opposition among church leaders, and they decided to silence the rebellious priest by assigning him to South America, where he reported for *Jesuit Missions*, a magazine he edited.

The move, however, stirred Catholic liberals, who demanded Berrigan's return, and within three months the church leadership relented. Berrigan wrote about his South American experience in his 1967 book *Consequences: Truth and . . .*, a work that criticized the United States for being more interested in supporting dictators than eradicating injustice.

In the fall of 1967, Berrigan moved to Ithaca, New York, to help lead the United Religious Work Program at Cornell University. Continuing his outspoken opposition to the war, he participated in the march on the Pentagon that October, and was one of several hundred demonstrators arrested. The following year, he traveled to Hanoi with leftist professor Howard Zinn and helped gain the release of three American prisoners of war. During his stay, he had to hide in bomb shelters in order to escape attacks by American planes. Later that year, he published an account, *Night Flight to Hanoi.*

Meanwhile, Philip Berrigan had staged a notorious antiwar protest at the customs house in Baltimore, Maryland, when he and three accomplices entered the Selective Service Office there and destroyed its files. While awaiting sentencing for his deed, he approached Daniel about staging another spectacular protest. Daniel agreed, and on 17 May 1968, after notifying reporters, they and seven fellow protesters walked into the Selective Service Office in Cantonsville, Maryland, and startled workers by grabbing hundreds of files, putting them in trash cans, taking them outside, and burning them with homemade napalm. There they joined hands, said prayers, and awaited arrest. In a statement, the protesters said:

> We are Catholic Christians who take our faith seriously. We use napalm because it has burned people to death in Vietnam, Guatemala and Peru and because it may be used in American ghettoes. We destroyed these records because they exploit our young men and represent misplaced power concentrated in the hands of the ruling class. . . . We believe some property has no right to exist. (Curtis 1974, 4)

The action by the Berrigans and their colleagues led to similar protests by other Catholics across the nation, including one in Chicago that destroyed 100,000 files.

Known as the Cantonsville Nine (and one year later immortalized in a play Berrigan wrote, *The Trial of the Cantonsville Nine*), the group faced charges of conspiracy and destroying government property. A jury found them guilty, and a judge sentenced Berrigan to three years in prison. But in April 1970, after his appeal failed, Berrigan went underground (as did his brother), convinced he could do considerable good as a radical slipping in and out of towns.

Much to the embarrassment of the FBI, whose agents were pursuing him, he appeared at a Methodist church on 2 August 1970 and presented a sermon in which he called for courageous actions to win the peace. Nine days later, however, the FBI captured him at Block Island, Rhode Island. His imprisonment lasted until 24 February 1972, after which he led rallies to help his brother, who was on trial for another incident. Since then, Berrigan has worked as a counselor to AIDS patients.

Although Berrigan's actions in the counterculture era resulted in criticism from moderates within and outside the Catholic Church, antiwar protesters praised him for his work in calling attention to the war's injustice.

See also Berrigan, Philip; March on the Pentagon, 1967; Zinn, Howard.

References Berrigan, Daniel, *Absurd Convictions, Modest Hopes: Conversations after Prison* (1973), *Consequences: Truth and . . .* (1967), *The Dark Night of Resistance* (1971), *False Gods, Real Men: New Poems* (1969), *Night Flight to Hanoi* (1968), *No Bars to Manhood* (1970), *Time without Number* (1957), and *The Trial of the Cantonsville Nine* (1970); Curtis, Richard, *The Berrigan Brothers: The Story of Daniel and Philip Berrigan* (1974).

Berrigan, Philip (1923–)

In the 1960s, Philip Berrigan and his brother Daniel, both Catholic priests, engaged in radical protests against the Vietnam War, an activity that made them the first clergymen sentenced to jail in the United States for political crimes.

Berrigan was born on 5 October 1923 in a small town, Two Harbors, Minnesota. In the 1930s, his father, a labor union organizer and dedicated socialist, moved the family to Syracuse, New York, where Philip went to high school and excelled in academics and athletics. After graduation in 1941, he worked for a year in a roundhouse, cleaning railroad locomotives in order to earn money for college. In 1942, Berrigan entered Saint Michael's College in Toronto, Canada, but within a few months the army drafted him.

World War II affected Berrigan deeply. For one, while training in the Deep South he witnessed so much white racism and black poverty that he determined this social injustice had to be corrected. For another, his battle experience in Europe, where he rose to the rank of second lieutenant, made him detest war.

Reverends Daniel, left, and Philip, right, Berrigan leave the Baltimore county jail on their way to trial in federal court on 7 October 1968. The brothers were among the nine Roman Catholic pacifists charged with destroying draft records.

After his return to the United States in 1945, Berrigan entered Holy Cross University, from where he graduated in 1950 with a bachelor's degree in English. He then decided to enter the priesthood and joined the Society of St. Joseph, an order dedicated to helping African Americans. He was ordained in 1955 and assigned to New Orleans, where he earned a B.S. degree in secondary education at Loyola University in 1957, and an M.S. degree at Xavier University three years later. While studying at Xavier, he taught at Josephite-run St. Augustine High School, located in a black district of New Orleans. There he worked hard to counteract what he considered to be a condescending attitude shown by most Josephites toward blacks, and did something many Josephites found unacceptable: he joined the civil rights protests then under way.

Berrigan gained notoriety in 1963 when he started out for a civil rights march in Jackson, Mississippi, with the intent of getting arrested during the demonstration and thus becoming the first Catholic priest to be thrown into jail. His superior, though, got wind of this and ordered Berrigan to end his trip. He did so, but not before telling newspaper reporters what had happened, a public revelation disliked by the Catholic leadership.

His actions caused the order to transfer him from New Orleans to the faculty of the Josephite seminary in Newburgh, New York. By this time, Berrigan, appalled at the threat of nuclear war, had become a pacifist, and his outspoken views, while earning him criticism from conservative Catholics, made him a sought-after speaker at numerous colleges and seminaries. He joined with his brother Daniel and another liberal Catholic, Thomas Merton, to found the Catholic Peace Fellowship, which over the next few months took out ads in publications, calling the Vietnam War morally unjustifiable and a violation of God's laws.

In 1965, Berrigan caused yet another stir when he addressed the Newburgh Community Affairs Council and linked the civil rights struggle to the war. He said the conflict in Asia was symptomatic of a racist society. That year he, his brother Daniel, and several other protesters signed a Declaration of Conscience, pledging their complete opposition to the war.

Once again his superiors decided to transfer him, this time to St. Peter Claver Church, a black inner-city parish in Baltimore, Maryland, under strict instructions that he not discuss the Vietnam War. Neither the move nor the instructions silenced him, and he formed clubs in ghetto neighborhoods through which blacks pressured landlords to repair buildings; held masses where he called the war racist; and started a new antiwar group, the Baltimore Interfaith Peace Mission.

In 1966, Berrigan and other clergymen drove to Washington, D.C., where they picketed Secretary of State Dean Rusk's house and that of Secretary of Defense Robert McNamara. Berrigan eventually got an audience with Rusk, but the secretary rejected the priest's ideas. After this, Berrigan led protests at Fort Myers, Virginia, in front of houses occupied by the military chiefs of staff.

With the Baltimore Interfaith Peace Mission, Berrigan escalated his protests after concluding that those who opposed the war must risk arrest and even death to stop it. On 27 October 1967, a few days after participating in a large march on the Pentagon, Berrigan and three other protesters entered the Baltimore Selective Service office carrying containers filled with blood, and as startled workers watched, they poured the contents onto hundreds of files. Berrigan explained:

> To stop this war I would give my life tomorrow, and I can't be blamed if I have little time for those who want to run ads in the *New York Times*. . . . In a word I believe in revolution, and I hope to continue a non-violent contribution to it. In my view, we are not going to save this country and mankind without it. And I am centrally concerned with the Gospel view that the massive suffering of this war and American imperialism around the world will only be confronted by the people who are willing to go with suffering as the first move to justice. (Curtis 1974, 82–83)

While awaiting sentence for his attack, Berrigan planned yet another spectacular protest: an assault on the Selective Service Office at Cantonsville, Maryland. His recruits included his brother Daniel, and on 17 May 1968 the group staged its raid. They grabbed hundreds of files, which they placed in trash baskets, took outside, and burned with homemade napalm. Then they joined hands, said prayers, and awaited their arrest.

The group, known as the Cantonsville Nine, was found guilty of conspiracy and destruction of government property. Philip Berrigan received a three-and-a-half-year sentence to run concurrently with the six years he had been given for his role in the Baltimore protest. In April 1970, while out on bail, and after his appeal failed, he went underground. FBI agents captured him on 21 April in New York City, and he was taken to the federal penitentiary at Lewisburg, Pennsylvania.

There, more trouble ensued when he began sending letters to a nun, Elizabeth McAlister, whom he had secretly married the previous year. The prison rules forbade him from engaging in correspondence, but a fellow inmate smuggled the letters out for him. In one letter, McAlister discussed an idea circulated by a few protesters to blow up some government buildings and kidnap presidential advisor Henry Kissinger in order to place him on mock trial for war crimes. Berrigan opposed the idea, but the FBI obtained copies of his letters from his fellow inmate, who turned out to be working undercover for the government. Berrigan, McAlister, and five others were then indicted on charges of conspiracy, and Berrigan and McAlister were charged with letter smuggling.

Except for the latter, the charges had little substance and represented part of a larger government effort to discredit protesters and embroil them in legal battles. The jury found Berrigan and McAlister guilty of the letter-smuggling charge, but it deadlocked on the others. Later, an appeals court overturned the conviction, and the government decided not to pursue a retrial on the conspiracy charges.

Berrigan received parole on 20 December 1972 and left the priesthood in 1973, shortly after making public his marriage. The former priest and his wife, along with their daughter, moved to a commune in a black neighborhood in Baltimore. Berrigan continued to work with peace groups while writing social commentaries, and he remains a controversial symbol of liberal Catholic radicalism.

See also Berrigan, Daniel.

References Berrigan, Philip, *No More Strangers* (1965), *Prison Journals of a Priest Revolutionary* (1970), and *A Punishment for Peace* (1969); Curtis, Richard, *The Berrigan Brothers: The Story of Daniel and Philip Berrigan* (1974).

The Bitter End

Located on Bleecker Street in New York City's Greenwich Village, the Bitter End presented comedy acts and folk singers. Many performers appeared there early in their careers, among them Bill Cosby; Richard Pryor; George Carlin; Peter, Paul, and Mary; and Bob Dylan. In the 1990s, the club continued to present musical and comedy acts.

See also Greenwich Village.

Black Is Beautiful

By 1966, the phrase "black is beautiful" had emerged as an expression of African American pride. For years, African Americans had been told by whites that black represented ugliness and inferiority. In the mid-sixties, however, African American cultural nationalism began challenging this view, demanding respect for black history, art, and literature. African Americans had nothing to be ashamed of, said the cultural nationalists, and they should stand dignified in asserting that black is beautiful. Proclaimed soul singer James Brown: "Say it loud—I'm black and I'm proud."

See also Black Power.

Black Muslims

Founded in the 1930s as an African American religious organization, in the 1960s the

Black Muslims contributed to the growth of "black power" through a separatist ideology.

Wallace D. Fard founded the Black Muslims, formally the Nation of Islam, in 1930, when he began a temple in Detroit, Michigan. Four years later, however, Elijah Muhammed assumed leadership, and would hold it until his death in 1975. Although not officially a part of Islam, Black Muslims followed many Islamic beliefs and rituals, including prayer five times daily and dietary restrictions. Their philosophy stressed creating black institutions separate from white ones, for they considered whites to be the devil, with whom any cooperation meant damnation. This black nationalism stood at odds with the mainstream civil rights movement, especially Martin Luther King's efforts at integration.

In the late 1950s and early 1960s, Malcolm X emerged as an outspoken Black Muslim leader, rallying followers around the message of whites as devils and the desire to create a separate black nation. Unlike King, who advocated nonviolent protest, Malcolm X called for advancing black goals "by any means necessary." By 1965, though, he had moderated his views—not completely dropping his separatist ideas, but refusing to equate whites with the devil. As he began to break with Elijah Muhammad, and in turn, pose a threat to Muhammad's power, several men said to be Black Muslims opened fire on him and killed him as he addressed an audience in New York City's Harlem district. Some African Americans considered Malcolm X a martyr, a leader who had stood tall in advocating black power and black pride.

Although the Black Muslims existed before the 1960s and remained separate from the radical organizations born amid that decade's tumult, their ideas foreshadowed the black power movement, with its emphasis on African American control of black neighborhoods, its distrust of whites, its promotion of black pride, and its rejection of King's "turn-the-other-cheek" philosophy. Although in several ways different

Black Muslim leader Malcolm X addresses a gathering in Birmingham, Alabama, 15 June 1963. In the 1960s, Malcolm X rallied Black Muslims in support of creating a separate black nation and called for advancing black goals "by any means necessary."

from the Black Muslims—such as in religious ideas and in not accepting complete separatism—many black power leaders idolized Malcolm X.

The Black Muslims have continued as an influential religious movement in the 1990s, despite suffering factional disputes. Louis Farrakhan has emerged as the group's leader and has raised enormous controversy with statements his critics call anti-Semitic.

See also Black Panthers; Black Power; Student Nonviolent Coordinating Committee.

References Lincoln, C. Eric, *The Black Muslims in America* (1994); X, Malcolm, with Alex Haley, *The Autobiography of Malcolm X* (1965).

Black Panthers

After developing a ten-point program in Oakland, California, Huey Newton and Bobby Seale founded the Black Panther Party for Self Defense, popularly referred to as the Black Panthers, in October 1966. This organization ranked among the more militant in the counterculture in fighting for black power and a socialist program.

Several different Black Panther groups formed at this time, such as the Black Panther Party of Northern California based in San Francisco. The Oakland organization, however, rejected cultural nationalism, the belief that whites should be condemned because of their race. Newton and Seale sought alliances with radical whites while promoting black self-determination. They supported black power with its pride for African American culture, but stressed politicizing the slogan to make it radical and claimed that the Panthers were not a racist organization "but a very progressive revolutionary party." Their ten-point program demanded freedom, full employment for blacks, decent housing and education, an end to capitalist exploitation and police brutality, the release of all blacks in jail, and a United Nations–supervised plebiscite so that blacks held as "colonial subjects" in the United States could determine whether they wanted to remain under its government. By 1970, the group had 30 chapters and several thousand members, largely in western and northern cities, and Newton insisted the Panthers would create a "democratic socialist society free of racism."

The Panthers established various self-help programs for African Americans in the ghettos, required strict discipline among their members—such as forbidding alcohol and drug use while doing party work—and ran candidates for political office. But they gained notoriety mainly for their militancy. The Panthers wanted a revolution to end political and economic oppression. They armed themselves with rifles, wore combat jackets, paraded militia-style, raised clenched fists, and shouted "Power to the people!" Riding in cars on armed patrol, they confronted police who arrested blacks and they tried to prevent brutality.

In May 1967, when the California Assembly debated a bill to make illegal carrying loaded guns in public, the Panthers staged a daring protest. They arrived at the state capital, M-1 rifles in hand and pistols strapped to their hips, sent Governor Ronald Reagan scurrying from a meeting he was holding outdoors with several young people, and marched onto the floor of the legislature. Although quickly ushered out, they gained the attention and earned the respect of many ghetto blacks.

Police harassment and internal problems hurt the Panthers. At various times, Newton and Seale were imprisoned, and the FBI and local police cooperated in extreme and even illegal actions, such as raids on the homes of Panther leaders that resulted in deaths. An attack by Chicago police on 4 December 1969 killed two prominent Panthers, Fred Hampton and Mark Clark. Three years later, a dispute between Newton and another Panther leader, Eldridge Cleaver, splintered the organization.

Newton redirected the Black Panthers to pursue reform rather than violent revolution. As a result, they focused on community organizing and tactics such as economic boycotts. The Panthers continued as a localized Oakland group in the 1980s, providing school programs and other social services, but then passed from the scene. Nevertheless, during the turbulent 1960s, they had advanced black pride, radicalized the countercultural attack on the establishment, and fomented distrust among many whites, who concluded that black radicals intended nothing less than to kill them.

See also Black Power; Cleaver, Leroy Eldridge; COINTELPRO; Newton, Huey; Seale, Bobby.

References Forman, James, *The Making of Black Revolutionaries* (1972); Haskins, James, *Profiles in Black Power* (1972); Meier, August, Elliot Rudwick, and John Bracey, Jr., eds., *Black Protest in the Sixties* (1991); O'Reilly, Kenneth, *"Racial Matters": The FBI's Secret File on Black America, 1960–1972* (1989).

Black Power

When Stokely Carmichael proclaimed "Black Power!" during a protest march in Mississippi in June 1966, he expressed a demand that stimulated controversy among African Americans and whites as to what it meant for society. A debate emerged, too, as to how the slogan originated, with most observers saying Carmichael first expressed it, but others insisting it had appeared a year earlier at a convention held by the Congress of Racial Equality (CORE).

Black Power meant that African Americans should unite, learn their heritage, define their own goals, lead their own organizations, and reject white racism. "The concept of Black Power," Carmichael insisted, "rests on a fundamental premise: Before a group can enter the open society, it must first close ranks." (Carmichael 1992, 44) Floyd McKissick, CORE's leader, defined black power in this way: "[It] means putting power in black people's hands. We don't have any, and we want some. That is simply what it means."

Black power insisted that African Americans know their historical past and not rely upon the white man's racist interpretation. Additionally, it professed that blacks should change society's values and political institutions while rejecting any desire to be like the bigoted, materialistic white middle class.

Black power rejected integration as racist because it required African Americans to lose part of their identity; and it demanded that blacks play a substantial role in decision making and end economic arrangements that made them subservient to whites. Charles Hamilton, a leading advocate, claimed that "Black Power clearly recognizes the need to perpetuate color consciousness, but in a positive way—to improve a group, not to subject it." (Meier 1991, 164)

In calling for self-determination and self-identity, black power expressed black nationalism, and this sometimes meant rejecting any white presence, at least in terms of leadership, in African American organizations, as happened with the Student Nonviolent Coordinating Committee. And even though many advocates warned against attaching black power to violent or physically threatening tactics, groups such as the Black Panthers did so, using it as the foundation for a paramilitary organization. As a result, to many whites, the phrase "black power" insinuated a race war. Thus, while black power promoted pride among African Americans, it promoted fear among whites that hardened race relations.

See also Black Panthers; Carmichael, Stokely.

References Hamilton, Charles V., "An Advocate of Black Power Defines It" in *Black Protest in the Sixties* (1991); Meier, August, Elliot Rudwick, and John Bracey, Jr., eds., *Black Protest in the Sixties* (1991); Ture, Kwame, and Charles V. Hamilton, *Black Power: The Politics of Liberation in America* (1992).

Blake, William (1757–1827)

In *Blake*, Peter Ackroyd says of William Blake, the English poet, painter, and engraver: "In [his] visionary imagination . . . there is no birth and no death, no beginning and no end, only the perpetual pilgrimage within time towards eternity." (17)

This *visionary imagination* connected Blake to the counterculture. "It began as a dream and ended as a legend," said Allen Cohen about his founding a hippie newspaper, the *San Francisco Oracle*. "I dreamt I was flying around the world. When I looked down, I saw people reading a newspaper with rainbows printed on it . . .

everywhere. A rainbow newspaper!" (Cohen 1991, xxiii) Visionary imagination permeated the hippies and permeated counterculture art—here lay Blake's appeal.

Blake was born on 28 November 1757 in London, England. His father, James Blake, worked as a tradesman. Young Blake early developed a desire to become a painter, and at age 14 went to drawing school and apprenticed as an engraver. Seven years later, after completing his apprenticeship, he studied briefly at the Royal Academy and then opened his own print shop. The enterprise failed, however, and he earned a living as an engraver and illustrator, spending many years on poverty's cusp.

Two contemporary philosophers and an earlier painter influenced Blake: Emanuel Swedenborg, Jakob Böhme, and Michelangelo. Swedenborg, a Swedish visionary, conversed with angels and spirits; he believed that upon death, human beings experienced a spiritual rebirth and existed in perfect human form. He asserted: "By reason that God is Man, all Angels and Spirits are Men in a perfect Form." (Ackroyd 1995, 104) Böhme rejected the supremacy of reason and postulated a mystical view of the world, describing seven "reference spirits" that through interaction perpetually create the cosmos. To Böhme, everything comes into existence through conflict, including man at war with himself. From Michelangelo's paintings, Blake learned a style Peter Ackroyd refers to as an exotic choice, since it was "considered to be hard, dry, almost 'Gothick,' and quite out of the contemporary fashion." (38)

Blake, who claimed at one point to have been visited by an archangel, published his first collection of poems in 1783 as *Poetical Sketches*, but is best known for *Songs of Innocence* (1789) and *Songs of Experience* (1794). *Innocence*, which he produced as an illuminated book with the help of his wife, Catherine, explored divine love, and *Experience*, which reflected his disillusionment with the human race, explored evil. In "The Shepherd," from *Innocence*, Blake writes:

> How sweet is the Shepherd's sweet lot!
> From the morn to the evening he strays;
> He shall follow his sheep all the day
> And his tongue shall be filled with praise.
> For he hears the lambs innocent call,
> And he hears the ewes tender reply.
> He is watchful when they are in peace,
> For they know that their Shepherd is nigh.

In *Experience*, Blake writes in "Ah! Sunflower":

> Ah Sun-flower! weary of time
> Who countest the steps of the Sun;
> Seeking after that sweet golden clime
> Where the traveller's journey is done,
> Where the Youth pined away with desire,
> And the pale Virgin shrouded in snow;
> Arise from their graves and aspire
> Where my Sun-flower wishes to go.

Innocence and *Experience* are meant to be read together as contrasts, and they express Blake's belief that innocence is impossible without experience transformed by imagination. From 1789 on, Blake wrote his *Prophetic Books*, long poems that used innovative free verse. He wrote, as well, essays in which he condemned political, social, and theological tyranny.

Blake included illustrations with his poems, using a unique technique he called illuminated painting. The figures he portrayed took on fantastic forms, again reflecting inner vision as his inspirational reference.

Blake had few followers in his day—most everyone rejected his work, except for several young artists near the end of his life. Who could foretell that after his death in London on 12 August 1827 his art would be resurrected? Over the years, it has gained a greater reputation, and its essential content earned him a following in the counterculture: his surrealistic engravings, for one, and the nonconformist philosophy that permeated his poems, for another.

Blake said that the soul that follows its imaginative instincts will be innocent and virtuous—law, custom, and reason are perversions. Freedom, he said, could come only through imagination, much as his images came not from life but from the mind. Nearly every aspect of his worldview, including his attacks against tyranny, corresponded with the cultural revolutionaries who populated the sixties.

More than coincidence, then, accounts for author Aldous Huxley naming his book *Doors of Perception* from Blake's visionary experiences and statement, "If the doors of perception were cleansed, everything would appear to man as it truly is, infinite." And beat countercultural poet Allen Ginsberg claimed that in 1948, while reading Blake's "Ah! Sun-flower," he heard a deep voice and recognized it as belonging to Blake. Ginsberg felt his body float and felt connected to the universal spirit.

See also Ginsberg, Allen; Haight-Ashbury; Hippies; Huxley, Aldous; *San Francisco Oracle*.

References Ackroyd, Peter, *Blake* (1995); Stevenson, W. H., *William Blake: Selected Poetry* (1988).

Blowing Someone's Mind (Mind Blowing)

By one definition, to blow a person's mind meant to bring about hallucinatory experiences, usually drug-induced, such as through the psychedelic LSD. Yet this phrase, which emerged around 1966, had a more general meaning as well: to provide a person with a pleasurable, surprising, or incredible experience. Hence, "That song blows my mind."

Blue Jeans

Little did Levi Strauss realize when he designed the first blue jeans in the mid–nineteenth century for miners that they would become, 100 years later, a rebellious symbol against traditional work values. When Strauss arrived in California in 1850 amid the gold rush, he realized that miners lacked adequate clothing, so, after consulting with a tailor in San Francisco, he began making pants from brown tenting canvas—pants that could withstand rigorous outdoor requirements. Soon, he changed the material to a tougher fabric, denim, and dyed it blue. He later added rustproof copper rivets, a stitched double-arc design on the back pockets, and a leather patch showing two horses trying to pull apart a pair of Levi's.

Blue jeans remained clothing for the labor class until the 1950s when urban youngsters began wearing them in rebellion against what their parents considered proper attire. Elvis Presley and other rock 'n' roll singers wore blue jeans, thus investing them with subversive connotations and undermining the work ethic Levi Strauss had intended them to serve.

During the 1960s, blue jeans soared in popularity among young people. To make them even more objectionable to parents, America's youth bleached them, battered them, and roughed them up. Leftist political activists equated blue jeans with a revolutionary outlook, since the pants had been worn for years by factory workers, supposedly an oppressed class. To the activists, whether Levi's or some other company manufactured the jeans meant little; in fact, they preferred unidentifiable army surplus jeans. By 1970, however, companies such as Levi's, Wrangler, and Lee had advertised their blue jeans heavily, and as a result consumers in ever larger numbers identified with a particular brand. Thus, these corporations integrated a counterculture symbol into mainstream society.

Reference Finlayson, Iain, *Denim: An American Legend* (1990).

Blue Unicorn

With a $100 investment in 1963, Bob Stubbs opened the Blue Unicorn, a hole-in-the-wall coffeehouse just north of Panhandle Park in San Francisco's Haight-Ashbury district. Initially, it attracted beatniks from nearby North Beach. Besides food and coffee, it offered used books, music, art, and companionship.

When hippies appeared on the scene in 1964, the Blue Unicorn served as a countercultural center befitting its owner, who looked upon Haight-Ashbury as a creative alternative to straight society's materialism and violence. LEMAR, the Legalize Marijuana organization, met here, as did the Sexual Freedom League. The

San Francisco Oracle, a hippie newspaper, frequently notified its readers about poetry readings at the coffeehouse, "open to all who want to read or listen." And the *San Francisco Examiner* described it as a place where you could get a meal in exchange for doing chores.

Trouble ensued in October 1965, however, when the city health department cited numerous code violations, especially complaining about used books being stored in a business that served food. Health officials eventually retreated from this position, and the Blue Unicorn corrected its other problems. Stubbs sold the coffeehouse in 1966, but it continued to operate until the hippie era in Haight-Ashbury ended.

See also Haight-Ashbury; Haight Independent Proprietors.

Blues

The sixties experienced a blues revival as this traditionally black music, descended from the days of slavery, influenced counterculture rock.

Young white musicians in Europe and America relished the blues for its heartfelt emotion, and they adopted its features as a basis for their own songs. The English bands of the mid-1960s, for example, displayed a blues influence that emanated not only from American recordings but also from a vibrant blues scene in London. The Rolling Stones covered many blues numbers and incorporated the blues style into their rock 'n' roll. The Paul Butterfield Blues Band, Canned Heat, Led Zeppelin, Jimi Hendrix, Janis Joplin, Eric Clapton, and numerous other rock performers in England and America also showed their attachment to the blues.

Young white musicians oftentimes frequented blues nightclubs, as they did in Chicago, where Butterfield, Elvin Bishop, and Mike Bloomfield jammed with Howlin' Wolf. White audiences listened to other African American blues artists, too, including Muddy Waters, Johnnie Lee Hooker, and B. B. King.

Bohemians

Bohemians have long existed in American society—people with artistic or literary interests who reject conventional values and standards of behavior. In the late 1940s and 1950s, bohemians emerged who influenced the 1960s counterculture. These bohemians adopted characteristics peculiar to their time: they criticized suburban conformity and its suit-and-tie, climb-the-corporate-ladder existence; they engaged in casual sex and took drugs, studied Eastern mysticism, pursued innovative literature and avant-garde art, and congregated in hip communities, such as North Beach in San Francisco and Greenwich Village in New York.

In their search for alternatives, these bohemians, called beats and beatniks, set examples for the countercultural hippies who adopted their attitudes toward drugs, sex, and philosophy, but had a more optimistic view regarding life than did their predecessors.

See also Beat; Beatnik; Hippies.

Bong

Some marijuana users in the counterculture preferred a water pipe, or bong, as a way to smoke marijuana or hashish. A bong removes carcinogens and cools the smoke, making it smoother and more refreshing, say its users, than a rolled joint.

Bonnie and Clyde

Released in 1967, the movie *Bonnie and Clyde* enthralled the counterculture generation with a fictionalized story about two infamous outlaws from the 1930s, Clyde Barrow and Bonnie Parker. Using sudden changes in mood, from violence to tranquil scenes punctuated by banjo music, director Arthur Penn kept his audience off balance. Film critic Pauline Kael noted the movie's effectiveness: "The brutality that comes out of the innocent 'just-folks' Barrow-family gang is far more shocking than the calculated brutalities of mean killers. . . . *Bonnie and Clyde* needs violence; violence is its meaning." (Kael 1995)

But equally important, the portrayal of Bonnie and Clyde as doomed outsiders and rebels against society—and perhaps victims of the capitalist-engendered Great Depression—captivated young moviegoers. For some, the outlaws assumed heroic proportions: one radical, writing in the leftist *Guardian*, called their activities consciousness-expanding, and another asked, "If a car full of revolutionaries like [Bonnie and Clyde] pulled up at the gas station where you pumped gas for a living, would you go off with them?" (Gitlin 1988, 15)

References Gitlin, Todd, "1968: The Two Popular Cultures," *Spectator*, Spring 1988, 8–17; Howard, Gerald, ed., *The Sixties: Art, Politics and Media of Our Most Explosive Decade* (1982); Kael, Pauline, "Bonnie and Clyde," *Cinemania 1996* (1995).

Boohoos

Arthur Kleps, a one-time graduate student in psychology and member of Timothy Leary's experimental LSD group at Millbrook, New York, organized the Neo American Boohoo Church in 1966 as a psychedelic religion. The Boohoos considered LSD a sacrament, and in using it tried to address epistemological questions, such as "What is thought?"

Yet Kleps rejected institutions as a barrier to understanding, so he infused his church with self-deprecating humor and satire. The *Boohoo Bible* contained cartoons and true-or-false tests, and he issued a psychedelic coloring book and a bulletin titled *Divine Toad Sweat*. The Boohoos used "Row, Row, Row Your Boat" as their hymn and coined a motto, "Victory Over Horse-Shit." They tried to get the legal system to recognize their use of LSD as protected by religious freedom, but the courts refused to take them seriously.

See also Leary, Timothy.

Boudin, Kathy (1943–)

She espoused Marxist revolution, built bombs, and robbed armored trucks. Such was Kathy Boudin in a life that took her from an intellectual family of comfortable means to the farthest reaches of New Left extremism.

Boudin was born in 1943 to Jean Boudin, a poet, and Leonard Boudin, a lawyer. Her father specialized in cases involving individuals whose constitutional rights had been violated by the government. Boudin grew up in New York's Greenwich Village and attended private schools that adhered to liberal values: the Little Red School House and Elizabeth Irwin School, where she excelled in academics and athletics.

In 1961, Boudin entered Bryn Mawr College in Philadelphia, Pennsylvania, where she served as president of a campus political discussion group and organized a conference on civil rights. In 1963, she was arrested for picketing in a civil rights protest and reacted with a statement that presaged her future political activities: "If desired ends cannot be achieved within law or by normally accepted methods of negotiation, then new methods must be adopted." (Castellucci 1986, 93)

Boudin did not know what course to follow after college—she felt attracted to a law career, but at the same time considered it a sellout to the status quo. In 1965, she began working for the Economic Research and Action Project, started by a New Left organization, Students for a Democratic Society (SDS), as an outreach program to help poor people. Boudin lived in a ghetto area of Cleveland, Ohio, where the hopelessness and poverty suffered by blacks touched her deeply and further convinced her that capitalism had produced an unjust society. In 1968, she participated in protest demonstrations at the Democratic National Convention in Chicago. That same year, she enrolled at Case Western Reserve University Law School in Ohio but soon dropped out, attracted to the expanding antiwar movement.

In 1969, a factional dispute erupted within SDS, and Boudin sided with a group called Weatherman, Marxist extremists who believed in street fighting to weaken the American government and ignite a revolution. In

Weather Underground leader Kathy Boudin, center, and other members of the Students for a Democratic Society hold a press conference in New York to announce a trip to Cuba in August 1969. Boudin and several other Weathermen took their Marxist revolution underground after she was arrested for her involvement in the "Days of Rage" rally in October 1969 in Chicago.

October, she helped coordinate National Action in Chicago, intended to rally working-class students behind Weatherman in a violent assault on property and police. Although Weatherman took to the streets in what newspapers called the "Days of Rage" and smashed windows while bloodying some cops and suffering numerous arrests, the action proved disappointing: only 600 Weathermen had assembled, and the working-class students were nowhere to be found.

The police arrested Boudin, but she failed to appear at her trial, for early in 1970 she and other Weathermen decided to take their revolutionary fight underground and launch terrorist attacks against government facilities. On 6 March 1970, Boudin and several Weathermen, including Terry Robbins, were in a townhouse on West Eleventh Street in New York City, planning an attack, when Robbins inadvertently short-circuited a timer and set off a bomb. The explosion destroyed the townhouse and killed three Weathermen, among them Robbins.

Boudin escaped—her clothes blown off, she went running to a neighbor's house before disappearing back into the underground. A short time later she wrote a poem titled "What It's Like To Be Inside an Explosion," in which she stated how amazing it was to be riding the subways and see her picture there, staring at her from police posters advertising her as a fugitive. That summer, the FBI placed her on its ten-most-wanted list.

Weatherman, or the Weather Underground as it began calling itself in 1970, claimed responsibility for 26 bombings from that year until 1976, none of which caused injuries or took lives. After Weather Underground dissolved in 1976, Boudin joined the May 19th Coalition (named after the birth dates of Ho Chi Minh and Malcolm X), which advocated continued terrorist attacks. On 20 October 1981, she and two other coalition members, along with members of the Black Liberation Army, robbed an armored Brink's truck in Nanuet, near New York City. The attackers got six bags filled with $1.6 million, but after dumping their car for a U-Haul truck and trying to complete their getaway, they wound up in a shoot-out. A guard was killed along with two policemen; Boudin was captured and the money recovered.

On 26 April 1984, she pleaded guilty to murder and robbery charges, and on 3 May received a sentence of 20 years to life. Boudin's odyssey as a revolutionary had come to an end.

See also Days of Rage; New Left; Students for a Democratic Society; Weather Underground.

References Castellucci, John, *The Big Dance: The Untold Story of Kathy Boudin and the Terrorist Family That Committed the Brink's Robbery Murders* (1986); Frankfort, Ellen, *Kathy Boudin and the Dance of Death* (1983).

Bread

"Got any bread, man?" In this case the word bread referred not to something made from wheat but to money. This meaning emerged in the early 1950s among beats and became widespread in the counterculture.

Brown Berets

"We found that the colleges were paying attention to the blacks because they were militant," said a Chicano activist in the late 1960s, "so we started to get as militant as the blacks." (Anderson 1995, 306) This statement bespoke an extremism among Mexican Americans as found in the Brown Berets, a leftist organization.

In 1969, as Chicano consciousness expanded, David Sanchez founded the Brown Berets in East Los Angeles, California, calling it a highly disciplined paramilitary organization committed to fighting police brutality. In some of its efforts to protest the oppression of Chicanos and the war in Vietnam, the Brown Berets allied with Students for a Democratic Society and the Black Panthers. As it did with other activist groups, the federal government infiltrated the Brown Berets and encouraged them to commit violent acts that would disparage the movement. In one famous incident, a Brown Beret, Eustacio Martinez, attacked a U.S. senator by kicking him and damaging his car. Martinez turned out to be an undercover agent.

See also Brown Power; Chavez, Cesar; COINTELPRO.

References Castro, Tony, *Chicano Power: The Emergence of Mexican America* (1974); Munoz, Carlos, Jr., *Youth, Identity, Power: The Chicano Movement* (1989).

Brown, H. Rap (1943–)

With fiery, militant rhetoric and violent acts, H. Rap Brown stirred black extremism in the sixties, inflaming racial animosities and arousing government recrimination.

Brown came from Baton Rouge, Louisiana, where he was born Hubert Geroid Brown on 4 October 1943. During World War II, his father fought overseas, and his mother, too poor to keep the family together, placed him in an orphanage, where he attended elementary school. After he left the orphanage and entered high school, he earned his nickname "Rap" from his bravado at "dozens," a game popular in the ghetto that involved one person trying to outdo another in exchanging insults.

Brown's horizons widened in 1963 when he spent the summer in Washington, D.C., with his older brother, a college student. Brown got involved in civil rights work and began reading W. E. B. Du Bois, Frederick Douglass, and Marcus Garvey. The following year, he traveled to Mississippi, where he participated in Freedom Summer, a project sponsored by the Student Nonviolent Coordinating Committee (SNCC) to register black voters. SNCC's dedication stirred him, as did the white opposition, often violent and in one instance resulting in the deaths of three civil rights workers. When the summer ended, he returned to

Washington where he continued to work for civil rights.

Brown never accepted the nonviolent philosophy preached by Martin Luther King, Jr., and by 1965 openly voiced his doubts. In May 1966, Stokely Carmichael, chairman of SNCC, chose Brown to direct a voter registration campaign in Alabama. The following May, Brown succeeded Carmichael as chairman.

Brown's speeches echoed the deepening discontent counterculture radicals felt toward the prevailing political structure, or establishment, which seemed determined to protect elite power and continue the Vietnam War. He specifically reflected black anger emanating from the ghettos, areas largely unimproved by King's civil rights campaign. Brown talked about going to war against whites, and in 1967 riots erupted after he made inflammatory speeches in Dayton, Ohio; East St. Louis, Illinois; and Cambridge, Maryland. In the latter incident, police arrested him for inciting a riot, claiming he had told blacks to get guns. While in jail, he wrote: "Black people . . . have known the real conspiracy in this country is to run us out, keep us down, or kill us, if we can't act like the honky wants us to act." (Haskins 1972, 228)

After his release on bail, Brown was arrested in September 1967 for transporting a gun from Louisiana to New York. A jury found him guilty, and in a harsh decision, the judge sentenced him to five years in jail. More trouble ensued when Brown, free while appealing his conviction, violated a previous bail provision by traveling to California. In several speeches he portrayed himself as the victim of political persecution. Whatever the case, he had certainly gained the nation's attention: in the 1968 Civil Rights Act, Congress made it illegal to cross state lines to incite a riot—a provision popularly called the "Rap Brown Amendment."

In addition to SNCC, Brown served as minister of justice for the Black Panthers, another militant group. As his trial on the Maryland charges approached in 1970, he suddenly disappeared, and in May the FBI placed him on its ten-most-wanted list. The New York City police captured him in October 1971, after a shoot-out during a bank robbery, and for this act he was sentenced to prison. Meanwhile, Maryland dropped its incitement charge.

Brown entered prison in 1973. Shortly thereafter, he converted to Islam and changed his name to Jamil Abdullah Al-Amin. Upon his release in 1976, he opened a grocery store in Atlanta and became leader of the Community Mosque. In that capacity, he earned a reputation for devotion, and the several mosques in Atlanta elected him their spokesperson.

He got into trouble with the law again, though, and the authorities arrested him in 1995 on assault and weapons-possession charges. As he awaited trial, friends labeled the accusations ridiculous and portrayed them as nothing less than a continuing government campaign to harass the former radical.

See also Black Panthers; Black Power; Carmichael, Stokely; Freedom Summer; Student Nonviolent Coordinating Committee.

References Brown, H. Rap, *Die, Nigger, Die!* (1969); Haskins, James, *Profiles in Black Power* (1972).

Brown Power

As the 1960s came to an end, many Chicanos embraced brown power—a pride in their heritage and physical appearance, and a desire to control their own communities.

Three main factors stimulated brown power: the countercultural challenge to mainstream ideas and institutions, Caesar Chavez's efforts to help Chicano farmworkers in California, and the example set by black power. One brown power activist said in 1969: "Our main goal is to orient the Chicano to *think* Chicano so as to achieve equal power with other groups, not to emulate the Anglo." (Anderson 1995, 306)

In its more extreme form, brown power manifested itself in the Brown Berets, a paramilitary organization similar to the Black Panthers. But brown power appeared in other less radical ways: the Chicano Youth Liberation Conference in Denver, Colorado, that attracted 1,500 delegates who promoted brown as beautiful and celebrated Chicano history; demands for bilingual education; proposals to recognize Mexican American contributions in textbooks; and calls for equal employment.

Not all Mexican Americans supported brown power (anymore than unanimity existed among other groups on other issues), for over the years significant numbers had achieved economic and political success. Many in this position considered the word *Chicano* derogatory and thought brown power had gone too far in criticizing America.

Brown power disintegrated in the early 1970s, a victim of government infiltration, disunity among protesters, and resistance by whites to what they perceived as attacks on their culture.

See also Black Power; Brown Berets; Chavez, Cesar.

References Acuna, Rodolfo, *Occupied America: A History of Chicanos* (1981); Anderson, Terry H., *The Movement and the Sixties* (1995); Castro, Tony, *Chicano Power: The Emergence of Mexican America* (1974); Munoz, Carlos, Jr., *Youth, Identity, Power: The Chicano Movement* (1989).

Bruce, Lenny (1925–1966)

A controversial, iconoclastic comic, Lenny Bruce skewered middle-class hypocrisies, awakening many to society's shortcomings but earning a reputation for obscene performances.

Born on 13 October 1925 in Mineola, New York, on Long Island, Bruce dropped out of school at age 16, left home, and worked on a farm. In 1942, he joined the navy, but when World War II ended, he decided to pursue acting and journeyed to Los Angeles, where he studied at the Geller Dramatic Workshop.

After this led only to unemployment, Bruce returned to New York and, at a club in Brooklyn, accidentally stumbled into comedy when, at the last minute, he substituted for an ill emcee and found that the audience laughed at his jokes. From there, Bruce began performing at local clubs, and he started hanging out at Hanson's Drug Store on West 51st Street, where comics gathered—sometimes accomplished ones, such as Milton Berle and Jackie Gleason, both of whom considered Bruce talented. At Hanson's he met Joe Ancis, a talkative neighborhood funny man who often held the young comedians spellbound with his improvisational stories—sharp, humorous attacks on society's conventions. Said one Hanson's regular about Ancis: "He talks like you'd pull the trigger on a machine gun." (Goldman 1971, 121) Bruce long remembered the Ancis style.

In 1947, Bruce won a contest on *Arthur Godfrey Talent Scouts*, a radio program, and soon began headlining at clubs in New York City. His act failed, however, when he took it outside New York, and as a result, he decided to join the Merchant Marine.

Bruce reentered show business in 1951, putting together an act with his wife (who did some singing) and playing small clubs. In his first days as a comedian his limited repertoire led him to perform mainly impressions, but this time around he developed a new style: ad-libbing, commenting on current events, ribbing customers . . . Joe Ancis style.

In 1958, Bruce began working the better clubs in San Francisco, and the hip crowd flocked to his performances—monologues filled with flashbacks, parallel constructions, associative montages—twisting and turning and riffing like jazz. He ridiculed religion, segregation, and most anything held dear by middle-class society. To Bruce, "whatever made you feel good *was* good," and he sprinkled his comments with profanity, insisting the words were not dirty, that the only thing making them dirty was what people thought of them, attitudes he intended to expose.

Bruce filled his sketches with references to masturbatory guilt, toilet training, infidelity, marital difficulties, and sex between parents; he criticized show-business stars and even other comedians, and jabbed at anyone who blindly followed authority figures. To critics who called his comedy tasteless, he replied:

> I've been accused of bad taste, and I'll go to my grave accused of it and always by the same people—the ones who eat in restaurants that reserve the right to refuse service to anyone. If you can tell me Christ or Moses, for instance, would say to some kid, 'Hey, kid, that's a *white* fountain, you can't drink out of there,' you're out of your skull. No one can tell me Christ or Moses would do that. And people who do aren't even agnostics. They're atheists. That's where the bad taste jazz comes from. (Carey 1975, 35)

Bruce's routine assured controversy and limited his appeal; in fact, many clubs explicitly advertised him as an "adults-only act," and he quickly got a reputation for being a "dirty comedian." Even so, in 1960 and 1961 he sold out Carnegie Hall in New York. The authorities in Philadelphia, however, did not appreciate his act in their city, and later that year they charged him with obscenity.

Although Bruce had a moral streak that his biographer Albert Goldman calls conservative in its attachment to marriage and family, young people in the emerging counterculture were attracted to the comedian's attacks against hypocritical leaders and institutions. The mainstream, meanwhile, continued to harass him. In 1964, a panel of judges in New York found him guilty of obscenity and sentenced him to a jail term, but Bruce returned home to California and obtained a court injunction preventing his imprisonment.

Still, his career quickly unraveled, damaged by the sentence, his uneven performances, and an addiction to methedrine. Throughout 1965, Bruce lived reclusively on little income. He gave his last performance on 25 June 1966 at San Francisco's Fillmore Auditorium, a place known for its hippie rock concerts. Bruce died on 3 August 1966 from a drug overdose, ruled to be accidental but called by some a suicide.

References Carey, Gary, *Lenny, Janis, and Jimi* (1975); Goldman, Albert, *Ladies and Gentlemen: It's Lenny Bruce!* (1971).

Buffalo Springfield

Generational differences and youthful angst obtained a powerful airing in the song "For What It's Worth," and revealed Buffalo Springfield's diverse rock sound and talented musicianship.

Although formed in Los Angeles in 1966, Canadians dominated the group. Stephen Stills and Neil Young provided vocals and guitars, Bruce Palmer played bass guitar, Richard Furay sang and played rhythm guitar, and Dewey Martin played drums. By and large, the band combined rock with country sounds. Buffalo Springfield had so much talent that its members eventually went on to form other highly successful groups: Crosby, Stills, Nash, and Young; Emerson, Lake, and Palmer; and Poco.

During its brief existence, Buffalo Springfield had only one commercial hit single, that being "For What It's Worth." Yet the group's blending of vocals and rhythms, along with its mix of acoustic and electric guitars, earned considerable acclaim and set a style other bands emulated for years to come. Further, in its proclamation that a chasm existed between young countercultural America and the older middle class, "For What It's Worth" provided a message as strong, if not stronger, than Bob Dylan's "The Times They Are A-Changing." Buffalo Springfield underwent several personnel changes in 1967, most notably when Jim Messina replaced Palmer. Differences took their toll, however, and in May 1968 the band split up.

See also Rock Music; Young, Neil.

Reference Ward, Ed, Geoffrey Stokes, and Ken Tucker, *Rock of Ages: The Rolling Stone History of Rock & Roll* (1986).

Bummer

The word *bummer* came directly from counterculture drug experiences. When it originated in 1967, it described a disappointing or bad trip on psychedelic drugs, such as LSD. Bummer soon came to mean a disappointing or bad experience of any kind: "How was the concert last night? A real bummer."

"Burn, Baby, Burn!"

The phrase "burn, baby, burn!" displayed the racial differences endemic to the mid-sixties. After black rioters set fire to Watts and ghetto areas in Detroit and numerous other cities, whites reacted with outrage. Radical African Americans reacted by saying let the whole nation, if necessary, explode into flames in order to achieve justice and revenge—that is, "burn, baby, burn!"

See also Watts.

Burroughs, William S. (1914–1997)

Known as a 1950s beat writer, William S. Burroughs actually went well beyond that genre to produce works heavy in mysticism, psychotic reactions, and scenes so sexually explicit they challenged what critics considered to be literature. His explorations into the irrational and absurd attracted many in the counterculture, including Harvard psychologist and LSD guru Timothy Leary who said, "Burroughs was Mr. Acid before LSD was invented." (Hodgson 1976, 325)

Born on 5 February 1914 in St. Louis, Missouri, Burroughs hailed from a wealthy family. His father, Perry Mortimer Burroughs, was the son of the man who invented the adding machine, and his mother, Laura Lee Burroughs, came from a prominent southern family. Burroughs attended John Burroughs School (named for his grandfather) and Taylor School in St. Louis, and continued his education at a prep academy in Los Alamos, New Mexico. As a young man, Burroughs developed a strong desire to become a writer, and so when he entered Harvard University he majored in English.

Soon after earning his B.A. in 1936, he moved to New York City, where he worked at various times as a bartender, exterminator, factory laborer, and advertising copy writer. He was drafted into the army in 1942 but was soon discharged for physical reasons.

In 1944, while struggling with his writing, he began his long addiction to morphine and heroin. He later claimed the experience damaged him by narrowing his perceptions—quite the opposite of his long-held desire to enhance his consciousness. From his torment, though, came elements that entered his novels: petty criminals, hustlers, and ne'er-do-wells—people with whom he had associated—and a realization of how damaging any addiction can be to the human spirit.

In the late 1940s, Burroughs established friendships with several writers, young intellectuals rebelling against the conformity prevalent in postwar society. These "beats," such as Allen Ginsberg and Jack Kerouac, challenged conventional writing techniques and in their stories emphasized living spontaneously and finding a mystical connection to the universe. Burroughs introduced Ginsberg to the works of earlier writers—Blake, Rimbaud, Kafka—and the psychoanalytical theories of Wilhelm Reich, who postulated that an energy permeated the universe and human beings must release it through sexual activity or risk suffering neuroses. Enthralled by Burroughs, Ginsberg considered him a brilliant antidote to middle-class blandness.

Like his friends, Burroughs traveled extensively to pursue new experiences and an elusive truth, a mystical revelation. While in Mexico, he wrote his first book, *Junkie*, published in 1953. At this time, he accidentally killed his wife while trying to shoot a glass from atop her head. After the tragedy, he traveled throughout South America and then moved on to Morocco. He corresponded extensively with Ginsberg, who, along with Kerouac, visited him. The writers discussed psychedelic drugs and the possible mystical connections these substances might evoke.

In 1957, Burroughs, wanting to concentrate on his writing, got help and ended his heroin addiction. Shortly after this, he completed his most famous novel, *Naked Lunch*, published in 1959. (Some sources attribute the title to Kerouac, who assisted Burroughs in putting the story together. Others attribute it to Ginsberg.) As *Naked Lunch* focuses on threats to individual identity and how needs can be destructive and all-consuming, it bounces like madness

William Burroughs, author of Naked Lunch *and* The Exterminator, *shown here in Paris, 1962*

from unpadded walls—echoing and reverberating, defying linear form or plot, encouraging the reader to enter at any point and plunge into the insane. Burroughs's technique involves frantic, surreal episodes and reflects his belief that standard sentence structure restricts the mind. Filled with graphic references to drugs, homosexuality, and sodomy, *Naked Lunch* received mixed reviews: praised for its innovations, condemned for its "filth."

Whatever the evaluation, the counterculture related to Burroughs's references to power that destroys people, and modern society's numbing depersonalization. To the counterculture, the government, the military, and big business exercised oppressive power. Further, Burroughs's nonlinear form corresponded with the countercultural search for alternatives to conventional thought and style.

Burroughs's later books continued his earlier themes: *The Ticket That Exploded*, *Nova Express* (which presents reality as a motion picture manipulated by a few insiders), *The Wild Boys*, *Cities of the Red Night*, and *The Place of the Dead Roads*. One critic called them "maps of Hell."

Burroughs developed a collage technique in the 1960s, by which he interspersed his own words with snippets from newspaper stories to reflect how the mind gathers information in nonlinear ways. He first used this approach in his book *The Exterminator*.

Burroughs did not accept all innovation in the 1960s, though. For example, he criticized the use of LSD and other psychedelic drugs. Although he believed they could help widen perception, he considered them dangerous, perhaps addicting people to an easy enlightenment or allowing malefactors to use them to control the masses.

Throughout the 1960s, Burroughs lived in England. He returned to the United States in 1974 and continued to write into the early 1990s. He died of a heart attack on 2 August 1997. Perhaps it is ironic that this grandson of the establishment man who invented the adding machine earned his notoriety by attacking rationality and developing a countercultural following.

See also Beat; Beatnik; Ferlinghetti, Lawrence; Ginsberg, Allen; Kerouac, Jack; Snyder, Gary.

References Burroughs, William S., *Cities of the Red Night* (1981), *The Exterminator* (1960), *Junkie: Confessions of an Unredeemed Drug Addict* (1953), *Naked Lunch* (1959), *Nova Express* (1964), *The Soft Machine* (1961), *The Ticket That Exploded* (1962), and *The Wild Boys: A Book of the Dead* (1971); Goodman, Michael B., *Contemporary Literary Censorship: The Case of Burroughs' Naked Lunch* (1981); Hodgson, Godfrey, *America in Our Time* (1976); Morgan, Ted, *The Life and Times of William S. Burroughs* (1988); Skerl, Jennie, *William Burroughs* (1985); http://www/hyperreal.com/wsb/.

The Byrds

In a country song, David Allan Coe once paid tribute to the Byrds when he sang, "Roger McGuinn had a twelve-string guitar and it was like nothing I'd ever heard." McGuinn's guitar and the Byrds' folk-rock sound burst onto the music scene in 1965, while the Beatles and other British bands had a seemingly unshakable grip on the top-ten list.

McGuinn organized the Byrds, originally called the Beefeaters, in 1964 because he had seen the Beatles and thought putting together a band using electric guitars would be fun. He had previously worked as a folk musician with the Chad Mitchell Trio. McGuinn recruited Gene Clark, who played guitar, harmonica, and tambourine; Chris Hillman, who played bass guitar; Mike Clarke, who played drums; and David Crosby, also a guitarist. The band recorded a song for Elektra Records in 1964 that flopped, and then switched to Columbia Records. For that company, they recorded Bob Dylan's "Mr. Tambourine Man." Actually, the band provided the vocals and McGuinn's 12-string guitar, while studio musicians provided the other instrumentation.

With "Mr. Tambourine Man," the Byrds embarked on a new musical form, folk-rock. The song topped the charts in both Britain and the United States, and thus temporarily dislodged the Beatles from their dominant position. The Byrds had one other million-seller the following year with "Turn, Turn, Turn," written by folk musician Pete Seeger. Late in 1965, Gene Clark left the group, and over the next few months the personnel changed often. In 1966, the Byrds released "Eight Miles High," a song about an airplane flight they took to London and their experiences overseas. Many radio stations, however, banned "Eight Miles High" from their play lists, claiming it glorified drug use. The Byrds split up in 1968, although the original band members reunited in 1973 and recorded one final album.

See also Rock Music.

Reference Ward, Ed, Geoffrey Stokes, and Ken Tucker, *Rock of Ages: The Rolling Stone History of Rock & Roll* (1986).

C

Camus, Albert (1913–1960)

Many young people in the 1960s avidly read works by French novelist and essayist Albert Camus, intrigued by his view that life was absurd, a view made poignant by his own tragic death as the decade began.

Born on 7 November 1913 in Mondovi, Algeria, Camus grew up in a working-class neighborhood. Although tuberculosis felled him in 1930, he still attended college and received a degree in 1936 from the University of Algiers. During World War II, he worked as a journalist and with the Resistance against Nazi Germany. In 1942, his first novel appeared, *The Stranger*, one that later had a great influence on the 1960s counterculture (as it did on the preceding decade's beat writers). His second novel, *The Plague*, appeared in 1947, followed by other brilliant novels, essays, and short stories in the 1950s. In 1957, Camus won the Nobel Prize for Literature. Then on 4 January 1960, he died in an auto accident when the car he was riding in as a passenger crashed into a tree on a wide, straight, nearly traffic-free road. The axle may have broken, or a tire may have blown at high speed.

Albert Camus, 1959

Camus's literary themes corresponded with countercultural ones. *The Stranger* portrays life as absurd; *The Plague* asserts the need to protect human dignity and community. To Camus the inevitability of death meant life must be enjoyed and lived intensely—as later hippies insisted, and he expressed an existential view that human beings must provide meaning to their existence and defend values such as truth and justice—a path later political activists pursued.

Todd Gitlin says in his book *The Sixties* that Camus's tragic death placed an aura around the novelist and led counterculture youths to believe "that rebellion is the essence of freedom because, after all, life is lived 'for keeps.'" (34) Indeed, Camus once said: "The struggle toward the summits itself suffices to fill a man's heart." Yet, the counterculture borrowed that which fit and discarded the rest, for Camus had also said that in seeking reform, extremism should be avoided.

References Camus, Albert, *The Plague* (1947) and *The Stranger* (1942); Gitlin, Todd, *The Sixties: Years of Hope, Days of* Rage (1987); Lottman, Herbert R., *Albert Camus: A Biography* (1979).

Carmichael, Stokely (1941–)

As he stood before a crowd in Greenwood, Mississippi, in 1966, Stokely Carmichael, leader of the Student Nonviolent Coordinating Committee (SNCC), expressed the idea that gained him widespread notoriety. "We been sayin' 'freedom' for six years and we ain't got nothin'," he declared.

Stokely Carmichael speaks at a civil rights gathering on 13 April 1970 in Washington, D.C. As a leader of the Student Nonviolent Coordinating Committee from 1966 to 1967, Carmichael shifted the organization from black integration to black liberation with his infamous "Black Power" speech.

"What we gonna start sayin' now is—Black Power!" (Viorst 1979, 374)

Carmichael was born on 29 June 1941 at Port-of-Spain, Trinidad. He attended Tranquillity Boys' School and obtained an education that he later insisted was flawed by its white biases. In 1962, he joined his parents in the United States. They had emigrated a few years earlier from Trinidad to Harlem.

Young Stokely thought that in America there would be equality, but instead he found racism and discrimination. Uprooted and restless, he joined a gang; yet, he had remarkable intelligence and scored well on an exam he took to enter the prestigious Bronx High School of Science. There, he associated with intellectual white kids and read extensively, especially the works of Leon Trotsky and Karl Marx. He joined the Young Socialists and hung out in the plush Park Avenue apartments where his friends lived. He later observed: "I was the good little nigger and everybody was nice to me."

That his friends applied socialist ideas to the problems facing white America but ignored black society disturbed him. Within a short time, he gravitated toward the writings of civil rights leader Bayard Rustin, who merged socialism with African American conditions. In his senior year, Carmichael avidly followed the lunch counter sit-in led by black college students in Greensboro, North Carolina. To him, it represented a new era in the fight for African American freedom. He joined the activist upsurge when he traveled to the nation's capital and helped picket the House Un-American Activities Committee, a zealous congressional body that believed Communists had infiltrated civil rights groups. When Carmichael graduated, he decided to attend predominantly black Howard University in Washington, D.C., a school known for its activism.

There, he joined a campus organization affiliated with SNCC.

Carmichael immersed himself in direct action when, in 1961, he joined the Freedom Rides, a campaign by blacks in the South to ride buses into various terminals and desegregate them. Whites attacked the riders, often beating them unmercifully. The police arrested Carmichael in Jackson, Mississippi, and he was sent to Parchman Prison, notorious for its harsh conditions. At one point, he angered the guards by leading his fellow imprisoned riders in spirited singing.

After his release, Carmichael joined SNCC and engaged in both sit-ins and a voter registration drive. During the 1964 Freedom Summer, he led a campaign to register black voters in the Mississippi Second Congressional District. Again the activists encountered massive white resistance and violent attacks, including beatings and shootings. In this setting, Carmichael, who had long distrusted the nonviolent strategy promoted by Martin Luther King, Jr., said blacks should carry weapons for self-defense.

Carmichael continued his studies at Howard and graduated in 1964 with a bachelor's degree in philosophy. The following year, he supervised a successful SNCC voter registration drive in Lowndes County, Alabama. Carmichael got 2,000 blacks to register where intimidation had previously kept the voting rolls all-white. In addition, he founded the Lowndes County Freedom Organization, an African American party intended to challenge the local Democrats. Although the group did not succeed in getting its candidates elected, it stimulated activism around a new symbol—a black panther. From this came its name, the Black Panther Party. (Other such parties, not linked to Lowndes County, organized later.)

In 1966, Carmichael won election as chairman of SNCC. This organization had pioneered direct action by youths, such as sit-ins. Originally, it embraced King's nonviolent, integrationist ideology, but Carmichael led SNCC in shifting from integration to liberation. In doing so, he represented SNCC's radical urban wing, based in the northern states. He ejected white members from SNCC and considered voter registration important not so much to increase the number of African American voters as to promote courage and pride that he believed would advance the black cause.

When Carmichael made his celebrated black power speech, he propelled the radicals to national attention. Never precise as to what black power meant, he nevertheless used it as an effective rallying cry, implying that African Americans needed to reject white assistance and develop their own institutions, a black nationalism akin to that of separatist Malcolm X. Carmichael said that "every Negro is a potential black man," and wrote: "Black Power . . . is a call for black people in this country to unite, to recognize their heritage, to build a sense of community. . . . It is a call to reject the racist institutions and values of this society." (Farber 1994, 164)

Carmichael made this declaration about the same time he journeyed to Havana, Cuba, where he expressed support for liberation movements against imperialism and observed that blacks in the United States were forming urban guerrilla groups. He adopted Pan-Africanism, expressing his belief that blacks in Africa and America should unite to end their oppression. He soon declared his opposition to the Vietnam War and criticized the Selective Service as "white people sending black people to make war on yellow people in order to defend the land they stole from red people." (Anderson, 1995, 158–159)

Carmichael left the SNCC chairmanship in 1967 and joined a new militant Black Panther Party organizing in Oakland, California. But Carmichael broke with the Black Panthers just months later, after they decided to seek alliances with white radicals. In 1969, he left the United States for Guinea, where he continues to live.

In his efforts, Carmichael challenged the traditional, mainstream civil rights movement and thus represented a countercultural rebellion against existing reform practices within the African American community. His radicalism displayed, too, the deepening countercultural discontent with institutions and leaders who opposed revolutionary change.

See also Black Power; Freedom Summer; Greensboro; Student Nonviolent Coordinating Committee.

References Anderson, Terry H., *The Movement and the Sixties* (1995); Carmichael, Stokely, *Stokely Speaks: Black Power to Pan-Africanism* (1971); Ture, Kwame, and Charles V. Hamilton, *Black Power: The Politics of Liberation in America* (1967); Viorst, Milton, *Fire in the Streets: America in the 1960s* (1979).

Cash, Johnny (1932–)

"Hello, I'm Johnny Cash."

With that statement, Johnny Cash opened all his concerts. Dressed in black and backed by minimal instrumentation, his songs of hardship and real people, tinged with cynicism, bridged musical genres—country, folk, and rock—and earned him a dedicated following within the counterculture.

Cash came from an impoverished southern background. He was born on 26 February 1932 in a three-room railroad shack near Kingland, Arkansas. His father picked cotton and worked on the railroad before getting his own farm in 1935 under a New Deal program. As a boy, Cash helped with the cotton picking, heard his parents sing Baptist hymns, and listened on the radio to Ernest Tubb, Hank Williams, and the Carter Family.

After graduating from high school in 1950, Cash enlisted in the air force and, while stationed in Europe, practiced his guitar. Soon after his discharge, he moved to Memphis, Tennessee, married, and sold appliances. The following year, he and two other musicians formed a trio, Johnny Cash and the Tennessee Two that auditioned for Sam Phillips at Sun Records. Phillips immediately liked Cash's musicianship and deep voice, and the band recorded "Hey Porter," released later that year.

Cash began touring, including opening for Elvis Presley, and in 1956 hit it big with two songs: "Folsom Prison Blues" and "I Walk the Line." This led to a lucrative contract two years later with Columbia Records and, in 1959, his first album release. At the same time, he appeared on many TV shows and grew popular overseas, especially in England.

In the early 1960s, though, his career suffered when he became dependent on tranquilizers. In 1965, he served one night in jail after his arrest at El Paso, Texas, for possession of Dexedrine. While he struggled with his addiction—and eventually conquered it—he made a comeback, experimenting with new sounds that appeared on his hit record *Ring of Fire*, recorded in 1963 with a Mexican brass effect.

In 1968, Cash married June Carter of the Carter Family, famous country performers whom he had listened to as a kid (his first marriage had ended in divorce a year earlier), and traveled to England, where he shattered the attendance record set by the Beatles at London's Palladium. His success came from transcending national boundaries, economic classes, ages, and musical categories, for his records sold well among fans of country, folk, and rock.

Several factors contributed to Cash's popularity with the counterculture: the sincerity in his songs reinforced by his using only a few instruments—usually a guitar, bass, and light drums; his siding with society's outcasts—evident not only in his music but also in the concerts he held for prisoners at Folsom Prison and elsewhere; his back-to-the-land mystique—that coincided with an antiurban attitude among many young people; and the counterculture's own exploration of rock 'n' roll's roots in country—where Cash's songs seemed richly rooted.

Cash strongly supported folk musician Bob Dylan, a favorite with the counterculture, and appeared on his album *Skyline.* In addition, rock musicians such as Roger McGuinn of the Byrds considered Cash among the significant influences on their work.

As the decade came to an end, Cash had yet another hit single, the humorous "A Boy Named Sue," recorded live at San Quentin Prison. His talent assured longevity in the music business, and he continued to record over the next two decades. Many producers in Nashville criticized Cash for not using more strings and other instruments, but he stayed with his minimalist style, the one that allowed him to transcend momentary stardom.

See also Dylan, Bob; Rock Music.

References Cackett, Alan, *The Harmony Illustrated Encyclopedia of Country Music* (1994); Cash, June Carter, *From the Heart* (1987).

Cassady, Neal (1926–1968)

By all accounts Neal Cassady burned with movement, action, energy . . . living the now while possessing a mystical—some said magical—connection to the cosmos. His life as a rebel inspired writers from both the 1950s and 1960s—Jack Kerouac, Allen Ginsberg, Ken Kesey—and his days as a hippie Merry Prankster thrust him into the counterculture.

From the start, Cassady lived unusually. He did not have roots, and this characterized his life as a man on the move. He was born on 8 February 1926 alongside a road in Salt Lake City. His father had, shortly before this, managed a barbershop in Des Moines but was now traveling the West. In the early 1930s, Neal, Sr. relapsed into drinking, and he and his son lived in a flophouse in Denver. The youngster went to school until the eighth grade, and after that only irregularly. While in his teens, Cassady traveled with his father to California, hopping freight trains or hitchhiking. The police arrested him numerous times, and he served several months in jail, but never for anything violent. He liked, for example, to steal cars.

By this time, Cassady's freewheeling behavior had become central to his life, and no more so than sexually. He had an uninhibited drive, losing his virginity at age 12 and using sex to gain favors, such as meals from women.

Cassady's importance to literary America, and his legendary status, began in 1947 when he met Jack Kerouac, a struggling writer. Kerouac marveled at Cassady's openness, his desire to just "go." The hard-jawed, muscled Cassady talked rapidly, bobbed his head about, and sparkled with an intensity geared toward meeting and using women.

Early in 1948, Cassady traveled with Kerouac to New York City and met poet Allen Ginsberg, who quickly fell in love with him. The two had a brief affair, but Cassady, preferring sex with women, headed back to Denver, leaving Ginsberg crestfallen and, for a while, angry.

Cassady inadvertently changed the course of American literature when he sent Kerouac a long, rambling letter in 1951. Kerouac considered the piece masterful and observed that Cassady had written it without revision while under a Benzedrine rush. This gave Kerouac the idea to write *On the Road*, a novel about his adventures with Cassady, Ginsberg, and others, in a similar way—no revision, written quickly, sometimes while doing drugs.

Although not published until 1957, *On the Road* gained widespread readership as a seminal work expressing the ideas and style of the beat generation. In addition, it brought Cassady to prominence as the main character in the story, Dean Moriarty. Kerouac later wrote *Visions of Cody*, which one analyst called a "paean" to Cassady.

Many beats considered Cassady saintly for his selfless attitude. He did, however, have his detractors, repulsed by what they called his irresponsibility, his readiness to sacrifice most anything for staying on the move. Cassady's unconventional behavior resulted in his arrest in 1958 for possession of marijuana, and he served two years at San Quentin.

In 1962, soon after his release, he traveled to Palo Alto, where he met Ken Kesey, the author of *One Flew over the Cuckoo's Nest*. As Cassady's second marriage unraveled in 1963, and Kerouac settled into a rut, he joined Kesey's Merry Pranksters, acid-dropping hippies one historian has called "a wilder, western, electronic, vastly more raucous version of the Beats." (Gitlin 1987, 207) In this way, Cassady moved into the sixties counterculture. In 1964, he drove the Pranksters' psychedelic bus, "Furthur," from California to New York.

The Pranksters looked up to Cassady. He seemed magically in synch with the cosmos—prescient and able to get away with things no one else could, such as his habitual wild drives through San Francisco's streets. He could carry on several conversations at the same time and resume them from the exact spot where, days earlier, they had ended. His friends called Cassady's quick impressionistic talk his rap: "Ten miles an hour, we're in a great four-wheeled drift, loose ya know, everybody in the audience has a right foot, but I can't heel and toe, I'm double left!" (Plummer 1981, 131)

Kesey admired Cassady for living by his wits. The author later observed: "I saw that Cassady did everything a novel does, except he did it better because he was living it and not writing it." (Plummer 1981) The counterculture took its toll on Cassady, though. He could not reconcile his habit to keep moving with the stability he desired and lost when his second marriage collapsed; he felt confined by his Prankster role, and he took more and more speed.

Early in 1968, Cassady left California for San Miguel, Mexico. On 4 February, he told a friend there he planned to walk along the railroad tracks and count the ties. Before doing so, he downed alcohol and the barbiturate Seconal. He was found the next morning along the tracks, comatose, and died a few hours later from overexposure. Legend has it that his last words were "64,928"—the number of railroad ties he had counted.

See also Beat; Ginsberg, Allen; Kerouac, Jack; Kesey, Ken.

References Gitlin, Todd, *The Sixties: Years of Hope, Days of* Rage (1987); Plummer, William, *The Holy Goof: A Biography of Neal Cassady* (1981); Wolfe, Tom, *The Electric Kool-Aid Acid Test* (1968).

Castaneda, Carlos (1925?–)

> "I say it is useless to waste your life on one path, especially if that path has no heart."
>
> "But how do you know when a path has no heart don Juan?"
>
> "Before you embark on it you ask the question 'Does this path have a heart?' If the answer is no, you will know it, and then you must choose another path." (160)

So says Carlos Castaneda in *The Teachings of Don Juan*. This and other Castaneda books won favor with countercultural youths seeking knowledge through mysticism.

Castaneda was born Carlos Cesar Aranha Castaneda in Cajamarca, Peru. Some sources list his birth date as 1925, others as 1931. He immigrated to the United States in 1951 and obtained a doctoral degree from the University of California–Los Angeles in 1970.

While a graduate student, he supposedly met don Juan, an old Indian "brujo," or sorcerer, living in the Southwest. Don Juan decided to convey his teachings to Castaneda, and he, in turn, to a larger audience through his books. *The Teachings of Don Juan: A Yaqui Way of Knowledge* appeared in 1968, presented by Castaneda as a true anthropological study. In it, he reveals don Juan's knowledge, a mystical journey into the mind, or "nonordinary reality," at many points aided by hallucinogenic drugs, namely peyote, jimsonweed, and psilocybin mushrooms.

Although it is debatable whether don Juan ever existed, Castaneda's concern with inner realities attracted countercultural audiences repelled by modern technology and scientific objectivity. Castaneda followed *The Teachings* with *A Separate Reality: Further Conversations with Don Juan* in 1971 and, a year later, *Journey to Ixtlan: The Lessons of Don Juan*, in which he details his own complete break with objective reality. He continued to write in the 1980s and 1990s, and his books attracted many in the New Age movement.

"For me there is only the traveling on paths that have heart, on any path that may have heart," don Juan told Castaneda.

"There I travel, and the only worthwhile challenge is to traverse its full length. And there I travel, looking, looking, breathlessly." (Castaneda 1968, 185)

References Castaneda, Carlos, *Journey to Ixtlan: The Lessons of Don Juan* (1972), *A Separate Reality: Further Conversations with Don Juan* (1971), and *The Teachings of Don Juan: A Yaqui Way of Knowledge* (1968); http://www.earth.com/castaneda/.

Catch-22

Catch-22 appeared first as a novel published in 1961, and then as a movie released in 1970. The novel, written by Joseph Heller, had the greater effect and displayed the higher quality. Set in World War II, Heller's story shows the insanity in military life, how bureaucracy stifles individuality through its rules, oftentimes inane. But, more than this, Heller uses the military as a metaphor for American society:

> There was only one catch and that was Catch-22, which specified that a concern for one's own safety in the face of dangers that were real and immediate was the process of a rational mind. Orr was crazy and he could be grounded. All he had to do was ask: and as soon as he did he would no longer be crazy and would have to fly more missions. Or be crazy to fly more missions and sane if he didn't, but if he was sane he had to fly them. If he flew them he was crazy, didn't have to; but if he didn't want to he was sane and had to. (47)

Heller's theme coincided with the countercultural belief that society had become so impersonal and hypocritical as to be grotesque. His influence can be seen in "catch-22" entering the vocabulary as a phrase indicating a difficult problem whose alternative solutions lacked logical validity and thus could not be attained; or, in other words, an absurd, senseless situation.

The movie *Catch-22*, directed by Mike Nichols, failed to effectively convey Heller's story. Audiences and critics found it long, ponderous, and preachy.

Chavez, Cesar (1927–1993)

Often described narrowly as a union leader, Cesar Chavez actually acted as a moral crusader. His goals: to organize and uplift migrant workers who toiled on farms for pay that permitted only miserable living conditions and to advance Chicano dignity.

Chavez was born on 31 March 1927 near Yuma, Arizona, where his father, Librado, owned a small gorcery store and auto repair shop. Librado lost the business during the Great Depression, and the young boy was forced to work with the rest of his family as a migrant farm laborer, picking fruits and vegetables and living in tar paper and wood cabins. As a result, he attended school only through the seventh grade and did not learn to read and write competently until years later.

While still a youngster, Chavez watched his father join various fledgling farmworkers' unions and participate in strikes, only to meet with failure. For two years, beginning in 1944, young Chavez served in the navy. When World War II ended, he returned to migrant farmwork, laboring in vineyards, cotton fields, and fruit orchards in Arizona and California, while getting married and raising a family.

Then, in 1952, the Community Service Organization (CSO) recruited Chavez to work among Mexican Americans. Begun by Saul Alinsky, a Chicago activist, the CSO sought to organize poor people so they could gain political and economic concessions. Chavez worked first as an unpaid volunteer, and later received a small monthly salary. As a CSO organizer, he led a successful voter registration drive in San Jose, California, and organized chapters in Oakland and various towns throughout the San Joaquin Valley.

Chavez quit the CSO, however, in 1962 over policy differences, and with his own money, a meager amount, founded the National Farm Workers Association (NFWA) as a union for migrant laborers. Organizing proved to be a tough, uphill battle. Chavez had to overcome not only resistance from growers but also from farmworkers demoralized by previous failed efforts.

By 1965, though, he had enrolled 1,700 families in the NFWA, and this provided

Farm labor leader Cesar Chavez leads a picket outside San Diego–area Safeway headquarters in this undated photograph. As a union leader and moral crusader, Chavez successfully led migrant laborers in a strike against grape growers in California that lasted from 1965 to 1969.

enough strength to win pay raises from growers in the area around Delano, California. He began, too, a credit union for the workers, along with a co-op store, newspaper, and insurance club. In fact, Chavez considered his effort more than a unionizing one, and he called it La Causa, or the movement, an attempt to activate and uplift an entire community.

Chavez wanted no more labor battles until he could get better organized, but in September 1965 another union with migrant Filipino workers went on strike over low wages, and he decided the NFWA had to join them. This began a long strike against grape growers in California's San Joaquin, Imperial, and Coachella Valleys.

Chavez pursued tactics similar to those used in the civil rights movement: sit-ins, marches, and support from the clergy. He even obtained help from activists sent in by the Congress of Racial Equality and the Student Nonviolent Coordinating Committee.

As the strike continued, Chavez merged the NFWA with the American Federation of Labor-Congress of Industrial Organizations, thus creating the United Farm Workers Organizing Committee (UFWOC). Although the UFWOC won contracts from 11 major wine grape growers, it failed to make headway against the table grape growers, those who provided the fruit sold in grocery stores and supermarkets.

Chavez thus decided in the spring of 1968 to boycott all table grapes grown in California. About 200 UFWOC members toured the United States and Canada, holding demonstrations to rally consumers and pressuring city governments to join the boycott.

Chavez went on a 25-day hunger strike to gain national attention. Senator Robert

Kennedy (D–New York) rallied to Chavez's cause, telling the labor leader he firmly supported the principles that led him to undertake his fast. In reaction to this strike, the growers labeled Chavez a Communist, recruited strike breakers, and pressured the federal government to allow more Mexican immigrants into the nation so they could be used to work the fields.

By the following year, the boycott had taken its toll. In July, several large growers, who produced half the state's table grapes, signed agreements with the UFWOC. Chavez followed this triumph with a lettuce boycott that also won concessions.

Chavez's efforts, although not exclusively geared to Mexican Americans, intensified Chicano awareness. Throughout the late 1960s, "brown pride" expanded, and in helping Chicanos economically, Chavez furthered this cause. The larger dimensions to his movement appeared when, in the early 1970s, he helped organize a Chicano march to oppose the draft and the Vietnam War, and in 1976 presented the presidential nominating speech for California governor Jerry Brown at the Democratic National Convention.

Chavez continued his work for the UFWOC, by now called the United Farm Workers (UFW), into the 1990s, and in 1992 helped organize a large-scale walkout by farmworkers in the Coachella Valley. In the spring of 1993, he began a fast to gain moral support for his effort to defend the UFW from a lawsuit filed against it by a large grower. He lost considerable strength and died on 23 April. In tribute, labor leader Lane Kirkland said that "the improved lives of millions of farm workers and their families will endure as a testimonial to Cesar and his life's work." (Griswold del Castillo and Garcia 1995, 173). And a colleague, Luis Valdez, stated about Chavez: "You shall never die. The seed of your heart will keep on singing, keep on flowering, for the cause." (174)

See also Brown Berets; Brown Power; Student Nonviolent Coordinating Committee.

References Dunne, John Gregory, *Delano: The Story of the California Grape Strike* (1967); Griswold del Castillo, Richard, and Richard A. Garcia, *Cesar Chavez: A Triumph of Spirit* (1995); Rodriguez, Consuelo, *Cesar Chavez* (1991); http://www.fiestanet.com/~www/8/chavez/index2.htm.

Chicago

See Democratic National Convention of 1968; Old Town.

Chicago Eight

After Richard Nixon became president, he and Attorney General John Mitchell decided to have the justice department prosecute eight leaders involved in the protests at the 1968 Democratic National Convention in Chicago. The media labeled the defendants, all charged with conspiring to riot, the Chicago Eight: Jerry Rubin and Abbie Hoffman of the Yippies; Dave Dellinger, Tom Hayden, and Rennie Davis of the National Mobilization Committee To End the War in Vietnam (MOBE); Bobby Seale of the Black Panthers; and two lesser-known activists who had worked as MOBE protest marshals, John Froines and Lee Weiner.

The sensational trial began in October 1969 and lasted into early 1970. From the start, judge Julius Hoffman, an older conservative stalwart, showed bias in the case—often deriding the defendants' testimony and the Chicago Eight proved uncooperative, sometimes shouting obscenities. At one point in the trial, Seale so strenuously objected to his not being able to serve as his own defense council that Judge Hoffman ordered him chained and gagged in the courtroom. When this led to numerous verbal outbursts by spectators, Hoffman declared a mistrial for Seale and sentenced him to an astonishingly long four and one-half years in prison for contempt of court. Seale's conspiracy trial continued at a later date, leaving the Chicago Eight as the Chicago Seven.

At best, the government had contradictory evidence to support its claim, and the indictments appeared aimed more at cowing protesters and making them seem disreputable than anything else—a move not hard to do, since public opinion polls showed most Americans condemning the demonstrations that had erupted at the Democratic Convention. Further, by forcing a trial, the government tried to keep these eight radical leaders separated from the protest movement and tried to drain their energies and money. In this repressive atmosphere, Vice President Spiro Agnew called the defendants "kooks" and "social misfits."

Outwitting Nixon and the justice department, the Chicago Seven managed to grab national headlines and communicate their ideas to a large audience. They accomplished this mainly by calling as defense witnesses prominent counterculture figures: poet Allen Ginsberg; singers Judy Collins, Phil Ochs, Arlo Guthrie, and Country Joe McDonald; LSD guru Timothy Leary; writer Norman Mailer.

A jury acquitted all the defendants of conspiracy, but Rubin, Hoffman, Dellinger, Hayden, and Davis were found guilty on a lesser count of rioting. They appealed their convictions, and in 1972 a higher court found such extensive bias on Judge Hoffman's part that it threw out the guilty verdicts. Still, the government continued its plan to harass the Chicago Eight and other dissenters, arresting them on flimsy pretexts, as when the police picked up Tom Hayden for resisting arrest; his real crime: sitting under a tree in a park.

See also Democratic National Convention of 1968; National Mobilization Committee To End the War in Vietnam.

Chicago Plaster Casters

Groupies abounded in the sixties, chasing after rock stars—but none equaled the Chicago Plaster Casters, two young women determined to make impressions of male genitals.

According to a writer in the *Realist*, an underground magazine, the Plaster Casters, ages 17 and 21, considered their work "a tribute to and reflection of the sexual revolution, a radical change in morality." They became legendary among the San Francisco bands and casted, as they called it, Jimi Hendrix and Noel Redding. The Plaster Caster technique required getting a man erect ("plating" him) and then carefully applying Vaseline followed by the plaster, which had to be removed before it got too hard. Rock musician Frank Zappa proposed having a Plaster Caster exhibit in an art show, but the collection never got big enough to permit it.

Civil Rights Movement

Ideology, tactics, and commitment—young people learned all three from the civil rights movement, and all three appeared in the counterculture.

In the 1950s, conformity enveloped society as Americans waged a cold war against the Soviet Union and the economy underwent tremendous growth. Fears about communism encouraged people to distrust reformers while the emergence of prosperous suburbs, where every house looked the same, everyone watched identical television shows, and everyone dressed alike, solidified conformist views. At least to most white Americans, the United States appeared to have conquered poverty and eliminated injustice; it was now essential to defend democracy against the Communist menace. Many a young person growing up in the fifties, the same youths who later joined the counterculture, adopted this view, or at least had it pounded into them by parents, schools, politicians, and the mass media.

But the civil rights movement assaulted this self-congratulatory outlook, making it clear that neither poverty nor injustice had been eradicated. The first crack in the facade appeared in 1954 with the bus boycott in Montgomery, Alabama, for it exposed a white commitment to racism in its most institutional form: Jim Crow laws that relegated blacks to an inferior position based on their color.

Other protests followed under Martin Luther King, Jr., who stressed nonviolent tactics whereby the protester encouraged the oppressor to commit violent acts in order to publicize the oppression but did not

Organized by the NAACP, 13 blacks protest the Katz Drug store segregation policy by sitting at the "white only" soda counter on 21 August 1958 in Oklahoma City. A similar demonstration at a Greensboro, North Carolina, lunch counter in 1960 led to the formation of the Student Nonviolent Coordinating Committee, which helped organize student marches, sit-ins, and boycotts.

carry weapons or at any time raise a hand in retaliation. King's strategy involving public marches and economic boycotts chipped away at the Jim Crow mentality and at the same time assulted white assumptions that all Americans enjoyed democracy and plenitude. Clearly, by the late 1950s, white kids who had been born soon after World War II perceived the contradiction between their suburban habitats and the larger reality that society had serious problems.

As these white suburban youths matured and reached high school age, the civil rights movement took another turn, influencing them all the more. This began in 1960 when African American college students staged a sit-in at a segregated lunch counter in Greensboro, North Carolina. In doing so, they took direct action and showed that young people could and would fight social injustice. After this protest, the college students formed the Student Nonviolent Coordinating Committee (SNCC) to organize and motivate people their age and promote direct action.

When, in the early 1960s, SNCC launched drives to register black voters, white college students joined them. Thousands traveled to Alabama, Mississippi, and other southern states where they learned organizing techniques and witnessed firsthand the racism that oppressed blacks. They experienced as well the reluctance of the federal government to support them. When the students returned to their campuses, they brought with them deep-seated dissatisfaction with their government and with the hypocrisies evident in the nation as a whole.

This meant that by 1964 a dramatic shift had occurred in the way some white youths viewed society. As a result of the civil rights movement they no longer saw America as democratic, and they believed that conservatives and liberals alike had created oppression. They no longer saw the economy as fair, but believed instead that an elite few dominated it for their own gain.

Disgust and disillusionment spread through young America, a malignancy eating at traditional values. This malignancy did not breed despair, however; it bred action. White college students did not forget the tactics learned from the civil rights movement, and political activists in the counterculture used them in attempting to cure the nation's ills. Students organized marches, sit-ins, and boycotts, whether fighting for free speech or against the Vietnam War.

Thus, in changing what young white Americans thought of their society and nation, the civil rights movement inadvertently set in motion events that went well beyond its original intentions. Indeed, it gave rise to both the politicized New Left, which wanted to dismantle corporate capitalism, and the hippies, who concluded that society could only be saved through psychedelics and a massive change in how people viewed life.

In addition to affecting whites, the civil rights movement fomented a counterculture among blacks. Increasingly, young African Americans considered King's philosophy and their own earlier tactics too timid and unrewarding. As a result, SNCC renounced nonviolence, and the Black Panthers appeared, replete with rifles and paramilitary training. Culturally, young African Americans declared, "black is beautiful!"

Although many ingredients entered the countercultural brew, the civil rights movement must be counted prominent among them. From it came ideas and tactics that combined with a youthful population, an unpopular war, and other factors to produce one of the most tumultuous periods in American history.

See also Black Panthers; Black Power; Free Speech Movement; Greensboro; New Left; Student Nonviolent Coordinating Committee.

Cleaver, Leroy Eldridge (1935–)

In 1968, Eldridge Cleaver, a leader in the Black Panthers, proclaimed at a rally: "Now all of you! You have to get into the political arena to articulate what's going on here. Power to the people! Pick up the gun. Don't stand in the middle wondering what to do. Be part of the solution!" (Rout 1991, 82)

Cleaver was born on 31 August 1935 in Wabbaseka, near Little Rock, Arkansas, but grew up in Los Angeles, where his father worked for the railroad, and his mother worked as a janitor in a public school. Before deserting the family in 1948, the elder Cleaver often beat Eldridge.

As a youngster, Cleaver got into trouble with the law and spent time in reform schools. After his release in 1952 from the Preston School of Industry, the police arrested him for drug possession, and he served more than two years at Soledad Prison. Racist conditions there, along with the intensifying civil rights movement outside the prison, awakened him to the oppression African Americans faced.

Cleaver received parole in 1957 and, by his own admission, soon began raping white women. Later in the year, he was arrested for assault with intent to kill and sentenced to San Quentin. While incarcerated, he began following the Black Muslims and identified strongly with Malcolm X. Through correspondence, he became acquainted with Beverly Axelrod, a lawyer. She knew the editor at *Ramparts* magazine and convinced him to read some essays Cleaver had written. The editor, in turn, had several prominent writers, including Norman Mailer, Leslie Fiedler, Norman Podhoretz, and Maxwell Geismar, evaluate the essay. They praised Cleaver's writing, and this, along with Axelrod's legal efforts, resulted in his release on parole.

A free man in 1966, Cleaver was shaken by the murder of Malcolm X. Searching for a role model, early in 1967 he developed a friendship with Huey P. Newton. Newton's bravado attracted Cleaver: his willingness to carry a loaded gun and stand up to the police. Cleaver soon called Newton the "ideological descendant, heir, and successor of Malcolm X."

Cleaver joined the Black Panthers, organized by Newton and Bobby Seale, and edited the Panther newspaper while still writing for *Ramparts*. The Panther commitment to black power and militancy, including paramilitary organization, did not put Cleaver in good standing with the authorities, although he made it a point to remain unarmed; nor did his appearance at a rally in San Diego on 15 April 1967, where he denounced the Vietnam War. In fact, this event evoked a sharp warning from his parole officer and convinced Cleaver that dissenters faced a chilling restriction on their freedom of speech.

After Newton was imprisoned in October, and with Seale already in jail, Cleaver emerged as the chief spokesman for the Panthers. He continued to develop his ideas based on several intellectual influences, particularly Robert Williams, a black protester who in the 1950s called on African Americans to meet white violence with an armed counterattack; Frantz Fanon, a black psychiatrist who considered violence to be necessary therapy for oppressed people; and Che Guevara, the Cuban revolutionary who stressed self-sacrifice in fighting imperialism.

In February 1968, Cleaver's *Soul on Ice* was published, a book that pleased radicals, enraged conservatives, and received glowing reviews for its style. The *New York Times* declared *Soul* the book of the year, and it ranked for several weeks as the number one nonfiction book, eventually selling 1 million copies. In this work, a collection of essays, Cleaver rails against an oppressive white society. He declares: "One tactic by which the rulers of America have kept the bemused millions of Negroes in optimum subjugation has been a conscious, systematic emasculation of Negro leadership." And proclaims: "We shall have our manhood. We shall have it or the earth will be leveled by our attempts to gain it."

Cleaver's cynicism toward America's leaders and institutions, past and present, corresponded with the cynicism found in the counterculture at large. Indeed, one essay in *Soul on Ice* praises white youth for their rebellion against an American way of life that Cleaver calls "a fossil of history." (81)

Cleaver faced prison again after a 90-minute gun battle broke out on 6 April 1968 between police and the Panthers. The shoot-out resulted in the death of Bobby Hutton, the Panther treasurer, and the wounding of four men, including Cleaver (who claimed he was unarmed). The Panthers charged that the police had surrounded them and initiated the fight. Whatever the case, the authorities rescinded Cleaver's parole. He remained in jail until 12 June, when a superior court judge released him on bail.

That fall, Cleaver ran for president of the United States as the nominee of the Peace and Freedom Party, which consisted of white and black radicals. He got only 30,000 votes but gained considerable attention for his militant views. Meanwhile, a higher court in California overruled the decision to grant Cleaver bail, and his rearrest appeared imminent. In November, after he exhausted all legal avenues, Cleaver fled the country. Some of his supporters considered his action foolish, one that would isolate him and destroy his political influence, but Cleaver was convinced if he went to jail, he would be murdered.

Carrying $15,000 he had received in royalties, Cleaver arrived in Canada and then took a freighter to Cuba. He expected a warm reception from Fidel Castro's government but got a cold one and quickly grew disenchanted after the Cubans refused to support his plans to organize a Black Panther center in Havana and begin radio broadcasts to the United States.

In July 1969, the Cuban government decided to expel Cleaver, and so it sent him to Algeria. The following year, he made a brief visit to North Korea and established contacts with North Vietnam. Meanwhile, back in the United States, the FBI acted to harass and destroy the Panthers. They encouraged police attacks on Panther members and sent forged letters to Cleaver, supposedly from fellow Panthers, warning him about a move by some within the organization to isolate him. At the same time, an undercover agent worked on Newton, convincing him that Cleaver intended to grab absolute power. (Newton had been released from prison and was once again the Panther leader.)

After the National Guard killed several students at Kent State University in Ohio and the police did the same at Jackson State College in Mississippi, Cleaver wrote that revolution had to be pursued—an immediate, armed insurrection. He claimed: "Pigs are carrying out a genocidal conspiracy of extermination against our people." (Rout 1991, 139–140) This stance, however, conflicted with Newton, who preferred a strategy emphasizing community education and self-help. When the FBI sent Newton a phony letter early in 1971 revealing a supposed plot by Cleaver to kill him, the exile was expelled from the Panther organization.

Meanwhile, Cleaver's financial situation worsened when the U.S. government withheld the royalty checks due him on his writing. In order to earn money, he and the small group around him in Algeria turned to trafficking in counterfeit visas and stolen cars from Europe. After a falling out with the Algerian government in January 1973, Cleaver moved to Paris and gained residency status. He felt isolated, however, with few people in America listening to him and his writing stagnating.

He then underwent a remarkable transformation. First, he talked about the need for the United States to be the strongest nation in the world militarily; then he agreed to return to America, and shortly after doing so, in 1975, announced his religious conversion as a born-again Christian. In 1977, he founded Eldridge Cleaver Crusades in California while, curiously, pushing his new design for men's pants: a zipper replaced by a pouch and tube for the testicles and penis—what he claimed to be the liberation of the male sex organ.

After prolonged legal maneuvering, in 1980 Cleaver was given probation for his earlier offense. His religious ideas continued to change: first he joined the Unification Church of Reverend Sun Myung Moon; then he claimed that God dwelled not in Mecca but in man's sperm; then he joined the Mormons. In 1984, he ran for Congress as an independent conservative against California Democrat Ron Dellums, an African American. After losing that race, in 1986 he entered the Republican Senate primary and called for an end to welfare and abortions, and vigorous enforcement of the death penalty. He again lost and was soon arrested for burglary and possession of cocaine, for which he received three years probation. In the 1990s, he professed allegiance to the Republican Party.

Critics claim that Cleaver never knew anything more than opportunism. In any event, few people listened to him after he fled the United States—his greatest influence came in the 1960s from his outspoken black power advocacy and uncompromising writing.

See also Black Panthers; Black Power; Newton, Huey.

References Cleaver, Eldridge, *Soul on Fire* (1978); *Soul on Ice* (1968), Rout, Kathleen, *Eldridge Cleaver* (1991).

COINTELPRO

In the 1960s, the FBI, under its director J. Edgar Hoover, aimed a powerful counterintelligence program, or COINTELPRO, against dissenters—militants, leftists, peace groups, antiwar activists, women's rights advocates, environmentalists . . . anyone who seemed to challenge what the federal government and Hoover considered to be acceptable behavior. COINTELPRO used surreptitious, violent, and illegal activities to achieve its ends.

The FBI employed 2,000 agents in COINTELPRO. Working undercover, they surveilled and infiltrated groups, often inciting them to criminal acts or sowing dissension within their ranks. COINTELPRO used numerous dirty tricks, such as leaking false information to newspapers (what it called "disinformation"), harassing financial contributors, wiretapping phones, and breaking into homes and offices.

COINTELPRO even encouraged and helped arrange political assassinations, such as those that involved the American Indian Movement and Black Panther Party. Concerning the latter, COINTELPRO agents infiltrated the Chicago Panthers in 1969. They instigated an armed clash between the Panthers and a street gang, the Rangers, and gathered information on Fred Hampton, a highly effective, charismatic Panther leader. In November 1969, COINTELPRO approached the Chicago police with a detailed diagram of Hampton's apartment and proposed a raid on the residence, ostensibly to confiscate illegal weapons but actually to kill Hampton. One police unit rejected the proposal, but another, the Special Prosecutions Unit, agreed.

As Ward Churchill and Jim Vander Wall detail in *Agents of Repression*, early on the morning of 4 December, Chicago police burst into Hampton's apartment. They shot one Panther, Mark Clark, point blank in the chest, killing him, and using submachine guns, sprayed bullets into the bedrooms. They seriously wounded Hampton, asleep in bed. Two agents then inspected him, and finding he was still alive, they fired two bullets point blank into his head. They then dragged his dead body by its wrists to an open doorway.

COINTELPRO helped the Chicago police concoct a story that the officers had fired in self-defense. In actuality, no shots had been fired by the Panthers. Not until years later, in 1983, did a court rule there had been an active governmental conspiracy to deny Hampton and other Panthers their rights. The court awarded $1.85 million to the survivors and families of those who had been killed. The damage, however, had been done, both in terms of lives lost and an organization destroyed, as the Panthers in Chicago collapsed.

Although few Americans in the 1960s knew about COINTELPRO, activists suspected its existence. Government undercover activities, by COINTELPRO, army intelligence, and the CIA, which under orders of President Richard Nixon began an illegal infiltration program called Operation Chaos, only deepened their distrust for the government and seemed to confirm their worst fears that oppression reigned.

See also American Indian Movement; Conus Intel.

References Churchill, Ward, and Jim Vander Wall, *Agents of Repression: The FBI's Secret Wars against the Black Panther Party and the American Indian*

Movement (1988); Donner, Frank J., *The Age of Surveillance: The Aims and Methods of America's Political Intelligence System* (1980).

Columbia University

For eight days in 1968 student demonstrators rocked the Columbia University campus in New York City, occupying buildings and taking a dean hostage before being arrested by police.

Several factors specific to Columbia, a highly selective private college, led to the protest. First, traditional rules still prevailed that allowed students little voice in campus affairs—the system of *in loco parentis* whereby administrators treated students as children, and the college assumed the role of authoritarian parent. Columbia's president, Grayson Kirk, supported this system and opposed any efforts to change it. Second, Columbia had a contract to engage in weapons research for the government through a program called the Institute for Defense Analysis (IDA). Third, for several years the college had been expanding outward from its campus at Morningside Heights into neighboring Harlem, in the process acquiring and leveling buildings that housed blacks and Hispanics. Columbia now had plans to build a gym in Morningside Park, a building that would scar the area, and this ignited strong opposition from Harlemites who believed the university did not respect their neighborhood. Finally, student activism had been increasing, with Students for a Democratic Society (SDS) demonstrating against the Vietnam War and the presence of military recruiters on campus.

Perhaps, then, it should not have come as a surprise when students began supporting Harlemites in a protest against Columbia. In April 1968, Mark Rudd, Columbia's SDS

A professor finds an entrance blocked during a student sit-in at Columbia University in April 1968. During the protest, Students for a Democratic Society and over 1,000 students occupied university buildings and took a dean hostage before being arrested by the police.

president, interrupted a college-sponsored memorial to Martin Luther King, Jr., when he shouted from the pulpit that racism characterized the college's policies. Soon after, six radicals protested Columbia's affiliation with the IDA by demonstrating inside Low Library, where President Kirk had his office.

Then, on 23 April, 500 activists from SDS, the Student Afro-American Society, and from more moderate groups held a rally on campus and marched to the gym construction site, which they occupied. Not stopping with that, they descended upon the administration building, Hamilton Hall, took a dean hostage, commandeered the offices, and renamed the structure Malcolm X Hall.

Other students occupied President Kirk's office and went through his files, discovering papers that revealed details about the IDA. Over the next two days, 1,000 students joined the original protesters, took over additional buildings, and created communes within them—groups dedicated to participatory democracy. On 26 April, one of Columbia's vice-presidents assured the students there would be no police attacks against them, but after negotiations to end the protest collapsed, President Kirk called in the police. On 30 April, they charged into the buildings, billy clubs flailing, leaving students' heads bloodied.

While this action received widespread support from the college trustees and from enraged suburbanites who watched the confrontation on television, it polarized the campus. Angered by the bloodshed, moderate students and many teachers joined the protest, boycotting classes and shutting down nearly the entire university. Columbia failed to resume a normal schedule that semester.

In the end, the protesters gained many concessions: President Kirk resigned, Columbia severed its ties with the IDA and promised not to build the gym without Harlem residents consenting to it, and the administration agreed to end its ban on indoor demonstrations and to allow students a voice in policy making. Although some New Left radicals considered the Columbia uprising a prelude to a greater, nationwide student revolution, few protesters wanted anything more than substantial changes in college policies. Thus, while radicals posted pictures of Che Guevara and Ho Chi Minh at Hamilton Hall, made speeches condemning American imperialism, and overturned some furniture, they fired no bullets, torched no buildings, and won few converts.

See also Dohrn, Bernardine; New Left; Rudd, Mark; Students for a Democratic Society.

References Caute, David, *The Year of the Barricades: A Journey through 1968* (1988); Kahn, Roger, *The Battle for Morningside Heights: Why Students Rebel* (1970); Kunen, James Simon, *The Strawberry Statement: Notes of a College Revolutionary* (1968).

Comix

Filled with cynicism, adult themes, and bizarre artistry, underground comix, an alternative form of comic book, captured the countercultural discontent with mainstream values and attacked them through humor.

The first comix appeared in 1963 when Jaxson (Jack Jackson) drew *God Nose*, but this innovative format did not become widespread until 1967, the year Robert Crumb produced *Zap Comix* and Jay Lynch and Skip Williamson produced *Bijou Funnies*. There soon followed many comix whose unusual names indicated they had something different to offer: *Spiffy Stories, Yellowdog, Moonchild, Fat Lip Funnies, Big Ass*.

Unlike mainstream comic books and the comic strips that appeared in traditional newspapers, comix do not usually present continuing stories, and they have an intense visual orientation, meaning the story line cannot exist apart from the drawings. Many underground cartoonists have experimented with drugs, and this shows in their bizarre renderings, sometimes mystical (an accomplishment made more noteworthy by the black-and-white format used in most comix). Further, comix deal with contemporary subjects and taboo ones, such as religion, death, sex, violence, and drugs; they contain obscene language; and they show human genitalia. They almost always have the label "adults only" on their covers, and some are exclusively sexual, such as Robert Crumb's publication, *Snatch*.

Crumb emerged in the 1960s as, by far, the most renowned and respected underground cartoonist. His drawings appeared in comic books and in underground newspapers, especially the *East Village Other*. Crumb's characters include Mr. Natural, a capitalistic guru; Flakey Foont, a city dweller preoccupied with sex; and Angelfood McSpade, a "child of nature" who stirs the repressed desires white men have for sex with black women. Crumb has been criticized for portraying women one-dimensionally and degrading them (a charge, in fact, leveled against comix in general), yet few doubt his artistic ability. "When *Zap* came out it blew my mind," said cartoonist George Metzger. "Eventually I went and saw Crumb. He's a weird guy but a genius . . . very aware; he draws what he sees—a fine cartoonist." (Estren 1974, 63)

In the sixties, comix circulated in San Francisco, New York, and other major cities. Their social satire poked fun at straight society but did not leave the radicals untouched; they attacked the prevailing belief that every drug is addictive, criticized those who perverted religious ideals or tried to push their religion on everyone else, and expressed disgust with the contradiction between America's self-proclaimed ideals and actual social conditions.

References Crumb, R., *R. Crumb's Head Comix* (1988); Daniels, Les, *Comix: A History of Comic Books in America* (1971); Estren, Mark James, *A History of Underground Comics* (1974).

Committee for a Sane Nuclear Policy

Founded in 1957, the Committee for a Sane Nuclear Policy (SANE) sponsored demonstrations against war and nuclear weapons. At several colleges, SANE attracted support through its student division, organized in 1958, and thus helped to break the campus quiescence dominant in the 1950s. SANE's activities included marches in the fall of 1961 to oppose President John Kennedy's decision to resume nuclear tests; and the following year, in February, SANE helped organize the largest student demonstration to date: a march on Washington that attracted several thousand protesters.

Such activities stirred young America's increasing discontent with Kennedy and traditional liberalism and contributed to the growth of a New Left, more radical than anything SANE wanted. In fact, when protests spread against the Vietnam War in 1964, SANE refused to endorse them, partly because it did not want to see its antinuclear message diluted by other concerns, and partly because it feared any affiliation with leftists that might be interpreted as supporting communism. SANE's conservative position caused it to lose members by 1966, as opposition to the Vietnam War intensified. When SANE refused to endorse the Mobilization, a massive antiwar protest in April 1967, it merely confirmed its decline among those in the counterculture.

See also New Left; Spock, Benjamin.

Commune

In 1970, residents of the Earth/Life Defense Commune in California issued a flyer, describing their vision:

> For us the future is in groups of people who establish more profoundly human relations with each other and their environment / those who return to the land and communal forms of living together / those who abandon ideologies so they can respond to ever-changing nature without preconceived notions . . . the communal decision is the result of our deep yearning to be together, to share our lives with others . . . to come to the country so our bodies can re-discover the feeling of freedom/because we yearn to live and be whole again. ("Only Human")

Thus, counterculture communes, where people shared their interests as an association committed to community, reflected a desire to escape middle-class society and create alternative ways of living.

Although counterculture communes first appeared in the early 1960s, they grew more numerous later in the decade as a back-to-the-earth movement emerged. Their growth coincided with a strong desire by young people to drop out of society—many of whom, disgusted with the Vietnam War, considered political protest fruitless. One communard said, "We are doing this, as much as possible, outside the existing structures, saying, as we progress, a fond farewell to the system, to Harvard, Selective Service, General Motors, Bank of America, IBM, A&P, BBD&O, IRS, CBS, DDT, USA, and Vietnam." (Anderson 1995, 270)

Visionaries joined communes, as did artists, ecologists, academicians, vegetarians, and Vietnam veterans. Largely in their twenties, with at least some college education and from the middle class, communards sometimes took over abandoned towns and formed new ones. In most instances, they began their communes with a few buildings located on several acres of land, in areas where farms or wide open spaces could be found: northern California, Colorado, New Mexico, Tennessee, Vermont. So many communes appeared that an underground directory began circulating. The Center for Communal Studies at the University of Southern Indiana claims that the number of communes in the late 1960s and early 1970s ranged from 10,000 to 100,000.

These communes exhibited many different social practices, all experimenting with liberation. Some developed around free love with group sex and bisexuality, others stressed monogamous relationships; some called themselves religious, others secular political, such as the Green Mountain Red Commune in Vermont, supportive of the black power movement and women's liberation; some followed anarchistic arrangements, others developed highly structured daily schedules. Overwhelmingly, they considered drugs, especially marijuana, an integral part of their communities, although some enforced antidrug rules.

In addition to those in rural areas, numerous urban communes emerged, where hippies gathered together in apartments or houses. These developed in cities with hip communities: San Francisco; Chicago; New York; Minneapolis; Austin, Texas; Boulder, Colorado; Eugene, Oregon; Lawrence, Kansas.

For all communes, economic survival posed a big challenge. Communards grew crops and engaged in bartering, raised livestock, or sold handicrafts to local stores. The Farm, a commune near Summertown, Tennessee, established a publishing and construction company, and a commune in Mendocino, California, linked itself to a rock band, the Grateful Dead.

Communes encountered another problem: whether to receive newcomers. A closed commune risked suffocation by isolating itself from fresh ideas; an open one risked being overwhelmed by persons not dedicated to its principles or mission. Freeloading, in fact, became a problem, and many communes erected fences and gates, and a few even posted guards.

All in all, residents found communal life difficult: hard work, disease, squabbles with fellow communards. Claimed one former resident: "I think people got tired of arranging things with people [they] didn't have a long-term commitment with." (Pollak 1995, D1) Another disagreed, however, insisting: "The division of labor gave you more free time to do things that you valued. People put in what they could afford." (ibid.) And Bob Courboin, the leader of an urban commune in Madison, New Jersey, said: "I look forward to the day when the whole world will be like this." (Buckley 1968, 41)

Communes varied in longevity, lasting anywhere from a few weeks to a few years, with a handful continuing into the 1990s. Many communards, though, measured success not by durability but in having experimented, and in doing so, having emerged the better for it. "Keeping low and close to the ground—like Indian or coyote—beginning again in the wilderness of Amerika [*sic*]," said the Earth/Life Defense communards, "we are re-discovered by stars—lost members of the cosmic community—surrounded on every side by friends and lovers!"

See also Hippies.

References Atcheson, Richard, *The Bearded Lady: Going on the Commune Trip and Beyond* (1971); Buckley, Tom, "Young Rebels Set Up Own Community in Jersey," *New York Times*, 26 August 1968, 41; Gardener, Hugh, *The Children of Prosperity: Thirteen Modern American Communes* (1978); Melville, Keith, *Communes in the Counterculture: Origins, Theories, Styles of Life* (1972); "Only Human," http://www.webcom.com/~enoble/diggers/elife.html; Pollak, Sally, "When Communes Were Common," *Burlington Free Press*, 13 August 1995, D1.

Communication Company

San Francisco's Haight-Ashbury district produced numerous hippie alternatives in the 1960s, among them the Communication Company, or com/co, begun in January 1967 by Chester Anderson and Claude Hayward. Anderson originated the idea for com/co. He wanted an instantaneous newspaper that could react to the rapid developments then happening in the Haight. Anderson considered the existing hippie newspaper, the *Oracle*, too predictable in terms of format and wanted com/co to publish literature written by Haight hippies; and he agreed to print flyers, for free, that the Diggers—a radical hippie group—planned to write.

Anderson and Hayward acquired a silkscreen stencil duplicator, an electronic stencil cutter, and a typewriter and went to work. In an early publication they derided Timothy Leary for his publicity-seeking antics. As the Summer of Love approached in 1967 and hordes of tourists and teenagers descended on the Haight, com/co urged calm. When the police sealed off Haight Street, com/co responded immediately with a flyer: "Stop, think peace, don't play their game."

Com/co did more than publish; as it grew in size, its members picketed events they thought overpriced or of poor quality, and Anderson did not hesitate to criticize the Haight—for example, often adding comments to Digger material calling readers' attention to its foolishness and producing a satire of the *Oracle* titled *The Electric Garden of Eden's Orifice*. Anderson disliked the chaos wrought by the Summer of Love and stunned many hippies by publishing a frank depiction of the Haight's deterioration:

> Pretty little sixteen-year-old middle-class chick comes to the Haight to see what it's all about and gets picked up by a seventeen-year-old street dealer who spends all day shooting her full of speed and again, then feeds her 3000 mikes [micrograms of LSD, 12 times the standard dose] and raffles off her temporarily unemployed body for the biggest Haight gang bang since the night before last.
>
> The politics & ethics of ecstasy. Rape is as common as bullshit on Haight Street. ("Uncle Tim'$ Children")

Anderson had a falling out with com/co during the Summer of Love, complaining the Diggers had taken over, and that it did not print enough artistic material. By this time, too, com/co had become a publishing arm for the Black Panther Party. The following year, com/co dissolved amid internal division and the general collapse of the Haight as a hippie community.

See also Diggers; *San Francisco Oracle*.

Reference "Uncle Tim'$ Children," http://www.webcom.com/~enoble/diggers/ccpaps2b.html.

Conus Intel

President Lyndon Johnson began Conus Intel, formally Continental U.S. Intelligence, as a top-secret program to spy on the American public. His successor, Richard Nixon, greatly expanded it. Conus Intel involved using about 1,000 U.S. Army agents to gather background information on civilians and put it on file. By the early 1970s, the military had dossiers on 25 million Americans. This activity, when revealed by the *New York Times* and congressional investigations, confirmed countercultural suspicions that a powerful government threatened democracy.

See also COINTELPRO.

Cool

Cool had several meanings. To keep one's cool meant to remain calm or tranquil.

Cool could also mean something pleasant or satisfying, as a "cool sound." The word had another meaning that emerged among bohemians in the late 1940s: being knowledgeable and hip to the alternative subculture, which in the 1960s meant being hip to the hippies or other aspects of the counterculture. To be cool in the sixties meant adopting the appearances and practices found in the counterculture, such as smoking pot, wearing long hair, and listening to certain rock bands.

Country Joe and the Fish

With roots in folk music, Joe McDonald organized Country Joe and the Fish to play political protest songs. In 1966, the band, based in Berkeley, California, and gaining popularity on the San Francisco countercultural scene, signed a recording contract with Vanguard Records.

Although Country Joe and the Fish never achieved tremendous commercial success with their albums, antiwar protesters treated their best-known song, "I-Feel-Like I'm Fixin' To Die Rag," as an anthem, and the band made a notable appearance at Woodstock in 1969 where they played the song and led the huge crowd in a "Gimme an F" cheer—400,000 voices spelling out an obscenity about the Vietnam War.

See also Rock Music.

Crash Pad

Young people in the 1960s often provided "crash pads" for friends seeking a place to sleep for a night or during an emergency. These crash pads—beds, mattresses, and blankets strewn about—served as places from which to escape parents and as safe havens to recover from drug trips.

Cream

The band Cream broke new ground by achieving commercial success before having a hit single. This obviously owed to their talent—an ability to fuse blues with rock that set them well above more pedestrian groups. All three members of Cream—Jack Bruce, Ginger Baker, and Eric Clapton—had experience in the British rhythm and blues movement.

Cream was formed in 1966 after Clapton, then playing guitar with the Bluesbreakers, met drummer Baker. They recruited Bruce for the new band, and over the next two years their LPs *Fresh Cream*, *Disraeli Gears*, and *Wheels* sold in the millions. Cream inspired other musicians to adopt blues techniques and paved the way for a new rock form, heavy metal.

Ego clashes and the desire to follow independent creative courses, though, made Cream short-lived. Late in 1968, they staged a farewell tour and after that broke up. The former members pursued successful solo careers, with Clapton in particular remaining popular into the 1990s.

See also Rock Music.

Reference Ward, Ed, Geoffrey Stokes, and Ken Tucker, *Rock of Ages: The Rolling Stone History of Rock & Roll* (1986).

Credence Clearwater Revival

Among the most dominant bands of the sixties, Credence Clearwater Revival combined country, blues, and rock with a tinge of bayou. This San Francisco–based band originated in 1959 as the Blue Velvets with John Fogerty on guitar, Doug Clifford on drums, and Stuart Cook on bass guitar and piano. A short time later, John Fogerty's brother, Tom Fogerty, joined them on guitar. Rooted in fifties rock, the blues, and country music, they struggled for years without success. In 1964, they changed their name to the Golliwogs and emulated the British sound, but still to no avail.

In 1967, however, the band again changed its name, this time to Credence Clearwater Revival (CCR), and decided to focus on John Fogerty's music. After modest success with a cover song, "Suzie Q," CCR scored a big hit with Fogerty's "Proud Mary." From there, popular albums and singles continued into 1970, as CCR presented a unique sound different

from the psychedelic music then played by most San Francisco bands. CCR disbanded in 1972, and its former members achieved little success in their solo pursuits until two albums by John Fogerty reached the top ten in the mid-1980s, *Centerfield* and *Eye of the Zombie*.
See also Rock Music.

Crystal
"Crystal" meant methedrine, a nerve-agitating stimulant that speeds up thought processes to the point that the brain receives images faster than it can handle them. Methedrine circulated among hippies, was manufactured in garage labs, and was sometimes mixed in with LSD.

D

Dashiki

A loose, brightly colored African tunic, the dashiki found favor with young African American men. They wore them to express their heritage and their pride in black culture at a time when the black power movement and expressions such as "black is beautiful" held appeal. Young whites sometimes wore dashikis to show their affinity for black culture and their sympathy with African American protest movements.

See also Black Is Beautiful; Black Power.

Davis, Angela (1944–)

As Angela Davis sat in a New York City prison shortly before Christmas Day 1970, she heard chants coming from outside, muffled by the thick concrete walls: "Free our sisters, free ourselves! Free Angela!" They filled her with excitement, with the possibility that the masses had heard her message, that they could be radicalized and tear down the oppressive social and political structure. A committed revolutionary, she wanted nothing less than a Communist future for America.

Davis was born on 26 January 1944 in Birmingham, Alabama. Unlike most African Americans in that heavily segregated city, she did not live in poverty. Her mother taught elementary school, and her father owned and operated a service station. Although as an infant she lived in the projects, at age four her family moved into a comfortable house on Center Street.

Despite Davis's economic situation, racism stung her. As a child, she heard a huge explosion when whites blew up a neighbor's house to protest the intrusion of African Americans into previously white areas. In subsequent years, she saw this vicious act repeated over and over again, and amid the racist atmosphere developed a deep dislike for segregation and envied the freedom whites enjoyed.

Racist Birmingham relegated her and the other African Americans in her neighborhood to Carrie A. Tuggle Elementary School, an all-black facility in complete disrepair. Her contact there with poor children caused her to realize the economic plight that other families faced.

The teachers told her and the other students to work hard and get ahead, but warned them that getting ahead would be more difficult for them than for the white kids. They taught her that the segregationist system would be permanent, and this she was not willing to accept. In middle school, her history books referred to the Civil War as the War for Southern Independence and portrayed blacks as preferring slavery. Such racist interpretations contributed to her discontent with the prevailing system.

She excelled in her studies, however, and through the American Friends Service Committee attended Elizabeth Irwin High School in New York City. There she heard teachers express socialist ideas. She read the *Communist Manifesto* and it enthralled her, and she attended meetings of Advance, a Marxist-Leninist youth organization.

In 1961, Davis received a full scholarship and enrolled at Brandeis University in Massachusetts. In her senior year, she veered from her concentration on literature and began studying philosophy under the renowned Marxist, Herbert Marcuse. She went to Germany in 1965 to pursue graduate studies in this field at Frankfurt. At the same time, her political activism stirred, and she joined demonstrations outside the U.S. Embassy in opposition to the Vietnam War.

In 1967, Davis continued her studies under Marcuse, who had relocated to the University of California at San Diego. That same year, she joined the Black Panther Party (BPP). With its headquarters in Los Angeles, the BPP operated independently from the Black Panthers in Oakland. She had become a revolutionary and later said: "For me revolution was never a 'thing-to-do' before settling down; it was no fashionable club . . . made thrilling by risk and confrontation, made glamorous by costume. Revolution is a serious thing, the most serious thing about a revolutionary's life. When one commits oneself to the struggle, it must be for a lifetime." (Davis 1974, 162)

In 1968, the BPP merged with the Student Nonviolent Coordinating Committee (SNCC) to form LA-SNCC. Davis traversed the black neighborhoods in Los Angeles, trying to build a mass movement while continuing work on her doctorate in San Diego. By the spring, she had formed a youth corps and a Liberation School, which she directed. Then the *Los Angeles Times* reported that LA-SNCC included a prominent member of the Communist Party, and the national SNCC decided to purge the local organization's leadership. Davis subsequently resigned from SNCC and joined the Communist Party, attracted to its "serious revolutionary" position.

Shortly after this, she joined the Oakland-based Black Panthers as well, but differences over policy soon caused her to leave that group. Davis traveled to Cuba in 1969, where on a farm she helped hoe the weeds around coffee plants and harvest sugarcane. The Cuban Revolution greatly impressed

Angela Davis, right, with American Indian Movement leader Clyde Bellecourt, center, and Rev. Ben Chavis, left, announces the formation of the National Alliance Against Racist and Political Repression, a Communist-affiliated group, at a Chicago news conference on 11 May 1973.

her and encouraged her revolutionary commitment.

When she returned to San Diego, the university hired her to teach philosophy, but after Governor Ronald Reagan and the board of trustees learned she was a member of the Communist Party, they fired her. Months later, the courts ruled unconstitutional the California law that barred Communists from teaching in state universities.

By this time, another adventure unfolded: in 1970, Davis organized a campaign to help George Jackson and two other men imprisoned at Soledad. This bleak fortress, bearing the Spanish name for solitude, had recently experienced considerable turmoil when Jackson led his fellow inmates in condemning the racism found there. Their protest led to a riot, the death of a guard, and charges against Jackson and his followers. Davis believed Jackson innocent, the victim of a government effort to punish him for his outspoken position.

Then, in August, Jonathan Jackson, George's brother, led a radical group in raiding a courthouse during a trial. They captured a judge, district attorney, and several jurors, whom they held as hostages. Jonathan intended to exchange them for George, and thus get his brother out of jail. The plan backfired when police attacked the assailants and a hail of gunfire resulted in several deaths, including Jonathan and the judge. Unfortunately for Davis, Jonathan's .380 automatic was registered in her name. The authorities considered her an accomplice and tried to arrest her. Davis went into hiding and eluded capture, but later in the year the FBI discovered her in New York City.

After several weeks' imprisonment, she was extradited to California, where she stood trial on charges of murder, conspiracy, and kidnapping. Throughout her confinement, she received strong support from both African American and white radicals, and even moderate observers considered the charges against her weak and perhaps part of a plan to persecute her. In 1972, after a three-month trial, a jury acquitted her.

Davis then toured the Soviet Union, East Germany, Bulgaria, Czechoslovakia, and Cuba, where warm receptions awaited. A few weeks later, she returned to the United States and formed the National Alliance Against Racist and Political Repression, a Communist-affiliated group that, she claimed, had chapters in 21 states and a diverse but small membership of African Americans, Chicanos, Puerto Ricans, Asians, and Indians.

In 1974, Davis wrote her autobiography and in the 1990s remains committed to radical social and political change, as evident in her writing and many speaking engagements. Her position in the 1960s had coincided with the counterculture's most extreme leftists.

See also Black Panthers; Black Power; Marcuse, Herbert.

Reference Davis, Angela, *Angela Davis: An Autobiography* (1974).

Davis, Miles (1926–1991)

Hailed by many as the twentieth century's greatest jazz musician, Miles Davis had an enormous influence on rock 'n' roll.

Davis was born on 25 May 1926 in Alton, Illinois, and as a young man began playing with jazz musicians in St. Louis. His father, a middle-class African American, sent him to the Julliard School in New York City, but the neophyte musician soon dropped out to pursue jazz.

Before long, Davis earned a reputation for the distinctive tone he imparted to his trumpet playing. After a bout with heroin addiction in the early 1950s, in 1955 he organized the Miles Davis Quintet, a group that explored improvisational techniques. In the sixties, Davis formed another quintet, and in 1968 combined jazz with rock on his album *Miles in the Sky*. There soon followed *Bitches Brew*, a two-LP set that featured Miles and what he called "the best damn rock and roll band in the entire world" jamming unrehearsed. For many rock musicians, Davis's fusion of their craft with jazz encouraged them to explore similar combinations.

Davis played to packed crowds in large venues during the late sixties and early seventies. After a car accident left him seriously injured, he returned to live performances in the 1980s, again selling out concerts in the United States and overseas. In 1990, he received the Grammy Award for Lifetime Achievement. He died on 28 September 1991 in Santa Monica, California.

Davis, Rennie (1941–)

A radical protester and one of the infamous Chicago Eight, Rennie Davis equated the struggle of America's New Left with Vietnam's National Liberation Front: a crusade to defeat imperialism and capitalism.

Davis was born on 23 May 1941 in Lansing, Michigan. His father, an economist, served as an advisor to President Harry Truman, and young Rennie grew up in metropolitan Washington and on a 500-acre farm in Virginia's Blue Ridge Mountains. He excelled academically in high school and played basketball. During his senior year, he took a trip to New York City that affected him greatly: seeing Harlem and the destitute in the Bowery opened his eyes to poverty and racism.

As a result, Davis decided to attend a liberal arts college, and in 1958 enrolled at Oberlin in Ohio. There he founded the Progressive Student League, a left-wing discussion group. In 1960, the sit-ins then under way at Greensboro, North Carolina, as a new phase of the civil rights movement, galvanized him. He watched them on television and committed himself to fight for social justice. He later said: "From 1960 onward, I considered myself a full-time activist in what was then called the 'student movement,' and later just the 'movement.'" (Viorst 1979, 177)

In 1961, Davis joined the recently formed Students for a Democratic Society (SDS), a New Left organization. Meanwhile, he continued his college studies, receiving his B.A. from Oberlin in 1962, and an M.A. from the University of Illinois the following year, before taking additional courses at the University of Michigan and University of Chicago.

Davis joined SDS's national council in 1963, and in 1964 directed the Economic Research and Action Project (ERAP) in Ann Arbor, Michigan, a program SDS started to help poor people in urban areas. Davis traveled with several other SDSers to Czechoslovakia in 1967 on a mission to meet with representatives from the Vietnamese National Liberation Front. From there he traveled to Hanoi. He said that while in North Vietnam he was impressed by "the magnitude of the war and the incredible human struggle. . . ." (Gitlin 1987, 272)

After this trip, he plunged into the antiwar movement, and in February 1968 he and activist Tom Hayden opened an office of the National Mobilization Committee To End the War in Vietnam (MOBE) in Chicago. From his position with MOBE, Davis began planning a massive protest to be held at the Democratic National Convention, scheduled for August in that city. Many in SDS objected to the plan—they feared violent clashes and worried that Davis intended such a confrontation. Indeed, although Davis insisted he wanted militant nonviolence, as plans for the convention proceeded he seemed to vacillate, and the many groups involved used divergent tactics.

As it turned out, violence did erupt from actions by both demonstrators and police. At one point, as the situation deteriorated, Davis urged protesters in Grant Park to remain calm, but cops assaulted the crowd and in the attack bloodied Davis by smashing his head with a billy club.

Unbowed, Davis organized a counter-inaugural for January 1969 in Washington, D.C., to be held opposite the presidential inauguration of Richard Nixon. More than 10,000 dissidents protested. This demonstration also deteriorated into violence when a mob rampaged through downtown Washington.

Later that year, Davis and seven other leaders of the protest at the Democratic

National Convention, a group known as the Chicago Eight, stood trial on charges of conspiring to incite a riot. Davis was found guilty of rioting (the conspiracy charge did not stick), but on appeal a higher court in 1972 overturned the verdict. That same year, Davis ended his political activities and adopted Eastern mysticism. In the 1970s, he joined the Divine Light Mission in Denver and sold life insurance. He has since become a national lecturer on meditation and self-awareness.

See also Democratic National Convention of 1968; ERAP; Hayden, Tom; National Mobilization Committee To End the War in Vietnam; Students for a Democratic Society.

References Gitlin, Todd, *The Sixties: Years of Hope, Days of Rage* (1987); Sale, Kirkpatrick, *SDS* (1973); Viorst, Milton, *Fire in the Streets: America in the 1960s* (1979).

Day-Glo

Day-Glo is a trademark referring to fluorescent coloring agents and materials. The counterculture adopted Day-Glo, primarily paints, as a means to break with the prevailing drab, conformist colors. Hippies liked Day-Glo because it replicated the vivid, swirling colors seen during certain drug trips. Day-Glo became so pervasive that the *New York Times* referred to the sixties as the "Day-Glo decade."

Days of Rage

In October 1969, a group called Weatherman rampaged along Chicago's streets, smashing windows and attacking police in an attempt to show revolutionary bravery and rally working-class students to its side. Weatherman called its outburst National Action, but newspapers called it Days of Rage.

Just a few months before, Weatherman, a radical faction, had taken control of Students for a Democratic Society (SDS), a prominent New Left organization. Where SDS had been loosely structured, Weatherman would be tight; where SDS had espoused diverse leftist ideologies, Weatherman would embrace Marxism; where SDS had primarily used peaceful protest, Weatherman would use violence. Weatherman believed imperialism and racism could be defeated only through militant struggle, and its members concluded that Chicago—site of the 1968 Democratic National Convention and the place where the trial of radicals associated with trying to disrupt the convention was about to begin—must be assaulted. The Chicago National Action, they believed, would ignite a nationwide revolution.

Thus Weatherman announced: "The action will start on Wednesday night, October 8, with a memorial rally for Che Guevara, who was murdered by the CIA pigs October 8, 1967, and Nguyen Van Troi, the Vietnamese hero murdered by the US October 15, 1964 for attempting to kill [secretary of defense] MacNamara [*sic*]." Weatherman thought National Action would attract working-class young people by the thousands, but it did not. In fact, only 600 radicals gathered to "ignite" the revolution.

Despite this, Weatherman acted. On day one, 8 October 1969, about 300 Weathermen marched from Lincoln Park—helmets fixed atop heads, clubs and chains in hand—and smashed the windows of businesses and cars. The police retaliated, hitting 6 Weathermen with buckshot and arresting 68 of them. Although not armed with guns, the Weathermen gave what they got, bloodying several cops, and Chicago's newspapers screamed headlines about the leftist rage under way.

On day two, a women's militia led by Bernardine Dohrn tried to attack and destroy an armed forces induction center. Only 70 women participated, however, and the police kept them from doing any damage, while arresting Dohrn and 11 others. Finally, on day three, Weatherman gathered at noon at Haymarket Square. Before they could get their rally started, police attacked several leaders with clubs, and a fight ensued, as did more arrests. After the melee, some 300 Weathermen peacefully paraded from the park, a planned activity for which they had a permit, but they soon broke through police lines and again smashed store windows.

One Weatherman proclaimed the Days of Rage a success—from a tactical standpoint, she said, 57 "pigs" had been hospitalized and extensive property damage inflicted; further, Weatherman had proved itself a fighting force and developed a committed cadre. Most other observers, even those within the New Left, disagreed with this. To them, Days of Rage had exposed Weatherman's limited support and fanned a conservative backlash against radical reforms. Several years later, James Mellen, a former Weatherman, said about Days of Rage: "We were hoping to find fifteen or twenty thousand people when we got [to Chicago]. What happened was that a lot of people rooted us on, and then didn't come themselves. We didn't have any working-class kids. We had ourselves, the Weatherman cadres, and almost nobody else. We didn't have a thousand people there. We failed abysmally." (Viorst 1979, 497)

See also Dohrn, Bernardine; Mellen, James; New Left; Rudd, Mark; Weather Underground.

References Jacobs, Harold, ed., *Weatherman* (1970); Sale, Kirkpatrick, *SDS* (1973); Viorst, Milton, *Fire in the Streets: America in the 1960s* (1979).

Dellinger, David (1915–)

An older political activist, David Dellinger took his previous experience with radical causes into the New Left where he gained prominence as chairman of the National Mobilization Committee To End the War in Vietnam (MOBE).

Dellinger was born 12 August 1915 into a leading family in Wakefield, Massachusetts. His father, Raymond Pennington Dellinger, was a Yale graduate and Boston lawyer. David also attended Yale, graduating from there *magna cum laude* in 1936. He studied at Oxford the following year, at Yale Divinity School from 1938 to 1939, and at the Union Theological Seminary in New York City from 1939 to 1940. Although an assistant minister when the United States entered World War II, and thus entitled to a deferment, Dellinger adhered to his strong pacifist principles and refused to register for the draft. As a result, he served three years in prison.

Dellinger adopted a Communist ideology—a "pure" one founded on true community, and not the kind practiced by the Soviet Union. In fact, as much as he disliked capitalism, he opposed the Soviets, insisting that Russia had "poisoned the left wing movement with dishonesty, opportunism, and violence." (Farber 1994, 61)

In 1948, Dellinger merged the Committee for Non-Violent Revolution, a leftist pacifist group that he led, with the Peacemakers, an organization dedicated to participatory democracy and civil disobedience to fight injustice. In 1956, he helped found a journal dedicated to radical leftist ideas, *Liberation*. At the same time, he journeyed to the South where he participated in numerous civil rights protests.

Dellinger opposed the Vietnam War as he did all wars, and in the mid-1960s began speaking at teach-ins on college campuses. In 1965, he called for the "immediate unconditional withdrawal" of American troops from Vietnam. The following year, he traveled to North Vietnam, in his first of several trips there, and back home, co-chaired the Spring Mobilization To End the War in Vietnam, which sponsored large demonstrations in 1967. One in New York City attracted 400,000 protesters, and 75,000 turned out in San Francisco.

In October 1967, during a march on the Pentagon, Dellinger, by this time an important leader within the New Left, discussed with activist Rennie Davis the possibility of staging a protest the following August in Chicago to coincide with the Democratic National Convention. Dellinger now chaired the mobilization group, recently renamed the National Mobilization Committee To End the War in Vietnam, or MOBE, and he and Davis, along with Tom Hayden, worked through this organization to plan for Chicago.

As August approached, Dellinger feared that Davis and Hayden intended violence in Chicago, and so he got them to pledge their commitment to a peaceful protest. Although militant himself in wanting to disrupt the war machine, Dellinger deplored bloodshed.

Despite these pledges, several developments indicated that peace would be impossible to maintain at Chicago. For one, MOBE was not a highly unified organization but a loose confederacy of political and antiwar groups, and some activists associated with these, and some completely outside the MOBE effort, wanted violence. For another, Chicago's political leader, Mayor Richard Daley, refused to allow any permits for demonstrations, making it clear he desired confrontation.

Violence began at the beginning of the Democratic National Convention, on 23 August, and continued throughout the conclave. At one point, Dellinger tried to calm a crowd at Grant Park by organizing it to march on the Amphitheater, where the Convention delegates were meeting, but bedlam and police opposition made a peaceful demonstration impossible. Dellinger later said: "We thought if we could hold the MOBE together, we could minimize the damage." (Gitlin 1987, 324)

A few months after Chicago, the federal government indicted Dellinger and seven others—whom the press called the Chicago Eight—for having conspired to riot. At his trial in 1969, Dellinger told the judge:

> You wanted us to be like good Germans supporting the evils of our decade and then when we refused to be good Germans and came to Chicago and demonstrated, now you want us to be like good Jews, going quietly and politely to the concentration camps while you and the court suppress freedom and the truth. (Dellinger 1993, 4)

In the end, a jury convicted him of rioting, although the conspiracy charge did not stick. Three years later, a higher court overturned the conviction. After the 1960s, Dellinger continued his commitment to pacifist and leftist causes, including in the mid-1980s when he led demonstrations protesting U.S. military intervention in Central America, and in 1992 when, in an attempt to secure "justice and peace in the Americas," he participated in a 42-day fast.

See also Davis, Rennie; Democratic National Convention of 1968; Hayden, Tom; National Mobilization Committee To End the War in Vietnam; New Left.

References Dellinger, David, *From Yale to Jail: The Life Story of a Moral Dissenter* (1993); Farber, David, ed., *The Sixties: From Memory to History* (1994); Gitlin, Todd, *The Sixties: Years of Hope, Days of Rage* (1987).

Democratic National Convention of 1968

"Confront the Warmakers!" declared a flyer released in 1968 by the National Mobilization Committee To End the War in Vietnam (MOBE)—and thousands responded. They converged on the Democratic National Convention in Chicago, intent on protesting the war and challenging the power structure. As a result, mayhem and bloodshed filled the city, and television broadcast a nation in disarray, in crisis, divided.

The idea to protest at the Democratic National Convention came from two different sources, often at odds with each other. Radical political activists provided one source. They met in January 1968 in New York City to plan a protest. This group included Rennie Davis, David Dellinger, Tom Hayden, several organizers from Chicago, and members of the liberal National Lawyers Guild, among them Bernardine Dohrn. Significant division, though, surfaced at this and other meetings of what became known as MOBE: the activists not only disagreed over tactics but also over whether to protest, for some feared that violence would erupt and give the antiwar movement a bad name.

On top of this, Dellinger distrusted Davis and Hayden, fearing they intended to promote a violent confrontation; and the largest New Left organization, Students for a Democratic Society, never liked the idea and never officially endorsed it (although numerous SDSers met with MOBE and eventually participated in the protest). Further, black radicals, such as the

Black Panthers, rejected the protest because they instead wanted to expose racist oppression. Yet MOBE carried on, and Davis and Hayden, given key organizing roles, fell in line with Dellinger and insisted that any protest should avoid violence and disruption, or else risk driving people away.

A second source for the protest emerged at the end of 1967 when Abbie Hoffman, his wife Anita, Jerry Rubin, Nancy Kurshan, and Paul Krassner gathered at the Hoffman apartment in New York City. They started talking about staging a festival at the Democratic National Convention, one that would include a free concert by rock bands and get extensive media coverage for Hoffman's street theatre: outrageous actions to expose straight society's absurdities. They wanted an irrational Festival of Life to confront what they called the Democratic war party, or the Convention of Death. As they discussed the possibilities, Krassner cried out "Yippie!," and they applied this name to their new organization.

The Yippies did not have a working relationship with MOBE, for they considered the group too politically dogmatic. For its part, MOBE criticized the Yippies as irresponsible and worried they would detract from the more serious antiwar protest.

As the August date for the Democratic National Convention approached, several developments indicated the protest might turn violent. In April, Chicago police launched an unprovoked attack on 6,000 antiwar marchers, clubbing them; an assassin killed Martin Luther King, Jr., worsening racial and political tensions; and in New York City student demonstrators took over several buildings at Columbia University, a move that indicated a turn by radicals toward militancy, confrontation, and violence. Then in June, Democratic presidential candidate Robert Kennedy fell to an assassin's bullet. Later in the summer, Richard Daley, mayor of Chicago, let it be known he would not tolerate the protesters. He did this through speeches and, even more tellingly, by refusing requests from MOBE and the Yippies for permits to march.

These developments set the nation on edge and caused many potential protesters to back away. They sensed a bad atmosphere. MOBE no longer hoped for 100,000 demonstrators; instead, it aimed for a few thousand, and to the media it de-emphasized numbers.

In the days before the convention, tension heightened. Mayor Daley put all 12,000 Chicago police on 12-hour shifts; the government mobilized 5,000 National Guardsmen; the FBI assigned 1,000 agents to Chicago; the army placed 6,000 troops in the suburbs, including the 101st Airborne; and radicals among the protesters itched for a confrontation, especially Hayden, who reversed his earlier position. He called the national government "an outlaw institution under the control of war criminals," and wanted it destroyed. (Farber 1988, 114) On 23 August, the Friday before the Convention, Jerry Rubin and the Yippies paraded Pigasus the Pig as their candidate for the presidential nomination. They had bought the 200-pound animal from a farmer; now they displayed it outside the Chicago Civic Center. The police, however, collared Pigasus and arrested Rubin.

The following afternoon, the Yippies held their Festival of Life at Lincoln Park, and it turned out to be a disaster. On the next day, Chicago's police disrupted the rock music by ordering the Yippies to remove a flatbed truck intended for use as a stage. Then, when an 11:00 P.M. curfew took effect, and many in the crowd refused to leave, the police charged, cracking heads with their clubs. Some among the 2,000 demonstrators relished the confrontation and fought back, and the cops responded with indiscriminate violence—clubbing a *Newsweek* reporter after he showed his credentials, beating an assistant U.S. attorney general dressed in suit and tie, attacking ministers, and lobbing tear gas. They did not clear the streets until 2:00 in the morning.

On Monday, 26 August, as the Democratic National Convention began, small groups reconvened at Lincoln Park and ran into the nearby streets, throwing rocks and bottles and smashing the windows of police cars. The cops closed the park that night, and when a hail of rocks greeted them, they again assaulted the crowd—with police badges and name tags removed so they could avoid identification. At one point, a policeman threw a black reporter to the ground, and, after the victim showed his credentials, the officer said, "That don't mean anything to me, nigger," and began beating him. (186)

On Wednesday, a protest crowd gathered around the band shell at Grant Park—an older group, many among them campaigners for presidential candidate Eugene McCarthy. When a teenage boy climbed a pole to lower the American flag, the police flailed away at protesters, clubs swinging. Meanwhile, several young people, including, as it turned out, an undercover agent, attempted to raise a red T-shirt on the flagpole, enraging the police again.

In the evening, protesters tried to march peacefully to the amphitheater where the convention delegates were meeting. The police, however, clubbed them and many bystanders—bloodying them, spraying them with Mace. When the assistant superintendent of Chicago's police tried to bring his men under control, they acted more violently, and some protesters retaliated by kicking and punching their assailants. Television cameras broadcast the melee as the crowd chanted "The whole world is watching! The whole world is watching!" (197–200)

Tear gas used against the protesters drifted into the amphitheater, choking some delegates, and as the fighting continued outside, Senator Abraham Ribicoff of Connecticut stepped to the podium, took the microphone, and denounced Mayor Daley for Gestapo tactics. Daley's face reddened, and he muttered, "You Jew son of a bitch." (Viorst 1979, 459)

The violence in Chicago left America divided. On the one hand, public opinion polls showed most people siding with the Chicago police and condemning the protesters. (Little did they know that one of every six protesters was an undercover agent.) On the other hand, many protesters considered the police violence indicative of an oppressive society. (Weeks later, a report issued by the National Commission on the Causes and Prevention of Violence concluded that a "police riot" had taken place.) Additionally, the turmoil may have contributed to the defeat of Democratic presidential candidate Hubert Humphrey, and the federal government arrested several of the protest leaders, known as the Chicago Eight, for conspiring to riot. Thus, the wounds proved deep and many doubted they could ever be healed.

See also Chicago Eight; Davis, Rennie; Dellinger, David; Dohrn, Bernardine; Hayden, Tom; Hoffman, Abbie; Krassner, Paul; National Mobilization Committee To End the War in Vietnam; Rubin, Jerry; Street Theatre; Yippies.

References Farber, David, *Chicago '68* (1988); Viorst, Milton, *Fire in the Streets: America in the 1960s* (1979).

Diggers

On a summer's day in 1966, the Diggers gathered in San Francisco's Haight-Ashbury district, where they set up a large orange scaffolding—what they called a "Free Frame of Reference"—and invited those who needed food to pass through it and receive a meal. Later, a reporter looked at this and other similar events and called the Diggers "a hip Salvation Army." No description could be more inaccurate, though, for unlike the Salvation Army, this hippie group rejected middle-class values and institutions and wanted to develop a communal society.

The Diggers emerged in the mid-1960s from a mime troupe in San Francisco. They took their name from a seventeenth-century radical group in England that had protested the monopolization of land by the wealthy. The protest involved laying claim to plots located on the commons atop Saint George's Hill in Surrey and working or "digging" them to grow food and distribute it to the needy. These early diggers emphasized sharing, condemned private property for promoting selfishness, and in their actions questioned the power structure.

Much like their English predecessors, the San Francisco Diggers considered private property injurious to social harmony, and in continuing their connection to their roots in mime, they used theatre and theatrics in the street to show the absurdity of conformist behavior. They promoted theatre as revolution—a way to get people to act and think radically different. For example, their Death of Money parade included three marchers who carried a silver dollar sign on a stick, and six pallbearers wearing Egyptian-like animal heads and carrying a black-draped coffin symbolizing the burial of greed. As one Digger pamphlet proclaimed: "Property is the enemy—burn it, destroy it, give it away. Don't let them make a machine out of you, get out of the system, do your own thing. Don't organize students, teachers, Negroes—organize your head." ("Digger Archives")

Many years later, a prominent ex-Digger said: "We saw ourselves as theatrical provocateurs of the psychedelic streets, challenging dropouts with visions of a creatively and sexually liberated, cooperative, and ecologically conscious social order to replace the one that was fighting the Vietnam War."

In line with this, the Diggers believed society could be changed by putting the word "free" in front of everything: free ideas, free bike, free boy, free girl, free love. This would bring liberation, as would the recognition that to make demands on authority only legitimated it and made those in power feel more powerful. Like many other hippies, the Diggers thus rejected politically oriented activities. To them, the New Left consisted of narrow-minded, spoiled white kids whose politics, like that of the older, ruling establishment, didn't solve anything and only created power games. Anarchistic at heart, they rejected all but the most informal organization.

The Diggers embraced existentialism and asserted that a person could and should take the initiative to improve himself. Liberation, they believed, began with the individual transcending society's strictures. Although the Diggers considered LSD beneficial in enhancing the appreciation of life's beauties, breaking suburban conformity, and showing how better conditions could be, they did not consider the drug a solution to problems or a foundation for the future.

The Diggers opposed the mass media, because of what it did to the hippie mecca, Haight-Ashbury. Reporters emphasized the sensationalist and the negative, and in doing so, the Diggers claimed, they created a poisonous environment that attracted people who had misconceptions about hippies or who had no attachment to true hippie values. The Diggers believed a person should not rely on experts for news, for they only restricted individual expression and freedom. Nevertheless, they were not adverse to occasionally using the media in order to display straight society's ludicrous arrangements.

True to their anarchistic individualism, the Diggers had no formal hierarchy and no chosen leaders. Any Digger could begin a project, and fellow Diggers were free to join or not join an activity. By 1967, numerous Digger groups existed in Haight-Ashbury, each usually unaware of what the other was doing. Nevertheless, two Digger activists exerted considerable influence: Peter Berg, a playwright, who at one point earned notoriety through a famous television appearance, and Emmett Grogan, a flamboyant ex-Brooklynite and founder of the group.

Berg displayed the Digger fondness for the outrageous when, on a TV talk show in New York City, he urged people to free themselves from their confinement, their boxes. He said he would show them how to do this and then walked to the studio exit door, opened it, told the viewers to get up and turn off their TV sets, and promptly walked out, leaving his host and the audience befuddled.

For his part, Grogan began free food distribution in Haight-Ashbury—in the afternoons Diggers at Panhandle Park distributed stew, cans of soup, and other items—promoted cooperative living, and developed plans to establish communal farms. (In fact, several Digger communes appeared within Haight-Ashbury.) He epitomized the Digger view when he expressed his idea of freedom: "Why can't I stand on the corner and wait for nobody? Why can't everyone?" and advised: "Do your own thing, what you are, and nothing will ever bother you."

See also Establishment; Haight-Ashbury; LSD; San Francisco Mime Troupe.

References Farber, David, ed., *The Sixties: From Memory to History* (1994); Gitlin, Todd, *The Sixties: Years of Hope, Days of Rage* (1987); "Digger Archives," http://www. webcom.com/~enoble/diggers/ diggers. html.

Direct Action

Counterculture political protesters frequently used direct action to further their aims. This meant marches, sit-ins, and boycotts as a means to gain media and public attention. Many political activists believed that more sedate measures, such as voting and sending letters to elected representatives, had little impact on an establishment unresponsive to minority concerns or issues of social injustice.

The counterculture learned many of its direct action techniques from the 1950s civil rights movement, particularly the efforts of Martin Luther King, Jr. His effective boycotts and marches in the South carried into protests organized by whites and blacks in the 1960s. Many white college students learned, too, from the lunch counter sit-ins staged by black college students in Greensboro, North Carolina, and elsewhere.

In addition to the civil rights movement, direct action tactics appeared in the movements against the Vietnam War and for women's rights, gay rights, Chicano rights, environmental protection, and many others. Occasionally, extremists took direct action to the point of committing violence, such as the bombing of federal facilities by Weatherman. Overwhelmingly, however, protesters rejected this approach.

Direct action promoted a belief that issues had to be dealt with now, and it encouraged a sense of community among the protesters. Todd Gitlin, a New Left activist, described the important connection between direct action and the 1960s political movement: "The movement didn't simply demand, it *did*. By taking action, not just a position, it affirmed a right to do so; by refusing to defer it deprived the authorities of authority itself. . . . Action in common was not just a means, it was the core of the movement's identity." (Gitlin 1987, 84–85)

See also Greensboro.

Reference Gitlin, Todd, *The Sixties: Years of Hope, Days of Rage* (1987).

Do Your Thing

"Do your thing" meant engage in whatever you want to . . . don't compromise or give in to those who oppose or criticize you.

Dohrn, Bernardine (1942–)

In 1968, Bernardine Dohrn declared herself a revolutionary Communist and shortly thereafter rose to prominence as a leader in Weatherman, a radical group committed to violence in the the name of change.

Born on 12 January 1942 in Chicago, Dohrn came from a middle-class family. Her mother worked as a secretary and her father as a manager in an appliance store. She pursued a college education and obtained bachelor's and master's degrees in the early 1960s from the University of Chicago. In 1964, she entered that college's law school, and, while studying there, joined Students for a Democratic Society (SDS), a New Left organization. She obtained her law degree in 1967, and then moved to New York City, where she worked for the National Lawyers Guild in organizing student resistance to the draft.

In 1968, Dohrn participated in a student strike at Columbia University, won election as interorganizational national secretary of SDS, made her declaration of commitment to revolutionary communism, and met in Yugoslavia with representatives of the Vietnamese National Liberation Front. By this time, warring factions had emerged within SDS, and Dohrn gravitated toward Third World Marxists, a group that considered racism and imperialism the chief causes of oppression. Third World Marxists wanted to overthrow capitalism through revolution and favored student street fighting to weaken the U.S. government.

By 1969, Third World Marxists had changed its name to Weatherman (after the lyrics in a Bob Dylan song), and Dohrn emerged as an important leader within it. In June, she attended the SDS National Convention in Chicago and advocated that the delegates expel Weatherman's main competition from the organization, a faction called Progressive Labor (PL). At one point, she rallied many delegates to her cause with an emotional, fiery speech in which she exclaimed: "We are not a caucus, we are SDS!" (Viorst 1979, 490) Then she marched back into the main meeting hall, declared PL expelled, and led Weatherman through the aisles, the group chanting "Ho, Ho, Ho Chi Minh, dare to struggle, dare to win!" (491)

In October 1969, Dohrn organized the Women's Militia at a protest in Chicago called by Weatherman. She intended to capture and destroy an armed forces induction center, but only 70 women turned out for the assault, and the police arrested her before any damage could be done.

Dohrn did not appear for her trial. In December 1969, she argued successfully at the Weatherman National War Council that the group go underground and conduct terrorist activities. Dohrn, now a leader in the Weather Underground, helped plan bombings against government facilities, and in 1970 appeared on the FBI's ten-most-wanted list.

In the mid-1970s, the Weather Underground divided into factions and collapsed, and in 1980 Dohrn surrendered to federal authorities. She was fined and received three years probation on charges of conspiracy. She then worked as a waitress in New York City; later, after being denied admission to the New York Bar, she worked as a paralegal.

See also Boudin, Kathy; Columbia University; New Left; Rudd, Mark; Students for a Democratic Society; Weather Underground.

Reference Viorst, Milton, *Fire in the Streets: America in the 1960s* (1979).

Donovan (1946–)

Referred to as the hippie madrigal, Donovan presented rock music that combined folk influences with mysticism. Born Donovan Leitch on 10 May 1946 in Glasgow, Scotland, Donovan first gained prominence in 1965 when he appeared as a regular on a British television rock show. Later that year, he made his debut in the United States at the Newport Folk Festival. Donovan combined his soft voice with acoustic guitar and sitars, flutes, cellos, and harps. His songs "Sunshine Superman" and "Mellow Yellow" in 1966 reached the top ten as listeners claimed they referred to psychedelic trips.

In 1967, Donovan traveled to India where he studied under the Maharishi Mahesh Yogi and renounced drugs. His 1968 hit "Hurdy Gurdy Man" reflected his hippie outlook tied to peace, and his lyrics "here comes the hurdy gurdy man singing songs of love" seemed to reflect his own life. After the hippie movement peaked in 1969, Donovan's musical career spiraled downward.

In the 1970s, he composed musical scores to three movies, recorded three albums, and wrote a book of poems, but few people noticed them. The following decade, his daughter Ione Skye appeared in the acclaimed movie *River's Edge*, and in the early nineties his son Donovan Leitch, Jr. gained considerable publicity as a model, actor, and singer in the rock band Nancy Boy. In 1996, Donovan recorded *Sutras*, his first new album in 12 years.

See also Maharishi Mahesh Yogi; Rock Music.

"Don't Trust Anyone over Thirty"

This phrase expressed both the youthful nature of the counterculture and the disdain many young people held toward the way adults were running the world. The first prominent use of the phrase goes back to Jack Weinberg, a civil rights organizer and student at the University of California–Berkeley. In 1964, he made the remark as administrators at the school acted to restrict free speech. Weinberg was not criticizing *their* duplicity but, rather, insisting that the student-organized Free Speech Movement distrusted older Communists and thus would not follow a Communist line.

His remark contained a greater meaning, however, in implying that he and many other students did not want to be restricted by rules from bygone battles or to be told the truth; instead, they wanted freedom and the latitude to discover truth on their own. In a humorous vein, one young writer went so far as to state: "As for this 'don't trust-anyone over-30' shit, I agree in principle, but I think they ought to drop the zero." (Anderson 1995, 264)

See also Free Speech Movement; University of California-Berkeley.

Reference Anderson, Terry H., *The Movement and the Sixties* (1995).

The Doors

Hello, I love you
Let me tell you my name . . .

A psychedelic rock band, the Doors produced music known for its darkness, often tied to themes of death and psychological neuroses. In this, they showed the inspiration provided by its leader and driving force, Jim Morrison, and developed into one of the most influential bands in rock.

Morrison, born on 8 December 1943 in Melbourne, Florida, had, in the early 1960s, attended Saint Petersburg Junior College, Florida State University, and the University of California–Los Angeles film school. An avid reader, influenced especially by Norman O. Brown's psychological *Life against Death*, which considers humankind as bent on self-destruction, Morrison wrote poetry and music. In 1965, while sitting on a beach, he showed these to Ray Manzarek. Morrison's works, loaded with mystical images, blew Manzarek away: "Once I had a little game/I like to crawl back in my brain/I think you know the game I mean/I mean the game called go insane."

Manzarek, who had played in a band called Rick and the Ravens, then proposed to Morrison that they start a rock band. Morrison, who had just dropped out of UCLA, agreed. After some initial personnel changes, the Doors consisted of Manzarek on organ, John Densmore on drums, Robby Krieger on guitar, and Morrison performing vocals. The band took its name from Aldous Huxley's book, *The Doors of Perception*, or as Morrison explained it: "There's the known. And there's the unknown. And what separates the two is the door, and that's what I want to be." (Hopkins and Sugarman 1980, 58)

The Doors recorded a demo tape in the summer of 1966, and then began working as the house band at the Whisky-A-Go-Go in Los Angeles. The gig ended four months later, however, after they performed "The End," an explicitly Oedipal song. By then Elektra Records had become interested in them, and in 1967 released the Doors' self-titled album, along with a single, "Light My Fire," both top-ten hits.

Counterculture audiences liked Morrison's dark, psychological explorations and the band's obvious psychedelic form propelled by Manzarek's organ. Morrison adopted shamanistic tendencies, and in the 1968 album *Waiting for the Sun* presented himself as the Lizard King.

On stage, the Doors reflected Morrison's infatuation with manipulating crowds, exploring group psychoses in a Norman O. Brown way, pushing crowds into a frenzy, even trying to foment riots. As a self-professed prophet, Morrison acted in ways that mainstream society, and even many in the counterculture, deemed outrageous. In December 1967, authorities in New Haven, Connecticut, arrested him for public

Known for dark psychedelic music, the Doors take a break at their 1968 open-air concert in Frankfurt, Germany. Band members, from left to right: organist Ray Manzarek, drummer John Densmore, singer and leader Jim Morrison, and guitarist Robby Krieger.

obscenity at a concert there; and in 1968 he was arrested for disorderly conduct aboard an airplane headed for Phoenix, Arizona.

His most sensational arrest, however, happened after a concert on 2 March 1969 at Dinner Key Auditorium in Miami, Florida. The authorities in that city charged him with "lewd and lascivious behavior in public by exposing his private parts and by simulating masturbation and oral copulation." (Burks 1969, 1) They charged him, too, with indecent exposure, public profanity, and public drunkenness. What happened at the concert that night remains disputed, especially since the charges were eventually dropped. All agree, however, that the Doors played an abysmal one-hour set during which Morrison, obviously drunk, shouted obscenities, talked drivel about nobody loving him, poured champagne over his own head, pretended to masturbate, and tried to get the crowd to riot. A reporter for the *Miami Herald* said, "I saw it all, and I wasn't offended at the obscenity. What *did* offend me was that he was trying to start a riot." (6)Witnesses disagreed as to whether Morrison actually exposed himself, and no photographic proof existed.

The contretemps greatly damaged the Doors, making it nearly impossible for them to get other concert bookings. Despite this, Morrison appeared at a show in Boston in May 1970 again drunk, throwing money from the stage, and asking the audience if they wanted to see his genitals.

Soon after the Doors released *L.A. Women* in 1971, Morrison took a leave from the band. Emotionally drained and decimated by drugs and alcohol, he traveled to Paris, France, where he and his wife lived in seclusion. On 3 July 1971, he died in his bathtub from heart failure.

The surviving Doors continued to record into 1973, but without Morrison they failed to make an impact. Interestingly, record sales for the Doors reached new heights in the 1980s and 1990s, after a Jim Morrison cult flourished, encouraged by biographies of him and by a major motion picture in 1991 produced by Oliver Stone. Strange circumstances surrounding Morrison's death, along with the singer's frequently expressed desire to drop out, assume a new identity, and start life over, have led to speculation that Morrison, like Elvis Presley, is still alive. "He was," his biographers say in *No One Here Gets Out Alive*, "gripped by the fact that [the poet Arthur] Rimbaud had written all his poetry by the age of nineteen and then disappeared into North Africa." (Hopkins and Sugarman 1980, 373)

See also Rock Music.

References Burks, John, "In the County of Dade," *Rolling Stone*, 5 April 1969, 1, 6; Densmore, John, *Riders on the Storm: My Life with Jim Morrison and the Doors* (1990); Hopkins, Jerry, and Danny Sugerman, *No One Here Gets Out Alive* (1980).

The Doors of Perception

In 1954, Aldous Huxley, the English intellectual and author, wrote *The Doors of Perception*. In it, he describes the mystical experience he encountered in his first experimentation with mescaline, a psychedelic drug. For Huxley, mescaline brought him into a realm where the ego had no control, where love took precedence, and where societal conditioning dissolved.

The Doors of Perception seemed to extol the use of psychedelics as a way to alter consciousness and improve the individual, and perhaps, in time, society. As a result, it gained a wide readership within the counterculture, especially among those hippies searching for a love-based alternative to conformist, impersonal society. *The Doors of Perception* exerted its influence in another way, too: a rock group adopted Huxley's title, calling themselves the Doors, and sang about breaking on through to another side of existence, a mystical realm, which previous generations had denied and even belittled as inferior to rationality.

See also The Doors; Huxley, Aldous.

Reference Huxley, Aldous, *The Doors of Perception* (1954).

Dope

Counterculture youth used the word *dope* in reference to drugs—everything from marijuana to LSD, speed, and cocaine. Attitudes surrounding the word displayed the great divide between countercultural and mainstream society. To discourage drug use among their children, older Americans repeated the refrain, "Why do they call it dope?"—implying a person must be stupid to use drugs. But youngsters considered the word dope alluring and preferred it to words such as grass in order to underscore their assault on traditional values. To say "I smoked dope" rather than "I smoked pot" had a more menacing, rebellious feel. "Dope is great, it's fun, it's healthy," said one hippie. "Get every creature so stoned they can't stand the plastic shit of American culture."

Dow Chemical

Antiwar protesters targeted Dow, a huge chemical company, because it was the largest maker of napalm, a gel-like mixture of gasoline, naphthenic acid, and palm oil. American military forces used napalm in Vietnam, dropping it from planes. When napalm hit a person's skin, it burned it off. Frequently, the Americans used napalm indiscriminately, killing and maiming civilians as well as combatants.

On college campuses, protests erupted against Dow, with students picketing to prevent the company from recruiting employees. At the University of Wisconsin, site of the most intense opposition, 300 students obstructed recruiters in 1967 while chanting "Down with Dow!" The police retaliated with tear gas and billy clubs, producing a bloody scene and polarizing the campus community.

Shortly thereafter, protests against Dow erupted at Harvard and over 20 other universities. A widely circulated activist flyer bore the phrase "Dow Shalt Not Kill."

Downer

In terms of drugs, downer meant a depressant, especially a barbiturate. However, the word came to mean any depressing development or experience.

Draft Resistance

As the Vietnam War intensified, and especially after the Tet Offensive early in 1968 revealed the futility of America's combat role, draft resistance skyrocketed. Middle- and upper-class men avoided the draft through several methods. Until 1968, enrollment as a college student brought automatic deferment. After that date, college graduates could avoid service by studying overseas, as did Bill Clinton, elected president in the 1990s. Deferments could also be obtained by working for defense industries. Some young men secured statements from family doctors attesting to flat feet and other medical problems, a tactic used by Rush Limbaugh, later a conservative political commentator.

Others joined the national guard or armed forces reserve units, knowing they would have to serve only six months on active duty. Numerous athletes followed this route, including ten players with the Dallas Cowboys football team, as did those from prominent families with political connections, such as Dan Quayle, who in the 1980s won election as vice-president. Draft resisters sometimes declared themselves conscientious objectors on religious grounds. Muhammad Ali, the world heavyweight boxing champion, took that route. If all else failed, a young man could flee to Canada. About 100,000 did so.

Some who resisted the draft on moral grounds engaged in public demonstrations. They participated in marches against the war, occupied selective service offices, and burned draft cards. Draft resistance coincided with a surge in military desertions and an increasing refusal by troops in Vietnam to fight.

Drugs and the Drug Culture

Hippie Erika Taylor talked about her transformation:

> Oh, marijuana, what's that all about? I'll never smoke grass. And then my younger sister turned me on. . . . The next week we took acid. A month later I moved away from home and lived up on this mountain. (Joseph 1974, 371)

An underground newspaper discussed the countercultural mentality: "That peace button . . . wasn't a cause, merely a symptom. The *cause*, nine times in ten, was grass, hash, acid, mescaline, peyote. . . ."

Did drugs have such a tremendous impact? Most definitely. They changed consciences and altered behavior, thus propelling and shaping the counterculture. Those who promoted psychedelics realized this; all along they were convinced that LSD and similar drugs could change individuals by placing them in contact with a universal oneness, a mystical union leading to kindness, harmony, and love. Any societal change, they believed, must be preceded by this individual one.

Drug use, of course, existed long before the counterculture. Prior to World War II, Americans in large numbers consumed alcohol, tobacco, and various so-called medicines that contained opium and codeine. In the 1950s, sales of tranquilizers and barbiturates skyrocketed within mainstream society, while a social substrata, mainly some blacks living in ghettos and white beatniks rebelling against conformity, smoked marijuana.

During that same decade a handful of psychologists, writers, and artists, along with the Central Intelligence Agency, experimented with LSD, a legal drug that had been developed little more than a decade earlier. A few persons took peyote or psilocybin mushrooms, other drugs used later in the sixties counterculture.

The answer as to why drugs flourished in the counterculture remains murky. Several factors, however, must be considered. Drugs such as LSD had their advocates, sometimes notorious ones. This description fits the Merry Pranksters. Bohemians with a carnival flair, they staged "Acid Tests," public parties at which they provided LSD to all comers. Add to this Harvard psychologist Timothy Leary, the High

Priest of Acid. He envisioned psychedelics as a way to re-create the world, and his phrase "turn on, tune in, drop out" aimed at getting millions of Americans to reject mainstream society with its selfishness and greed.

In addition to the Pranksters and Leary, an entire experimental community adopted LSD: Haight-Ashbury in San Francisco. Hippies in the Haight hoped to create a self-sufficient settlement around psychedelic visions of peace and love. They failed in their endeavor but not before many youngsters, those lonesome and confused, and those disgusted with mainstream society's own failings imbibed the message from Haight-Ashbury and the sensational stories in the media about LSD and love-ins.

At the same time, psychedelia exploded into rock music. The San Francisco sound suggested what LSD and marijuana could do, and Jefferson Airplane, the Grateful Dead, and many bands outside San Francisco keen to this music spread the drug message. When the Beatles sang about Dr. Roberts or intoned "I get high with a little help from my friends," young people grew more and more curious and more and more stoned.

Drugs, in fact, achieved ritualistic status. They separated countercultural youths from straight society and hit the older generation where it hurt the most: their sons and their daughters beyond their command and doing drugs. "Marijuana and music became a collective ritual," said political activist Todd Gitlin. Rolling a joint, tokes, giggles, munchies, free associations, linear thought shattered—these produced bonding made even stronger by the illegal scene. Once a youngster smoked pot, immersion into the counterculture likely followed, for getting high often met getting hip to society's hypocrisies and cruelties.

Drugs did not treat all partakers the same, and if the counterculture thought marijuana, LSD, and their companions offered a panacea, the offer proved deceptive. The 1967 Summer of Love showed this when thousands of youngsters, high school age and younger, crowded the Haight and took drugs, not to develop alternative communities but to escape. Predators plied the scene, too, selling adulterated drugs and ripping off customers. Writing in *Storming Heaven*, Jay Stevens says that "instead of creating a taste for enlightenment, LSD was promoting a love of sensation." (342) This story repeated itself across the nation.

Haight-Ashbury, rock music, and youthful bonding and rebellion all promoted drug use, along with the older generation that set an example by downing pills in response to pressures, professing democracy but practicing racism, and promoting a murderous war in Vietnam. Could there have been a counterculture without drugs? Of course, but not in the same form, not with the psychedelic aura that surrounded it. At their best, drugs helped promote ideals worth achieving; at their worst, they encouraged mindlessness, selfishness, and destruction.

See also Acid Tests; Haight-Ashbury; Kesey, Ken; Leary, Timothy; LSD; Marijuana; Peyote; Speed.

References Joseph, Peter, *Good Times: An Oral History of America in the 1960s* (1974); Stevens, Jay, *Storming Heaven: LSD and the American Dream* (1987); http://www.hyperreal.com/drugs/psychedelics/.

Dude

In the counterculture movie *Easy Rider*, Jack Nicholson puzzles over having been called a dude by two hippie-type motorcyclists. "What does that mean?" he asks. The reply: a regular person, nothing phony or pretentious. To be called a dude was complimentary; to be called a cool dude even more so.

See also Cool; *Easy Rider*.

Dylan, Bob (1941–)

Folk-rock musician Bob Dylan is often identified with the counterculture through the words contained in his 1964 song "The Times They Are A-Changin'"—words that declare sons and daughters to be no longer under their parents' control. He has been hailed as among the most influential of all American pop musicians and certainly the most influential musician of the 1960s. Dylan's work reshaped Western culture.

Dylan was born Robert Allen Zimmerman on 24 May 1941 in Duluth, Minnesota. In the late 1940s, he moved with his parents to Hibbing, a predominantly Catholic small town where his was one of only a few Jewish families. As a child, Dylan liked to write poetry, and in the mid-1950s he began listening to country music, especially Hank Williams. At the same time, he idolized movie star James Dean, the symbol of youthful rebelliousness in a placid decade, and adopted his mannerisms in trying to redefine himself.

In 1956, Dylan began listening to rock 'n' roll and joined a high school band in which he played piano. Shortly thereafter, he learned to play the guitar and formed several different bands over the next few years, the Shadow Blasters being among the first and the Golden Chords the most prominent. Withdrawn in school, he was outgoing on stage. In 1958, Dylan formed the band Elston Gunn and the Rock Boppers, thus obtaining his first stage name and a poor reception when the audience at the St. Louis County Fair in Hibbing booed him.

In 1959, for reasons unclear but perhaps related to his frequenting bohemian hangouts in Minneapolis, Dylan switched from rock to folk music. That same year, he enrolled in the arts college at the University of Minnesota and began playing at a coffeehouse, the Ten O'Clock Scholar, near campus. This was when he changed his name to Dylan, presumably derived from the poet Dylan Thomas.

A few months later, Dylan left college and, after brief stops elsewhere, arrived in New York City's Greenwich Village, a beatnik enclave known for its artists and hip coffeehouses. He played at the Café Wha? during an amateur night, and soon started performing there on a regular basis for little pay. He frequently visited folk music legend Woody Guthrie, at the time hospitalized with a serious disease, and met many prominent musicians who gathered at the home of a Guthrie friend.

After Café Wha?, Dylan played at other coffeehouses, especially Gerde's Folk City, a cradle of musical creativity. He quickly improved his harmonica and guitar skills while infusing traditional folk songs with rhythm and blues. His approach, including his talking blues style, emulated Guthrie's and displayed the influence of Jack Elliott, a leading folk performer in Greenwich Village. At this point, Dylan's songs displayed little originality, but by the fall of 1961, he had begun diversifying, with one newspaper critic saying "he had learned to churn up exciting, bluesy, hard-driving, harmonica-and-guitar-music." (Heylin 1991,63) In September, Robert Shelton gave him such a good review in the *New York Times* that Columbia Records signed him to a contract.

His first LP, *Bob Dylan*, released in 1962, contained only two originals but nevertheless showed he had considerable talent. Also that year he wrote his first protest song, presented at a benefit for the Congress of Racial Equality, and introduced his masterful "Blowin' in the Wind." This song appeared on his album *The Freewheelin' Bob Dylan*, and Peter, Paul, and Mary made it a top-ten hit.

Dylan caused controversy in 1963 when he backed out of an appearance on the *Ed Sullivan Show* after the CBS television network refused to let him sing a protest song he had written, "Talkin' John Birch Society Blues," for fear it would offend conservative viewers. Dylan's action made him a hero among folk music fans and within the hip community at large.

Later that year, he played at the Newport Folk Festival for the first time and wrote "The Times They Are A-Changin'," the song that castigated politicians and others who did not understand social reform and youthful efforts to remake America. Many young people interpreted the song as referring to generational conflict, although Dylan insisted he meant it to be about the difference between "aliveness and deadness." (86–87) In any event, college students within an emerging radical political movement identified

American folk singers Bob Dylan and Joan Baez, 27 April 1965

with Dylan. Activist Todd Gitlin said: "The tiny New Left delighted in one of our own generation and mind singing earnest ballads about racist murderers, the compensatory racism of poor whites, cold-war ideology . . ." (Gitlin 1987, 197) Indeed, some activists believed that social injustice could be ended by exposing it in such songs.

But Dylan soon considered protest music too limiting, and according to his own account, in 1965 he felt burned out. He intended to quit playing altogether and pursue a writing career, until he composed "Like a Rolling Stone" (this after he had just scored a top-40 hit with "Subterranean Homesick Blues," and the Byrds had achieved success with his "Mr. Tambourine

Man"). This song rejuvenated him, and he included it on a new album, *Highway 61 Revisited.* In *Bob Dylan: Behind the Shades,* Clinton Heylin says that with this recording Dylan "reinvented rock and roll in a way perhaps only half a dozen albums have done in the forty-year history of the art . . . No one had ever written lyrics like these for a rock and roll album." (146–147) At the recording session, Dylan decided to mix organ with guitar in a musical style called folk-rock. While recording this work in July 1965, Dylan appeared at the Newport Folk Festival with an electric guitar and backed by the Paul Butterfield Blues Band. Many in the crowd booed him for supposedly defiling folk music.

After a world tour that ended early in 1966, Dylan completed *Blonde on Blonde,* which he had begun recording the previous fall. The LP included the masterpieces "Visions of Johanna," "Stuck Inside of Mobile with the Memphis Blues Again," "Just Like a Woman," and "Rainy Day Women #12 & 35."

On 29 July 1966, Dylan crashed his motorcycle while riding it near his home in upstate New York and suffered a concussion, several broken neck vertebrae, and lacerations of the face and scalp. The injuries left him in critical condition for a week. During his recovery, he and the rock group the Band recorded several tracks soon famous as *The Basement Tapes.*

Dylan returned to the studio in 1968 to record *John Wesley Harding* with its puzzling ballad "All Along the Watchtower." The album marked a return to a simple, clean sound with country music overtones. In 1969, his *Nashville Skyline* showed a distinct turn toward country and featured "Lay Lady Lay," and "Girl from the North Country" recorded with Johnny Cash.

Dylan continued making records in the 1970s, and in 1976 appeared in the Band's farewell concert movie, *The Last Waltz.* Three years later, he announced his conversion to born-again Christianity. In 1989, he was inducted into the Rock and Roll Hall of Fame, but his career drifted, marred by several poorly received albums and concert tours. Then, in the mid-1990s, his concerts showed new life, and younger musicians took a greater interest in his early works as foundations of contemporary rock. Certainly, Dylan's contributions to both folk and rock music cannot be overstated. In the sixties, he broadened folk music's appeal, and as he changed his style he infused rock 'n' roll with social consciousness previously lacking. Thus, he bridged the vacuous rock music produced in the early 1960s with the more complex arrangements appearing at mid-decade. Dylan helped shape counterculture experimentation, its challenges to conventional forms, and spoke for a generation that questioned the values handed down by the middle class.

See also Rock Music.

References Cott, Jonathan, *Dylan* (1984); Dylan, Bob, *Bob Dylan in His Own Words* (1993); Gitlin, Todd, *The Sixties: Years of Hope, Days of Rage* (1987); Heylin, Clinton, *Bob Dylan: Behind the Shades* (1991); Humphries, Patrick, *Absolutely Dylan* (1991); Riley, Tim, *Hard Rain: A Dylan Commentary* (1992); Scaduto, Anthony, *Bob Dylan* (1971); Shelton, Robert, *No Direction Home: The Life and Music of Bob Dylan* (1986).

E

Earth Day

Earth Day was first celebrated on 22 April 1970: time set aside to show concern for the natural environment; in effect, a moratorium akin to the ones used in the antiwar movement, but this time proposed by the "establishment" itself.

The idea for Earth Day came from two liberal politicians, Senator Gaylord Nelson of Wisconsin and Representative Pete McCloskey of California, who proposed a special day for people to meet and discuss environmental issues. From this, Dennis Allen Hayes, a young activist who had hitchhiked around the world, coordinated a national program.

But the recognition of Earth Day took many local forms, some trivial and some important, and went well beyond discussions. For example, Girl Scouts in canoes removed garbage from along the Potomac River; thousands of citizens picked up trash from roadways in Vermont; blacks in St. Louis conducted street theatre, dramatizing health problems caused by lead paint; thousands of people attended teach-ins around the San Francisco Bay Area; and 5,000 gathered at the Washington Monument to sing along with Pete Seeger and Phil Ochs, followed by a protest march on the Interior Department.

Although Nelson and McCloskey proposed Earth Day, its emergence reflected environmental concerns that had been building throughout the 1960s, articulated in works such as Rachel Carson's *Silent Spring* and Barry Commoner's *The Closing Circle* and displayed in the popularity of *The Whole Earth Catalog*, the development of communes by hippies, and the expanding back-to-the-earth movement. Environmental awareness and demands that something be done about an ecological crisis had been a central element of the counterculture with hippies and other young people joining or allying with the Sierra Club, Ecology Action Council, and similar groups in ever larger numbers. Long before Earth Day they had proposed an Earth People's Park for New Mexico or Colorado—open to all, for free.

Some activists complained that Earth Day diverted attention from more radical reforms needed to protect the environment. But before and shortly after Earth Day, Congress passed a record number of clean air and water acts, and many states passed favorable legislation. The politicians counted heads: public opinion surveys showed the environment to be a big issue, and more than 20 million people had participated in Earth Day activities.

See also *Silent Spring; The Whole Earth Catalog.*

East Village

In addition to Greenwich Village, New York City's East Village was an important hippie center. At Tompkins Square Park, along Tenth Street, there occurred frequent smoke-ins, rock concerts, and spontaneous gatherings. Long-haired hippies in colorful garb congregated there, as did Hare Krishnas. The Cave, a popular coffeehouse, and The Something!, a luncheonette, also attracted many hippies. In addition, the village housed Fillmore East, Bill Graham's enormously successful rock music hall.

The East Village hippie scene flourished in 1966 and 1967, but the following year it declined as many hippies moved to the countryside or gave up flower power for political revolution. "The heroes aren't Timothy Leary and Allen Ginsberg anymore," said Jeffrey Shero, editor of the *East Village Other*, an underground newspaper, in 1968. "They're Che Guevera and Eldridge Cleaver of the Black Panthers."

See also Flower Power; Greenwich Village; The Something!

Crowds throng New York's Fifth Avenue in celebration of the first Earth Day on 22 April 1970.

East Village Other

Oklahoman Walter Bowart began the *East Village Other*, an underground newspaper, in October 1965 that appealed to bohemian readers in New York City's Lower East Side—refugees from Greenwich Village. An *EVO* editor later explained: "We founded [the newspaper] because the Establishment press had entirely copped out. After ten years, the *Village Voice* had too."

Many observers considered *EVO* leftist, but Bowart was a libertarian, a free thinker who desired diverse coverage. As was the style in the underground, *EVO* used subjective reporting. The paper covered local culture; contained raunchy comix and explicit personals; often criticized mainstream cultural institutions, such as art galleries; wrote about alternative artists, among them Andy Warhol; and carried a regular column written by the guru of LSD, Timothy Leary. *EVO* reflected the drug culture with its psychedelic images, and in 1967 it went color—a move that influenced the underground *San Francisco Oracle* to do likewise.

See also Comix; *San Francisco Oracle;* Underground Newspapers; *Village Voice.*

Reference Peck, Abe, *Uncovering the Sixties: The Life and Times of the Underground Press* (1985).

Easy Rider

Movie critic Roger Ebert said of the film *Easy Rider*: "Nobody went to see *Easy Rider* only once. It became one of the rallying points of the late sixties, a road picture and a buddy picture, crossed with sex, drugs, rock and roll, and the heady freedom of the open road." (Ebert 1995) This low-budget production emerged as the most expressive movie of the sixties counterculture.

Several factors make it so. First, it does not seem pretentious, a fact attributable to its status as a "B" film. Second, it uses rock music, such as that by Jimi Hendrix and the Band. The director, Dennis Hopper, took this approach because he did not have enough money to develop an original soundtrack. Third, Hopper employs an innovative style to minimize the barriers between the camera and the audience. This is evident in the realistic scenes set amid natural surroundings and in the occasional use of amateur rather than professional actors. Fourth, the movie's themes express the countercultural worldview: a desire for the open road, a longing for simplicity and companionship as an antidote to scientific technology and impersonal relations, and a belief that mainstream society will destroy anything unconventional. The latter appears most strongly in two scenes: the deaths of the main characters, and Jack Nicholson's fireside dialogue about how people talk about freedom, but when they come face-to-face with it, it scares them.

Released in 1969, *Easy Rider* stars Peter Fonda, Dennis Hopper, Jack Nicholson, and Karen Black. The movie follows Fonda, Hopper, and Nicholson as they ride about the countryside on motorcycles, heading for Mardi Gras in New Orleans. The minimal plot reveals visits with a New Mexican farmer and communards, conflicts with southern rednecks, and a harrowing drug trip in New Orleans.

For all its countercultural reflections, the movie does not portray the youthful movement uncritically; rather, it provides an ambiguous ending, implying that excesses, even countercultural ones, can be harmful. Fonda related to this in an interview with *Rolling Stone* magazine, when he explained the movie's title:

> "Easy Rider" is a Southern term for a whore's old man, not a pimp, but the dude who lives with a chick. Because he's got the easy ride. Well, that's what's happened to America, man. Liberty's become a whore, and we're all taking an easy ride. (Campbell 1969, 18)

The movie propelled Fonda, Hopper, Nicholson, and Black to stardom, and in particular saved Nicholson's fledgling career, earning him an Academy Award nomination for Best Supporting Actor. "Open your mind. Find your own freedom," said a writer for the underground *Miami Daily Planet*. "Get off on Easy Rider." (Donahue 1969)

References Campbell, Elizabeth, "Easy Rider," *Rolling Stone*, 6 September 1969, 18–20; Donahue, Tommy, "Easy Rider," *Miami Daily Planet*, 24 October 1969; Ebert, Roger,"Easy Rider," *Cinemania 1996*, Microsoft Corporation, 1995.

Economic Research and Action Project

See ERAP.

Education

Counterculture youths exhibited an ambivalent attitude toward higher education: attending universities, getting degrees, pursuing graduate schools—but criticizing colleges for their impersonal atmosphere and mindless routines, and labeling the educational system an establishment game.

Young people in the 1960s attended colleges in record numbers—some 50 percent of them earned their diplomas—and during this decade the United States became the first society in world history to have more college students than farmers. With this, colleges expanded their staffs and facilities at a record pace, hiring more teachers and constructing buildings, labs, and stadiums. Yet expansion often brought conditions in which students found themselves herded into large classes—100, 150, 200 and more in a room—and treated as computer cards. This led to a student demand: "Don't fold, spindle, and mutilate me."

Many students disliked another aspect of college: overbearing rules that restricted their constitutional right to freedom of speech, as evident in restrictions on discussing issues that might challenge the administration or middle-class sensibilities.

The impersonal environment and oppressive rules led to the Free Speech Movement (FSM) at the University of California–Berkeley, which ignited similar protests at other colleges. The FSM leader, Mario Savio, declared: "In California, the privileged minority manipulates the university bureaucracy to suppress the student's political expression." (Anderson 1995, 87)

Savio's statement linked the situation at Berkeley with society at large and showed how many students believed that oppression on campus reflected a greater problem with oppression across the nation. In short, they viewed college as a microcosm and did not like what they saw.

This generated extremism among some young people—disillusioned with college and with society, they dropped out and urged others to do likewise, to wake up, to see college as nothing more than legitimating America's ludicrous ideas and institutions. Jerry Rubin, a founder of the Yippies, expressed this view when he wrote:

> The classroom is an authoritarian environment. Teacher up front and rows of students one after another. . . .
>
> The class struggle begins in class. . . .
>
> Scratch a professor and find a pig. . . .
>
> Schools—high schools and colleges—are the biggest obstacle to education in Amerika today.
>
> Schools are a continuation of toilet training. Taking an exam is like taking a shit. You hold it in for weeks, memorizing, just waiting for the right time. Then the time comes, and you sit on the toilet.
> Ah!
> Um!
> It feels so good.
> You shit it right back on schedule—for the grade. . . .
>
> School addicts people to the heroin of middle-class life: busy work for grades (money) stored in your records (banks) for the future (death). We become replaceable parts for corporate Amerika.
>
> DROP OUT!
> (Albert 1984, 446–447)

See also Free Speech Movement; Rubin, Jerry; Yippies.

References Albert, Judith Clavir, and Stewart Edward Albert, eds., *The Sixties Papers: Documents of a Rebellious Decade* (1984); Anderson, Terry H., *The Movement and the Sixties* (1995); Rubin, Jerry, *Do It! Scenarios of the Revolution* (1970).

Edwardian

Among the eclectic styles adopted by hippies in the mid-1960s, Edwardian clothing (originally prominent during the reign of England's King Edward VII in the nineteenth century) bespoke a break with mass-produced consumerism. Hippies often made these clothes themselves and considered them attractive, elegant, and in keeping with their desire to be different.

Electric Circus

Around 1964, Stanley Tolkin converted an auditorium located in New York City's Greenwich Village into a night club that at one point featured the Fugs rock band. He then rented it to pop artist Andy Warhol, who called it the Exploding Plastic Inevitable, a forerunner to 1970s disco. Here the Velvet Underground appeared. After that, Tolkin converted the club into the Electric Circus, and it gained notoriety for its loud rock music, dances, flashing lights, and merry-go-round. The club closed for good in 1971.

See also The Fugs; Greenwich Village; Velvet Underground; Warhol, Andy.

Reference Miller, Terry, *Greenwich Village and How It Got That Way* (1990)

The Electric Kool-Aid Acid Test

The Electric Kool-Aid Acid Test, published in 1967, captures in every hallucinogenic detail the restless, pulsating search by Ken Kesey and the Merry Pranksters, indeed by hippies everywhere, for a post-suburbia, postmind-numbing life. Critics have hailed this book as the most penetrating and revelatory account of the counterculture.

Tom Wolfe, a writer and journalist, wrote *Acid Test* in 1967 as a factual, eyewitness account, compiled from interviews and his own association with the Merry Pranksters in the mid-1960s. His style reflects the widespread countercultural challenge to traditional art forms; intent on going beyond objectivity, he writes *Acid Test* from the standpoint of the Merry Pranksters enwrapped in their psychedelic journey.

Or as Wolfe later said: "I . . . tried not only to tell what the Pranksters did but to re-create the mental atmosphere and subjectivity of it." A reader accustomed to traditional writing confronts perplexing passages such as this:

> Christ, man! It's too much for us even! We wash our hands of this : : : :
> Atrocity : : : :
> : : : what . . . exactly have we done? and : : : :
> : : : : even to some Pranksters, the anti-Babbs faction, the Test was a debacle. (Wolfe 1968, 253)

Thus, Wolfe presents, best as he can, the psychedelic world, its drugs, relationships . . . the entire mindset that goes with it, verbal associations smashed and with them the cultural patterns that cement middle America.

See also Hippies; Kesey, Ken; New Journalism.

Reference Wolfe, Tom, *The Electric Kool-Aid Acid Test* (1968).

Ellsberg, Daniel (1931–)

A war hawk who initially supported U.S. intervention in Vietnam, Daniel Ellsberg changed his position and, to generate antiwar sentiment, leaked secret documents to the press in the early 1970s that revealed how American officials had deceived the public.

Nothing in Ellsberg's background, except a strong commitment to integrity, indicated he would oppose American militarism. Born on 7 April 1931 in Chicago, Ellsberg grew up in Detroit, where he attended an exclusive prep school. After graduation, he received a scholarship to Harvard, majored in economics, and obtained his B.A. Following this, he studied advanced economics in England at Cambridge University, and then returned to Harvard for a master's degree.

Ellsberg joined the Marine Corps in 1954. After leaving the service, he worked on a doctorate at Harvard. In 1959, he joined the Rand Corporation, a prestigious California-based research organization, and in the early 1960s participated in high-level policy discussions with government officials in Washington concerning Cuba and Vietnam.

In 1964, Ellsberg joined the staff of the assistant secretary of defense for international security affairs and helped shape President Lyndon Johnson's decision to escalate the American military presence in Southeast Asia. Later in the decade, though, he grew disillusioned with the civilian deaths in Vietnam and the corrupt nature of the South Vietnamese government. In 1967, the secretary of defense asked Ellsberg to help write a history of the war. He agreed, and his findings reinforced his disillusionment. He concluded that the war had been caused by the United States and that it reflected excessive and often devious presidential power. This written history, later called the *Pentagon Papers*, received a top-secret classification.

Bothered by what he had uncovered and by his earlier support of the war, Ellsberg decided in 1969 to convince government leaders that the United States should withdraw its troops. His efforts met with considerable resistance, and the Rand Corporation forced him to quit his job there. Ellsberg then decided to photocopy the *Pentagon Papers* and leak them to the *New York Times*.

The *Times* began publishing excerpts on 13 June 1971, startling revelations that showed government lies about the war. At that point, the Nixon administration obtained an injunction to prevent further publication of the papers, but the Supreme Court later sided with the *Times*, basing its decision on First Amendment freedom.

Meanwhile, the federal government obtained indictments against Ellsberg for conspiracy and theft, and he went on trial in May 1973. But he soon got all the charges dismissed when the judge cited the government for duplicitous acts: Ellsberg's phone had been illegally wiretapped, the office of his former psychiatrist had been broken into by secret agents, and the judge himself had been offered the directorship of the FBI in a blatant attempt by President Nixon to affect the trial.

The counterculture considered Ellsberg a hero, and both the revelations concerning Vietnam and the actions taken against him supported its assertion that government leaders could not be trusted, that the political establishment reeked with excessive power and lies.

References Ellsberg, Daniel, *Papers on the War* (1972); Salter, Kenneth W., *The Pentagon Papers Trial* (1975); Ungar, Sanford J., *The Papers and the Papers: An Account of the Legal and Political Battle over the Pentagon Papers* (1989).

ERAP

Inspired by the community action projects of the Student Nonviolent Coordinating Committee (SNCC), members of Students for a Democratic Society (SDS) organized ERAP, formally the Economic Research and Action Project. They began it in 1963, and the following year several hundred SDSers entered white and black ghettos in Newark, Chicago, Cleveland, Philadelphia, and other northern cities. They had as their goal organizing poor people to stand up for their rights and exert pressure to obtain political and economic gains. In Newark, for example, SDSers put together rent strikes and got the city to repair ghetto roads.

But ERAP ran into problems. For one, many blacks distrusted the SDSers, mostly white college students, whom they considered out of touch with the poverty and despair that overwhelmed the ghettos. For another, poor people had little experience in the structure and tactics needed to fight city hall. In addition, SDS had hoped to unite poor blacks and poor whites in a common, class-based cause, but racial antagonisms kept the two apart. Beset by these difficulties and then the riots that erupted in northern cities, ERAP collapsed in 1968. Yet for many organizers a true spirit of unity survived, as did a realization that helping the disadvantaged required confronting the power structure. These influences carried into their political crusades and often made sixties politics principled and volatile.

See also New Left; Student Nonviolent Coordinating Committee; Students for a Democratic Society.

Reference Gitlin, Todd, *The Sixties: Years of Hope, Days of Rage* (1987).

Establishment

Counterculture protesters used the word "establishment," often appearing capitalized, to refer to the political and military establishment, in a derogatory, though imprecise, way. Mainly it referred to traditional institutions and people within them who wielded substantial power. Writer and social critic Paul Goodman described the establishment as "the clubbing together of the secular and moral leaders of society—in industry, the military, labor unions, the cities, sciences and arts, the universities, the church, and state—to determine not only the economy and policy but the standards and ideals of the nation. The role of an Establishment is to tell what is right, accredited, professional . . . and to rule out what is not." (Collier 1969, 347)

Protesters considered the establishment to be antipopular and antidemocratic. Exactly what the establishment was, however, varied. Student demonstrators at a university, for example, might consider the establishment to mean the college administration. Antiwar demonstrators might consider it to mean the national government—Congress, the president, the courts, the military.

When, in the broadest sense, people referred to the counterculture versus the establishment, they pictured the latter to include national political institutions, large corporations, and anyone who cooperated with them to maintain their power. The mentality behind this, evident in remarks such as "He's just part of the establishment," encouraged a divisive situation. To the counterculture, the establishment could not be trusted.

"Eve of Destruction"

"You're old enough to kill but not for votin'," sang Barry McGuire in "Eve of Destruction," which in August 1965 topped the record charts, just five weeks after its release. Rock music had never seen a song like it in terms of its brooding voice, its sharp, foreboding condemnation of society. Many radio stations banned "Eve of Destruction" when conservative groups called it a Communist perversion.

To the emerging counterculture, though, it was a clarion call and a song that struck at the frustrations and deepest feelings coursing through a generation disgusted with hypocrisy, violence, and war. New visions, new policies, a new society had to be created—or else the eve of destruction would become the day of destruction.

A 19-year-old, P. F. Sloan, wrote the song for his own enjoyment. After it came to the attention of Dunhill Records, the company's owner asked McGuire, a former lead singer with the New Christy Minstrels, a folk group, to record it. Activist Todd Gitlin later claimed: " 'Eve of Destruction' seemed to certify that a mass movement of the American young was upon us." (Gitlin 1987, 197)

See also Rock Music.

Reference Gitlin, Todd, *The Sixties: Years of Hope, Days of Rage* (1987).

Evergreen Review

Published by Grove Press, *Evergreen Review* provided a sanctuary for dissenting ideas in the 1950s when conformity ruled, and in the 1960s added its voice to the New Left. In the earlier decade, *Evergreen Review* published works that brought beat writers a wider audience. Many counterculture political activists read the beats along with various political commentaries and counted *Evergreen Review* among the early influences in their ideological development.

Existentialism

Existentialism, the belief that a person or people collectively have freedom of choice and can rise above limitations and reshape the world, acted as a great wellspring in the counterculture.

New Left activists and hippies both embraced it. Existentialism, for example, appeared in sit-ins, which always entailed more than a demand—those engaged in them believed if they suffered long enough, the world would change to the way they envisioned it should be.

On a literary level, erudite persons in the counterculture read existentialist writers such as Albert Camus. Although the counterculture had its fatalists, by and large it believed limits could be transcended by thinking and acting past them.

See also Camus, Albert.

The Family Dog

In October 1965, four residents of San Francisco organized a promotion business they named "The Family Dog" to bring rock 'n' roll dance concerts to their city. In doing so, they popularized the psychedelic movement.

The founders of The Family Dog—Luria Castell, Ellen Harmon, Al Kelly, and Jack Towle—lived together in a house on Pine Street in San Francisco's Haight-Ashbury district. After their involvement in helping to open the hippie Red Dog Saloon in Virginia City, Nevada—where lights, bands, drugs, and wild costumes held sway—they conceived the idea to promote dances and have fun with rock music. They particularly desired venues where young people could cut loose. Castell observed that "Rock 'n' roll is the new form of communication for our generation," and she believed San Francisco could become another Liverpool.

The Family Dog—a name chosen in tribute to their dog, recently run over by a car—promoted their first dance concert with a poster that read:

THE FAMILY DOG PRESENTS
A Rock 'n' Roll Dance and Concert
THE JEFFERSON AIRPLANE,
THE MARBLES,
THE GREAT SOCIETY
And in high gear
Those CHARLATANS Announce
Their arrival
Oct. 16
9 to 2
Longshoreman's Hall

This building rented by The Family Dog and located near Fisherman's Wharf had recently been used for jazz shows. KYA radio promoted the dance concert, and The Family Dog distributed some silk screen posters, created by Jefferson Airplane's Marty Balin. Several hundred young people responded, decked in riotous, colorful clothing. They wore Edwardian designs, capes, velvet, SNCC and peace buttons—and with loud psychedelic rock music echoing in the acoustically poor hall, lights flashing to a beat, they danced hours on end, holding hands, snaking through the crowded dance floor in a form one observer called "orgiastic, spontaneous . . . completely free-form." Intent on being participants, not just promoters, The Family Dog joined in.

Several weeks later, the original Family Dog members left San Francisco for Mexico, and Chet Helms, manager of the band Big Brother and the Holding Company, reorganized the group. Helms considered himself a producer and "taste maker," and in January 1966 held his first concert at California Hall, featuring Jefferson Airplane and the Charlatans. In February, he sponsored a dance, "The Tribal Stomp," at the Fillmore, where promoter Bill Graham also held shows. The two men soon had a falling out, and Helms moved The Family Dog dance concerts to the Avalon Ballroom. He began using poster art, with its psychedelic designs and colors, on a regular basis, along with bigger light shows.

In 1967, Helms expanded The Family Dog to Denver—establishing a facility complete with recording studio and dance floor. Helms, however, had overextended himself and serious financial problems arose. In 1969, heavily in debt, he reorganized The Family Dog as The Associated Rubber Dog, but the ledger book and trends worked against him, for rock had moved away from the relatively small, participatory dance concerts to expensive shows in large auditoriums and stadiums.

Some criticized Helms for deserting the original Family Dog desire for fun over profits and becoming too much the businessman; others said he lacked enough business acumen. Whatever the case, The Family Dog collapsed and lay sleeping until the 1990s when it resumed promoting concerts.

See also Avalon Ballroom; Edwardian; Fillmore; Graham, Bill; Helms, Chet; Red Dog Saloon; Rock Music.

References Gleason, Ralph J., *The Jefferson Airplane and the San Francisco Sound* (1969); Perry, Charles, *The Haight-Ashbury: A History* (1984); http://www.familydog.com/.

Fanon, Frantz (1925–1961)

A black psychiatrist and social analyst, Frantz Fanon influenced the counterculture's political side with his attacks against colonialism and his call for violent revolution.

Fanon was born in 1925 on the small Caribbean island of Martinique. He served in the French army during World War II and, after it ended, studied psychology and medicine at the University of Lyon. From 1953 until 1956, he headed the psychiatry department at Blida-Joinville Hospital in French-controlled Algeria. His book *Black Skin, White Masks* appeared in 1952, presenting his critique of racism.

At Blida-Joinville he solidified his views on colonialism and psychology. Fanon considered Western civilization decadent, infused with a hypocrisy that praised human beings while actually degrading them. He said: "[In] Europe . . . they are never done talking about Man, yet murder men everywhere they find him, at the corner of every one of their own streets, in all the corners of the globe." Fanon believed colonialism was not only oppressive in terms of political rights but also damaging psychologically, contributing to neuroses.

In 1954, Fanon joined the National Liberation Front (FLN), which was seeking to end French rule in Algeria, and two years later edited *El Moudjihad*, the rebel newspaper published in Tunis. His book *The Wretched of the Earth*, written shortly before his death, won a wide readership. In it, he calls for colonial peoples to rebel violently against their rulers to end foreign domination and purge societies of alien practices. Political, economic, and psychological bondage, all intertwined, have to be removed, he writes; rebellion, an existentialist act of the highest calling, will produce psychic liberation.

Fanon died from cancer while in Washington, D.C., on 6 December 1961, but in America during the 1960s, political radicals embraced his works. Many in the New Left believed the United States promoted colonial oppression—talking human rights but crushing them in the name of defeating communism. To them, Fanon stood alongside Che Guvera, Fidel Castro, and Mao Tse-tung as a hero.

Among African Americans, Fanon's ideas encouraged the Student Nonviolent Coordinating Committee to adopt militancy, and the Black Panthers considered him essential reading. James Forman and Stokely Carmichael, two prominent radicals, attributed their ideological growth in part to Fanon.

See also Black Panthers; Black Power; Carmichael, Stokely; Forman, James.

References Fanon, Frantz, *Black Skin, White Masks* (1967) and *The Wretched of the Earth* (1963).

Far-Out

Although *far-out* first appeared in the American vocabulary in 1954, it was not popularized until the 1960s. Hippies and other young people in the counterculture used it to mean excellent or splendid. Hence a rock song could be described as "far-out," usually in an exclamatory tone.

Feiffer, Jules (1929–)

A cartoonist and writer, Jules Feiffer emerged in the late 1950s as a talented social commentator whose critiques concerning racism, nuclear tests, and the Vietnam War earned a large following among liberals and activists.

Feiffer was born on 26 January 1929 in Bronx, New York, the son of David Feiffer and Rhoda Davis Feiffer. His father worked as a salesman and his mother as a fashion designer. Feiffer graduated from Monroe High School in the Bronx, and then pursued his desire to be a cartoonist by attending drawing classes at Pratt Institute in New York City.

In 1951, he was drafted into the army, and during his stint worked in a cartoon animation unit at a film center. After his discharge in 1953, he tried in vain to find employment as a cartoonist or writer and had to take odd jobs. Then, in 1956, after some success working for a comic book publisher, he took his cartoons to a recently founded alternative newspaper, the *Village Voice*. The newspaper printed his panels, titled *Sick, Sick, Sick*, on a nonpay basis, and they proved to be highly popular with its readers, generally a hip crowd. Feiffer later said his cartoon "was designed as a weekly satiric comment on the people I knew, the young urban middle class, their work habits, sex urges, and family antagonisms. You must remember that this was another time. Sex was treated as either dirty or discreet, not right as material for humor in family newspapers or on TV." (Feiffer with Heller 1982, 10)

Feiffer drew simple figures, such as his first two prominent characters, Bernard Mergendeiler, an urban liberal who suffered from anxiety attacks, and the Dancer, Mergendeiler's female counterpart who, through all her difficulties, maintained her faith. His various characters engaged in soliloquies and showed the stress generated by a cold-war, atomic-bomb society. Little action appeared in his works, reflecting his technique of writing the captions first and then drawing the picture, as in the following, which appeared around 1967, and in cartoon form shows a black man's face, dark sunglasses shading his eyes, Afro atop his head:

> I dug jazz
> And whitey picked up on it
> I dug hip
> And whitey picked up on it
> I dug rock
> And whitey picked up on it
> I dug freedom
> And finally lost whitey. (111)

Feiffer's cartoons criticized nuclear tests and political leaders and exposed society's hypocrisies. He did not shy from tackling conformity and sacrosanct images—as when he implied that Superman's wearing a cape might make him a transvestite. His work inspired college students who, in the early sixties, began breaking the political lethargy that dominated on campuses by leading protests against nuclear weapons.

In 1958, McGraw-Hill published Feiffer's work *Sick, Sick, Sick: A Guide to Non-Confident Living*, and within a short time it sold over 100,000 copies. In the sixties, his cartoons circulated widely through syndication, providing a prominent liberal critique, and he was at the forefront among editorial cartoonists in criticizing the Vietnam War. Feiffer supported antiwar protesters, and in 1968 won selection as a Eugene McCarthy delegate to the Democratic National Convention. In addition to his drawings, Feiffer has written plays and novels and still produces his cartoons, which appear weekly in syndication.

See also *Village Voice*.

References Feiffer, Jules, *Feiffer's Album* (1963); Feiffer, Jules, with Steven Heller, ed., *Jules Feiffer's America: From Eisenhower to Reagan* (1982).

The Feminine Mystique
See Friedan, Betty.

Ferlinghetti, Lawrence (1919–)

Lawrence Ferlinghetti promoted an alternative beat literary style in the 1950s and 1960s by publishing new authors, selling their works in his bookstore, and writing his own poetry. His efforts helped foment discontent with middle-class conformity and thus stirred the counterculture.

Ferlinghetti was born on 24 March 1919 in Yonkers, New York. He spent much of his childhood in Bronxville but suffered considerable instability and unhappiness when he was shifted from his mother, to an orphanage, to an aunt, to other families. Ferlinghetti attended Mount Hermon, a private high school in Massachusetts, where literature enthralled him and he hoped to become a journalist. He graduated from there in 1937 and four years later obtained his bachelor of arts degree from the University of North Carolina-Chapel Hill.

Shortly thereafter, he joined the navy and served as a commanding officer in 1944 during the invasion at Normandy. The following year, when World War II ended, Ferlinghetti moved to Greenwich Village. He studied English and literature at Columbia University, where, in 1947, he obtained his M.A. He then moved to Paris and studied at the Sorbonne. Soon after writing his dissertation on modern urban poetry and receiving his doctorate, he returned to the United States and settled in San Francisco.

In that city, Ferlinghetti met writers who, like him, explored new styles and challenged the oppressive materialism and suburban conformity that dominated the 1950s. These writers, known as beats, pursued honesty, spontaneity, and mysticism in their lives and works. They congregated in San Francisco's North Beach, where they developed a bohemian following. For his part, Ferlinghetti believed that "style is a feeling for the weight and arrangement of words on a page" (Cherkovski 1979, 71), and he sought to arrange his poems so that the way they looked facilitated the message.

Ferlinghetti promoted the beat movement when, in 1953, with $1,000 in capital, he opened the nation's first all-paperback bookstore. At City Lights, as he named it, beats participated in poetry readings and gathered to exchange ideas. In 1955, Ferlinghetti began publishing the City Lights Pocket Book Series with his own collection of poems, *Pictures of the Gone World*. The following year, he released *Howl*, a poem by Allen Ginsberg, but the authorities in San Francisco deemed the work obscene and arrested Ferlinghetti for having published it. He successfully defended himself, however, based on First Amendment rights, and the controversy made *Howl* a best-seller—unusual for poetry.

Ferlinghetti continued to publish and edit City Lights Books (by the end of the 1950s he had over 13 titles in the Pocket Poets Series and 23 on the entire City Lights list) while editing *City Lights Journal*. He continued his own poetry, too, most prominently his 1958 work, *A Coney Island of the Mind*. Unlike other beat poets, Ferlinghetti related his poems to painting, in which he had received training. He made frequent references to painters and sculptors, and stressed imagery over ideology. He considered the subject less important than what he, as a poet, wanted to say. This quality, along with his attacks on conformity, appears in his poem *In Goya's Greatest Scenes We Seem To See*. He begins with a direct reference to the great painter, and then jabs at society when he compares middle-class Americans to Goya's figures:

> They are the same people
> only further from home
> on freeways fifty lanes wide
> on a concrete continent
> spaced with bland billboards
> illustrating imbecile illusions of happiness
>
> (Ferlinghetti 1958, 9)

As the beatnik era gave way to the hippies, many in the counterculture related to Ferlinghetti's themes, his informal style, and imagery that conflicted with the rationality so prominent in a technological society. And Ferlinghetti related to them. He had great hopes for the counterculture, believing it might bring an end to nation-states and remake the world in a harmonious way.

Ferlinghetti joined political protesters in the counterculture when he marched against the Vietnam War and nuclear weapons. In 1967, he was arrested and served time in prison for his participation in a protest at California's Oakland Army Induction Center. Ferlinghetti read frequently at demonstrations and even at rock concerts, experimented with LSD, and later wrote "Mock Confessional" about it. In addition to poems, he authored an experimental novel *Her*, several plays, and made films.

See also Beat; Beatnik; Ginsberg, Allen; Kerouac, Jack; Snyder, Gary.

References Cherkovski, Neeli, *Ferlinghetti: A Biography* (1979); Ferlinghetti, Lawrence, *A Coney Island of the Mind* (1958), *Endless Life: Selected Poems* (1981), *Her* (1960), *Howl of the Censor* (1961), *Open Eye, Open Heart* (1973), and *Starting from San Francisco* (1961); Smith, Larry R., *Lawrence Ferlinghetti: Poet-At-Large* (1983).

Fillmore

To San Franciscans in the 1960s, "Fillmore" meant either the large black district and its main thoroughfare, which bordered Haight-Ashbury, or the old brick auditorium that stood on the corner of Geary and Fillmore Streets, where counterculture youths gathered for psychedelic rock 'n' roll dance concerts.

Fillmore Auditorium had long been important to the black community. An African American businessman, Charles Sullivan, owned it and had staged blues shows there with prominent artists, such as Ray Charles. The building, entered by climbing a stairway tucked between storefronts at street level, housed a stage, a large wooden dance floor (hence, the Fillmore's reputation as a ballroom), and at the rear and along one wall a spacious balcony from which observers could look onto the crowd below or frequent a café-bar tucked in its recess.

The Fillmore proved well suited for the dance concert scene that gained popularity; in fact, rock promoter Bill Graham considered it ideal, and on 10 December 1965 held a concert there to benefit the San Francisco Mime Troupe. The bill featured area bands, including Jefferson Airplane and The Great Society. Ken Kesey and the Merry Pranksters staged an Acid Test there in January 1966, and Chet Helms and The Family Dog used the site for concerts until Graham signed an exclusive three-year lease with Sullivan early that spring. The Fillmore's proximity to Haight-Ashbury meant it drew young people from the hippie district.

Graham ended his concerts at Fillmore Auditorium after altercations erupted between whites and neighborhood blacks. The last rock concert was held there on 4 July 1968, featuring Credence Clearwater Revival. Graham took the Fillmore name with him, however, and called his new venue (formerly the Carousel) Fillmore West to distinguish it from Fillmore East, another site he had recently opened at the old Village Theatre in New York's East Village on Second Avenue and Sixth Street, near New York University.

Both Fillmores continued to draw crowds attracted by the rock bands and light shows until 1971, when the trend shifted from dance concerts to elaborate shows at large stadiums. By this time, too, Graham had tired of promoting the Fillmores. He closed Fillmore East on 27 June 1971 and Fillmore West in early July, after a spectacular weeklong series of rock concerts.

See also Acid Tests; The Family Dog; Graham, Bill; Kesey, Ken.

Flashback

In counterculture parlance, flashback referred to the aftereffects from psychedelic drugs, notably LSD. Some users claimed that long after taking acid, they had hallucinogenic experiences at unexpected times.

Flower Power

The term "flower power," originally coined by the poet Allen Ginsberg, referred to hippies who wore flowers to symbolize their attachment to peace and love. Supposedly these hippies, and the counterculture in general, represented a new force capable of changing the world through peaceful means—spreading flowers—rather than through violence. The term flower power, though, had wider use in the mainstream media (as did "flower children," the phrase used in reference to counterculture youths) than it did among hippies.

Rock promoter Bill Graham talked critically about flower power when he said: "For a period . . . there was an escape from reality. Which was a fantasy. Which was flower power. 'Oh, aren't the streets beautiful?' No, they have shit in them! 'Well, I'll just dance on the shit then.' No! Try to clean it. 'Oh, no no. That's work. That's reality.'" (Joseph 1974, 347–348)

Reference Joseph, Peter, *Good Times: An Oral History of America in the 1960s* (1974).

Fluxus

Fluxus emerged as an experimental art group and style in the early 1960s, created by George Maciunas, an eccentric artist who owned a gallery in New York City. Maciunas never precisely defined fluxus; some said he used it to simply mean change, or flux; others said it reflected his humor and that he used it satirically to mean clearing the bowels. Fluxus art represented the counterculture attack on traditional standards—it treated as art that which people wanted to call art, and thus democratized and liberated the field. Anyone could be an artist. In many ways, fluxus resembled the 1910s international Dada movement—an antiart, poised against all conventions and rooted in an anarchistic attitude, the whimsical, fantastic, and absurd.

Maciunas applied the word "fluxus" not only to specific works of art but also to the group of artists who identified with him. He and his followers gave exhibitions of whatever items they found, staged concerts around the themes of everyday life, and mass-produced drawings and paintings, much as Andy Warhol later did. In *Greenwich Village 1963*, Sally Banes quotes a fluxus leader:

> Fluxus invites each human, every human to come forward, to work or to play. The ritual is interactive, the audience can address, transform, change. Whoever picks up a box of cards by George Brecht, by Takehisa Kosugi, by Robert Watts, can make the art. Whoever wants to look at some shoes by Alison Knowles or Aktual clothing by Milan Knizak can also make, sign and have. (65)

See also Ono, Yoko; Performance Art.

References Banes, Sally, *Greenwich Village 1963* (1993); Kirby, Michael, *Happenings* (1965); Morgan, Robert, *Conceptual Art: An American Perspective* (1994).

Folk Music

In the early sixties, a folk music revival enraptured young people and helped to stimulate the counterculture. The Newport Folk Festival in Rhode Island drew considerable attention; but more than this, folk music concerts appeared on college campuses. Bob Dylan, Joan Baez, Phil Ochs, and others used topical songs, and this appealed most to those seeking music that addressed social issues. Many persons who later worked as political activists in the counterculture claimed that folk music stirred their awareness of racism, poverty, and war and inspired them to seek change.

See also: Baez, Joan; Dylan, Bob; Guthrie, Arlo; Guthrie, Woody; Newport Folk Festival; Ochs, Phil; Rock Music; Seeger, Pete.

References Cantwell, Robert, *When We Were Good: The Folk Revival* (1996); Rodnitzky, Jerome L., *Minstrels of the Dawn: The Folk-Protest Singer as a Cultural Hero* (1976).

Fonda, Jane (1937–)

An actor and political activist, Jane Fonda said about American society in 1970: "If you strip away the facade and false sense of freedom and social justice and comfort that lulls the white middle class into thinking they're safe, you can see the system for what it is: racist, oppressive, totalitarian, and monstrous." (Davidson 1990, 142)

Fonda was born on 21 December 1937 in New York City to Frances Seymour Brokaw Fonda and Henry Fonda, a movie and stage actor. Because of her father's profession, she lived at various times on the East Coast and in California. She received her primary and secondary education at the Brentwood Town and Country School in Los Angeles, the Greenwich Academy in Greenwich, Connecticut, and the Emma Willard School in Troy, New York. Fonda formed few friendships with her fellow students and had a difficult relationship with her father, who remained distant and aloof. Tragedy struck on 25 April 1950 when her mother, then suffering from depression at a psychiatric hospital, committed suicide by slitting her throat with a razor blade.

In 1955, Fonda graduated from the Emma Willard School and obtained a small role in a play that starred her father. That fall, she enrolled at Vassar College, and the following summer worked as an apprentice actor at the Cape Playhouse in nearby Dennis, Massachusetts. Although she returned to Vassar in 1956, she showed little interest in her studies and exhibited substantial restlessness, probably resulting from loneliness and bulimia. As a bulimic, she obsessively feared becoming fat and engaged in eating binges follwed by compulsive vomiting.

In 1957, Fonda convinced her father to send her to Paris, where she could paint and study art. Once there, she did little of either and instead partied with jet-set playboys. Tired of this scene, however, she returned to the United States and studied at Lee Strasberg's Actors Studio in New York City. There she met and fell in love with Andreas Voutsinas, a wealthy Greek and fellow student who guided her early career. Fonda made her Broadway debut in 1959 with a part in *There Was a Little Girl*, and her film debut in 1960 when she starred opposite Tony Perkins in *Tall Story*.

Several more movies followed, but she gained her largest following within the counterculture when she starred in *Barbarella*, a 1968 film directed by Roger Vadim, whom she had married three years earlier. This comedic science-fiction movie presents Fonda amid psychedelic trappings as a forty-first century space adventurer who triumphs over a sadistic world. The opening scene in *Barbarella* shows Fonda removing her space uniform in a striptease. At the time of the movie's release, she said: "I don't think of it as an erotic film. It's just funny and free and nice." (123)

Soon after, though, she criticized it as sexually exploitive. Fonda acted in other prominent movies in the mid to late 1960s: *Any Wednesday*, *Barefoot in the Park*, *Cat Ballou*, *The Chase*, *La Curee*,

Jane Fonda inspects the damage of the U.S.–bombed Bach Mai Hospital in Hanoi, Vietnam, in this undated photo.

Hurry Sundown, *Spirits of the Dead*, and *They Shoot Horses, Don't They?*

As the decade ended, Fonda developed a radical social consciousness. The reasons for the change are not clear, but several influences deserve mention: her father's New Deal liberalism, her desire for acceptance and camaraderie, the student riots she witnessed during her trips to France, the vivid scenes of destruction she saw—including atrocities by American soldiers—on the news film from Vietnam broadcast by French television, a trip she made to India during which she witnessed considerable poverty, and demonstrations within the United States. Fonda later stated:

> The most specific thing I can remember was watching television when there was a march of a half-million people on the Pentagon. That had a profound effect on me, because I suddenly realized to what degree the country had changed since I'd been away. I watched women leading marches. I watched women getting beaten up. I watched women walking up to the bayonets that were surrounding the Pentagon and they were not afraid. It was the soldiers who were afraid. I'll never forget that experience. It completely changed me. It began my searching for what was behind it all. (132)

Thus started her radical efforts working for numerous causes. She plunged into this in 1970, when she supported Indian protesters at Alcatraz who were trying to reclaim the island from the federal government. She seemed at first to know little about the issues involved but worked hard to learn them. In addition to the Indian movement, she supported the Black Panthers and antiwar protesters, and began a grueling speaking schedule to convey her message.

Fonda's actions brought considerable publicity and earned her a place on President Richard Nixon's "enemies list," those he considered a threat to his power. The FBI subsequently labeled Fonda an anarchist and began harassing her. The government wiretapped her phone; illegally investigated her bank account; wrote an anonymous letter, approved by FBI director J. Edgar Hoover, to a newspaper columnist, accusing her of saying Nixon had to be killed (the columnist never used the letter); and, claiming she possessed drugs, stopped her during a return trip from Canada. The drugs turned out to be vitamin pills.

Fonda made a controversial trip to North Vietnam in July 1972 at a time when the war, which had killed over 40,000 American soldiers and 1.2 million Vietnamese, was slowly winding down. While there, she criticized Nixon as a liar and made a radio address to American soldiers, telling them their bombs had destroyed hospitals and their attacks had violated international agreements. She returned to the United States after two weeks, amid intense criticism that she had committed treason. One newspaper, New Hamphshire's archconservative *Manchester News Leader*, called for her to be shot. A government official later admitted, however, that "Fonda was saying what she thought was true. She caused no desertions. As far as giving aid and comfort to the enemy was concerned, who was the enemy? We had never declared a state of war with North Vietnam." (176)

Fonda's trip effectively halted her acting career as few studios would hire her. Her radical involvement continued when, in 1972, she married Tom Hayden, a founder of Students for a Democratic Society and a high-profile antiwar and social activist. The following year, she sued the federal government for having violated her rights with its harassment campaign. An out-of-court settlement did not bring her a damage award, but the government did admit its wrongful doings.

Fonda returned to the screen with a successful movie in 1977, *Fun with Dick and Jane*. That year, she organized her own production company, intended to make movies largely dealing with social topics. These included *Coming Home* (1978), about the wife of a Marine captain fighting in Vietnam, and *The China Syndrome* (1979), about a reporter investigating a meltdown at a nuclear power plant—a story some critics called far-fetched until shortly after the movie's release a partial meltdown occurred at Three Mile Island in Pennsylvania.

In the late 1970s and 1980s, Fonda sold millions of exercise books, records, and videotapes. Her marriage to Hayden ended as the eighties came to a close, and in the 1990s she married Ted Turner, a wealthy media mogul, and produced movies through his Turner Pictures and her own Fonda Films Company. Critics accused her of selling out; others debated whether her earlier activism had any attachment to principles or whether it merely represented a passing phase. Whatever the case, this academy award–winning actor had been, in the sixties, Hollywood's preeminent activist.

See also Hayden, Tom.

Reference Davidson, Bill, *Jane Fonda: An Intimate Biography* (1990).

Forman, James (1928–)

As black power swept the civil rights movement in the mid-1960s, James Forman, a leader in the Student Nonviolent Coordinating Committee (SNCC), expressed a radical ideology.

Born on 5 October 1928 in Chicago, Forman spent his early childhood on his grandmother's farm in Mississippi. At age six, he moved back to Chicago, where he lived with his parents and attended Roman Catholic and public schools. He graduated from Englewood High School in 1947, entered the air force, and then briefly attended the University of Southern California. He continued his college education at Roosevelt University in Chicago, from where he graduated in 1957. The civil rights movement had affected him greatly, and in 1956 he wrote stories for the *Chicago Defender* about the desegregation battle under way in Little Rock, Arkansas.

In the 1960s, his fight against racial injustice intensified. After suffering arrest during the Freedom Rides in Monroe, North Carolina, he was, in 1961, appointed executive secretary of SNCC. Shortly thereafter, he participated in nonviolent demonstrations to desegregate public facilities in Albany, Georgia, and Danville, Virginia. Forman criticized President John Kennedy for moving too slowly on civil rights and for failing to provide federal protection for the movement's workers; at one point he accused him of "double-dealing."

In 1964, Forman developed radical views after taking a trip overseas to Guinea. He returned convinced that blacks in America must join with those in Africa to end white oppression, promulgate Marxist ideas, and develop black cultural identity. He equated American blacks with exploited colonial subjects and helped plan a political protest at the Democratic National Convention in which members of the Mississippi Freedom Democratic Party, a largely black group committed to civil rights, challenged the seating of the state's all-white segregationist delegation. This protest, however, resulted in few concessions.

The following year, Forman guided SNCC in a cooperative project with the Southern Christian Leadership Conference to register black voters in Selma, Alabama. After state and local authorities blocked a protest march to Montgomery, Forman participated in demonstrations there. The futility he encountered deepened his anguish. In 1966, SNCC replaced him with Stokely Carmichael as executive secretary. Forman supported Carmichael and the shift to a strident black power strategy, and convinced SNCC to stop using integrated units in the freedom struggle—blacks, he believed, could best lead blacks.

As director of international affairs for SNCC, he sought to build contacts with African nations. In 1968, SNCC expelled him while the organization underwent internal turmoil and disintegrated, and he joined the League of Revolutionary Black Workers.

In 1969, Forman wrote a controversial document, "The Black Manifesto." In it, he decries racism and demands money from churches and synagogues as reparation for slavery. When, in 1972, he authored *The Making of Black Revolutionaries*, he offered no retreat from his radical ideology.

Forman later obtained a master's degree in African American history from Cornell University and a doctorate from the Union of Experimental Colleges and Universities.

See also Black Panthers; Black Power; Student Nonviolent Coordinating Committee.

Reference Forman, James, *The Making of Black Revolutionaries: A Personal Account* (1972).

Freak

The word *freak* appeared in the early twentieth century and meant a person with an intense interest or involvement in something. In the 1960s, *freak* and the drug culture merged, so that a person might be described, for example, as a speed freak—someone addicted to STP, a potent psychedelic; or freak might mean a person who experienced hallucinations through psychedelic drugs.

Freak took on additional meaning, though, and referred to hippies and others who challenged or did not fit the social norms. Thus, one person might describe another as a "real freak," a term many counterculture youths considered an honor, indicating successful rebelliousness. In fact, many freaks exhibited pride in calling *themselves* freaks. In 1968, the student government president at Ohio State University described himself and his supporters as "freaks, not radicals." (Anderson 1995, 244)

Reference Anderson, Terry H., *The Movement and the Sixties* (1995).

Freak Out

"Freak out" emerged as a phrase in 1966 and referred to a person experiencing a hallucinatory or strong emotional experience, either under the influence of drugs or straight: "I was crossing the street, man, and saw this dude I hadn't seen for years. He looked so different—long hair, groovy clothes—it just freaked me out."

Free Speech Movement

In 1964, the Free Speech Movement (FSM) erupted at the University of California-Berkeley—the first massive countercultural protest by college students. Few expected it, and even fewer realized it would ignite other campuses.

Students at Berkeley had, for some time, felt constrained by university regulations that restricted political expression. They had only one place outside the classroom where they could present their ideas: a small piece of land, called a free speech area, at the entrance to the college on Bancroft Strip. There they made speeches and distributed pamphlets. On 14 September 1964, however, the university announced it would end this free speech zone. The decision came after several students picketed the nearby *Oakland Tribune*, claiming it had engaged in racial discrimination. This action caused the newspaper's owner to complain about students fomenting radicalism, and so the administration decided to crack down.

The campus seethed with anger as students claimed the episode proved that the university, and American society as a whole, wanted to crush dissent. Then on 1 October, the tense situation boiled over when university police arrested a student, Jack Weinberg, for violating the restrictions on political speech. Dozens of students immediately gathered in front of Sproul Hall, the main administration building, where they surrounded the police car holding Weinberg. Mario Savio, a philosophy student, addressed the crowd and won recognition as the leader of the protest. About 200 students soon occupied Sproul Hall, began a sit-in, and did not disperse until the administration promised to establish a committee, which would include faculty and students, to study college rules. The protest became known as the Free Speech Movement later that week, after representatives from several student clubs met and established a formal organization.

On 20 November, the Board of Regents eased the speech restrictions and the crisis appeared to be over. Several days later, however, the administration announced it would prosecute the protest leaders. On 2 December, new sit-ins occurred at Sproul Hall, with 400 students occupying the building until riot police dragged them out; at the same time, graduate teaching assistants went on strike, and in the turmoil, the college canceled many classes. On 8 December, the faculty agreed, in general, with the students' demands, and the Regents decided to further extend free speech rights.

In all, the students sought freedom of political expression and some educational reforms, and for the most part were neither ideologues nor under the control of outside agitators. They presented, one analyst observed, "a clear-eyed and courageous response to concrete, felt injustices." (Wolin and Schar 1970, 41) Perhaps most importantly, in America's increasingly technological society, they wanted to feel human. About Clark Kerr, the university chancellor, the students insisted: "By our action we have proved [him] wrong in his claim that human beings can be handled like raw material without provoking revolt. We have smashed to bits his pretty little doll house. The next task will be to build in its stead a real house for real people." (Draper 1965, 225)

On campuses across the nation students held Berkeley-style protests in reaction to oppressive conditions. Most universities reformed, but often minimally. Meanwhile, the FSM splintered, with some stressing the speech issue and others launching a broad attack on society as sterile and oppressive. Within a short time, the Vietnam War emerged as the overriding concern. By 1966, the FSM ended, replaced by radicalized movements disgusted with liberal moderation, and by hippie cultural influences that rejected political action as futile.

See also Savio, Mario; University of California-Berkeley.

References Draper, Hal, *Berkeley: The New Student Revolt* (1965); Wolin, Sheldon, and James H. Schar, *The Berkeley Rebellion and Beyond: Essays on Politics and Education in the Technological Society* (1970).

Free University

Emulating the freedom schools that had been founded in the South by civil rights activists, and responding to the call for liberated universities issued during the free speech movement at the University of California-Berkeley in 1964, Free University attempted to promote a radical, socialist alternative to existing colleges.

In 1965, James Mellen, a leader within the May 2nd Movement, an antiwar group, joined with friends from Progressive Labor, a pro-Chinese Marxist organization, to begin Free University in New York's Greenwich Village at Fourteenth Street between Fifth Avenue and University Place, where it occupied two large rooms on the second floor of a loft building. FUNY, as it called itself in derision of mainstream education's presumptuous titles, offered courses such as Marxist Geography, Life in Mainland China Today, Poetry and Revolution, Art and Communism, Imperialism in Latin America, and the Instruments of Imperialism. Mellen, FUNY's secretary-treasurer, set tuition at $8 per course.

He later called FUNY "a serious intellectual undertaking," but unusual events happened, too: petition drives, peace demonstrations, and hippies coming in to play rock music. Before internal bickering caused FUNY to disintegrate in 1966, it had by example encouraged free universities to open in other locations, including Chicago, Detroit, and Gainesville, Florida.

See also May 2nd Movement; Mellen, James; New Left.

Reference Viorst, Milton, *Fire in the Streets: America in the 1960s* (1979).

Freedom House

When, in the early 1960s, the Student Nonviolent Coordinating Committee (SNCC) sent volunteers into the South to register black voters and lead sit-ins, it often established freedom houses. A converted private residence, the freedom house served as local headquarters for a campaign. Usually filled with typewriters, mimeograph machines, charts, and notices, freedom houses served as refuges for blacks and whites who faced a hostile environment in trying to advance civil rights. SNCC members held meetings at the freedom houses, gatherings that involved everything from planning strategy to singing songs as a means to motivate people and maintain their confidence.

See also Student Nonviolent Coordinating Committee.

Freedom Schools

As young student activists galvanized the southern civil rights movement in the early and mid-1960s, they established freedom schools, particularly in Mississippi and Alabama. Through them, they intended to build awareness among blacks as to what could be done about oppression. The schools were operated by the Council of Federated Organizations, or COFO, that consisted of the Congress of Racial Equality, the National Association for the Advancement of Colored People, the Southern Christian Leadership Council, and the Student Nonviolent Coordinating Committee. The last group most actively founded the freedom schools to accompany its voter registration drives.

In Mississippi, some 700 volunteers, both white and black college students, opened 47 such schools during Freedom Summer of 1964 and enrolled 2,000 African Americans. Some schools lasted several months, others merely weeks. They had few amenities—often just a single-room structure with inadequate plumbing, heat, or electricity. The volunteers lived precariously, always wondering if white reactionaries would assault them, fearful that someone might lob a bomb into the schoolhouse or at the residences where they lived.

But they persevered. In the freedom schools they taught blacks of all ages. At first, they emphasized reading and writing skills for older African Americans to enable them to vote, and they held classes on constitutional rights. Then they expanded their curriculum and taught the need for social change; they taught children as young as four and led discussion groups for teenagers. In addition to academics, the schools provided recreational activities.

White attitudes toward the freedom schools displayed ingrained racism. For example, the mayor of Ruleville, Mississippi, complained about two volunteers, white female college students from the North: "They've sent some of the trashiest people down here. Those . . . little girls over there now don't represent American womanhood. . . . Wallowing around Negro men who need a bath is degrading to their sex." (Meier 1991, 87)

The freedom schools challenged segregation and activated thousands to fight social injustice. They represented an attempt to spark grassroots activism through education, part of the countercultural impulse that the masses could work outside the system to change it.

See also Student Nonviolent Coordinating Committee.

Reference Meier, August, Elliot Rudwick, and John Bracey, Jr., eds., *Black Protest in the Sixties* (1991).

Freedom Summer

In 1964, the Council of Federated Organizations (COFO), consisting of the National Association for the Advancement of Colored People, the Congress of Racial Equality, the Southern Christian Leadership Conference, and the Student Nonviolent Coordinating Committee (SNCC), pondered what action to take after a largely successful drive the previous year to register black voters in Mississippi. COFO, dominated by SNCC, did not want the enthusiasm that had been stirred to fade and the fight for black rights to lose momentum, and thus it launched Freedom Summer.

At a meeting in Greenville, Mississippi, David Dennis of SNCC proposed to 45 delegates that a Freedom Summer campaign be aimed primarily at expanding the voter registration drive, taking it into areas of the state where opposition and hostility ran high. The delegates immediately debated whether they should recruit white college students from the North to help in the effort. Many in SNCC believed that Freedom Summer should be all-black; this, they insisted, would promote black leadership. Further, these delegates did not like the attitude of whites who had previously come south to help, one bespeaking superiority.

When civil rights leader Bob Moses arrived at the meeting, he helped persuade the delegates to recruit the white students. "Look, I'm not going to be part of anything all-black," he insisted. "I always thought that the one thing we can do for the country that no one else can do is to be above the race issue." He realized, too, that the presence of white students would increase media coverage and assure federal protection for civil rights workers.

Such protection proved meager, however, and even before the campaign began in June, extensive violence had erupted as local whites assaulted blacks. When the SNCC volunteers arrived—more than 800 who had met at the Western College for Women in Oxford, Ohio, to plan their strategy the violence continued unabated. Freedom Summer included a tragedy: three students, one black and two whites, were brutally killed near Philadelphia, Mississippi, by whites. One observer estimated that by summer's end, whites had killed 3 additional volunteers, beaten 80, shot at 35, burned over 30 churches to the ground, and bombed about 30 buildings.

Freedom Summer greatly affected SNCC and the civil rights movement: the violence radicalized blacks, even to the point that some rejected nonviolence and armed themselves for protection. The white students returned home convinced that American society was not only undemocratic but also cruel and barbaric, and they felt betrayed by the federal government and its liberal supporters for having done little to protect the volunteers and, in the case of the FBI, having even sympathized with the white attackers. These students constituted an activist minority that expressed disgust with the status quo and through the counterculture challenged the major political parties, the Vietnam War, poverty, the entire economic structure.

Freedom Summer registered black voters (although, due to white resistance, only in small numbers) and led to an important confrontation at the Democratic National Convention when the recently organized Mississippi Freedom Democratic Party challenged the all-white delegation from that state. Perhaps more importantly, Freedom Summer had exposed injustice and thus left an indelible imprint on the emerging counterculture.

See also Student Nonviolent Coordinating Committee.

Friedan, Betty (1921–)

"It is twenty years now since *The Feminine Mystique* was published," Betty Friedan observed in 1983. "I am still awed by the revolution that book helped spark." *The Feminine Mystique* had indeed set a spark, and Friedan's efforts as a writer and feminist changed the status of women in American society.

Friedan was born Betty Naomi Goldstein on 4 February 1921 in Peoria, Illinois, to Harry Goldstein and Miriam Horowitz Goldstein. Her father, an immigrant Jew, owned a jewelry store and the family lived comfortably. As a child, two experiences stung Friedan and shaped her consciousness, making her uneasy with some middle-class values: the anti-Semitism she experienced from the people in Peoria, and her mother's discontentment with having given up her work as a journalist in order to get married.

After high school, where she had excelled academically and founded a literary magazine, Friedan entered Smith College in Massachusetts. There she edited the student

Betty Friedan, founder of the National Organization for Women, pictured here in 1970

newspaper and majored in psychology. She graduated *summa cum laude* in 1942 and accepted a research fellowship to study at the University of California-Berkeley. After one year there, she moved to New York City, where she worked as a journalist and met Carl Friedan, a theatre producer, whom she married in 1947. Two years later, she took a maternity leave to have her first child.

A personal experience in 1954 stirred Friedan's dissatisfaction with society's treatment of women: she requested a second maternity leave, only to be fired from her job. Rather than protest, though, she retreated to her family's home along the Hudson River and tried to be what 1950s society expected of women: a happy, suburban homemaker. At the same time, she wrote articles on a freelance basis. These portrayed women as satisfied and fulfilled in their duties as housewives, but Friedan realized this theme did not hold true for her. She wondered about other suburban women, whether they were happy, and in 1957 decided to find out by interviewing and surveying her former Smith College classmates.

She published the findings in her 1963 book, *The Feminine Mystique*. This work immediately earned a wide readership because it expressed the frustration felt by many women, and it coincided with an emerging social and political activism that in two years would develop into a full-fledged counterculture. Without a doubt, Friedan's book contributed to the ferment.

Friedan's phrase, "feminine mystique," refers to the idealization of the traditional female role of wife and mother. The place in the home where society expects women to stay, she claims, both frustrates and oppresses many women and represents a male conspiracy to limit competition from the opposite sex. In *Mystique*, Friedan discusses "the problem that has no name" as gnawing at women. "As she made the beds, shopped for groceries, matched slipcover material, ate peanut butter sandwiches with her children, chauffeured Cub Scouts and Brownies, lay beside her husband at night" Friedan says in referring to a typical suburban woman, "she was afraid to ask even of herself the silent question—'Is this all?'" (Norton 1989, 390) Friedan continues: "Gradually I came to realize that the problem that has no name was shared by countless women in America. . . . The women who suffer this problem have a hunger that food cannot fill." (392–393) Friedan insists:

> If I am right, the problem that has no name stirring in the minds of so many American women today is not a matter of loss of femininity or too much education, or the demands of domesticity. It is far more important than anyone recognizes. . . . It may well be the key to our future as a nation and a culture. We can no longer ignore that voice within women that says: "I want something more than my husband and my children and my home." (393–394)

Although Friedan received widespread favorable reaction to her book, some men reacted negatively, and some women reacted defensively—even fervently opposing her position. Amid the debate she had stimulated, she toured the nation, making speeches and appearing on television.

Friedan decided that advancing women's liberation required political action. Thus, in 1966, she founded the National Organization for Women (NOW), devoted to obtaining equal rights. This, she believed, could be accomplished by enforcing existing legislation, such as the 1964 Civil Rights Act that made sexual discrimination in employment illegal, and by amending the Constitution.

Divisions within NOW hampered Friedan's efforts, however, for as the counterculture expanded, younger, radical women joined the organization and fought with her over issues. Whereas Friedan sought to form alliances with men who supported the cause, these radicals considered all men enemies and opposed all cooperation with them. They raised sexual issues, too, that Friedan thought alienated many women: rights for lesbians and complete rejection of the family unit as dysfunctional and oppressive. Many radicals, such as those affiliated with the group Redstockings, criticized Friedan for selling out to the male "bourgeois world."

The infighting grew so intense that Friedan decided not to seek reelection in 1970 as NOW president. She did, however, organize a rally that year, in August, to demand equal rights with men. The considerable turnout in Washington, D.C., and elsewhere made it the largest women's rights rally in many decades.

In the 1970s, Friedan worked for the right to safe and legal abortions. An organization she had founded in the late 1960s, the National Abortion Rights Action League, led the effort. In 1971, Friedan joined with feminists Gloria Steinem, Bella Abzug, and Congresswoman Shirley Chisholm and founded the National Women's Political Caucus, dedicated to encouraging women to seek political office.

When much of the counterculture lost its momentum in the early 1970s, Friedan helped keep the women's liberation movement alive at the local level. She did this by organizing and directing the First Women's Bank and Trust Company in New York City. At the same time, she tried, unsuccessfully, to begin a new group that could counteract the radicalism in NOW. After the requisite number of states failed to ratify the Equal Rights Amendment, she criticized NOW for having caused the defeat by alienating mainstream society.

In the 1980s and 1990s, Friedan continued to lecture, and she wrote two books, *The Second Stage* and *The Fountain of Age*. She remains best remembered, however, for the revolution she stimulated in the 1960s that not only changed women's place in society but also fostered a continuing debate over how men and women should relate to each other.

See also Morgan, Robin; Redstockings; Steinem, Gloria; Women's Movement.

References Friedan, Betty, *The Feminine Mystique* (1963), *It Changed My Life: Writings on the Women's Movement* (1985), and *The Second Stage* (1981); Norton, Mary Beth, ed., *Major Problems in American Women's History* (1989).

Frisbee

At parks, beaches, and on college campuses, young people in the 1960s threw Frisbees. Hippies, long-haired guys and girls, straight and stoned, threw them. The first Frisbees actually appeared in the 1920s, when students at Yale University threw tin pie plates manufactured by the Frisbee Pie Company in New Haven, Connecticut. In 1948, Fred Morrison picked up the idea and developed a plastic disk that he first called the Flying Saucer and then, in 1951, Pluto Platter. Four years later, he sold his patent to the Wham-O Company that, in 1959, named his invention the Frisbee.

Students at Columbia High School in Maplewood, New Jersey, invented the game Ultimate Frisbee, a team sport, in 1967. But for the most part, Frisbee players in the sixties contented themselves with casual rather than competitive tossing.

The Fugs

Singing such songs as "Coca-Cola Douche," the Fugs never appeared on the *Ed Sullivan Show*, nor did their records get air time on top-40 radio. Led by Ed Sanders, from New York City's hippie Lower East Side, the Fugs played rock music dedicated to sex and revolution. They appeared at numerous antiwar protests, including the notable march in 1967 on the Pentagon. By 1968, the Fugs had recorded two record albums and developed a following in San Francisco, but their sparse air time and inability to develop more than a garage-band sound kept their appeal limited. Besides leading the Fugs, Sanders operated a bookstore and wrote poetry—reflections on penises, vaginas, and sexual acts.

See also March on the Pentagon, 1967; Rock Music.

Fuller, R. Buckminster (1895–1983)

Counterculture hippies and environmentalists admired Buckminster Fuller for his projects and proposals to use the earth's energy and resources efficiently and wisely. Fuller pursued his quest working as an engineer, inventor, designer, architect, writer, educator, and philosopher.

Fuller was born in Milton, Massachusetts, on 12 July 1895 and attended Harvard University from 1913 to 1915 before he was expelled for low grades. After serving in the navy during World War I and afterward holding odd jobs, he founded the Dymaxion Corporation in 1932 to produce his inventions, among them an inexpensive portable house, doughnut-shaped.

In 1947, he developed his most publicized invention: the geodesic dome. This half-sphere had an internal network of interconnected four-sided pyramids that formed a grid with a high strength-to-weight ratio, making it an economical structure. A plastic or fiberglass skin covered the grid. Most notably, Fuller designed a dome for the American pavilion at the 1967 World's Fair in Montreal, Canada. The military and many industries used his dome, too, and they appeared on hippie communes.

Over the years, Fuller, who held a chair as research professor at Southern Illinois University in Carbondale, authored more than 25 books. His *Nine Chains to the Moon*, written in 1938 and reissued in 1963, and *Operating Manual for Spaceship Earth*, published in 1969 warning about the planet's dwindling resources, had the greatest impact on the counterculture that, despite its distrust of technology, saw in Fuller an alternative to mainstream society's wasteful practices. *The Whole Earth Catalog*, bible of the hippie back-to-the-earth movement, said: "Fuller's lectures have a raga quality of rich nonlinear endless improvisation full of convergent surprises." (Brand 1971, 3)

Fuller received 39 honorary doctorates and, in 1983, the Presidential Medal of Freedom. He died on 1 July 1983 in Los Angeles from a heart attack.

References Brand, Stewart, ed., *The Whole Earth Catalog* (1971); Fuller, R. Buckminster, *Nine Chains to the Moon* (1938, reprinted 1963, and *Operating Manual for Spaceship Earth* (1969); Hatch, Alden, *Buckminster Fuller: At Home in the Universe* (1974); Pawley, Martin, *Buckminster Fuller* (1990).

Fuzz

The word *fuzz* emerged around 1930 in reference to the police, and young people used it extensively in the fifties and sixties. Thus, "The fuzz busted me" or "The fuzz searched my room."

Garcia, Jerry

See Grateful Dead.

Gas

Counterculture youths equated the word *gas* with something entertaining, amusing, fun, or exciting. "Jumping Jack Flash, it's a gas, gas, gas," sang the Rolling Stones.

Gaye, Marvin (1939–1984)

A prominent rock singer in the sixties, Marvin Gaye earned renown as the "Prince of Motown," a tribute to his importance in the recording company that brought black music to white suburbia.

Gaye was born in 1939 in Washington, D.C., the son of a minister. He grew up singing gospel and playing the organ; in high school he diversified his musical taste and played piano, guitar, and drums. Gaye sang in the late 1950s with a rock group called the Moonglows, but he soon decided to work as a soloist, and in 1962 Berry Gordy, Jr., founder and president of Motown Records, heard him sing at a party and offered him a recording contract.

Gaye subsequently moved to Detroit and developed the mainstream soul sound that Gordy liked. He recorded his first hit, "Stubborn Kind of Fellow," in 1962, and followed it with "Hitch Hike" and "Pride and Joy." His 1965 single "How Sweet It Is To Be Loved By You," made the top 20.

While recording additional hits in the mid-1960s, Gaye married Gordy's sister Anna. At the same time, he formed a singing duo with Tammi Terrell, and they recorded "Your Precious Love," and "Ain't Nothing Like the Real Thing." Gaye had become crucial to Motown's success and a Gordy favorite, but he began to rebel against the company's restrictions, which, as laid out by Gordy, prohibited the artists from having any creative input.

In 1967, Gaye suffered a tragedy when, while singing on stage at Hampden-Sydney College in Virginia, Terrell collapsed in his arms from a brain tumor. In 1968, Gaye scored a hit with his solo recording, "I Heard It through the Grapevine." At the same time, he worked diligently to help Terrell recover, but in 1970 she died. This affected him deeply and caused him to stop touring.

Gaye's ability to infuse his music with 1960s-style social issues was evident on his 1971 album *What's Going On*, which included "Mercy, Mercy, Me," a song about threats to the ecology, and "Inner City Blues," about problems facing blacks living in ghettos. The album broke radically with the Motown sound and reflected Gaye's decision to distance himself from Gordy's staff and produce his own material.

In the mid-1970s, his personal and professional career hit a rough period, evident with his divorce and his declining record sales. In 1982, however, he made a comeback with the LP *Midnight Love* for Columbia. The following year, he toured the nation and won two Grammies for his work: best male rhythm and blues vocal performance, and best rhythm and blues instrumental performance.

The comeback proved short-lived, however. Gaye died in Los Angeles on 1 April 1984, shot dead by his father during a domestic argument.

See also Motown.

Reference Ritz, David, *Divided Soul: The Life of Marvin Gaye* (1985).

Gerde's Folk City

In the early sixties, Gerde's Folk City ranked among the premier clubs in New York for established and aspiring folk singers. Bob Dylan and Phil Ochs both got their early breaks there.

Gerde's had existed for many years as a family restaurant in New York City's Greenwich Village at Mercer and Third, owned and operated by William Gerde. In 1957, Mike Porco bought Gerde's, and it continued to prosper; but in 1960, the city leveled a nine-square-block area that dislocated so many residents Gerde's business declined. After moving to Fourth Street in 1961, Porco reopened the restaurant, but it still fared poorly. He tried to attract customers with live jazz, but this did not work.

Then two promoters, Izzy Young and Tom Pendergast, approached him about staging folk music at Gerde's. At first, Porco demurred, knowing nothing about folk, but then he decided to try it—maybe he could save his restaurant. The initial shows, with the establishment renamed the Fifth Peg, attracted only a few additional customers. After Young and Pendergast pulled out, Porco went back to the name Gerde's and continued to book acts. His Monday open mike nights, known as Hootenanny at Gerde's Folk City, in time attracted hundreds of people enticed by free admission and beer at 50 cents a bottle.

Gerde's success corresponded with a nationwide folk revival as young people sought music that addressed social issues. In addition to Bob Dylan and Phil Ochs, Peter, Paul, and Mary and other rising folk artists appeared at Gerde's, and the club continued presenting folk music long after the revival had ended.

See also Dylan, Bob; Ochs, Phil.

Ginsberg, Allen (1926–1997)

Bearded, wearing flowing robes, and tapping tiny cymbals attached to his fingers, Allen Ginsberg appeared at many hippie scenes. A poet who first gained notoriety in the 1950s, Ginsberg bridged the beats and the counterculture, and within the latter bridged the hippies and political protesters.

Born on 3 June 1926 in Newark, New Jersey, Ginsberg grew up in a family environment that deeply affected his later literary career. His father taught high school and wrote poetry, and this encouraged Ginsberg's writing ambitions; his mother, an émigré from Russia, went mad, and this fueled Ginsberg's fears about psychosis, which appeared as a prominent theme in his poems. He later remarked: "I already had my mind caved in when I was about ten, in terms of ability to reexamine things for what was what and what was not. . . . I knew craziness was a family matter, a human matter, rather than something you swept under the carpet." (Viorst 1979, 60)

Ginsberg graduated from high school in Paterson, New Jersey, in 1943 and went to Columbia University on a scholarship. There he majored in English, joined the debating team, and won a prize for poetry. He ran into trouble, however, for misbehavior in the dorms, and the college suspended him in 1945. He then took an adventurous route. He worked as a welder, night porter, and dishwasher before entering the Merchant Marine Academy for a brief stint. From there, he hitchhiked to Denver, then to Texas, and then took a freighter to France and Africa. Ginsberg returned to Columbia, worked part-time as a file clerk, and graduated in 1948 with a bachelor's degree.

That year, he got involved with a friend in a petty theft scheme, was arrested, and sentenced to a psychiatric ward, where he underwent eight months of Freudian psychoanalysis. After his release, he suffered enormous depression but maintained an ongoing friendship with writers William Burroughs and Jack Kerouac. That summer, he experienced mystical visions while pondering "Ah! Sun-flower," a poem by the eighteenth-century English writer, William Blake. He felt he understood more than the poem—he understood life itself. Ginsberg later commented: "I suddenly realized that this . . . was the moment I was born for. This initiation. Or this vision or this consciousness of being alive unto myself, alive myself unto the Creator. As the son of the Creator—who loved me." (Stevens 1987, 111)

This epiphany later contributed to his break with traditional poetry and stimu-

Outside the Women's House of Detention in New York City's Greenwich Village, poet Allen Ginsberg leads a group of demonstrators advocating the legalization of marijuana, 11 February 1965.

lated his experimentation. At about the same time, he fell in love with Neal Cassady, one of Kerouac's friends. Kerouac says about them in his book *On the Road*: "They rushed down the street together, digging everything in the early way they had, which later became so much sadder and perceptive and blank." In fact, Cassady rejected Ginsberg, and in the aftermath the poet's verses displayed intense self-disgust and a great desire for love.

For two years, from 1951 to 1953, Ginsberg worked as a market researcher, first in New York City and then—after brief sojourns to Key West, Cuba, and Mexico—in San Francisco. His move to the latter location rejuvenated his writing and relationships. For one, he met Peter Orlovsky, and they became lovers. Then, dissatisfied with his job, Ginsberg left it after receiving advice from a psychoanalyst to pursue his desires. He soon formed friendships with other writers who influenced him, especially Zen Buddhist poet Gary Snyder, and plunged into an intellectual and bohemian community that congregated at North Beach, a district dotted with bookstores and coffeehouses. Ginsberg, in turn, affected the literary circle known as the beats.

These writers rebelled against the conformist materialism found in 1950s society. As Ginsberg once said, "I knew about *Time* [magazine] as a social phenomenon in the early 1950s. It delivered a funny, phony, CIA version of cleanliness. . . . This was a vast propaganda effort to fake a personal consciousness in America and to present a fake personal consciousness as the real, internal, sensitive self." The beats sought a higher consciousness, and to pursue it they experimented with Judaism, Zen Buddhism, yoga, and drugs. Snyder turned Ginsberg on to Zen, meditation, and two mystical works, *The Tibetan Book of the Dead* and *Tibetan Buddhist Documents*.

Ginsberg met another beat poet, Lawrence Ferlinghetti, and frequented his City Lights bookstore. Ferlinghetti provided an enormous boost to Ginsberg's writing: he heard him read his poem *Howl* and decided to publish it. Ginsberg wrote the first portion of *Howl* quickly, put it aside for a couple of weeks, and wrote the remainder while under the influence of peyote.

Howl has been called Ginsberg's "most passionate" poem. This work combines his personal conflicts—his struggle, for example, with homosexuality—with the conformity threatening to devour America, particularly his generation's brightest minds. Hence, Ginsberg compares American society to Moloch, the Old Testament god to whom people made sacrifices. The modern Moloch threatened to destroy visionary imagination:

> Moloch whose eyes are a thousand blind windows! Moloch whose skyscrapers stand in the long streets like endless Jehovahs! Moloch whose factories dream and croak in the fog! Moloch whose smokestacks and antennae crown the cities! (Sullivan 1978, 669)

Ginsberg concludes his poem with a call for everyone to recognize love as existing within everything.

Mainstream society condemned *Howl* for its vulgar language and supposed indecency. Ginsberg, however, considered his style essential in attacking falsity. The police in San Francisco arrested Ferlinghetti for publishing *Howl*, and banned its sale on the grounds it contained obscenities. A judge, however, ruled the poem not obscene and released Ferlinghetti. All the attention made *Howl* a best-seller (unusual for a poem). Ginsberg followed *Howl* with *Kaddish for Naomi Ginsberg*, which enhanced his reputation as a poet.

In 1960, Ginsberg traveled with Gary Snyder to Japan and India, seeking greater spiritual enlightenment, and claimed to have experienced a mystical revelation while riding on a train near Tokyo. He returned to the United States in 1963, fully attached to Zen Buddhism and convinced he had reached cosmic consciousness. Shortly after this, the hippies emerged in San Francisco, and they considered Ginsberg—arguably the leading beat writer—a pioneer in a spiritual quest.

Ginsberg believed LSD an important drug that could be used to remove societal conditioning (although he believed meditation more authentic than any drug), and the hippies, already using acid to create a psychedelic community, agreed. They liked, too, his Eastern mysticism as they looked toward Hinduism, Buddhism, and Taoism for spiritual guidance. Like the hippies, Ginsberg believed that "society could be redeemed only by the cumulative transformation of individuals to a higher sense of self." (Viorst 1979, 77) In these ways, then, the beat poet bridged the 1950s rebels and those a decade later.

In addition, Ginsberg bridged the hippies and political protesters in the counterculture, as evident in his belief that meditation and finding personal identity should precede any engagement in politics, and in his many appearances at counterculture events in which he combined this philosophy with activism—for example, when he chanted mantras at antiwar demonstrations. In 1967, Ginsberg helped inspire the Human Be-In, a major counterculture event in San Francisco, and in New York City he participated in protests against the Vietnam War.

Ginsberg wrote poetry into the 1990s, continuing his "life's work," as he called it, until a day or two before his death. He died on 5 April 1997. In remembrance, the Associated Press called his influence "almost inestimable," and the *New York Times* labeled him "the poet laureate of the Beat generation."

See also Beat; Burroughs, William S.; Ferlinghetti, Lawrence; Kerouac, Jack; Snyder, Gary; Zen Buddhism.

References Cassady, Carolyn, *Off the Road: My Years with Cassady, Kerouac, and Ginsberg* (1990); Ginsberg, Allen, *Howl and Other Poems* (1956); Miles, Barry, *Ginsberg: A Biography* (1989); Schumacher, Michael, *Dharma Lion: A Critical Biography of Allen Ginsberg* (1992); Stevens, Jay, *Storming Heaven: LSD and the American Dream* (1987); Sullivan, Nancy, ed., *The Treasury of American Poetry* (1978); Viorst, Milton, *Fire in the Streets: America in the 1960s* (1979); http://www.levity.com/corduroy/ginsberg.htm.

Gitlin, Todd (1943–)

An important leader in counterculture political protests, Todd Gitlin organized peace rallies and demonstrations against the Vietnam War and served as president of Students for a Democratic Society (SDS), the nation's leading New Left organization.

Gitlin was born on 6 January 1943 in New York City to Max Gitlin and Dorothy Siegel Gitlin, both schoolteachers. Liberal in his political views, as a teenager Gitlin considered the 1950s oppressively conformist, and he criticized its conservative leaders. At a later date, he said:

> I read the *New York Times* and my parents were liberal. I stayed up late on election nights and rooted for Democrats almost as passionately as I followed the New York Giants baseball team. I thought Dwight Eisenhower was a genial deadhead, a semi-literate fuddy-duddy who deserved to be chastised as much for excessive golfing and tangled sentences as for embracing *Generalissimo* Franco. I thought Richard Nixon was sinister. . . . I delighted in Julius Feiffer's worldly spoofs of Eisenhower's syntax, the phone company's arrogance, and middle-class clichés. . . . My closest friends, the children of Jewish civil servants and skilled workers, held similar opinions. (Gitlin 1987, 1)

Whatever faith Gitlin may have had in liberalism began fading when, in 1956, he entered the Bronx High School of Science, a school for gifted students interested in scientific careers. Although Gitlin liked calculus more than any other subject, politics attracted him, and in 1958 he attended a socialist rally near his school. He came away from it impressed with the critique of capitalism.

After obtaining his high school diploma, Gitlin enrolled at Harvard. Here, his political radicalization grew as his disillusionment with President Kennedy intensified. He disliked Kennedy's decision to isolate Fidel Castro's regime in Cuba, and he joined Tocsin, an organization formed to protest nuclear weapons. Gitlin helped organize the first large-scale peace march on Washington that brought together college students willing to challenge the political establishment and break with the placid 1950s. The demonstration in February 1962 attracted several thousand protesters. Later that year, the Cuban missile crisis further estranged Gitlin from Kennedy and liberalism—he thought the president had overreacted and taken a belligerent stance because Cuba, a small nation, had dared to defy the United States.

At this time, Gitlin met members of the newly organized SDS whose Port Huron Statement—a declaration that criticized American society for being oppressive and undemocratic—enthralled him. Gitlin believed that only a movement led by students could reform the nation in any meaningful way. After obtaining his B.A. from Harvard in 1963, he entered graduate school at the University of Michigan, a hotbed of SDS activity. He attended SDS meetings and felt invigorated by its ideology and sense of common purpose. "Everything these people did," Gitlin said, "was charged with intensity." (105) That June, the delegates at the SDS national convention elected him president, a position he held for two years.

Gitlin helped organize a large march on Washington in 1965 to protest the Vietnam War and worked in urban slum neighborhoods under an SDS-sponsored project to help the poor. In 1967, one year after receiving his master's degree, Gitlin traveled to Cuba as part of an SDS delegation. Soon after his return, he moved to California and plunged into the radical and violent demonstrations there. He remarked: "If balls are not equivalent to revolution—they are not—they are prerequisite to an honorable resistance." (252)

He participated, too, in the demonstrations at the 1968 Democratic National Convention in Chicago, but by the following year had grown disenchanted with many in the New Left. SDS had collapsed, and he criticized Weatherman, a radical faction within SDS, for having hastened its demise and for having adopted turgid extremist rhetoric steeped in irrelevant Marxism that meant nothing in an environment neither prepared for, nor receptive to, revolution. To Gitlin, there no longer existed a difference between the establishment "death culture" and the student movement. He did not abandon his principles or his criticism of the political system—but he felt betrayed.

In 1969, Gitlin worked as a reporter for the *San Francisco Express Times*. He lectured at San Jose State University in 1970 and, at the same time, studied for his doctorate in sociology at the University of California-Berkeley, receiving his degree in 1977. Since then, Gitlin, a professor of sociology and director of the mass communications program at Berkeley, has written numerous articles and books on how the mass media affects society.

See also New Left; Port Huron Statement; Students for a Democratic Society; Tocsin.

Reference Gitlin, Todd, *The Sixties: Years of Hope, Days of Rage* (1987).

Goodman, Mitchell (1924–1997)

A writer and teacher, Mitchell Goodman gained renown in the counterculture as a prominent leader of antiwar protests.

Born in Brooklyn, New York, in 1924, Goodman served as an artillery officer in World War II and received his bachelor's degree from Harvard University in 1946. He then began studying for a doctorate in economics, but after meeting a young English poet, Denise Levertov, whom he later married, he left graduate school and turned to writing.

In the 1950s, he wrote magazine articles and held several teaching positions. His first book, *The End of It*, appeared in 1961 to wide acclaim, and today some critics consider it among the finest antiwar novels ever written.

Originally apathetic toward the Vietnam War, by 1965 Goodman experienced a change of heart and became a protester. In March 1967, he led 50 people in a walkout at the National Book Award ceremonies in New York while Vice-President Hubert H. Humphrey addressed the crowd. This disruption gained national attention. Several weeks later, he led a protest march down Fifth Avenue in Manhattan, which concluded with military veterans gathering at Union Square, where they burned their discharge papers.

Later that year, he organized a protest in Boston that involved collecting draft cards and burning them. This violated federal law, and the government arrested him and other prominent protesters, among them Dr. Benjamin Spock, a pediatrician and writer, and Rev. William Sloan Coffin, Jr., chaplain at Yale University. The ensuing trial resulted in guilty verdicts for Spock, Coffin, and Goodman, but on appeal a higher court reversed the decisions, dismissing the charges against Spock outright, while deciding that Coffin and Goodman could be tried again. The government, however, dropped the case.

The "Spock Trial," as it was called, made the defendants martyrs and thus propelled Goodman into prominence within the counterculture. In 1970, he showed his sympathy for countercultural ideas when he compiled primary materials, such as articles from underground newspapers, and presented them in his book *The Movement toward a New America: The Beginnings of a Long Revolution*. Goodman continued to speak out against the war into the early 1970s while holding the Chair of Ideas at Mankato State University in Minnesota. He left that position around 1980 and settled in Maine, where he wrote poetry and campaigned against nuclear weapons. Goodman died on 1 February 1997 from cancer.

See also Spock, Benjamin.

References Goodman, Mitchell, *The End of It* (reprint 1980) and *The Movement toward a New America: The Beginnings of a Long Revolution* (1970).

Goodman, Paul (1911–1972)

A prolific writer and a lay psychotherapist, Paul Goodman developed a counterculture audience when he criticized modern society for its oppressive conformity.

Goodman was born in New York's Greenwich Village on 9 September 1911. His father deserted the family when Goodman was still an infant, leaving him to be raised by his mother, Augusta. Goodman graduated from Townsend Harris High School in 1927 and from the College of the City of New York in 1931. Later in the decade, he entered graduate school at the University of Chicago, but in 1940 dropped out. He eventually returned to his studies, received his doctorate degree in 1955, and held teaching positions at the University of Chicago and the University of Wisconsin.

Although Goodman wrote extensively, he received little recognition until 1960 with his book *Growing Up Absurd*. In it, he argues that America's youth feels alienated because they have been separated from nature and honest work, and he proposes camps for young people where they would be able to experience the natural world and learn jobs that would benefit society. To the emerging counterculture, though, his book was most appealing for its portrayal of modern society as conformist and commercialized. In several essays, he returned to this theme frequently:

> Every element of [President Lyndon Johnson's] . . . Great Society, including its war on poverty and its conservation, is contaminated by, compromised by, and finally determined by lust, greed, and fear of change. . . . The drive to schooling . . . is not to liberate the children and to insure that we will have independent and intelligent citizens (this was the educational aim of Jefferson); it is apprentice-training of the middle class for the corporations and military, a desperate attempt to make slum children employable and ruly. . . .
>
> The Great Society is to aggrandize the Establishment, the education barons, the broadcasting barons, the automobile barons, the shopping center barons. (Collier 1969, 344–345, 348)

Counterculture youths, especially those within the New Left who considered liberalism a sellout to the corporate military state, agreed with Goodman, and he became a sought-after lecturer and consultant.

In 1964, Goodman wrote *Compulsory Mis-education*, attacking progressive educators for weakening standards. At the same time, he participated in several antiwar demonstrations. Despite this, Goodman often disagreed with the counterculture, for he believed it contributed to a decline in education fortified by destructive anti-intellectualism, a view he expressed in his 1970 work, *New Reformation: Notes of a Neolithic Conservative*.

Overall, Goodman wrote more than 40 books, plays, and short stories, along with essays and poems. These included *Communitas* (1947), a nonfiction work about urban planning coauthored with his brother Percival Goodman; *Gestalt Therapy* (1951), written with Frederick Perls and Ralph Hefferline; *The Structure of Literature* (1954); and *The Empire City* (1959). Goodman died at his farm in North Stratford, New Hampshire, on 2 August 1972.

See also Education; New Left.

References Collier, Peter, ed., *Crisis: A Contemporary Reader* (1969); Goodman, Paul, *Compulsory Mis-education* (1964), *Growing Up Absurd: Problems of Youth in the Organized System* (1960), and *New Reformation: Notes of a Neolithic Conservative* (1970); Goodman, Paul, and Percival Goodman, *Communitas: Means of Livelihood and Ways of Life* (1947).

The Graduate

"A landmark film," "A formative influence on the counterculture"—these words have been used to describe *The Graduate*. Released in 1967 and directed by Mike Nichols, *The Graduate* stars Anne Bancroft, Katharine Ross, and in his first major role, Dustin Hoffman.

The story, based on a novel by Charles Webb, develops a generation-gap theme that shows young people, in this case a recent college graduate, Benjamin Braddock (as played by Hoffman), in conflict with an older generation corrupted by materialism and cynicism. Braddock is seduced by a middle-age woman, but then falls in love with her daughter, whom he saves from an ill-advised marriage. The ending, however, leaves it questionable as to whether Braddock, and by implication young America, will succeed in creating anything better.

Many youths flocked to this movie, drawn by the story and the soundtrack, songs by Simon and Garfunkel. Yet while *The Graduate* criticizes middle-class values, it panders to them. Benjamin Braddock comes from a wealthy family, and his rebelliousness never threatens his material comfort, a fact many in the audience appreciated. Contrast *The Graduate* with *Easy Rider*, released two years later: drug-oriented, grittier, much more at odds with straight society.

Graham, Bill (1931–1991)

Impresario Bill Graham helped define the counterculture by promoting rock at Fillmore West, Fillmore East, and Winterland.

Born into a Jewish family in Germany on 8 January 1931, Graham's original name was Wolfgang Grajonca. The boy never knew his father, who died while Graham was still an infant, and in 1939 Graham's mother sent him away to avoid persecution by the Nazis. In September 1941, after the Nazis killed his mother, Graham arrived in New York City and lived for several weeks at an orphanage in Poughkeepsie, until his great-uncle's family adopted him and took him to the Bronx.

Graham attended DeWitt Clinton High School and in the late 1940s enrolled at Brooklyn College while working part-time for a jewelry company. In 1950, he legally changed his name to William Graham. That same year, the army drafted him, and he served in the Korean War. After his return in 1952, he worked at several resort hotels in New York's Catskill Mountains, where he earned a reputation for supporting unionization and being a free spirit, or as one associate said: "He was *anti*. He was anti-*everything*. Anti-establishment all the way." (Graham and Greenfield 1992, 86)

Through the 1950s, Graham displayed a restless spirit, bouncing from job to job and back and forth between New York and California. He tried to break into acting and at one point auditioned to costar in a network television series, for which he ended up a finalist. After Graham learned that he did not get the part because the director did not like the way he looked, he decided to quit acting.

Again, he kicked around at various jobs until 1965, when he began working for the newly formed San Francisco Mime Troupe. He drove the group's truck, sold tickets, and promoted their shows. Graham liked the Mime Troupe's commitment to theatre as a public platform from which to expose racial injustice and the Vietnam War.

In November 1965, Graham organized a party to raise funds for the Mime Troupe, and it turned out to be a big success, both in monetary terms and in bringing together San Francisco's hip artists, everyone from the poet Lawrence Ferlinghetti to the rock band Jefferson Airplane. One Trouper, Peter Berg, said: "Those Mime Troupe benefits were the towering cultural events leading to the Haight-Ashbury." (125) And with them, Graham experienced a personal change, moving into the counterculture, although always maintaining a distance, always remaining attached to business.

For a second benefit, a dance concert in December 1965, he rented the Fillmore Auditorium near the hippie Haight-Ashbury district. He then began to use the auditorium on a regular basis for rock concerts (eventually getting an exclusive contract). This drew him away from the Mime Troupe, one of whose members later said: "From the get-go he was a businessman. Unfortunately, we never changed him. What we never did was convince Bill Graham that art and social change were more important then money." (132)

On 20 January 1966, Graham sponsored the Trips Festival at Longshoremen's Hall in San Francisco with Stewart Brand, who had originated the idea. This exposed Graham to the acid culture for the first time. He, however, rejected drugs and complained that the Acid Tests had a central fallacy in assuming everyone could handle LSD.

Soon after the Trips Festival, Graham organized his first concert on his own. He featured Jefferson Airplane and showed he could adopt the psychedelic scene: he lined the walls at the Fillmore with bedsheets, and as the band played, projectors flashed images from slides, films, and glob-liquid concoctions. Graham set up a few chairs at the show, but as was typical for the time, the main floor was largely vacant so people could dance or just hang out.

By 1967, Graham was staging concerts at the Fillmore and at another auditorium nearby, Winterland. He booked all the major rock acts: Janis Joplin, the Doors, Cream, Jimi Hendrix, the Paul Butterfield Blues Band, Traffic, the Who, Procul Harum, and Santana (for whom he provided their first big break). The musicians considered it a great learning experience, despite Graham's sometimes overbearing personality. Known for frantically moving about during a concert with clipboard and checklist in hand, Graham demanded that bands appear on time, that few people be allowed in free, and that the show run smoothly and professionally.

His success at the Fillmore convinced him to open Fillmore East, which he did in 1967 after buying and refurbishing the Village Theatre on Second Avenue and Sixth Street in New York City's Lower East Side. A few months later, in June 1968, he moved Fillmore West, as he then called it, from the Fillmore Auditorium, a dangerous site due to gangs that roamed the neighborhood, to the old Carousel Theatre, also in San Francisco.

In 1971, Graham decided to close both Fillmores. Even though they still turned a good profit, he disliked traveling between California and New York. In June, he held a huge final concert at Fillmore East, recorded on an album and on film. Fillmore West closed its doors in July.

This did not end Graham's promotional business; in fact, in the second half of 1971, he grossed $250,000 from concerts in the Bay Area and remained San Francisco's "most prolific producer." In addition, he maintained his lease at Winterland.

Graham continued to promote rock concerts into the 1990s, staging shows at large auditoriums and stadiums: the Rolling Stones; Bob Dylan; George Harrison; and Crosby, Stills, Nash, and Young. He put together a rock concert in the Soviet Union featuring Santana and the Doobie Brothers, and an Amnesty International tour that included the band U2.

On 25 October 1991, after attending a concert that night in San Francisco,

Graham boarded a helicopter, headed for his home in Marin County. Despite low clouds and heavy rain that shrouded the sky and reduced visibility, Graham's pilot decided to fly. Shortly after takeoff, the copter struck an electric transmission tower, instantly killing Graham and the others on board.

Soon after, Albert Ertegun, cofounder of Atlantic Records, said about Graham: "Nothing fazed [him]. Nothing. . . . Undaunted, like a champion warrior, he faced all calamity and walked through. Unions and tough guys and this and that. Because of his incredible vitality and force as a person, I consider him one of the great legends of rock and roll. An immigrant who came to America with a lot of ideas and hopes and who found an incredible niche. He built a place for himself." (235)

See also Fillmore; Rock Music; San Francisco Mime Troupe; Trips Festival.

Reference Graham, Bill, and Robert Greenfield, *Bill Graham Presents: My Life inside Rock and Out* (1992).

Grass

Grass meant not a lawn but marijuana.

See also Marijuana.

Grateful Dead

The Grateful Dead rock band emerged from the psychedelic atmosphere in San Francisco's Haight-Ashbury district, exuding counterculture improvisation and experimentation, and earning a dedicated following of "Deadheads."

The story of the Dead, as they were called by fans, is inextricably tied to its leader, Jerry Garcia. Born in 1942 in San Francisco, Garcia grew up listening to bluegrass music, rock 'n' roll, and the beat poets who populated North Beach. He got his first electric guitar at age 15, and along with it came a driving ambition to change rock and make it more artistic.

After listening to the Beatles and Bob Dylan, he took an acoustic band he had formed and changed its personnel and style to play electric rock. The Warlocks, as he called them, began performing in the Bay Area in 1964, with Garcia joined by Bill Kreutzmann on drums; a classically trained musician, Bob Weir, on guitar; Phil Lesh on bass guitar; and Ron "Pigpen" McKernan on keyboard. Later in the year, Garcia changed the band's name to the Grateful Dead, when the phrase caught his eye after he opened a big Oxford dictionary. About this time, the Dead made a connection that altered their music when Merry Prankster Ken Kesey invited them to be the house band for experimental LSD celebrations, or Acid Tests. In their book *Acid Dreams*, Martin A. Lee and Bruce Shlain describe the tests as "weird carnivals with videotapes, flashing strobes, live improvised rock and roll . . . lots of costumes, and dancing." (125)

The Dead accepted Kesey's invitation and took LSD themselves. Their music, transformed, emerged psychedelic and improvisational, and listening to it, or at least listening to it effectively, required a fellowship and common experience that encouraged the audience to consume LSD—the music and drugs together known as the Grateful Dead trip.

The Dead played numerous free shows in Haight-Ashbury, along with commercial gigs at the Avalon Ballroom and the Fillmore, known for their light shows and freewheeling dance-concerts. Although the Dead wanted success, they did not want to sell out, and in this and their antiauthoritarianism, loose style, commitment to principles, and periodic self-indulgence, they reflected countercultural values.

Rather than pander to the crowd, the Dead made their music and waited for audiences to come to them. Perhaps for this reason, in the sixties they never had a hit record, and remained first and foremost a live band, a style conducive to their improvisational music. The Dead rejected standard play lists, and the audience could never be sure which way the music would go or where it would take them.

In 1970, the band recorded its biggest-selling album in the counterculture era, *Workingman's Dead*, soon followed by their

Jerry Garcia, joined by fellow members of the Grateful Dead, speaks at a press conference on 5 October 1967. The band complained that the marijuana raid on their pad was police harassment and was "out of touch with reality." Notorious for their psychedelic and improvisational music, the Grateful Dead emerged from San Francisco's Haight-Ashbury district, a counterculture mecca, in the 1960s and went on to earn a dedicated following of "Deadheads."

critically acclaimed *American Beauty*. The Dead did not score a top-ten hit until the late 1980s with their single "A Touch of Grey." They kept playing into the nineties, drawing large audiences, with their followers, or Deadheads, developing into a musical and social cult. Garcia's popularity led him to design neckties in the 1990s, and Ben & Jerry's Ice Cream created its most popular flavor, Cherry Garcia.

On 9 August 1995, Garcia died from a heart attack while at Forest Knolls, a drug and alcohol treatment center. He had experienced drug problems for years, and although he had recently gone clean, they had worn him down. In a memorial to Garcia, *Rolling Stone* magazine summarized the Dead's legacy:

> Long after the Haight's moment had passed, it would be the Grateful Dead—and the Dead alone among the original San Francisco bands—that would still exemplify the ideals of fraternity and compassion which most other 60s-bred groups had long relinquished, and many subsequent rock artists repudiated, in favor of more corrosive ideals. (Gilmore 1995, 49)

References Gans, David, *Conversations with the Dead: The Grateful Dead Interview Book* (1991); Gans, David, and Peter Simon, *Playing in the Band: An Oral and Visual Portrait of the Grateful Dead* (1996); Gilmore, Mikhail, "Jerry Garcia," *Rolling Stone*, 21 September 1995, 44+; Greene, Herb, *Book of the Dead: Celebrating 25 Years with the Grateful Dead* (1990); Harrison, Hank, *The Dead Book: A Social History of the Grateful Dead* (1973); Jackson, Blair, *Grateful Dead: The Music Never Stopped* (1983); Lee, Martin A., and Bruce Shlain, *Acid Dreams: The CIA,*

LSD, and the Sixties Rebellion (1985); Troy, Sandy, *One More Saturday Night: Reflections with the Grateful Dead, Dead Family, and Deadheads* (1991); http://www.rockument.com/haimg.html; ftp://gdead.berkeley.edu/pub/gdead/.

The Greening of America

Written in 1970 by Yale professor Charles A. Reich, *The Greening of America* reached the best-seller lists by asserting that the counterculture had created a new era, Consciousness III, with spiritual community ascendant over technology.

In *Greening*, Reich sees rock music, marijuana, and communes as representing a shift in how people perceive reality. With Consciousness III led by youths, he writes, society will overcome war, violence, poverty, and individual powerlessness. "The extraordinary thing about this new consciousness," he says, "is that it has emerged out of the wasteland of the Corporate State, like flowers pushing up through the concrete pavement. Whatever it touches, it beautifies and renews: a freeway entrance is festooned with happy hitchhikers, the sidewalk is decorated with street people, the humorless steps of an official building are given warmth by a group of musicians." (Reich 1970, 429)

Thus, the counterculture did not, as many middle-class Americans feared, signal moral decay but rather a new hope. "What is coming is nothing less than a new way of life and a new man—a man with renewed energies and imagination—a man who is part of the living world." (380–381) He concludes: "For one who thought the world was irretrievably encased in metal and plastic and sterile stone, it seems a veritable greening of America." (430)

Reference Reich, Charles A., *The Greening of America* (1970).

Greensboro

On 2 February 1960, the *New York Times* reported: "A group of well-dressed Negro college students staged a sit-down strike in a downtown Woolworth store . . . and vowed to continue it in relays until Negroes were served at the lunch counter." This confrontation in Greensboro, North Carolina, radicalized the civil rights movement, led to black power, and stimulated white protests against injustice.

Weeks before the sit-in, Ezell Blair, Jr., Franklin McClain, Joseph McNeill, and David Richmond, freshmen at North Carolina Agricultural and Technical College, an all-black school in Greensboro, discussed their desire to take action amid hope and frustration: the civil rights movement had scored important victories but still encountered great resistance. For example, the National Association for the Advancement of Colored People (NAACP) had obtained court decisions ending several racist laws including, in 1954, *Brown v. Board of Education* that struck at segregated schools; and Martin Luther King, Jr. had acted to change the racially segregated public bus system in Montgomery, Alabama. But despite these developments, the South remained committed to white supremacy.

Adding to the situation, more and more young blacks had entered college, where they experienced new ideas and expressed their restlessness and their discontent with oppression. In Greensboro, racism seemed unshakable—whites controlled a paternalistic system that maintained segregation, even in the public schools.

Thus on 1 February 1960, Blair, McClain, McNeill, and Richmond staged their daring sit-in, one day after McNeill had been denied service at the local bus depot. Blair later said about Woolworth's: "The waitress stared at me as if I were from outer space." They stayed until the store manager closed the lunch counter, one hour later. But blacks did not accept this rejection. The next day, 27 students joined the 4 original crusaders to continue the sit-in; on day three, the number increased to 63; on day four, to 100; and by week's end, some 1,000 protesters had descended on Woolworth's and the nearby S. H. Kress store.

Newspapers and television stations broadcast pictures, energizing black America—North and South. One Harlem resident observed that blacks in Greensboro had shed obsequiousness for determination. Boldness spread: within two weeks, African Americans repeated the Greensboro strategy in 15 cities across five southern states. By 1961, sit-ins had occurred involving 50,000 protesters and resulting in 3,000 arrests. As a consequence, several hundred restaurants desegregated, including the lunch counters in Greensboro.

The sit-ins marked a new era in the civil rights movement and stimulated the 1960s counterculture. Although both the Congress of Racial Equality and the NAACP had used this tactic in the 1940s and 1950s, they had done so sparingly. At Greensboro, young blacks proclaimed they would take charge with bold actions, and their sit-in led them to form the Student Nonviolent Coordinating Committee (SNCC), committed to high-profile, public demonstrations. Indeed, several of SNCC's future leaders watched the Greensboro protest on TV and later stressed not civil rights but black power, calling on African Americans to reject all racist institutions and define their own goals.

In challenging the strategy set out by their elders, the Greensboro protesters assaulted traditional practices within the civil rights movement. Further, these young blacks awakened white youths to injustice, forcing them to see beyond the nation's material wealth and democratic platitudes. At the same time, Greensboro showed college students, white and black, how to use public protest to obtain humane ends.

See also Black Power; Civil Rights Movement; Student Nonviolent Coordinating Committee.

References Carson, Clayborne, *In Struggle: SNCC and the Black Awakening of the 1960s* (1981); Wolff, Miles, *How It All Began: The Greensboro Sit-Ins* (1971); Young, Andrew, *The Civil Rights Movement and the Transformation of America* (1996).

Greenwich Village

Long a bohemian center, New York City's Greenwich Village contributed to the counterculture from the early 1960s onward with its political and artistic challenge to middle-class values.

Located in lower Manhattan, Greenwich Village teemed with alternative political organizations: the Greenwich Village Peace Center, New York School of Marxist Studies, Militant Labor Forum, American Humanist Association, Students for Democratic Reform, Lower Manhattan Branch of the Socialist Party, Village-Chelsea Women Strike for Peace, and a chapter of Americans for Democratic Action, among others.

Besides this, coffeehouses and discos appeared, such as Bitter End, Café Wha?, and Gerde's Folk City, where many aspiring folk singers, including Bob Dylan, got their start. On Sheridan Square stood the offices of the *Village Voice*, a pioneer in underground journalism. The Living Theater sponsored poetry readings and film showings, and painters, poets, and writers congregated in various restaurants and bars.

Most importantly, the village's substantial artist community blazed new ground, developing an avant-garde style whose influence spread and helped shape countercultural attitudes across the nation. These sixties artists brought into their work themes central to the counterculture: people in ordinary life, freedom from rules, sexuality, and playfulness. They transmitted democratic, liberating values, sometimes by exploiting modern technology, as Andy Warhol did with his Pop Art, and at other times by taking the products of mass culture and using them to criticize it, as in fluxus and Yoko Ono's performance art.

According to Sally Banes in *Greenwich Village 1963*, these avant-garde artworks "were not just 'reflections' of society; they helped shape the very form and style of political and cultural protest in the Sixties." (9)

See also The Bitter End; Dylan, Bob; *East Village Other;* Electric Circus; Fluxus; Gerde's Folk City; Ono, Yoko; *Village Voice;* Warhol, Andy.

Reference Banes, Sally, *Greenwich Village 1963* (1993).

Groovy

The word "groovy" first appeared in 1944, and in the 1960s it gained widespread use within the counterculture. The word meant anything exciting, enjoyable, excellent, or pleasurable. Often hippies linked the word to drugs, using it to mean a pleasant high. Groovy seemed everywhere—in literature, advertising, and music. One pop song contained the lyrics a "groovy kind of love."

Guthrie, Arlo (1947–)

Arlo Guthrie achieved countercultural fame when his song "Alice's Restaurant" derided establishment hypocrisy.

Guthrie was born on 10 July 1947 in Brooklyn, New York, the son of Marjorie Mazia Greenblatt Guthrie, a dancer and teacher with the Martha Graham Company, and Woody Guthrie, the legendary folk singer. He grew up surrounded by his father's songs and by visits from folk greats Pete Seeger, Lee Hays, Jack Elliott, and Leadbelly. Guthrie played harmonica at age three, and at age six began learning the guitar.

Four years later, at age ten, he appeared on stage at Gerde's Folk City in Greenwich Village. Guthrie attended music camps and private schools, obtaining his secondary education at Stockbridge School in Massachusetts, after which he decided to develop his music rather than go to college.

In 1965, Guthrie visited his friends Alice and Ray Brock in Stockbridge, Massachusetts, and there began an adventure that inadvertently made him famous. The Brocks had been Guthrie's teachers at the Stockbridge School, but at this time Alice ran a restaurant while they both cared for several young people in an abandoned church, a commune of sorts. On Thanksgiving Day, Guthrie attempted to unload some garbage at the town dump, only to find it closed. So he instead left it in a nearby gully. After the police tracked him down and gave him a ticket, he decided to relate the episode, his other disagreements with authority, and his life with the Brocks in "Alice's Restaurant." In it, he satirically criticized his draft board: "You want to know if I'm moral enough to join the Army, burn women, kids, houses, and villages after being a litterbug?"

After Guthrie played the song on WBAI radio in New York City, people called in to hear it again. He subsequently recorded it and in 1967 placed it on his first album, *Alice's Restaurant*. Two Hollywood producers and director Arthur Penn then decided to make the song into a movie starring Guthrie. Although released in 1969 to mixed reviews, counterculture audiences embraced it for using subtle humor in expressing discontent with hypocritical mainstream practices.

Guthrie continued to record after the sixties, appeared at concerts, including many dedicated to social causes, and wrote a book in 1995 about moose. He now lives with his wife and children on a farm in Massachusetts.

See also *Alice's Restaurant;* Guthrie, Woody.

Reference Cronkite, Kathy, *On the Edge of the Spotlight: Celebrities' Children Speak Out about Their Success and Struggles* (1981).

Guthrie, Woody (1912–1967)

The great folk musician Woody Guthrie wrote more than 1,000 songs, along with an autobiography and several magazine articles. In these and in sketches that he drew, he provided a left-wing critique, sympathized with the oppressed, and spoke the common person's feelings. His work stimulated a folk music revival in the early 1960s and made him a hero to those in the counterculture who embraced reform.

Woodrow "Woody" Guthrie was born on 14 July 1912 in Okemah, Oklahoma, to Charles Guthrie and Nora Belle Tanner Guthrie. Guthrie's father bought and sold real estate, played professional guitar, and held local office as a Democrat—in fact, the Guthries named their son after Democratic presidential candidate Woodrow Wilson. Young Woody grew up listening

American folk singer Woody Guthrie

to the songs his mother sang, songs from England and Ireland that had been passed down through the family, songs about everyday people involved in love, war, joy, and heartache.

For part of Woody's childhood, the family prospered, but in the 1920s a seemingly endless string of tragedies struck: his father went bankrupt and then suffered severe burns in a fire, his sister was killed in an oil stove explosion, fire destroyed two family houses, a cyclone destroyed a third, and his mother had a mental collapse and ended up in an asylum. In his teens, Woody earned money delivering milk, shining shoes, and working at other odd jobs. Around 1928, while living in Pampa, Oklahoma, he learned from an uncle how to play guitar. Soon after the Great Depression began, Guthrie, who never went beyond the tenth grade but read avidly and, over time, developed an impressive knowledge of psychology, religion, and Eastern philosophy, headed west, hitching rides on freight trains and earning money by painting signs and singing in saloons.

In California, he teamed up with his cousin, Jack Guthrie, who wanted to become the next singing cowboy sensation. In July 1937, they started their own radio show on KFVD in Los Angeles. They received no pay, but that did not bother Jack; he, after all, used the program strictly for promotional purposes. Seldom did Woody sing solo; his cousin dominated the show, which soon expanded from airing once to airing twice a day. Jack, however, did not have enough money to continue, and so he soon quit. Woody stayed on the air but made changes: he dropped the cowboy songs, which he never liked anyway, and sang mountain ballads, hymns, and hillbilly tunes.

At this time, Guthrie witnessed migrant laborers and the unemployed suffering amid the Great Depression. His songs stood up for them. He sided with labor organizers, and he performed at leftist rallies, even writing a column for *People's World*, a Communist newspaper. While in California, Guthrie established a friendship with stage actor Will Geer, who had close ties with the Communist Party. The two performed together at migrant labor camps and then headed east.

Guthrie appeared on numerous radio shows in New York City and for the first time in his life earned enough money to buy a new car and move his family from Oklahoma to be with him. He never compromised his principles, though, and quit the radio circuit after producers censored his songs. He joined the Almanac Singers, a group that performed in union halls, and toured Mexico with folk singer Pete Seeger. In 1943, E. P. Dutton and Company published Guthrie's autobiography, *Bound for Glory*, illustrated with his own sketches. The book sold well and received good reviews.

During World War II, Guthrie served in the Merchant Marine and, briefly, in the army. In the early 1950s, he traveled from coast to coast, making concert appearances and writing articles for newspapers and magazines. He continued to communicate folklore and the travails of ordinary people in a voice that sounded like the subjects he sang about.

Then, in 1955, Guthrie suffered from dizziness and headaches. An examination revealed he had contracted Huntington's chorea. The prognosis was not good: doctors told Guthrie he would lose control over his mind and body as his brain gradually died, leaving him in a vegetative state. From 1956 until his death, he spent most of his time hospitalized.

Other folk singers visited Guthrie, keeping him company and paying homage, Bob Dylan among them. One of Guthrie's sons, Arlo, began singing, and shortly before Woody died, he heard Arlo's hit song "Alice's Restaurant."

Guthrie passed away on 3 October 1967, hardly cognizant of the counterculture and the many young people who admired him. His commitment to protest, principles, and the common folk made him an icon. His music reverberated through Dylan, Phil Ochs, Joan Baez, and other counterculture singers, and enraptured college students who protested against nuclear weapons, war, and injustice. Guthrie felt the oppressed, their fears, their hopes—and the counterculture listened.

See also Dylan, Bob; Guthrie, Arlo.

References Guthrie, Woody, *Bound for Glory* (1943); Klein, Joe, *Woody Guthrie: A Life* (1980).

H

Haight-Ashbury

Haight-Ashbury, often called "Hashberry," emerged in the 1960s as the "capital of the hippie world" and the "headquarters of the counterculture." One hippie commented: "The Haight-Ashbury had four or five grapevines cooking at all times, and the two words that went down the wire most in those days were *dope* and *revolution*. Our secret formula was grass, LSD, meditation, hot music, consolidation, and a joyous sexuality."

In the 1950s, this roughly 40-block working-class district in San Francisco, adjoining Golden Gate Park, showed its decay with boarded up storefronts and a high crime rate. But by the mid-1960s, students from nearby San Francisco State College along with refugees from North Beach—the old beatnik center recently commercialized—and other bohemian types had discovered the Haight and transformed it into a hippie settlement. A person walking the streets in 1965 or 1966 could not escape noticing this dramatically changed scene.

The Haight's dilapidated shops had come to life; they displayed multicolored psychedelic-looking signs and sold used books, handcrafted belts and wristbands, clothing, incense, posters, and drug paraphernalia—rolling papers, roach clips, water pipes. Coffeehouses and small restaurants specializing in vegetarian and natural foods dotted the landscape. These hippie businesses bore what a straight observer would consider strange names: The Blue Unicorn (a coffeehouse), The Psychedelic Shop (a drug paraphernalia or "head" shop), The Drogstore (a café), Mnasidika (a boutique), Garbanza's Bead and Storm Door Co. (bead stringer's supplies). Their owners let people hang out, so these stores actually served as crucial gathering spots, symbols and vehicles of community.

Seemingly strange young people walked the streets. They wore mod styles, miniskirts, Beatle boots, colorful paisley prints, Edwardian and velvet clothes, or perhaps Buddhist robes or flowing capes; they often acted as if in another realm, while marijuana smoke drifted around them; and they sometimes panhandled, sometimes chanted or played flutes. The Haight had few bars, theatres, or other entertainment spots—the hippies relied on drugs and sensual explorations in their own homes. They lived in the old Victorian houses—paint peeling and roofs the worse for wear—that lined the residential streets. Hippies liked these buildings for their low rents and "groovy" architecture and decorated them with patterned Indian blankets, wind chimes, and god's eyes: wooden crosses covered with multicolored yarn. In 1966, some 15,000 hippies, largely California natives, lived in Haight-Ashbury.

But more than physical aspects made the Haight unique. Psychedelics permeated the entire scene. Hippies considered LSD, or acid, an avant-garde tool—it elicited spontaneity, the ability to see previously hidden connections, and feelings of oneness with the universe. Hippies believed in spreading love, freedom, peace, sincerity, and creativity, and they considered acid essential in doing this. Once a person took LSD and experienced the mystical, life appeared radically different, which is what the hippies wanted . . . a change in individual consciousness to affect the larger world.

Despite their disagreements, such as personality conflicts and disputes between shop owners and communards, the hippies believed that LSD brought them an underlying unity. And they believed that through psychedelics they could create a true community, a haven freed from straight society's conformity, selfishness, and greed.

Beyond psychedelics and hippie ideals, other influences permeated the Haight. Drug money primed its economy as many hippies worked as dealers, selling to middle-class kids from suburbia who would rather procure marijuana or acid in the Haight than in some scary slum. Political dropouts arrived jaded by middle-class society's rejection of their antiwar efforts. The radical Diggers promoted street acting as the key to societal salvation.

Intellectual influences also permeated the Haight: Zen Buddhism, Gestalt therapy, the *I Ching*, and the writings of Ken Kesey, Buckminster Fuller, and Marshall McLuhan. Concepts percolated, so feverishly they went well beyond straight society's ability to comprehend them.

Historian Charles Perry asserts in *The Haight-Ashbury: A History* that the hippies originally had noble intentions in trying to deal with the problems of war, technology, human nature, and "the great issues directly raised by the completely uncharted world of psychedelics." (275)

In 1967, however, hippie Haight-Ashbury experienced a crisis from which it never recovered. The media had discovered the scene, and unwilling or unable to understand it, reporters portrayed Haight-Ashbury simplistically, either as a sinkhole of degradation or a naive haven for free love. Stirred by this exposure, by the call of some hippies for the Haight to serve as the center for a Summer of Love, and by such popular rock songs as "San Francisco (Be Sure To Wear a Flower in Your Hair)," thousands of lost and confused kids, high-school age and even younger, descended on the Haight. So, too, did gawking tourists who ate "love burgers," often ridiculed

Flower children of the famed Haight-Ashbury district hold their Death of Hippie ceremony on 9 October 1967. A "dead" hippie is carried on a slab, followed by a symbolic 25-foot casket and a sign that reads "The Brotherhood of Free Men Is Born." The hippies held the ceremony in an attempt to rid themselves of the hippie image following negative media coverage and an influx of gawking tourists.

the hippies, and treated the district as a zoo for their amusement. Grey Line even operated a bus tour, called the Hippie Hop, although some hippies retaliated by running alongside the buses and holding mirrors to the windows so the tourists would see only themselves.

The young newcomers that summer knew nothing about the avant-garde or intellectual concerns; they did not see LSD as a vehicle to altering society. Instead, they donned love beads in trying to copy a hippie look and took acid as an escape. Unemployment, homelessness, food shortages, and self-indulgent drug trips plagued the Haight. Traffic slowed to a crawl, tempers flared, and a producer shot a cheap exploitation movie, *The Love-Ins*, that featured a girl freaking out on acid. In August, police discovered a grizzly murder scene: a known LSD dealer, in his apartment, stabbed through the heart 12 times, his right arm hacked above the elbow and missing. They arrested a motorcycle racer, after finding in his car the victim's gun, $2,600, and a severed arm wrapped in blood-soaked cloth.

While the hippies endured the Summer of Love, they faced stepped-up harassment from the authorities. Health and building inspectors issued warnings, often on dubious grounds, and the police raided parties and busted street people. Amphetamine and heroin use spread, along with reports, some exaggerated, of outsiders drugging young girls and raping them.

Many hippies left, fleeing the crowds, crime, and commercialism for small towns and farms in northern California, Colorado, New Mexico, and elsewhere. By summer's end, the Haight no longer reigned as the hippie capital. The tremendous influx of people had killed Haight-Ashbury; add to that the media, police actions, and the failure of hippies to adequately prepare for the summer invasion or to understand the ramifications of psychedelics on young kids.

In October, some Haight residents walked mournfully through the streets in a symbolic Death of Hippie ceremony that concluded with burying the Psychedelic Shop sign. Early the following year, tensions exploded between Haight residents and police with several riots breaking out, and in April, after the assassination of Martin Luther King, Jr., angry blacks smashed store windows. Many businesses had closed the previous fall—now more did. Thirty-six shops stood vacant in 1969, and those that survived looked like fortresses with metal bars over their windows.

Yet the Haight's earlier hippie culture still vibrated through society. Drug use, fashions, and psychedelic art and music all reflected the Haight, as did the central message: the world needed less greed, less violence, more togetherness, more love.

See also Diggers; Fuller, R. Buckminster; Hippies; *I Ching;* Kesey, Ken; LSD; McLuhan, Marshall; Summer of Love; Zen Buddhism.

References Anthony, Gene, *The Summer of Love: Haight-Ashbury at Its Highest* (1980); Gaskin, Stephen, *Haight-Ashbury Flashbacks* (1990); Perry, Charles, *The Haight-Ashbury: A History* (1984); Thompson, Hunter S., *The Great Shark Hunt: Strange Tales from a Strange Time* (1979).

Haight Independent Proprietors

In November 1966, the *San Francisco Examiner* announced:

> The hip purveyors of paintings, poetry, handcrafted leather and jewelry along Haight Street, having been blackballed by the Haight Street Merchants' Association, have formed their own Haight Independent Proprietors. That's HIP for short. (Burton Wolfe 1968, 60)

Thus, the hippie merchants had united. For two years, the Haight-Ashbury district had been undergoing substantial change from a downtrodden neighborhood with many boarded up storefronts to a thriving, colorful bohemian settlement. In the transformation, hippie merchants opened shops, such as the Psychedelic Shop begun by Ron and Jay Thelin, and In Gear, a clothing store owned by Tevi Strauch. Tension soon arose, though, between them and longtime merchants in the area. Opposition appeared from outside Haight-Ashbury, too, as city officials criticized the hippies and encouraged the police to harass hippie shops.

At this point, the hippie merchants sought support. They got some from professors, college students, and other liberally oriented people in the Haight. But they needed more and sought to join the existing Haight Street Merchants' Association. These mainstream shop owners, however, wanted nothing to do with the newcomers. Said one: "The biggest moan and groan from us is hippies blocking the sidewalk and scaring away customers." (59)

Tevi Strauch then got the idea for a hippie business association, and with the support of the Thelins founded HIP. Some 25 hippie merchants joined, and they opened the organization to everyone doing business in the Haight, including artisans and rock bands. Although beset with internal differences and confrontations with radicals such as the Diggers—who opposed private businesses as antithetical to a new, postcapitalist society—HIP provided the community with leadership during trying moments, such as during the 1967 Summer of Love, and committed itself to the vision of an artistic, freethinking Haight that would be an alternative to mainstream society.

See also Haight-Ashbury; Psychedelic Shop; Summer of Love.

References Perry, Charles, *The Haight-Ashbury: A History* (1984); Wolfe, Burton, *The Hippies* (1968).

Hair

On 29 April 1968, the play *Hair* opened at the Biltmore Theater on Broadway and revolutionized musicals with its topical subject, rock-style numbers, and nudity.

Hair presented countercultural values on a commercial level. The producer called *Hair* a "tribal love-rock musical" about the "dawning of the Age of Aquarius" when "peace will guide the planets and love will steer the stars." The play predicted a new era of "harmony and understanding." Written by Gerome Ragni and James Rado, with the music scored by Galt MacDermot, *Hair* opened with what *Rolling Stone* magazine called "a slow ballet of bodies, young bodies exulting at the possibilities of being alive" (Carney 1968, 21), and in one scene the entire cast, men and women, stripped naked and paraded about, dancing and singing joyously.

A tremendous hit with audiences, the play led to a successful Broadway-cast record album and several songs recorded by cover artists that reached the top ten: "The Age of Aquarius/Let the Sunshine In" by the Fifth Dimension, "Easy To Be Hard" by Three Dog Night, "Good Morning Sunshine" by Oliver, and "Hair" by the Cowsills.

The play's producer, Michael Butler, said:

> What *Hair* did was, at a time when musicals, when the theater was pretty well controlled and handled by formula musicals, very dull, very boring, *Hair* suddenly came out and really said something in a very strong way and got through. A new format was used; a new approach. It just looked like incredible chaos, but it was *organized* chaos. It was really an expanding, mind-blowing experience for people who saw it because they had never seen anything like it before. (Joseph 1974, 423)

See also Age of Aquarius.

References Carney, Leigh, "Hair Rock," *Rolling Stone*, 7 December 1968, 21; Joseph, Peter, *Good Times: An Oral History of America in the 1960s* (1974).

Happening

In the art world, "happenings" first appeared in the late 1950s and referred to any presentation lacking a developmental sequence, one that might occur anywhere at anytime, that might or might not be planned, that used free association and artistry in action. Artists might hold happenings in their lofts, as they did in Greenwich Village in the 1960s, or they might be held in auditoriums or on college campuses. The word *happening* eventually took on a broader meaning, and people used it to describe a spontaneous spectacle, such as the coming together of bands, dancers, and participants in a park.

See also Fluxus; Ono, Yoko.

Happening House

As the Summer of Love approached in 1967, Happening House prepared to meet the throngs of young people headed for San Francisco by expanding its role as a "psychedelic outreach" program.

Leonard Wolf, a writer and English professor at San Francisco State College, founded Happening House in the Haight-Ashbury district shortly before the Summer of Love. Happening House provided classes in alternative culture—practices alien to most middle-class young people, for example, lessons on the sitar, yoga, bread making, weaving, and natural childbirth.

At first, Wolf presented his classes in the streets and at Panhandle Park. Later, he obtained an actual house at 409 Clayton Street. Wolf envisioned a new society with a culture expressing the emerging alternative community, one founded on a postcapitalist communal arrangement. Happening House, however, did not survive to the end of the decade.

See also Haight-Ashbury; Hippies; Summer of Love.

Reference Perry, Charles, *The Haight-Ashbury: A History* (1984).

Hare Krishna

Some hippies pursued spiritual enlightenment by joining the Hare Krishnas. Swami Prabhupada (1896–1977), a Sanskrit scholar from Calcutta, India, introduced the Hindu sect Hare Krishna to the West in 1965. The sect's formal name is the International Society for Krishna Consciousness, or *Gaudiya Vaisnavism*, with the name Hare Krishna derived from its member's chant: "Krishna, Krishna, Hare Krishna."

Hare Krishnas believe they must chant the mantra and meditate on it to achieve enlightenment and remove themselves from the cycle of reincarnation. They must also live ascetic lives, refusing meat, eggs, alcohol, tea, coffee, and drugs, and engaging in sexual relations only within marriage and only for procreation.

The Harrad Experiment

Written by Robert H. Rimmer, *The Harrad Experiment* received considerable attention when it first appeared in 1966. The novel describes an experimental school, Harrad College, that encourages young men and women to live together. Besides premarital sexual relations, the story delves into student interests in philosophy, politics, and religion.

Readers in the 1960s considered *Harrad* quite revelatory about young people's ideas and desires, and the book sold more than 3 million copies. Perhaps liberated sex meant more than carnal love, as when the author describes the actions of two young men at Harrad:

> Sheila, in a shorty night gown, opened the door, snapped on the lights, and stared at us unbelievingly.
>
> "Oh, my good lord," she gasped, unable to stop laughing. "Look at the two of you! Naked as jaybirds."
>
> "We came to warm your belly," Stanley said. . . .
>
> "See," I said. "No subtlety. No symbols. No secrets."
>
> Stanley grabbed her and pushed her into the bedroom. "Since you really can't make up your mind, get in bed. We're both going to sleep with you."
>
> And we did! Wedged between us, Sheila finally stopped laughing and solemnly kissed us each good-night.
>
> "Thank you, Harry. Thank you, Stanley," she said.
>
> "For what?"
>
> "For caring." (121)

Reference Rimmer, Robert H., *The Harrad Experiment* (1966).

Harris, David (1946–)

"We will renounce all deferments and refuse to cooperate with the draft in any manner, at any level. . . . The War in Vietnam is criminal and we must act together, at great individual risk, to stop it. Those involved must lead the American people, by their example, to understand the enormity of what their government is doing." So wrote David Harris and his colleagues in their first public announcement for The Resistance, an antiwar, antidraft group. Harris helped found The Resistance, and he shaped it into an influential, highly respected protest organization.

Harris was born in 1946 in Fresno, California, where his father worked as an attorney. He attended Fresno High School, did well academically, played on the football team, and was named "Fresno High School Boy of the Year" in 1963. He graduated that spring and went on to Stanford University in Palo Alto.

The following year, the civil rights movement attracted Harris, and he traveled to Mississippi, where in October he helped the Student Nonviolent Coordinating Committee organize black voters in Quitman County, on the delta. Within days the dangerous situation facing civil rights workers hit him full force when two men emerged from a pickup truck, walked over to him, stuck a shotgun against his neck, and warned: "Nigger lover, we're givin' you five minutes to get out of town." (Harris 1993, 83) Despite this, he continued his scheduled weeklong effort in Mississippi.

After returning to Stanford, Harris gradually involved himself in the antiwar movement and participated in his first protest in the fall of 1965 when he marched with 6,000 other demonstrators from Berkeley to Oakland. In 1966, he entered the race for student body president at Stanford; not expecting to win a position normally held by fraternity men, he did so anyhow by using radical speeches. At one point he declared, "Students are niggers here," and condemned both the college administration and the war in Vietnam as oppressive.

Soon after Harris received his draft notice in January 1967, he addressed a student rally at Stanford and called on his audience to resist conscription and, if necessary, go to jail. The following month, a few weeks before he graduated, Harris resigned from his position as student body president. He devoted his time outside class to the Peace and Liberation Commune, a dozen people living in three houses in East Palo Alto and involved in activities ranging from Buddhist meditation to political protest; and to The Resistance, which he cofounded with activist Dennis Sweeny. This organization, which initially numbered only four students, set a date, 16 October, on which men from all over the nation were to gather in public and return their draft cards to the government.

Throughout that summer and fall, The Resistance grew and developed a national network with chapters in several cities, despite criticism from the leading New Left organization, Students for a Democratic Society, whose leaders considered the upstart group too intent on martyrdom. As it happened, many protesters admired The Resistance for its principled stand.

October 1967 turned out to be filled with antiwar protests, including demonstrations at the Oakland induction center in California and a large march on the Pentagon. As planned, on 16 October, Harris led The Resistance demonstration on the steps of San Francisco's Federal Building. About 2,000 people gathered there, and when he passed around a basket asking young men to turn in their draft cards so they could be delivered to the federal attorney's office, 400 did so. Similar demonstrations led by The Resistance in 17 other cities resulted in hundreds more breaking the law by giving up their cards, and the group held another round of draft card returns early in December.

By this time, Harris had met with folk singer Joan Baez and received her support for The Resistance. As his trial date neared, they fell in love and married—a highly publicized union that lasted three years before ending in divorce.

Harris made many appearances on college campuses, eventually giving hundreds of speeches in his effort to build opposition to the war. As part of its COINTELPRO program, the FBI followed him closely and compiled a lengthy dossier on his activities.

Harris's trial for violating the selective service law began on 27 May 1968 and lasted two days, during which he insisted he was not guilty because the Vietnam War was unconstitutional and unjust. When the jury indicated it could not reach a decision, the judge reminded it that refusing to submit to an induction order in and of itself proved illegal intent and purpose. The jurors then returned a guilty verdict.

Harris appealed his case, and at the same time continued to work for The Resistance, which participated in the protest at the 1968 Democratic National Convention in Chicago and, in November, held another draft card return. In January 1969, however, The Resistance collapsed, torn apart by factional fighting of the type that damaged many New Left political groups: militants argued with those who wanted to drop out, end political protests, and form an alternative community in New Mexico or some other rural location.

Harris began serving his sentence on 15 July 1969, and while in jail continued his opposition to the draft by staging a hunger strike. In all, he served two years at La Tuna Federal Correctional Institution in Texas. Shortly after his parole on 15 March 1971, he helped found another antiwar group, the Peoples Union, and two years later, when the Paris Peace Agreement signaled an end to the American troop presence in Vietnam, he began a career in journalism. He remarried in 1977, and in the 1970s and 1980s wrote several books and magazine articles.

See also Baez, Joan; New Left; Students for a Democratic Society.

Reference Harris, David, *Dreams Die Hard: Three Men's Journey through the Sixties* (1993).

Harvard University

Harvard University in Cambridge, Massachusetts, ranked among the most politically active college campuses in the 1960s, one where student protests began early in the decade. Tocsin, for example, formed in cooperation with students at nearby Radcliffe in 1960 as a peace organization intended to promote discussion about nuclear weapons. Tocsin members formed study groups, handed out leaflets, and lobbied congressmen. At the same time, other Harvard students engaged in civil rights activities in the South and elsewhere.

Antiwar protests also emerged early at Harvard. These included in 1965 some of the nation's first teach-ins, where professors discussed with students the American involvement in Vietnam. Two years later, protest intensified into resistance, and radicals appeared who advocated a complete refusal to abide with the war; they destroyed draft cards and disrupted campus recruiters from Dow Chemical, a company that made napalm. In one episode, members of Students for a Democratic Society invaded Harvard in 1969. They marched on the Center for International Affairs, seized University Hall, and forcibly expelled the administrative staff. The protestors had little student support until police attacked them. This sparked a student strike.

Activism at Harvard continued into the early 1970s when students demonstrated for stronger environmental laws and protested workplace discrimination against women, an inequity evident in the few female teachers and the disparity in wages between men and women at all levels.

See also Weather Underground.

Reference Rosenblatt, Roger, *Coming Apart: A Memoir of the Harvard Wars of 1969* (1997).

Hashish

THC, or tetrahydrocannabinol, comes from the female marijuana plant, and its most potent form, concentrated in the plant resin, is known as hashish. Some eight times stronger than regular marijuana, hashish usually produces in the partaker an intense euphoria, and this made it attractive to hippies. They heard, too, of the drug's reputation (one highly debatable) as an aphrodisiac. A famous Arabic poem begins:

> The member of Abu'l-Haylukh remained
> In erection for 30 days, sustained
> By smoking hashish
> Abu'l-Haylukh deflowered in one night
> Eighty virgins in a rigid rite
> After smoking hashish (Masters 1967)

An expensive drug, hashish never attained widespread use in the counterculture as did marijuana.

See also Marijuana.

Reference Masters, R. E. L., "Sex, Ecstasy, and the Psychdelic Drugs," November 1967; http://www.hyperreal.com/psychedelics/ (15 March 1997).

Hayden, Tom (1940–)

As riots erupted and tear gas drifted along the streets of Chicago, outside the Democratic National Convention in 1968, Tom Hayden declared: "The city and the military machinery it has aimed at us won't permit us to protest in an organized fashion. Therefore . . . we must turn this overheated military machine against itself. Let us make sure if blood flows, it flows all over the city."

Hayden seemed everywhere in the decade's radicalized politics and emerged as perhaps the most prominent New Left leader—helping organize Students for a Democratic Society, writing the initial Port Huron Statement, working in northern ghettos, making highly publicized trips to Cuba and North Vietnam, and enduring arrest for his part in the Chicago protests. Hayden expressed the discontent, idealism, and occasional fury of young radicals while conservatives targeted him for vilification, including harassment by the government.

Born on 12 December 1940 in Royal Oak, Michigan, Hayden spent part of his childhood in San Diego, California, where his father served in the navy. At Royal Oak High School his interest turned to journalism, and he gained a reputation for having a feisty, rebellious attitude. As a senior, he wrote an editorial criticizing overcrowding in the school and so positioned the first letters of the lead words in the subheads to spell "GO TO HELL."

Hayden entered the University of Michigan in 1957 with hopes of obtaining a degree in journalism and becoming a foreign correspondent. The rebelliousness he displayed in high school carried over to college as he was immediately turned off by the authoritarian policies of the administration that, not unusual for those days, set strict rules for students and allowed them little participation in campus governance.

The bigger picture in America influenced Hayden as well. He disliked the materialistic conformity that characterized the 1950s and started reading Jack Kerouac, whose novel, *On the Road*, fed Hayden's rebellious instinct. In June 1960, during the summer break, Hayden hitchhiked to California thinking he might live the type of dropout existence portrayed in Kerouac's story.

He, however, was much too political for that. In fact, his journey was prompted in part by a protest that had occurred a month earlier in San Francisco at which college students from Berkeley demonstrated against hearings held by the House Un-American Activities Committee. The police had reacted by hosing down the peaceful demonstrators, forcing them from the stairways in city hall. After this confrontation, the committee called the protesters Communists. To Hayden, the episode displayed oppression and a callous disregard for the ideas of students.

Hayden's politics grew more radical during his California trip. He stayed with people who showed him the poverty suffered by farmworkers—a contrast to the pleasant images of suburbia prevalent on television—and taught him about nuclear research under way at Livermore. Then, in August, he covered the Democratic National Convention in Los Angeles for the *Michigan Daily*, the student newspaper at his college, and had his first contact with the civil rights movement when he met protesters there. In the stories he sent back, Hayden called for student activism, a message university officials disliked.

In his senior year, Hayden served as editor of the *Michigan Daily*. His activism expanded when Al Haber, a political leader in Students for a Democratic Society (SDS), convinced him to help the Student Nonviolent Coordinating Committee (SNCC) in its civil rights efforts. Consequently, after Hayden graduated in 1961,

During the 1968 Democratic National Party Convention, Tom Hayden uses a megaphone to talk to a group gathered in Lincoln Park on 8 October.

he worked as a field-worker for SDS and a volunteer for SNCC in Georgia and Mississippi. He thus saw racism firsthand, and grew angry when President John Kennedy seemed to hold back from pushing a civil rights agenda.

With SDS, Hayden had found an outlet for his protest and his desire to change American society. In 1962, he wrote the draft version of the Port Huron Statement, a manifesto expressing the criticisms, ideals, and principles of SDS. The Port Huron Statement attacked both liberalism and right-wing anticommunism. The former it saw as having sold out to a big military state, and the latter as promoting extremism to the point of stifling dissent. The manifesto called for a new, participatory democracy, a political system no longer dominated by the elite but expressive of community and individual rights.

From 1962 to 1963, Hayden served as president of SDS while completing his master's degree in sociology at the University of Michigan. The following year, he helped begin the Economic Research and Action Project (ERAP), an SDS program intended to help poor people in the nation's cities. Hayden opened an ERAP office in the all-black Central Ward of Newark, New Jersey, and, like other ERAP volunteers, lived in the decrepit housing that characterized the area. He and his 30 or so coworkers put together rent strikes and pressured the local government to repair neighborhood streets. He later recounted: "We believed that people can solve problems by themselves." (Findley 1972, Part 1, 44) Yet he found it difficult to organize the residents, many of whom considered him a white interloper.

Near the same time, Hayden participated in protests against the Vietnam War. In 1965, at the invitation of Staughton Lynd, a left-wing historian, Hayden made his first of several trips to North Vietnam. He did so with reservation, wondering if he were a traitor, but finally concluding the best way to support American soldiers would be by ending the war. Hayden praised the stamina of the Vietnamese people and the integrity of their revolutionary fight. Back in the United States, in 1966 and 1967, he spoke at campus teach-ins aimed at protesting the war. In the latter year, he traveled to Cuba and expressed admiration for Fidel Castro.

Hayden left Newark in 1967, after the ghetto exploded into riots. He dedicated himself full-time to the antiwar movement. Earlier, in 1965, he had participated in an SDS-sponsored protest march in Washington, and he now began planning a large-scale demonstration to be held in 1968 at the Democratic National Convention in Chicago. Amid this, Hayden involved himself in a student strike that broke out in the spring of 1968 at Columbia University. He helped hold together one of the student protest groups, although some leftists accused him of grandstanding. One protester commented: "Like the Lone Ranger, he didn't even wave goodbye, but quietly slipped away, taking his silver protest button to another beleaguered campus." (Kunen 1968, 36)

Still planning for Chicago, Hayden worked with representatives from other radical groups that had organized the National Mobilization Committee To End the War in Vietnam (MOBE). Hayden and MOBE (which included activists Rennie Davis and David Dellinger) organized the protest despite warnings that fringe groups committed to violence would likely show up, and that the Chicago police would crush any demonstrations, peaceful or otherwise. He later stated that the assassination of Robert Kennedy that year had affected him deeply, reinforcing his belief that a violent society only understood force.

Hayden took an ambivalent position in the Chicago protests—stating he had no desire for violence but also expressing a desire to shut down the Democratic Convention and "confront" the oppressors. Shortly before the protest, he said the national government must be destroyed and claimed: "The government of the United States is an outlaw institution under the control of war criminals." (Farber 1988, 114)

When the Chicago protest deteriorated into rock and bottle throwing and heavy-handed use of tear gas and billy clubs by the police, Hayden made his pronouncement calling for retaliation. Evidence uncovered later found that the government had infiltrated the protest movement, and secret agents may have provoked at least some of the violence.

Soon after Chicago, the government arrested Hayden and seven other radicals for having planned and incited a riot—newspapers called them the Chicago Eight (on trial as the Chicago Seven after one defendant was granted a separate hearing). In February 1970, Hayden was found guilty, but two years later the Seventh Circuit Court of Appeals overturned the conviction on the grounds that the presiding judge had displayed bias against the defense. Looking back on his involvement, Hayden said: "Chicago was part of a decisive upsurge which, we thought, faster than any of us could predict, was going to bring down the American government." (Findley 1972, Part 1, 48)

In the early 1970s, Hayden and his then wife, Jane Fonda, engaged in several efforts to end America's continuing presence in South Vietnam. Additionally, Hayden wrote articles for *Ramparts* and *Rolling Stone*, and a book recounting his Chicago experience. In 1976, he ran for the U.S. Senate from California but lost in the Democratic primary. In the 1980s and 1990s, he served in the California legislature, and in 1997 ran for mayor of Los Angeles but lost.

During the 1960s, Hayden worked day and night to promote change. When a friend once asked him where he got his energy, he replied; "I have an ideology." (Hayden 1988, 172) He refused to compromise his radicalism or to support the hippies, at one point criticizing them as escapists. The antiwar movement, he said years later, had been right.

See also Chicago Eight; Democratic National Convention of 1968; ERAP; Fonda, Jane; Gitlin, Todd; National Mobilization Committee To End the War in Vietnam; Port Huron Statement; Students for a Democratic Society.

References Farber, David, *Chicago '68* (1988); Findley, Tom, "Tom Hayden Rolling Stone Interview Part 1," *Rolling Stone*, 26 October 1972, 36–50, and "Tom Hayden Rolling Stone Interview Part 2," *Rolling Stone*, 9 November 1972, 28–34; Hayden, Tom, *The American Future: New Visions beyond Old Frontiers* (1980), *The Love of Possession Is a Disease with Them* (1972), *Reunion: A Memoir* (1988), and *Trial* (1970); Kunen, James Simon, *The Strawberry Statement: Notes of a College Revolutionary* (1968).

Head

Head referred to a habitual drug user. Depending on the drug, a person might, for example, be known as an "acid head" or "pot head." The word stemmed from the effect drugs had, changing thought patterns and causing the user to live inside the mind, or head, at least while on a trip, if not also after. In fact, the counterculture differentiated between "body" drugs and "head" drugs. The former, such as heroin, opium, tranquilizers, and alcohol, depressed the senses; the latter, including LSD, mescaline, psilocybin, and speed, intensified them.

Head Shop

With drugs extensive in the counterculture, "head shops" appeared in hip areas. These shops sold drug paraphernalia: rolling papers, roach clips, pipes, and bongs. They also sold items related to drug trips, among them incense, posters, and black lights, and, in some instances, hippie-style clothes and jewelry. A few head shops dealt in illegal, under-the-counter drug sales.

Head shops bore names such as The Entrepreneur in Chicago; Drog Shop and Psychedelic Shop in San Francisco; Pipefitter in Madison, Wisconsin; Third Eye in Los Angeles; The Trance in Columbia, Missouri; and OZ in Miami. Some proved lucrative, most barely turned a profit. Entering one, its muted atmosphere saturated with incense, separated a person from mainstream society, as if opening a door into a subterranean realm where everyone knew that everyone knew they smoked dope and marched to a different drummer.

See also Marijuana; Psychedelic Shop; Roach.

Headband

Headbands worn around the forehead to keep hair out of the eyes first became popular during the 1920s, primarily among women. In the sixties, however, many counterculture male youths joined the females and wore headbands to hold back their long hair, then in style. Headbands came in different materials, but hippies favored leather.

Hell's Angels

They weren't just sixties counterculture—they were counterculture, period. And they took it to the extreme, these Hell's Angels; so extreme that some youths romanticized them, as Americans have done with other outlaws in other times.

Founded in Fontana, California, a town east of Los Angeles, in 1950, the Hell's Angels quickly gained a reputation as a dangerous motorcycle club, filled with vulgar criminals who, at one slight, one wrong look, would stomp a person senseless. The Angels did not disown this image, as one said: "I don't really care if people think we're bad. I think this is what really keeps us going. We fight society and society fights us." (Thompson 1966, 149)

The Hell's Angels emblem, or the group's "colors," consisted of an embroidered patch that displayed a winged skull wearing a motorcycle helmet, below the wing the letters "MC," and over that, the words "Hell's Angels." This patch was usually sewed to a sleeveless denim jacket, which contained other patches, including one bearing the local chapter name. Angels preferred to keep their clothes, and their bodies, unwashed; they wore beards, long hair, and sometimes belts made from motorcycle drive chains—an instant weapon, if needed. They rode, almost exclusively, Harley-Davidsons and considered themselves extreme nonconformists, complete rebels:

> We're the one percenters, man—the one percent that don't fit and don't care. . . . We've punched our way out of a hundred rumbles, stayed alive with our boots and fists. We're royalty among motorcycle outlaws, baby. (13)

When the Angels rumbled along a highway on a "run," they struck fear in middle-class motorists—fear evoked by the Angels' huge motorcycles, or "hogs"; by their jackets undone and flapping in the wind; by their bare chests and tattoos. The mainstream press carried several stories in the mid-1960s attesting to the Angels' barbarity: upstanding citizens assaulted, teenage girls raped, small towns terrorized. A report by the California attorney general in 1965 detailed these atrocities, but the Angels only numbered a few hundred, and Hunter Thompson, in his classic work *Hell's Angels*, calls the stories exaggerated.

Whatever the numbers, the Angels rode into the 1960s counterculture. Mean and snarling, they never did like hippies. For one thing, these fascists at heart hated the peace-and-love message; for another, they equated hippies with antiwar activism, and the Angels staunchly defended the Vietnam War—despite their nonconformity, they hated anyone who disparaged the American flag or manliness. At one point, at an antiwar demonstration in Oakland, California, they stomped several protesters.

Yet the Angels' mystique appealed to some in the counterculture, and the outlaws could be seen frequently in San Francisco's hippie Haight-Ashbury district, sometimes welcome, although just as often feared. Two contacts between the sixties counterculture and the Hell's Angels gained notoriety. The first happened in 1965 when Ken Kesey and the Merry Pranksters decided to experiment and see if they could expand the Angels' minds and, they hoped, mellow them out. They invited the Angels' San Francisco chapter to an Acid Test at Kesey's home in La Honda. The Angels downed LSD and, for the most part, reacted as the hippies wanted, grooving on the scene contentedly. The first party went so well that others soon followed (not ending until the Oakland stomping, mentioned above).

A second contact turned bad. In December 1969, the Rolling Stones and their promoters invited the Angels under their leader Sonny Barger to patrol the Altamont Rock Concert. Loaded on beer and drugs, the Angels went into a violent frenzy, beating spectators with lead-weighted pool sticks, kicking them, and in one instance knifing a black man to death. For the counterculture a tragedy, for the Hell's Angels just another visitation.

See also Altamont; Kesey, Ken.

Reference Thompson, Hunter S., *Hell's Angels: A Strange and Terrible Saga* (1966).

Helms, Chet (1942–)

Chet Helms emerged as an important figure on the San Francisco rock scene, managing Big Brother and the Holding Company, operating The Family Dog, and staging concerts at the Avalon Ballroom.

Helms was born on 2 August 1942 in Santa Maria, California, but as a kid lived mainly in Missouri, where his grandfather, a fundamentalist Baptist minister, raised him. Helms attended the University of Texas-Austin for one year, then dropped out and roamed Mexico before moving in 1962 to San Francisco. There, he supported himself with a small Mexican import business and joined in the hippie counterculture emerging in the Haight-Ashbury district. He started hanging out at 1090 Page Street, a huge Victorian mansion occupied by several musicians and other bohemian types. In the summer of 1965, he organized jam sessions in the mansion's basement ballroom, to which he admitted people for 50 cents.

Later that year, Helms played an integral role in putting together a rock band, Big Brother and the Holding Company, whose concerts incorporated a new technique promoted by him: flashing film and slide projections intended to replicate a psychedelic experience. Early in 1966, Helms adopted the name The Family Dog for his emerging rock promotion business—a name originally held, but since abandoned, by another group of promoters. He sponsored successful dances and concerts at the Fillmore: the Tribal Stomp, featuring Big Brother, and the King Kong Memorial Dance, both in February, and, in March, another that featured the Butterfield Blues Band. The shows attracted many young people from Haight-Ashbury.

Helms complained, however, about unfair treatment in his dealings with Bill Graham, a rock promoter who controlled the Fillmore, and in mid-1966 he began sponsoring dances and concerts at the Avalon Ballroom. At this time, he used Stanley Mouse and Alton Kelley to produce publicity posters based on his concepts. They created psychedelic imagery so popular that people started yanking the posters down almost as quickly as Helms could put them up.

In the fall of 1967, Helms purchased a dance hall in Denver, Colorado, and it opened as The Denver Dog, featuring Blue Cheer and Big Brother. Other headliners that year included the Grateful Dead, the Doors, and Buffalo Springfield. Helms, though, had overextended himself; The Denver Dog lost money, and he soon closed it.

Through the remainder of the decade, Helms continued sponsoring concerts. He left the Avalon late in 1968 when the city revoked his permit. From then until 1970, he presented shows at an old beachfront dance hall, competing with the Fillmore and another site operated by Graham, Winterland. Graham considered Helms lazy and a sloppy planner. "People loved Chet and he was a very nice man," Graham later said. "But he didn't have a sense of responsibility." (Graham and Greenfield 1992, 148–149) Another observer who worked with Helms criticized him for hiring too many people and for letting friends and friends of friends into concerts free.

In the dichotomy between hippie and businessman, Helms indeed leaned toward the hippie side—as opposed to Graham who never quit hustling. Helms failed to achieve Graham's financial success but denied it had anything to do with laziness. He worked 18-hour days and produced 500 evenings of entertainment at the Avalon and elsewhere. His problems, he claimed, came from being undercapitalized.

Despite Helms's limitations, even Graham admitted that "The pure hippie of the day thought of the Avalon as the *real* church. Mine [the Fillmore] was the commercial church." (149) After The Family Dog, Helms ran an art gallery. In the mid-1990s, he revived The Family Dog and sponsored concerts in San Francisco before again leaving and returning to his art gallery.

See also Avalon Ballroom; The Family Dog; Fillmore; Graham, Bill.

Reference Graham, Bill, and Robert Greenfield, *Bill Graham Presents: My Life inside Rock and Out* (1992).

Hendrix, Jimi (1942–1970)

Mike Bloomfield of the Butterfield Blues Band remarked about the day he first saw rock guitarist Jimi Hendrix in concert:

> In front of my eyes, he burned me to death. I didn't even get my guitar out. H-bombs were going off, guided missiles were flying—I can't tell you the sounds he was getting out of his instrument. He was getting every sound I was ever to hear him get right there in that room. . . . I didn't even want to pick up a guitar for the next year. (Shapiro and Glebbeek 1990, 104)

Bloomfield was not alone: Hendrix combined blues and psychedelic music with a guitar style that left most in awe.

Hendrix was born Johnny Allen Hendrix on 27 November 1942 in Seattle, Washington. His name was soon changed to James Marshall Hendrix. As a kid, Hendrix's parents, mainly black but partly Cherokee Indian, took him to a Pentecostal church, where he joined them in singing gospel songs. By age 8, he had become obsessed with playing the guitar, although for years he could not afford one and had to use imaginary strings on a broom. Finally, at age 11, his father bought him an inexpensive acoustic guitar, and soon after the youngster got his first electric one.

Hendrix quit Garfield High School during his senior year, worked as a handyman for a while, and then in 1963 joined the army. A back injury he suffered during a parachute jump led to his early discharge from the service. He then played with several different rhythm and blues bands before making his way to New York City's Greenwich Village, where an active music scene revolved around several new coffeehouses and clubs. In 1966, he formed his first band, bought his first Fender Stratocaster guitar, and tried out his material at Café Wha? There, he got to know other young musicians, such as Bob Dylan and Bruce Springsteen, and developed the talent of playing his Stratocaster while holding it upside down.

During his engagement at Café Wha? Chas Chandler, bass player with the rock band the Animals, caught his act. At this time, the Animals were breaking up, and Chandler wanted to find a musician he could manage back home in England. He convinced a skeptical Hendrix that he could make him a star, and so in 1966 the young American headed overseas and at Chandler's suggestion changed the spelling of his first name to "Jimi" to make him more distinctive.

Once in England, Hendrix formed a band with bass guitarist Noel Chandler and drummer Mitch Mitchell, called the Jimi Hendrix Experience. Only six weeks after leaving New York and just four days after forming the band, Hendrix opened at the Olympia in Paris, France, a major venue. Then he toured Europe, with the Experience breaking attendance records, including sellout crowds at the Sports Arena in Copenhagen and the Seville Theater in London. True to Chandler's expectations, Hendrix had quickly emerged as a star.

In 1967, after recording several hit records and an album in England, Hendrix returned to the United States, and the Experience made its American debut on 18 June at the Monterey International Pop Festival in California. The audience sat

Singer Jimi Hendrix performs on 31 December 1969.

mesmerized during Hendrix's performance, which included his favorite song "Wild Thing," and watched in disbelief as Hendrix played his Stratocaster behind his back, and at the end of his show set the guitar afire.

Hendrix had presented an electrifying soul and psychedelic performance filled with a sensuality that characterized his stage presence, what one observer called "the voodoo child run wild in electric ladyland!" He did not lack critics, however, such as San Francisco journalist Ralph Gleason, who found him boring, and Robert Christgau, a writer for *Esquire*, who called him "a psychedelic Uncle Tom." (Ward, Stokes, and Tucker 1986, 376) Still, his single "Purple Haze" and LP *Are You Experienced?* climbed the record charts. In 1968, *Rolling Stone* magazine named him Performer of the Year.

In 1969, however, personal disagreements caused the Experience to split up. Hendrix played at the Fillmore in San Francisco with a new group, A Band of Gypsys, and appeared in August at Woodstock. "'Scuse me while I kiss the sky . . . don't know if I'm comin' up or down," he sang—but, over all, his music drifted, and he expressed dissatisfaction with his work. Hendrix got back together with the Experience, but differences remained, and he played with them only sporadically.

In 1970, Hendrix told an interviewer for *Melody Maker*, a British pop newspaper, "You know the drug scene . . . was opening up things in people's minds, giving them things that they just couldn't handle. Well, music can do that, you know, and you don't need any drugs." ("Jimi" 1970, 8) Shortly after, on 18 September 1970, he was found dead in his London apartment. The official coroner's report ruled out suicide and said his death had resulted from "an inhalation of vomit due to barbiturate intoxication." (Shapiro and Glebbeek 1990, 475)

Writing in *Rolling Stone*, John Burks said that Hendrix, more than any other guitarist, had "brought the full range of sound from all the reaches of serious electronic music—a wider palette of sound than any other performing instrumentalist in the history of music ever had at his fingertips—plus the fullest tradition of black music—from Charley Patton and Louis Armstrong all the way to John Coltrane and Sun Ra—to rock and roll." (Burks 1970, 8)

See also Monterey Pop Festival; Rock Music.

References Burks, John, "An Appreciation," *Rolling Stone*, 15 October 1970, 8; Hopkins, Jerry, *Hit and Run: The Jimi Hendrix Story* (1983); "Jimi," *Rolling Stone*, 15 October 1970, 1, 6–8; Shapiro, Harry, and Caesar Glebbeek, *Jimi Hendrix: Electric Gypsy* (1990); Ward, Ed, Geoffrey Stokes, and Ken Tucker, *Rock of Ages: The Rolling Stone History of Rock & Roll* (1986).

Hippies

A leading symbol of the counterculture, hippies espoused love, peace, drugs, and community. Despite this common ideology, and media generalizations about naive flower children, hippies lived in many different ways and their society changed over the decade.

The true hippie, if such a person existed, could perhaps be found in San Francisco's Haight-Ashbury district around 1965. That is when this deteriorating neighborhood experienced a bohemian invasion filled with challenges to mainstream society. And it is also when Michael Fallon, a reporter for the *San Francisco Chronicle*, coined the word *hippie* in a story he did about a coffeehouse in the Haight, called the Blue Unicorn. Fallon likened the strange denizens there to the beatniks and hipsters who had recently inhabited nearby North Beach. Like their predecessors, this new group turned away from middle-class society, but they were optimistic, attached to ideals such as love and peace, and expressed themselves linguistically and physically in vivid colors—hence not full-blown hipsters, said Fallon, but hippies. Hippies never did like the word, but it stuck.

The hippies in Haight-Ashbury set the tone for hippies elsewhere. The Haight hippies considered mainstream society false, or plastic; they rejected its preoccupation with material goods, its manipulations, its vacuous politics; they rejected its eight-to-five job routine, its conformist suburbs, its impersonal technology. The hippies rejected mainstream values, such as Christianity, nationalism, and chastity. They believed not in the goodness of all but in the value of all as human beings, and that people should do what they want as long as they did not hurt others. "The chief characteristic of hippie activity," says Leonard Wolf in *Voices from the Love Generation*, "is that it is imaginative, spontaneous, charged with energy—and sporadic." (xlvi)

Drugs were essential to hippie life—marijuana and, more importantly, LSD. Influenced by Aldous Huxley's book, *The Doors of Perception*, hippies considered acid a means by which to separate the individual from mainstream indoctrination—a deprogramming, in a way, but one heavily mystical in pursuing heightened consciousness. In the Haight, hippies sought a true psychedelic community that rejected private property and the power game found in politics. They had no desire to take to the streets and march against the Vietnam War or, in a larger quest, reform society. Protest, they believed, only enhanced the feeling of power in those who had it, and thus played into the establishment's hands. The hippies did not want to protest or blow up the establishment, but love it to death; they preferred dropping out and indulging in an LSD experience that would tear down ingrained beliefs and categories and infuse their lives with an intense sensory experience—"an overwhelming, pulsating, vibrant mixture of sight, sound, and feeling." (Irvin 1977, 95–96)

Consequently, hippie art reflected intuition and texture over rational analysis and linear construction, and hippie psychedelia permeated rock music, influencing young people throughout the nation. Soon, emphasis on the visual, the colorful, the sensate affected mainstream society and appeared in everything from clothing to television ads.

Hippies rejected the establishment—mainstream society's eight-to-five jobs, its preoccupation with material goods, suburbs, and impersonal technology—in favor of ideals such as love, peace, and heightened consciousness, often reached through the use of drugs. Here, an unnamed hippie dances at Detroit's first love-in on 30 April 1967.

Hippies abhorred such commercialization, particularly evident in the 1967 Summer of Love. This largely media-promoted event brought thousands of young people to the Haight, where they searched for an elusive togetherness that proved even more elusive when they engaged in wanton drug use and fell prey to hustlers and criminals.

Hippies lived in many different ways, even in the Haight, where some sold crafts or opened businesses, and others, such as the radical Diggers, sought a true communal settlement based on sharing. Outside Haight-Ashbury, some hippies lived in communal houses or in the countryside on communal farms.

Throughout the 1960s, the hippie ranks grew, enlarged by young people disgusted with the mainstream establishment's intransigence toward reform. Many political radicals, for example, gave up the fight against the Vietnam War, racial injustice, and other social problems and joined the hippies in dropping out.

Although some hippies read authors whose works encouraged them to seek alternative ways—writers such as Henry David Thoreau, Paul Goodman, and David Riesman—most had only to live through the sixties and see how the establishment acted in order to conclude that straight society had little to offer. In *The Movement and the Sixties*, historian Terry H. Anderson states: "The behavior of the [mainstream] culture boosted the counterculture. Without racism, war, and campus paternalism, the population of hippiedom would have been proportionately about the same size as that of the Beats in the postwar society." (248)

Yet for every true hippie who did drop out, many more youths adopted only hippie appearances and mannerisms. Not every young person who wore beads and bell bottoms (and for the guys, long hair), smoked pot, and flashed a peace sign was a hippie. Plastic hippies and weekend hippies abounded—those, for example, who went to college or held regular jobs, or still had some faith in the middle-class ethic but took drugs and communed in parks on sunny weekends.

With this said, caution must be used in trying to define who was or was not a hippie. A person did not have to completely drop out to be a hippie, or take drugs, or renounce all mainstream values. Being a hippie meant, more than anything else, embracing a state of mind liberated from mainstream routines. This usually caused a person to reject the values found in straight society and to live in ways older Americans found incomprehensible and even contemptible. Middle America condemned hippies and "longhairs" (they equated these two) and harassed counterculture youths. Police raided hippie houses for containing psychedelic posters, and the governor of Tennessee declared: "It's war. We want every long-hair in jail or out of the state." (250)

As the sixties ended, the hippie movement experienced great strains. Hippie practices could not endure the invasion of young people into certain areas, such as Haight-Ashbury, nor could they withstand the media coverage and commercial exploitation noted above. Hippiedom required small settlements and contact with mainstream society on hippie terms. For this reason, many hippies fled Haight-Ashbury in 1967, and with their counterparts elsewhere in the nation, gravitated toward rural areas. Other hippies, as they got older, confronted practical problems—such as needing insurance and money to educate their children—by entering the mainstream.

In the short term, though, Haight-Ashbury's unraveling did not mean the end to hippies—their numbers actually increased into the mid-1970s. Even later, some hippies remained true to their original ideals, and irrespective of numbers, hippie society left an indelible imprint on greater America.

"All you need is love," said the Beatles affected by the hippies, and said the hippies to the world.

See also Commune; Diggers; Haight-Ashbury; Huxley, Aldous; LSD.

References Anderson, Terry H., *The Movement and the Sixties* (1995); Braden, William, *The Age of*

Aquarius: Technology and the Cultural Revolution (1970); Howard, Gerald, ed., *The Sixties: Art, Politics and Media of Our Most Explosive Decade* (1982); Irwin, John, *Scenes* (1977); Miller, Timothy, *The Hippies and American Values* (1991); Roszak, Theodore, *The Making of a Counterculture: Reflections on the Technocratic Society and Its Youthful Opposition* (1968); Stevens, Jay, *Storming Heaven: LSD and the American Dream* (1987); Von Hoffman, Nicholas, *We Are the People Our Parents Warned Us Against* (1968); Wolf, Leonard, ed., *Voices from the Love Generation* (1968); Yablonsky, Lewis, *The Hippie Trip* (1968); http://www. rockument.com/links.html.

Hitchhiking

A popular rock song in the sixties joyously proclaimed "Ride, ride, ride, hitching a ride!" Before roadside muggings and murders took hold, hitchhiking flourished as an enjoyable alternative way to travel, bonding young people together in a generational community. For a freak driver to see hitchhiking freaks, or a longhair driver to see hitchhiking longhairs, and give them a lift created a common identity. Not infrequently, the driver and hitchhiker would pass a joint, further solidifying their sense of togetherness in a world different from the mainstream.

Hitchhiking might mean catching a ride to school, to the local head shop, or to see friends. Or it could mean donning a backpack and thumbing across the nation, as many hippies and other young people did. Nobody knows for sure how many hitchhiked these long distances, but it probably numbered over 2 million. Often, hitchhikers stayed at communes that welcomed them.

The hitchhiking scene deteriorated in the 1970s as stories circulated about people being robbed or assaulted, and many communes closed their gates to hitchhikers in order to discourage freeloaders.

See also Commune; Freak.

Reference Weiss, Walter F., *America's Wandering Youth: A Sociological Study of Young Hitchhikers in the United States* (1974).

Hoffman, Abbie (1936–1989)

A brilliant, satirical person driven to revolutionize American society, Abbie Hoffman moved through the counterculture first as a political radical and then as a promoter of street theatre. He gained prominence for his outrageous acts, meant to call attention to injustices, and for founding the Yippies. Hoffman's mentality is best summed up in the testimony he offered in 1969 at his trial for conspiring to riot:

> Attorney Weinglass: Would you state your name?
>
> Witness: My name is Abbie. I'm an orphan of America.
>
> Attorney: Where do you reside?
>
> Witness: Woodstock nation.
>
> Judge: What state is that in?
>
> Witness: The state of mind. It's a nation of alienated young people which we carry in our minds, just as the Sioux Indians carried around the Sioux nation in their minds. (Handelman 1989, 49)

Hoffman was born 30 November 1936 in Worcester, Massachusetts. As a high school student, he once got into trouble for striking a teacher, but he did well enough in his studies to enroll at Brandeis University in Waltham, Massachusetts, from which he received his B.A. in 1959. Hoffman continued his education at the University of California–Berkeley, and the following year obtained his master's degree in psychology. He then began working as a psychologist at the Massachusetts state hospital.

By this time, Hoffman had adopted radical political views, which he later attributed not only to social injustice but also to his Jewish heritage and the lesson he learned from the failure of Jews in 1930s Germany to forcefully fight their oppression. He said: "Six million dead and except for the Warsaw ghetto hardly a bullet fired in resistance." (Hoffman 1980, 15) Rejecting what he saw as his ancestors' passivity, he intended to stand up to oppression in America and the insanity of war.

Hoffman claimed his real birth occurred in May 1960 when two "generation-shaking" events "mold[ed] my consciousness forever." (39) The first was a protest he joined in California against the death penalty. The second happened a few days later when he demonstrated in San Francisco

With fist raised, Abbie Hoffman speaks at a rally on 1 May 1970. Hoffman, one of the seven prominent protesters known as the Chicago Seven, stood trail in 1969 for having conspired to riot during the Democratic National Convention.

at hearings held by the House Un-American Activities Committee and watched the police attack him and other demonstrators with clubs and water hoses.

Back in Massachusetts, Hoffman worked for the civil rights movement in Worcester as an activist with the National Association for the Advancement of Colored People, and in the summers of 1964 and 1965 traveled to Mississippi, where he helped the Student Nonviolent Coordinating Committee (SNCC) register black voters. That year, too, he had his first experience with LSD, acquired for him by a friend working in a CIA-funded project. The following year, he moved to New York City and operated Liberty House, a SNCC store that sold goods handmade by a black cooperative in the South.

In 1967, after SNCC decided to eject its white workers, Hoffman plunged into street theatre, first developed by a San Francisco hippie group, the Diggers. Street theatre involved staging outrageous acts in order to get media attention and expose straight society's absurdities. While it had a political goal—revolutionizing society—it emphasized cultural activities and so rejected picketing and sit-ins. Hoffman saw street theatre as a creative way to make statements against oppression without relying on wordiness, and a way to bring the hippies, who rejected political activity, into a greater crusade to change America—a bridge, in effect, between the political radicals and the cultural ones. "I always held my flower in a clenched fist," he said. "A semi-structure freak among the love children, I was determined to bring the hippie movement into a broader protest." (Gitlin 1987, 233)

With regard to media appeal, Hoffman stated: "I trained for the one-liner, the retort jab, or sudden knockout put-ons."

(ibid.) Hoffman exploited television interview shows intent on ridiculing him, and turned the tables through stunts, such as when, during the David Susskind program, he let loose a duck wearing a sign reading "I AM A HIPPIE." "The goal of this nameless art form—part vaudeville, part insurrection, part communal recreation—was to shatter the pretense of objectivity," he later said. "We learned to sneak onto the airwaves with Conceptual Art pieces that roused viewers from their video stupor." (Hoffman 1980, 114)

Hoffman staged his first widely reported put-on early in 1967 when he threw dollar bills from the balcony of the New York Stock Exchange to the floor below, causing stockbrokers to scramble after the money in a chaotic frenzy that paralyzed the Exchange for several minutes. He claimed that this act said "more than thousands of anti-capitalist tracts and essays." (Albert and Albert 1984, 420)

In October 1967, he and Jerry Rubin worked together to enliven the antiwar march on the Pentagon. They led a band of self-proclaimed witches, wore outlandish outfits, and declared their intention to levitate the Pentagon and purge its evil spirits. Needless to say, the press widely publicized the weird antics.

The following month, Hoffman organized a "War Is Over" demonstration at Washington Square in New York City. About 3,000 young people gathered and on cue ran down the streets from Grand Central Station to Times Square and back, shouting "the war is over!" They wanted straight society to think about Vietnam and how liberating it would be to end the war.

In December 1967, on New Year's Eve, Hoffman, Rubin, and several other friends decided to plan a street theatre action to be held at the Democratic National Convention scheduled for August in Chicago. They called it the Festival of Life to contrast with their name for the Democratic Party's meeting: the Convention of Death. They formed an organization to promote their concept: the Yippies. Hoffman later called the Yippies a myth formulated to manipulate the media. "How do you do this starting from scratch, with no organization, no money, nothing?" he said. "Well, the answer is that you create a myth. Something that people can play a role in and relate to." (419)

In the spring and summer, Hoffman publicized the Yippies by distributing buttons bearing the word *Yippie!* in pink psychedelic letters set on a purple background and by staging several events to excite people, to get them and the media involved. For example, the Yippies held a Yip-in at Grand Central Station, a largely unorganized party that attracted several thousand.

At Chicago, however, Hoffman and the Yippies failed to pull off the Festival of Life. In fact, the entire scene quickly deteriorated into violence due to several factors, including tension between Hoffman and Rubin over tactics; differences between the Yippies and other protesters, most notably the National Mobilization Committee To End the War in Vietnam, which wanted a more serious political demonstration; and the decision by the Chicago police to use brute force. Shortly after this, Hoffman made another controversial move when he answered a subpoena to appear before the House Un-American Activities Committee by showing up wearing boots, buckskin pants, and an American flag shirt.

Within weeks after Chicago, the federal government arrested Hoffman and seven other prominent protesters for having conspired to riot during the Democratic National Convention. The press called this group the Chicago Eight. At his trial in 1969, known for its counterculture celebrity witnesses, uproarious actions by the defendants, and intolerant decisions by the judge, Hoffman professed his innocence. Although a jury did not find him guilty of conspiracy, he was convicted of rioting. Three years later, however, a higher court overturned the conviction.

In 1973, undercover cops in New York City arrested Hoffman for selling cocaine. Rather than face the charges, he disappeared from view. Living in upstate New York under the alias Barry Freed, he wrote and worked as an environmentalist. In typical Hoffman outrageousness, he disguised himself and pulled off an appearance before a U.S. Senate subcommittee as Freed.

Through the 1980s, he never deserted his earlier social commitment; always the activist, he said: "Democracy is not something you believe in or a place you hang your hat, but it's something you do. You participate. If you stop doing it, democracy crumbles." (Handelman 1989, 49)

On 12 April 1989, Hoffman was found dead in his motel room in New Hope, Pennsylvania. He had taken an overdose of phenobarbital. Hoffman had, for some time, suffered from manic depression, and the authorities ruled his death a suicide.

See also Democratic National Convention of 1968; Diggers; Krassner, Paul; Rubin, Jerry; Street Theatre; Yippies.

References Albert, Judith Clavir, and Steward Edward Albert, eds., *The Sixties Papers: Documents of a Rebellious Decade* (1984); Gitlin, Todd, *The Sixties: Years of Hope, Days of Rage* (1987); Handelman, David, "Abbie Hoffman," *Rolling Stone*, 1 June 1989, 49; Hoffman, Abbie, *Revolution for the Hell of It* (1968), *Soon To Be a Major Motion Picture* (1980), *Steal This Book* (n.d.), and *Woodstock Nation: A Talk-Rock Album* (1969); Jezer, Marty, *Abbie Hoffman: American Rebel* (1992); Raskin, Jonah, *The Life and Times of Abbie Hoffman* (1997).

Hootenanny

In 1963, ABC television launched *Hootenanny*, a weekly show that exploited the folk-music revival then sweeping the nation's college campuses. *Hootenanny* (the word means an informal presentation by folk singers) featured prominent folk musicians, and about 10 million people watched it each week. Nearly all the acts, however, were those carefully groomed and packaged rather than those found in coffeehouses.

The show encountered problems when ABC banned renowned folk singer Pete Seeger from appearing, claiming his leftist politics showed disloyalty toward America. The ban caused several folk singers, including Joan Baez and the trio Peter, Paul, and Mary, to boycott *Hootenanny*. This controversy and declining ratings brought the show to an end in September 1964.

See also Baez, Joan; Dylan, Bob; Guthrie, Arlo; Guthrie, Woody; Ochs, Phil; Seeger, Pete.

Humor

Counterculture humor differed from that found in mainstream society by its witty freak critiques and by its drug themes. That is to say, counterculture humorists embraced the weird. They scribbled graffiti that said, "Give me librium or give me meth," "People who live in glass houses shouldn't get stoned," "People who live in grass houses must get stoned," and "A friend with weed is a friend indeed." (Dorson 1973, 296)

Freaks engaged in numerous pranks and put-ons, as evident in street theatre and in such antics as challenging the mayor of Ithaca, New York, to an arm-wrestling match because they believed in "armed struggle," advocating a loot-in at Macy's Department Store, and distracting ROTC cadets during their drills by blowing bubbles or playing leapfrog on the training field.

Drug experiences permeated counterculture folklore and jokes, such as these:

> A concerned father came home to find his daughter and her friends smoking marijuana. Grabbing the pot out of her mouth, he exclaimed: "What's a joint like this doing in a nice girl like you?"
>
> What is better than LSD? Sex, if you have the right pusher.
>
> There were two hippies in a room and they were smoking pot and taking LSD. And one hippie turned to the other and said, "Hey man, go turn on the radio." So the hippie got up, walked over to the radio, and facing it he said, "I love you." (297–298)

No matter how good, or bad, the jokes, this humor displayed the difference between counterculture youth and straight society.

See also Freak; Street Theatre.

Reference Dorson, Richard M., *America in Legend: Folklore from the Colonial Period to the Present* (1973).

Huxley, Aldous (1894–1963)

An English intellectual and prolific writer who moved to the United States, Aldous Huxley pursued mysticism through religion and drugs. His use of psychedelics and the prominence he accorded them influenced the counterculture generation.

Huxley was born on 24 July 1894 at Godalming, Surrey, to a notable family. His father, Leonard Huxley, was an educator, writer, and editor of *Cornhill* magazine. His mother, Julia Arnold Huxley, was an educator, too, and founded a girls' school.

Aldous Huxley graduated from Balliol College, Oxford, in 1916, the same year he published his first book. This tall, gangly, and nearly sightless young man quickly gained a reputation for his intellect and erudition. He ranged widely, developing, over the years, interests in molecular biology, psychology, and art, while producing poems, short stories, essays, biographies, and novels.

Huxley's poetry appeared shortly before 1920, and in 1921 he authored his first novel, *Crome Yellow*. He usually wrote in an intellectual style, but in 1932 produced *Brave New World* that resembled popular fiction and attracted many college students. This novel depicts a future world corrupted by misguided technology and excessive government control, and its pessimistic tone reflects Huxley's despondency about mankind.

At about this time, Huxley began a mystical search to find an ultimate beauty and oneness, and embraced a school of thought that argued human beings can reach cosmic consciousness. He developed a philosophy that the wise person should participate actively in life but maintain an emotional and material detachment to permit moments of great revelation.

Huxley wanted to expand the brain's use—to activate more neurons and override barriers that restricted perception. Toward this end, he expressed his willingness to take a drug, asserting he would agree "to sniff or swallow something that would, for five or six hours each day," transport him to a paradise. (Stevens 1987, 41)

In 1937, Huxley moved permanently to Los Angeles after having lived in several European countries. He continued to write novels and essays and studied Eastern religions. Then he read an article by Humphrey Osmond and John Smythies, two psychologists, that discussed mescaline, and he invited Osmond to visit him. In March 1953, Huxley had his first mescaline experience, with Osmond carefully supervising the adventure. Huxley then wrote about the need for an educational system that would include mescaline or some other substance as a means to promote insight, inspiration, and an awareness "of other things than those enumerated in the Sears-Roebuck catalogue." (45)

Within weeks after his mescaline trip, Huxley wrote *The Doors of Perception*, a book-length essay in which he describes his experience (or describes it the best he can given the limits of the English language in communicating the irrational). He tells how he had entered a realm where the ego had no control, where temporal and spatial considerations lost all importance. "The mind was primarily concerned," he writes, "not with measures and locations, but with being and meaning." (Huxley 1954, 20)

Many literary critics disliked *Doors*—after all, it endorsed mescaline, at least for intellectuals. For his part, Huxley remained dissatisfied because he had not obtained the mystical level reached by some of his friends who had tried the drug. This changed two years later when during a mescaline trip he reached religious ecstasy and experienced "love as the primary and fundamental cosmic fact." In December 1955, he took LSD for the first time, and the following year wrote another essay, *Heaven and Hell*, to describe his more recent experiences and to account for the unpredictability of mescaline and LSD trips, in which some partakers obtained mystical enlightenment and others endured hell.

A thinker filled with contradictions—an intellectual who questioned intellect, a rationalist who pursued mysticism—Huxley produced works that many in the 1960s counterculture read and reread, especially *The Doors of Perception*, a book that even convinced a rock group to adopt the title—they called themselves the Doors. Huxley died in Los Angeles on 22 November 1963, unable to witness the hippies who continued the mystical search for harmony through psychedelic drugs.

See also Leary, Timothy; LSD; Mescaline.

References Bedford, Sybil, *Aldous Huxley: A Biography* (1974); Clark, Ronald W., *The Huxleys* (1968); Huxley, Aldous, *Brave New World* (1932), *The Doors of Perception* (1954), and *The Doors of Perception and Heaven and Hell* (1956).

I

I and Thou Coffee House

David Rothkop, a former teacher at San Francisco Sate College, opened the I and Thou Coffee House in Haight-Ashbury early in 1966, and it soon emerged as a hangout for hippies and other young people. The I and Thou encouraged its patrons to relax over coffee and discuss ideas, and it sponsored frequent poetry readings.

See also Haight-Ashbury.

I Ching

An ancient Chinese book, the *I Ching* (pronounced yee-jing) emerged a favorite among hippies who saw in it an alternative to linear, rational thought. *I Ching* means "book or oracle of change," and when consulted, it can reveal the workings of the hidden world in a person's life, as well as knowledge of the unconscious self. The *I Ching* advises when to proceed with particular actions and when to abandon others.

Infused with Confucianism and Taoism, the *I Ching* teaches that the superior person recognizes the primacy of "the cosmic forces of the universe"; this, in turn, provides mastery over fate. (Douglas 1971, 30) The oracle is divined, and the book thus used, by asking questions and then casting either yarrow stalks, coins, or wands and reading the hexagons formed by them. One commentator in the 1960s claimed that the popularity of the *I Ching* had expanded due to the "dangerous times." (Kemp 1970, 17)

See also Hippies.

References Douglas, Alfred, *How To Consult the I Ching, The Oracle of Change* (1971); Kemp, Dan, "I Ching," *Rolling Stone*, 9 July 1970, 17; Walker, Brian Browne, *The I Ching or Book of Changes* (1992).

Invisible Circus

The Diggers, a San Francisco hippie group, intended the Invisible Circus to be a radical artistic offering, one that would contrast with the recent Human Be-In, which they criticized as a media event.

Emmett Grogan and other Diggers developed the idea in 1966 to pool their resources with those of the Artists' Liberation Front and stage a massive three-day affair where the audience could participate in pursuing fantasies. The Diggers got permission to use the Glide Church near Haight-Ashbury, and then went about converting individual rooms into different fantasy scenes. As guests entered the basement, they immediately sank into a three-foot-high layer of shredded plastic and had to wade through it to reach the activities. In the recreation room, loud rock music blared, and a punch bowl contained Tang mixed with water and LSD. Several rooms were called "love making salons"—each with candles, incense, body lubricants, and mattresses situated on the floor and covered with colorful spreads from India. An obscenity conference, as the Diggers called it, featured a naked couple screwing on a canopied mattress while belly dancers gyrated nearby.

Upstairs, several couples had sex on the church altar while, above them, a naked weight lifter, his muscles bulging, masturbated and conga drums beat incessantly. Off in separate corners, drag queens kissed and an albino lashed a black transvestite with a whip. As smoke swirled from incense sticks, an old man with a flowing white beard walked about and introduced himself as God.

The circus lasted only eight hours—ended by the police who shut it down for violating the fire code—but within that time about 20,000 people entered, watched, and participated. The event showed how far some in the counterculture would go in challenging mainstream values and practices.

See also Diggers; Haight-Ashbury.

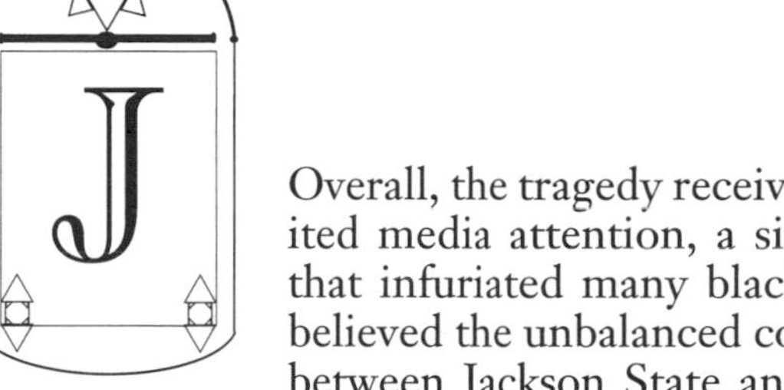

Jackson State

On 14 May 1970, just five days after National Guardsmen shot several college students at Kent State University, police opened fire at Jackson State College, a predominantly black school in Jackson, Mississippi. The shooting reflected the explosive situation on many campuses after Kent State and reinforced the view held by counterculture youth that the establishment intended to use the police to kill college students.

Unlike Kent State, the Jackson State carnage did not stem primarily from antiwar sentiment, although that was a factor. Rather, it resulted from racial tension between whites and blacks in Jackson. On the evening of the shooting, students set fire to a dump truck on campus and pelted passing cars with rocks. As a result, the police moved in, but a crowd started throwing rocks at them, too, and the situation grew extremely tense. After someone threw a bottle, the police responded by firing shotguns, pistols, and rifles, raking a women's dormitory and people outside it with bullets. They killed 2 students and wounded 12 others.

Although the police claimed they had been assaulted by sniper fire, no independent evidence ever arose to support this assertion, and a federal investigative commission reported it could find "no physical evidence of small arms fire" in the area around the dormitory. (Spofford 1988, 156) *Time* magazine said about the event:

> No tear gas was used; there was no warning given to the crowd. [Police] shotguns were loaded with deadly 00 buckshot rather than anti-riot birdshot. . . . The five-story building was spattered indiscriminately with gunfire from top to bottom. Every window on that end of the dorm was shattered. No effort had been made to fire warning shots or shoot over the crowd's heads. ("The South," 1970, 22)

Overall, the tragedy received limited media attention, a situation that infuriated many blacks who believed the unbalanced coverage between Jackson State and Kent State underscored society's racism.

See also Kent State.

References "The South: Death in Two Cities," *Time*, 25 May 1970, 22–23; Spofford, Tim, *Lynch Street: The May 1970 Slayings at Jackson State College* (1988).

Jefferson Airplane

Before Jefferson Airplane developed its psychedelic sound, it formed in 1965 as a folk-rock group. Marty Balin, who managed a folk club on San Francisco's Fillmore Street, founded the band, which took its name from a member's pet dog. At the same time, another band formed in San Francisco: Great Society, with lead singer Grace Slick. The following year, Slick joined Jefferson Airplane.

The band's following remained limited until its appearance in January 1967 at the San Francisco Be-In. By this time it had shifted to psychedelic music, in keeping with the Bay Area's countercultural use of LSD and other hallucinogenic drugs. Slick's vocals, and the band's unusual musical intervals and guitar lines, attracted attention. Balin explained the style:

> Like lots of times we'll be playing a song that might be three or four minutes long. We'll go to the guitar break, you know, and Jorma [lead guitarist Jorma Kaukonen] will just start creating then and there. And we all hear it, we know it. And so we'll just go on with it. Nobody says anything, nobody worries. And when he's finished his idea, maybe somebody else can take it up. (Gleason 1969, 102)

Although the band's first album *Jefferson Airplane Takes Off* failed to, their second, *Surrealistic Pillow*, reached the top ten in 1967, along with the single "Somebody To

Love." Slick's "White Rabbit" puzzled older people, but the counterculture fully understood its drug references and criticism of mainstream society when she sang, "the pills that mother gives you don't do anything at all."

Jefferson Airplane underwent a change in personnel in 1972 when Balin left; in 1974, the group changed its name to Jefferson Starship and continued to record successfully into the 1980s.

See also Rock Music.

Reference Gleason, Ralph J., *The Jefferson Airplane and the San Francisco Sound* (1969).

Jesus Freaks

Searching for answers, some countercultural youths turned to Christianity and worshipped it fervently. These "Jesus freaks" adopted a peculiar mix, part fundamentalist and part liberal. They proclaimed their born-again status but began communes and coffeehouses, listened to rock music, and in some instances took drugs. They established, too, about 50 underground newspapers and numerous organizations on college campuses.

See also Freak.

Joint

Joint meant a marijuana cigarette. For some in the counterculture, being able to make or roll a joint showed real talent, sought after at parties. One person with this ability said: "I like rolling joints. It is a very visceral pleasure; you get to play with the nifty green stuff and it gives your hands something to do."

See also Marijuana.

Joplin, Janis (1943–1970)

An emotional singer, Janis Joplin captivated audiences with her hard-driving blues and rock songs that often expressed an inner torture—one so intense it led to her death.

Joplin was born on 19 January 1943 in Port Arthur, Texas, into a middle-class family. As a teenager, she grew disenchanted with school and rebelled against conformity by reading poetry, listening to folk music, and unlike most white kids, listening to the blues. She left home at age 17 and sang with a country music band in Houston, Texas. Various singing jobs followed over the next few years, and in 1965 she made her way to San Francisco, where she performed in folk clubs and bars. At one show a rock promoter, Chet Helms, heard her and came away impressed.

Janis Joplin

Joplin returned home to Texas in 1966, dejected over her inability to advance, but then she received a phone call from Helms, who wanted her to join a new band, Big Brother and the Holding Company. She agreed and returned to California, where at the Monterey Pop Festival in the summer of 1967 she made a sensational appearance, rocking the audience with her rough blues voice, and won national recognition.

Of another appearance, *Time* magazine reported:

> When she stomps, quivers, flails her arms, tosses her mane of hair and swoops through a vocal chorus with hoarse croons and piercing wails, few listeners fail to get the message. Last week at the Newport Folk Festival, a crowd of 17,800 clapped and roared for encores until 1:00 A.M. ("1960s Highlights—Folk and Rock" 1995)

She and Big Brother recorded the album *Cheap Thrills* in 1968 that earned a gold record. Later that year, though, she quit Big Brother and formed another group, the Kozmic Blues Band. In 1969, her album *I Got Dem Ol' Kozmic Blues Again Mama!* went gold.

Joplin then began recording *Pearl* but never completed it: she died on 4 October 1970 from a heroin overdose. Unstable emotionally, she had for years abused drugs and alcohol in an attempt to obliterate the loneliness and boredom she felt when away from her music. *Pearl* was released posthumously, and "Me and Bobby McGee," a single from the album, written by Kris Kristofferson, reached the top ten. Ironically, the song made reference to a needle used in shooting up heroin.

See also Helms, Chet; Monterey Pop Festival; Rock Music.

References Amburn, Ellis, *Pearls: The Obsessions and Passions of Janis Joplin: A Biography* (1992); Dalton, David, *Piece of My Heart: The Life, Times, and Legend of Janis Joplin* (1985); Friedman, Myra, *Buried Alive: The Biography of Janis Joplin* (1973); Joplin, Laura, *Love, Janis* (1992); "1960s Highlights—Folk and Rock Music," *Time Almanac of the 20th Century* (1995); http://www./rockument.com/haimg.html.

Karenga, Ron Ndabezitha (1941–)

Shortly after the Los Angeles community of Watts erupted into riots and flames in 1965, Ron Ndabezitha Karenga emerged as the city's most influential black leader, advocating cultural separatism from whites.

Karenga was born Ron Everett in Maryland on 14 July 1941. He obtained his college education at the University of California–Los Angeles (UCLA), where he received a master's degree in political science. He went on to continue his studies there, intending to earn a doctorate in languages, when the riots broke out in Watts. An intelligent, well-spoken, and charismatic figure (also somewhat mysterious—he has always refused to divulge much information about his upbringing), Karenga reacted to Watts by forming an organization, US, which he claimed stood for United Slaves. He immediately gained a following among young blacks in Watts who felt exploited by whites and bypassed by the efforts of Martin Luther King, Jr.

Karenga believed that the riots showed how little the civil rights movement had accomplished. To him, and many other black ghetto residents, integration, the right to use the same facilities as whites, meant nothing when unemployment and poverty remained so high. Blacks, he insisted, needed to liberate themselves by embracing African culture, emphasizing cultural revolution before political revolution, and establishing an African American cultural nation within the United States.

US wanted black self-determination, he said, and with this position he reflected the black power movement then emerging and evident in such groups as the Black Panther Party. Despite this similarity, Karenga had a major difference with the Panthers: where they argued that racism resulted from economics, and thus economics must be addressed first, Karenga argued that racism transcended economics and had become the number one international issue; and where the Panthers sought alliances with white groups, Karenga rejected any such arrangements.

Karenga told blacks that to achieve liberation they must first erase their Negro mentality—he defined Negro in these terms:

> The "Negro" is made and manufactured in America;
>
> The "Negro" works on a two-fold economy. He buys what he wants and begs what he needs.
>
> "Negroes" want to be like Jesus; blond hair, blue eyes, and pale skin. (Haskins 1972, 205–206)

In addition to his separatism, Karenga took a militant position. He did not advocate that blacks go out and shoot whites, but made clear his belief that weapons had a place in making progress. Love and picketing, he said, had not worked for blacks—they will have to defend their communities with "force, intelligence, and deception." He urged that 1970 be the year for separation from white domination, and 1971 the year for defensive guerrilla action.

Karenga shaped US to educate blacks in African culture. He changed his name to an African one and urged others to do the same. Fluent in Swahili, he insisted that blacks learn the language. He dressed in a "buba," a togalike garment he likened to African style, and important, he believed, as a symbol for his program.

Karenga's differences with the Black Panthers boiled over into violence. Early in 1969, the Panthers and US engaged in a minor shoot-out in Los Angeles. Later that year, the two groups vied for control of the Black Students Union at UCLA. At one point, members of US marched into the student cafeteria where several Panthers had gathered. They pulled out their guns, and in a hail of bullets killed two of the Panthers. The incident greatly damaged US and contributed to its collapse in the early 1970s. At a later date, Karenga described the failure of the black power movement as follows: "The presumption that the people who hold power are moral rather than amoral [was] the fatal flaw. . . . [We depended] so much on the good will of the oppressor and [our]white allies." (Gates 1996, 60)

See also Black Panthers; Black Power.

References Gates, Henry Louis, Jr., "After the Revolution," *New Yorker,* 29 April/6 May 1996, 59–61; Haskins, James, *Profiles in Black Power* (1972).

Kathmandu

Hippies from the United States and European countries flocked to Kathmandu, the capital of Nepal. This city offered several attractions: a beautiful setting with tall, snowcapped Himalayan mountain peaks jutting into the sky; a simple environment without Western technology and urban hassles; a Buddhist influence that shrouded the city in mysticism; and access to drugs from Asia.

Some hippies came for brief periods, others for much longer—in the 1990s, hippies still lived there—and hippie craft shops and communes appeared. The Nepalese, however, often complained about Westerners disrespecting their culture and hippies refusing to work.

Keep on Truckin'

As the 1960s ended, the phrase "keep on truckin'" appeared, meaning to persevere. A person might be told to keep on truckin' as a sign of encouragement. Although the origin of the phrase is obscure, many attribute it to Robert Crumb, an underground artist who produced Zap Comix.

See also Comix.

Kennedy and King Assassinations

President John F. Kennedy, Senator Robert Kennedy, and civil rights leader Martin Luther King, Jr. so touched young America with their moral commitment, their dedication to building a just society, that their assassinations not only traumatized the nation but also radicalized the counterculture.

When John Kennedy (born in 1917), a Democratic senator from Massachusetts, won the presidency in 1960, America's youth, and many political analysts, considered it a break with the past, with the old politics characterized by Dwight Eisenhower, the elderly departing president. Eisenhower seemed opposed to any bold initiatives at a time when society needed to confront pressing issues, such as racism, poverty, and nuclear proliferation. He seemed to reflect 1950s society: maintain equilibrium and ignore any problems that indicated prosperity and democracy did not exist for all. Kennedy himself noted his own commitment to change when, at his inauguration in January 1961, he proclaimed that "the torch has been passed to a new generation." (Viorst 1979, 127)

The young, talented president surrounded himself with young, talented advisors, energizing the White House. When Kennedy established the Peace Corps and recruited America's youth to fill its ranks and help poor societies overseas, he projected an idealism that captivated the younger generation then growing in ever greater numbers, filling the nation's public schools and colleges, a direct result of the "baby boom" immediately after World War II.

Yet some older baby boomers, political activists who were leftist in their politics or becoming so, soon grew disenchanted with Kennedy. The president displayed cold-war rhetoric equal to his predecessors and, in addition, endorsed nuclear testing, tried an unsuccessful invasion of Cuba, and expanded the American military presence in Vietnam. Then came the Cuban missile crisis in 1962 that brought the nation to the brink of nuclear war with the Soviet Union. Some activists said the president had engaged in reckless policies that risked destroying the world. On the domestic front, these activists thought Kennedy too slow in pursuing civil rights, and they chas-

The funeral procession for civil rights leader Dr. Martin Luther King, Jr. in Atlanta, Georgia, 9 April 1968, drew thousands of followers. King's assassination led to a violent uproar as African Americans rioted in 110 cities.

tised him for appointing conservative judges to the federal courts.

All in all, without a change in course—and Kennedy might have changed as evident in his strengthening commitment to civil rights legislation—had the president lived, he may have found himself losing his following among young people. Yet for all that Kennedy's policies did in stirring youthful opposition to the government, his death did even more. First, the assassination on 22 November 1963 as the president rode in a motorcade in Dallas, Texas, shattered the hopes many young people had that the system could work and bring substantial reform . . . their hero, as many still considered him, had been killed. Second, the sloppy inquiry by the Warren Commission, appointed to investigate Kennedy's death, raised the possibility that the government had lied or engaged in a cover-up by proclaiming Lee Harvey Oswald the lone gunman. This raised questions as to whether government officials could ever be trusted. Finally, the assassination, coming amid violence in the civil rights movement as whites assaulted blacks, indicated a sickness in America, that society as it then existed had to be reformed, or even replaced with something better.

When King (born in 1929) learned of Kennedy's assassination, he remarked that he, too, would likely be killed, victimized by the social sickness. His prescient observation came true on 4 April 1968 when James Earl Ray fired a rifle at King as the civil rights leader stood on the balcony outside his hotel room in Memphis, Tennessee. The bullet tore through the right side of his face, knocking him to the floor, leaving a huge hole in his body and fracturing his spine. Efforts to revive him at a hospital failed.

Although King had always preached nonviolence, his death brought the opposite:

African Americans rioted in 110 cities, setting fires and looting buildings. The riots killed 39 people, mostly blacks, and the authorities had to call out 75,000 federal troops and National Guardsmen to quell the disturbances. The worst rioting erupted in Washington, D.C., and lasted three days.

To many African Americans, and many whites as well, King's death proved the activist-critics correct: America would never accept blacks in powerful leadership positions, especially those who proposed great changes, as King had when he talked about the need to lessen society's disparity in income and wealth and to get American troops out of Vietnam. Black power advocate Stokely Carmichael said: "When white America killed Dr. King, she declared war on us." (Oates 1982, 475) White America had killed King, thought many blacks; sick America had killed King, thought many young activists.

One last hope existed that the political system could be responsive to blacks, ethnic minorities, the poor, and those who opposed the war in Vietnam. One last hope that there could be meaningful reform: the election of Robert Kennedy to the presidency. Kennedy (born in 1925), John Kennedy's younger brother and a Democratic senator from New York, had, in the spring of 1968, entered the race for his party's presidential nomination. Although the more radical activists did not like Kennedy, thinking him an opportunist and another in a long line of liberals who talked compassion but failed to show it, many other youths rallied behind him.

Through the spring primaries, Kennedy battled another favorite among the young, Minnesota senator Eugene McCarthy. As the political contest seesawed, the candidates entered the crucial California primary. On 5 June 1968, Kennedy defeated McCarthy by a narrow margin. That night, he addressed his cheering supporters in a hotel ballroom and, in reference to the upcoming Democratic National Convention in Illinois, declared: "On to Chicago and let's win there!" As he left the podium and entered the kitchen area behind the ballroom, Sirhan Sirhan shot him in the head, leaving stunned onlookers crying in grief. Kennedy died within hours.

Mercy Ann Wright, a young political worker for Kennedy, said: "I knew it was all over, that there was no more reason for hope, because there wasn't anybody else on the scene." (Joseph 1974, 359) Tom Hayden, a radical activist who had opposed Kennedy, nevertheless paid his respects to him as the fallen leader lay in state, and commented that the coffin contained "all that remained of last night's hopes of the poor. Nothing left of that hope now. . . . I started to cry hard." (Miller 1996, 238) Another activist, Todd Gitlin, said: "We still wanted the system to work, and hated it for failing us." (Gitlin 1987, 310)

A sick society. The system had failed. No more hope. What more could be done? To counterculture youth the answer blew in the wind: get radical, even revolutionary, or drop out—from politics and from mainstream society.

See also Hippies; New Left.

References

John Kennedy assassination: Belin, David, *Final Disclosure: The Full Truth about the Assassination of President Kennedy* (1988); Epstein, Edward Jay, *Inquest: The Warren Commission and the Establishment of Truth* (1966); Morrow, Robert D., *Betrayal* (1976); Scheim, David E., *Contract on America: The Mafia Murder of President John F. Kennedy* (1983); Viorst, Milton, *Fire in the Streets: America in the 1960s* (1979).

Robert Kennedy assassination: Gitlin, Todd, *The Sixties: Years of Hope, Days of Rage* (1987); Moldea, Dan E., *The Killing of Robert F. Kennedy: An Investigation of Motive, Means, and Opportunity* (1995); Turner, William W., *The Assassination of Robert F. Kennedy: A Searching Look at the Conspiracy and Cover-Up, 1968–1978* (1978).

Martin Luther King assassination: Andrews, Robert, *Death in a Promised Land* (1993); Melanson, Philip H., *The Martin Luther King Assassination: New Revelations on the Conspiracy and Cover-Up, 1968–1991* (1991); Oates, Stephen B., *Let the Trumpet Sound: The Life of Martin Luther King, Jr.* (1982); Pepper, William, *Conspiracy: The Truth behind Martin Luther King Jr.'s Murder* (1995).

All three assassinations: Goode, Stephen, *Assassination! Kennedy, King, Kennedy* (1979); Scott, Peter Dale, Paul L. Hoch, and Russell Stetler, eds., *The Assassinations: Dallas and Beyond: A Guide to Cover-Ups and Investigations* (1976).

Kent State

In *Fire in the Streets*, Milton Viorst writes:

> The 1960s ended in a small town in Ohio called Kent. It happened on May 4, 1970, in the bright sunshine, just after midday, at a campus demonstration which was like so many others except that, in thirteen crackling seconds of gunfire, four students were killed and nine were wounded. What passion remained of the 1960s was extinguished in the fusillade. (507)

The antiwar movement had actually receded in the days before the shooting at Kent State University. Then, President Richard Nixon announced on 30 April 1970 an invasion, or what he called an incursion, into Cambodia, a nation neighboring Vietnam. This widening of the war, he said, was necessary to show the world that the United States would not be defeated.

Nixon equated the need to stand firm overseas with the need to do likewise at home against protesters on the nation's college campuses. In fact, some analysts believe his move into Cambodia emerged as much from a desire to show he could wield power domestically as it did to attack North Vietnamese bases. Henry Kissinger, the president's main foreign policy advisor, years later called Nixon's speech delusional.

Nixon certainly did his most to keep tension high within the United States. He had previously sent his vice-president, Spiro Agnew, on a national tour to condemn antiwar protesters. Agnew used some of the most vitriolic language ever heard from a person in his position. At the same time, Nixon himself ranted to his aides about protesters who had used violence, calling them bums. For the president, though, nothing separated good protesters from bad ones—anyone who challenged his authority fit the enemy category.

More than the "bums" protested Nixon's speech. The *New York Times*, *Wall Street Journal*, and *Washington Post* all objected to his action. Many ordinary citizens demonstrated, and on college campuses the antiwar movement regained its vibrancy. At Kent State University, in northern Ohio, students attacked businesses downtown and set fire to the campus ROTC building. (There is evidence that the fire may have been set by an undercover government agent, although student radicals certainly joined in burning the building, an old structure scheduled to be torn down. At the very least, the authorities let the building be set afire, probably to create an excuse for calling in the National Guard.) Meanwhile, the state's governor, James Rhodes, playing to conservative voters, called the demonstrators "the worst type of people we harbor in America" and said he would "eradicate the problem." (Miller 1996, 293)

With that, he sent the National Guard to Kent State. The soldiers arrived feeling on edge, partly because they had just finished patrolling a violent strike involving the Teamster's Union. On 4 May, about 3,000 demonstrators held a peaceful rally on campus. As it drew to a close, guardsmen, wearing gas masks and carrying M-1 rifles, moved forward to break up the crowd. Troop G, about 30 men, moved up a hill and for reasons still unclear lowered their rifles at the protesters and fired, killing four students and wounding others. Since that time, many analysts have called it highly unlikely that the guardsmen would have acted as they did, nearly in unison, without an order being given or some prior arrangement being made—indeed, some eyewitnesses assert the men had plotted their move several minutes earlier.

Two of the dead had been passersby, walking to class at the time. Despite this, Nixon showed no remorse and Agnew called the deaths "predictable" given the "traitors and thieves and perverts in our midst." (ibid.) Many Americans agreed with this view, but college students reacted with anger, and the nation seemed to be verging toward an internal war.

Tension ran so high on campuses that 450 colleges closed, either voluntarily or because student strikes shut them down. Eighty percent of the nation's campuses experienced protests after Kent Sate and 58 percent of the students participated in them. A special federal commission appointed to investigate Kent State called the killings "unnecessary, unwarranted, and inexcusable." An FBI report concluded that "No Guardsmen were hurt by flying rocks or projectiles and none was in danger of his life." The report labeled as fabrication a story by guardsmen that they had been threatened by the student protesters.

In Ohio, the National Guard took no disciplinary action against the men involved; on the contrary, it promoted them. For its part, the state not only refused to indict any guardsmen, it pursued indictments against the demonstrators.

One admirer in California wrote the conservative county prosecutor to wish him more power and advise him to keep his "chin up." The federal government did not bring indictments against any guardsmen until 1974. At that time, several were charged in the killings, but a judge released all the defendants on a technicality. The families of those killed and injured at Kent State won a suit for damages in January 1979, but the court awarded little money.

Mainstream America had sided with the National Guard, and while this may seem to have been based on the events at Kent State alone, other factors actually entered the situation: conservatives disliked everything about the counterculture—its hair, clothes, music, hippies, and activists, and now they at last had a way to express their disapproval in caustic terms. Kent State was a referendum drenched in hatred and blood.

References Davies, Peter, *The Truth about Kent State: A Challenge to the American Conscience* (1973); Gordon, William A., *Four Dead in Ohio: Was There a Conspiracy at Kent State?* (1995), and *The Fourth of May: Killings and Coverups at Kent State* (1990);

Clasping her head in anguish, a coed reacts to the shock of seeing the body of a fellow student who was shot and killed by National Guardsmen during a Vietnam War protest at Kent State University on 4 May 1970. The slain student was one of four killed during the rally.

Kelner, Joseph, and James Munves, *The Kent State Coverup* (1980); Michener, James A., *Kent State: What Happened and Why* (1971); Miller, Douglas T., *On Our Own: Americans in the Sixties* (1996); Stone, I. F., *The Killings at Kent State: How Murder Went Unpunished* (1971); Viorst, Milton, *Fire in the Streets: America in the 1960s* (1979).

Kerouac, Jack (1922–1969)

A prominent beat novelist, Jack Kerouac infused his writing with spontaneity and adventures so at odds with mainstream America that two generations of young people admired his prose and life: those of the 1950s beatnik movement and those of the counterculture a decade later. They wanted to hang loose, break through constraints, and find value in living for the moment—and Kerouac epitomized the desire. "It was drizzling and mysterious at the beginning of our journey. I could see that it was going to be all one big saga of the mist," Kerouac intones in *On the Road*. He continues:

> "Whooee!" yelled Dean. "Here we go!" And we hunched over the wheel and gunned her; he was back in his element, everybody could see that. We were all delighted, we all realized we were leaving confusion and nonsense behind and performing our one and noble function of the time, *move*. (Charters 1995)

Kerouac was born on 12 March 1922 in Lowell, Massachusetts. According to his own account, as a child he kept diaries and wrote novels. Kerouac attended St. Joseph's Parochial School, Lowell High, and Horace Mann, a preparatory school for boys. An intense person, he read extensively—greatly attracted to Thomas Wolfe and Ernest Hemingway—excelled in his studies, and participated in sports—mainly football, baseball, and track. As a result, he obtained an academic and athletic scholarship from Columbia University and arrived there in the fall of 1940, determined he would become a writer.

Kerouac, though, did not stay in college long. In his third game on the freshman football team he broke his leg, and he found his formal studies to be less exciting than the reading and writing he did on his own. He quit Columbia and enlisted in the navy. A few weeks later, however, he obtained a psychiatric discharge, went on to odd jobs, and then joined the Merchant Marine. After Kerouac sailed the North Atlantic, he decided to resume his college education, and in the fall of 1942 returned to Columbia. Once again, he grew disenchanted with academic life and spent his time hanging out at his apartment with other nonconformist artists and intellectuals. This was when he met Allen Ginsberg, an aspiring poet and later a prominent one. The two frequented bars in Harlem—digging jazz and black culture, which they praised for its soul.

From 1943 until 1950, Kerouac roamed the United States and Mexico, sometimes with Ginsberg and another friend, Neal Cassady, in an adventure that provided material for his writing. He returned to Lowell before relocating to New Jersey, where he lived with an aunt. In 1949, Harcourt Brace published Kerouac's first novel, *The Town and the City*, written over a three-year period, during which he made numerous revisions and cast it in a traditional style. Many reviewers hailed the book as evidence of a promising new writer.

Shortly after this, in 1951, Kerouac jettisoned his write-and-revise approach and composed his next novel, *On the Road*, in spontaneous fashion over a mere three weeks. He typed the manuscript on huge rolls of paper that he pasted together, and made few revisions. Viking Press published the novel in 1957, and critics considered it an important contribution to beat literature.

In *On the Road*, Kerouac just goes—riding buses and boxcars, hitchhiking—living for the moment, linked closely to the character Dean Moriarty (in real life, Cassady), a totally spontaneous, rather crazy, and not altogether trustworthy character. One reviewer called the novel "a tone poem to Cassady . . . and the electrifying effect his personality had on Kerouac and Ginsberg." As it rejected literary convention and traditional plot—Kerouac called it "bop prosody"—*On the Road* reached biblical proportions among beatniks, thus influencing nonconformists who, in turn, influenced young people in the 1960s. In fact, *On the Road* remained an attractive symbol of rebellion into the counterculture decade.

By the mid-1950s, Kerouac had popularized the phrase "beat generation." He described it as follows:

> It never meant juvenile delinquents, it meant characters of a special spirituality who didn't gang up but were solitary Bartlebies staring out the dead wall window of our civilization—the subterranean heroes who'd finally turned from the "freedom" machine of the West and were taking drugs, digging bop, having flashes of insight, experiencing the "derangement of the senses," talking strange, being poor and glad, prophesying a new style for American culture, a new style completely free from European influences . . . a new incantation. (559)

Kerouac continued writing novels, poems, and essays. "Always considered writing my duty on earth," he said. "Also the preachment of universal kindness, which hysterical critics have failed to notice beneath frenetic activity of my true-story novels about the 'beat' generation." (xxv) In 1952 and 1953, while working as a brakeman in California, he wrote *Doctor Sax*, *Maggie Cassidy*, and *The Subterraneans*—all not published until after *On the Road* appeared.

In 1954, he began studying Buddhism in New York and California, an influence that coexisted with his long-held Catholicism and appeared in his novel *Dharma Bums*, which he wrote in 1957 while living in Florida. This novel follows two young men searching for truth as they roam America. Kerouac's other works included *Visions of Cody*, *Desolation Angels*, *Tristessa*, *Big Sur*, *Satori in Paris*, and *The Book of Dreams*—all completed in the 1950s and early 1960s. Amid the counterculture in 1967, he completed *Vanity of Dulouz*.

For all his spontaneity and rebelliousness, Kerouac changed in the 1960s. Oddly, as rebellious hippies and political activists appeared, Kerouac turned traditional in his approach to writing and criticized the counterculture. He did not get along with Timothy Leary, the LSD guru who claimed, "Jack Kerouac was scary. Behind the dark good looks of a burly lumberjack was a New England mill-town sullenness, a Canuck-Catholic soggy distrust. This is one unhappy kid, I thought." (Leary 1983, 65)

Kerouac lashed out at his old friend Ginsberg as a dangerous atheist, and in 1964 at a party where he met Ken Kesey, novelist and leader of the hippie Merry Pranksters, the tension ran high. Kerouac stayed only a few minutes and left after folding an American flag that he felt the Pranksters had disrespected. Writer Tom Wolfe later recounted the scene: "It was like hail and farewell. Kerouac was the old star. Kesey was the wild new comer from the West heading christ knew where."

Kerouac suffered from alcoholism, and on 21 October 1969—a little more than one year after Neal Cassady's death—he died in Saint Petersburg, Florida.

See also Beat; Beatnik; Burroughs, William S.; Cassady, Neal; Ginsberg, Allen; Kesey, Ken.

References Challis, Chris, *Quest for Kerouac* (1984); Charters, Ann, *Kerouac: A Biography* (1973) and *The Portable Kerouac* (1995); Clark, Tom, *Jack Kerouac* (1984); French, Warren G., *Jack Kerouac* (1986); Gifford, Barry, and Lawrence Lee, *Jack's Book: An Oral Biography of Jack Kerouac* (1978); Kerouac, Jack, *Big Sur* (1962), *Book of Dreams* (1961), *The Dharma Bums* (1958), *Doctor Sax* (1959), *Maggie Cassidy* (1959), *On the Road* (1957), *Satori in Paris* (1966), *The Subterraneans* (1958), *The Town and the City* (1950), *Tristessa* (1960), *Vanity of Duluoz* (1968), and *Visions of Cody* (1959); Leary, Timothy, *Flashbacks: An Autobiography* (1983); McNally, Dennis, *Desolate Angel: Jack Kerouac, the Beat Generation, and America* (1979); Nicosia, Gerald, *Memory Babe: A Critical Biography of Jack Kerouac* (1983); http://www.cmgww.com/historic/kerouac/kerouac.html.

Kesey, Ken (1935–)

A novelist most noted for *One Flew over the Cuckoo's Nest*, Ken Kesey embraced the hippie side of the counterculture, rejecting his all-American upbringing to adventure into psychedelics with the Merry Pranksters.

Most everything in Kesey's youth appeared to indicate a future firmly rooted in society's mainstream. He was born on 17 September 1935 in La Junta, Colorado, where his parents owned a dairy farm. When Kesey was in the third grade, his family moved to Springfield, Oregon, so his father could manage a milk cooperative. Kesey attended Springfield High School, making good grades and participating on athletic teams. Robust, strong, and with a compact build, the young man excelled as a wrestler. But beneath this highly visible and seemingly practical personality existed a vibrant imagination, attracted to reading comic books.

Ken Kesey

Kesey attended the University of Oregon and again earned a reputation as an outstanding wrestler. He graduated in 1957, got small parts acting in Hollywood movies, and then returned to Springfield to begin writing a novel. The following year, he arrived at Stanford University in California on a Woodrow Wilson Fellowship to study writing. Stanford's program in that discipline had an excellent reputation, and Kesey lived in a cottage on Perry Lane, a small writer's colony. He wrote *Zoo*, a novel about the son of a rodeo star who lived in bohemian North Beach, California.

Then, in 1959, Kesey participated in something that reshaped his life and led to his most notable novel: he volunteered to be a subject in an experimental program at Veterans Hospital in Menlo Park, California—a program involving the psychedelic drug LSD. Kesey got paid $75 per day for his participation. When the program ended, he worked as a night attendant in the hospital mental ward, where he had access to mescaline and other drugs and consumed them regularly.

The LSD took Kesey deeper into his unconscious, deeper into a search for a mystical communion with the universe, and intensified his rebelliousness. His stint in the mental ward provided the setting and story line for *One Flew over the Cuckoo's Nest*, part of which he wrote while tripping on LSD.

When Kesey's novel appeared in 1962, it received outstanding reviews. Observers noted its comic-book quality and its criticism of conformity. In the novel, the mental ward replicates the confinement found in society at large, and the villain, "Big Nurse," represents power bent on stifling individualism for the sake of order. The narrator of the story is an Indian nicknamed Chief, and the novel can be read as an allegory about the subjugation of the Indians by white men who sacrificed an entire native culture with its attachment to nature for the sake of "advancing" Western civilization. *Cuckoo's Nest* sold well and boosted Kesey to literary importance. Several years later, the story was made into a movie—one which Kesey disliked but nevertheless boosted the sales of his book.

To gain background material for his second novel, *Sometimes a Great Notion*, Kesey worked as a logger near Florence, Oregon. The story, published in 1964, involves a young man, Lee Stampers, who returns from his studies at Yale University to manage his family's logging company amid labor strife. Initially, the intellectually oriented Lee conflicts with his older brother, but in time the two develop a close relationship. Kesey cast the novel in a more serious vein than *Cuckoo's Nest*, intending it to reach Faulkner-like proportions, but most reviewers agreed it had not.

Kesey then largely turned his back on writing, producing only occasional articles. He immersed himself in living life comic-book fashion, prodding mainstream America to accept alternatives, encouraging individuals to change their personalities, and in the process, he hoped, getting society to reject material conformity and hate. Kesey believed that since the world forces people into a game both mad and unfair, he was better off inventing his own game. He had moved to La Honda, south of San Francisco (where he wrote *Sometimes a Great Notion*), and bohemians and LSD-consuming hippies gathered at his house. As Kesey later described it, after taking LSD, "We were beautiful. Naked and helpless and sensitive as a snake after skinning but far more human than that shining knightmare that had stood creaking in previous parade rest. We were alive and life was us." (Lee 1985, 120)

In 1964, he purchased an old International Harvester school bus, painted it in psychedelic colors, wired it with speakers and sound, and traveled from San Francisco to the World's Fair in New York City (where there was to be a party for the release of *Sometimes a Great Notion*). He took with him a band of Merry Pranksters, as they called themselves. Along the way, they engaged in antics intended to expose middle-class absurdities. In fact, they considered LSD, which they consumed in prodigious quantities, a deprogrammer to rid individuals of their addictive conformist behavior and open new doors of perception—ones that would reveal life's beauty. Unlike psychedelic guru Timothy Leary, though, Kesey and the Pranksters rejected religious texts or any guides through the mystical realm; they lived by the dictum, "Go with the flow . . . freak freely." (Stevens 1987, 236)

The differences between the two psychedelic approaches appeared stark when, during the 1964 journey, Kesey and the Pranksters visited Leary and his followers at Millbrook, New York. The Pranksters couldn't wait to leave—they considered the scene boring and called it "the crypt trip."

The Merry Pranksters came to view themselves as part of a new generation rejecting traditional society and merging with a greater cosmic consciousness. Kesey and the Pranksters held Acid Tests in 1964 and 1965 where they invited people to listen to rock bands—often the Grateful Dead—dance amid psychedelic lights, and drink Kool-Aid or other beverages laced with LSD (at the time a legal drug). Kesey considered the Acid Tests an art form, a total experience "with all the senses opened wide—words, music, lights, sounds, touch . . . lighting." (248) The author Tom Wolfe claimed, "The Acid Tests were the *epoch* of the psychedelic style and practically everything that has gone into it." (Wolfe 1968, 223)

At one point, Kesey invited the Hell's Angels to an LSD gathering at La Honda. He wanted to see if the drug could produce a beautiful mystical experience among this violence-soaked group. The Pranksters decorated the trees outside Kesey's house—tucked away in a valley—with Day-Glo colors; they hung speakers from the branches, played rock music, and scared the neighbors with a huge banner that they put up, bearing the message "Welcome Hell's Angels." The Angels seemed temporarily transformed by the LSD, diverted from their fury.

Kesey's adventures, however, eventually got him into trouble with the authorities when they busted him for possessing marijuana. After fleeing to Mexico, he returned to the United States, and in 1967 served time in jail.

By decade's end, Kesey had turned away from LSD and in vague terms talked about the need to alter consciousness by going beyond the acid experience. In 1969, he returned to his farm in Oregon and refused to accompany the Merry Pranksters to

Woodstock. His era with the group had ended, although he and several Pranksters remained close friends.

In 1973, he issued a collection of his writings under the title *Ken Kesey's Garage Sale*. His works in the 1980s and 1990s included *The Demon Box*, *The Further Inquiry*, *Sailor's Song*, and *Last Go Around*.

See also Acid Tests; *The Electric Kool-Aid Acid Test;* Leary, Timothy; LSD.

References Kesey, Ken, "Excerpts from Kesey's Jail Diary," *Ramparts*, November 1967, *Ken Kesey's Garage Sale* (1973), *One Flew over the Cuckoo's Nest* (1962), and *Sometimes a Great Notion* (1964); Lee, Martin A., and Bruce Shlain, *Acid Dreams: The CIA, LSD, and the Sixties Rebellion* (1985); Leeds, Barry H., *Ken Kesey* (1981); Porter, M. Gilbert, *The Art of Grit: Ken Kesey's Fiction* (1982) and *One Flew over the Cuckoo's Nest: Rising to Heroism* (1989); Stevens, Jay, *Storming Heaven: LSD and the American Dream* (1987); Tanner, Stephen L., *Ken Kesey* (1983); Wolfe, Tom, *The Electric Kool-Aid Acid Test* (1968); http://www.key-z.com/.

The Kinks

The Kinks ranked among the most innovative rock bands in the counterculture era. Four English youths formed the group in 1961: Ray Davies, his brother Dave Davies, Michael Avery, and Peter Quaife. Originally called the Ramrods and then the Ravens, in 1963 they changed their name to the Kinks and signed a contract with Pye Records.

The Kinks hit number one on the British charts in 1964 with a Ray Davies song, "You Really Got Me"—and its hard-driving sound and tough vocal inflection made it a top-ten hit in the United States, too. This style foreshadowed hard rock that Led Zeppelin and other bands produced in the 1970s. Two other hits soon followed: "All Day and All of the Night" and "Tired of Waiting for You." Then came their classic "A Well Respected Man," a harsh ballad about a suburban commuter.

In the late sixties, the Kinks' singles and albums sold unevenly, and the band never reached the popularity achieved by some other British groups. This came in part from their image, one which they cultivated: tough guys who would do what they wanted no matter what others thought. The band members engaged in fistfights with one another and on more than one occasion showed their dislike for American audiences. Their brawling caused the American Federation of Musicians Union to ban them in the late sixties from concerts in the United States. (Some observers, though, believe the union's dislike for British pop artists may have been equally the cause.)

The Kinks reversed their fortunes in 1970 with their creative album *Lola versus Powerman and the Moneyground*, from which came a hit single, "Lola," about a transvestite. The band continued to record and perform concerts all the way into 1996, by which time Ray Davies had achieved the status of a rock 'n' roll icon.

See also Rock Music.

References Davies, Dave, *Kink: An Autobiography* (1997); Mendelssohn, John, *The Kinks Kronikles* (1985); Savage, Jon, *The Kinks: The Official Biography* (1984).

KMPX Radio

When in February 1967, Larry Miller, a guitarist from Detroit, began his stint as a DJ on station KMPX, he revolutionized commercial radio by presenting a new format called "hip rock." KMPX was soon transformed into a freewheeling hippie radio station, replete with dope dealers for salesman and DJs whose outrageous comments caused continual controversy.

Prior to Miller's arrival, KMPX, a stereo FM station, had struggled to survive. Located in San Francisco, with its studio in an old waterfront warehouse near Telegraph Hill, KMPX mainly broadcast instructional foreign-language programs. Miller signed on to do a show from midnight to 6:00 in the morning, believing he could present music that youths in tune with the hippie counterculture wanted but could not find on AM radio. He faced, though, a great challenge, for at the time few people in San Francisco, or elsewhere for that matter, listened to FM, which mainly broadcast classical and jazz.

Miller arrived at the station to find it owned only 50 records, so he brought his own, combining rock and folk with other hip sounds—he played Bob Dylan, the Beatles, and Ravi Shankar ragas, and had no play list, no catchy jingles, no attachment to 45-rpm singles. Young people listened to his show in increasing numbers, especially those in the hippie Haight-Ashbury district.

In April 1967, KMPX expanded hip rock when Tom Donahue began airing his show immediately before Miller's, replacing a Chinese-language program. Donahue, the station's program director, developed a rapport with his audience and, like Miller, dispensed with a play list. He too played folk and rock but placed a greater emphasis on the latter; and he played album cuts, an innovative practice. At the same time, KMPX broke ground in yet another way: it hired female engineers, a first in the Bay Area.

As hippies and other young people listened to Donahue, they sent him beads, bells . . . and dope. During the Summer of Love in 1967, Donahue served as an informal counselor when youngsters on bad drug trips called his show and asked that he talk them down.

By September, KMPX had become the highest-rated radio station in several time periods. One fan told Donahue: "Now that I listen to Underground Radio every morning I find myself completely losing track of time, oblivious to changes in climate . . . and so turned on I am unable to turn off in order to make the change from personal and private to public and businesslike." (Kreiger 1979, 41)

These developments did not occur without problems, most notably an eight-weeklong strike in 1968 by the DJs, who complained about stagnant salaries and new restrictions on what music they could play. The DJs set up picket lines, and several bands entertained bystanders, including Credence Clearwater Revival, the Grateful Dead, and Blue Cheer. Most of the strikers voted to leave KMPX, and they followed Donahue to another station in the area, KSAN.

Despite this, KMPX had set a style that many commercial FM stations emulated throughout the nation. Hip radio lasted until the early 1970s, at which time market surveys and play lists took over, aimed at target audiences.

See also Rock Music.

Reference Kreiger, Susan, *Hip Capitalism* (1979).

Krassner, Paul (1932–)

Writer, editor, and humorist Paul Krassner published the alternative magazine *The Realist* and gained notoriety for coining the name of a protest group, the Yippies.

Krassner was born 9 April 1932 in New York City, where his father worked as a printer. In 1950, he enrolled in the City College of New York, and while still a student, began doing standup comedy at small clubs. At the same time, he wrote freelance material for a magazine whose humor and irreverence impressed him, *Mad*. Soon after he left college with a degree in journalism, he sold sketches to comedian Steve Allen's popular television comedy show.

In 1958, Krassner began publishing and editing *The Realist*, intended to be a lively, free-thought periodical. *The Realist* presented both serious and satirical articles from a leftist perspective, digging at society's absurdities. Krassner later said that, among other features, his magazine served as "a clearinghouse for bizarre news items sent in by readers. I reprinted unusual material from medical journals—on fracture of the penis; on the caloric content of semen; on objects found in the rectum." (Krassner 1993, 50) With its humor, bluntness, and often explicit language, *The Realist* attracted many young readers disgusted with 1950s conformity (its total circulation may have reached over 80,000)—readers who later incorporated *The Realist*'s style into the counterculture.

In 1967, Krassner published his most controversial *Realist* article. "The Parts Left Out of the Kennedy Book" purported to be a passage written by William Manchester, an author who wrote about President

John Kennedy's assassination. Krassner presented the material in Manchester's style, leaving the impression Manchester had written it, and refused to confirm that the piece was satirical. The story described how, as Air Force One left Dallas and headed back to Washington with Kennedy's body on board, the new president, Lyndon Johnson, defiled the corpse.

On 31 December 1967, at a New Year's Eve gathering at Abbie and Anita Hofmann's apartment, Krassner helped develop the idea and name for a new group that would combine political protest with street theatre, the Yippies. Krassner's account—one of several that provide somewhat different details as to what actually happened—is as follows:

> Our working title was the International Youth Festival. But the initials YIF were meaningless. . . . But what could make YIP? Now *that* would be ideal because the word Yippie could be derived organically from YIP. "Yippie" was a traditional shout of spontaneous joy. We could be the *Yippies!* It had just the right attitude. Yippie was the most appropriate name to signify the radicalization of hippies. What a perfect media myth that would be—the Yippies! And then working backwards it hit me. Youth International Party! Of course! (156)

Although the Yippies were under the leadership of Abbie Hoffman and Jerry Rubin, Krassner played a role in the group's plans and participated in its protest at the 1968 Democratic National Convention in Chicago.

In the 1970s, *The Realist* published details about the Watergate break-in at a time most newspapers ignored the crime. In the 1980s and 1990s, Krassner continued to write and perform standup comedy, and after a hiatus resumed publishing *The Realist.*

See also Yippies.

References Krassner, Paul, *Confessions of a Raving, Unconfined Nut: Misadventures in the Counterculture* (1993); http://www.primenet.com/~lippard/realist.html.

L

Laing, R. D. (1927–)

When R. D. Laing, a Scottish psychiatrist, wrote *The Politics of Experience*, he produced a work that resonated throughout the counterculture, one that merged with feelings of alienation and a desire for transcendental experiences.

In 1927, Laing was born into a working-class family in Glasgow, Scotland. As a young man, he liked literature, music, and philosophy. Laing attended the University of Glasgow, decided to continue there as a graduate student in psychiatry, received his M.D. in 1951, and then served for two years as a psychiatrist in the British army. Laing disliked the military and spent most of his time associating with his patients. Through his work, he questioned traditional assessments regarding schizophrenia and concluded it was not always bad, that it and other delusional behavior could be therapeutic.

After his army stint, Laing worked at the Glasgow Royal Medical Hospital and taught in the Department of Psychological Medicine at the University of Glasgow. In 1956, he began doing clinical research at Tavistock Institute in London. The following year, he wrote *The Divided Self*, published in 1960, and, a year later, *The Self and Others*.

Laing applied his unconventional ideas when, in 1965, he helped found Kingsley Hall in London. At this psychiatric center, patients and doctors lived in the same quarters and related informally within a self-governing communal arrangement. Laing wanted those considered mad to experience their madness without being subject to coercive techniques or drugs. He believed madness could be as much breakthrough as breakdown, as much liberation as enslavement.

By this time, the counterculture was emerging in both Europe and America, and Laing found a receptive audience for his unconventional methods and views. He considered schizophrenia potentially beneficial and likened psychosis to a psychedelic trip where a person confronted the self and life's meaning. His 1967 work *The Politics of Experience* sold widely on college campuses as many young people found themselves relating to his observations regarding alienation. In this book he discusses the inability of one person to know another, for, he says, as human beings all we can really know is our own experience. Laing concludes that this makes us "invisible men."

Like many in the counterculture, Laing often attacked middle-class society. We have become, he claimed, entombed in a world where we strive to conform; where public education teaches children to hate but disguises it as love; where we are told to distrust spirituality. By the time a child is 15, "we are left with a being like ourselves, a half-crazed creature more or less adjusted to a mad world."

The clinically mad, Laing believed, could reach transcendence, a state where the ego is pushed aside, allowing the mind to enter other worlds. Madness is not for everyone, however—nor is it always beneficial, believed Laing. Other routes to transcendence exist, some perhaps spiritual. He experimented with Buddhism and Hinduism and, as evident in his prose poem "The Bird of Paradise," which appeared in *The Politics of Experience*, with psychedelic drugs. Although Laing condemned irresponsible use of mescaline and LSD, he believed they could provide trips into the inner self.

Some saw Marxism in Laing's politics, but he decried any one political doctrine and insisted reform needed to begin first with the individual and the family. In this, in his search for new ways to structure society, in his journeys seeking transcendence, he influenced the counterculture.

See also Huxley, Aldous; Leary, Timothy; LSD.

References Laing, R. D., *The Divided Self: An Existential Study in Sanity and Madness* (1960), *The Politics of Experience* (1967), *The Politics of the Family and Other Essays* (1971), and *The Self and Others* (1961).

Laugh-In

A television show that premiered in 1968 on NBC, *Laugh-In* featured topical humor, colorful sets, and fast-paced action created by piecing together snippets of videotape filled with sight gags, skits, and one-liners.

Produced by George Schlatter and hosted by comedians Dan Rowan and Dick Martin, *Laugh-In* reflected the quickness evident in sixties developments, and it challenged conventional comedy. The show featured "no swiveling chorus lines, no tuxedoed crooners," said *Time* magazine. "Just those quick flashes of visual and verbal comedy, tumbling pell-mell from the opening straight through the commercials." ("1960s Highlights—Colorful Television" 1995) *Laugh-In* won huge audiences and awards for excellence before it ended its run in 1973.

Reference "1960s Highlights—Colorful Television," *Time Almanac of the 20th Century* (1995).

League for Spiritual Discovery

Former Harvard psychologist Timothy Leary founded the League for Spiritual Discovery in 1966 after a trip to India and conversion to Hinduism and after his arrest for possession of marijuana. He considered the League a religious sect dedicated to altering consciousness and exploring mysticism through psychedelic drugs, primarily LSD. Beyond this, he intended the League to provide a rationale that would allow him to avoid conviction for his arrest: namely, that he used drugs as religious sacraments.

Leary toured the nation promoting his organization through "psychedelic religious celebrations" that involved reenacting the lives of the world's great religious leaders—Buddha, Christ, and Mohammed. With lights and music, Leary tried to replicate an LSD trip and show the religious revelation psychedelics could bring.

See also Drugs and the Drug Culture; Leary, Timothy; LSD.

Leary, Timothy (1920–1996)

In the 1960s, Harvard psychologist Timothy Leary promoted psychedelic drugs as a means to expand consciousness, change personalities, and reform society. His sensationalist comments earned him a reputation as the "high priest of LSD."

Leary was born on 22 October 1922 to Abigail Ferris Leary and Tote Leary in Springfield, Massachusetts. His father was a captain and post dentist at West Point. After inheriting some money 12 years later and giving small sums to Abigail and Timothy, Tote deserted his family. Leary's mother enrolled the youngster at Classical High School in Springfield, where he earned a reputation as a socializer and served as editor of the student newspaper. He received mediocre grades and in his senior year skipped several classes. This caused him to miss out on gaining acceptance to an Ivy League college. Consequently, in 1938 he enrolled at Holy Cross.

Leary soon grew disenchanted with the traditional curriculum and strict Jesuit atmosphere. He managed to gain admittance to West Point in 1940 but did not stay long. His fellow cadets subjected him to the silent treatment for having lied, so they said, about an incident in which he was drunk. Although found innocent of the charge, Leary resigned from the academy in August 1941. Nevertheless, his days there had not been totally wasted—while in isolation he had read Eastern philosophy, particularly Buddhism.

He next enrolled at the University of Alabama, where he pursued psychology, history, and literature. He read James Joyce's *Ulysses*, whose stream-of-consciousness technique floored him, but his tendency toward rebelliousness again got him into trouble, and he was expelled for violating visitation rules in a women's dorm. He obtained his bachelor's degree in psychology from the university while serving in the army during World War II. When the war ended, he continued his education, obtaining his master's degree at Washington State University, followed by a doctorate in psychology from the University of California–Berkeley. In 1950, the university appointed him to an assistant professorship. From 1955 to 1958, he worked as the research director of the psychiatric clinic at Kaiser Hospital in Oakland.

Leary soon won accalim for his examination of personality assessment, *The Interpersonal Diagnostic of Personality*, published in 1957. He studied behavior modification, too, and criticized psychotherapy as ineffective. Then, in 1958, Leary's wife committed suicide, and he felt ready to explore new avenues.

Leary traveled with his two children to Europe. In 1959, as his funds ran low, Harvard recruited him for its psychology program. He arrived in Cambridge and plunged into existential transactional psychology. This field believes you cannot know another person's reality but that people can be helped to find meaning in life through work or religion. Leary's learning and confidence impressed the younger graduate students, as did his criticism of conformist, middle-class society and his conclusion that social interaction and personal behavior consisted of stylized games.

The following year, Leary began a psilocybin research project, using a chemical compound synthesized by Sandoz Laboratories. Months earlier, Leary had traveled to Mexico, where he consumed the psilocybin found in "magic mushrooms" and experienced, he said, an enlightening, mystical revelation. Now he wanted to see if psilocybin could alter personalities in profound ways by stimulating unconscious searches for union with the greater universe, attaining a cosmic consciousness.

Leary discussed his research with Aldous Huxley, author of *The Doors of Perception*. The men disagreed about how widely psychedelic drugs should be circulated, with Huxley arguing they should be restricted to an elite intelligentsia and Leary advocating their widespread use. Both men desired, however, to liberate society from its stifling conformity and violent barbarity.

Leary's research soon evolved into weekend gatherings where students and artists took psilocybin. Another professor, Richard Alpert, joined Leary in the project, and both men claimed the future belonged to drugs that could change behavior. As Leary's work evolved into a holy crusade (he later referred to himself as a "visionary prophet"), his critics attacked him for sloppy procedures, and the psilocybin project split the psychology department into warring camps. Leary agreed to relinquish his drug supply to the university health service, but Harvard did not realize he had already found a new psychedelic to use in his experiments, LSD.

Late in 1961, Leary violated his agreement with Harvard when he helped administer psilocybin to 20 theology students in an attempt to see if a mystical religious experience could be replicated. This incident at Marsh Chapel produced two results: for one, it reinforced Leary's belief in the positive benefits of psychedelics as nearly all the partakers reported deeply transcendent experiences that changed their views of life; for another, it convinced Harvard that Leary could not be trusted to contain his adventuresome behavior.

Tired of the Harvard setting and wanting to proselytize his psychedelic message, Leary returned to Mexico in 1962, where he and several followers gathered at a hotel situated along a dirt road in Zihuatanejo and took LSD to explore the unconscious. He hoped to create a community founded on spiritual brotherhood rather than individual egos, for he believed that once psychedelic substances could be handled without damaging side effects, the human brain could be used to its fullest. Leary read *The Tibetan Book of the Dead* and concluded that its description of the postdeath passages experienced by the soul could be applied to the psychedelic trip. Later that year, he founded the International Foundation

Harvard psychologist Dr. Timothy Leary stands under the Village Theater marquee in New York City on 19 October 1966, the venue where he presented "The Reincarnation of Jesus Christ." Leary used the event to explain his League for Spiritual Discovery, which he called an orthodox, psychedelic religion.

for Internal Freedom (IFIF) to train guides in psychedelic exploration, supply them with LSD (at the time, along with psilocybin, a legal drug), and get them to form small groups to continue the research.

Leary decided to leave Harvard in June 1963, but before he could do so the university, appalled by his unconventional practices, including providing drugs to students, fired him and Alpert. That summer, Mexican authorities ordered Leary and his IFIF to leave the country. Leary found a new home, however, when a wealthy benefactor allowed him to use an estate in Millbrook, New York. The land, dotted with woods, ponds, and streams and the main house, 64 rooms in all, soon accommodated a research institute and monastery for mystics. Although IFIF folded in November 1963, Leary continued his Millbrook experiments in LSD and, after a trip to India in 1965, which converted him to Hinduism, founded the League for Spiritual Discovery, dedicated to mystical explorations.

In 1967, Leary, still at Millbrook but living in a teepee, claimed he had dropped out of society completely. He had little money and presented lectures for a fee. His appearances earned him notoriety as, barefoot and dressed in white trousers and Indian silk shirts, Beatles music playing in the background, he urged young people to "turn on, tune in, and drop out"—meaning, turn on to mystical experience (likely through LSD), tune in to the message, and drop out of the mainstream. He proclaimed that America "will be an LSD country within fifteen years." (Roszak 1968, 168) Despite this, many hippies rejected Leary's proclamation; they considered him too preoccupied with publicity. One hippie in Haight-Ashbury later remarked: "It isn't true that people like Timothy Leary were listened to. They weren't . . . ever." (Von Hoffman 1968, 23)

Like the hippies, though, Leary rejected politics as a dead end. In San Francisco, at the offices of the *Oracle*, an underground newspaper, he depicted leftist radicals as follows: "They are repeating the same dreary quarrels and conflicts for power of the Thirties and Forties . . . of Trotskyism and so forth. I think they should be sanctified, drop out, find their own center, turn on, and above all else, avoid mass movements, mass leadership, mass followers. I see that there is a great difference—I say incompatible difference—between the leftist activist movement and the psychedelic religious movement." (Cohen 1991, 151)

To some observers in 1968, Leary seemed disjointed. Millbrook deteriorated into an anarchic mix of drug escapists. The local police harassed the residents, setting up roadblocks and conducting raids. Added to this, Leary inexplicably reversed his position regarding politics, and in 1970 entered the California governor's race. His campaign ended, however, after a judge in that state sentenced him to ten years in prison on a marijuana possession charge, to be served consecutively with a ten-year sentence in Texas, where he had been arrested in 1965 after accepting responsibility for marijuana found in his daughter's possession.

Leary entered a minimal security correctional facility located near San Luis Obispo. On 13 September 1970, during the night, he inched his way along a wire that extended from a telephone in the compound to one just outside a fence and escaped. "Neck arching, shoulders thrusting, body wiggling, legs kicking, shoulders pushing propelled by uterine squeeze," Leary recalled. "My glasses fell but my arms smoothly reeled cable. Thus I butted head first sweating wet into a new life." (Leary 1983, 295) Leary fled to Algiers, where for a brief period he stayed with radical Black Panthers living in exile, most notably Eldridge Cleaver.

He then journeyed to Switzerland and lived there from 1971 to 1973 before traveling to Afghanistan. Upon his arrival, government officials in Kabul turned him over to the U.S. Embassy. Leary spent the rest of that year and part of 1974 in Folsom Prison before being transferred to a facility in Vacaville, California. He remained in prison until 1976.

Leary wrote several books in the 1960s that conveyed his psychedelic message, including *The Politics of Ecstasy*, *High Priest*, *Psychedelic Prayers*, and an edited work, *The Psychedelic Reader*. In the 1980s, he lectured on college campuses—including a tour with Watergate conspirator G. Gordon Liddy—and resumed writing, producing six new books and some 50 articles. He remained resolute regarding his ideas and proclaimed: "I vigorously oppose laws prohibiting American citizens from altering their nervous systems. Still 100 percent in favor of the moderate, intelligent use of drugs, I am increasingly convinced that the individual's right of access to his or her own brain has become the most significant political, economic, and cultural issue in America today." (371)

In the 1990s, he hailed computers as the new avenue to mind expansion and started a software company. He suffered setbacks in his personal life, though, with a divorce from his fourth wife and the suicide of his daughter. Leary's health deteriorated in 1996 as prostate cancer gripped his body; he died on 31 May. In a fashion true to his character, shortly before his death Leary requested that his body be cremated and his remains sent into space. This was done on 21 April 1997 when a rocket carrying his ashes, and those of 23 others, was launched in the Canary Islands. "I can hear Timothy laughing," said a friend. "He would have loved to have seen this."

See also Alpert, Richard; Drugs and the Drug Culture; Huxley, Aldous; League for Spiritual Discovery; LSD; Psilocybin.

References Cohen, Allen, *The San Francisco Oracle, Facsimile Edition: The Psychedelic Newspaper of the Haight Ashbury, 1966–1968* (1991); Leary, Timothy, *Confessions of a Hope Fiend* (1973), *Flashbacks: An Autobiography* (1983), *High Priest* (1968), *Jail Notes* (1970), *The Politics of Ecstasy* (1970), and *Psychedelic Prayers* (1966); Leary, Timothy, Ralph Metzner, and Richard Alpert, *The Psychedelic Experience* (1970); Lee, Martin A., and Bruce Shlain, *Acid Dreams: The CIA, LSD, and the Sixties Rebellion* (1985); Roszak, Theodore, *The Making of a Counterculture: Reflections on the Technocratic Society and Its Youthful Opposition* (1968); Stevens, Jay, *Storming Heaven: LSD and the American Dream* (1987); Von Hoffman, Nicholas, *We Are the People Our Parents Warned Us Against* (1968); http://www.leary.com.

Led Zeppelin

Although music critics gave Led Zeppelin mixed reviews, the band pioneered heavy metal with a style that influenced many other bands.

Late in the summer of 1968, Jimmy Page sat in his home near London, England, and worked to put together a new rock band. Until a few weeks earlier, he had been a guitarist with the now defunct Yardbirds. At first Page's efforts went nowhere, but a call to a friend produced a recommendation for a vocalist: Robert Plant, then singing for an obscure band, Hobbstweedle. Page went to hear Plant and immediately liked his strong, emotional voice, one filled with soul.

Plant subsequently joined Page and suggested that John Bonham be hired as a drummer. Page agreed and then invited John Paul Jones, a bass guitarist who worked as a studio musician, to round out the group. They called themselves the New Yardbirds until Keith Moon, drummer for the Who, jokingly suggested the name Led Zeppelin. In October 1968, they recorded their first album, self-titled. For the most part, it relied on the band's raw sound rather than extensive dubbing, and as with most of their music, displayed a strong attachment to the blues mixed with guitar distortion and filled with Plant's intensity. To accompany the album's release early in 1969, the band toured the United States for the first time. *Led Zeppelin* reached the American top ten that spring, soon followed by *Led Zeppelin II* that included "Whole Lotta' Love," "Bring It on Home," and "What Is and What Should Be." This success brought contracts for more tours and records, and the band members quickly grew wealthy.

Led Zeppelin released an untitled album in 1971 that contained "Stairway to Heaven," and followed this two years later with *Houses of the Holy*. Their tour that year broke box office records throughout the United States, and by 1975 they had achieved worldwide stardom. Other albums followed: *Physical Graffiti*, *Presence*, *The Song Remains the Same*, and *In through the Out Door*. But personal problems struck, among them the

Led Zeppelin, clockwise from top: John Bonham, Jimmy Page, John Paul Jones, and Robert Plant

tragic death of Plant's six-year old son, and, as the band planned another tour in 1980, the alcohol-related death of Bonham.

At this point, the group decided to disband. Plant and Page went on to record solo albums in the 1980s and 1990s, and the surviving members reunited on three occasions, the last time in 1995 when they played at the Rock and Roll Hall of Fame.

See also Rock Music.

Reference Cole, Richard, *Stairway to Heaven: Led Zeppelin Uncensored* (1992).

Liberation News Service

The Liberation News Service (LNS), founded by two radicals, Marshall Bloom and Ray Mungo, emerged in October 1967 as an underground newspaper network formed to circulate syndicated columns and distribute radical news. Although the member papers included hippie editors who preferred stories about cultural change, the LNS tended to attract the politically oriented, those seeking to communicate leftist ideas.

In fact, at the conference of editors in Washington, D.C., that led to the formation of LNS, many participants criticized newspapers such as the *East Village Other* for dominating the recently organized Underground Press Syndicate and favoring a hippie drop-out-of-society approach.

LNS distributed packets containing news stories and features, with topics that plumbed the countercultural mindset: resisting unjust laws, the right to an abortion, drugs, Karl Marx, imperialism, and capitalism. The network strongly supported self-determination in third-world nations, particularly the socialist revolution in Cuba.

In 1968, though, LNS split apart, shattered by an internal struggle between nonviolent leftists and militant Marxists, and undermined by secret government plots initiated by the FBI. This federal agency wanted to destroy the New Left and took advantage of the split by sending inflammatory letters to the warring parties and their various supporters or opponents. LNS limped into the early 1970s and then finally collapsed.

See also Underground Newspapers; Underground Press Syndicate.

References Mungo, Ray, *Famous Long Ago: My Life and Hard Times with the Liberation News Service* (1970); Peck, Abe, *Uncovering the Sixties: The Life and Times of the Underground Press* (1985).

Life against Death

Some critics condemned Norman O. Brown's book *Life against Death* as farfetched, but its Freudian interpretations attracted countercultural youths. Brown, who was born in 1913, received his doctorate from the University of Wisconsin in 1942, taught classics at various colleges, and wrote *Life against Death* in 1959. In it, he describes human beings as self-repressive and suggests that humankind inevitably moves toward its own destruction. He calls society morbid for its "incapacity to accept death," and says the creation of culture leads to a "neurotic obsession with the past and the future." Brown praises instinct over intellect and advocates receptivity to all forms of sexual experience—two views prevalent in the counterculture.

Some analysts consider Brown one of the important intellectual foundations of the counterculture. Among those who read *Life against Death* was Jim Morrison of the rock band the Doors, who tuned into Brown's assertion that repression caused neurosis at a societal level. Morrison concluded that crowds could have sexual neuroses similar to those of individuals, and he may have used this belief in his attempts to manipulate audiences.

In any event, Brown's outlook complemented the counterculture. Many young people in rejecting modern technology agreed with him when, shortly after writing *Life against Death*, he said: "The power which makes all things new is magic. What our time needs is mystery: what our time needs is magic. Who would not say that only a miracle can save us?" (Goodman, Mitchell, 1970, 630)

See also The Doors.

References Brown, Norman O., *Life against Death: The Psychoanalytical Meaning of History* (1959); Goodman, Mitchell, ed., *The Movement toward a New America: The Beginnings of a Long Revolution* (1970).

Lid

To the counterculture, *lid* meant an ounce of marijuana, as in "We had a lid of Acapulco Gold."

Longhair

A longhair meant more than a male who wore his hair long; it implied a cool person. As rock singer Stephen Stills explained, in the sixties you knew that a guy who had long hair was with it, that he knew the scene regarding drugs, the war, the entire countercultural opposition to straight society. In fact, many in the counterculture considered long hair on guys to be a "freak flag."

See also Freak.

Los Angeles Free Press

Many historians claim that underground newspapers began with the *Los Angeles Free Press*. Certainly its founder, Art Kunkin, intended his publication to be innovative.

A socialist intellectual active in the pre–World War II Old Left and a former tool-and-die maker, Kunkin wanted to develop in Los Angeles a newspaper with features similar to the recently formed *Village Voice* in New York City, a publication that appealed to bohemians. He desired, however, to be more political and advocate radical change, particularly after mainstream newspapers denounced the Free Speech Movement, a student protest at the University of California–Berkeley. He later acknowledged: "I wanted the *Free Press* to build a local movement base."

In 1964, Kunkin printed and distributed the *Faire Free Press* at a Renaissance festival sponsored by a local radio station. This eight-page, black-and-white paper was a takeoff on the Renaissance but included stories about jazz music and folk singer Joan Baez, then protesting the Vietnam War by refusing to pay her federal taxes.

After this debut, Kunkin obtained financial help from socialists—in the amount of $700—and free office space in a coffeehouse. He used these to begin the *Los Angeles Free Press*. Modern technology helped him, too, since recently developed offset techniques enabled him to produce the newspaper at a cost lower than he could with the old letterpress printing method.

In 1969, *Freep*, as it was affectionately called, sold 100,000 copies as a weekly and employed 150 workers. Kunkin, who breathed and ate journalism, had created the biggest underground newspaper in the nation. *Freep*'s topics and style set the underground tone by rejecting what it called false objectivity, the kind found in the mainstream press. Early on, *Freep* included African American perspectives, and while it called the destructive Watts riot of 1964 unfortunate, it blamed public officials for not heeding long-festering problems, and claimed that the rioting represented a black referendum on white America.

Freep won the enmity of conservative extremists, who at one point firebombed its offices, and the federal government, which spied on its reporters in an effort to close the publication. Kunkin's demise as the owner of *Freep* came in 1973—not through outside interference but through his own mismanagement.

He got into financial trouble when he invested in a four-color press and discovered that in order to cover his substantial outlay he had to keep the machine running almost constantly. This requirement consumed his time in obtaining printing contracts at the expense of properly supervising *Freep*. Kunkin went bankrupt, and a new ownership removed him. *Freep* stumbled along for a short while and then collapsed. At its height, though, *Freep* had redefined newspaper reporting and provided a model for the underground press.

See also Liberation News Service; Underground Newspapers; Underground Press Syndicate; *Village Voice*.

References Leamer, Laurence, *The Paper Revolutionaries: The Rise of the Underground Press* (1972); Peck, Abe, *Uncovering the Sixties: The Life and Times of the Underground Press* (1985).

Love

Other than the single "My Little Red Book," recorded in 1966, the Los Angeles–based rock band Love never had a hit record. Yet led by Arthur Lee, Love's music influenced other groups, notably the Doors. Love recorded long, reflective songs that paved the way for psychedelic rock. "If there hadn't been a San Francisco," say the authors of *Rock of Ages*, "Love might have invented it." (336)

See also Rock Music.

Reference Ward, Ed, Geoffrey Stokes, and Ken Tucker, *Rock of Ages: The Rolling Stone History of Rock & Roll* (1986).

The Love Book

In 1966, *The Love Book*, poems written by Lenore Kandel, stirred a sensational controversy. On 15 November, police raided the Psychedelic Shop, located in San Francisco's Haight-Ashbury district, and arrested the store clerk, Allen Cohen, for selling obscene material, namely *The Love Book*. The raid puzzled a few people, for although the poems contained four-letter and slang words in reference to genitalia, excerpts from Kandel's work had been selling without a problem in an anthology, and other writings conveying explicit sexual scenes could be bought in San Francisco stores.

Adding to the controversy, the police raided City Lights Bookstore, a beatnik hangout in North Beach, just days after the bust at the Psychedelic Shop, also for selling *The Love Book*. Why, then, the crackdown? Speculation centered on several possibilities: the police wanted to harass the emerging hippie community in Haight-Ashbury, they wanted to intimidate the entire avant-garde scene—at North Beach and in the Haight—and they wanted to get back at Ron Thelin, part owner of the Psychedelic Shop, and Allen Cohen for their publishing and editing the *Oracle*, a hippie newspaper. The *Oracle* had recently printed a story about a man who claimed to have been beaten by the police after a drug bust.

Whatever the explanation, the arrests reflected a polarization in American society between the conventional mainstream and the alternative counterculture. Earlier in November, California voters had elected Ronald Reagan their governor, and he promised to control radicals and all threats to middle-class morals.

After the crackdown against *The Love Book*, six defiant English professors from San Francisco State College held a public reading of it, attended by several hundred people. Lenore Kandel reacted to the arrests at the bookstores by asserting, "Any form of censorship whether mental, moral, emotional, or physical, whether from the inside out or from the outside in, is a barrier against self-awareness." (Cohen 1991, xxxix) In May 1967, a jury found *The Love Book* obscene, reinforcing the counterculture's view that oppression characterized America.

On appeal, a higher court threw out the conviction as violating the First Amendment. For Kandel, the controversy proved somewhat rewarding—sales of *The Love Book* skyrocketed, and she promised to donate a small portion of the profits to the Police Retirement Association!

See also Beat; Beatnik; Haight-Ashbury.

Reference Cohen, Allen, *The San Francisco Oracle, Facsimile Edition: The Psychedelic Newspaper of the Haight Ashbury, 1966–1968* (1991).

Love Grass

Sometimes a counterculture youth shared or gave marijuana to another person to enjoy—a high provided out of affection, friendship, or what was considered humanitarianism. The term love grass referred to this gift.

See also Grass.

Love-In

A gathering of countercultural young people to celebrate peace and community was called a love-in. These events were synonymous with be-ins. The first gathering specifically called a love-in may have been one held in Los Angeles in March 1966. To middle-class Americans, the long-haired youths dressed in tie-dye shirts, bell bottoms, beads, and listening to rock music seemed a strange, threatening collection. Straight society often used the term love-in derisively, as in the movie *Easy Rider* when a redneck stared at the three hippie-like characters played by Peter Fonda, Dennis Hopper, and Jack Nicholson and called them "refugees from a gorilla love-in."

See also Be-In.

Love Pagent

For hippies in San Francisco's Haight-Ashbury, the sixth of October 1966 loomed as a menacing, dark threat, for on that day a California law was to take effect making LSD illegal. As the date neared, and as tension mounted between police and hippies, Michael Bowen, a painter, and Allen Cohen, editor of the *Oracle*, an underground newspaper, decided to defuse the situation with the Love Pageant—a coming together that they envisioned not so much as a protest but, as Cohen put it, a celebration of "transcendental consciousness, the beauty of the universe, the beauty of being." (Lee and Shlain 1985, 149)

In flyers announcing the Love Pageant to be held at Panhandle Park, its promoters called themselves the Psychedelic Rangers and declared that mankind's inalienable rights included freedom of the body, pursuit of joy, and expansion of consciousness. They declared their love for all the "hate-carrying" men and women in the world and invited San Francisco's mayor to the event.

The mayor didn't show, but several thousand other people did, mainly hippies, but tourists and reporters, too. Rock groups performed on a flatbed truck—the Grateful Dead, Big Brother and the Holding Company with Janis Joplin, Wild Flower—and drugs circulated freely. The *Oracle* reported "Beautiful People" at the Panhandle, "ecstatically costumed and handing out flowers to friends and FBI agents." From this event, Bowen got the idea to promote a Be-In, held just weeks later.

See also Be-In; Haight-Ashbury; LSD; Psychedelic Rangers.

Reference Lee, Martin A., and Bruce Shlain, *Acid Dreams: The CIA, LSD, and the Sixties Rebellion* (1985).

Lovin' Spoonful

The Lovin' Spoonful had only a brief existence in rock music's top ten, but made a notable contribution by incorporating a jug-and-folk-band style into rock 'n' roll and by imparting the upbeat, feel-good days of the counterculture. Formed in 1965 by John Sebastian and Zal Yanovsky, the Lovin' Spoonful began their career in New York's Greenwich Village. The band had its first big hit later that year with "Do You Believe in Magic?" Over the next two years they recorded additional hits: "You Didn't Have To Be So Nice," "Daydream," "Did You Ever Have To Make Up Your Mind?" "Summer in the City," "Rain on the Roof," "Darling Be Home Soon," "Nashville Cats," and "Six O'clock."

Then the roof fell in. Many young people protested when two members of the band, Yanovsky and Steve Boone, avoided drug prosecution by turning in an acquaintance. To the counterculture, this represented a betrayal. After the band's record sales plunged in 1968, they split up.

See also Rock Music.

Lowenstein, Allard (1929–1980)

A civil rights activist, crusader for liberal causes within the Democratic Party, opponent of the Vietnam War, and one-term congressman, Allard Lowenstein gained notoriety for successfully leading a seemingly impossible campaign in 1968 to dump President Lyndon Johnson from the Democratic ticket. Despite Lowenstein's accomplishment in removing a counterculture nemesis, many political radicals distrusted him—he seemed too close to the liberal political establishment.

Lowenstein was born in 1929 in Newark, New Jersey, and grew up in Westchester County, New York, where his father, a former doctor, worked as a restaurateur. After completing his secondary education at Horace Mann School, Lowenstein attended the University of North Carolina–Chapel Hill (UNC), and in his sophomore year went to his first convention of the National Student Association (NSA), a group that included representatives from college student governments across the nation. Shortly after his graduation in 1950, he won election as president of NSA and enrolled in Yale Law School, from which he earned a degree three years later. He then entered graduate school at UNC, where he studied history for a year before enlisting in the army for a two-year stint.

Lowenstein served as a foreign-policy assistant to Senator Hubert Humphrey in 1959, a job that sent him on a fact-finding trip to South Africa. There he analyzed the oppressive system of apartheid and wrote about his experience in *Brutal Mandate*, published later that year. In 1961, he taught political science and worked as an assistant dean at Stanford University in California before returning to North Carolina to teach at the State College of Agriculture and Engineering in Raleigh.

In 1963, Lowenstein applied his concern for social justice to the expanding civil rights movement and worked as a lawyer representing demonstrators in Mississippi who had been sponsored by the Student Nonviolent Coordinating Committee (SNCC). The rough treatment meted out by whites to the civil rights workers shocked him, and later in the year he traveled to Stanford and Yale to recruit volunteers to work with SNCC. He helped organize the Mississippi Summer Project of 1964 to register black voters, but soon had a falling out with SNCC as that organization radicalized and announced it would no longer allow whites in its leadership positions.

In 1966 and 1967, Lowenstein gathered hundreds of signatures from student leaders for a letter that he sent to President Johnson protesting the Vietnam War. Many radical students criticized this as a feeble attempt, but Lowenstein soon went further and joined with Curtis Gans, a lobbyist with the liberal Americans for Democratic Action, to put together a dump Johnson movement. As was his style, Lowenstein traveled the nation, getting support for his effort. A main stumbling block appeared, however, in his inability to find someone to challenge Johnson for the Democratic presidential nomination—few people thought it possible to deny an incumbent president the nomination from his own party. Lowenstein approached Robert Kennedy, but the senator refused. Finally, Senator Eugene McCarthy of Wisconsin agreed, and Lowenstein supported him, although his heart remained with Kennedy.

The impossible transformed into reality in February 1968 when Johnson fared poorly against McCarthy in the New Hampshire primary and, in March, decided to withdraw from the race. With Johnson out, newspapers called Lowenstein "the original dump Johnson apostle." (Viorst 1979, 237) Soon, Robert Kennedy entered the race, posing a predicament for Lowenstein: should he stay with McCarthy or work for Kennedy?

He reacted by doing neither—instead he ran for Congress. Scoring an upset that November, he won and represented New York's Fifth Congressional District on Long Island. Two years later, he lost his bid for reelection. In the 1970s, he worked as an attorney and served in several government positions, including as a delegate to the United Nations under President Jimmy Carter, while trying unsuccessfully to win a congressional seat.

Tragedy struck on 14 March 1980 when a deranged former activist who had worked with Lowenstein during the civil rights campaign in Mississippi, Dennis Sweeny, entered Lowenstein's office and shot him. Lowenstein died from multiple wounds a few hours after the attack.

Over the years, radicals in the black and antiwar movements had criticized Lowenstein, calling him too moderate and suspecting he may have had connections with the CIA. But unlike them, he had faith in the political system, always dedicating himself to rational analysis, the Constitution, and enlightened self-interest. If nothing else, his efforts had resulted in what Milton Viorst in *Fire in the Streets* calls "one of the stunning episodes of the 1960s." (386)

See also McCarthy, Eugene; New Left; Students for a Democratic Society.

References Harris, David, *Dreams Die Hard: Three Men's Journey through the Sixties* (1993); Viorst, Milton, *Fire in the Streets: America in the 1960s* (1979).

LSD

A legal drug until 1966, and used despite its illegality thereafter, lysergic acid diethylamide tartrate, popularly known as LSD, or acid, brought psychedelics to the counterculture and greatly affected mainstream society.

LSD was invented, or synthesized, in the late 1930s by Albert Hofmann, a chemist working for Sandoz Pharmaceutical Laboratories in Switzerland. Hofmann, however, did not learn about LSD's hallucinogenic qualities until 16 April 1943, when he accidentally spilled a minuscule amount of the drug on his skin. Over the next few days he experimented with small doses and reported both a "terrifying" experience in which objects "assumed grotesque, threatening forms," and an amazingly pleasant sensation during which "kaleidoscopic, fantastic images surged," and "every sound generated a vividly changing image, with its own consistent form and color." Hofmann later proclaimed: "I see the true importance of LSD in the possibility of providing material aid to meditation aimed at the mystical experience of a deeper, comprehensive reality. Such a use accords entirely with the essence and working character of LSD as a sacred drug." (Hofmann 1980)

The mystical experience, the possibility that somehow LSD could break down the ego and end the prevailing confrontational attitude most Westerners had toward the natural environment, led some Americans to experiment with the drug. LSD first arrived in the United States in 1949, and in the 1950s psychologists began treating patients with it, attempting to see if mental disorders could be cured. They had limited success in that regard, but many patients experienced a mystical enlightenment, one that caused them to change their lives; often they turned contemplative and rejected competitive materialism. The actor Cary Grant claimed after an acid trip: "I have been born again. . . . I found I was hiding behind all kinds of defenses, hypocrisies, and vanities. . . . With me there came a day when I saw the light." (Stevens 1987, 64–65) While these developments unfolded, the CIA got involved with LSD. In searching for a "mind control" drug, the agency (along with the military) administered LSD to unsuspecting prisoners and mental patients—even to fellow agents within the organization, dosed in the CIA coffee room. This super secret program, called MK-ULTRA, did not become known to the public until years later.

By the 1960s, LSD had seeped into bohemian communities, where artists and intellectuals used it to tap into the unconscious. Sometimes people had bad trips with the drug, but by and large they reported a greater realization of a universe bound together by love. When the hippies began emerging in San Francisco's Haight-Ashbury district in 1965, they embraced LSD as a way to transform individuals and destroy conformity and a technocracy that said all truth resided in expert, rational pursuits. Most of these hippies took LSD to reach a mystical state—thus they studied Eastern religions and read works dealing with visionary experiences, such as books by Aldous Huxley and eighteenth-century poems by William Blake.

LSD gave rise to a psychedelic influence in popular culture. Rock music replicated the acid trip with hallucinatory sounds and lyrics. Art, particularly poster art, presented vivid colors and distorted images. Clothes sported these colors—a jarring new concept for men, especially. Even Madison Avenue joined the psychedelic explosion, with advertisements showing a product's ability—whether it be mouth freshner or bubble gum—to take its user into a surrealistic realm.

A portentous controversy affected LSD's proponents: who, exactly, should take the drug? Huxley argued that its consumption should be limited to an elite; any widespread use without proper mindset and calculated setting could produce disastrous results. Harvard psychologist Timothy Leary, on the other hand, argued for millions of Americans to take the drug, although responsibly, as part of a process to change personality through mystical experiences. The author Ken Kesey provided a more extreme answer: he, along with his Merry Pranksters, held Acid Tests in various locations in which they administered LSD en masse.

Attempts to create a psychedelic community in Haight-Ashbury collapsed in 1967, amid the type of consumption Huxley feared. That summer, young people converged by the thousands on the hippie district. They pursued love, companionship, and drugs. The latter, however, they did not regard as a route to mystical enlightenment. Rather, these kids, many in their midteens, took LSD simply to see wild colors. They took it too frequently, and often consumed impure mixtures laced with other chemicals that produced unexpected side effects. In short, they abused the drug, immersed themselves so totally in it that they could not function on a normal basis—such as holding jobs or acquiring food or housing. The mass media consequently portrayed LSD in the worst terms, as a drug that without exception ruined people's lives.

Reacting to this onslaught of irresponsible youths, media attention, and the crime that accompanied the entire scene, most hippies fled Haight-Ashbury and headed for rural communes. There, LSD use continued. But so, too, did its abuse among young people in suburbia. Rather than raising consciousness, LSD oftentimes dulled it, as many considered the drug an answer to whatever problems confronted them. In *The Making of a Counterculture*, Theodore Roszak observes: "The psychedelics, dropped into amorphous and alienated personalities . . . diminish consciousness by way of fixation." (160) As the drug spread, Albert Hoffman worried about the damage it could do, although he insisted: "If people would learn to use LSD's vision-inducing capability more wisely, under suitable conditions, in medical practice and in conjunction with meditation, then in the future this problem child could become a wonder child." (Hofmann 1980)

See also Alpert, Richard; Drugs and the Drug Culture; Huxley, Aldous; Kesey, Ken; Leary, Timothy.

References Hofmann, Albert, *LSD: My Problem Child* (1980); Roszak, Theodore, *The Making of a Counterculture: Reflections on the Technocratic Society and Its Youthful Opposition* (1968); Solomon, David, ed., *LSD: The Consciousness-Expanding Drug* (1966); Stevens, Jay, *Storming Heaven: LSD and the American Dream* (1987).

Lynd, Staughton (1929–)

In the 1960s, Staughton Lynd adhered staunchly to his Quaker principles and applied them in his fight for righteousness as a historian, civil rights worker, and New Left activist.

Lynd was born on 22 November 1929 in Philadelphia, Pennsylvania. A bright child, he benefited from the intellectual orientation of his parents and his family's Quaker heritage. His father, Robert Staughton Lynd, taught as a professor of sociology at Columbia University in New York City. His mother, Helen Merrell Lynd, also held a degree in sociology and rank as a professor, in her case at Sarah Lawrence College in Bronxville, New York. In 1929, the Lynds published *Middletown: A Study in Contemporary American Culture*, today considered a classic in sociology.

Young Staughton received his education at Ethical Culture School in Manhattan and Fieldston School, a private institution in the Bronx, New York. In the late 1940s, he attended Harvard University on an academic scholarship and while there joined left-wing political groups, at one point affiliating with a Communist organization. After graduating from Harvard in 1951 with a degree in history, he entered graduate school at the University of Chicago. Two years later, however, the army drafted him. This caused a problem for Lynd: on the one hand, his devout Quaker beliefs made him a pacifist; on the other, he did not want to avoid all military service while men his age were fighting in Korea. As a result, he accepted induction but took a noncombatant assignment. One year later, however, he received a dishonorable discharge because of his affiliation with Communists during his days at Harvard. This government action took place during the Red Scare, a time when people who held, or once held, Communist beliefs, or leftist beliefs of any kind, faced retribution.

After his discharge, Lynd and his wife moved to a commune in Georgia. In 1958, they relocated to New York City, where Lynd engaged in community work on the Lower East Side. The following year, after a Supreme Court ruling overturned his dishonorable discharge, changing it to an honorable one and making him eligible for GI benefits, he entered graduate school at Columbia University. In 1962, Lynd received his doctorate in American history and began teaching at Spelman College in Atlanta, Georgia. At the same time, he engaged in civil rights demonstrations, then spreading across the South. Among his activities, he headed the Freedom Schools project in Mississippi.

Lynd remained dedicated to his scholarly work and produced several impressive articles and books for academic publishers and a wider audience. His *Anti-Federalism in Dutchess County, New York: A Study of Democracy and Class Conflict in the Revolutionary Era* won favorable reviews in 1962, and articles he wrote appeared in *Commentary*, *The Nation*, and *New Republic*.

In 1964, Yale University hired Lynd to teach American history, and he moved to Connecticut, from where he entered the antiwar movement to protest the American involvement in Vietnam. In April 1965, he and several other protesters were

Staughton Lynd (second from right) marches in a protest against U.S. policy in Vietnam on 28 December 1965. Lynd, an American history professor at Yale University, created controversy with The Other Side, *a book that compared the Vietnamese revolution to democracy in the United States.*

arrested in Washington when they tried to enter the floor of the House of Representatives.

Later that year, in December, Lynd took a trip to North Vietnam that raised a storm of controversy. He traveled there with Tom Hayden, a left-wing activist prominent with Students for a Democratic Society, and Herbert Aptheker, a pronounced Communist. Lynd worried about traveling to North Vietnam with Aptheker, fearing it would make him look like he endorsed communism, when, in fact, he did not; but the North Vietnamese had issued the invitation and set the rules: a Communist must accompany him.

Lynd sincerely believed his journey could lead to successful negotiations between the United States and North Vietnam to end the war, but this did not occur. Instead, the trip changed his career. While in North Vietnam, Lynd, although wary of his hosts' deceit about the war, compared the Vietnamese revolution with democracy in the United States. In *The Other Side*, a book he wrote with Hayden (and which he later criticized as awful), he states: "We suspect the colonial American town meetings and current village meetings . . . have much in common, especially the concept of 'grass-roots' or 'rice-roots' democracy." (Gitlin 1987, 266)

On an even more controversial note, while in North Vietnam he pronounced the American military presence immoral and antidemocratic. This assessment received wide press coverage in the United States and produced an outcry by conservatives, especially wealthy alumni at Yale. When Lynd returned home, he found his job in jeopardy. Officially, he took an extended leave of absence; but unofficially, Yale's administration had let it be known he would not be welcomed back.

Although rejected by Yale and widely criticized by others, Lynd emerged a hero and a leading figure in the developing New Left movement. Searching for a place in academia, he applied for teaching positions at other colleges—at first to no avail. Finally, Chicago State University agreed in 1967 to hire him for one year. Lynd moved to Illinois, only to see the Board of Governors of State Colleges and Universities refuse to grant him a contract, basing its decision on his antiwar activity in North Vietnam. Lynd then sued the Board, a move that resulted in its members relenting and allowing him to be hired.

In 1968, Lynd's contract at Chicago State expired, and as expected, Yale, the institution from which he was on leave, announced he would not be granted tenure, despite his scholarly achievements. He formally resigned and focused on his antiwar activities, and that same year produced two historical works praised by academics: *Class Conflict, Slavery, and the United States Constitution*, and *Intellectual Origins of American Radicalism*. Written from a New Left viewpoint, these works established Lynd's credentials as a radical historian.

Lynd participated in the antiwar demonstrations held at the 1968 Democratic National Convention in Chicago and was arrested. Several months later, he testified on behalf of the Chicago Seven—Hayden and six other radicals who were on trial for conspiring to incite a riot outside the Convention—and favorably compared what the radicals had done to what the resistance movement had done against Britain during the American Revolution.

Nevertheless, Lynd had serious misgivings about the New Left: ever since 1966 he had been disenchanted with its internal divisiveness and its tendency toward repeating Communist dogma and resorting to violence. As a result, he decided to concentrate on local organizing. Further, since he had no hope of getting hired by a college, he decided to change professions. In 1973, he enrolled in law school at the University of Chicago, and after graduating three years later began working as a labor lawyer, representing workers.

In the 1980s, Lynd continued his law career and wrote a book about the steel industry and labor's place in it. He never relinquished the principles and humanitarianism that he embraced as a young man and that had contributed significantly to the 1960s counterculture.

See also Chicago Eight; Freedom Schools; Hayden, Tom; New Left.

References Gitlin, Todd, *The Sixties: Years of Hope, Days of Rage* (1987); Lynd, Staughton, *Anti-Federalism in Dutchess County, New York: A Study of Democracy and Class Conflict in the Revolutionary Era* (1962) and *Intellectual Origins of American Radicalism* (1968); Lynd, Staughton, ed., *Non-Violence in America: A Documentary History* (1966) and *Reconstruction* (1967); Lynd, Staughton, and Tom Hayden, *The Other Side* (1966).

M

Macbird

A play by Barbara Garson presented on stage in 1966, *Macbird* reinforced the image many countercultural political activists had of President Lyndon Johnson as an uncouth, deceitful politician. Garson modeled *Macbird* after Shakespeare's *Macbeth* and implied Johnson had used palace intrigue and murdered John Kennedy.

McCarthy, Eugene (1916–)

Eugene McCarthy captivated college students in 1968 when he began what many people considered an impossible quest: a campaign to unseat incumbent president Lyndon Johnson and capture the Democratic presidential nomination, and the presidency, as a peace candidate committed to getting the United States out of Vietnam.

McCarthy hailed from Watkins, Minnesota, where he was born on 29 March 1916. He graduated from Saint John's Preparatory School in 1932 and then entered Saint John's University in Collegeville, Minnesota. After obtaining his bachelor's degree in 1935, he enrolled in graduate school at the University of Minnesota, and while continuing his studies there, taught social science in the public high schools. One year after receiving his master's degree in 1939, McCarthy began teaching economics and education at Saint John's University, a position he held until World War II, when he worked as a civilian technical assistant to the Military Intelligence Division of the War Department.

In 1946, McCarthy chaired the sociology department at the College of Saint Thomas in St. Paul, Minnesota. He entered politics and won election as a county chairman of the Democratic Farmer-Labor Party. This led to his running in 1948 under that party's banner for Congress. He won and held the seat for ten years before winning election to the Senate.

In a losing effort, McCarthy supported Lyndon Johnson over John Kennedy for the Democratic presidential nomination in 1960, a move that many young activists, who supported Kennedy, could never fathom. For this reason, and because of his diffidence as a political leader—given more to writing poetry than struggling for power—he seemed an unlikely person to challenge Lyndon Johnson. By 1967, though, he had grown disenchanted with the Vietnam War and realized that antiwar liberals within the Democratic Party had begun an effort to dump Johnson. Hence, on 30 November 1967, McCarthy announced he was running against Johnson as an antiwar candidate. Hardly anyone took him seriously —Johnson held enormous power, and never in modern history had a sitting president been denied his own party's nomination. In addition, McCarthy had no organization and little money.

Despite this, a secret weapon helped him: thousands of college students poured into New Hampshire, the first primary state, and went door to door in the cold, snowy weather, promoting McCarthy with the voters. Their effort coincided with an uprising in Vietnam, the Tet Offensive, that indicated the United States remained further than ever from victory in the war. Then it happened: McCarthy stunned the nation by winning 42 percent of the New Hampshire primary vote and 20 of that state's 24 convention delegates—a crushing defeat for Johnson.

McCarthy's upset victory exposed Johnson's vulnerability, and within a few days Robert Kennedy announced he would seek the Democratic presidential nomination. Then, in late March, Johnson declared he would not serve another term as president.

McCarthy and Kennedy battled for the nomination, with Kennedy gaining the upper hand. But in June, an assassin killed Kennedy, turning the nomination campaign into a race between McCarthy and Johnson's vice-president, Hubert Humphrey. Most young political activists despised Humphrey, or the "Hump," as they called him, for supporting the war and being close to Johnson. McCarthy's campaign, however, sagged as the senator seemed more and more reluctant to continue the race after Kennedy's death. On top of that, Johnson controlled the Democratic National Convention and had no intention of letting McCarthy win. Thus, Humphrey secured the nomination in August 1968 and went on to lose the general election by a narrow margin to the Republican candidate, Richard Nixon.

McCarthy left the Senate in 1970 and campaigned again for president in 1976 as an independent but received only 1 percent of the vote. He remained an ineffectual force in politics in the following two decades, largely retired from the scene while teaching and writing. But many remembered him as the giant killer, the senator who brought down the sitting president from his own party and, in addition to Robert Kennedy, the establishment politician who had given college students some hope in 1968 that the system could end the war and bring substantial reform.

See also Democratic National Convention of 1968; Lowenstein, Allard; New Left.

Reference McCarthy, Eugene, *The Year of the People* (1969).

McKissick, Floyd (1922–)

As a college student, Floyd McKissick committed himself to advancing the African American cause, and never slackened his fight. Upon assuming leadership of the Congress of Racial Equality (CORE) in the 1960s, he radicalized it, moving the organization from civil rights to black power.

McKissick was born on 9 March 1922 in Asheville, North Carolina. His father, head bellhop at the Vanderbilt Hotel there, encouraged him to get an education and avoid being, as he phrased it, an Uncle Tom to the white man. Through high school, McKissick earned money delivering ice on a wagon and shining shoes. After graduation, he joined the army and served in Europe during World War II. When the war ended, he enrolled at Morehouse College in Atlanta, and then transferred to North Carolina College in Durham. Throughout this time, McKissick worked hard for civil rights. He joined the National Association for the Advancement of Colored People (NAACP) and directed its youth program in North Carolina. He worked also for CORE, a group founded in 1942 to engage in nonviolent protest. In 1947, he participated in bus rides sponsored by CORE that aimed to desegregate southern terminals. For the first time, he encountered brutal white opposition.

Floyd McKissick, leader of the Congress of Racial Equality during the 1960s, carries a "black power" sign in a demonstration protesting the drafting of blacks to fight in Vietnam.

McKissick wanted to study law at the University of North Carolina in Chapel

Hill. The law school there, however, followed a segregationist policy and would not admit him. With the help of Thurgood Marshall, a prominent black lawyer, McKissick went to court and in 1949 obtained an order allowing him to enroll in the law school. Three years later, he gained admittance to the North Carolina bar and practiced law in Durham. He succeeded in the 1950s at winning court cases that resulted in the desegregation of several schools in the state.

Then the civil rights movement took a new turn in 1960: African American college students began staging sit-ins at segregated lunch counters. As confrontations increased, McKissick represented demonstrators arrested in these and other protests.

Two years later, as national chairman of CORE, McKissick announced his support for more direct action. In 1966, CORE's members elected him national director, their top position. When black power emerged as a prominent concept and slogan that year, McKissick supported it enthusiastically. To him black power meant breaking with white liberals, who seemed to support African American rights only when they did not infringe on their power, and it meant promoting African culture and establishing black control in black neighborhoods.

When riots broke out in several urban ghettos, McKissick said they had resulted from an oppressive system under which African Americans received low wages, if they held any jobs at all, and paid exorbitant prices for food and rent. After the Detroit riots of 1967, he demanded that all persons arrested be released—he claimed they were political prisoners. That same year, McKissick announced that CORE had no room for whites in its leadership positions, and he rejected Martin Luther King's call for nonviolent protests, desiring instead to pursue black economic and political power through such tactics as rent strikes. At about the same time, he earned the enmity of President Lyndon Johnson when he criticized the Vietnam War, calling it a disgrace that blacks should die overseas when they did not have democracy at home.

McKissick took a leave of absence from CORE later in 1967 to start a project to help the ghetto poor. He remained influential in the black power movement, though, and in 1969 wrote *Three-Fifths of a Man*, a call for blacks to gain control of their own communities.

See also Black Power; Carmichael, Stokely.

References Haskins, James, *Profiles in Black Power* (1972); McKissick, Floyd, *Three-Fifths of a Man* (1969).

McKuen, Rod (1933–)

Rod McKuen entered show business in the 1950s, but his years as a celebrity came when his singing and poetry appealed to the sixties counterculture.

McKuen was born in a Salvation Army hospital in Oakland, California, on 29 April 1933. He dropped out of school at age 11 and in the 1940s worked at odd jobs. In 1953, he was drafted into the army. Two years later, after his release, he began performing as a folk singer in San Francisco. In the late 1950s, McKuen appeared in several low-budget movies. The following decade, he sang in France, where his pop songs hit the record charts.

At the same time, McKuen's poems found a wide audience in the United States. His collections *Stanyan Street and Other Sorrows*, *Listen to the Warm*, and *Lonesome Cities* all reached the best-seller lists. McKuen honed another talent, too, as a songwriter. He composed the musical score for *The Prime of Miss Jean Brodie*, a 1969 movie, and many singers covered his songs. He himself recorded *The Sea, The Earth, and The Sky*, a popular three-disc LP on which he narrates his own poems accompanied by instrumental music.

McKuen's works emphasized love, loneliness, and what his publisher called "the alienation of our present era and the need of people to reach one another." The *Los Angeles Herald Examiner* hailed him as among the finest lyrical poets. Another reviewer, though, described his work as not even good enough to be trash. Many critics believed McKuen had tapped into and exploited the shallowest part of the countercultural search for love.

References McKuen, Rod, *Listen to the Warm* (1967), *Lonesome Cities* (1968), and *Stanyan Street and Other Sorrows* (1966).

McLuhan, Marshall (1911–1980)

Whether breaking through linear thought processes and developing psychedelic newspapers or using the media for outrageous declarations, the counterculture showed its indebtedness to Marshall McLuhan, a popular communications theorist.

Herbert Marshall McLuhan was born on 21 July 1911 in Edmonton, Alberta, Canada. His father, Herbert Ernest McLuhan, worked as a real estate and insurance salesman, and his mother, Elsie Hall McLuhan, was an actress. While young McLuhan was still a boy, his family moved to Winnipeg, where he grew up. He entered the University of Manitoba intending to major in engineering, but quickly switched to English literature, in which he received his B.A. in 1933 and his M.A. the following year.

He then traveled to England and studied at Cambridge. While working on his dissertation, he began his teaching career in the United States at the University of Wisconsin. In 1937, he left there to teach at Saint Louis University, and in 1944, two years after obtaining his doctorate from Cambridge, he returned to Canada and taught at Assumption University in Windsor, Ontario. McLuhan made one final career move in 1946 when he began teaching at the University of Toronto, a position he held for 34 years.

McLuhan wrote his first book, *The Mechanical Bride*, in the early 1950s. Although it received little attention, his conclusions presented the foundation for his future works: that industrial civilization has produced an unbalanced, inhumane society in contrast to the agricultural past and has changed the psychic structure of all who live under its influence. The later counterculture expressed a similar critique in calling technocratic society cold, impersonal, and inhumane, thus McLuhan's ideas would eventually find wider acceptance.

The Canadian's second book did not appear until 1962: *The Gutenberg Galaxy*. Here he shows how the invention of movable type in the fifteenth century has affected the psyche and promoted linear thought. This development has moved society away from oral tradition and has produced self-centeredness while destroying the unity of the senses. Stream-of-consciousness techniques, though, have mollified this, and electronics, he argues, has restored some tribal ways in developing what he calls a "global community."

Two years later, McLuhan's *Understanding Media* appeared; it continued the theme found in *The Gutenberg Galaxy* and introduced the phrase "the medium is the message," meaning that the form of communication alters the psyche and so contains in itself the means to alter consciousness. McLuhan writes:

> In a culture like ours, long accustomed to splitting and dividing all things as a means of control, it is sometimes a bit of a shock to be reminded that, in operational and practical effect, the medium is the message. This is merely to say that the personal and social consequences of any medium . . . result from the new scale that is introduced into our affairs by each extension of ourselves, or by any new technology. (McLuhan 1964, 23)

Although some reviewers criticized McLuhan for unsubstantiated assertions and sloppy reasoning, his works generated debate about the connections among media, human thought, and societal structure. Media students flocked to his message, while many other young people challenged traditional means of communication. The underground press, for example, experimented with noncolumnar layouts, vivid colors, and strangely shaped lettering.

Activists absorbed McLuhan as well, realizing they could use the television media to shock audiences and get them to reevaluate social standards. In *Soon To Be a*

Major Motion Picture, Abbie Hoffman, a leader of the Yippies, declares: "*Understanding Media* became a guide for comprehending the electronic world. I wasn't sure I understood McLuhan any more than I did [Herbert] Marcuse, but his thinking made me focus on those psychedelic news images that instantaneously seemed to penetrate our fantasy world." (85)

McLuhan lectured widely in the late 1960s, and his jargon, filled with such words as "probe," "implosions," and "interface," became known as McLuhanisms. His followers, called McLuhanites, considered him a prophet. In 1967, he won the Molson prize for outstanding achievement in the social sciences by a Canadian, followed by a one-year appointment to the Albert Schweitzer Chair of the Humanities at Fordham University in New York.

But McLuhan's prominence quickly faded after the 1960s. He continued teaching and writing until he retired in June 1980 after suffering a severe stroke. He died later that year, on 31 December, in Toronto. Interestingly, the spread of computers in the 1990s and communication systems such as the Internet has regenerated talk of a "global community" and debate about the media-society relationship raised by McLuhan in the sixties.

See also Hoffman, Abbie; *San Francisco Oracle*; Yippies.

References: Hoffman, Abbie, *Soon To Be a Major Motio Picture* (1980); McLuhan, Marshall, *Counterblast* (1969), *Culture Is Our Business* (1970), *The Gutenberg Galaxy: The Making of Typographic Man* (1962), *The Mechanical Bride: Folklore of Industrial Man* (1951), *Understanding Media: The Extensions of Man* (1964), and *War and Peace in the Global Village: An Inventory of Some Current Spastic Situations That Could Be Eliminated by More Feedforward* (1968); McLuhan, Marshall, and Quentin Fiore, *The Medium Is the Message: An Inventory of Effects* (1967); Marchand, Philip, *Marshall McLuhan: The Medium and the Messenger* (1989); Wolfe, Tom, *The Pump House Gang* (1968).

Macrobiotic Diet

Nutrition did not escape the countercultural rebellion. The macrobiotic diet attracted some people in the sixties, partly in response to Hindu strictures against eating the flesh of any living thing, and partly from a general conclusion that eating meat was unhealthy. A macrobiotic diet presumably promoted longevity with its emphasis on whole grains, vegetables, and fish. In several instances, countercultural youths interpreted the diet incorrectly and suffered life-threatening malnutrition.

See also Organic Food.

Mad

Mad magazine, graced by Alfred E. Neuman's cockeyed face, had an immense impact on those young people in the 1950s who, in the following decade, constituted the counterculture generation. Women's liberationist Gloria Steinem has observed: "There was a spirit of satire and irreverence in *Mad* that was very important, and it was the only place you could find it in the '50s." (Reidelbach 1991, 132)

Publisher Bill Gaines started *Mad* as a comic book in 1952, part of his EC Publications that included horror and war comics for kids. The first issue, under editor Harvey Kurtzman II, satirized the very comic books EC and others produced. *Mad* sold poorly until the fourth issue, when young readers devoured its takeoff on Superman, titled "Superduperman." Sixties activist Paul Krassner, writing in *Confessions of a Raving, Unconfined Nut*, recalls, "What a kick to see Clark Kent going to a phone booth to change into his Superman outfit, only to find that Captain Marvel was already there." (Krassner 1993, 36)

As *Mad*'s readership expanded, the publication encountered problems with comic-book censors who considered its content unfit for its young audience. At that point, Gaines decided to convert *Mad* into a bimonthly magazine, and the first issue appeared in this format, priced at 25 cents, during the summer of 1955.

Under Kurtzman's guidance, the revamped *Mad* evolved from parodies about comics to parodies about television and movies. One issue, for example, presented

"Howdy Dooit," a mean-looking Howdy Doody-like puppet who demanded that kids drag their parents to the TV set and force them to watch commercials.

Initially, *Mad* presented little political satire, but this changed later in 1955, after Al Feldstein succeeded Kurtzman as editor. Youngsters who eventually filled the counterculture ranks absorbed these digs at conformist society, and they appreciated *Mad* poking fun at itself and its readers, as in this advice about "How To Be Smart":

> Now many people are under the impression that the world is a pretty dumb place and there aren't many smart people around nowadays. To foolishly say whether there *are* lots of those dumb people will not be the purpose of this article.
>
> To *help* all those millions of people will be the purpose of this article.
>
> And with smartness in the minority, let's face it . . . you are probably one of "those" . . .
>
> Especially since you're reading this magazine. (Reidelbach 1991, 100)

Another article lampooned psychiatrists and their therapy sessions. "If you are in group therapy it is important that you attend every session," *Mad* inveighed. "Because if you are absent, guess who they will talk about!" (104) An article that appeared in 1957 presented a 1960s countercultural outlook long before the counterculture began:

> The American brags about being an individualist, when actually he's the world's *least* individual person. The guy who has been taken in by this philosophy is the guy who really believes that contemporary people are slim, and clean-limbed, and they're so much fun to be with . . . because they drink Pepsi-Cola. . . .
>
> Once a guy starts *thinking*, once a guy starts *laughing* at the things he once thought were very real . . . he's making the transition from "Day People" to "Night People." And once this happens, he can never go back! (102)

The "Night People" would soon appear and infuse the counterculture with prankster tricks and hippie attitude.

In 1966, Gaines permitted a producer to stage an off-Broadway play based on the magazine. *Mad*, the play, appeared to favorable critical reviews, and over a two-year period its 900 shows entertained audiences with quick one-liners and a set in which actors and props moved constantly.

As to how *Mad* treated the sixties, it spared no one from its satire, neither counterculture nor establishment. One issue featured Alfred E. Neuman on the cover, dressed to look like a hippie, with a phrase encircling his image: "Turn On, Tune In, Drop Dead." In *Completely Mad*, the magazine's historian, Maria Reidelbach, states that "no president was exempt from *Mad*'s sledgehammer humor, no movement or institution safe from *Mad* jabbing a finger at its excesses and inconsistencies, laughing fiendishly." (132)

In response to all critics, Alfred E. Neuman responded, "What—Me Worry?" This fictitious gap-toothed kid with big ears, stupid smile, freckles, and eyes misaligned so that one sat slightly above the other first appeared on the cover of a *Mad* anthology and then in the comic book. He made his first full-page appearance in the magazine in 1956, the year he initially ran for president under the slogan, "You could do worse and always have!" (138–139) (He has "run" for president every election since!) At first, Neuman did not have a name, then it was, briefly, Melvin Coznowski and, after that, Mel Haney. The readers finally started calling him Alfred E. Neuman after a joke on a radio program.

But *Mad* did not invent Neuman's image; it had been circulating in advertisements and on billboards and postcards since the late 1800s. Feldstein thought it odd enough to use, and in 1956 hired Norman Mingo to create a modern, color portrait. That year, Neuman first appeared on the *Mad* cover, and he has been there ever since.

For many in the counterculture, irreverence began in childhood, reading *Mad* and staring at the big-eared, gap-toothed kid.

References Jacobs, Frank, *The Mad World of William Gaines* (1972); Krassner, Paul, *Confessions of a*

Raving, Unconfined Nut: Misadventures in the Copunterculture (1993); Reidelbach, Maria, *Completely Mad: A History of the Comic Book and Magazine* (1991).

Magic Mushrooms

In the late 1950s, psychedelic adventurers pursued magic mushrooms found in Mexico. More than a decade earlier, botanist Richard Evan Schultes had begun a seminal investigation of vision-inducing plants held sacred by Indian tribes in Mexico and South America, including southern Colombia, where there exists in the Sibundoy hills the largest concentration of hallucinogenic plants on earth.

Schultes's scholarly writings (that in the 1960s influenced the drug culture) encouraged Gordon Wasson, an investment banker, to undertake a similar search. For several years, he and his spouse, Valentina, had been investigating their thesis that some religious experiences in Europe emanated from the hallucinogenic qualities of mushrooms. Expanding their research across the Atlantic, in 1952 the couple traveled to Mexico, pursuing mushroom folklore. Three years later, in the central Mexican highlands, they discovered a mushroom cult that, as in ancient Indian civilization, consumed a native mushroom, genus *Psilocybe*. Gordon Wasson consumed the mushroom and reported reaching an ecstatic mystical state.

The Wassons made several more journeys to Mexico, allowing only a few people to know about their discovery, most notably a photographer who took pictures of the cult's mushroom ceremony, and the director of the French National Museum of Natural History, who shipped a mushroom to Albert Hofmann, the chemist noted for having recently synthesized LSD. Hofmann isolated the mushroom's hallucinogenic element and reproduced it as a new chemical, psilocybin.

In 1957, Gordon Wasson made his discovery public when he reported it to *Life* magazine. That July, *Life* printed a 17-page story replete with color photographs. The article presented a highly favorable report about the mushroom's hallucinogenic qualities, and this led to several hundred Americans venturing south to procure the "magic mushroom." Among the many who read the article in *Life* was a clinical psychologist, Timothy Leary. In 1960, he consumed a mushroom and, like Wasson, reported a mystical experience. In a short while, he obtained psilocybin and began a research project at Harvard University. This, in turn, led to his experiments in LSD. Thus, in several different ways magic mushrooms gave birth to the psychedelics that flowed through America's counterculture like a great wellspring.

See also Drugs and the Drug Culture; Leary, Timothy; LSD; Psilocybin.

Maharishi Mahesh Yogi (1911?–)

An Indian guru dressed in a white robe, his face bedecked with a long gray beard, Maharishi Mahesh Yogi attracted thousands in the sixties with his transcendental meditation, a way to be one with and at peace with the universe.

Little is known about Maharishi's early life. Born in India around 1911, the son of a government official, he graduated from Allahabad University around 1940 with a degree in physics. He then spent 13 years studying under Guru Brahamamamda Saraswati, also known as Guru Dev, from whom he learned Hindu transcendental meditation, or TM. Shortly before Guru Dev died in 1952, he told Maharishi to continue his mission. Maharishi prepared to do this by retreating into meditative seclusion in the Himalayas. He emerged in 1955, and the following year organized a Spiritual Development Movement.

Maharishi traveled throughout India in 1958, spreading his TM message, claiming it would free individuals from tension and bring them bliss. Early in 1968, he announced the formation of a worldwide Spiritual Regeneration Movement to help humankind, and in 1959 he began his international mission in California. After a brief return to India, he continued his world tour in 1962, and again in 1963, the year he wrote *Science of Being and Art of Living*.

Maharishi emphasized that he taught a technique, not a religion, although a technique closely connected to Hinduism. His greatest renown, and controversy, came when the Beatles, along with Mick Jagger of the Rolling Stones, joined his movement. In February 1968, the Beatles journeyed to Maharishi's retreat at Rishekesh, in north India. They traveled by plane to Delhi, then by taxi, then jeep, and when the road worsened, by donkey. At Maharishi's ashram, they spent mornings attending lectures, afternoons practicing meditation, and evenings writing music, producing a large number of songs.

After several weeks, though, the Beatles, one by one, returned home. Neither Ringo Starr nor Paul McCartney could understand or relate to TM, and although John Lennon and George Harrison adopted parts of Maharishi's philosophy, tension arose between the Beatles and the guru when he seemed to be capitalizing on their fame to help himself. Maharishi, in fact, had embraced the material world, with an elaborate house, helicopter pad (if the Beatles had only known, they would not have needed the donkeys!), and efforts to obtain some of the Beatles' income, 10 to 25 percent.

Maharishi's falling out with the Beatles hurt his reputation, and a world tour he conducted in 1971 attracted sparse audiences. Nevertheless, the following year he announced an international plan to reorganize society and solve the basic problems facing humankind, and in 1974 his efforts received support when several scientists announced that TM could improve a person's life. Certainly, in the 1960s and early 1970s, many young people thought so, having adopted it as an alternative to what they considered ineffectual Christian beliefs. TM thus represented a countercultural infatuation with Eastern mysticism as an antidote to rational, technocratic Western society. In the 1990s, Maharishi continued to lead his worldwide organization.

References Jefferson, William, *The Story of Maharishi* (1976); Maharishi Mahesh Yogi, *Meditations of Maharishi Mahesh Yogi* (1968) and *Science of Being and Art of Living* (1963).

Mailer, Norman (1923–)

An author often associated with the beats, an activist often associated with liberal causes, Norman Mailer attracted many young people in the 1960s with his intelligent, frequently acerbic attacks on technocracy and conformity.

Mailer was born on 31 January 1923 in Long Branch, New Jersey, to Isaac Barnett Mailer and Fanny Schneider Mailer. Shortly after World War I, Mailer's father had emigrated from South Africa to England, and then to the United States, where he earned a modest living as an accountant. In 1927, the family moved from New Jersey to Brooklyn, New York, and young Norman excelled in his schooling, first at P. S. 161, and then at Boys' High School, where he developed an interest in aeronautics.

Mailer entered Harvard University in 1939, planning to become an engineer, but that winter he plunged into reading modern American literature and developing his writing in pursuit of the literary career he had desired since age 16. He wrote several short stories and won *Story* magazine's annual college contest in 1941 with his work "The Greatest Thing in the World."

While working for *Harvard Advocate*, the undergraduate literary magazine, he completed a novel, *No Percentage*, that displayed the influence of Ernest Hemingway. Mailer later called this unpublished work "terrible." He worked at a state hospital in Boston during the summer of 1942 and used his experience there as the basis for yet another unpublished novel, *A Transit to Narcissus*.

A more notable experience propelled Mailer into creating a masterful book. In 1943, he enlisted in the military and served as an infantryman in the Philippines

Controversial author Norman Mailer, right, and former boxer José Torres, center, attend a rally at the Village Gate in 1969.

during World War II. When the war ended, he served with the occupation forces in Japan before returning home, settling in New York City, and, in 1946, writing *The Naked and the Dead*. The publication of this book two years later won him literary acclaim and commercial success. At 25 he had arrived in the world of letters.

The Naked and the Dead portrays GIs in World War II, situated on a mythical island. Beneath the war story there unfolds a searing criticism of America in the 1940s. Each character displays a personality twisted into grotesque form by society, and one, General Cummings, through his naked grasp of power, represents the inhumanity that had overtaken the nation. From Mailer's viewpoint, an impersonal technocracy had ruined America with its cold rationality and conformist materialism. In the process, society had fallen victim to indecency caused by brutality and cynicism.

This theme appeared time and again in Mailer's writings and won him a wide audience among young radicals in the 1950s and 1960s. They agreed with his condemnation of technocracy as dehumanizing, his criticism of bleak architecture as reflective of a declining spirituality, and his warnings about despoiling nature and laying it to waste.

In 1957, he wrote "The White Negro," an essay that appeared in *Dissent*. One critic later called its influence on conscientious young Americans "so deep as to be well-nigh incalculable." (Scott 1973, 46) In it, Mailer defines the hipster (akin to poet Allen Ginsberg's "angel-headed hipsters") as one who lives with death as an immediate danger and rejects the conformist fascism of the technocracy in order to express selfhood; a person who lives by instinct and may even resort to murder in order to purge hatred from the soul; a person committed to "the rebellious imperatives of the self." (48) Mailer considered the Negro as the source of hip because the Negro lives with danger.

In his works, Mailer looked not toward a new politics to save America but toward a new humanism, and this could be gained, he believed, only by using creative powers. In this sense, Mailer had something in common with beat writers such as Jack Kerouac and Allen Ginsberg, who in the 1950s rebelled against conformity.

Unlike such 1950s beats, however, Mailer rejected the tendency to drop out and shun mainstream society. He envisioned life as war—and he would follow an activist route, battling through his writings and his political efforts to shape society, to create a new, revolutionized form (a position that later endeared him with the political activists in the counterculture). Thus, back in the 1940s, he dabbled with communism before rejecting it. In 1955, he joined Daniel Wolf and Edwin Francher to found *The Village Voice*, an alternative newspaper that covered the hip scene in Greenwich Village and political topics ignored by the mainstream press. Five years later, he attended the Democratic National Convention that nominated John Kennedy for the presidency.

Then as the Vietnam War expanded in the 1960s, he protested against it while writing *Cannibals and Christians*, a collection of essays that appeared in 1966 and warned about a totalitarian plague. He recounted his role in helping to lead the 1967 march on the Pentagon (and his subsequent arrest for attempting to enter the building) in an autobiographical piece, *The Armies of the Night*, which the following year won the Pulitzer Prize for nonfiction. In this book, he sees the young in an ambiguous role: warring against what technology had wrought but consumed by drugs and the technological, TV world they criticized. He intones: "The same villains who . . . had gorged on LSD and consumed God knows what essential marrows of history, wearing indeed the history of all eras on their back as trophies of gluttony, were now going forth . . . to make war on those other villains, who were destroying the promise of the present in their self-righteousness and greed and lust . . . for some sexo-technological variety of neofascism." (93) Overall, Mailer's ideology, infused with irrationality and instinct, appealed to an emerging counterculture that saw itself at odds with middle-class conformity.

Shortly after the 1967 Pentagon march, Mailer wrote *Why Are We In Vietnam?* a critical view of the war, and *Miami and the Siege of Chicago*, which covers the 1968 Republican and Democratic National Conventions. In his political activism, he rankled liberals by criticizing them for participating in building the technocratic state, and he garnered ridicule for his own unsuccessful run, in 1969, for mayor of New York City. Central to his campaign, he proposed that the city secede from New York and become the nation's fifty-first state.

Mailer lived in controversy, constantly at war with those around him. This included a difficult period in the late 1950s when he battled drugs and depression and, at a party, stabbed his wife with a penknife, and it included egotistical pronouncements and running battles with the press. Mailer continued writing essays, novels, and nonfiction literature into the 1970s and the following two decades. His works included the highly acclaimed account of murderer Gary Gilmore, *The Executioner's Song*. Yet his greatest literary success and influence with young America spanned the 1950s and 1960s when he both fed and absorbed the beat rebels and counterculture protesters.

See also Beat; March on the Pentagon, 1967.

References Adams, Laura, *Existential Battles: The Growth of Norman Mailer* (1976); Bufithis, Philip H., *Norman Mailer* (1978); Ehrlich, Robert, *Norman Mailer: The Radical as Hipster* (1978); Glenday, Michael K., *Norman Mailer* (1995); Mailer, Norman, *Advertisements for Myself* (1959); *An American Dream* (1965), *The Armies of the Night: History as a Novel/The Novel as History* (1968), *Barbary Shore* (1951),

Cannibals and Christians (1966), *The Deer Park* (1955), *Miami and the Siege of Chicago* (1968), *The Naked and the Dead* (1948), *Of a Fire on the Moon* (1970), *The Short Fiction of Norman Mailer* (1967), *The White Negro: Superficial Reflections on the Hipster* (1957), and *Why Are We in Vietnam?* (1967); Manso, Peter, ed., *Mailer: His Life and Times* (1985); Merrill, Robert, *Norman Mailer* (1978) and *Norman Mailer Revisited* (1992); Mills, Hilary, *Mailer: A Biography* (1982); Poirier, Richard, *Norman Mailer* (1972); Rollyson, Carl E., *The Lives of Norman Mailer: A Biography* (1991); Scott, Nathan A., Jr., *Three American Moralists: Mailer, Bellow, Trilling* (1973); Wenke, Joseph, *Mailer's America* (1987).

Make Love Not War

At first hippies, and then other countercultural young people, used the phrase "make love not war" to express their desire for an alternative to straight society's attachment to violence and war. "Make Love Not War" appeared on protest placards and, in commercialized form, on posters.

The Mamas and the Papas

With their roots in folk music, the Mamas and the Papas produced eight top-30 rock singles in the sixties, enrapturing audiences with imaginative songwriting and beautifully blended harmonies. Their biggest hit, "California Dreamin'," reached the top ten after an unusual circumstance.

The Mamas and the Papas comprised John Phillips, his wife Michelle Phillips, Denny Doherty, and "Mama" Cass Elliot, each of whom had been members of folk groups. In 1965, they met Barry McGuire in Los Angeles. McGuire had just recorded a hit single, "Eve of Destruction," and asked them to back him on an album he was completing for producer Lou Adler at Dunhill Records. They agreed, and while in the studio they auditioned for Adler. Riveted by their performance, he immediately signed them to a contract.

Meanwhile, they completed singing backup on McGuire's album, including the cut "California Dreamin'," which John Phillips had written. After hearing the song, Adler decided it could be a big hit for the Mamas and the Papas, and although he left "California Dreamin'" on McGuire's album, he rushed the new group back into the studio to record it. In order to save money, however, he did not start from scratch but rather edited McGuire's voice from the tape and had the Mamas and the Papas add more of their own vocals. His hunch proved correct, and in 1966 "California Dreamin'" hit the top ten.

The Mamas and the Papas followed this with additional big-selling singles and albums, such as "Monday, Monday" on *If You Can Believe Your Eyes and Ears* and "I Saw Her Again" on *The Mamas and the Papas*. Each song seemed to exceed the other in its elaborate harmonies.

The Mamas and the Papas helped organize the highly successful 1967 Monterey Pop Festival, at which they appeared. The group split up the following year, with only Mama Cass Elliot scoring hits in a solo singing career. John Phillips re-formed the Mamas and the Papas with new personnel in 1971, but it failed. Elliot died of a heart attack on 29 July 1974. Michelle Phillips, divorced from John Phillips, had some success as an actress in the late seventies and early eighties.

See also "Eve of Destruction"; Monterey Pop Festival; Rock Music.

References Phillips, John, *Papa John: An Autobiography* (1986); Phillips, Michelle, *California Dreamin': The True Story of the Mamas and the Papas* (1986).

Mandala

Many a mandala graced hippie walls in the sixties. These geometric designs symbolize the universe and are used in Hinduism and Buddhism as an aid to meditation. Eastern religions appealed to the counterculture as mystical alternatives to Christianity.

Manson, Charles (1934–)

A psychotic murderer, Charles Manson committed a heinous crime that mainstream society pointed to as exemplifying a counterculture gone wrong. "Blood orgy," one newspaper called it; "Ritual killings," said another about the Tate-LaBianca slayings.

Manson's childhood portended trouble. He was born on 12 November 1934 in Cincinnati, Ohio, the illegitimate son of 16-year-old Kathleen Maddox. In 1939, she and a brother robbed a gas station, and during her subsequent five-year prison sentence an aunt and uncle raised Manson in McMechen, West Virginia. He lived with his mother again after her release on parole in 1942, but four years later she placed him in a school for boys.

Manson, though, ran away and began burglarizing stores. He committed his first armed robbery at age 13 and as a result was sentenced for three years to the Indiana School for Boys in Plainfield. Once again he escaped, and in 1951 fled to California, where he resumed his burglarizing. After his capture later that year, he was sent to the National Training School for Boys in Washington, D.C. A counselor there described him as antisocial, restless, and moody. In February 1952, Manson assaulted a boy at the training school, and the authorities, who considered him dangerous, transferred him first to Federal Reformatory at Petersburg, Virginia, and then to a high-security prison in Chillicothe, Ohio.

Manson compiled a good conduct record at Chillicothe and received parole in May 1954 at age 19. Crime, however, continued to be his life, and after he got married early in 1955, he returned to California. Over the next five years, Manson stole cars, worked as a pimp, and forged checks, leading to yet another arrest. In 1960, he began serving time at a federal

Psychotic murderer and hippie cult leader Charles Manson is brought to court on 15 January 1971 to hear the final arguments in the Tate-LaBianca murders. Manson and several of his "family members" were found guilty and sentenced to life imprisonment.

penitentiary on McNeil Island in Washington State. A psychiatric examination concluded Manson wanted to gain attention through negative acts and that he sought to find himself by pursuing different religious philosophies, such as Scientology and Buddhism. From these, though, he picked up only a few phrases and ideas.

In 1963, Manson's wife divorced him, and the following year, while still in prison, he obsessively followed a rock 'n' roll band, the Beatles. As parole approached, Manson begged the authorities to let him stay in prison, claiming he could not function in the outside world. They rejected his plea, and in March 1967 he returned to the larger society he found so alien.

By this time, the hippie counterculture had gained media attention, and Manson started hanging out in Haight-Ashbury, San Francisco's bohemian enclave. There during the Summer of Love, Manson found young people looking for someone and something to believe in, and through his pseudoreligious babble he developed a group of followers, the Manson Family—so tightly under his control that, in time, they would carry out his orders to kill.

The Manson Family moved about, and at one point stayed at the home of musician Dennis Wilson, who played with a prominent rock band, the Beach Boys. Wilson gave Manson money and even had some of his rock music recorded—Manson envisioned himself an artist who could rival the Beatles. After several months, Wilson evicted the Manson Family, and later said; "I'm the luckiest guy in the world, because I got off only losing my money." (Bugliosi and Gentry 1974, 251) He lost some sleep, though—on more than one occasion Manson threatened him.

Shortly before the Tate-LaBianca murders, Manson and his followers resided at the Spahn Ranch, about ten miles east of Beverly Hills. George Spahn, 81 years old and nearly blind, let the Manson Family use his ranch, unaware of Manson's doings, or even how many people Manson had brought with him. The Manson Family, numbering more than 20, comprised a few men, and many more women, joined together in part by drugs, more so by sex, and mostly by Manson's mysterious power—an ability to break down other peoples' values and replace them with his own.

On 9 August 1969, early in the morning, Manson and several family members entered a house rented by Sharon Tate, a movie actress married to famed director Roman Polanski (then away on location). There they found Tate; her ex-boyfriend Jay Sebring, an internationally renowned hair stylist; and two friends, Voytek Frykowski and Abigail Folger, heiress to a coffee empire. They tortured and killed all four—hanging the pregnant Tate from a rafter before finally stabbing her to death. Sometime during the crime, a teenage boy inadvertently stumbled onto the murderers, and they killed him, too. The next day, police officers found a gruesome scene, with the word "PIG" scrawled on a wall in blood.

The Manson Family struck again the following night, murdering Leno LaBianca and his wife, Rosemary, at their home. He was president of a supermarket chain in Los Angeles. Again, the police found a grisly scene, with the bodies bound and as at the Tate residence, mutilated—Leno LaBianca's body had a fork protruding from it and the word WAR carved into its stomach, and Rosemary LaBianca's body had 41 stab wounds. On a refrigerator door, the phrase "Helter Skelter" had been written in blood.

Initially, a motive for these murders remained elusive, and, in fact, one did not become clear until evidence at the two crime scenes led to the Manson Family and resulted in the police questioning them. The motive: Manson wanted to liberate whites and had ordered the murders hoping people would believe they had been committed by blacks; this, in turn, would lead to a race war. Manson believed that blacks would win the war, but once in power they would not know how to rule, or as he put it, "The only thing blackie knows is what whitey has told him." (247) At this point, he and his followers would emerge from hiding, take power, persecute blacks, and rule the world.

Manson based his belief on a strange reading of the Bible and of songs by the Beatles. He treated the Beatles' *White Album* as prophecy. For example, he believed "Blackbird" referred to blacks ready to arise, and he interpreted "Helter Skelter" as meaning his family would assume power and "Revolution 9" as proclaiming an impending Armageddon. In the Bible, the Book of Revelation attracted him: he considered the four angels to be the Beatles, and members of his family believed Manson to be the fifth angel.

Manson's arrest, and that of others in the family, caused a nationwide sensation and newspapers labeled him the "hypnotic hippie." This distorted the meaning of "hippie" and ignored substantial differences between most hippies and the Manson Family. For one, Manson said that he placed his faith in violence. For another, Manson and his followers came from unhappy homes and suffered from mental illness. A sociopath, Manson had frequently stopped priests in the street to tell them he was Jesus. (During his murder trial, he petitioned the judge for release, using the name Jesus Christ.) Manson, then, was less a hippie than an incorrigible, disturbed convict pulled into the alternative scene.

In an interview with *Rolling Stone* magazine, Manson said:

> If God is one, what is bad? Satan is just God's imagination. Everything I've done for these nineteen hundred and seventy years is now in the open. I went into the desert to confess to God about the crime I, you, Man has committed for 2,000 years. And that is why I'm here. As a witness. ("An Audience with Charles Manson" 1970)

Yet while the mainstream press used Manson's crime to smear hippies, some radicals contributed to the middle-class dislike for the counterculture by identifying with Manson as a persecuted individual. Jerry Rubin, for one, expressed his support for the murderer.

Manson's trial in 1970 resulted in a guilty verdict (handed down early in 1971), and he and several family members continue to serve time in prison for their role in the murders. (Manson was denied parole in the early 1990s.) In the sixties, some observers considered the Manson murders and the violence at the Altamont Rock Festival, which had happened at about the same time, as signs that excess had overtaken the counterculture and killed it.

See also Altamont.

References "An Audience with Charles Manson, aka Jesus Christ," *Rolling Stone*, 25 June 1970, 35+; Bugliosi, Vincent, and Curt Gentry, *Helter Skelter: The True Story of the Manson Murders* (1974); Sanders, Ed, *The Family: The Story of Charles Manson's Dune Buggy Attack Battalion* (1971).

March on the Pentagon, 1967

On 21 and 22 October 1967, antiwar protesters marched on the Pentagon in a demonstration signaling a new militancy. The National Mobilization Committee To End the War in Vietnam (MOBE) coordinated the march—if coordinated is the proper word, for many groups participated, and MOBE left each to pursue its own tactics. Thus, the demonstrators included famous writers and political ideologues, as well as people dressed as witches, wearing black-magic garb, who surrounded the Pentagon and chanted in an attempt to levitate the building and expel its evil spirits.

For the most part, the march, which attracted about 100,000 protesters, turned out to be peaceful. Notably, a small contingent walked up to the bayonet-wielding soldiers who guarded the Pentagon and placed flowers in their rifle barrels. But militants made their presence felt; some tried to break through the lines and enter the building. These included the noted author Norman Mailer, who recounted his experience in *The Armies of the Night:*

> "Go back" [an MP] said hoarsely to Mailer. . . .
> He had a quick impression of hard-faced men with grey eyes burning some transparent

> flame, and said, "I won't go back. If you don't arrest me, I'm going to the Pentagon," and he knew he meant it, some absolute certainty had come to him, and then two of them leaped on him at once in the cold clammy murderous fury of all cops at the existential moment of making the bust. (Mailer 1968, 130–131)

Still others, numbering a few hundred, gathered illegally in a parking lot near the building. And when several thousand protesters refused to leave the Pentagon grounds at curfew, federal marshals cleared them out with clubs and tear gas. In all, the authorities arrested more than 800 demonstrators.

The march signified a militancy born from frustration. Earlier protests against the war had been ineffective, and, in fact, the government had sent more troops to Vietnam. Within the counterculture this escalation indicated a bigger problem than the war itself: the entire system seemed unresponsive and corrupt, and the protests had to be intensified.

See also Hoffman, Abbie; Mailer, Norman; New Left; Rubin, Jerry.

Reference Mailer, Norman, *The Armies of the Night: History as a Novel/The Novel as History* (1968).

Marcuse, Herbert (1898–1979)

A Marxist philosopher, Herbert Marcuse served as an intellectual and spiritual leader to the New Left as it sought revolutionary change.

Marcuse was born into a wealthy family on 19 July 1898 in Berlin, Germany. He attended the University of Berlin and after obtaining his undergraduate degree, continued his studies at the University of Freiburg, where in 1922 he received a doctorate. He then researched and taught at the Institute of Social Research in Frankfurt until 1933, when Hitler closed it. Marcuse fled the Nazis and in 1934 immigrated to the United States. He taught at Columbia University and later, Harvard, Brandeis, and the University of California at San Diego.

In his two most prominent works, *Reason and Revolution*, published in 1941, and *One Dimensional Man*, published in 1964, Marcuse expounds a revised Marxist ideology. He rejects the notion of workers as the vanguard of a proletarian revolution and criticizes technocracy—domination by machines and elite experts—as repressive for regimenting people, whether within a socialist or capitalist system. The true revolutionary leaders against exploitive capitalism, he believes, will emerge from young college students, urban blacks, and third-world peoples. He considers the laboring class in America too numbed by materialism to revolt. Revolutionary ideals, he says, should not be compromised, and toward this end the young must refuse capitalism and consumerism.

Marcuse's works had an enormous impact on the radical New Left; many in the movement read *Reason and Revolution* and *One Dimensional Man* avidly, coming away convinced that society could be improved only through revolution. While at San Diego, Marcuse inspired one of his students, Angela Davis, who soon embraced black militancy. Shortly before his death, Marcuse, unchanged in his views, looked back on the 1960s and declared that the leftist movement had failed not because of ideological deficiencies but because the national government had "murdered" it.

See also Davis, Angela; New Left; Students for a Democratic Society.

References Marcuse, Herbert, *One Dimensional Man: Studies in the Ideology of Advanced Industrial Society* (1964) and *Reason and Revolution: Hegel and the Rise of Social Theory* (1941).

Marijuana

Marijuana—hemp, pot, weed, bhang, ganja—captivated the counterculture. Psychologist Timothy Leary, writing during the sixties in the *Marihuana Papers*, says:

> The number of pot smokers worldwide is larger than the population of the United States of America. It is safe to say that there are more pot smokers than there are members of the middle class throughout the world. Indeed, we have the astonishing spectacle of a middle-class minority, tolerant to alcohol and addicted to bureaucracy, passing laws against and

interfering with the social-religious rituals of a statistically larger group! Think about that one. (Solomon 1966, 87)

A worldwide use of marijuana? For centuries, human beings have cultivated this plant, *cannabis sativa*, in China, India, Africa, Europe, and later, the Americas. The male plant provides a fiber called hemp, used to make rope and cloth. (British colonists harvested this back in the eighteenth century, George Washington among them.) The female plant yields from its flowers tetrahydrocannabinol, better known as THC. Ingested through smoking or eating, THC alters the consciousness. At least 1,600 years ago Hindus in India used marijuana for enlightenment, and Indian religious philosophy has long been tied to the plant.

THC comes in different forms: bhang, lowest in potency and most known in the United States; ganja, more potent, from higher-quality plants; and hashish, concentrated in the plant resin and eight times more powerful than marijuana THC. Whatever the form, marijuana is illegal in the United States, a result of legislation in 1937 passed after exaggerated stories scared the public into thinking marijuana deranged people mentally.

To many young people in the sixties, these stories only showed the deceit and hypocrisy of the older generation. Marijuana, they insisted, produced euphoria without the toxic or addictive harm obtained from alcohol. (Actually, it can cause psychological dependence.) How could older Americans, they questioned, berate marijuana while at the same time consume alcohol?

Typically found in the 1950s only in black urban areas and among beatniks, a decade later, marijuana emerged as the drug of choice, after alcohol, among college students. While they consumed pot for its euphoric effect, something else made it central to the counterculture: a shared experience, and an illegal one at that. Sitting together, hand-rolling a joint, passing the water pipe, the Beatles or Neil Young playing in the background resulted in bonding. Writing in *Acid Dreams*, Martin A. Lee and Bruce Shlain state: "Dope was an initiation into a cult of secrecy, with blinds drawn, incense burning to hide the smell . . . as the joint was ritualistically passed around a circle of friends." (129) The underground press advertising roach clips, the Zig Zag man, what do you do at Itchycoo Park . . . you get high there—young people shared what their parents did not.

In a sense, the mainstream establishment had it correct: marijuana could corrupt. A youngster smoking pot was more receptive to countercultural ideas that challenged prevailing practices. As a leader of the Free Speech Movement said: "When a young person took his first puff of psychoactive smoke, he . . . drew in the psychoactive culture as a whole, the entire matrix of law and association surrounding the drug, its induction and transaction. One inhaled a certain way of dressing, talking, acting, certain attitudes. . . . You couldn't smoke dope without being an outlaw and being against the state, because the state was out to get your ass." (ibid.)

See also Acid; Hashish; Leary, Timothy.

References Lee, Martin A., and Bruce Shlain, *Acid Dreams: The CIA, LSD, and the Sixties Rebellion* (1985); Lindesmith, Alfred R., *The Addict and the Law* (1965); Solomon, David, ed., *The Marihuana Papers* (1966); Tart, Charles T., *On Being Stoned* (1971).

Marrakech

Marrakech, Morocco's second largest city, and known for its abundant and relatively cheap supplies of marijuana and hashish grown in the Rif Mountains near the Mediterranean Sea, thrived as a destination point for American and European hippies. Teahouses dotted the city, as they had for generations, where Moroccans gathered to smoke hashish stuffed in tiny pipes. Now the counterculture joined them.

Marvel Comics

During the 1950s, Marvel Comics created superhero legends that influenced many youngsters who, a decade later, constituted the counterculture.

Martin Goodman, a publisher of pulp magazines, began Marvel Comics in 1939. Marvel's first superhero characters, the Human Torch and Sub-Mariner, launched an entire line of similar figures, including Captain Marvel, and helped propel the company into a dominant position within the comic-book industry.

In the 1950s, Marvel's stories reflected cold-war anxieties, namely the threats from communism and nuclear weapons. Captain America and other characters stood tall against these threats, and in fighting for goodness, meaning the American way, they presented a simplistic picture that infatuated young people.

While Marvel's readers liked the moral stories these works contained, they liked, too, their fantastic and bizarre tales. In fact, these themes so permeated the comics that the government investigated Marvel and other companies. This, however, only attracted more kids—something neat had to be going on, they figured, if adults were considering censorship.

Although the comic-book companies subsequently sanitized and homogenized their material, their mythic heroes still possessed unique qualities that said people could succeed without embracing every adult value. Their simplistic stories said that the older generation had messed up the world. The counterculture took them to heart.

See also *Mad.*

References Benton, Mike, *The Comic Book in America: An Illustrated History* (1989); Daniels, Les, *Marvel: Five Fabulous Decades of the World's Greatest Comics* (1991).

Max, Peter (1937–)

Blue, pink, yellow, electric flowers and star-studded skies—psychedelic electric . . . this characterized the designs created by Peter Max, a pop culture artist who captured the counterculture visual style.

Max was born on 19 October 1937 in Berlin, Germany, but when World War II erupted, he moved with his family to Shanghai, China. There his father prospered as a pearl merchant, and young Max spent considerable time with Buddhist monks. In 1950, his family moved again, this time to Israel. A third move occurred in 1953, to the United States, where Max attended Lafayette High School in Brooklyn, New York. He developed an interest in art, and studied for five years at the Art Students League, the Pratt Graphic Arts Center, and the School of Visual Arts, after which, in 1962, he and a partner founded the Daly-Max Studio, a graphic arts business. Max achieved immediate success designing illustrations for record albums and book jackets.

But in 1965, he quit his business and began a two-year hiatus, accepting few commissions and delving instead into Eastern mysticism, studying with a Hindu holy man and learning yoga. He emerged from this stage rejuvenated and in 1967, began making designs, usually from crayon or felt pen, applied to tableware, book covers, fabric, rugs, and other mass-produced items. Young people liked his psychedelic style that used stars, bold letters, and numerous colors to convey love and joy. By 1968, a company had begun marketing his posters, selling more than a million per year.

At the same time, Max won a commission from the Metro Transit Advertising Company to provide posters for the buses and subways that used the company's advertising services in New York City, Chicago, and other locations. Max considered this a way to bring art to the masses. Some critics called him little more than a smart commercial businessman, but others hailed his boldness and his ability to maintain an inner peace based on his continued involvement with Eastern religion.

See also Warhol, Andy.

Reference Max, Peter, *The Peter Max Poster Book* (1970).

May Day Protest

By 1970, the Vietnam War had so disrupted and demoralized most Americans that they wanted the United States to withdraw its troops. This atmosphere produced record turnouts that year for antiwar demonstrations, overwhelmingly peaceful in character. One in particular, though, resulted in violence: the May Day Protest. Activist Rennie Davis and about 30,000 protesters camped in the nation's capital at Potomac Park, calling themselves the May Day Tribe and proclaiming their intention to disrupt the government.

President Richard Nixon decided to act first and arrested several hundred protesters in their encampment. Then on Monday, 3 May, the Tribe set up barricades and blocked traffic. Nixon immediately sent 10,000 troops into the city, where, carrying machine guns, they patrolled the streets and perched on the rooftops of government buildings. Mass arrests followed—the government detained about 12,000 people at the Washington Coliseum and in a fenced-off field near RFK Stadium. At the same time, Nixon's officials labeled the protesters dangerous traitors and denied claims that the president intended to run a police state.

Nixon's real objective may have been to tie up dissident leaders in court, a tactic he had used before as a way to keep such people too occupied with their own defense to plan any further demonstrations. The trials involving the May Day protesters resulted in only 63 guilty verdicts out of 12,000 arrests, and later the protesters filed a class-action suit against the federal government for violating their rights and won.

See also Davis, Rennie.

May 2nd Movement

The May 2nd Movement (M-2-M), named after the date of a street demonstration in New York City, emerged as an offshoot to the Progressive Labor (PL) organization and advocated a third world–style revolution in the United States, an uprising by the oppressed through guerrilla activity.

PL, which promoted a pro-Chinese Marxist ideology, organized M-2-M in 1964 to agitate on college campuses against the Vietnam War. Among its activities, M-2-M circulated a "We Won't Go" petition, calling on students to refuse service in the military.

A small group never numbering more than a few hundred, M-2-M believed that Third World Marxist revolutions would play a crucial role in destroying American imperialism. But despite this ideology, M-2-M soon had a falling out with PL. From PL's standpoint, M-2-M had embraced ideological impurities, meaning an incorrect Marxism. Part of the acrimony, however, came from M-2-M's disenchantment with PL's centralized leadership, which sought to dictate all policy, and PL's criticism of M-2-M members for adopting long hair, drugs, and sexual freedom that separated them from the industrial workers—important people in any socialist advance. As a result, in February 1966, PL disbanded M-2-M. Subsequently, several M-2-M activists went on to help found an anti-PL group, Weatherman.

See also Mellen, James; New Left; Progressive Labor; Students for a Democratic Society; Weather Underground.

Reference Jacobs, Harold, ed., *Weatherman* (1970).

Means, Russell (1940–)

A leader in the American Indian Movement (AIM), Russell Means worked to protect Indian treaty and civil rights against government oppression and exploitation.

Born on the Pine Ridge Reservation of South Dakota in 1940, Means was raised in the Oakland, California, area by his father, part Oglala and part Irish, and his mother, a Yankton Sioux. He held several jobs, among them rodeo rider and public accountant, before joining AIM around 1970. In 1972, Means led a protest in Gordon, Nebraska, that resulted in the police arresting two white men involved in the murder of an Indian.

The following year, Means and 200 other AIM protesters held a press conference at Wounded Knee on the Pine Ridge Reservation and, in the wake of continued injustices against Indians, demanded recognition as a sovereign nation. The protesters found themselves surrounded by police allied with a corrupt Sioux tribal president, Dickie Wilson, and by federal marshals. Means and the others reacted by taking over a trading post and confiscating its rifles and ammunition. A long siege began, and before it ended in May, several gunfights erupted, leaving two AIM protesters dead and a federal marshal wounded. Means stood trial on ten felony counts, but the prosecution so flagrantly violated the rules of legal conduct that the judge threw out the charges.

Means ran against Wilson for the tribal presidency in 1974 but lost in a close election noted for Wilson's ballot tampering. Tension continued on the Pine Ridge Reservation between Wilson and Means, and numerous confrontations eventually led to Means's arrest and sentence to one year in prison on an assault charge. After his release, Means continued in the 1980s to work for Indian rights. He left AIM in 1988, claiming it had accomplished its goals, and four years later he played the role of Chingachgook in the movie *The Last of the Mohicans*.

See also American Indian Movement; Banks, Dennis; Peltier, Leonard.

Mellen, James (1935–)

James Mellen held prominent positions within several New Left organizations, including Students for a Democratic Society (SDS) and Weatherman, in which he promoted revolutionary Marxism.

Born in Los Angeles, California, in 1935, Mellen was raised by his mother, who worked as a drugstore clerk. In the mid-1950s, he attended community college and then enrolled at the University of California-Los Angeles but dropped out. He spent several years wandering, selling portrait photography before reading Jack Kerouac, whose beatnik style intrigued him. In 1959, he moved to San Francisco and lived as a bohemian. More politically minded than most beatniks, however, Mellen gravitated toward the emerging protest movement in the Bay Area.

In 1960, he enrolled at San Francisco State College, excelled in political science, and received a scholarship to graduate school at the University of Iowa. There, among the placidity of midwestern values, his radicalism developed. He joined the Socialist Discussion Club, which exposed him to Marxism and activism. In 1964, he graduated with a doctorate in political science, moved to New York City, and taught foreign affairs at Drew College in Morristown, New Jersey.

At this time, Mellen attended meetings of a small Maoist party, Progressive Labor (PL), that supported China in its dispute with the Soviet Union and advocated Communist revolution in the United States. He soon joined the May 2nd Movement (M-2-M), an organization formed by PL to activate college students against the Vietnam War. In 1965, Mellen and several others founded Free University (FUNY) in New York's Greenwich Village. An alternative college, FUNY offered radical courses on China, Marxism, and revolution. Mellen served as FUNY's secretary-treasurer, but the school folded within two years.

After PL disbanded M-2-M in 1966, Mellen traveled to Africa, where he taught at the University of Dar es Salaam in Tanzania and learned about third-world conditions, including the harm caused by U.S. imperialism. Upon his return to America in April 1968, Mellen helped form Third World Marxists as a faction within SDS to offset PL's influence within that organization. Within a few months, Third World Marxists controlled one of SDS's national offices.

Mellen wanted to change SDS into a completely Marxist revolutionary organization committed to street fighting as a way to weaken American imperialism by weakening the government. This, he believed, would help third-world nations and eventually end capitalism. But he believed that in order to succeed, he had to get PL expelled from SDS. Mellen and his supporters in Third World Marxists, now known as Weatherman after the lyrics in a Bob Dylan song, accomplished this in June

1969 at an acrimonious SDS National Convention in Chicago. The expulsion, however, shattered SDS—a result Mellen neither intended nor desired.

Mellen objected to Weatherman's having alienated moderate activists and having hastened SDS's demise. He subsequently maintained an ambivalent relationship with Weatherman, heading its efforts in Michigan but keeping his distance from the national leadership. His failure to recruit working-class youths in Detroit hindered a showdown Weatherman scheduled for Chicago in October 1969, called National Action.

Weatherman intended National Action to ignite a revolution by showing the group's bravery through violence. Much to Mellen's dismay, when he and several hundred Weathermen arrived at Chicago they found few other supporters. Despite this, the group went ahead and rampaged through Chicago's streets over a three-day period that newspapers called the Days of Rage. (Interestingly, Weatherman still showed some restraint by refusing to acquire and use guns.)

Mellen escaped arrest. When, early in 1970, Weatherman decided to take its activities underground and engage in terrorist attacks against government buildings, he broke with his colleagues. "I was reluctant to quit. I couldn't give in," he said later. But he felt demoralized, and so while other Weathermen busied themselves detonating bombs, he quit the movement.

See also Boudin, Kathy; Days of Rage; Dohrn, Bernardine; Free University; May 2nd Movement; New Left; Rudd, Mark; Students for a Democratic Society; Weather Underground.

References Sale, Kirkpatrick, *SDS* (1973); Viorst, Milton, *Fire in the Streets: America in the 1960s* (1979).

Merry Pranksters

See Kesey, Ken.

Mescaline

A hallucinogenic or psychedelic drug, mescaline provided the trip recounted in Aldous Huxley's seminal work, *The Doors of Perception*, and those in the counterculture seeking mysticism embraced it. Mescaline can be obtained in two ways: from the mescal plant, a cactus found in Mexico and the southwestern United States, or from synthesizing the drug in a lab. Mescaline was first produced this way by a German scientist in 1919.

Huxley, a British author who, in the 1930s, wrote *A Brave New World*, brought mescaline to prominence among artists and intellectuals after he took it for the first time in 1953 and wrote *Doors*. Huxley called his drug trip "without question the most extraordinary and significant experience this side of a Beatific Vision." (Lee and Shlain 1985, 46) He insisted that a person who steps through the door in the wall and enters a mystical realm "will never be quite the same as the man who went out. . . . He will be . . . better equipped to understand the relationship of words to things, of systematic reasoning to the unfathomable Mystery which it tries, forever vainly, to comprehend." (Huxley 1954, 79) Although within the counterculture LSD emerged as the psychedelic drug of choice for trying to overcome conformity and the ego and establish connection with a cosmic consciousness, some preferred mescaline, insisting it produced a more contemplative experience.

See also Alpert, Richard; Drugs and the Drug Culture; Huxley, Aldous; Leary, Timothy; LSD; Magic Mushrooms; Psilocybin.

References Huxley, Aldous, *The Doors of Perception* (1954) and *The Doors of Perception and Heaven and Hell* (1956); Lee, Martin A., and Bruce Shlain, *Acid Dreams: The CIA, LSD, and the Sixties Rebellion* (1985).

Midnight Cowboy

Released in 1969, the motion picture *Midnight Cowboy* reflects a deepening countercultural discontent with American society.

The movie stars Dustin Hoffman as Ratso Rizzo and Jon Voight as Joe Buck. Rizzo, a street hustler, and Buck, a dishwasher from a small town in Texas, meet in New York City, where they live together in a dilapidated apartment. Buck intends to survive by providing sexual favors for rich women, but he fails.

Director John Schlesinger portrays New York City, and by extension, society at large, as predatory and cruel—an emphasis so intense that film critic Pauline Kael remarked: "The point of the movie must be to offer us some insight into two derelicts . . . but Schlesinger keeps pounding away at America, so determined to expose how horrible people are . . . [that] his spray of venom is just about overpowering . . . ." (Kael, "Midnight Cowboy" 1995)

Young people flocked to the movie for its explicit sexual content—itself indicating how public morality had changed during the 1960s—and its bleakness that seemed to complement their feelings about a society torn by war, racism, and riots. . . . in short, a nation near collapse.

Reference Kael, Pauline, "Midnight Cowboy," *Cinemania 1996* (1995).

Miniskirt

The miniskirt that ended well above the knee appeared in 1962 and remained popular with younger women through the decade. French designer Andre Courreges introduced the miniskirt, and two English designers helped popularize it, Mary Quant and John Bates, the latter lifting the hemline yet higher. "Recently imported from Paris," said *Time* magazine in 1965, "the short, short skirt has been gleefully adopted by the avant-garde among U.S. teen-agers and coeds as the perfect complement to patterned stockings and leather boots—usually white." The magazine continued:

> From San Francisco coffeehouses to Manhattan discotheques, girls are beginning to reveal more thigh than they have stocking to cover, and American males are scrambling for the best vantage point. ("1960s Highlights—Fashion" 1995)

The miniskirt reflected liberated sexual attitudes evident in other public forms, from movies and books to topless bathing suits and see-through pants. Yet many women did not "gleefully" accept miniskirts; instead, they disliked them for exposing unattractive knees and considered them awkward and uncomfortable. When a woman wearing a miniskirt sat down, she had to struggle in order to limit the exposure.

See also Topless Bathing Suit.

Reference "1960s Highlights—Fashion," *Time Almanac of the 20th Century* (1995).

MOBE

See National Mobilization Committee To End the War in Vietnam.

Mod

Mod emerged in the mid-sixties as a shortened version of the word modernist. For young people, it meant those who wore hip, modern-style clothes. This entailed colorful shirts or blouses; tight, hip-hugging jeans held up by wide belts; and boots. Girls might forego the jeans for miniskirts, and mod boys wore their hair Beatles-style.

The clothes indicated an attitudinal difference from other youths; where mods congregated they listened to the hippest rock music. In some locations, antagonism existed between mods and surfers, with the former considering surf music and the beach scene as gauche. The mod category, however, quickly dissolved as the hippies and other manifestations of the counterculture reached beyond California and spread across the nation.

The Monkees

If anyone needed an example of the mainstream establishment co-opting the counterculture, they got it with the Monkees. The group did not exist until two television producers decided to create a rock band around which a series could be built and money generated. In September 1965, the producers advertised for "four insane boys, aged 17 to 21." They selected Mickey Dolenz, Peter Tork,

Robert "Mike" Nesmith, and David Jones. Don Kirschner, president of Colgems Records, trained the young men, who had some previous musical experience, in singing and working together as a band.

In August 1966, the Monkees scored a hit with their first single, "Last Train to Clarksville." Interestingly, because they had not yet jelled as a band, they sang the vocals on the record but did not play the instruments. Colgems released the group's first album, *The Monkees*, in September to coincide with the premier of their television show, which bore the same name. In its style, the show copied *A Hard Day's Night*, the Beatles' hugely successful movie.

The Monkees, both album and show, attracted teeny-boppers and provided the vehicle for selling Monkees merchandise: clothing, key chains, lunch boxes, ad infinitum. The band's success revealed rock as an industry, geared to promotion and profits—social consciousness smothered, lyrics sanitized, commercialism fulfilled. (Although in a peculiar twist, one of the Monkees donated money to a hippie underground newspaper.)

The Monkees had a short life, however, with their TV show and records fading from the scene after 1968. The group minus Mike Nesmith got together in 1986, played concerts, and released a new record that sold moderately well. They toured again in 1996.

See also Rock Music; Teeny-Bopper.

Monterey Pop Festival

Great music, peace, and tremendously good vibes characterized the 1967 Monterey International Pop Festival in California, the first rock festival of the counterculture.

The idea for this event came from Ben Shapiro, a Los Angeles promoter, who had been impressed by the Human Be-In held earlier that year in San Francisco and thought the format could be modified into a profit-making venture. He and his partner, Alan Pariser, raised some money, leased the Monterey County Fairgrounds near San Francisco, and signed Indian musician Ravi Shankar. But Shapiro and Pariser lacked the funds needed to lure additional acts, at which point John Phillips, of the Mamas and the Papas rock group, and singer Paul Simon convinced them to make the event an artist-run nonprofit festival. The two promoters and their publicist, Derek Taylor, agreed, and Lou Adler, Phillips's manager, stepped in, took over the bookings, and defrayed expenses by negotiating a contract with ABC television to film the event.

Monterey turned out to be a tremendous success: many unknown bands received exposure; crowds teemed among the fairgrounds and nearby Monterey Peninsula College, where additional facilities had been leased; and harmony prevailed. On Friday, 16 June, the festival began with Eric Burdon and the Animals, along with Beverly (a folk singer), the Association, the Paupers, Johnny Rivers, and Simon and Garfunkel. In addition to the main show, a stage had been built where impromptu acts appeared, rooms had been set aside where meditation and a music industry colloquium were held, and camping areas had been hastily arranged for the many people who stayed overnight.

On Saturday morning, 17 June, the crowd surpassed 60,000—many dressed in bell bottoms, leather vests, and joyful colors—Diggers (a hippie group from San Francisco) gave away free fruit, and the Beatles conveyed a message: "Love to Monterey from Sgt. Pepper's Lonely Hearts Club Band." (Perry 1984, 206) Other than Canned Heat, a group from Los Angeles, San Francisco bands dominated the Saturday afternoon show: Big Brother and the Holding Company, Country Joe, Paul Butterfield, Quicksilver Messenger Service, Electric Flag, and Steve Miller. Outside the fairgrounds, the Grateful Dead and others staged free all-day jam sessions, while in the evening, inside the fairgrounds, Moby Grape, Jefferson Airplane, Buffalo Springfield, Booker T. and the MGs, Hugh Masekela, and Otis Redding performed.

Sunday afternoon featured Ravi Shankar, and that night's grand finale featured a return by Janis Joplin with her group Big Brother and the Holding Company, along with the appearance of a largely unknown English band called the Who, the Jimi Hendrix Experience, the Byrds, the Mamas and the Papas, Scott McKenzie, and the Grateful Dead, whose rhythm guitarist Bob Weir advised the audience to fold up its folding chairs and dance . . . and they did.

At a press conference during the festive weekend, Monterey police chief Frank Marinello praised the peaceful gathering and said: "I feel the hippies are my friends, and I am asking one of them to take me to the Haight-Ashbury." (209) Many police officers adorned their motorcycles with flowers. On a more practical level, Monterey led to several bands receiving national recording contracts and made Otis Redding, the Who, and Jimi Hendrix national acts. The 1968 movie *Monterey Pop*, filmed at the concert, drew large audiences across the nation.

See also: Be-In; Rock Music.

Reference Perry, Charles, *The Haight-Ashbury: A History* (1984).

Moody Blues

The Moody Blues rock band began as a British rhythm and blues group, but achieved its greatest success when it switched to a new form, psychedelic classical-rock.

The Moody Blues emerged in 1964, created by musicians who had experience with other bands, mainly in Birmingham, England. After signing a contract with Decca, the Moody Blues recorded a single that flopped and another, "Go Now," that in 1964 reached the top ten in both Britain and the United States.

Their album *Go Now: The Moody Blues #1*, released the following year, sold well, but it remained for *Days of Future Past*, released in 1968, to signal a different direction in their music and an even greater recognition. They recorded *Days* after a change in personnel that led to the idea for a classical-rock fusion, one emphasizing selling the album rather than a single. This LP included "Nights in White Satin," recorded with the London Festival Orchestra (a song unsuccessful as a single until its re-release in 1972). The Moody Blues got to record *Days* only after they convinced Peter Knight, the orchestra's conductor, to change his plans and abandon a strictly classical album to one using their music. Actually, the group only had enough songs for half an album, but Knight added classical links between the songs that filled it out.

After *Days*, the Moody Blues had three additional hit LPs in the late 1960s and early 1970s: *In Search of the Lost Chord*, *On the Threshold of a Dream*, and *Seventh Sojourn*. This band paved the way for other classical-rock, or art-rock, performers, a style that dominated the industry in the early 1970s with Pink Floyd, Yes, and similar groups. The Moody Blues continued performing concerts and recording music into the 1990s, their classical rock style largely unchanged.

See also Rock Music.

Moore, Barrington, Jr. (1913–)

College political activists looked up to Barrington Moore, Jr. in the sixties, a sociologist who wrote a monumental comparative history and insisted that sometimes revolution's benefits outweighed its detriments.

Moore was born in 1913 in Washington, D.C., the son of a wealthy Boston banker. He studied Greek and Latin at Williams College in Williamstown, Massachusetts, and received his doctorate in sociology from Yale. During World War II, he worked as a political analyst in the Office of Strategic Studies and in the Department of Justice. After the war, he taught briefly at the University of Chicago before moving in 1948 to Harvard. Beginning in 1951, he worked at Harvard's Russian Research center, and his earliest monographs analyzed developments in the Soviet Union.

Moore started writing his most important book in the mid-1950s and completed it ten years later. Titled *Social Origins of Dictatorship and Democracy*, it has been hailed as an intellectual work fully the equal in stature to Max Weber's *Protestant Ethic* and Emile Durkheim's *Suicide*. In *Social Origins*, Moore studies how the landed upper class and peasantry in selected American, European, and Asian societies contributed to modernization, and he studies the political systems that emerged from the process—both democratic and totalitarian.

In terms of the United States, he focuses on the Civil War and its aftermath, and concludes that the conflict only indirectly resulted from slavery; the main difference involved Northern industrial democracy versus Southern aristocratic agrarianism. A Southern victory, he says, would have legitimated an antidemocratic aristocracy. Instead, the Northern triumph made competitive democratic capitalism ascendant.

The conclusion in *Social Origins* that most appealed to college intellectuals dealt with revolution, in which Moore states that both Western liberalism and Soviet communism had evolved into obsolete systems used to justify oppression. Establishing a free society, he believes, requires revolutionary force, although as a last resort.

In the sixties, Moore appeared at several rallies against nuclear weapons and war. He criticized traditional pacifist tactics, such as those emphasizing the horrors of war, as failing to get at the root problems in society. Although Moore rejected Marxism and accepted democracy, even one built on capitalism, he claimed that the United States had developed into a reactionary nation oppressing third-world peoples, and that ending this system required extreme protest. He told college students: "The attempt to make practical proposals, constructive proposals, moderate and realistic proposals, is the most unrealistic thing you can do at this point." (Gitlin 1987, 100) He called, instead, for simultaneous revolutions in the United States and the Soviet Union. Moore's analysis caused some politicized students to conclude that peace could not be obtained within existing institutions, that salvation required revolution—not necessarily violent but certainly drastic.

References Gitlin, Todd, *The Sixties: Years of Hope, Days of Rage* (1987); Moore, Barrington, Jr., *Social Origins of Dictatorship and Democracy: Lord and Peasant in the Making of the Modern World* (1966); Smith, Dennis, *Barrington Moore: Violence, Morality, and Political Change* (1983).

Moratorium

On 16 October 1969, the *New York Times* carried the following headline on its front page:

> Bells Toll and Crosses Are Planted Around U.S. as Students Say "Enough!" to War

The accompanying story described how, on the previous day, there had occurred a massive, nationwide protest against the Vietnam War. Sam Brown and David Hawk, formerly associated with Senator Eugene McCarthy's 1968 presidential campaign, had developed the idea, called it the "Moratorium," and promoted the protest as a peaceful way to pressure Congress and President Richard Nixon to bring American troops home quickly. The Moratorium, which involved more than students, relied mainly on people ceasing their normal activities for one day: not going to work or class, for example, and instead going to church services for peace or participating in marches.

Americans did so by the millions. They wore black armbands and held vigils; over Boston, a skywriter wrote a peace symbol; Vassar College coeds walked onto the grounds at West Point and handed flowers to the cadets; nearly all the high school students in New York City stayed away from classes, as did many teachers; and 600,000 protesters gathered on the Mall in Washington, D.C.

Although Nixon declared himself unmoved, not willing to be pushed around by "the rabble in the streets," and instructed his vice-president, Spiro Agnew, to viciously criticize protesters as Un-American, the Moratorium boosted the antiwar movement and, unlike violent protests that had erupted earlier, won the hearts and support of people from many walks of life. One public opinion survey found Americans agreeing in overwhelming numbers with the statement "I am fed up and tired of the war." (Anderson 1995, 331)

Nixon had already declared Vietnamization—turning the American war effort over to the South Vietnamese. Now the pressure to quicken the pace and steady the resolve intensified.

See also Days of Rage; Democratic National Convention of 1968.

References Anderson, Terry H., *The Movement and the Sixties* (1995); Small, Melvin, *Johnson, Nixon, and the Doves* (1988).

Robin Morgan

Morgan, Robin (1941–)

A writer and activist, Robin Morgan described herself in the late 1970s as a "radical feminist" and as "one of the women who helped start this wave of feminism back in the Pleistocene Age of the middle and late 1960s." (Morgan 1977, 3)

Born in 1941 in Lake Worth, Florida, Morgan grew up in a one-parent family. Her parents divorced while she was still an infant, so her mother, Faith Berkely Morgan, raised her. She graduated from Columbia University in the early 1960s, married a poet, Kenneth Pitchford, and worked as a lexicographer for a book publisher while doing freelance editing.

Morgan participated in civil rights and antiwar demonstrations, and in the mid-1960s, as she adopted a socialist ideology, wrote many articles for New Left publications, among them *Liberation*, *Win*, *Rat*, and *The Guardian*. Yet something seemed wrong, something discriminatory and oppressive. She discovered that the New Left, much as mainstream society, relegated women to secondary positions.

As her feminist consciousness developed, she helped organize New York Radical Women, a group that initiated the idea to protest the 1968 Miss America Pageant in Atlantic City, New Jersey. According to Morgan, "Each work meeting with the organizers of the protesters was an excitement fix: whether we were lettering posters or writing leaflets or deciding who would deal with which reporter requesting an interview, we were affirming our mutual feelings of outrage, hope, and readiness to conquer the world." (62) Mutual feelings, solidarity, feminism—the protest called national attention to the commercial and sexual oppression of women. "It announced our existence to the world," Morgan said, "and is often taken as the date of birth of this feminist wave." (ibid.)

Morgan claimed she never deserted the New Left but wanted to take it further and confront sexism. She did so pointedly when, late in 1969, she announced she would cease writing for the leftist publication *Rat* because she could no longer tolerate its sexist hierarchy. A few months later, in January 1970, she supported feminists who forcibly took over the paper, and she wrote an article for *Rat*, a subsequently widely quoted tract in the women's movement: "Goodbye To All That." In it she says:

> White males are most responsible for the destruction of human life and environment on the planet today. Yet who is controlling the supposed revolution to change all that? White males. . . . It just could make one a bit uneasy. It seems obvious that a legitimate revolution must be led by, *made* by those who have been most oppressed: black, brown, and white *women*—with men relating to that the best they can. . . .
>
> Goodbye, Goodbye. The hell with the simplistic notion that automatic freedom for women—or nonwhite peoples—will come about ZAP! with the advent of a socialist revolution. . . . Two evils predate capitalism and have been clearly able to survive and post-date socialism: sexism and racism. . . .
>
> We are rising with a fury older and potentially greater than any force in history, and this time we will be free or no one will survive. *Power to all the people or to none*. All the way down, this time. (123–130)

In 1970, Morgan edited *Sisterhood Is Powerful: An Anthology of Writings from the Women's Liberation Movement* that includes historic documents from feminist activism and numerous articles pertaining to sexism. Her book influenced many women both within and outside the movement, opening their eyes to oppression in its many facets. Morgan, in fact, claimed *Sisterhood Is Powerful* deeply affected her, for as she toured the nation to speak with women about it, she discovered their widespread work on issues such as child care and abortion. "I felt as if I had discovered a whole new continent," she said, "the authentic Women's Movement." (120)

She encountered another influence too: *The Dialectic of Sex* written by Shulamith Firestone that criticized the National Organization for Women (NOW), a moderate women's rights group. Consequently, Morgan considered NOW's approach inappropriate, as wanting only limited reforms in women's second-class citizenship. She defined her radical feminism as a drive to uproot oppression and prevent it from continuing to "put forth the branches of racism, class hatred, ageism, competition, ecological disaster, and economic exploitation." (9)

Morgan continued to write into the 1990s, including poetry—notable for its militancy—*The Anatomy of Freedom*, an exploration of feminist consciousness, and *Sisterhood Is Global*, about international solidarity. Thus, she maintained her countercultural commitment to radical feminism.

See also Friedan, Betty; *Rat;* Redstockings; SCUM; Steinem, Gloria; Women's Movement.

References Firestone, Shulamith, *The Dialectic of Sex: The Case for Feminist Revolution* (1970); Morgan, Robin, *The Anatomy of Freedom: Feminism, Physics, and Global Politics* (1982), *Going Too Far: The Personal Chronicle of a Feminist* (1977), *Sisterhood Is Global: The International Women's Movement Anthology* (1984), and *Sisterhood Is Powerful: An Anthology of Writings from the Women's Liberation Movement* (1970).

Morrison, Van (1945–)

Reclusive, enigmatic, and seldom a big hit on the record charts, Van Morrison nevertheless shaped rock music through his diverse style and his influence on other musicians, a feat that made him rank among the foremost artists.

Morrison's interest in music came from his family background. He was born on 31 August 1945 in Belfast, Northern Ireland, to a mother who performed as a singer and to a father who collected blues and jazz records. Morrison began playing the guitar, saxophone, and harmonica early in his teens, and at age 15 quit school to join a rhythm and blues band that toured Europe. While in Germany, he acted in a movie, playing the roll of a jazz musician. He then returned to Belfast and formed the band Them, which attracted a local following and, by 1965, a following throughout Britain with its singles "Here Comes the Night" and "Gloria," the latter written by Morrison. After "Gloria" reached the record charts in the United States, Morrison embarked in 1966 on his first concert tour there.

Soon after returning to Britain, Morrison disbanded Them, went solo, and reached the top ten in 1967 with the single "Brown-Eyed Girl." In 1968, he completed his album *Astral Weeks*, recording it in just two days. Although *Astral Weeks* sold poorly, critics praised it for its Irish romantic mysticism, and many still consider it his best work. Music critic Greil Marcus said: "With *Astral Weeks*, Morrison opened the way to a new career, and established himself as a rock performer who deserved to be ranked with the creators of the very best rock and roll music." (Ward, Stokes, and Tucker 1986, 456) He had greater commercial success with his next album, *Moondance*, in 1970 and with the singles "Domino" and "Blue Money."

Morrison appeared on stage infrequently—he had a quirky, temperamental style and if upset, would sometimes leave the stage in midact. He professed no desire for creating an image: "I don't want to have one," he said. "I'm not interested in it. I went through that when I was a teenager. . . . Everybody's got different sides to them, but an image is like taking one thing and saying a person is *that*." (Cott 1978, 54)

Morrison's tendency to withdraw caused him to stop recording for long periods, sometimes two or three years. He kept making records in this sporadic fashion into the 1990s, displaying an amazing virtuosity with musical instruments and an eclectic taste that incorporated rock, blues, hymns, and traditional Irish folk music. His vocal style and articulate lyrics influenced musicians as diverse as Bruce Springsteen and Elvis Costello.

See also Rock Music.

References Cott, Jonathan, "Van Morrison," *Rolling Stone*, 30 November 1978, 50-54; Ward, Ed, Geoffrey Stokes, and Ken Tucker, *Rock of Ages: The Rolling Stone History of Rock & Roll* (1986).

Moses, Robert Parris (1935–)

With charisma and humility, Robert Moses helped organize the Student Nonviolent Coordinating Committee (SNCC) into a leading civil rights group that represented younger blacks and their desires.

Born on 23 January 1935 in New York City, Moses lived as a child in a public housing project near the Harlem River. He graduated from Stuyvesant High School in 1952, went from there to Hamilton College in Clinton, New York, where he received his B.A., and then on to Harvard, where, in 1957, he obtained a master's degree in philosophy.

Moses returned to New York City and taught at Horace Mann High School. At this time, the civil rights movement attracted him, and in 1960 he spent the summer in Atlanta, Georgia, working for the Southern Christian Leadership Conference (SCLC). Later that year, he recruited for a new organization, SNCC. This group took a more radical position toward the civil rights movement than the SCLC—it stressed sit-ins and similar activities involving primarily black college students.

In August 1961, Moses traveled to Mississippi, where in McComb he established the headquarters for a SNCC voter registration drive. To complement this, he set up a citizens' school whose teachers instructed blacks about the intricacies of registering to vote and boosted their morale. Moses experienced numerous hardships in Mississippi: he was brutally beaten by whites in the town of Liberty, and in October 1961 the police arrested him on trumped-up charges, forcing him to serve four months in jail.

Throughout this, his dedication won him many admirers, as did his belief that power should flow upward from the grass roots. Thus, he never sought personal aggrandizement; the reward, he believed, came in empowering local communities.

In 1964, Moses and another activist, Jim Forman, developed a plan to fight racism at the Democratic National Convention. Consequently, the Mississippi Freedom Democratic Party (MFDP) tried to oust the all-white Mississippi delegation (which had been chosen through segregated voting procedures). The plan faltered, however, when President Lyndon Johnson refused to back the MFDP. He did offer Moses a compromise: the right to seat two members of the MFDP as at-large delegates. Moses, however, recoiled at this. "We are here for the people," he said, "and . . . they don't want symbolic votes. They want to vote for themselves." (Viorst 1979, 267–268)

In 1964 and 1965, Moses participated in demonstrations against the Vietnam War, but the defeat of the MFDP so discouraged him that he wanted nothing more to do with whites. Coupled with this, new leaders within SNCC, particularly Stokely Carmichael, criticized Moses for not being forceful enough, and they believed the MFDP plan had been a naive one in relying on white liberal support. With these factors in mind, and with the possibility he might be drafted to fight in Vietnam, Moses left the United States for Canada in 1966. Two years later, he moved to Tanzania to teach at a rural school. Moses returned to the United States in 1976 and later studied philosophy at Harvard under a MacArthur Foundation Award.

See also Baker, Ella; Carmichael, Stokely; Student Nonviolent Coordinating Committee.

References Burner, Eric, *And Gently He Shall Lead Them: Robert Parris Moses and Civil Rights in Mississippi* (1994); Viorst, Milton, *Fire in the Streets: America in the 1960s* (1979).

Mother's

The first psychedelic nightclub in San Francisco, Mother's opened in the summer of 1965 with the Lovin' Spoonful, a band then riding high with a hit record. Tom Donahue established Mother's in North Beach, an old beatnik hangout. A 400-pound man who went by the nickname "Big Daddy," Donahue worked as a disk jockey on radio station KYA, managed several local bands, and promoted rock shows at the cavernous Cow Palace.

To make Mother's psychedelic, Donahue recruited artists and poets who painted huge murals and adorned even the bathrooms with artwork. Plastic paneling embedded with electric lights covered the walls and pulsated to the beat of rock music. With additional equipment, Mother's presented the first light show in a San Francisco nightclub.

The location of Mother's, however, was a disadvantage—young people avoided North Beach because it attracted too many tourists and was too distant from the hippie activity in Haight-Ashbury. As a result, although the Lovin' Spoonful packed Mother's, the crowds soon declined, and within a few months the nightclub closed.

See also The Family Dog; Rock Music.

Motown

Berry Gordy founded Motown records in Detroit, Michigan, and developed it into a highly profitable black-owned business, one that added a rock beat to rhythm and blues and produced a commercially appealing sound.

Gordy, a songwriter, started Motown in 1959 when he borrowed money to release two singles under the company's Tamla label. The records sold modestly, but in 1960 Gordy signed several acts that brought him greater success: the Marvalettes, the Temptations, and the Miracles. The latter group recorded under Gordy's Motown name and produced his first top-ten release. In 1964, Motown competed well with the British music invasion and scored hit after hit with yet more black performers appealing to white audiences, singers such as Mary Wells, the Four Tops, and the Supremes. Two years later, Gordy lured the Isley Brothers and Gladys Knight and the Pips from rival companies, and he bought out competing labels in Detroit.

Yet some chafed under Gordy's leadership. He established strict rules, keeping his writers and performers on a tight leash and limiting their royalties. This caused several top writers to leave the company in 1967 and contributed to a plunge in Motown's sales in the late sixties. As the decade came to an end, however, Gordy signed a new act that soon eclipsed all his other stars: the Jackson Five.

Motown continued to thrive in the 1970s, boosted by Stevie Wonder's popularity, and Gordy expanded the company to engage in film production. But it suffered new reverses in the eighties when the singers Marvin Gaye and Diana Ross left, and its original entertainers grew older. In 1988, Gordy sold Motown to MCA Records.

Despite its commercialism, the "Motown Sound" appealed to counterculture youths, much as Gordy had expected in pursuing his plan to produce black crossover hits. Sometimes it appealed in unusual ways, as when white radicals adopted a song by Martha and the Vandellas, "Dancing in the Street," as an anthem—a little rhythm to accompany a barricade.

See also Gaye, Marvin.

References Allyn, Douglas, *Motown Underground* (1993); Benjaminson, Peter, *The Story of Motown* (1979); Estleman, Loren D., *Motown* (1991); George, Nelson, *Where Did Our Love Go? The Rise and Fall of the Motown Sound* (1985); Gordy, Berry, *To Be Loved: The Music, the Magic, the Memories of Motown: An Autobiography* (1994); Taraborrelli, J. Randy, *Hot Wax, City Cool and Solid Gold* (1986); Waller, Don, *The Motown Story* (1985).

The Movement

When counterculture activists talked about the movement, they meant the efforts to reshape the American political system—efforts emanating from the civil rights crusade, and then expanding into a radical agenda. But in the late 1960s, the term took on an ambiguous meaning—sometimes referring only to political protests, at other times referring to the entire counterculture itself as a vast cultural, social, political challenge to mainstream society.

Even when speaking only of politics, the word "movement" reveals an incredible array of ideas and actions, usually equated with the New Left. Some political groups wanted to decentralize institutions and thus weaken the nation's corporate, military, and bureaucratic elite and empower people in their local communities—those usually ignored by the decision makers . . . such as blacks, Chicanos, and the poor. Other groups pursued specifically socialist, Marxist, or Maoist agendas. Movement organizations read like an ideological laundry list: Students for a Democratic Society, the Black Panthers, Progressive Labor, Third World Marxists, the Brown Berets, and many others—some focused on draft resistance or ending the war, others on black power or brown power, others on women's liberation, gay rights, or environmentalism.

Political groups in the movement adopted confrontational tactics from the belief that the establishment had developed into an unresponsive Goliath, as witness elections in which Republicans and Democrats offered no real choices. Movement activists thus engaged in picketing, sit-ins, marches, rent strikes, and economic boycotts. But just as the movement disagreed on ideology, it disagreed over tactics—how militant they should be, how much violence should be encouraged or used.

Given its diversity, the political movement never came together as a single force, despite the desires of radical leaders to mold it into a coordinated revolutionary upheaval. This turned out to be both its weakness and strength: on the one hand, movement groups often fell far short of their goals because they worked at cross-purposes; on the other, diversity allowed many different groups to express their desires unfettered by attachments to others.

By the late 1960s, the political movement had broadened and diversified to the extent that it had merged into the larger counterculture and could not be easily distinguished from cultural challenges to the mainstream, such as the formation of underground newspapers, the development of communes, and the use of street theatre. Thus, "movement" as a societal development and defining word grew more imprecise and encompassed anyone in the counterculture who strove to change society. One civil rights activist later said:

"Above all, the term 'movement' was self-descriptive. There was no way to join; you simply announced or felt yourself to be a part of the movement. . . . Almost a mystical term, 'the movement' implied an experience, a sense of community and common purpose." (Anderson 1995, xv–xvi)

Although weakest in the southern and Rocky Mountain states, and always a minority elsewhere, the movement appeared throughout the nation and affected all regions. It challenged nearly all institutions: churches, governments, corporations, the military—producing enormous confrontations between new and traditional ideas, the counterculture and middle America.

See also New Left.

Reference Anderson, Terry H., *The Movement and the Sixties* (1995).

Munchies

Munchies referred to marijuana-induced hunger pangs. A pot party ran the risk of inducing incredible raids on the refrigerator.

Muste, A. J. (1885–1967)

A curious mixture of pacifism and revolutionary Marxism, A. J. Muste gained the admiration of countercultural political activists for his principled stand against war.

Muste was born in the Netherlands in 1885 but in 1891 immigrated with his family to Grand Rapids, Michigan. He graduated from Hope College in Holland, Michigan, and in 1913 received a Bachelor of Divinity Degree from Union Theological Seminary in New York City. When the United States entered World War I, Muste took a pacifist stand.

In the 1930s, Muste founded the American Workers Party, a revolutionary Marxist group, and during World War II his pacifism led him to help find alternative service jobs for conscientious objectors. His activities in the 1950s brought him to the attention of young people who later constituted the counterculture. During that decade, Muste chaired the Committee for Nonviolent Action and opposed nuclear arms testing.

When, in the 1960s, college students began protesting the Vietnam War, Muste lent his support, and he wholeheartedly endorsed the most prominent New Left organization, Students for a Democratic Society. At one point, he traveled to Hanoi with two other clergymen to meet with North Vietnam's leaders and discuss the possibility of ending the war. A few weeks after the trip, on 11 February 1967, Muste died.

See also Students for a Democratic Society.

Reference Muste, Abraham John, *The Essays of A. J. Muste* (1967).

N

Nader, Ralph (1934–)

A pioneer consumer rights advocate, Ralph Nader first gained national attention in his battle with car manufacturers to get them to make safe vehicles. His efforts reinforced countercultural beliefs that corporate America cared only for itself in pursuing profits.

Ralph Nader was born the son of Lebanese immigrants on 27 February 1934 in Winsted, Connecticut. His father, strong-willed and self-righteous, instilled in him a commitment to justice, and in the evenings led family debates about responsibility to society. After graduating in 1951 from Winsted's Gilbert School, Nader enrolled in the Woodrow Wilson School of Public and International Affairs at Princeton University. There he displayed his trademark: battling the authorities, in this instance over the spraying of campus trees with DDT. He tried to get the university to stop using the chemical but failed.

Nader graduated *magna cum laude* from Princeton in 1955 and then entered Harvard Law School, where he won appointment as editor of *Harvard Law Review* and used the publication as a forum for social issues. He received his law degree in 1958 and after a brief stint in the army, began a small private practice in Hartford, Connecticut. At the same time, he traveled as a freelance writer to the Soviet Union, Africa, and South America, trips that exposed him to the great disparity in wealth between haves and have-nots and convinced him that American corporations, who wielded much power overseas, acted oppressively.

In 1964, Nader moved to Washington, D.C., where he worked as a staff consultant on highway safety to Daniel Patrick Moynihan, an assistant secretary of labor. Here Nader delved into automobile manufacturers and discovered they made unsafe cars for the sake of speed and appearance. His book *Unsafe at Any Speed*, published in 1965, recounted his findings and reached the best-seller list. General Motors, whom Nader criticized for making the dangerous Chevrolet Corvair, hired detectives to secretly investigate and harass him. They put together a dossier about his personal life but found nothing scandalous. When uncovered, the corporation's actions raised a brouhaha and assured passage of the Traffic and Motor Vehicle Safety Act of 1966 that set safety standards for cars sold.

The episode made Nader a hero to many Americans, especially young people already discontent with an impersonal and exploitive society. Nader's unorthodox way of living made him attractive, too: he resided in an efficiency apartment, owned no car, and used only $5,000 per year to meet his personal expenses.

After his successful battle with General Motors, in which sales of the Corvair plunged 93 percent and the company had to remove the car from the market, Nader embarked on other consumer campaigns. He toured the nation speaking about consumer rights, recruiting ordinary citizens to fight abuses by government and business, and motivating many law students to think about social issues rather than corporate jobs. He urged workers to become "whistle-blowers" and expose immoral or illegal acts by corporations. His statement that "there is a revolt against aristocratic uses of technology and a demand for democratic uses" (Anderson 1995, 345) corresponded with the counterculture's distaste for a technocratic society where experts had tremendous authority and the average citizen little.

Through Nader's efforts, Congress passed legislation establishing meat inspection and setting safety standards for natural gas pipelines. In 1969, he helped found the Center for the Study of Responsive Law in Washington, D.C., which investigated the influence wielded by corporations over federal regulatory agencies intended to protect the public. In 1970, Nader began the Public Interest Research Group to work for consumer reform, and the following year Public Citizen, a consumer lobbying organization intended to counteract corporation lobbies. He and his associates, dubbed "Nader's Raiders," exposed many unsafe corporate practices and various government failings. His actions helped shape or create several regulatory agencies, such as the Occupational Safety and Health Administration, the Environmental Protection Agency, and the Consumer Product Safety Commission.

Although his popularity and influence waned in the late 1970s, Nader continued into the 1990s as a fighter for consumer rights, and in 1996 ran unsuccessfully for president on the Green Party ticket.

References Anderson, Terry H., *The Movement and the Sixties* (1995); Nader, Ralph, *Unsafe at Any Speed: The Designed-In Dangers of the American Automobile* (1965).

Nark

The word *nark*, or *narc*, was short for narcotics officer. Hippies and other countercultural youths often used the term in fear, suspecting that the person next to them in beads and bell bottoms could be a nark. Or they used it in derogation, despising narks because of their devious ways.

National Mobilization Committee To End the War in Vietnam (MOBE)

Using the slogan "Confront the Warmakers!" the National Mobilization Committee To End the War in Vietnam, more popularly called MOBE, coordinated protests at the Pentagon in 1967 and at the 1968 Democratic National Convention in Chicago. MOBE evolved from the National Coordinating Committee To End the War, formed in 1965 as a loose alliance of pacifist and antiwar organizations.

MOBE's outspoken leader, David Dellinger, insisted that the organization should aim to "disrupt and block the war machine." (Farber 1994, 69) After activists Rennie Davis and Tom Hayden proposed demonstrations in Chicago, meetings to formulate a plan began in January 1968 in New York City. These and subsequent planning sessions held in various locations included representatives from several prominent groups opposed to the Vietnam War, among them The Resistance, the National Lawyers Guild, and the Socialist Workers Party.

MOBE neither functioned smoothly nor put together a coordinated protest at Chicago to build on the success at Washington. Many disputes erupted within MOBE as to tactics, and friction existed between MOBE and the Yippies, committed to street theatre, and Students for a Democratic Society, the nation's leading New Left organization, which refused to officially endorse the protest. After the Chicago demonstrations turned violent, divisions deepened in American society, not only between radicals and moderates but also within the radical movement itself.

See also Dellinger, David; Democratic National Convention of 1968; March on the Pentagon, 1967; Street Theatre; Yippies.

References Farber, David, ed., *The Sixties: From Memory to History* (1994); Halstead, Fred, *Out Now! A Participant's Account of the American Movement against the Vietnam War* (1978).

Nehru Jacket

The Nehru jacket had a brief fling in the late sixties as an alternative to the traditional suit jacket. The Nehru replicated that worn by Jawaharlal Nehru, who served as prime minister of India from 1947 to 1964: slim, hip-length, and buttoned in front to a straight, standing collar.

New Journalism

New journalism emerged as a part of the countercultural challenge to traditional literary forms. The new journalists believed that standard reporting, with its supposed objectivity and detached voice, neither interested readers nor revealed the fullness or true conditions of events. In terms of style, the new journalists wanted their stories to read like fiction. As Tom Wolfe writing in *The New Journalism* observes: "The idea was to give the full objective description, plus something that readers had always had to go to novels and short stories for: namely the subjective or emotional life of the characters." (21)

New journalists focused on detail to convey fullness; they used different and sometimes shifting points of view—perhaps the narrator's or the main participant's, or somebody else in the event—and they treated realism as central to the story to give it immediacy and build character and believability. Often, they included the reporter's own travails in obtaining the story as part of the account, sometimes founded on the belief that the reporter must experience that being reported to really know it. Thus, for example, George Plimpton wrote his book about quarterbacking a pro football team by actually working out in the Detroit Lions training camp and playing the position in a preseason game. In his book *Paper Lion* he says: "I came off the bench slowly, working my fingers up into my helmet to get at my ears. As I crossed the sidelines I was conscious then not only of moving into the massive attention of the crowd, but seeing ahead out of the opening of my helmet the two teams waiting." (230–231)

Four devices characterized new journalism: scene-by-scene construction (Gay Talese was noted for this, trying to bring out every point he wanted to make through a scene rather than through chronological narration); realistic dialogue; scenes presented through the eyes of a particular character; and everyday gestures, mannerisms, and accoutrements recorded to show how they symbolized a person's status. These devices, particularly the novel-like dialogue, appear in Gay Talese's *The Overreachers*, about a play opening on Broadway, where he writes:

> "Darling," said Nedda, her voice coming through over the clinking of glasses from Sari's, "darling, Dick Rogers wants to speak with you."
> "Hello, Josh?"
> "Hello, Dick!"
> "Now, listen, Josh, this thing you got here tonight, no crap, Josh, it was marvelous!"
> Logan seemed unable to speak. (Wolfe 1973, 78)

Truman Capote's *In Cold Blood* describes the town of Holcomb, Kansas, in engaging detail: "After rain, or when snowfalls thaw, the streets, unnamed, unshaded, unpaved, turn from the thickest dust into the direst mud. At one end of the town stands a stark old stucco structure, the roof of which supports an electric sign—dance—but the dancing has ceased and the advertisement has been dark for several years." (3–4)

Despite its commonalties, new journalism went in different directions with unique characteristics developed by its major practitioners, writers such as Talese, Wolfe, Capote, Terry Southern, Norman Mailer, and Joan Didion. Hunter S. Thompson wrote what he called Gonzo journalism—it communicated the essence of a situation by using contrived events, blurring the line between what "really" happened and what did not. Many traditionalists reacted to the new journalism by considering it an undisciplined form, well beneath them; but in portraying realism in different ways, the new journalists oftentimes pursued their subjects with greater intensity than found in the standard approach.

See also *The Electric Kool-Aid Acid Test;* Thompson, Hunter S.

References Capote, Truman, *In Cold Blood* (1965); Didion, Joan, *Slouching toward Bethlehem* (1968); Mailer, Norman, *The Armies of the Night: History as a Novel/The Novel as History* (1968); Plimpton George, *Paper Lion* (1965); Southern, Terry, *Red-Dirt Marijuana and Other Tastes* (1967); Talese, Gay, *The Overreachers* (1965); Thompson, Hunter S., *Fear and Loathing on the Campaign Trail '72* (1973) and *Hell's Angels: A Strange and Terrible Saga* (1966); Wolfe, Tom, *The Electric Kool-Aid Acid Test* (1968),

The New Journalism (1973), *The Pump House Gang* (1968), and *Radical Chic and Mau-Mauing the Flak Catchers* (1970).

New Left

"We have spoken at last with vigor, idealism, and urgency, supporting our words with picket lines, demonstrations, money, and even our own bodies. . . . Pessimism and cynicism have given way to direct action," so proclaimed Al Haber, a radical leader, in 1960 as the New Left emerged. (Anderson 1995, 61) No one at the time could precisely define New Left, and it took on several manifestations, but in general, New Leftists represented the politics of the counterculture, born on college campuses and committed to reforms, often radical, that would restore community and uplift the individual.

In the 1950s, an Old Left occupied liberalism's radical side. This group had matured during the Great Depression and had linked its crusades to labor unions, then fighting for recognition. Old Leftists widely debated Communist ideas and in a few instances embraced them and the class analysis they entailed. After World War II, young radicals considered the Old Left irrelevant, exhausted by attacks from conservatives during the Second Red Scare, also known as McCarthyism, and dispirited by overwhelming social conformity. In 1956, an article in the *National Guardian*, "The New Left: What Should It Look Like?" reinforced the belief that liberalism needed rejuvenation. Younger radicals sought fresh ideas and, most importantly, renewed action.

Al Haber, son of a prominent professor, sensed this discontent, not only in others but also in himself; as a college student at the University of Michigan he realized that the campuses, with their rapidly increasing enrollments, could serve as a vanguard for reform. In 1959, he convinced the League for Industrial Democracy, an Old Left organization, to change the name of its youth group to Students for a Democratic Society (SDS).

Haber recruited bright, motivated students into SDS, people such as Sharon Jeffrey, Robert Ross, and Tom Hayden. Although small in membership, SDS quickly emerged as the preeminent New Left organization.

At the same time, other changes external to the New Left affected its development. The first massive civil rights sit-in occurred in 1960 at Greensboro, North Carolina, initiated and led by black college students. And at Harvard and a few other universities, students participated in protests against nuclear weapons. These stirrings of politically minded young people infused the New Left with ideas and tactics.

Two years later, Tom Hayden and his SDS colleagues compiled the Port Huron Statement, considered to be the New Left manifesto. In it, they criticized society for its racism, poverty, and conformist oppression, and called for enhanced individual rights, community, and participatory democracy, which would lessen the power of the elite.

The New Left thus took on the tone of disenchanted white college students, raised in America's suburbs amid material comfort, who realized this comfort did not extend to all Americans. While they rejected class analysis, they employed its rhetoric and saw themselves as being readied to enter a new oppressed class: white-collar professionals programmed to make money for big corporations. The New Left realized, too, the glaring contradictions between prevailing democratic ideals and the existing racial segregation and corporate political power, along with a technocracy that said only experts know what is best for America.

New Leftists criticized both conservatives and liberals—the former for McCarthyism and the latter for selling out to a military state. To many young people, the Free Speech Movement at the University of California-Berkeley in 1964 revealed the oppression enforced by these groups. Both appeared united in keeping students from exploring divergent ideas.

Although white, largely male college students founded the New Left, the movement soon diversified, and the term itself described many different groups with many different liberal ideologies: the Student Nonviolent Coordinating Committee, the Black Panthers, the American Indian Movement, Chicano organizations, and women's liberationists. Although these groups often stood at odds with one another, to middle-class America they represented a uniform radical assault on traditional values and institutions. Yet despite the movement's influence and the fears it generated within the mainstream, one survey found that, in the late 1960s, only 3 percent of noncollege youth and only 13 percent of college students identified with the New Left.

In *We Are the People Our Parents Warned Us Against*, Nicholas von Hoffman calls the New Left an emotional political movement, operating on gut feeling and with "unqualified conviction" that gave it little desire to compromise. (132) Theodore Roszak in *The Making of a Counterculture* sees personal commitment as the hallmark of New Leftists. These factors appeared evident in the boldness and intransigence that characterized civil rights protests, antiwar marches, and the infamous demonstrations at the 1968 Democratic National Convention in Chicago.

Overall, the New Left shunned ideology, or at least refused to place it on a level higher than the individual. In fact, the SDS slogan "One man, one soul" proclaimed the dignity of each person to be more important than doctrine. But as the decade drew to a close, some groups rejected peaceful protest and wrapped themselves in self-proclaimed ideological purity (for example, Lenninism or Maoism) as they embraced class consciousness. In doing so, they distanced themselves from any who disagreed, and thus shattered the already decentralized New Left. Theodore Roszak notes that an "ideological drift toward righteous violence" resulted in part from "extremist Black Powerites and a romanticized conception of guerrilla warfare." (Roszak 1968, 60) A New Left group proclaimed: "We reject the elitist, technocratic bullshit that tells us only experts can rule, and look instead to leadership from the people's war of the Vietnamese." (Jacobs 1970, 70)

Talk of revolution filled the air and encouraged factional disputes and violence. Most prominently, a group called Weatherman broke away from SDS and pursued tactics such as bombing government buildings. Between September 1969 and May 1970, radicals, some associated with Weatherman, others not, bombed or attempted to bomb several hundred facilities, including draft boards and induction centers.

As the 1970s began, the New Left, like the Old more than a decade earlier, stood exhausted, torn by internal disputes, by rising middle-class opposition to extremism, and by government surveillance and harassment. Added to this, other developments within the counterculture overwhelmed the political activists—more young people turned their backs on politics and took to communes, travel, rock, and drugs. Indeed, many New Left organizations found themselves disoriented by this freewheeling cultural revolution.

Writing in *The Movement and the Sixties*, Terry H. Anderson says that "in a sense dope clouded the political focus." (290) Activist Jerry Rubin declared at the time that "grass destroyed the left," and a leader in SDS observed: "the ideals of the New Left have now merged into whole new cultural situations . . . the youth communities outside the system which may or may not have coherent politics." (ibid.)

Yet the New Left had activated many youths to work for change, and in the process it advanced civil rights, raised opposition to the Vietnam War, and produced a fundamental rethinking about the American political system.

See also Free Speech Movement; Hayden, Tom; Lynd, Staughton; The Movement; Students for a Democratic Society; Weather Underground.

References Anderson, Terry H., *The Movement and the Sixties* (1995); Bacciocca, Edward, Jr., *The New*

Left in America: Reform to Revolution, 1956 to 1970 (1974); Breines, Wini, *Community and Organization in the New Left, 1962–1968: The Great Refusal* (1989); Gitlin, Todd, *The Sixties: Years of Hope, Days of Rage* (1987) and *The Whole World Is Watching: Mass Media in the Making and Unmaking of the New Left* (1980); Isserman, Maurice, *If I Had a Hammer: The Death of the Old Left and the Birth of the New Left* (1987); Jacobs, Harold, *ed., Weatherman* (1970); Miller, James, *Democracy Is in the Streets: From Port Huron to the Siege of Chicago* (1987); Roszak, Theodore, *The Making of a Counterculture: Reflections on the Technocratic Society and Its Youthful Opposition* (1968); Unger, Irwin, *The Movement: A History of the American New Left, 1959–1972* (1974); Von Hoffman, Nicholas, *We Are the People Our Parents Warned Us Against* (1968).

New Mexico

Why did so many hippies move to New Mexico in the late sixties? The open spaces, the beautiful scenery, an atmosphere quite different from other states with its Chicano and Indian pueblo cultures—all attracted the counterculture. So, too, did a desire by hippies to leave the cities, where cops hassled them and urban crowds stifled them. So they settled in Santa Fe, Taos, Aspen Meadows. They opened macrobiotic restaurants, organic food stores, pottery shops, and yoga centers. In the countryside they went into farming and ranching, either individually or communally.

One hippie observer, writing in 1969, said: "The Longhair, at his very best, attempts to synthesize the virtues of the Indian and Chicano ways of life." (Goodman, Mitchell 1970, 702) He went on to say that difficulties faced even the "most enterprising freaks" from antihippie attitudes stirred by a few inconsiderate hippies who disrespected the local culture.

See also Back-to-the-Earth Movement; Macrobiotic Diet; Organic Food.

Reference Goodman, Mitchell, ed., *The Movement toward a New America: The Beginnings of a Long Revolution* (1970).

Newport Folk Festival

For folk musicians, a successful performance at the Newport Folk Festival meant widespread recognition and recording contracts. This was particularly true during the early sixties, when a folk music revival swept the nation's college campuses and attracted young listeners.

The festival, held annually at Freebody Park in Newport, Rhode Island, had an intimate atmosphere, at least in comparison to the large rock concerts that appeared a few years later. Only about 15,000 people could fit into the main stage area, and over three days the event usually drew only 25,000 or so. In fact, many of the better concerts occurred at small venues away from center stage and at those held in the afternoons before the nighttime feature performances.

Today, most people recall Newport as the place where Joan Baez and Bob Dylan appeared early in their careers, and where the latter received a hostile reaction when, in 1965, he used an electric guitar to supplement his acoustic one.

See also Baez, Joan; Dylan, Bob.

Newton, Huey (1942–1989)

"The first lesson a revolutionary must learn," Huey Newton said in 1973, "is that he is a doomed man. Unless he understands this, he does not grasp the essential meaning of his life." (Albert and Albert 1984, 169) Newton applied this philosophy in helping to found the militant Black Panthers, a group dedicated to advancing black power and a socialist agenda.

Born on 17 February 1942 in New Orleans, Newton grew up in Oakland, California, where his father worked as a laborer for the city. He barely graduated from high school, but decided to overcome his poor academic record and enrolled at Merritt College, a two-year school, where he studied liberal arts and read avidly. After his friend Bobby Seale introduced him to *The Wretched of the Earth*, a book by the black psychologist Frantz Fanon, Newton supported the idea that violence could educate oppressed people and develop leadership.

Raised in Oakland's ghettos, Newton had already proven himself a tough street fighter. Now he extended his prowess to politics. While at Merritt, he organized the

Soul Students' Advisory Council, through which he advocated that oppressed blacks defend themselves with guns and develop a revolutionary program to dismantle capitalism and establish socialism. Most of the group's members rejected his call concerning guns, and disagreement arose over cultural nationalism—the idea that whites should be condemned for being white. Newton opposed such racial determinism and insisted that alliances could be forged with radical whites who wanted to advance leftist revolution.

In October 1966, Newton huddled with Seale, and the two men wrote a ten-point program that included demands for freedom, black self-determination, and the end to police brutality. They adopted the name Black Panther Party and opened an office in Oakland on 1 January 1967, with Newton as minister of defense and its primary leader. Shortly after this, Newton declared that to be a "revolutionary nationalist" one would "have to be a socialist."

The Oakland police strongly disliked a tactic initiated by Newton: armed patrols to monitor arrests of blacks. Newton, though, understood his rights—California law allowed the carrying of loaded guns, and he was determined to use the patrols in order to reduce police brutality.

The Panthers wore combat jackets, raised clenched fists, and shouted "Black Power!" and "Power to the People!" Newton talked about "revolutionary suicide," meaning the revolutionary must act against reactionaries even at the risk of death. Then, in October 1967, shortly after the Panthers had staged a sensational demonstration in the state legislature, two policemen, one notorious for his poor relations with ghetto residents, stopped Newton and a friend. A struggle ensued between one of the cops and Newton, and the policeman's gun went off, killing him and wounding Newton.

The Black Panther's subsequent arrest brought widespread protests from radicals and even moderates who considered him a political prisoner. Newton was tried for murder and found guilty of manslaughter. In May 1970, however, a higher California court set aside Newton's conviction and released him.

By this time, the FBI and police had weakened the Panthers through harassment and raids so intense that, later, one of Newton's close friends claimed they changed the Panther leader's personality, making him forever paranoid. A dispute between Newton and another prominent Panther, Eldridge Cleaver, contributed to the turmoil. In 1971, Newton announced that the Panthers would forego guns and revolution in favor of education, community programs, and nonviolent protests.

Newton still faced retrial for his confrontation with the Oakland police, but the state failed to get a guilty verdict. In 1974, facing trial on charges of murdering a prostitute and illegally possessing weapons, Newton fled the country. He returned, however, in July 1977 and was acquitted on the murder charge. At the time, Newton suffered from drug and alcohol abuse but still managed in 1980 to earn a doctorate in social philosophy at the University of California–Santa Cruz. His legal problems continued, and he was imprisoned at San Quentin in 1987 for nine months, a result of the weapons charge, and was convicted early in 1989 for misappropriating public funds used in a Panther school project. On 22 August 1989, an assailant killed Newton on a ghetto street in Oakland.

See also Black Panthers; Cleaver, Leroy Eldridge; Seale, Bobby.

References Albert, Judith Clavir, and Stewart Edward Albert, eds., *The Sixties Papers: Documents of a Rebellious Decade* (1984); Newton, Huey P., *Revolutionary Suicide* (1973) and *To Die for the People: The Writings of Huey P. Newton* (1972); Pearson, Hugh, *The Shadow of the Black Panther: Huey Newton and the Price of Black Power in America* (1994); Seale, Bobby, *Seize the Time: The Story of the Black Panther Party and Huey P. Newton* (1970).

Nudity

No question about it—lots of young people bared all in the sixties. As the counterculture in general attacked traditional standards and, specifically, promoted toleration in all forms of sexuality, practices regarding public nudity changed. Sometimes nudity simply brought to the surface male erotic desires, as in the explicit photographs of women appearing in *Playboy* magazine and the increasing number of men's publications available in general circulation, such as *Screw* (followed, a decade later, by magazines catering to women with photographs of nude men, namely *Playgirl*), and the greater availability of pornographic movies. In 1964, buxom Carol Doda caused a sensation at the Condor Club in San Francisco when she performed a dance called the "swim"—topless. This led to hundreds of other topless nightclubs opening in California and elsewhere, and to businesses such as Off Broadway and the Cellar, also in San Francisco, where waitresses who served lunch wore only bikini underpants and high-heeled shoes.

At other times, nudity reflected not so much an erotic pursuit than a countercultural attitude that naked bodies, male or female, young or old, fat, slim, or in between, should be accepted—in short, puritanical notions about sin should not condemn human bodies to clothes. Naked couples holding hands and singing, people sunbathing in the nude, skinny-dipping as at Woodstock—the counterculture asked, "What was there to hide?" and answered by disrobing. Thus, nudity in Hollywood motion pictures (geared also to selling tickets), in Broadway plays such as *Hair* and *Oh! Calcutta!*, and in fashion, such as with the topless bathing suit.

Nude hippie communities and nude beaches and bathing areas appeared—a few with legal sanction but mainly surreptitiously, with or without mainstream society's acquiescence. Most were located in California, which had a widely used nude beach in 1965 and where, in 1972, the state supreme court declared "nude is not lewd." Black's Beach in San Diego emerged as perhaps the leading "swimsuit optional" area in the state. (Joseph 1974, 64)

To some, nudity was therapeutic, as at the Elysium Institute in Los Angeles that advertised "nude psychotherapy—a scientifically conducted weekend session." To others, it was a crusade, as with the Om United Nude Brigade that appeared sporadically on the streets of San Francisco, walking the streets naked (and ending up in jail swaddled in prison clothes). The Omists insisted: "There are so many reasons nudity is important. It's healthful, it breaks down barriers between people. . . [it relieves] mankind of 6,000 years of the sexual guilt burden, the first original sin." ("Om United Nude Brigade" 1970, 8)

See also *Hair; Oh! Calcutta!;* Topless Bathing Suit.

References Joseph, Peter, *Good Times: An Oral History of America in the 1960s* (1974); "Om United Nude Brigade," *Rolling Stone*, 23 July 1970, 8.

Ochs, Phil (1940–1976)

Phil Ochs first made his mark as a topical folk singer whose political commentary about nuclear weapons and war placed him alongside Joan Baez, Bob Dylan, Arlo Guthrie, and Pete Seeger as a counterculture troubadour.

Ochs was born on 19 December 1940 in El Paso, Texas, where his father, Jacob Ochs, was stationed in the army. During World War II, the elder Ochs, a doctor, served as a combat medic. After the war, the family returned to its home in Far Rockaway, New York. As a child, Philip showed a talent for music and in grade school began playing the clarinet. Beginning in 1956, he attended Stanton Academy, a military school, in Virginia. There he played in the school band and listened to Johnny Cash, Faron Young, Buddy Holly, and Elvis Presley—important influences on his developing musical interest.

Ochs entered Ohio State University in 1958, wearing his James Dean–style red jacket, but dropped out after a few months to pursue his music in Miami, Florida, where he kicked around at odd jobs and found no one wanted him. Penniless, he returned to Ohio State. Suddenly, he delved into politics, reading Marx, Engels, Mao Tse-tung, Thomas Jefferson, John Adams, Tom Paine, and the *Federalist Papers*. From friends he learned how the United Fruit Company, a large American corporation, exploited workers in Latin America, and he learned, too, about the assaults in the United States by the House Un-American Activities Committee against free speech. Ochs decided to major in journalism, and after a falling out with the campus newspaper over political issues, started his own publication, *The Word*.

At Ohio State, a friend, Jim Glover, introduced Ochs to the songs of Pete Seeger and the Weavers, and to the guitar, which Ochs learned quickly. This led the two young men to form a short-lived folk duo, the Sundowners. Ochs began writing music, topical folk songs based on his reading of newspaper articles, compositions such as "Bay of Pigs." He again dropped out of college and this time headed for New York City, where in 1962 he began performing during open mike night at Gerde's Folk City, an up-and-coming club in Greenwich Village. He received his first formal gig at Gerde's in March 1963 and played to a standing ovation.

At the same time, Ochs helped edit *Broadside*, a new Pete Seeger publication that published topical folk songs. In an essay he wrote titled "The Need for Topical Music," Ochs said: "Every newspaper headline is a potential song, and it is the role of an effective songwriter to pick out the material that has the interest, significance and sometimes humor adaptable to music." (59)

As a folk revival swept the nation's young people, Ochs landed a recording contract with a major label, Elektra Records, and many hailed him as the next Bob Dylan. Early in 1964, he recorded his first LP, *All the News That's Fit To Sing*. One reviewer called it "as important in 1964 as Bob Dylan's *Freewheelin'* album was in 1963." (85) Ochs achieved widespread recognition when Joan Baez covered one of his songs, and it made the national charts. His best-selling album soon followed, *In Concert*, which included "When I'm Gone" and "Love Me I'm a Liberal," a sharp, satirical jab at liberals who listened to all the Pete Seeger songs but wouldn't risk anything to fight social injustice.

In 1967, Ochs signed with A & M Records and recorded *Pleasures of the Harbour*, a new direction in his music. With it, he moved from topical to a contemplative and poetical style. The album included "Crucifixion," a song about John Kennedy and one that fused folk with rock. Politically, Ochs helped lead demonstrations against the Vietnam War, and he sang at several rallies. He played a minor role in planning the Yippie demonstration at the 1968 Democratic National Convention in Chicago, and sang during that tumultuous protest. He later testified at the trial of the protest leaders, who were dubbed the Chicago Eight.

For Ochs, 1968 and 1969 were difficult years: his albums sold poorly, attendance at his live performances fell, and audiences booed his rock 'n' roll medleys, wanting, instead, his previous style. Tragedy struck in 1973 during a tour in Africa. While walking along the beach one evening in Tanzania, three black men attacked him; one of the attackers held him tightly around the neck, and when Ochs tried to scream, he ruptured his vocal chords. He never recovered his ability to sing high notes.

His singing hampered, his songwriting deteriorating, Ochs drank heavily and gained weight. In the few concerts he gave, he often appeared on stage drunk. Ochs was found dead at his sister's home in New York on 7 April 1976, having committed suicide by hanging.

See also Chicago Eight; Democratic National Convention of 1968; Dylan, Bob; Gerde's Folk City.

Reference Eliot, Marc, *Death of a Rebel* (1979).

O.D.

The word *O.D.* entered the vocabulary in 1960 as an abbreviation for "overdose," meaning an overdose, often fatal, of drugs. A verb appeared in 1969: OD'd. Thus, the explanation: "The victim OD'd on heroin."

Oglesby, Carl (1935–)

Born on 30 July 1935 in Akron, Ohio, Carl Oglesby served as president of the nation's leading New Left organization, Students for a Democratic Society (SDS), and guided it to a larger membership.

The son of an Ohio rubber worker, Oglesby graduated from Kent State University, and in the early 1960s worked as a technical writer in Ann Arbor, Michigan. After he wrote an article in the fall of 1964 criticizing American policy in Southeast Asia, members of the recently formed SDS asked him to join them. He did so and advised the organization to establish a research, information, and publication bureau. SDS agreed and, in turn, hired Oglesby to head it.

In June 1965, the SDS national convention elected Oglesby president, and although he served in that position for little more than one year, under his guidance membership rapidly increased, and SDS emerged at the forefront of campus protests against the Vietnam War. On 27 November 1965, Oglesby delivered the most effective speech at a large rally in Washington, D.C., sponsored by the Committee for a Sane Nuclear Policy and supported by SDS. He called the Vietnam War a result of liberalism defending corporate capitalism. Oglesby said:

> The original commitment to Vietnam was made by President Eisenhower, a moderate liberal. It was intensified by the late President Kennedy, a flaming liberal. Think of the men who now engineer the war—those who study maps, give the commands, push the buttons and tally the dead. . . . They are not moral monsters. They are all honorable men. They are all liberals. (Viorst 1979, 400)

In making this statement, Oglesby articulated the distrust that the New Left had toward liberals, whom they believed had sold out to an economic and political elite.

After leaving office in September 1966, Oglesby coauthored a book criticizing U.S. foreign policy, and in 1967 served on the International War Crimes Tribunal, a private antiwar project sponsored by British philosopher Bertrand Russell. The following year, he took another active role in SDS as a member of its National Interim

Committee, but in 1969 the organization split into factions. Although Oglesby left SDS, he continued to write political articles.

See also Students for a Democratic Society.

Reference Viorst, Milton, *Fire in the Streets: America in the 1960s* (1979).

Oh! Calcutta!

After *Hair* shocked Broadway with a scene depicting complete nudity, *Oh! Calcutta!* opened in 1968 with a sexually explicit theme, even more nudity, and simulated sex acts. There was a major difference between the two plays: *Hair* did not focus on nudity, nor did it present itself as a sex play; *Oh! Calcutta!* did both.

The play reflected greater sexual permissiveness in the arts, a trend that led to complaints from traditionalists about declining moral values. Drama critic Eric Bentley, however, waxed effusive, calling the naked actor a social savior, a person who amid a confining urban civilization "asserted the claims of natural man, the claims of the body. . . . I don't think our soul is going to be saved until our body is joined to it again." (Braden 1970, 247)

See also *Hair*.

Reference Braden, William, *The Age of Aquarius: Technology and the Cultural Revolution* (1970).

Old Town (Chicago)

Chicago's Old Town developed a bohemian atmosphere in the 1920s, when artists began converting its flats and Victorian houses into studios. In the sixties, it emerged as the center of Chicago's counterculture and sported art and poster shops in abundance.

An underground newspaper, *Seed*, known as the voice of Old Town, had its headquarters there. The Second City Theater, an improvisational outfit, also flourished, and cafes and bars sprung up along Piper's Alley. Most of the countercultural businesses were located on Wells Street. During the 1968 Democratic National Convention, demonstrations and violence spilled into Old Town's streets.

See also *Seed*.

Olympics, 1968

By 1968, a great divide had developed in the United States between black radicals and mainstream whites, and the resulting tension carried into that summer's Olympics, held in Mexico City, when two African American athletes used the medal ceremonies to protest oppression in their home country.

Tommie Smith shocked an international audience first by breaking the world record and winning the 200 meter dash, and then by wearing a black glove on his right hand when he received the gold medal for his accomplishment. As the national anthem played, Smith, while looking down, stabbed his arm into the air, keeping it raised toward the sky, his hand clenched in a black power salute. John Carlos wore a black glove and struck the same pose when he received his bronze medal.

The all-white U.S. Olympic Committee suspended Smith and Carlos from the games for advocating a political cause, and the two athletes apologized to Mexico for their behavior. Their stand ignited enormous controversy in the United States and generated greater attention for the black power movement. Many whites felt outrage and television sportscaster Howard Cossell reported receiving hate mail for having interviewed Smith about the protest. African Americans, on the other hand, often applauded Smith and Carlos, and black power leader Stokely Carmichael stated: "That one act communicated to all of us, and we knew precisely what it said." (Anderson 1995, 231)

Controversy about symbols at the medal ceremonies did not strike the Olympics again until the 1990s. This time the disputes involved what corporate logos athletes should wear and when they should wear them in light of their having signed lucrative contracts with companies.

See also Black Power.

Reference Anderson, Terry H., *The Movement and the Sixties* (1995).

Om Festival

On 20 August 1967, chants descended from Mount Tamalpais, near San Francisco—sounds of the Om Festival. This event, also called the Summer of Love Festival of Lights, attracted 2,500 people. They listened to the Grateful Dead, until the band's generator burned out; sang together while beating on garbage cans; and then late in the night, chanted Om and lit candles. Fire rangers eventually evicted the crowd from the state park for not having the requisite permit. Despite this, participants considered the event a success—amid the hectic Summer of Love an attempt at community, free entertainment, and spiritual harmony.

See also Summer of Love.

Ono, Yoko (1933–)

Most people remember Yoko Ono as the wife of musician John Lennon, yet Ono contributed artistically to the counterculture in her own right as an avant-garde painter, musician, and writer.

Born on 18 February 1933 in Tokyo, Ono came from a wealthy, elite Japanese family. For a short time, immediately before the U.S. entry into World War II, she lived in New York City, where her father worked as an investment banker, but in the spring of 1941 her family returned to Japan. All through her childhood her mother, Isoko, and father, Yeisuke, failed to develop a close relationship with her. Ono later recounted how, in order to see her father, she would have to make an appointment at his office. During these years, she developed a liking for writing, music, and painting and received tutoring in English, the Bible, and Buddhism.

After the war, Ono attended Gakushuin University in Tokyo but left there in 1951 when her family moved back to the United States and settled in Scarsdale, New York. She continued her higher education at Sarah Lawrence College but preferred writing short stories and practicing her music to attending classes. Ono left the college without receiving her degree, married Toshi Ichiyanagi, a young classical composer, and moved to New York City. Thorough him, she made contacts in the avant-garde art world.

Another composer, John Cage, greatly influenced Ono with his experimental music. Cage believed that all forms of noise along with silence should be used by a composer. Hence, his pieces included the sound of opening and closing a piano lid and the coughing, whispers, and so on from the audience. Ono liked the spontaneity involved and how it reconceptualized art.

In 1958, Ono began to display her artwork in her loft in Greenwich Village, but although several persons prominent in the avant-garde turned out, Cage among them, critics either ignored or panned the showings. Two years later, she along with several other artists developed modern performance art. In demanding audience participation, in which the participant helped create the work, this new technique further redefined what constituted art.

One of Ono's performance art pieces, called "Stone Show," required the observer to enter a small white room and crawl into a black nylon bag; there the observer, now participant, would strip and stand, crouch, or sit while lights flashed and loud speakers filled the room with different sounds. Thus, with performance art the originating artist develops the concept, which then must be completed by the observer-participant who, in the act, becomes an artist.

Since her art continued to receive a poor response, Ono decided in 1962 to return to Japan. Dejected, she attempted suicide by taking an overdose of sleeping pills, and while recovering, awoke to find herself in a mental hospital, where she stayed for several weeks.

The times soon coordinated with Ono's work: in 1964, the year she divorced her

Yoko Ono with John Lennon during their "bed-in" in Montreal on 8 October 1969

first husband and returned to the United States, the popular arts movement spread as part of the emerging counterculture. As a result, more and more artists experimented with new forms. Given this development, Ono thought her book *Grapefruit* would earn her acclaim. The work consisted of Zen-like paragraphs that presented instructions for creating artistic events—for example, "Steal a moon on the water with a bucket. Keep stealing until no moon is seen on the water."

Still, few people paid attention and she remained a minor avant-garde figure until a counterculture icon entered her life, John Lennon. The two met in November 1966 at an exhibition of Ono's art in London. Although Lennon did not know Ono, she certainly knew about him, his money, and his success. Thus, the first encounter between the two was a chance one only from Lennon's side—Ono and her husband Tony Cox had used connections to get Lennon to see the exhibition. Soon after Lennon arrived, he stopped beside a white ladder. Above it, Ono had mounted a black canvas with a tiny white dot in the center. A magnifying glass on a chain hung from the picture. Lennon climbed the ladder, looked through the spy glass, and discovered, in tiny letters, the word "yes."

Ono then met him at the bottom of the ladder and handed him a card that said "breathe." From there, a conversation began. In *Yoko Ono*, Jerry Hopkins says, "Both John and Yoko said later that they were drawn together immediately, recognizing something of themselves in each other—a common, turn-around sense of humor, a peculiar yet somewhat intellectual sense of the ridiculous side of art." (63) Ono sought to develop a friendship with Lennon, get him interested in her art, and get his financial backing. She succeeded in all three areas, and the relationship with Lennon soon went further than she likely anticipated, although perhaps not beyond what she had planned, for she aggressively pursued Lennon, sending a copy of *Grapefruit* to him at his Abbey Road studio; bringing him into a cooperative art project; showing up unannounced at his home and standing outside it, near the driveway, from early morning until late at night; forcing herself into his Rolls-Royce while he and his wife were driving home from a lecture; and writing frequent notes intended to entice him.

In 1968, after Ono and Lennon left their spounses and lived together, tension arose between him and the other Beatles. Although several factors contributed to the friction within the band and its breakup the following year, observers agree that Ono's presence caused great discord. The other Beatles, Paul McCartney, George Harrison, and Ringo Starr, disliked her and her presence in the Abbey Road studio during recording sessions. Beyond that, public criticism engulfed Ono and Lennon with observers deriding them for acting weird and for treating their spouses cruelly. The criticism grew worse after Ono and Lennon released a record album, *Unfinished Music No. 1: Two Virgins*, with its cover showing them both nude. Lennon responded: "When people attack Yoko and me, we know they're paranoiac, we don't worry too much." (82–83)

Lennon obtained a divorce from his wife late in 1968, and Ono obtained one from her husband a few weeks later. In March 1969, Lennon and Ono married and then held what they called an "open honeymoon" in Amsterdam, inviting reporters to visit them.

Shortly after this, they held a "bed-in" for peace in a hotel room in Toronto, Canada, to which they again invited reporters and numerous celebrities. Ono and Lennon led their visitors, among them LSD guru Timothy Leary, in a recording session in their hotel room, with everyone singing "Give Peace a Chance." The record reached the top ten, and the couple included the song in a concert they performed at the Toronto Rock 'n' Roll Festival with their new group, the Plastic Ono Band. A recording of the concert appeared on their album *Live Peace in Toronto*, released early in 1970. An entire side of *Live Peace* has Ono singing, or more accurately, screaming a simple song about her daughter and Lennon.

Ono and Lennon made several other albums in the late sixties and early seventies, including *Unfinished Music No. 2: Life with the Lions*, *Fly*, *Yoko Ono: Plastic Ono Band*, *John Lennon: Plastic Ono Band*, and *Sometime in New York City*. Ono's music offered no melody or lyrics—only wailing intended to express her inner feelings. A single they released in 1972 caused controversy with its lyrics and title: "Woman Is the Nigger of the World." Over all, these albums sold poorly.

Ono made several controversial films, too: *Bottoms*, which presented over 365 bare rear ends; *The Ballad of John and Yoko* and *Cold Turkey*, both personal montages; *Smile*, which captured Lennon smiling for 45 minutes; and *Fly*, which showed a women's naked body from the vantage point of a fly. Many critics again condemned her work, although in 1971 *Fly* received a standing ovation at the Cannes Film Festival.

That year, the couple moved to New York City, at first living in West Village and then at an old but exclusive apartment building, the Dakota. Soon, their marriage entered a rocky period, and in 1973 they separated. Lennon returned to Ono in 1975 and continued working on albums with her while they both lived reclusively. As the decade neared its end, Lennon withdrew to the point that he stopped recording, and Ono handled nearly all the couple's business affairs. In 1980, though, Lennon returned to the studio and he and Ono put together a new album, *Double Fantasy*.

On 8 December, before the album's release, Mark David Chapman called out to Ono and Lennon as they left a car around 11:00 P.M. and headed to the entrance of the Dakota. Lennon turned to look, at which point Chapman shot and killed him.

In the 1980s and 1990s, Ono continued to run her late husband's business affairs, supervised the release of songs he had recorded, contributed heavily to charities, and revived her own musical career, including, in 1996, a concert in New York City. During these two decades, her earlier work, such as *Grapefruit*, gained more favorable reviews from critics, and historians recognized her as a pioneer in performance art.

See also The Beatles; Fluxus; Performance Art.

Reference Hopkins, Jerry, *Yoko Ono* (1986).

Orange Sunshine

In the sixties, LSD was produced in various qualities, and "orange sunshine" was considered a premium kind.

See also LSD; Stanley, Augustus Owsley III.

Organic Food

The countercultural attraction to organic food began primarily in the late sixties as a rebellion against mass-produced, chemically adulterated products that harmed people physically and psychologically. Organic food is grown with fertilizers and mulches consisting only of animal or vegetable matter; no manufactured chemicals or pesticides are used. In its processed form, organic food does not contain preservatives. "Food is another terrible thing we have been programmed to believe in," said Ron Thelin, co-owner of The Psychedelic Shop. "The markets are filled with food that has preservatives and junk in it. . . . Organic food that grows up from Mother Nature, the way Mother Nature intended it to grow, *really* affects your consciousness." (Von Hoffman 1968, 139)

To raise or eat organic food seemed to be stepping back from technology to a simpler existence, and thus the popularity of organic food coincided with the back-to-the-earth movement. Some people talked about living an organic lifestyle, meaning in harmony with nature.

See also Back-to-the-Earth Movement; Macrobiotic Diet.

Reference Von Hoffman, Nicholas, *We Are the People Our Parents Warned Us Against* (1968).

The Organization Man

Written by William H. Whyte, Jr., *The Organization Man* won an audience among college students in the early sixties for criticizing post-World War II society as stifling in its conformity. The book first appeared in 1956, and in it Whyte, an editor at *Fortune* magazine, portrays corporate power and government bureaucracies as creating a closed hierarchy that threatens to crush individualism. He derides college students for their passivity, a conservatism not philosophical but rooted instead in accepting the status quo. Universities feed students into the corporate bureaucracy and the students, he says, accept it willingly. Whyte observes:

> The urge to be a technician, a collaborator, shows most markedly in the kinds of jobs seniors prefer. They want to work for somebody else. . . .
>
> Students are still interested in security but they no longer see it as security *versus* opportunity. Now when they explain their choice, it is that the corporation is security *and* opportunity both. (68, 72)

In the early sixties, many college students rejected this arrangement; they agreed with Whyte that oppression accompanied security and, consequently, they rebelled.

Reference Whyte, William H., Jr., *The Organization Man* (1956).

The Other America

When it first appeared in 1962, Michael Harrington's book *The Other America* exposed how the nation's affluent society had bypassed farm laborers, unskilled urban workers, the elderly, and most blacks. The book thus ran counter to the conformist 1950s and helped middle-class citizens realize that poverty existed in their nation. In his work, Harrington talks about an invisible America, the oppressed, cloaked by television shows that depicted only the white middle-class, by supermarkets loaded with bounty, by suburbs that bespoke prosperity. "The new poverty," Harrington says, "is constructed so as to destroy aspiration; it is a system designed to be impervious to hope." (11)

In awakening the middle class, *The Other America* eventually helped stimulate reforms in the mid-1960s known as the War on Poverty. But it did more than that in making many college students realize society's shortcomings and the need to change them through political action, sometimes drastic.

Reference Harrington, Michael, *The Other America: Poverty in the United States* (1962).

Out of Sight

The phrase "out of sight" first appeared in the late 1800s. Within the counterculture, as in its previous existence, it meant superb, terrific, exciting—often too wonderful to be described. Hence, "The new Beatles album is out of sight!"

Owsley

See Stanley, Augustus Owsley III.

Paisley

Many young people wore paisley shirts and blouses, which they liked for their Asian-derived patterns: colorful swirls in abstract, curved shapes.

Participatory Democracy

When the New Left organization Students for a Democratic Society (SDS) issued its Port Huron Statement in 1962, it demanded participatory democracy. SDSers wanted to involve more people in politics, such as African Americans who had traditionally been denied the vote through restrictive laws or practices. But participatory democracy meant more than voting—it meant bringing people together in their localities (and thus fostering community) to make decisions for themselves.

In impoverished areas, for example, poor people would be encouraged to establish their own organizations to pressure government and businesses for changes and to determine the types of governmental assistance needed in their neighborhood. SDS complained that the War on Poverty and other liberal programs gave government bureaucrats too much power. Indeed, participatory democracy intended, overall, to restrict the political and corporate elite throughout the nation.

SDS never came to grips with the mechanics needed to implement participatory democracy beyond the position that it required assertion by college students, sharecroppers, the poor, and industrial workers. For a while in the mid-1960s, SDS organized poor people in urban ghettos through its Economic Research and Action Project (ERAP). They achieved some temporary gains, such as improved streets and, through rent strikes, concessions from landlords, but ERAP did not last long, and SDSers bickered over what route to follow in going beyond the failed program—would it take socialism or even communism to develop true participatory democracy? Would, in fact, capitalism have to be torn down?

Whatever disagreements existed, the drive toward participatory democracy stemmed from a deeply held belief that American society as developed in the 1950s and imparted to the younger generation in the 1960s was restrictive, impersonal, and oppressive. The Port Huron Statement asserted: "Loneliness, estrangement, isolation describe the vast distance between man and man today." (Gitlin 1987, 106) This necessitated change, perhaps revolutionary.

See also ERAP; New Left; Port Huron Statement; Students for a Democratic Society.

References Gitlin, Todd, *The Sixties: Years of Hope, Days of Rage* (1987); Hayden, Tom, *Reunion: A Memoir* (1988); Sale, Kirkpatrick, *SDS* (1973).

Paul Butterfield Blues Band

Paul Butterfield organized his band in Chicago where blues clubs thrived in the early sixties. Butterfield, a white musician, jammed with blacks and put together a biracial band that obtained a recording contract with Elektra Records and played numerous shows in San Francisco, helping to propel a blues revival among white youth.

Peace Symbol

The peace symbol pictured at right appeared on placards, posters, flags, clothes, and pendants, and seemed so integral to the counterculture that some people thought hippies had invented it. Actually, it first appeared in 1958 at an antinuclear demonstration in Britain. Most sources attribute its creation to Bertrand

Russell and claim it was formed by placing the signs N and D (for nuclear disarmament) from the international marine signaling system on top of each other and a circle around them.

See also Russell, Bertrand.

Reference Liungman, Carl G., *Dictionary of Symbols* (1991).

Peltier, Leonard (1944–)

A charismatic leader in the American Indian Movement (AIM), Leonard Peltier fought for Indian treaty and civil rights until his arrest and conviction, after a controversial trial, for killing two FBI agents.

Born on 12 September 1944 in Grand Forks, North Dakota, Peltier, an Ojibway Indian, grew up in poverty, moving with his family from one mining and logging camp to another. At age 14, he left home and worked at odd jobs until the mid-1960s, when he owned an auto body shop in Seattle, Washington.

In 1970, Peltier joined AIM, an organization recently formed to protect Indian rights through an activist and, at times, militant strategy modeled after the Black Panthers. Peltier became friends with Dennis Banks, an AIM founder, and helped raise money for the organization. He took part in several AIM protests, among them the "Trail of Broken Treaties" caravan that, in 1972, traveled to Washington, D.C. Peltier was among the 400 protesters who occupied the Bureau of Indian Affairs (BIA) building after officials reneged on a promise to meet with them.

By this time, the FBI had started an extensive program to infiltrate, harass, and destroy AIM, and tension mounted on the Pine Ridge Reservation in South Dakota, where federal officials in the BIA allied with a corrupt Sioux Indian faction under Dickie Wilson. The officials intended to cooperate with white interests to obtain reservation land and get concessions that would allow the national government to mine for uranium.

This situation led to violent confrontations between AIM on one side and the federal government–Wilson alliance on the other. On 26 June 1975, federal agents, joined by Wilson's men, attacked an AIM encampment near the reservation village of Oglala. The firefight that ensued resulted in the deaths of one AIM member and two FBI agents. Immediately after, the government pursued Peltier, along with Bob Robideau and Darrelle Butler, as the men who had killed the agents. Fearing he would not get a fair trial, Peltier fled, at first hiding with friends at Pine Ridge and then slipping into Canada. He was captured early the following year, however, and extradited to the United States, perhaps illegally.

Most observers believe that the prosecutors and judge validated Peltier's fears about his trial. Highly dubious judicial rulings disallowed Peltier from using a self-defense presentation—one that in an earlier trial had led to Robideau and Butler obtaining acquittals. Further, the judge allowed the prosecution to submit questionable evidence. At the trial, held in Fargo, North Dakota, in 1977, a jury found Peltier guilty of murder, and he received two consecutive life terms. On appeal, a court upheld the conviction, although the government has since admitted that it has no idea who killed the agents.

Today, Peltier languishes in the federal penitentiary at Marion, Illinois. Many activists consider him to be a political prisoner, a talented leader persecuted because he did not fit the compliant Indian model federal officials mandate on the reservations. In 1997, a campaign continued to get President Bill Clinton to pardon Peltier.

See also American Indian Movement.

Reference Matthiessen, Peter, *In the Spirit of Crazy Horse* (1991).

People's Park

Tear gas, gunshots fired into an unarmed crowd—this behavior by the authorities erupted in Berkeley, California, months before a more prominent conflict at Kent State University. The turmoil accompanied an attempt by hippies, radicals, and "straights" to build a community park on land owned by the University of California.

Early in 1968, the university purchased a three-acre plot along Telegraph Avenue, the road leading to the college's south entrance, on which several buildings rested: a bookstore, coffee shop, and old houses. The university then tore down the buildings as part of a plan to build dormitories and a parking lot. The construction, however, did not begin immediately, and the land lay dormant, dotted with garbage and broken glass. When this situation continued, students, nonstudents, and neighborhood residents pooled their resources, and in April 1969 began building a public park. They removed the debris, planted grass and trees, and erected swings and slides. People's Park, as they called it, even had a community vegetable garden. A flier claimed:

> A long time ago the Costanoan Indians lived in the area now called Berkeley. They had no concept of land ownership. They believed that the land was under the care and guardianship of the people who used it and lived on it. . . .
>
> We are building a park on the land. We will take care of it and guard it, in the spirit of the Costanoan Indians. When the University comes with its land title we will tell them: "Your land title is covered with blood. We won't touch it. Your people ripped off the land from the Indians a long time ago. If you want it back, now, you will have to fight for it again." (Goodman, Mitchell 1970, 505)

That is exactly what happened. At 5:00 A.M. on 15 May 1969, without notice, the police moved in, followed by a construction crew that erected a fence around the entire park, closing it. When word of this action spread, about 3,000 people marched down Telegraph Avenue toward the park—a diverse crowd that included counterculture youths but also cheerleaders, athletes, fraternity boys, and neighborhood residents. When the crowd started throwing rocks, the police charged it, detonating tear gas and then firing shotguns. This stunned many protesters who did not believe live ammunition would be used. The buckshot wounded 30 and killed 1 person, 26-year-old James Rector.

Governor Ronald Reagan praised the police, and as the battle continued during the next week, he sent in the National Guard and helicopters that unleashed tear gas on demonstrators and the campus. The demonstrators, in turn, grew more violent. When the tear-gas clouds cleared, the authorities stood triumphant, but the conflict had widened the gulf between mainstream and counterculture and set the nation on edge.

See also University of California-Berkeley.

Reference Goodman, Mitchell, ed., *The Movement toward a New America: The Beginnings of a Long Revolution* (1970).

Performance Art

Performance art in the 1960s, as developed by Yoko Ono and several other artists, made the observer a participant. According to this approach, the originating artist developed a concept and presented it to an audience to complete. Performance art also involved using nontraditional media, such as objects found in the home, multimedia, and the artist's body as a medium. In one performance art work, Yoko Ono placed pieces of blank canvas on the floor and waited for people to walk on them; in a second instance, she had people come forward with scissors and snip away her clothing, bit by bit; and, in yet another, an observer was instructed to get inside a black nylon bag, undress, and assume various positions while lights flickered and music filled the room . . . the piece thus completed.

See also Fluxus; Ono, Yoko.

Peyote

Peyote refers either to a small, spineless cactus found in Mexico and the southwestern United States or to the mushroom-shaped tops of the cactus. These tops are also called mescal buttons. Mescal is the psychoactive agent in peyote. Some Indians have used peyote in their religious rites since pre-Columbian times.

The use of peyote by bohemians began in the early 1900s, when it appeared in the artistic and intellectual subcultures of London, Paris, and New York City's Greenwich Village. The poet Antonin Artaud wrote about peyote's mystical qualities in *The Peyote Dance*, claiming it produces a visionary state of mind. In 1919, a German chemist, Ernst Spath, produced the first synthetic version of peyote. In the 1950s, a bookstore in Greenwich Village sold peyote buttons and displayed them in its front window. During the following decade, hippies and others searching for mystical transcendence took peyote, but its side effect—a wrenching nausea—dismayed many.

See also Drugs and the Drug Culture; LSD; Mescaline.

Pig

Counterculture youths used the word *pig* derisively, usually meaning a policeman, although sometimes referring to anyone in authority. During the turmoil surrounding the 1968 Democratic National Convention in Chicago, protesters chanted "Pigs eat shit! Pigs eat shit!"

Among some radicals, *pig* took on a different meaning. For Weatherman, an extremist group, it meant the enemy—be it policeman, politician, or reactionary opponent. When Bernardine Dohrn, a leading Weatherman, praised Charles Manson and his followers for murdering Sharon Tate, a movie actress, and several of her friends, she exclaimed: "Dig it, first they killed those pigs, then they ate dinner in the same room with them, and then they even shoved a fork into the victim's stomach! Wild!" (Viorst 1979, 502)

In 1968, a radical newspaper in Richmond, California, ran a headline proclaiming "Today's Pig Is Tomorrow's Bacon." (Gitlin 1987, 287)

References Gitlin, Todd, *The Sixties: Years of Hope, Days of Rage* (1987); Viorst, Milton, *Fire in the Streets: America in the 1960s* (1979).

The Pill

Did the birth-control pill, nearly 100 percent effective when taken according to directions, cause the 1960s sexual revolution? Only in a limited way, for as historian Beth Bailey notes in *The Sixties: From Memory to History*, the revolution required, foremost, changes in cultural attitudes that made it more permissible for unmarried women to request the pill. Nevertheless, the pill had a role, an important one, in making more possible premarital sex with a greatly reduced risk of pregnancy. Whether this sexual liberation meant liberation for women is highly debatable, however; for while the pill allowed more sexual activity and perhaps fulfillment, it may have encouraged men to be more aggressive in demanding sex.

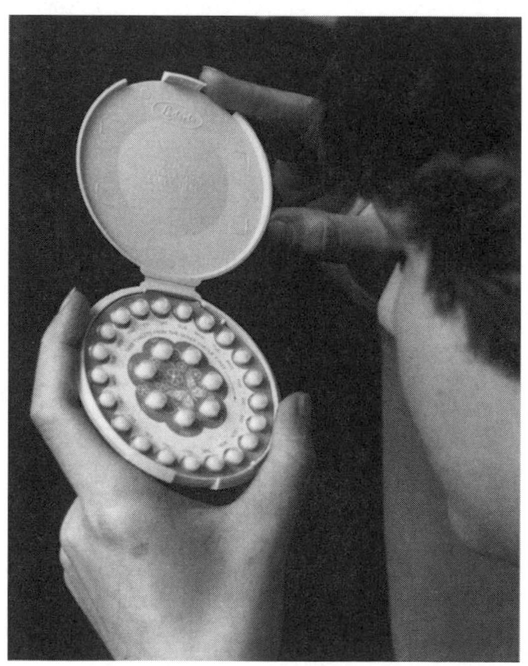

The pill hit the retail market in 1960, and by 1967 more than 7 million American women were using the new form of birth control.

The pill first hit the retail market in 1960; it cost little more than one penny to manufacture, and a month's supply could be purchased for $2. By 1967, it had been taken by about 7 million American women. *Time* magazine stated that in a few cases the pill may have promoted sexual promiscuity, "but the consensus among both physicians and sociologists is that a girl who is promiscuous on the pill would have been promiscuous without it." ("The Sexual Revolution" 1995)

See also Sex.

References Farber, David, ed., *The Sixties: From Memory to History* (1994); "The Sexual Revolution," *Time Almanac of the 20th Century* (1995).

Pine Street

Pine Street runs through San Francisco's Haight-Ashbury district, and in the 1960s it emerged as a hippie center. Wealthy people inhabited the area to the north and poor blacks the area to the south. The hippies consequently served as a line of demarcation.

Pine Street was the place to dress in Edwardian or colorful clothes, purchase and indulge in drugs, and otherwise flaunt the straight world. There emerged here, too, a commune whose bohemian residents helped shape the hippie culture: Luria Castell, for example, who founded The Family Dog, promoters of rock concerts; and Jim Gurley, an original in the band Big Brother and the Holding Company.

See also Haight-Ashbury; Hippies.

Plastic

To the counterculture generation, the word *plastic* meant artificial, insincere, false, or fake. A plastic hippie, for example, dressed like a hippie and had hippie mannerisms but remained integrally connected to mainstream society. When Frank Zappa and his rock group the Mothers of Invention criticized the middle class for its hypocrisy, they did so through a song called "The Plastic People."

Poor People's Campaign

In 1967, civil rights leader Martin Luther King, Jr. stated that in order to eliminate inequality, Americans would need to undertake a "radical reconstruction of society itself." (Miller 1996, 229) With this in mind, he developed plans for a Poor People's Campaign, open to all races, that would begin in the spring of 1968 with a march to Washington, D.C., followed by an encampment there. A few weeks before the march could begin, however, an assassin killed King in Memphis, Tennessee. This led to riots in many urban ghettos that stirred a white backlash against the entire civil rights movement.

Despite this chaotic environment, Dr. Ralph Abernathy, King's chief lieutenant, proceeded with the Poor People's Campaign. Inadequately planned, few participated in it, even though it represented a radical new direction for the civil rights movement, namely an attack on class differences. The marchers set up a shantytown, called Resurrection City, near the Lincoln Memorial, but it turned into a muddy mess, and the government soon arrested several leaders and forced the demonstrators out.

The *New York Times* said the Poor People's Campaign "was planned to probe the essence of the American system, to see whether it could make a massive material and spiritual readjustment to change the lives of its poverty-stricken millions and construct a rational future where base poverty would not coexist with stupendous wealth." (Meier, Rudwick, and Bracey 1991, 297) In this, both the campaign and society failed.

References Meier, August, Elliot Rudwick, and John Bracey, Jr., eds., *Black Protest in the Sixties* (1991); Miller, Douglas T., *On Our Own: Americans in the Sixties* (1996).

Port Huron Statement

Issued by Students for a Democratic Society (SDS), the Port Huron Statement acted as a declaration of principles for that organization and a broad statement of counterculture political ideas. Historians who study the 1960s consider the statement an essential document in trying to understand the decade.

In June 1962, 49 SDS members and a few nonmembers gathered at a retreat owned by the American Federation of Labor–Congress of Industrial Organizations at Port Huron, near Detroit. As one of their leaders, Tom Hayden, later said, they came to found a movement and "declare a crossroads in history." More specifically, they came to discuss a 75-page draft document written the previous December by Hayden. (Hayden 1988, 85) After he presented it, the participants broke into small study groups—sitting under trees, taking notes, drinking coffee, and, for five days, debating.

The resulting Port Huron Statement outlined what had drawn the group together, and it critiqued cold-war society. "We are people of this generation, bred in at least modest comfort, housed now in universities, looking uncomfortably to the world we inherit," the statement declared before clarifying what had shaken this generation out of its complacency: the civil rights struggle and fears that the cold war might lead to nuclear devastation.

The Port Huron Statement offered few concrete proposals, but it attacked both liberalism and right-wing anticommunism. The former it portrayed as in league with those who desired a militaristic society and wanted to protect the political status quo, and the latter it portrayed as promoting oppressive extremism. In *The Sixties*, Todd Gitlin states that "what haunted this generation was not the specter of communism but the force and mood of McCarthyism." (121) The Port Huron Statement showed how the image of democracy contrasted with the reality of racism, the image of peace with huge military budgets, and the image of equality with poverty. Individual rights, the SDSers proclaimed, had been eroded and power concentrated in an elite. The manifesto called for a new democracy:

> We would replace power rooted in possession, privilege, or circumstance by power and uniqueness rooted in love, reflectiveness, reason, and creativity. . . . We seek the establishment of a democracy of individual participation, governed by two central aims: that the individual share in those social decisions determining the quality and direction of his life; that society be organized to encourage independence in men and provide the media for their common participation. (Miller 1996, 189)

Toward this end, the document emphasized the need for immediate reform in an intransigent society: "In this is perhaps the outstanding paradox: we ourselves are imbued with urgency, yet the message of our society is that there is no viable alternative to the present." (Findley, 1972, 37)

Whereas in the past, Old Left liberals had sought to form labor unions and promote reform through them, the Port Huron Statement looked toward college students as the primary agents of change. Hayden believed students would be the ones to "awaken other classes of people to participate in the democratic process." (Miller 1996, 189) As if to emphasize this, after liberals tied to the labor movement reacted negatively to the Port Huron Statement, SDS committed itself to a complete break with the Old Left.

Later that summer, SDS delegates distributed mimeographed copies of the Port Huron Statement to those attending the National Student Association meeting in Columbus, Ohio. Over the next few years, thousands of copies circulated on college campuses. Despite this, relatively few young people read the document, and it failed to impress those in the counterculture who rejected politics, particularly the hippies.

Still, the Port Huron Statement summarized a generation's discontent and provided a grand, sweeping vision—an idealistic naiveté that radical change could occur peacefully. Further, the statement excited those who participated in the original conference. As the meeting concluded, the participants walked along Lake Huron's shore to watch the sun rise and contemplate the future: "It was exalting," said one. "We thought that we knew what had to be done, and that we were going to do it."

See also Hayden, Tom; New Left; Students for a Democratic Society.

References Anderson, Terry H., *The Movement and the Sixties* (1995); Findley, Tim, "Tom Hayden Rolling Stone Interview Part 2," *Rolling Stone*, 9 November 1972, 28–34; Gitlin, Todd, *The Sixties: Years of Hope, Days of Rage* (1987); Hayden, Tom, *Reunion: A Memoir* (1988); Miller, Douglas T., *On Our Own: Americans in the Sixties* (1996); Miller, James, *Democracy Is in the Streets: From Port Huron to the Siege of Chicago* (1987); Sale, Kirkpatrick, *SDS* (1973).

Poster Art

Eye-catching and psychedelic, poster art first emerged in San Francisco to advertise rock dance-concerts. These posters placed the commercial message second in importance to the design.

The most original poster art at first came from Chet Helms for the dance-concerts he sponsored beginning in 1966 through his promotion business, The Family Dog. Helms usually conceived the ideas and sometimes supplied the art in posters produced by Wes Wilson. Helms, for example, created The Family Dog logo, an Indian with long hair, a stovepipe hat, and a large cigarette dangling from its mouth, all beside a motto: "May the Baby Jesus Shut Your Mouth and Open Your Mind." Wilson provided the lettering for these posters, using freehand to create distorted shapes, which he initially produced in one color. This design resulted in crowded-looking posters, difficult to read. But rational acts, such as reading, meant little in psychedelia—images carried the day.

For a while, Wilson worked both for Helms and for Bill Graham, a competing concert promoter in the hippie Haight-Ashbury district. Graham, however, preferred more straightforward posters with limited imagery. In addition to Wilson, Helms employed Stanley "Mouse" Miller to create posters. Miller used varied, colorful imagery involving pop art, collages, cartoons, and surrealism. Meanwhile, by 1967, Wilson had developed roller lettering, even more distorted than that used previously. Also by this time, the posters had attained so much popularity that young people removed them from walls and utility poles as quickly as they could be put up. Helms and Graham then began distributing extra posters to those who attended their dance-concerts.

This creative work in posters quickly received recognition as a legitimate art form. The Oakland Art Museum displayed a collection in 1966, soon followed by the San Francisco Art Institute, and then a large showing at that city's Moore Gallery, complete with rock music provided by Country Joe and the Fish.

Poster art lost its popularity when the counterculture faded, but its influence continued, and several poster artists designed album covers and T-shirts for rock bands.

See also The Family Dog; Graham, Bill; Helms, Chet.

Pot

To the counterculture, *pot* meant marijuana.

See also Marijuana.

The Power Elite

Although C. Wright Mills (1916–1962) wrote *The Power Elite* in the mid-1950s, it affected the counterculture a decade later. In this book, Mills, a sociologist, criticizes American society as an undemocratic oligarchy conforming to a corporate state. He says: "The life-fate of the modern individual depends not only upon the family . . . but increasingly upon the corporation in which he spends the most alert hours of his best years." (6)

His observations seemed valid in the 1960s to both the radical political activists who considered the United States undemocratic (many of whom had read Mills in college) and the hippies disgusted with society's conformity.

Reference Mills, C. Wright, *The Power Elite* (1956).

Power to the People

Political activists in the counterculture used the phrase "power to the people" to express their desire for democratization in a society they considered elitist. The words carried more than political implications, however, and reflected a broader view that society should as a whole reflect the people's desires.

Procol Harum

In Latin, *procol harum* means "beyond these things," and this rock group produced a hit record in 1967 that expressed the "beyond" in psychedelics: "A Whiter Shade of Pale." John Lennon of the Beatles called it the perfect LSD song.

Before Procul Harum even existed, Keith Reid, an Englishman, wrote the poem that provided the song's lyrics. He then met Gary Brooker, an unemployed musician, who set it to music. From there, they formed a band with organist Matthew Fisher, guitarist Roy Royer, bassist Dave Knights, and drummer Bobby Harrison. In recording "Whiter Shade of Pale" they used Bachian organ riffs. Decca Records released it on 12 May 1967, and it quickly hit the charts in the United States, Britain, and France.

In all, Procul Harum recorded ten albums, but in 1977, after several personnel changes, the band broke up.

Progressive Labor

One of the great struggles for power within the New Left involved Progressive Labor (PL). The group emerged in 1962 as a small Maoist party, siding with China during the Sino-Soviet split. Even though young activists in increasing numbers gravitated toward the New Left in the early 1960s, PL failed to attract them; as a result, in 1966, it decided to work within the most prominent New Left organization, Students for a Democratic Society (SDS), and gain control of it. PL wanted to move SDS away from its emphasis on building a student power base and toward a broader following.

PL espoused a strident Marxist-Maoist line, and unlike SDS as a whole, it enforced strict discipline on its members. Consequently, what PL did not have in numbers it had in commitment, and the group managed to cause a huge ruckus.

PL's grab for power encouraged another faction to form: Third World Marxists, many of whose members had formerly cooperated with PL. The Third World Marxists advocated student street action to help bring down the U.S. government, but PL disagreed, insisting that such tactics would cause a conservative reaction among industrial workers and hurt the prospects of a socialist revolution.

As it increasingly stressed the role of the proletariat in overthrowing capitalism, PL shifted its ideological position away from Chinese communism, which emphasized third-world peasant revolts, to orthodox Marxism immersed in authoritarian control, akin to Stalinism in the Soviet Union. (Although in a peculiar twist, the group still pronounced its admiration for Mao.)

However confusing and withered the ideological disputes between Third World Marxists and PL may seem today, at the time they assumed momentous proportions for these two groups as they struggled to control SDS. The final showdown occurred in June 1969 at the SDS National Convention in Chicago. By that time, the Third World Marxists had adopted the name Weatherman (after the lyrics in a Bob Dylan song). They ridiculed PL's position that racism and male chauvinism were less important than the class struggle, and one Weatherman speaker called PL "armchair Marxists" who had yet to take the struggle into the streets. PL delegates shouted down these remarks and tempers flared.

After a Black Panther representative demanded PL be expelled from SDS, Weatherman held a rump session and did so. PL then faded from radical prominence, although it continues today as a small, ineffective organization.

See also May 2nd Movement; New Left; Students for a Democratic Society.

Reference Sale, Kirkpatrick, *SDS* (1973).

Psilocybin

Psilocybin is a chemical compound derived from the mushroom, *Psilocybe mexicana*. In 1958, Albert Hofmann, a chemist who had synthesized LSD, extracted the compound and replicated it at the Sandoz Pharmaceutical Laboratories in Switzerland. In its manufactured form, psilocybin assumed a central role in the 1960s drug culture.

In 1960, Timothy Leary, a psychologist at Harvard, first took psilocybin mushrooms while on a trip to Mexico. He reported a spiritual revelation whereby he realized that beauty and sensuality resided within him. After he returned to Harvard, Leary began an infamous experimental program. In one instance, he administered psilocybin to inmates at the Massachusetts Correctional Institute, and the project resulted in a sharp drop in recidivism. In yet another, he gave the drug to ten theology students, nine of whom reported an intense mystical religious experience.

Proponents of psychedelic drugs within the counterculture considered psilocybin, along with LSD, as able to alter personalities for the better and as a result radically improve society.

See also Alpert, Richard; Drugs and the Drug Culture; Huxley, Aldous; Leary, Timothy; LSD; Magic Mushrooms; Mescaline; Peyote.

Reference Lee, Martin A., and Bruce Shlain, *Acid Dreams: The CIA, LSD, and the Sixties Rebellion* (1985).

Psychedelic

In 1957, the psychologist Humphry Osmond, a Briton who had immigrated to Canada, introduced the word "psychedelic" to a meeting of the New York Academy of Sciences. Shortly before this, he and the British author Aldous Huxley had taken mescaline and LSD. They disliked the prevailing terms used in psychological circles to describe the mystical trip experienced on these drugs—words such as hallucination and psychosis. Huxley originally coined "phanerothyme" as a descriptive, and sent the following couplet to Osmond:

> To make this trivial world sublime,
> Take half a gramme of phanerothyme.

To which Osmond replied:

> To fathom hell or soar angelic
> Just take a pinch of psychedelic.
> (Stevens 1987, 57)

To the counterculture, the word meant not only the actual hallucinogenic experience but also the events, art, music, and so forth that replicated the drug-induced distortions.

See also Drugs and the Drug Culture; Huxley, Aldous; LSD; Mescaline.

Reference Stevens, Jay, *Storming Heaven: LSD and the American Dream* (1987).

Psychedelic Art

Psychedelic art emerged in the counterculture to convey the hallucinatory images and emotions experienced while using LSD and similar drugs. The paintings displayed intense colors, kaleidoscopic swirls, and distorted shapes and forms. With this style, the drug acted as the agent in the artistic process, the artist its medium. The paintings of Isaac Abrams gained considerable renown.

The Psychedelic Experience

See Leary, Timothy.

Psychedelic Rangers

Everyone considered John Starr Cooke mysterious. A wealthy man who gravitated to the occult, Cooke traveled to Algiers, where polio confined him to a wheelchair, and where he supposedly obtained a miraculous ability to touch people and infuse them with energy. With this background, he formed the Psychedelic Rangers to initiate people in LSD.

As Haight-Ashbury teemed with hippies, Cooke lived in Cuernavaca, Mexico, where he gathered his Psychedelic Rangers and sent them on a mission: provide LSD to selected individuals so they could discover its revelatory power, its ability to connect human beings with the universal oneness. The Psychedelic Rangers supposedly gave LSD to activist Jerry Rubin and comedian Dick Gregory, along with a reporter for *Life* magazine. Cooke and his group played a leading role in organizing the Human Be-In at San Francisco in 1967 as part of their plan to psychedelicize the world and liberate it.

See also Be-In; Haight-Ashbury.

Reference Lee, Martin A., and Bruce Shlain, *Acid Dreams: The CIA, LSD, and the Sixties Rebellion* (1985).

Psychedelic Shop

Begun by Ron and Jay Thelin on 3 January 1966, the Psychedelic Shop emerged as a prominent countercultural business in America's hippie center, Haight-Ashbury, a district in San Francisco. The Thelins, who once owned a parking lot and boat and umbrella rental business at Lake Tahoe, were turned on to LSD in the mid-sixties and developed the idea of bringing together under one roof books about psychedelia and the occult, Indian records, incense, and drug paraphernalia. In short time, their small store (located on the corner of Haight and Ashbury) added posters, American Indian fabrics, clothing, and tickets for dances and rock concerts. The dark meditation room in the rear gained a reputation as a place where couples could engage in sex.

Some hippies, especially Emmett Grogan, criticized the Thelins for commercializing the psychedelic revolution. But while the brothers wanted to make a profit, they operated the shop in an unconventional way: they agreed with other Haight businesses not to carry items, such as handcrafted hippie goods, that might compete with those carried in a competitor's store, and they contributed generously to community projects. The Thelins envisioned a cooperative, self-sufficient setting where the Haight could exist independent of straight society.

The Psychedelic Shop served as more than a store—hippies gathered there and sometimes sat in chairs located in the front window, facing the street, from which they could gaze at the people outside. A community bulletin board—the first in Haight-Ashbury—allowed people to leave messages.

In short time, though, the Thelins encountered harassment from the authorities. First, building inspectors charged them with allowing too much loitering; then in November 1966, the police raided the shop for selling a supposedly obscene collection of poems, Lenore Kandel's *The Love Book*.

As with most businessmen in the Haight, the 1967 Summer of Love proved to be a bust, and the shop reported a debt totaling $6,000. That October it closed, and Ron Thelin joined a hippie group, the Diggers. The Psychedelic Shop's demise coincided with Haight-Ashbury's decline as an idealistic enclave founded on psychedelics, love, and community.

See also Haight-Ashbury; Head Shop; Hippies; *The Love Book*.

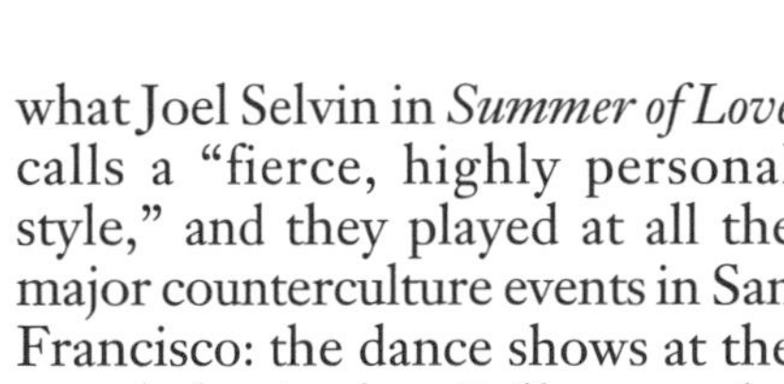

Quicksilver Messenger Service Although they never had a number one hit record, Quicksilver Messenger Service emerged in the mid-sixties as San Francisco's first prominent rock band, one that developed the psychedelic sound.

Quicksilver came about when David Freiberg, excited by the Byrd's song "Turn, Turn, Turn," joined John Cipollina, a guitarist who had played on the Bay Area's folk music circuit, and Jim Murray. They then recruited Gary Duncan as a rhythm guitarist and Greg Elmore as a drummer. The group coined their name based on the astrological dominance of Mercury among them. They first appeared as Quicksilver in December 1965 at a party thrown by an improvisational comedy troupe in North Beach, their pay $200 and two ounces of marijuana.

Within the next few months, Quicksilver had improved considerably, producing what Joel Selvin in *Summer of Love* calls a "fierce, highly personal style," and they played at all the major counterculture events in San Francisco: the dance shows at the Fillmore and the Avalon Ballroom, the Human Be-In, and Winterland, among others.

Quicksilver recorded its first album in 1968, self-titled, and *Happy Trails* in 1969, a highly acclaimed live LP. Three other albums followed in 1970 and 1971, but by then the band had changed personnel, and shortly thereafter it broke up. Today, critics generally consider Quicksilver Messenger Service along with the Grateful Dead as the two most influential bands in the San Francisco counterculture.

See also Rock Music.

References Selvin, Joel, *Summer of Love: The Inside Story of LSD, Rock & Roll, Free Love and High Times in the Wild West* (1994); http://www.penncen.com/quicksilver/.

Ram Dass
See Alpert, Richard.

Ramparts
In May 1962, *Ramparts* magazine appeared, a radical publication edited by Catholic laymen in San Francisco. *Ramparts* dedicated itself to presenting fiction, poetry, art, criticism, and essays representing, it asserted, "those positive principles of the Hellenic-Christian tradition which have shaped and sustained our civilization for the past two thousand years."

As the Vietnam War, counterculture, and protest movements intensified in the 1960s, *Ramparts* developed a political voice, attacking those who supported the war, including businessmen and clerics. Although not an underground newspaper, it gained inspiration from them and frequently published startling exposés. In 1967, for example, *Ramparts* revealed that the National Student Association, a nationwide organization of college student governments, had for years obtained money from the CIA.

In other issues, the magazine presented evidence that questioned the official government investigation of President John Kennedy's assassination, and it carried the writings of Black Panther Eldridge Cleaver and leftist leader Tom Hayden who, in referring to the radical takeover at Columbia University in 1968, called for "two, three, many Columbias." *Ramparts* last appeared in the mid-1970s.
See also Underground Newspapers.

Rap
Rap meant to talk casually, usually at great length. Thus, "Let's sit down and rap about life."

Rat
Displaying its logo, a rodent carrying a rifle, *Rat* emerged in March 1968 as an underground newspaper devoted to leftist revolutionary change. Jeff Shero founded *Rat* at a time when protests were sweeping the nation's college campuses, with one of the most infamous at Columbia. There, radical students stormed and captured the administration building. *Rat* supported the student takeover and the theft of files from the president's office that showed Columbia's involvement in research to produce weapons of war and its ownership of slum property. The newspaper printed some of the stolen files, and its May 1968 issue bore the headline "Heil Columbia" and a drawing of the college library topped by a huge, swastika-inscribed steel helmet.

Soon, a feminist rebellion rattled *Rat*. Women at the newspaper (and women throughout the underground press) disliked their relegation to a secondary status among reporters and editors, and they chastised their male colleagues for writing sexist stories. So, in January 1970, they commandeered *Rat* and secured the right to put out their own issue. In one article, Robin Morgan ripped the New Left for its traditional male sexism. *Rat* soon changed its name to *Women's Liberation*, and then in the early 1970s collapsed amid disagreements within the leftist movement.
See also Morgan, Robin; Underground Newspapers.

The Realist
See Krassner, Paul.

Rebel without a Cause
Released in 1955, *Rebel without a Cause* deeply affected the 1960s counterculture

in the critical way it portrayed middle-class society.

Directed by Ray Nichols, the movie stars James Dean as the rebel Jim, whose parents fail to provide him with the guidance he needs. His mother dominates the household, and in this environment his father lacks masculinity—he has even taken to wearing a woman's apron when cooking meals. Disgusted with this weakness and his parents' belief that by providing him with material goods they have provided him with everything he needs, Jim rebels and is picked up by the police for being drunk and disorderly.

Later, he falls in love with Judy (Natalie Wood), a lonely girl who cannot relate to her parents, and the couple befriends Plato (Sal Mineo), whose family is always traveling and leaving him in the care of a housekeeper. First Jim, and later Judy and Plato, get into trouble with a gang, and this tension drives the movie's plot.

In the 1950s, young people flocked to see *Rebel* and especially James Dean who—with his practiced off-cadence speech, sullen expression, good looks, and belief in living for today—epitomized cool. Parents, though, criticized *Rebel* for promoting violence and for condemning the older generation.

Rebel gained notoriety as one of the first major motion pictures to present teenage America from a teenage viewpoint. Many young people who later participated in the counterculture, mainly those involved in its early phase, related to James Dean and the movie. Bob Dylan read stories about Dean in magazines. David Wellman, a New Left leader, tried in the late fifties to copy Dean's haircut and supported *Rebel*'s critique of society. These people related as well to Dean's death in an automobile crash shortly after he finished *Rebel*. The tragedy made Dean a cult hero and exposed mortality in a society that wanted to sanitize life for its youth.

See also Beat; Beatnik.

References Alexander, Paul, *Boulevard of Broken Dreams: The Life, Times, and Legend of James Dean* (1994); Dalton, David, *James Dean, The Mutant King: A Biography* (1974).

Red Dog Saloon

Located in Virginia City, Nevada—a former silver boomtown geographically far removed from San Francisco and its hippie scene—the Red Dog Saloon thrived as a psychedelic hangout, where drugs, music, colors, and clothes expressed a countercultural style.

The idea for the Red Dog Saloon originated with Mark Unobsky, who provided the main capital for the venture; Chan Laughlin, who once owned a coffeehouse in San Francisco; and Don Works, who owned a mine. They originally wanted to open a bar that would draw folk musicians traveling between New York and California, but their plan changed after George Hunter, an experimenter with light-and-sound shows, convinced them to hire a rock band called the Charlatans. This group had never before played in public, but Hunter liked the way they looked—Edwardian garb, then popular among hippies, mixed with cowboy outfits, which made them appear as if they had stepped out of the Old West.

The saloon opened on 29 June 1965 in the historical Comstock House building. Red walls bordered in black, velvet curtains, and Victorian furniture greeted visitors. Throughout the summer, thousands flocked from San Francisco to the saloon, where they listened to the Charlatans—who even displayed some musical ability—and reveled in marijuana, LSD, and the innovational color light show devised by Bill Hamm.

Yet Red Dog Summer, as many called it, came to a crashing end. The locals complained about drugs and "long-haired freaks," and after the Charlatans were busted by police for marijuana possession, the saloon's owners fired them.

Unobsky closed the Red Dog for a while but reopened it in 1966. Rock bands appeared again that summer, most notably Big Brother and the Holding Company. But the scene had calmed considerably, and despite a visit by Ken Kesey and the Merry Pranksters, most hippies went elsewhere. The saloon was soon converted into Kitty's

Long Branch, a Western bar. Nevertheless, in its heyday the Red Dog had promoted psychedelia, and several persons involved in the venture, including the founders of The Family Dog, which promoted rock concerts in San Francisco, took their experiences and ideas with them to California—the music, the costumes, the freedom, the adventure—all essential elements in the counterculture.

See also The Family Dog; Haight-Ashbury; Hippies.

Redstockings

Shulamith Firestone and Ellen Willis organized Redstockings in 1969 as a radical feminist group dedicated to addressing women's issues apart from any connection with the male-dominated New Left. They issued the Redstockings manifesto that declared:

> Women are an oppressed class. Our oppression is total, affecting every facet of our lives. We are exploited as sex objects, breeders, domestic servants, and cheap labor. . . .
>
> We identify the agents of our oppression as men. Male supremacy is the oldest, most basic form of domination. All other forms of exploitation and oppression (racism, capitalism, imperialism, etc.) are extensions of male supremacy. . . . *All men* have oppressed women. . . .
>
> We call on all our sisters to unite with us in struggle.
>
> We call on all men to give up their male privileges and support women's liberation in the interest of our humanity and their own.
>
> In fighting for our liberation we will always take the side of women against their oppressors. We will not ask what is "revolutionary" or "reformist," only what is good for women.
>
> The time for individual skirmishes has passed. This time we are going all the way. (Morgan 1970, 598–602)

See also Women's Movement.

Reference Morgan, Robin, ed., *Sisterhood Is Powerful: An Anthology of Writings from the Women's Liberation Movement* (1970).

Reichian Psychology

Reichian psychology involved a controversial theory developed by psychoanalyst Wilhelm Reich (1897–1957). Reich, born, raised, and professionally trained in Austria, moved to the United States in 1939 and advocated his orgone energy theory. He said that orgone permeated the universe, including human beings, and they must release it through sexual activity or suffer neuroses. To support his research, he founded the Orgone Institute, and to help in the energy release he invented the orgone box.

Many colleagues ridiculed Reich, and he served two years in jail for making fraudulent claims in his practice. Yet his ideas found a home with some in the counterculture who believed that sexual repression caused psychological problems and that irrational forces operated in the universe.

References Cattier, Michel, *The Life and Work of Wilhelm Reich* (1971); Reich, Ilse Ollendorff, *Wilhelm Reich: A Personal Biography* (1969); Reich, Wilhelm, *Passion of Youth: An Autobiography, 1897–1922* (1988).

Roach

A roach was not a bug but a butt—a marijuana cigarette butt, that is. Oftentimes, smokers saved roaches and used the accumulated marijuana to make a new joint.

Rock Music

Eclectic and innovative, sexual and political, popular and pervasive, rock 'n' roll defined the counterculture. "For our generation, music is the most vital force in most of our lives," said activist John Sinclair. (Anderson 1995, 246) This influence resulted from rock expressing a mentality that challenged the very foundations supporting mainstream society. Sex, drugs, and rock 'n' roll reached a combustible level.

Rock 'n' roll emerged as a distinct musical form in the early 1950s. With its doo-wop sound, the connection between it and sixties rock may seem slight, but in actuality while counterculture rock broke new ground, it continued many early developments. From its beginning, rock symbolized youth culture and rebellion, and adults considered it too primitive, too sexual, and too African American. Indeed, rooted in the blues and country sounds that emanated from blacks and poor southern whites, rock connected middle-class youngsters to a subculture quite different from the suburbs in which they lived. As a result, rock became a way to challenge conformity, to break the constraints imposed by suburbia and the adults who ruled it.

Whatever rebelliousness existed in rock, however, encountered a leavening influence, namely business. Performers and record companies did not exist simply to entertain but to make money. This required appealing to a young audience, but doing so in a way that would not cause adults to shut down the industry. Thus, from the start rock musicians censored their lyrics to reduce sexuality, and when controversy arose, such as when politicians and parents complained about too many black influences, the record companies sanitized the trade. They did this by promoting clean-cut white kids who recorded songs produced assembly-line style and puppy love in content. Bobby Vee, Bobby Rydell, and countless others fulfilled this requirement with their bland sounds and letter-sweater looks. Even Elvis Presley, provocative in his early days, appeared greatly tamed by the late fifties.

In the early 1960s, many young people began rejecting this format as unexciting, conformist, and irrelevant. They wondered how music supposedly created for them could ignore developments increasingly important to their generation—the civil rights protests, the nuclear arms buildup, an expanding war in Vietnam. As their consciousness stirred, they turned to a musical form that had, for years, treated social problems and war seriously, namely folk music. Pete Seeger, Joan Baez, and Phil Ochs appeared before large audiences in coffeehouses and on college campuses. So, too, did Bob Dylan, who would alter the course of rock.

At the same time, and in partial contradiction to these developments, young people tuned in to the Beatles. When this British band arrived in New York on 7 February 1964 aboard Pan Am Flight 101, they brought with them music far removed from social issues—songs such as "I Wanna' Hold Your Hand" and "She Loves You." They appealed in part to the innocence and good times American youngsters sought after the shocking assassination of President John Kennedy. The Beatles provided escape. Yet they provided, too, a rejuvenated rebelliousness. As trite as their lyrics may have been, their music had a beat, the Liverpool sound, that challenged assembly-line American rock, and the band's long hair made a statement (much as had Presley's sideburns a decade earlier) that young people would set their own standards.

A year later, folk social consciousness and rock sounds converged, with Dylan and the Beatles at the forefront but with other artists contributing substantially. Some observers trace this to the 1965 Newport Folk Festival when Dylan appeared for the first time on stage playing an electric guitar. While this upset folk purists, it widened Dylan's audience, and more youths than ever before heard his lyrics criticizing middle-class conformity. Political activist Todd Gitlin said about his fellow college students: "We admired Dylan's ability to smuggle the subversive into mass-culture trappings." (Gitlin 1987, 197)

During this year, and more so the next, the Beatles experimented, too, evolving into a more mature, introspective band influenced by social changes and drugs. This showed itself in their albums *Revolver* and *Rubber Soul* with songs such as "Dr. Roberts," "Nowhere Man," and "Norwegian Wood."

At about the same time, the Byrds popularized Dylan's song "Mr. Tambourine Man" with its nonlinear form and drug implications. And Barry McGuire condemned mainstream society's decay in his powerful "Eve of Destruction." Suddenly rock appeared countercultural rather than just subcultural, offering values that challenged the mainstream to its core.

The San Francisco sound that burst onto the national scene in 1966 and remained prominent until decade's end reinforced this challenge. Jefferson Airplane, Quicksilver Messenger Service, the Grateful Dead, and others developed psychedelic music, with simple melodies and electronic distortion, attuned to the influences then emerging from the LSD experience in the hippie Haight-Ashbury district. These sounds influenced rock bands outside the area, as it did the Beatles who recorded *Sgt. Pepper's Lonely Hearts Club Band*. Released in 1967, this album's path-breaking format united the songs within it to a common theme and displayed the band's immersion in psychedelia. Notably, *Sgt. Pepper's* release coincided with Beatle Paul McCartney signing a full-page ad in the *London Times* that called marijuana laws immoral and unworkable.

Although politics and drugs characterized a new stage in rock, the music maintained its attachment to sexuality. The Rolling Stones typified this with their sensual songs and lead singer Mick Jagger's stage antics. Of course, rock bands did not always fit neatly into one musical style, and many combined sex with politics and drugs—the Stones, for one, and to a greater extent the Doors, a Los Angeles–based band whose prominence owed in part to lead singer Jim Morrison's eroticism and mysticism.

In fact, mysticism flowed through counterculture rock and converged with idealism, at least until the late sixties. Whereas a decade earlier rock artists had sung about puppy love, now influenced by psychedelics, they sang about communal love, about humankind, brothers and sisters getting together and loving one another. A mystical harmony, the music said, must and will replace the cold, impersonal society the younger generation had inherited.

New York City policemen attempt to restrain hordes of teenagers—mostly female—from piling into the hotel where the Beatles were staying. At a time of social unrest, the Beatles' music and innocent lyrics provided American teenagers with an escape. Later in the decade, rock bands such as Jefferson Airplane and the Grateful Dead would bring psychedelic music to the forefront.

In terms of musicians, whites dominated psychedelic rock. Only Jimi Hendrix and Sly and the Family Stone provided notable exceptions. As in the 1950s, though, rock connected white society with black, in this instance through a blues revival. Numerous white musicians learned from African American blues masters, and although many bands that used the blues failed to rise above mediocrity, others performed well: the Jeff Beck Group; Electric Flag; the J. Geils Band; Traffic; and Blood, Sweat, and Tears.

By the late 1960s, rock music had hardened, once again reflecting changing social conditions. In 1968, the assassinations of Martin Luther King, Jr. and Robert Kennedy, and the violence at the Democratic National Convention, indicated to the counterculture that the system would not accept radical change, or any change that might effectively represent young America's views. The rock bands Steppenwolf and MC5 presented a highly politicized anticapitalist message, and angry themes from them and others surged to the fore.

Yet, conversely, some people searched for the mellow, as in Dylan's change to a country sound and in the placidity found in Crosby, Stills, Nash, and Young (at least prior to the shootings at Kent State University). Hope for flower power had faded, though, and the journey into the mellow represented escape—a kind that corresponded with the back-to-the-earth movement and its bucolic vision.

An inner tension has always existed in rock music between authenticity and commercialism. In the sixties, rock grew bigger as a business, and record companies rushed to exploit the hottest sound, be it psychedelic or some other style. By the early 1970s, many young people considered rock too packaged and predictable, much as the previous generation had felt about it a decade earlier. From this arose punk rock, although rock music went in many other directions as well.

Whatever rock's commercial aspects, for the 1960s counterculture the music had held a promise—that it would reflect countercultural desires and in the end free society. Many youths considered rock a liberating force, either culturally, politically, or both. Rock expressed feelings, ideals, and practices at odds with the mainstream. Of course, how far any young person went in adopting countercultural values as a result of rock music varied. But whatever similarities it may have had to its earlier form, counterculture rock expressed something different: that its audience would listen and come away changed—and the old society would crumble.

See also Avalon Ballroom; Baez, Joan; The Beatles; The Doors; Dylan, Bob; Fillmore; Grateful Dead; Haight-Ashbury; Hendrix, Jimi; Jefferson Airplane; Ochs, Phil; Quicksilver Messenger Service; The Rolling Stones; Sly and the Family Stone.

References Anderson, Terry H., *The Movement and the Sixties* (1995); Gitlin, Todd, *The Sixties: Years of Hope, Days of Rage* (1987); Selvin, Joel, *Summer of Love: The Inside Story of LSD, Rock & Roll, Free Love and High Times in the Wild West* (1994); Ward, Ed, Geoffrey Stokes, and Ken Tucker, *Rock of Ages: The Rolling Stone History of Rock & Roll* (1986).

Rolling Stone

Ideas, mood, and music—*Rolling Stone* magazine communicated countercultural developments in these areas using a style similar to the underground press but more commercial and less political.

Jann Wenner, a college dropout, borrowed $7,500 in 1967 to begin *Rolling Stone*. Wenner, then only 21 years old, had dabbled in journalism at the University of California–Berkeley, where he wrote a rock music column for the campus newspaper. Infatuated with rock 'n' roll, he immersed himself in the emerging San Francisco music scene, forming a friendship with Ralph Gleason, a longtime music critic for area newspapers, and attending dance-concerts at the Avalon Ballroom. In 1966, Wenner was hired to edit *Sunday Ramparts*, a spin-off of *Ramparts* magazine, and applied his pen to discussing rock's revolutionary aspects.

That same year, *Crawdaddy!* appeared, a magazine that treated rock as intrinsically important rather than peripheral to other issues. Wenner liked the concept but disliked the magazine's style. Influenced by what he saw in underground newspapers and by their founders who had started them with little money, Wenner believed he could begin his own rock magazine on a shoestring. Thus, *Rolling Stone* made its debut on 18 October 1967, with Wenner and his friend Gleason going from business to business in San Francisco, selling ads to radio stations and head shops. An early issue of *Rolling Stone* offered a free roach clip with every new subscription. This blatant appeal to the drug culture angered Gleason, but Wenner decided to run the magazine as he saw fit.

By early 1968, he had obtained advertising from major record labels, and later that year scored a controversial breakthrough when the manager of the Beatles agreed to have *Rolling Stone* publish a photograph of John Lennon and his wife, Yoko Ono, in the nude.

As *Rolling Stone* grew, Wenner lived lavishly, partying with rock stars and spending money on limousines, clothes, and drugs. He had little use for politics and considered his magazine a profit-making venture rather than one geared toward social reform. According to Laurence Leamer in *The Paper Revolutionaries*, Wenner's publication smoothed the counterculture's radical edges "to make it manageable and neutral." (166)

Wenner attracted writers to *Rolling Stone* who treated journalism experimentally and creatively. They rejected the objectivity found in mainstream newspapers as devious subterfuge used for communicating mainstream establishment ideas. At first, the magazine covered only the San Francisco scene, but soon it carried articles about bands on the East Coast, such as the Velvet Underground, and it interviewed notables—John Lennon, Mick Jagger, Jim Morrison, and Bob Dylan—thus earning a reputation for penetrating analysis. Young, talented writers flocked to *Rolling Stone*, and Wenner helped shape them, or at least gave them room to express themselves as they desired: Tim Cahill, Cameron Crowe, Greil Marcus, Hunter S. Thompson.

Still, in 1970, *Rolling Stone* neared collapse. Wenner claimed he had $100,000 in the bank, but he actually had nowhere near that. His profligacy—while most on the staff lived close to the bone—had contributed to the crisis. Wenner subsequently invoked an austerity budget and in another coup, obtained an exclusive interview with John Lennon that caused two issues in December 1970 to sell out. With these moves, *Rolling Stone* not only survived, it went on to prosper. What Wenner called "a little rock and roll newspaper from San Francisco" lived beyond the counterculture, moved its headquarters to New York City, and developed into the leading commercialized magazine for young America.

Activist Abbie Hoffman said about *Rolling Stone:* "The ease with which the larger society absorbed and diluted hippie culture I still regard as a defeat. . . . The spontaneity of the counterculture press was absorbed by *Rolling Stone* and hip capitalism became the sponge used to mop up hippie originality." (Hoffman 1980, 124)

See also Underground Newspapers.

References Draper, Robert, *Rolling Stone Magazine: The Uncensored History* (1990); Hoffman, Abbie, *Soon To Be a Major Motion Picture* (1980); Leamer, Laurence, *The Paper Revolutionaries: The Rise of the Underground Press* (1972).

The Rolling Stones

In contrast to the Beatles when they arrived in America, the Rolling Stones presented themselves as the bad boys of rock—the kind that no parent would want their daughter to be near. They parlayed this image and remarkable musical talent into becoming a rock 'n' roll institution.

In the early 1960s, three young musicians began sharing a squalid apartment in London: Mick Jagger (a student at the London School of Economics), Keith Richards, and Brian Jones. Together with drummer Tony Chapman, and under Jones's leadership, they formed a band and

Members of the Rolling Stones, aboard a boat on the Hudson River, 24 June 1966. Band members, from left to right: Bill Wyman, Brian Jones, Mick Jagger, Keith Richards, and Charlie Watts.

cut a demo tape—promptly rejected by record companies (with one critic advising them to get rid of the big-lipped Jagger as too ugly).

When Chapman left the band to attend art school, Jagger, Richards, and Jones added Dick Taylor on bass and Mike Avory on drums, and at Jones's suggestion began calling themselves the Rolling Stones, after a Muddy Waters song. Presently, Taylor and Avory were replaced by guitarist Bill Wyman and a new drummer, Charlie Watts, who had played for a band called Blues, Inc., but at the time was working for an advertising agency. Ian Stewart played piano and, as the only band member with a steady job, provided needed financial support.

In 1963, Andrew Loog Oldham began managing the Rolling Stones. Amid the English craze for the Beatles, he molded them into a moody, ill-behaved alternative (forcing out the mild-looking Stewart, who worked from then on as a road manager and studio musician). Unlike the Beatles, the Stones in their early existence did not write their own music, and they displayed a greater blues influence. In December 1963, they made the British top 20 with "I Wanna' Be Your Man," a song written by the Beatles' John Lennon and Paul McCartney. They first toured the United States in June 1964, soon after the Beatles had appeared on American television, and they had their first big American hit that November with "Time Is on My Side."

Thereafter, Mick Jagger and Keith Richards wrote nearly all their music. In 1965, they composed a song that expressed youthful frustration and that the counterculture adopted en masse: "I Can't Get No Satisfaction." Numerous top-ten hits followed during that year and the next, including "Get Off of My Cloud," "As Tears Go By," "Mother's Little Helper," and "Have You Seen Your Mother, Baby, Standing in the Shadows?" The last two slammed the older generation's hypocrisy, with "Mother's Little Helper" declaring "What a drag it is getting old."

When the Beatles moved toward diverse, complex songs, the Stones did, too, showing a strong Eastern influence in, for example, "Painted Black." They caused a sensation in 1967 when they appeared on the *Ed Sullivan Show* and had the word "night" censored from their song "Let's Spend the Night Together." To Sullivan, the word implied sexuality that should not be on commercial TV.

After the Beatles released *Sgt. Pepper's Lonely Hearts Club Band* in 1967 to tremendous commercial and critical success, the Stones tried desperately to release a similar, history-making work. The Beatles had, for the first time, compiled an album that contained a unified theme, used instrumentation and sound effects in innovative ways, and blended rock with Eastern and drug-induced mysticism. The Stones responded in December with *Their Satanic Majesties Request*, replete with a three-dimensional album cover. Unfortunately for them, critics universally panned it as an indecipherable mess, and it sold poorly. Their foray into psychedelic rock seemed a disaster.

After Richards insisted the Stones get back to basics, they recovered in May 1968 with "Jumpin' Jack Flash," a hard-driving rocker that reached the top ten, and another album, *Beggar's Banquet*, which critics hailed. In June 1969, Brian Jones quit the band over artistic differences. The Stones hired Mick Taylor to replace him. Just one month later, in July, Jones was found dead in his swimming pool after having overdosed on drugs.

That summer and fall, the Stones toured the United States, and although fans crowded the concerts and cheered their music, including their latest hit "Honky Tonk Woman," critics claimed that the band had displayed selfish, egotistical behavior—fits of jealousy, for example, when the opening acts received great reviews—and had charged exorbitant ticket prices. In November, the Stones responded by announcing a free concert in San Francisco. Mick Jagger and company hoped to replicate the peace and good times that had recently occurred at Woodstock. Held at the Altamont Raceway, the concert, which included several other bands, proved to be a disaster, marred by people on bad drug trips, short tempers, poor planning by the Stones, and runaway Hell's Angels—hired to serve as security—who beat persons in the audience with lead-tipped pool cues and knifed and stomped a black youth to death. With songs such as "Sympathy for the Devil," which they had played shortly before the knifing incident, the Stones had built a satanic image—now they paid the price, and criticism engulfed them as the ugly scene at Altamont seemed to signal the end to the ideals that had fueled the counterculture.

The Stones showed their resiliency, however, and during the 1970s they recorded numerous hit albums and singles while engaging in three successful American tours. The band underwent some personnel changes, too. During the 1980s, the Stones recorded additional hit albums, but nothing approaching the originality found in their earlier works. In the late 1980s, the band went dormant as Jagger and Richards quarreled and released solo albums, and it looked like the Stones had come to an end.

In 1989, however, the Stones released a new album and again toured the United States, breaking attendance records. Yet another concert tour followed in 1992—the band members by then in their fifties. Their status as an institution well established, the Stones' creativity resided largely in the tumultuous sixties, a decade that, with their help, had taken rock 'n' roll in new directions.

See also Altamont; Rock Music.

References Booth, Stanley, *Dance with the Devil: The Rolling Stones and Their Times* (1984); Norman, Philip, *Symphony for the Devil: The Rolling Stones Story* (1984).

Rubin, Jerry (1938–1994)

A leader in the Yippies and other activist groups, Jerry Rubin displayed the countercultural crosscurrents of politics and culture. Beginning as a political protester, he later declared "revolution is theater-in-the-streets" and advocated attacks on culture to reveal society's injustices and absurdities. (Albert and Albert 1984, 443)

Rubin grew up in Cincinnati, Ohio, where he was born on 14 July 1938. His parents, both Jewish, differed in a noticeable way: his mother was well educated, while his father drove a truck and worked as a business agent for the Teamsters Union. They provided their son with a comfortable upbringing and the opportunity for a college education. In the late 1950s, Rubin enrolled at the University of Cincinnati. He graduated in 1961 and worked as a newspaper reporter in his hometown.

Rubin read widely, especially politics, and developed an interest in socialist ideas. Late in 1961, he went to Israel and began graduate studies in Jerusalem. As he surveyed the scene there, he found himself identifying more and more with the Palestinians and, at the same time, associating with socialists who deepened his discontent with capitalism.

In 1964, Rubin left Israel for the University of California–Berkeley, where he began studying for a doctorate in sociology (which he never completed). The timing could not have been more propitious given his newfound ideology, for that fall the Free Speech Movement broke out on campus, and Rubin, attracted to the fight against societal oppression, joined it.

The following year, Rubin helped organize Berkeley's first teach-in against the Vietnam War. From there, he founded the Vietnam Day Committee (VDC) that attracted college militants and held several highly publicized confrontations. In one instance, VDC members laid across railroad tracks in Oakland, California, in an attempt to stop troop trains carrying soldiers bound for the war.

Rubin typified New Left activists in his belief that Vietnam exposed an oppressive capitalist society that needed revolutionary change. Many New Leftists admired him for his ability to create visual action that communicated more effectively than speeches. For example, the VDC protested the manufacture of napalm by painting an old truck dark gray, placing a large bright yellow sign on it that warned "Danger, Napalm Bombs Ahead," and then using it to follow napalm delivery vehicles.

Increasingly, Rubin talked about exploiting the popular media to change consciousness, and with that he began to move toward cultural radicalism and the street theatre tactics developed by the Diggers in San Francisco's Haight-Ashbury district. This entailed staging outrageous stunts to draw media attention and show society its absurdities. In 1966, for example, he answered a summons to the House Un-American Activities Committee by appearing in the uniform of an American revolutionary soldier.

The following year, Rubin did an about-face and mounted a serious campaign for mayor of Berkeley. If anyone thought he had entered the mainstream, however, they were sadly mistaken. After losing, he totally rejected traditional politics, and his association with hippies convinced him that the entire social system should be jettisoned in favor of a new one.

At this time, David Dellinger, chairman of the National Mobilization Committee To End the War in Vietnam (MOBE), asked Rubin to direct an antiwar march in Washington, D.C. He agreed and joined his new friend, Abbie Hoffman, in injecting street theatre into it. Thus, the demonstration included a rock band—the Fugs—and an attempt to levitate the Pentagon and remove its evil spirits.

As 1967 ended, Rubin joined Hoffman and several others in forming the Yippies. They intended to stage an outrageous protest, the Festival of Life, at the 1968 Democratic National Convention in Chicago. Disagreement surfaced on two fronts, however. For one, tension existed between Rubin and Hoffman, with Rubin stressing politics while Hoffman preferred less-serious street theatre. For another, differences erupted between the Yippies and MOBE, with the latter fearing the Yippies would detract from a serious antiwar protest.

In any event, circumstances at the Convention in late August contributed to violence, and the Festival of Life never got off the ground. Rubin, however, managed to make a sensational appearance a few days before the Convention began when he paraded outside the Chicago Civic Center with "Pigasus," a 200-pound pig that he and the Yippies declared as their presidential nominee. The event drew enormous media coverage, in line with what Rubin thought about television and demonstrations in general, as he states in his book *Do It!*:

> Have you ever seen a boring demonstration on TV? Just being on TV makes it exciting. Even picket lines look breathtaking. Television creates myths bigger than reality.
>
> Demonstrations last for hours, and most of that time nothing happens. After the demonstration we rush home for the six o'clock news. The drama review. TV packs all the action into two minutes—a commercial for the revolution. (442)

Soon after Chicago, the federal government arrested Rubin, Hoffman, and six other prominent protesters on grounds of conspiring to riot. The media called them the Chicago Eight. At his trial in 1969, Rubin put together his defense. He was found guilty of rioting, although not conspiracy. Three years later, a higher court overturned the verdict.

In the 1980s, Rubin returned to Wall Street, capital of the capitalism he earlier attacked, worked as a stockbroker, and said he had no apologies for making money. He had learned, he said, that in order to change the world, he first had to have cash. Secretly, he may still have been committed to his counterculture principles, for he had once stated, "Every guerrilla must know how to use the terrain of the culture that he is trying to destroy." (443) Most observers, though, believed he had sold out.

In 1991, Rubin moved to Denver, Colorado, and worked as a distributor for Wow!, a nutritional drink company. While crossing a street in November 1994, a car struck and killed him.

See also Diggers; The Fugs; Hoffman, Abbie; National Mobilization Committee To End the War in Vietnam; Street Theatre; Yippies.

References Albert, Judith Clavir, and Stewart Edward Albert, eds., *The Sixties Papers: Documents of a Rebellious Decade* (1984); Farber, David, *Chicago '68* (1988); Rubin, Jerry, *Do It! Scenarios of the Revolution* (1970) and *Growing (Up) at Thirty-Seven* (1976).

Rudd, Mark (1947–)

As chairperson of the leftist Students for a Democratic Society (SDS) at Columbia University, Mark Rudd sparked a long, divisive student strike in 1968, and the following year rose to prominence in the revolutionary group Weatherman.

Born in 1947, Rudd grew up in Maplewood, New Jersey, amid the tree-shaded streets of an upper-middle-class neighborhood where conditions bespoke a placid future for him. In 1966, he enrolled at Columbia University in New York City, and within two years chaired the college SDS chapter. On the surface, Columbia appeared to be a benign institution, but students grew disenchanted with three prominent policies: severe limitations on student participation in college governance; college ties to war industry, primarily through the Institute for Defense Analysis; and the administration's decision to build a gym in Harlem without consulting the residents there. In addition, many students had reached total disgust with the expanding war in Vietnam.

Then in April 1968, Rudd disrupted a university memorial service to Martin Luther King, Jr., the civil rights leader who had been slain just days earlier. The SDS chairman seized the pulpit and denounced Columbia as hypocritical for pretending to care about blacks while disrupting their neighborhoods in Harlem and paying black workers practically nothing; he singled out, too, the college's relationship with the Institute for Defense Analysis. His denunciations led to students seizing campus buildings and beginning a strike. Over a two-day period in late April, about 1,000 students joined the occupation. They demanded numerous changes, and after a prolonged and bloody encounter that included massive arrests by the police, they obtained concessions. Soon after this, Rudd dropped out of Columbia to work as a full-time political organizer.

In 1969, Rudd allied with Third World Marxists, a faction within SDS formed to battle another faction, Progressive Labor (PL), for control of the national organization. That summer, he helped lead the successful effort to boot PL from SDS. Third World Marxists, in turn, evolved into Weatherman, dedicated to revolution, and Rudd won election as its national secretary. In October, he helped lead the Days of Rage, an assault against police and property in Chicago. At one point in the upheaval, the cops attacked and arrested him.

Along with other Weathermen, Rudd considered the organization a separate entity from SDS—now in its last throes—and grew disenchanted with SDS's campus chapters. "I hate SDS," he proclaimed. "I hate this weird liberal mass of nothingness." (Gitlin 1987, 392–393) He wanted action, he wanted violence to tear down the capitalist system. Late in 1969, he declared: "It's a wonderful feeling to hit a pig. It must be a really wonderful feeling to kill a pig or blow up a building." (399)

He soon got his chance. Facing charges from the Days of Rage for conspiring to riot, Rudd and most other Weathermen went underground, and in the early 1970s they bombed government facilities. Rudd surrendered himself to the authorities in 1977 and, for his actions in Chicago, was sentenced to two years' probation.

See also Columbia University; Days of Rage; Progressive Labor; Students for a Democratic Society; Weather Underground.

Reference Gitlin, Todd, *The Sixties: Years of Hope, Days of Rage* (1987).

Rules for Radicals

Battling racial and economic discrimination, environmental pollution, misleading advertising, and shoddy consumer goods entailed organizing, and in *Rules for Radicals*, published in 1971, author and activist Saul Alinsky provided original strategy by which to advance what he called the second American Revolution. "In the world of give and take," Alinsky writes, "tactics is the art of how to take and how to give. Here our concern is with the tactic of taking; how the Have-nots can take power from the Haves." (126)

Both *Rules for Radicals* and Alinsky's earlier *Reveille for Radicals* served as guides for activists fighting social injustice. The former book, however, assumed special importance for two reasons. First, it helped propel protest in the early 1970s as the counterculture began to lose steam and organizational efforts shifted from the national level to the local one. Second, it advanced a tactic called proxy power, whereby activists purchased stock in a corporation so they could gain entry into the annual meeting of the board of directors.

Alinsky did not propose using proxies to elect members to the board, for he considered that a useless effort; rather, he wanted to use them to publicize harmful practices and activate a demoralized middle class. Thus, in 1970, proxies attended the annual board meeting of a giant utility in Chicago, Commonwealth Edison, that had been polluting the air with its soft-coal burning plant. At that meeting, author Studs Terkel led 800 protesting proxies in a chant, "Let us breathe!" These and other tactics led to concessions by the utility.

Alinsky says in his book: "The vast majority of Americans, who feel helpless in the huge corporate economy, who don't know which way to turn, have begun to turn *away* from America, to abdicate as citizens. . . . Proxies can be the mechanism by which these people can organize, and once they are organized they will re-enter the life of politics." (178)

Reference Alinsky, Saul D., *Rules for Radicals: A Practical Primer for Realistic Radicals* (1971).

Russell, Bertrand (1872–1970)

The famous British philosopher and mathematician Bertrand Russell influenced the counterculture primarily through his pacifism, socialism, and views regarding sex.

Born in Trelleck, Wales, on 18 May 1872, Russell obtained his higher education at Trinity College, Cambridge University. After graduation in 1894, he traveled throughout Europe and to the United States, and upon his return to England began teaching at his alma mater. Among his early works, he wrote, in collaboration with Alfred North Whitehead, the three-volume *Principia Mathematica*, today considered a classic in mathematics.

Philosophically, Russell expounded realism, a belief that objects perceived by the senses exist independent of the mind. This rationality and his faith in scientific methods conflicted with the later counterculture, which often took a mystical course, but other ideas held by Russell corresponded with countercultural developments. For one, he promoted socialism, favored in the 1960s by many New Leftists, although he disliked the kind practiced in the Soviet Union. For another, after his own mystic experience, he embraced pacifism (deserting it only during World War II) and opposed nuclear weapons. In the late 1950s, in fact, he advocated unilateral nuclear disarmament by Britain. Finally, he attacked organized religion in his book *What I Believe* and advocated sexual freedom in *Marriage and Morals*.

Russell remained politically active in the 1960s and was imprisoned at age 89 for his actions during an antinuclear demonstration. He opposed the Vietnam War and organized an international tribunal to gather evidence about American war crimes in Southeast Asia. Russell died in Britain on 2 February 1970.

References Clark, Ronald W., *Bertrand Russell and His World* (1981); Russell, Bertrand, *The Autobiography of Bertrand Russell* (1967–1969); *Marriage and Morals* (1929), and *What I Believe* (1925).

"San Francisco (Be Sure To Wear Some Flowers in Your Hair)"

Scott McKenzie's hit song "San Francisco" floated through the 1967 Summer of Love, calling young people to the hippie Haight-Ashbury district. An anthem, it portrayed the hippie movement at its honest and joyful best. McKenzie sang: "If you're going to San Francisco / Be sure to wear some flowers in your hair . . ." (Ward, Stokes, and Tucker 1986, 372)

John Phillips, leader of the Mamas and the Papas rock group, wrote the song and produced the record, which stayed on the charts for 12 weeks and sold 7 million copies. The song was rereleased in 1977 on its tenth anniversary.

See also The Mamas and the Papas; Rock Music.

Reference Ward, Ed, Geoffrey Stokes, and Ken Tucker, *Rock of Ages: The Rolling Stone History of Rock & Roll* (1986).

San Francisco Mime Troupe

Avant-garde artists committed to theatre as social protest, the San Francisco Mime Troupe served as a seedbed for the countercultural revolution that swept Haight-Ashbury.

Ronnie Davis founded the Mime Troupe in the mid-1960s as an alternative to the established San Francisco art scene. Always involved in more than mime, the troupe staged plays, parades, and music that emphasized satire and protest. Their promoter and business manager, Bill Graham, said:

> What was most obvious and what lured me to these people was that they were involved with an attempt at making changes in society. They weren't just actors. . . . They were expressing their problems with society through theater by taking *commedia del l'arte* and updating the dialogue to relate to the strife of the day, be it the Vietnam War or civil rights. They were really the very first radicals I had ever met, in the sense of using theater as a public platform to make a statement about what was going on in the world. (Graham and Greenfield 1992, 119)

In forming the Mime Troupe, Davis did not believe in accepting government funds, which he felt always had restrictions attached, and he wanted to bring art directly to the people, with performances in city parks and on the streets. In fact, he advocated guerrilla theatre whereby the audience, motivated by political and social issues, would participate in the performance and feel liberated. In the fall of 1965, he had a confrontation with the authorities over a play he presented: the city parks and recreation department called it obscene (it included four-letter words) and revoked his permit. Davis considered the move a political one to silence leftist views and later was arrested for ignoring the officials when, despite the sanction against him, he presented a performance in a public park.

In 1966, the Mime Troupe staged several activities that showed its satirical challenge to tradition. One play took sharp digs at the mayor's race then under way in Berkeley, another derided the police who had intimidated hippies, and the Gargoyle Sisters, as they called themselves, sang Christmas carols outside a topless bar in North Beach, dressed up like dwarfs and cripples from the Middle Ages. The Mime Troupe participated in Haight-Ashbury's Death of Money Parade and held tie-dyeing classes. That year, Davis organized the Artists' Liberation Front, a third of whose members came from the troupe.

Clashes among creative minds long typified the Mime Troupe, but in 1966 the situation grew more serious when a deep split occurred after some members organized as the Diggers and combined cultural with political and economic radicalism. The Diggers rejected hierarchy, organization, and money, and their protests often angered the hippie merchants in Haight-Ashbury.

As the Mime Troupe splintered, its influence diminished, but the group's impact proved far-reaching. For one, protesters, such as Jerry Rubin, who at Ronnie Davis's suggestion appeared before a hearing of the House Un-American Activities Committee dressed in Revolutionary War garb, adopted street theatrics; for another, the Mime Troupe at one point included several persons who played prominent roles in the counterculture: Emmett Grogan, a Digger activist; Peter Berg, a Digger leader and prominent playwright; and as its business manager, Bill Graham, who eventually promoted rock shows.

In a broad sense, the Mime Troupe combined the cultural with the political—art expressing politics and politics expressing art—that permeated the counterculture.

See also Diggers; Graham, Bill; Haight-Ashbury; Hippies; Performance Art.

References Graham, Bill, and Robert Greenfield, *Bill Graham Presents: My Life inside Rock and Out* (1992); Perry, Charles, *The Haight-Ashbury: A History* (1984).

San Francisco Oracle

Published in the Haight-Ashbury district in San Francisco, the *Oracle* revolutionized the underground press with its colors, images, free-flowing stories—its commitment to the mind, not in an intellectual sense but in a psychedelic one. Allen Cohen, the paper's founder and editor, called it "a journal of arts and letters for the expanded consciousness." (Cohen 1991, xxxi)

The idea for the *Oracle* came to Cohen in a dream, one in which he saw people all over the world reading a newspaper filled with rainbow colors. In 1966, he approached Ron and Jay Thelin, owners of the Psychedelic Shop in the Haight, and they supported his idea with capital. When Cohen gathered a group to discuss the newspaper's format, a serious division separated those who wanted to emphasize politics from those who preferred emphasizing cultural change as found among the hippies in the Haight who used LSD and lived communally.

From this meeting came *P. O. Frisco*, a political newspaper in traditional columnar format that rehashed leftist articles about the government readying internment camps to hold dissidents and that presented a bland piece about the joy of masturbation. Greatly disappointed, the Thelins insisted on a different newspaper, and Cohen kept pursuing his dream. He edited the third issue, printed in September 1966, and it appeared as the *San Francisco Oracle*, featuring an article on the upcoming Love Pageant Rally—a far cry from leftist diatribe.

Assisted by the painter Gabe Katz, Cohen soon produced the *Oracle* with a free-flowing format rather than linear columns and with artwork that reflected psychedelics. Cohen recalled that he and the staff wanted the newspaper "to provide guidance . . . for the journey through the states of mind that the LSD experience had opened up." (xxvii)

In January 1967, the *Oracle* offered four-color swirls through its slit-fountain process, using different colored inks on the ink fountains of the printing press. Mind-blowing images appeared: mandalas, Indians, naked men and women, sexual scenes, abstractions. In one instance, the staff splattered pages with ketchup as the paper rolled off the press; in another, they sprayed them with jasmine perfume.

Later in the year, the *Oracle* moved from its first offices behind a poster shop called the Print Mint to larger quarters on Haight Street, near the Masonic Lodge, and remained open 24 hours a day to help those needing food or suffering from bad drug trips. By this time, the paper ranged from the psychedelic to the occult as the *Oracle* staff, who considered mainstream society hopelessly corrupt, sought a spiritual transformation to advance economic justice and peace.

The newspaper carried stories about Ken Kesey and drug busts; spiritual messages; poster art; poetry; love-ins; police reactions; cultural events, such as coffee house activities and rock concerts; and ads from craft shops, head shops, and numerous other hippie businesses. The *Oracle* even developed theme issues, with its first one about the Age of Aquarius.

In a controversial move, Cohen promoted the Summer of Love, a call to America's young people in 1967 to converge on Haight-Ashbury and experience the hippie scene. Some hippies criticized him, claiming he really did not want to spread love but wanted to improve business for the shopkeepers. Whatever the case, young people heeded the call, and the crowded streets that summer boosted the *Oracle*'s circulation to over 100,000. As August began, crime and drug rip-offs, along with threatening scenes involving the Hell's Angels, made a mockery of the love message. Cohen still promoted marijuana and LSD as beneficial—even while his plans to publish the *Oracle* on a regular monthly basis, rather than continuing its irregular appearance, fell victim to staff members spaced out on drugs.

The Summer of Love ruined the hippie community in Haight-Ashbury, and as it quickly declined so, too, did the *Oracle*. In February 1968, the *Oracle* made its last appearance. Only the echo of Cohen's words lingered: "We, the Aquarian youth, shall begin the new tribal culture where peace and love will reign."

See also Haight-Ashbury; Liberation News Service; Summer of Love; Underground Newspapers; Underground Press Syndicate.

References Anthony, Gene, *The Summer of Love: Haight-Ashbury at Its Highest* (1980); Cohen, Allen, *The San Francisco Oracle, Facsimile Edition: The Psychedelic Newspaper of the Haight Ashbury, 1966–1968*, (1991); Peck, Abe, *Uncovering the Sixties: The Life and Times of the Underground Press* (1985).

San Francisco State College

See Third World Strike.

Savio, Mario (1942–1996)

In 1964, Mario Savio, angry and defiant, led the first large political protest by white college students when the Free Speech Movement erupted at the University of California–Berkeley.

Born on 8 December 1942 into a Catholic Italian-American working-class family in New York City, Savio attended Queens College until his junior year, in 1963, when, after his parents moved to Los Angeles, he transferred to Berkeley. As with many political activists in the counterculture, Savio worked in the civil rights movement, teaching during the summer of 1964 at a freedom school for black children in McComb, Mississippi. The experience affected him deeply, stirring his anger, he said, about racism and oppression in a nation that proclaimed itself free.

This anger extended to his experiences at Berkeley. As he continued to study for a degree in philosophy, the impersonal red tape at the university and its restrictions on speech disturbed him, a concern reinforced and intensified when he read Karl Marx's assertion that alienation emerged as a response to bureaucratic institutions. In the fall of 1964, Savio, who had worked briefly in the Young People's Socialist League, won election as chairman of the University Friends of the Student Nonviolent Coordinating Committee, and thus remained active within the civil rights movement.

He was in that position when conflict erupted on campus over the university administration's refusal to let students use a narrow strip of sidewalk at the south entrance as a place where they could recruit volunteers for off-campus social causes, especially civil rights activities. Savio and several student leaders opposed the ban and formed the United Front to set up tables and defy it.

The administration reacted on 1 October 1964 by suspending Savio and seven other students. Later that afternoon, police arrested a member of a civil rights organization for sitting at a table near the administration building. Students then surrounded a police car that had arrived and prevented it from leaving. As the crowd reached several thousand, Savio climbed atop the car and gave a speech that catapulted him into a leadership position.

Savio had an ability to combine rational argument with angry epithets, long analytical statements with terse metaphors. He called the administrators a "bunch of bastards" and said about the police: "They have a job to do! . . . Like Adolph Eichmann. He had a job to do. He fit into the machinery." (Rorabaugh 1989, 22)

As the sit-down continued, Savio played only a minor role in the negotiations to end the crisis, for he had little talent as a mediator. An agreement reached on 2 October between the students and administration ended the sit-down. Soon after, Savio won election to the steering committee of the Free Speech Movement (FSM), formed to protect the right of students to express their ideas and organize as they desired.

In late November, after the Board of Regents made clear its intention to continue restrictions on student advocacy, and after the administration brought charges against Savio for his actions during the sit-down, FSM called a mass rally. More than 6,000 students turned out on 2 December, at which time Savio spoke and encouraged the crowd to occupy the administration building, Sproul Hall. He and about 800 demonstrators stayed the night there, and the following morning police and state troopers evicted and arrested them.

On 3 December, a campus strike began that lasted five days. During it, on 7 December, when Savio approached a microphone to address a rally of more than 18,000, campus police grabbed him and

Leader of the Free Speech Movement, Mario Savio speaks at a rally at the University of California at Berkeley on 4 January 1965.

forced him from the stage. They relented, however, after the crowd grew angry. Savio and FSM gained concessions later that month when the Board of Regents agreed to recognize First Amendment rights governing speech and assembly as primary.

In June 1965, Savio and 154 other students were convicted on charges relating to their political protests, and he served some time in jail. The university refused to readmit him in November 1966, because as a nonstudent he had violated rules by distributing leaflets on campus. Later that month, he participated in a sit-in to protest the administration's refusal to allow nonstudents to set up an antiwar table at the student union. Soon after this, he largely withdrew from politics.

Savio earned his bachelor's degree in 1984 from San Francisco State University, and shortly after that, a master's degree in physics from the same college. In 1995, Savio, a mathematics and critical thinking professor at Sonoma State College in California, organized the Campus Coalitions for Human Rights and Justice. The group had as its main goal to oppose those seeking to end affirmative-action programs.

Savio labeled House Speaker Newt Gingrich and North Carolina Senator Jesse Helms "crypto-fascists" and proclaimed his countercultural concerns alive and well. He said: "Occasionally something comes down the pike that is just so horrible, that you . . . have to do something." Savio died on 6 November 1996 after moving furniture at his house. He had for years suffered from a weak heart. (Mehren 1995, 4)

See also Free Speech Movement; University of California–Berkeley.

References Mehren, Elizabeth, "Radicals of '60s Preserve the Spirit," *Eugene (Oregon) Register-Guard*, 6 August 1995, 1, 4; Rorabaugh, W. J., *Berkeley at War: The 1960s* (1989).

Screw

As society exhibited sexual permissiveness in movies, books, and underground publications, *Screw* appeared. This weekly New York City sex tabloid, founded by Jim Buckley and Al Goldstein in November 1968, contained interviews with pimps, prostitutes, rock singers, and movie stars. *Screw* carried explicit sex ads and articles about sex. With its lewd visual references to "Tricky Dick" Nixon and its "Peter Meter" movie reviews, *Screw* quickly obtained a circulation of 150,000.

The publication's success reflected Goldstein's vision; as a former editor of underground newspapers he had seen how many people purchased the *East Village Other* for its sex ads. *Screw*, he decided, would move the sexual to the forefront and aim its appeal primarily at men—thus *Screw*'s contribution to the widening countercultural assault on middle-class values.

See also *East Village Other;* Underground Newspapers.

SCUM

As the women's movement expanded, a small, unusual group appeared on its extremist fringe: SCUM, the Society for Cutting Up Men. Led by Valerie Solanas (infamous for her attempt to kill artist Andy Warhol), SCUM wanted to eliminate men, whom it considered vile oppressors and the source of humankind's major evils, such as war, conformity, prejudice, hate, violence, disease, and death. "The male," said SCUM in its manifesto, "has made the world a shitpile." (Morgan 1970, 581)

How to proceed? SCUM claimed that through modern technology it was possible to reproduce without males and to reproduce only females. This must be pursued, they advocated, along with killing men or cutting off their genitals. "SCUM will not picket, demonstrate, march, or strike," claimed the organization. "Such tactics are for nice, genteel ladies who scrupulously take only such action that is guaranteed to be effective. . . . If SCUM ever strikes, it will be in the dark with a six-inch blade." (578) Solanas continued to lead SCUM in the 1990s, and in 1997 Orion Pictures released a move about her, *I Shot Andy Warhol.*

See also Women's Movement.

Reference Morgan, Robin, ed., *Sisterhood Is Powerful: An Anthology of Writings from the Women's Liberation Movement* (1970).

SDS

See Students for a Democratic Society.

Seale, Bobby (1937–)

Michael Tigar, a radical activist, described Bobby Seale and his Black Panther organization: "The Panthers started with the notion of the gun and the law book together. That's what Bobby and [Huey] Newton were really about. . . . You could organize all you want and be represented in court, but people first had to know you were serious." (Joseph 1974, 406) Seale communicated this seriousness by leading the Black Panthers and shaping them into a stridently militant group.

Seale was born on 22 October 1937 in Dallas, Texas, but grew up in Oakland, California. Discontent with high school, he dropped out and joined the air force. His stint, however, did not last long—after a fight with an officer, he was dishonorably discharged. He then enrolled in night classes, obtained his high school diploma, and in 1965 entered Merritt College, a small two-year school on the edge of the Oakland ghetto where he lived. Seale immersed himself in the writings of left-wing radicals and black nationalists, especially Frantz Fanon and Malcolm X. While at Merritt he met Huey Newton, and they exchanged ideas and shared their anger about oppression.

Seale helped Newton organize the Soul Students' Advisory Council and advocated a militant revolutionary agenda that espoused opposition to capitalism and insisted blacks should arm themselves for self-defense. When many in the group opposed this position, he and Newton wrote a ten-point program, and in October 1966 founded the Black Panther Party. Seale and Newton demanded freedom for blacks, economic improvements, socialist development, and the end to police brutality. Seale served as the group's chairman and Newton as minister of defense.

The two men antagonized the police when they organized armed patrols to monitor arrests in the ghettos and prevent brutality. Seale gained nationwide attention for the Panthers in May 1967 when he protested a legislative proposal to prohibit the carrying of guns in public by leading several Panthers—armed with rifles, shotguns, and pistols—on to the floor of the California Assembly in Sacramento. Panther membership subsequently surged, although the authorities arrested Seale for disrupting the legislature, and he served six months in jail.

After his release, he helped forge ties with white radicals and joined them in forming the Peace and Freedom Party, under whose banner Newton ran for president in 1968. That same year, Seale joined a protest outside the Democratic National Convention in Chicago and was arrested for inciting a riot based on an emotional speech he had presented to a crowd in which he condemned oppression. He stood trial with seven other radicals, a group newspapers called the "Chicago Eight." During the proceedings, Seale protested so vociferously that the judge ordered him gagged and bound to a chair, declared a mistrial in Seale's case, and sentenced him to four years in jail for contempt. The charge, however, was later dropped.

With Newton in jail from 1968 to 1970, Seale assumed greater power in the Panther organization. By this time, the FBI had infiltrated the group with spies and agent provocateurs, and in cooperation with local police departments it launched violent and illegal attacks on the Panthers. Seale acted to purge the government spies, but this produced schisms within the group and distrust mounted. In 1971, he went on trial for supposedly ordering the execution, two years earlier, of a Panther who was

Bobby Seale, leader of the militant Black Panther organization, addresses a rally outside Chicago's Federal Building on 9 April 1969 after he and several other protest leaders pleaded innocent to federal charges that they entered into a conspiracy to incite riots at the Democratic National Convention in 1968. Thomas Hayden, also indicted, stands at Seale's left.

actually a government informer. Radicals considered this an attempt by the authorities to silence Seale by putting him away in prison. The government failed to get a conviction.

Back in Oakland, with the Panthers in disarray, Seale and Newton de-emphasized militancy and developed neighborhood programs. In 1973, Seale ran for mayor of Oakland, and although he lost, he won many votes in the ghetto.

After the Panthers faded in the 1980s, Seale engaged in social work to help ghetto youth. In 1987, he published a cookbook, *Barbecue with Bobby*, a best-seller, and in the 1990s he worked in Philadelphia, Pennsylvania, as a recruiter for the African American Studies Program at Temple University.

See also Black Panthers; Black Power; Chicago Eight; Newton, Huey.

References Joseph, Peter, *Good Times: An Oral History of America in the 1960s* (1974); Marine, Gene, *Black Panthers* (1969); Seale, Bobby, *A Lonely Rage: The Autobiography of Bobby Seale* (1978) and *Seize the Time: The Story of the Black Panther Party and Huey P. Newton* (1970).

The Second Sex

When in the late 1940s, Simone de Beauvoir (1908–1986), the French novelist and philosopher, wrote *The Second Sex*, she created a work that later influenced the countercultural women's liberation movement.

In *The Second Sex*, de Beauvoir emphasizes the importance of equality for men and women and analyzes women's place in society. She bases her conclusions on an existentialist view, believing the only meaning to life is that which individuals give it. Women, she says, must transcend themselves or else suffer powerlessness and dependency on men; they must claim their place in the world as individuals seeking transcendence beyond their child-bearing and child-rearing functions. Toward this end, they must break the masculine code that oppresses them (as it does men). She laments: "The majority of women resign themselves to their lot without attempting to take any action."

De Beauvoir does not believe that liberation from oppression would mean a loss of femininity for women; she says if men would accept women as equals, women would not be preoccupied with their femininity and would "gain in naturalness." In the 1960s, one feminist said about de Beauvoir's work:

> For many of us . . . *The Second Sex* changed our lives. This book was written at a time when feminism had been thoroughly discredited as a movement, and women were being shuttled back into domestic slavery. . . . *The Second Sex* is still the most intelligent, human, and thorough document written on female oppression and masculine supremacy." (Redstockings n.d., 19)

See also Friedan, Betty; Redstockings; Steinem, Gloria; Women's Movement.

Reference Beauvoir, Simone de, *The Second Sex* (1953); Redstockings, *Feminist Revolution* (n.d.).

Seed

An underground Chicago newspaper founded in 1967 by Don Lewis, an artist, and Earl Segal, a store owner, *Seed* combined hippie cultural views with leftist politics and mixed colorful psychedelics with community news. In doing so, it emulated the *San Francisco Oracle*, perhaps the nation's premier hippie publication. (In fact, like the California hippies, Lewis and Segal organized a Be-In and called it a "unity of love.") In its first months, the *Seed* exuded an idealistic communal message; as one of its founders explained: "We were less organizers than liberals and freaks in the middle of a magical tour." (Peck 1985, 89)

After the traumatic Democratic National Convention in 1968, however, *Seed* took a serious political turn, covering black and student protests and draft resisters, while calling for unified efforts between hippies and the New Left. In 1970, the newspaper dropped its hippie orientation altogether and promoted a socialist future, heaping praise on leftist guerrillas fighting in Latin America. Three years later, beset by financial problems and declining readership, *Seed* collapsed.

See also *San Francisco Oracle;* Underground Newspapers.

Reference Peck, Abe, *Uncovering the Sixties: The Life and Times of the Underground Press* (1985).

Seeger, Pete (1919–)

Pete Seeger stands alongside Woody Guthrie as the most influential modern folk musician, and his liberal politics committed to social causes made him a luminary within the counterculture.

Born on 3 May 1919 in New York City to Dr. Charles Louis Seeger, a conductor, educator, and musicologist, and Constance de Clyver Edson Seeger, a violinist and teacher, Seeger inherited a rich musical tradition. After attending a private boarding school at Avon, Connecticut, he entered Harvard University in 1936. He quit, however, two years later and traveled the New England countryside painting watercolors.

By this time, folk music had already attracted him, and as he improved his banjo playing, he listened to Woody Guthrie and Huddie Ledbetter (Leadbelly), who influenced him greatly. So, too, did Dr. John Lomax and his son Alan through their work at the Archive of American Folk Songs in Washington, D.C., where the elder Lomax was curator. Seeger spent many hours listening to recordings there while working as an assistant.

In 1940, Seeger toured the nation with Woody Guthrie as part of a folk group, the Almanac Singers, and developed a repertoire of labor and topical songs. With Guthrie, he sang at migrant labor camps and union halls, and they collaborated in writing music. Seeger served in the military during World War II, entertaining troops as part of the Special Services.

After the war, he founded People's Songs that issued a songbook containing topical music, and he held weekly hootenannies (informal folk concerts). Seeger helped stimulate a folk music revival when, in 1948, he founded a quartet, the Weavers. They sang on radio, and by the 1950s their record sales had exceeded 4 million.

Because Seeger's songs criticized racism and nuclear weapons, in 1955 the House Un-American Activities Committee, investigating what it said were Communist influences, called him to testify. Seeger appeared before the committee but refused to answer questions, claiming he had never engaged in any subversive conspiracy and that the Constitution protected his freedom of speech. Congress subsequently indicted him for contempt, and at his trial in 1961 a jury found him guilty. He received a one-year prison sentence, but on appeal a higher court reversed the conviction.

Despite this decision, Seeger, who had started a solo career in 1957, found himself blacklisted by radio and television stations as a subversive. When the folk music program *Hootenanny* made its debut on ABC television in 1963, the network banned Seeger from it. Joan Baez and many other folk musicians consequently boycotted *Hootenanny*. This caused ABC to say it would allow Seeger to appear if he signed an affidavit about his political affiliations, but he refused, claiming the requirement violated his constitutional rights. Seeger later said that the persecution did not hurt him: "I had a small circle of friends who kept me singing. I'd sing for the students in some little college and they'd pass the hat." (Hood 1986, 30)

Seeger's liberalism and his battle against the authorities made him a favorite among college students, an audience that had turned to folk music in the early sixties as an alternative to rock 'n' roll whose vacuity held little appeal. They liked, too, Seeger's peculiar banjo playing, his "basic strum." As he explained it:

> You pluck up on a melody string . . . with your first finger. Half a beat later, you strum down across one, or two, or three, or four, or even five strings with the back of your fingernail. Now that can be the back of your ring finger or the back of your first finger. You get a slightly different effect depending on which finger you pluck up with and which finger you pluck down with. This coming up on the downbeat and brushing down on the offbeat is the essential part of this particular strum. (31)

Seeger wrote several songs in the sixties that sold well, recorded not only by him but also by other singers. These included "Where Have All the Flowers Gone?" "If I Had a Hammer," and "Turn, Turn, Turn." As the Vietnam War expanded, he opposed it strenuously and appeared at many antiwar rallies.

Seeger continued to make records (over 60 albums in his career) into the 1990s and remained active on the concert circuit.

See also Guthrie, Woody.

References Dunaway, David King, *How Can I Keep from Singing: Pete Seeger* (1981); Hood, Phil, ed., *Artists of American Folk Music* (1986).

710 Ashbury

The Grateful Dead rock band used a huge Victorian house at 710 Ashbury, two blocks up a hill from Haight Street in San Francisco's hippie Haight-Ashbury district, as a home base. Most of the band moved into it during the winter of 1966. They practiced there and hosted members from other bands, such as with a huge Thanksgiving Eve party in 1966 that included Quicksilver Messenger Service and Jefferson Airplane.

See also Grateful Dead.

Sex

A sexual revolution swept society in the sixties, one so intense that it went well beyond the counterculture and affected the mainstream. At one point, the sexual revolution's youthful progenitors considered it powerful enough to alter the political system.

As with so many other countercultural developments, changes in sexual attitudes and behavior had their origin back in the 1950s. Although people imagine that decade as staid and morally pure, such views emanate from a contrived persona, whether it be the contemporary television programs, such as *Leave It to Beaver* featuring the fictional Cleaver family, that refused to show married couples in other than twin beds, or later nostalgic ones, such as *Happy Days*, that submerged all personal problems beneath ice-cream parlor sundaes. In actuality, dissonance existed between public images and private practices. The Kinsey surveys of American sexuality in the late 1940s and early 1950s showed, for example, that men and women engaged in premarital sex frequently enough to make mother June Cleaver's hair stand on end.

To young people who reached sexual maturity in the early 1960s, these contradictions seemed hypocritical and injurious because they caused tension that harmed individuals psychologically. End the hypocrisies, they said. This could have meant enforcing puritanical standards, but other forces worked to make the response a permissive one.

In addition to hypocrisy, publications in the 1950s influenced sexual attitudes and behavior. Beat writers Allen Ginsberg and William Burroughs, among others, presented explicit scenes that ran the gamut from heterosexuality to homosexuality to bestiality. On the more commercial side, *Playboy* appeared as a mass-circulation magazine. Taken together, these works presented liberal, if not libertine, attitudes toward sex, and in the case of *Playboy* glamorized freewheeling sex as fun.

This situation, then, greeted the sixties, as did a technological change with sweeping implications: the birth-control pill. The pill, which first appeared as a prescription drug in 1960 and soon gained widespread use, meant less worry that sexual intercourse would lead to pregnancy.

No other technological development could have better complemented the emerging hippie belief in free love. And no other belief could have best expressed the revolutionary nature of sex in the sixties. Building on the attacks beats had leveled against mainstream society's values, and on the sexual freedom leagues that had appeared in San Francisco and New York City, hippies insisted that nothing should impede sexual enjoyment; on the contrary, people should emphasize that which helps it.

Thus, in the mid-1960s, when hippies discussed drugs, they linked them to sex, believing that marijuana, for example, worked as an aphrodisiac. And as hippies listened to rock music, they linked it to sex as well, considering its beat liberating, embracing its message that declared sex primary over oppression, even over death. "Get it while you can," Janis Joplin sang . . . for tomorrow what would there be? "Sex, drugs, and rock 'n' roll" went the saying, expressing quite perceptively the connections.

Were it only hippies who adopted these sexual attitudes and behavior, the term *revolution* would be inappropriate. But the changes spread. Cultural and political activists recognized how sex could alter society and the bigger picture. "How can you separate politics and sex?" asked radical Jerry Rubin. (Farber 1994, 257) Sex could lure young people into a revolutionary cause, sell a revolutionary consciousness—that sexual oppression came from an authoritarian system oppressive in many other ways—and weaken the middle class by assaulting a core value. Thus, sex evolved into more; it challenged mainstream culture and politics—the sexual as the political.

Although it would be a stretch to say that sexual attitudes and behavior caused the New Left to attack the political system—for many additional factors propelled political activists—New Leftists recognized the connection. Thus, to foster unity and revolutionary consciousness and to weaken individualism and male dominance, the extremist group Weatherman developed collectives that ended monogamous relationships. Couples, for example, could be separated by the collective and men ordered to sleep with men, women with women, men with a variety of women, and women with a variety of men.

The changes in sexual attitudes and behavior affected college students. As enrollments burgeoned on campuses, students began demanding that rules setting curfews and limiting male-female visitations in dormitories be rewritten or abolished. As colleges complied, the opportunities for sexual intercourse increased. Off campus, young men and women cohabited more frequently, and the new sexuality affected teenagers in high school as well. A sociologist told the *New York Times*: "My own sense of the situation . . . is that behavior is catching up with values, and that there really is more overt sexuality among young people." (Stern 1968)

The effects went well beyond the younger generation, and as the sixties continued, older, mainstream Americans in greater numbers engaged in premarital, extramarital, and gay sex. And commercialism took over with explicit movies, topless dances, and sex shows, with *Playboy* joined by *Penthouse* and those by *Screw*, *Suck*, and *Hustler*.

Whether the sexual revolution liberated people is highly debatable. Many women, for one, considered themselves more exploited, more readily seen as sex objects, and they protested this situation. Whatever the case, the counterculture had questioned and altered the basic principles behind sexual morality.

See also New Left; The Pill; Weather Underground; Women's Movement.

References Farber, David, ed., *The Sixties: From Memory to History* (1994); Stern, Michael, "Teen-Age Revolt: Is It Deeper Today?" *New York Times*, 7 October 1968, 49, 67.

Sex and the Single Girl

Written by Helen Gurley Brown and published in 1962, *Sex and the Single Girl* earned notoriety for approving the increasingly popular practice of women staying single for a long period and engaging in premarital sex. In her book, Brown claims that "nice, single girls *do*."

See also Sex.

Reference Brown, Helen Gurley, *Sex and the Single Girl* (1962).

Shankar, Ravi (1920–)

A talented classical sitarist, Ravi Shankar infused rock music with Far Eastern sounds largely through his association with George Harrison of the Beatles.

Shankar, born on 7 April 1920 in Benares, India, studied classical Indian music in the 1930s and 1940s under a fellow countryman, Ustad Allauddin Khan, a guru who had mastered all the Indian musical instruments. Shortly after World War II, Shankar began performing on his own, contributed music to Indian films, and served as musical director of All-India Radio. In 1956 and 1957, determined to take Indian music into the West, he toured Britain and the United States, playing his sitar and generating interest in the raga—melodic rising and falling movements consisting of an octave or a series of five or six notes. Each raga conveys a specific mood, such as devotion, eroticism, or tranquillity. While in the United States, Shankar recorded two albums with other musicians.

Shankar's greatest recognition in the West, though, came in the mid-sixties when George Harrison of the Beatles studied under him. Harrison played the sitar in 1965 when the Beatles recorded the song "Norwegian Wood." The entrancing sound started a sitar craze among rock musicians. They found, however, that the sitar could not be easily mastered. A 700-year-old instrument, the sitar originated in India and typically is more than four feet long with a teakwood neck, tuning pegs, and two resonators, one on each end, made from dried gourds. The sitar has 6 or 7 main strings and 13 drone strings that vibrate. Sitar music is improvisational and complex. To make playing the instrument easier while maintaining its basic sound, in 1966 a guitarist invented an electric sitar, subsequently used by several rock musicians.

In May 1967, Shankar opened the Kinnara School of Music in Los Angeles (a branch of his school in Bombay, India), and later that year performed at the Monterey Pop Festival. Shortly after this, he recorded two highly acclaimed albums, *Portrait of a Genius* and *Ravi Shankar in New York*. In 1969, he played at Woodstock.

Two years later, at Shankar's urging, Harrison, by then an ex-Beatle, organized an all-star concert at New York City's Madison Square Garden to help famine victims in Bangladesh. Shankar's performance appeared on the 1971 album *Concert for Bangla Desh*. In the 1970s, Shankar recorded for Harrison's own label. His influence on rock continued in the 1990s while he found himself in demand among listeners of New Age music.

See also The Beatles; Monterey Pop Festival; Rock Music.

Silent Spring

When author and scientist Rachel Carson (1907–1964) wrote *Silent Spring* in the early 1960s, she stirred an environmental awareness that carried into the counterculture. Her book questioned the use of chemical pesticides, especially DDT, showing their damage to water, wildlife, and human beings. Shortly before Carson wrote *Silent Spring*, 600 million pounds of pesticides were being applied in the United States, and by the early 1960s DDT spraying was producing malformed animals. When *Silent Spring* appeared in 1962, it caused enormous controversy, with chemical companies condemning it. But the book, well researched and built on numerous scientific studies, found a wide audience with its revelations and literary style.

In *Silent Spring*, Carson writes:

> For the first time in the history of the world, every human being is now subjected to contact with dangerous chemicals, from the moment of conception until death. In the less than two decades of their use, the synthetic pesticides have been so thoroughly distributed throughout the animate and inanimate world that they occur virtually everywhere. . . . They destroy the very enzymes whose function is to protect the body from harm, they block the oxidation processes from which the body receives its energy, they prevent the normal functioning of various organs, and they may initiate in certain cells the slow and irreversible change that leads to malignancy. (15–17)

Carson's book gave rise to the modern environmental movement that emerged within the counterculture; it led to new regulations, such as the ban on DDT in 1972; and it stimulated organic farming and the back-to-the-earth movement, which many young people in the sixties embraced as an alternative to modern technology.

See also Back-to-the-Earth Movement; Earth Day; Organic Food.

Reference Carson, Rachel, *Silent Spring* (1962).

Simon and Garfunkel

Folk music's strong influence on rock appeared prominently in the duo Simon and Garfunkel. Paul Simon and Art Garfunkel first met in public school, and while teenagers growing up in wealthy Forest Hills near New York City, they started singing together. As the duo Tom and Jerry, they had a moderately successful record in 1957, "Hey Schoolgirl," and appeared on Dick Clark's television show, *American Bandstand*.

But then their musical career stagnated, and Simon went to New York University and Queen's College, where he studied music and English, while Garfunkel went to Columbia University, where he studied mathematics and education. They still dabbled at performing, however, and Simon edged into the top 100 in 1962 with the band Tico and the Triumphs, and again the following year under the name Jerry Landis. At this time, he changed his musical style to folk and recorded an acoustical album with Garfunkel, *Wednesday Morning, Three A.M.*, on the Columbia record label. The LP included "The Sound of Silence" that had obscure, poetic lyrics, such as "The words of the prophet are written on the subway walls." After the album sold poorly, the two musicians went their separate ways.

Then came a strange development: as folk music spread, several radio stations in New England began playing "The Sound of Silence." A producer at Columbia heard the song, liked it, ordered musicians into the studio to dub in an electric guitar, and late in 1965 rereleased it. "The Sound of Silence" reached number one on the record charts early in 1966, much to Simon and Garfunkel's surprise, and made *Wednesday Morning, Three A.M.* a hit album.

The duo quickly got back together and recorded another LP, *The Sound of Silence*, containing songs written mainly by Simon. His music writing, effective vocals, and instrumentation, combined with Garfunkel's high, velvety voice, led to more hit singles over the next year, especially "Homeward Bound" and "I Am a Rock."

Simon and Garfunkel recorded another album in 1966, *Parsley, Sage, Rosemary, and Thyme*, and followed it, two years later, with their biggest single to that time, "Mrs. Robinson." When this song and others by the duo were included in the hit motion picture *The Graduate*, released as a soundtrack album, their popularity soared, and they recorded *Bookends*.

Then, amid Garfunkel's appearance in the movie *Catch-22*, came the duo's megahit: "Bridge over Troubled Water," written by Simon and carried by Garfunkel's stunning vocals. Simon and Garfunkel broke up in the early 1970s, however, and pursued solo careers.

The more versatile Simon had the greater success, beginning with his album *Paul Simon*, released in 1972. He followed this with several other popular and innovative albums into the early 1990s, notably *Graceland*. Simon and Garfunkel occasionally reunited for live performances in the late 1980s, but as a duo their main contribution had been to fuse folk with rock and touch the counterculture's self-doubts and idealistic hopes.

See also Rock Music.

Sinclair Incident

A *cause celebre* within the counterculture, John Sinclair's conviction on marijuana charges seemed to display not only straight society's unfairness but also its vengeance.

After his arrest in Detroit, Michigan, in 1970 for selling two joints to an undercover agent, a jury found Sinclair guilty and the judge sentenced him to ten years in prison. As far as the counterculture was concerned, for Sinclair to have received such a harsh sentence displayed injustice and more. Sinclair had been a radical activist. He had founded a commune in Detroit; managed the rock band MC-5, controversial for its obscene language and politicized message; and organized the White Panther Party, a cultural revolutionary group. Thus, many in the counterculture, and a substantial number outside it, believed the sentence represented less a concern with drugs and more a desire to punish Sinclair for his beliefs and silence him.

The counterculture rallied around Sinclair and raised money for his appeal. John Lennon and Yoko Ono, for example, participated in a large rally. The federal courts finally threw out his case, but not until he had spent two years in prison.

See also Rock Music; White Panther Party.

Sly and the Family Stone

Sly and the Family Stone followed Jimi Hendrix's success in combining black music with psychedelia. They scored big hits with "Everyday People," the number one song for several weeks early in 1969, and their album *Stand!* released the same year.

Sylvester Stewart, who used Stone as his air name when he worked as a rhythm and blues DJ and then carried it over to the stage, organized the band in 1967. They gained substantial notice that year when they played at Winchester Cathedral, a nightclub in Redwood City, California. Stone called his music "psychedelic soul."

See also Hendrix, Jimi.

Snyder, Gary (1930–)
With his attachment to Zen Buddhism, American Indian tradition, and environmental issues, Gary Snyder, a prominent poet, had a considerable influence on 1950s beat writers and the 1960s counterculture. His heritage, he claimed, went back to the magic of shamans and the mysteries of the earth.

Snyder was born on 8 May 1930 in San Francisco, but at age 2 his family moved to Washington State, where they worked as farmers. As a child, he read extensively, wrote poems, and began hiking—activities that remained prominent throughout his life. In 1942, Snyder's family moved to Oregon, and the youngster avidly pursued backpacking and mountain climbing; at age 15 he obtained membership in an exclusive outdoors organization consisting of persons who had scaled at least one snow-capped peak.

In 1947, Snyder enrolled at Reed College in Oregon and four years later received a bachelor's degree in anthropology and literature, reflecting his interests in writing and the study of American Indian societies. He then decided to concentrate on Zen Buddhism and poetry, and in 1952 began his graduate studies in Oriental languages at the University of California–Berkeley. He earned money through various odd jobs and worked during the summers for the U.S. Forest Service.

His demeanor and philosophical outlook made him influential with the beats in San Francisco—writers who were challenging materialist conformity and literary traditions. Poet Allen Ginsberg later claimed that Snyder introduced him to *The Tibetan Book of the Dead* and *Tibetan Buddhist Documents*, a fact confirmed by novelist Jack Kerouac, who said that Snyder infused him, Ginsberg, and many in the beat movement with Zen Buddhism. Snyder encouraged Ginsberg's writing and was in the audience at the Six Gallery in North Beach when his friend first read *Howl*, a poetic jab at American oppression.

Snyder's attachment to the mystical, to the irrational that courses through nature, found a heightened outlet in 1956 when he won a scholarship to study Zen Buddhism in Kyoto, Japan. With a few interruptions, he lived there for nearly 12 years, studying in a Buddhist monastery and learning directly from a Zen master. He worked for several months aboard a tanker that sailed from Yokohama around the world, and in 1961 traveled to India with, among others, his wife and Ginsberg. Snyder journeyed back to California in 1964 and taught English at Berkeley while hosting a program on Eastern religion for public television. Shortly thereafter he returned to Japan, where he began living with a communal group on an island near Kyushu. In 1965, his first volume of poems, *Riprap*, was published.

He soon wrote two more volumes of poems; *The Back Country* appeared in 1968, near the time he returned to the United States for good. By now, the counterculture had emerged, and Snyder believed the artificial, plastic suburban kids had to be saved. His poems, reflecting Zen and nature, provided guidance toward personal salvation and advised that the old order be destroyed. For example, in *A Curse on the Men in Washington, Pentagon*, he writes about killing the white "American" in himself so that the America of grass and streams—Indian America—can be returned.

On several occasions, Snyder hailed the counterculture as an extension of centuries-old tribal mysticism but disagreed with LSD guru Timothy Leary on an important point: whereas Leary condemned the political Left for engaging in useless crusades, Snyder believed there existed areas where political radicalism and the psychedelic subculture could converge, particularly on the issue of love and peace that circulated in both movements.

Snyder feared, too, that Leary's message to America's youth, that they should "drop out," contained a danger because so many young people did not know how to substitute the prevailing culture with something more rewarding. To Leary he said: "If you're going to talk this way you have to be able to specifically [respond] to somebody in Wichita, Kansas who says, 'I'm going to drop out. How do you advise me to stay living around here in this area which I like?'" Snyder's own answer: "I say, okay, get in touch with the Indian culture here. Find out what was here before. Find out what the mythologies were. Find out what the local deities were." (Cohen 1991, 161)

Snyder helped organize the Human Be-In, held at Golden Gate Park in January 1967, and blew a conch shell to open this hippie celebration of life. Further, he spoke out prominently on environmental issues.

Snyder continued writing after the 1960s while living on a secluded mountain ridge some 100 miles from San Francisco, and in 1975 his collection *Turtle Island*, which portrayed a simplistic life, one respectful toward nature, won the Pulitzer Prize for poetry.

See also Beat; Ginsberg, Allen; Kerouac, Jack; Watts, Alan; Zen Buddhism.

References Cohen, Allen, *The San Francisco Oracle, Facsimile Edition: The Psychedelic Newspaper of the Haight Ashbury, 1966–1968* (1991); Halper, Jon, ed., *Gary Snyder: Dimensions of a Life* (1991); Snyder, Gary, *The Back Country* (1968), *Earth House Hold: Technical Notes and Queries to Fellow Dharma Revolutionaries* (1969), *Myths and Texts* (1960); *Riprap* (1965), and *Turtle Island* (1974); Von Hoffman, Nicholas, *We Are the People Our Parents Warned Us Against* (1968).

Sock It to Me

As a comical expression, "sock it to me," used humorously on the TV show *Laugh In* by various guests, including Richard Nixon in 1968, meant "to give the speaker something." Exactly what was to be given depended on the situation, but the phrase had enough ambiguity to imply sex.

The Something!

In 1967, The Something!, a luncheonette in New York City's East village, at Avenue A and East Tenth Street, teemed with hippies. There they drank coffee and discussed psychedelics. Outside, on the corner, they smoked pot and slept on the sidewalk. The Cave, a dark coffeehouse, was located in the luncheonette's basement. Both businesses closed during the summer of 1968 when many hippies left New York City for the countryside.

Speed

References to speed appeared around 1967 as an amphetamine drug, usually methamphetamine. Most hippies considered speed dangerous because it kept the user up without sleep for a long period and induced hallucinations that were often paranoid and violent.

See also STP.

Spock, Benjamin (1903–)

A pediatrician and author of the world's biggest-selling book on child care, Benjamin Spock shaped the counterculture in two important ways: through his advice to parents and his antiwar activism.

Spock was born on 2 May 1903 in New Haven, Connecticut, silver spoon in mouth: his father worked as a corporate lawyer for the New Haven Railroad. After two years of college preparatory work at the exclusive Phillips Academy in Andover, Massachusetts, Spock enrolled at Yale University, where he excelled academically and earned recognition as an oarsman on the crew that won a gold medal at the 1924 Olympics in Paris.

Spock obtained his B.A. degree the following year and enrolled at the Yale Medical School and later, the Columbia University College of Physicians and Surgeons, from which, in 1929, he obtained his M.D. He then completed his residencies, trained at the New York Psychoanalytic Institute, and began a private practice in pediatrics. The parents who brought their children to his office in New York City praised the way he could set the youngsters at ease.

Spock served in the navy during World War II as a psychiatrist in the medical corps. During this time, he began writing his monumental book, *Baby and Child Care* (originally titled *Common Sense Book of Baby and Child Care*). First published in 1946, it instructed mothers to create a warm, intimate atmosphere for their children and advised parents to use reasoned discussion rather than physical punishment to enforce discipline.

Critics labeled Spock's book instructions in permissiveness, and in reaction to this, he wrote a revision in which he insisted that parents deserved respect from their children and that there should be firm parental standards. Later, in the 1960s, critics of the counterculture blamed youthful rebelliousness on Spock's influential book (as if the upheaval could be held apart from the influences of economic prosperity and social problems). They claimed Spock had created a spoiled, irresponsible generation. Whatever the case, between its first appearance and the mid-1960s, *Baby and Child Care* outsold every other book except the Bible.

Spock's moneyed background indicated he would be conservative politically. And at first he was; he considered, for example, nuclear arms important in order to contain the Soviet Union. But he changed his views in the early 1960s, when he opposed nuclear testing, and nuclear weapons in general, as a threat to children. He joined the National Committee for a Sane Nuclear Policy (SANE) in 1962 as a member of its national board. He later said he took this action "because I was reluctantly convinced we had to have a test-ban treaty. Otherwise more and more children would be born with mental and physical defects. So, I thought it was a pediatric issue." (Joseph 1974, 153)

As Spock recalled, another turning point came after President Lyndon Johnson betrayed him and the nation by sending American troops to fight in Vietnam despite assurances he would never do so. Spock decided to protest the war and led numerous demonstrations. In 1967, his cooperation with New Left groups brought criticism from SANE, and although he remained a member of that organization, he resigned as its cochairman.

Spock's most notorious political involvement came in late 1967, when the Department of Justice decided to prosecute him and four other prominent activists for having encouraged young men to resist the draft and burn their draft cards. Spock had helped to write, and he signed, a "Call To Resist Legitimate Authority." Formally charged with aiding violations of the Selective Service Act, Spock and the other defendants were tried, and in June 1968 found guilty. Spock received a two-year prison sentence, but he appealed his case and a higher court reversed the convictions, claiming the presiding judge had improperly instructed the jury, thus making a fair trial impossible. The case stirred enormous controversy, partly because Spock's views drove a wedge between those who supported and those who opposed the Vietnam War, but also because the government had clearly selected a few high-profile activists to prosecute, out of thousands who could have been brought to trial, in an attempt to intimidate others into silence.

Spock always strenuously condemned the Vietnam War as unconstitutional, illegal, and unjust. But, he said, his radicalism grew incrementally, in which every action "was a relatively small step following another. It started with what I thought was a pediatric concern." (156)

See also Goodman, Mitchell.

References Bloom, Lynn Z., *Doctor Spock: Biography of a Conservative Radical* (1972); Joseph, Peter, *Good Times: An Oral History of America in the 1960s* (1974); Spock, Benjamin, *Common Sense Book of Baby and Child Care* (1968) and *Dr. Spock on Vietnam* (1968).

Stanley, Augustus Owsley III (1935–)

"Mr. LSD," "The Henry Ford of Acid," and "The LSD King"—the hippie counterculture assigned these titles to Augustus Owsley Stanley III, the legendary manufacturer of the hallucinogenic drug LSD . . . not just any LSD but the finest that could be found.

As with so many counterculture rebels, Owsley, as he was called, came from a middle-class family. Sketchy biographical information reveals that he was born in 1935 in Arlington, Virginia, the son of a government attorney. He attended various prep schools, where he displayed substantial intelligence and considerable rebelliousness. He then entered the University of Virginia, but after a short while dropped out and headed for California. In 1956, Owsley entered the air force and learned electronics. After returning to civilian life in 1958, he held various broadcasting and engineering jobs.

The most momentous change in Owsley's life occurred in the early 1960s when, in a second college sojourn, this time at the University of California–Berkeley, he met a chemistry major, a young woman, who helped him set up a laboratory in a vacant store. There he began experimenting with chemical mixtures and produced LSD in liquid form. By 1965, he had moved to Los Angeles, where he manufactured blue, red, and green aspirin-sized LSD tablets, then legal, that retailed on the street for $2 each. His production reached 10 million tablets, making him a millionaire. At the same time, he gave substantial amounts of LSD away. Owsley provided most of the acid consumed in San Francisco's Haight-Ashbury district and considered himself part of a grand experiment to see if LSD could change the world into a more beautiful place.

"Owsley really has dynamite, righteous acid," hippies said. (Dorson 1973, 285) Owsley Acid had a potency and purity that other LSD failed to attain, and in making the drug, Owsley did much to popularize it, taking it beyond the intellectual elite, people such as the author Aldous Huxley who had been using it since the 1950s. Owsley is credited with providing LSD for the first Trips Festival in San Francisco in 1966 and for supplying it to the Grateful Dead rock band. For a short time, he provided them with money they needed to buy amplifiers and other equipment.

Whenever the Acid King—Owsley—appeared at a party, he received an ovation, and his fame among hippies generated many spectacular, apocryphal stories about him. One told how he once dressed as a minister and visited some activists in jail. Standing before them, he opened his Bible and began tearing out its pages, handing them to the prisoners. They looked at him with puzzled expressions, until he calmly explained that each page had been dipped in acid.

Owsley's reign as Acid King ended, though, soon after the government made the drug illegal. He continued to manufacture it, but in December 1967 federal agents raided his lab. In 1969, a federal court sentenced him to three years in prison. While out on bail, he was arrested two more times, once in New Orleans and once in Oakland, California, for possessing marijuana and LSD. The federal court then revoked his bail, and in 1971 he began serving his prison sentence at Terminal Island in Los Angeles.

See also Acid; Huxley, Aldous.

References Dorson, Richard M., *America in Legend: Folklore from the Colonial Period to the Present* (1973); Lee, Martin A., and Bruce Shlain, *Acid Dreams: The CIA, LSD, and the Sixties Rebellion* (1985).

Stash

"Where's your stash?" meant where are your drugs. Stash could be marijuana, LSD, or any combination of drugs.

Steinem, Gloria (1934–)

A leading feminist, journalist, and founding editor of *Ms.* magazine, Gloria Steinem, activated by the counterculture, helped change the status of women in American society.

Steinem was born on 25 March 1934 in Toldeo, Ohio. Her father, Leo Steinem, worked at one point as an antique dealer and operated a summer resort, but for the most part he lived as an itinerant and traveled in a house trailer with his family, barely able to keep finances together. In 1946, he and Steinem's mother, Gloria Nunevillar Steinem, divorced, and young Gloria then lived with her mother in a poor district of East Toledo. For years she took care of her mother, a near invalid who suffered from anxiety and depression. As a teenager, Steinem tap-danced at the neighborhood Elks Club and entered and won a local television talent contest, hoping this might lead to an escape from her environment in Toledo.

Then, in 1952, she gained acceptance to Smith College in Massachusetts. She worked hard, won scholarships, and graduated *magna cum laude* in 1956 with a degree in political science. That summer, Steinem traveled to India under a fellowship she had received to study in Delhi and Calcutta. Little did she realize the trip would transform her, helping shape her social outlook. In fact, the journey proved so eventful that, in *The Education of a Woman*, her biographer, Carolyn G. Heilbrun, says Steinem discovered in India "the political focus of her life," namely, a strong concern for the disadvantaged. (69) Steinem found, too, that, as she published freelance articles in Indian newspapers, she could earn a living through writing and advocacy.

Upon her return to the United States in 1958, Steinem tried to find work as a reporter but to no avail. She eventually was hired as codirector of the Independent Research Service in Cambridge, Massachusetts. This organization operated in conjunction with the National Student Association (NSA), which brought together leaders in college student governments. When, in the sixties, it turned out that the NSA had received money from the CIA, Steinem's enemies accused her of having been a government spy. This charge, however, amounted to no more than political mudslinging.

Steinem landed her first job with a magazine in 1960, but did not have her first article published until two years later when *Esquire* carried her story about the sexual revolution. In 1963, Steinem wrote an article that appeared in *Show*, based on her work as an undercover Playboy bunny. The article preceded her conversion to feminism by six years, but it presaged her later observations that women were sex objects, worth something to men only as bunnies.

Writer and critic Gloria Steinem

Steinem's writing gained little recognition after that, however, until, beginning in 1968, her City Politic column appeared in *New York* magazine. According to Heilbrun, with this column Steinem "was on her way to becoming a serious journalist, reporting events affecting women, as well as other dispossessed groups, but not noticing that she was noticing women in any special way." (137)

The counterculture affected Steinem greatly, stimulating a feminist outlook. This appeared in March 1969 when she attended a meeting on abortion organized by the radical feminist group Redstockings. Steinem spoke out and confessed she had once had an abortion, and she said that women should not have to feel criminal about undergoing the procedure.

Following this meeting, Steinem wrote an article, "After Black Power, Women's Liberation," in which she took an openly feminist stand. Her writing ability and the knack she had for presenting ideas without being confrontational moved her to the forefront of the emerging women's liberation movement. In 1971, she joined Betty Friedan, Bella Abzug, and Congresswoman Shirley Chisholm in founding the National Women's Political Caucus (NWPC), which recruited women to run for public office.

At the same time, her journalistic career took a new turn when she worked to found a feminist magazine. At first, she doubted she would get any advertisers for the project, but her enthusiasm grew when she contacted women editors, journalists, and opinion makers and found them all supportive. Publisher Clay S. Felker then agreed to run a 30-page sample publication, called *Ms.*, as an insert in the December 1971 issue of his magazine, *New York*. After this proved successful, he financed the first full issue of *Ms.*, which appeared in January 1972, with Steinem serving as editor, as she had for the supplement. The issue contained a petition for legal abortions.

During the following summer, *Ms.* Ap peared on a regular monthly basis and featured articles such as "Down with Sexist Upbringing" and "Why Women Fear Success." Within a few months, the magazine's circulation reached half a million.

Steinem believed that the oppression of women prevented men from living fuller lives, and she carried this view into her work at *Ms.* She believed, as well, that men and women should share equal responsibility for child rearing and household obligations, that women who hold jobs should not be expected to handle all the cooking, housecleaning, and the like.

In 1972, Steinem campaigned to get the necessary number of states to ratify the Equal Rights Amendment, an effort that eventually failed. At the same time, radicals within the women's liberation movement, primarily Redstockings, attacked her and *Ms.* for selling out to male-dominated corporations. She, however, continued to edit *Ms.* In the 1980s and 1990s, she worked as a contributing editor at Random House publishers.

An articulate voice for feminism, by keeping the women's movement alive, Steinem helped propel the counterculture into the early 1970s at a time when many other of its aspects—the antiwar movement and black power, for example—had lost their momentum.

See also Friedan, Betty; Redstockings; Women's Movement.

Reference Heilbrun, Carolyn G., *The Education of a Woman: The Life of Gloria Steinem* (1995).

Steppenwolf

Hermann Hesse's novel *Steppenwolf*, written in 1927, obtained a wide readership among intellectual counterculture youths. Hesse's appeal came from his pacifism and his search for values to replace traditional ones no longer valid in the modern world. Hesse, born in Germany in 1877 but a Swiss citizen from 1923 until his death in 1962, had been deeply disillusioned by World War I, and this shaped his outlook and his writing. *Steppenwolf* portrays a hero, a spiritually lonely artist, part human and part wolf in character, whose internal conflict symbolizes the greater conflict between individualism and conformity within a capitalist society.

Hesse's *Siddhartha*, published in 1922, also attracted counterculture readers with its Eastern mysticism.

References Hesse, Hermann, *Siddhartha* (1951) and *Steppenwolf* (1963).

Stone, I. F. (1907–1989)

As an iconoclastic liberal journalist, I. F. Stone appealed to many activists in the countercultural New Left.

Isidor Feinstein Stone was born on 24 December 1907 in Philadelphia, Pennsylvania, where his Jewish immigrant parents owned a dry-goods store. He developed an interest in journalism and liberal ideas while still a child, and in high school published his own monthly newspaper that contained editorials supporting Gandhi, Woodrow Wilson, and the League of Nations. After graduating from the University of Pennsylvania in 1928, Stone worked as a reporter in New Jersey for the *Camden Courier-Post* and briefly joined the Socialist Party.

Stone moved to New York City in 1933 and worked as an editorial writer for the *New York Post.* Six years later, he became Washington editor for the *Nation*, a leading liberal weekly. After World War II, he took positions that endeared him to disaffected young people—namely his criticism of American cold-war policy as preventing peaceful coexistence with the Soviet Union. Stone did not support communism, and he frequently attacked the Soviet government as tyrannical, but he insisted the United States could best work its influence and avoid nuclear war through more cooperative efforts.

In 1952, Stone wrote *The Hidden History of the Korean War*, in which he blamed the conflict not on aggression by Communist North Korea but on a conspiracy between South Korea and the United States. This radical departure from standard interpretations brought him considerable notoriety, as did his frequent exposures about what he claimed to be Pentagon lies.

The following year, Stone began his own publication, *I. F. Stone's Weekly*. He researched, wrote, and edited the *Weekly*, and it quickly gained a substantial liberal audience. Politically minded college students read this work in the 1960s, and it stimulated their opposition to cold-war policies. Activist Todd Gitlin recounted: "We applauded I. F. Stone when he came to [Harvard] to speak with . . . sympathy about Castro's Cuba, and I subscribed to his beacon *Weekly*, which taught me, as it taught many of my contemporaries, that the government lied." (Gitlin 1987, 90) Al Haber, founder of Students for a Democratic Society, the leading New Left organization in the sixties, also read Stone's publication. (Stone once described himself as "New Lefty before there was a New Left.")

Stone early opposed the U.S. military involvement in Vietnam and appeared at numerous antiwar rallies. He wrote three books widely read by student activists: *The Haunted Fifties*, about McCarthyism and the Eisenhower administration; *In a Time of Torment*, about the Vietnam War and black revolution; and *The Killings at Kent State*, about how those responsible for the shootings at that university got away with murder. Stone discontinued the *Weekly* (by then actually a biweekly) in 1972 but continued writing books and newspaper articles. He died on 18 June 1989 in Boston.

See also New Left; Students for a Democratic Society.

References Gitlin, Todd, *The Sixties: Years of Hope, Days of Rage* (1987); Stone, I. F., *The Hidden History of the Korean War* (1952), *In a Time of Torment* (1967), *The Killings at Kent State: How Murder Went Unpunished* (1971), *Polemics and Prophecies, 1967-1970* (1970), and *The Truman Era* (1953).

Stoned

In the sixties, the word *stoned* did not mean throwing rocks at someone. Rather, it meant being high, usually from drugs but sometimes without them, as with a "naturally stoned" person.

Stonewall

Blacks, Chicanos, Indians, Asian Americans, women—all protested in the 1960s as discontentment and assertiveness surged across the nation. This rebelliousness stirred yet another group, a sexual minority: gays. Discriminated against and relegated to a secretive existence, homosexuals stood up for their dignity during a confrontation at a bar in New York City's Greenwich Village, the Stonewall Inn.

The showdown occurred on the night of 27 June 1969. For several years, gays had been working toward their liberation, most notably in 1965 when they staged a "sip-in" at nightclubs in New York to protest a rule established by the state liquor authority that no more than three homosexuals be allowed in a bar at any one time, and shortly thereafter when they organized the Student Homophile League at Columbia University, followed by another at New York University. This activity, and the public profile taken by some gays as the counterculture took the position that individuals should be able to live as they wanted without harassment, caused the police to react, raiding gay bars and closing them down. When they moved against the Stonewall Inn, they expected gays would simply take their arrests without complaint, as they had usually done in the past. Not so this time—gays fought back rather than submit, and a melee resulted in injuries to four policemen.

The Stonewall Inn closed, but when the police returned to the neighborhood the following night and made additional raids, a crowd of 400 young men and women appeared, hurling bottles at them and chanting "gay power!" The *Village Voice* newspaper called the events "a kind of liberation, as the gay brigade emerged from the bars, back rooms, and bedrooms of the Village and became street people." (Miller 1996, 304–305)

After Stonewall, gays formed the Gay Liberation Front (GLF) and demanded an end to discrimination based on sexual preferences. The GLF picketed companies that refused to hire homosexuals, and in June 1970 organized Gay Pride Week to commemorate the first anniversary of Stonewall. About 10,000 gays marched in New York City, displaying the pride, assertion, and liberation already evident in their other endeavors, including magazines and newspapers committed to gay life and gays marching in antiwar demonstrations under banners proclaiming "Homosexuals against the War."

References Adam, Barry D., *The Rise of a Gay and Lesbian Movement* (1987); Duberman, Martin, *Stonewall* (1993); Katz, Jonathan, *Gay American History: Lesbians and Gay Men in the U.S.A.: A Documentary* (1976); Miller, Douglas T., *On Our Own: Americans in the Sixties* (1996).

Stop the Draft Week

In 1967, the nation's college campuses teemed with antiwar activity, and it reached its height with Stop the Draft Week that began on Sunday, 15 October. The protest showed the widening appeal of the antiwar movement when its culminating event, the March on the Pentagon, which occurred on 21 October, attracted demonstrators from beyond the campuses: writers, civil rights workers, federal employees, Vietnam veterans, and many others.

See also March on the Pentagon, 1967.

STP

A chemist at Dow Chemical Company first synthesized STP (2,5 dimethox-4-methylphene-thylamine), a potent psychedelic, in 1964 and provided it to the U.S. Army for use in an experimental program intended to find an incapacitating drug. The CIA also tested it. Three years later, the formula for STP ("Serenity, Tranquillity, Peace," hippies called it) circulated publicly, and its street manufacture coincided with the Summer of Love in San Francisco. The drug spread through the Haight-Ashbury scene, producing many bad hallucinations. One user remarked: "Acid [LSD] is like being let out of a cage; STP is like being shot out of a gun." (Lee and Shlain 1985, 187)

The author Ken Kesey took STP, which acquired the nickname "speed," and claimed he had lost part of an inexplicable something that made him human. Indeed, a typical STP trip lasted three days, and while some users reported pleasant experiences, many described hellish encounters. Young people tripping on the super-psychedelic flooded the free medical clinic in Haight-Ashbury, seeking help. Before summer's end, most hippies were warning against taking STP, and the slogan "Speed kills!" appeared.

See also Drugs and the Drug Culture.

Reference Lee, Martin A., and Bruce Shlain, *Acid Dreams: The CIA, LSD, and the Sixties Rebellion* (1985).

The Strawberry Statement

Many counterculture youths read *The Strawberry Statement*, written in 1968 by James Simon Kunen, a 19-year-old student at Columbia University. He composed the book as diary entries that describe the bloody strike and protests at his college that year and what had motivated him, and others, to participate in them. His account offers a keen insight into the counterculture, largely because Kunen, although left-of-center in his politics, was not a member of Students for a Democratic Society, the group that led the strike. "That's why I can't be too close with the radicals sometimes," Kunen writes. "I just don't feel as sure of myself as they seem to feel about themselves." (102) Not radicalism, but disgust over the war, accompanied by a feeling that something had gone wrong in America and that this something permeated Columbia, motivated Kunen. He writes:

> Thursday, June 27: I don't understand why our government has us fight the war. . . . How can [President] Johnson sleep? How can he go to bed knowing that 25,000 American boys—and countless Vietnamese—have died because of his 'policies.' . . . It's in me that my friends every day hear gunfire and see others fall and hate the enemy. But when they see the ground spin up at them and feel the wetness of their own blood, whom do they think they hate then? These kids who were and were being and were going to be, suddenly find themselves ending. (59)

Beyond this, *The Strawberry Statement* shows a protester torn between dissent and respect for the traditional middle-class values he had been raised with, and it shows a college student's everyday musings while growing up in the sixties: from the trivial, such as the joy at using a fresh tube of toothpaste, to the significant, such as relations with his parents and falling in love with Laura, a fellow student.

New York magazine and *The Atlantic Monthly* published portions of *The Strawberry Statement*, and Kunen appeared on several radio and television talk shows to explain the situation at Columbia. Combining innocence with weariness, and seriousness with humor, *The Strawberry Statement* tells a story that, today, makes it essential reading for anyone trying to understand the counterculture from a human rather than political perspective.

"I declare," says Kunen, "that the meaning of the Columbia uprising is that one too many persons has been educated, and one too many wires has linked people's thoughts together, for power to breed power anymore." (150)

See also Columbia University.

Reference Kunen, James Simon, *The Strawberry Statement: Notes of a College Revolutionary* (1968).

Street Theatre

Street theatre involved developing public consciousness through outrageous displays and put-ons. Abbie Hoffman first brought this technique to national attention, but he adopted the idea from the Diggers, a hippie group in San Francisco's Haight-Ashbury district. The Diggers had evolved from a mime troupe and equated life with theatre. Thus, they considered themselves Life Actors, taking their props, costumes, skits, and improvisations into the streets to act in and act out the struggle under way in Haight-Ashbury and elsewhere between counterculture and mainstream culture. Their actions, they hoped, would cause people in the straight world to reevaluate their institutions and behavior.

Abbie Hoffman used street theatre in 1967 when he and his followers marched in a "Support Our Boys in Vietnam" parade—bedecked in long hair and flowers. In another outrageous act, he joined an official tour of the New York Stock Exchange and threw dollar bills from a balcony onto the floor below. This sent stockbrokers scrambling after the money and disrupted all business for five minutes—Hoffman had made his point about greed, its overwhelming presence, and its ability to cause chaos.

To protest the war in Vietnam, Hoffman favored street theatre over picketing. He believed that absurd, weird, colorful behavior would draw bigger media attention; thus his attempt to levitate the Pentagon at a peace march in 1967 and his plan to hold a Festival of Life, replete with poets and rock bands, at the 1968 Democratic National Convention in Chicago.

See also Democratic National Convention of 1968; Diggers; Hoffman, Abbie; March on the Pentagon, 1967; San Francisco Mime Troupe.

Student Nonviolent Coordinating Committee (SNCC)

When African American college students organized the Student Nonviolent Coordinating Committee (SNCC), little did they realize that the group would depart from the mainstream civil rights movement to pursue black power.

SNCC emerged in 1960 from sit-in demonstrations begun by black college students in Greensboro, North Carolina, to protest racial segregation. As the protests spread, Ella Baker, 57-year-old executive director of the Southern Christian Leadership Conference (SCLC), convinced her organization to sponsor a meeting of the sit-in leaders and arranged for her alma mater, Shaw University in Raleigh, to provide the facilities. The meeting began in April 1960; Baker expected about 100 students, but more than 200 turned out.

These students expressed impatience with the leading civil rights organizations, including the SCLC and its leader, Martin Luther King, Jr., for having relied too heavily on court proceedings; they wanted quicker results through civil disobedience, such as sit-ins, and rejected token gains and detailed organization. They feared, too, that King and other leaders would manipulate them. Baker agreed they should separate from the SCLC, and at a second meeting in May, they opened an office in Atlanta.

In October, they declared SNCC a permanent organization and voiced nonviolent ideas similar to those held by King, but they relied more on enthusiasm, an existentialist, almost romantic faith in their ability to change conditions. Their chairman, Charles McDew, expressed their intent to proceed forcefully when he said, "Instead of sitting idly by, taking the leavings of a sick and decadent society, we have seized the initiative, and already the walls have begun to crumble."

At this time, segregation remained largely intact in the South, and the Deep South in particular displayed a total unwillingness to allow blacks equal rights. In states such as Alabama and Mississippi, few African Americans could vote, and most lived in dire poverty. SNCC decided to strike these states directly, and in August 1961 the organization opened its first voter registration school in McComb, Mississippi. At the same time, SNCC continued its direct action campaign, staging additional sit-ins in the South.

Mississippi whites reacted with violence, beating blacks and their white supporters, and on 12 June 1963 a white reactionary killed civil rights worker Medgar Evers. The following year, SNCC began its Mississippi Freedom Summer Project—a bigger attempt to register blacks. The plan angered many in the civil rights movement who believed it would produce a white backlash in the South, and perhaps elsewhere, and thus damage Lyndon Johnson's chances to win election. Johnson had succeeded John Kennedy as president and had worked hard to get civil rights legislation through Congress.

SNCC rejected this argument, and its more radical members made clear their determination to challenge basic American ideas and institutions. James Forman declared that SNCC "argued for a . . . revolution in American society." (Forman 1972, 361) SNCC had no more than 150 formal members at its peak, but it recruited many volunteers, such as during Mississippi Freedom Summer, when over 1,000 helped with the campaign. They worked on voter registration, established the Mississippi Freedom Democratic Party (MFDP) to challenge the existing, lily-white Democratic Party, organized freedom schools to teach black heritage, and began community centers and libraries.

Mississippi Freedom Summer had an enormous impact on SNCC, the civil rights movement, and the counterculture. The volunteers included many northern white students who returned to their campuses after experiencing oppression

The Student Nonviolent Coordinating Committee established the Mississippi Freedom Democratic Party (MFDP) in 1964, challenging the white-dominated Democratic Party with their mission to register blacks to vote. Here, 68-year-old Tom Flowers registers to vote at the Panola County Courthouse after the MFDP marched in Batesville, Mississippi, on 11 June 1969.

firsthand and learning about direct action. They subsequently expressed their view that America had failed to develop an equitable, democratic society, and in protesting injustices they used tactics such as marches and sit-ins.

For their part, many blacks in SNCC resented the whites who seemed to exhibit a superior attitude and tried to dominate leadership positions. Dissension tore at SNCC as a struggle erupted between those who saw the white volunteers as making a valuable contribution and those who believed the movement should be exclusively in black hands in order to promote African American skills and independence.

As in SNCC's previous efforts, the Mississippi Summer Project resulted in violence, most notably the killing of three civil rights workers, two of whom were white. That the FBI investigated primarily because whites had been murdered infuriated many blacks. So too did the FBI's refusal to protect civil rights workers and its intimation that Communists controlled SNCC. The failure of the summer project to register many blacks added to the anger. Consequently, many in SNCC rejected nonviolence and argued that blacks should arm and protect themselves.

At the same time, formation of the MFDP widened the gulf between SNCC and other civil rights groups. At the 1964 Democratic National Convention in Atlantic City, the MFDP tried to get itself seated in place of the regular all-white Mississippi delegation. When President Johnson refused more than a token, nonvoting presence for the MFDP—an arrangement supported by King and many other civil rights leaders who did not want to weaken Johnson's campaign—SNCC denounced the action and claimed it proved that the Democratic Party had no desire to end white oppression. Said one SNCC leader: "After Atlantic City, our struggle was not for civil rights, but for liberation." (Sitkoff 1981, 185)

From then on, SNCC radicalized rapidly. Riots in Watts in 1964, the death of Malcolm X in 1965, and the widening Vietnam War produced a sense of urgency and crisis. In January 1966, SNCC criticized the war—the first civil rights organization to do so. The American government, SNCC claimed, protected an illegitimate regime in South Vietnam while doing nothing to protect blacks in America. SNCC then engaged in antidraft protests.

In 1967, SNCC declared itself an organization promoting human rights throughout the world. As such, it pledged to support struggles against colonialism, racism, and economic exploitation, and declared its opposition to apartheid in South Africa. By this time, SNCC had completely ended its support of nonviolence and ejected its white volunteers. The group's leader, Stokely Carmichael, talked about "offing pigs," and his successor, H. Rap Brown, instructed blacks to shoot whites.

SNCC allied itself with the black power movement and promoted it. SNCC never clarified what the phrase meant, but used it to express frustration and assert that there should be no compromise with white leaders.

Radicalization, though, hurt SNCC—it halted white financial support, and mainstream civil rights organizations wanted nothing to do with the group. At the same time, the U.S. government infiltrated and harassed SNCC, with agent provocateurs stirring its extremism.

By 1972, SNCC collapsed. As one analyst and participant in SNCC reported about the group: "They nurture a vision of a revolution beyond race, against other forms of injustice, challenging the value-system of the nation and of smug middle-class society everywhere." (Zinn 1964, 216) When SNCC radicalized, it reflected the counterculture's tendency to react against the deepening Vietnam War and society's intransigent conservatism with extreme, sometimes violent, measures, while its internal divisions exhibited the counterculture's diffuse and often contradictory nature.

See also Baker, Ella; Brown, H. Rap; Carmichael, Stokely; Forman, James.

References Carson, Clayborne, *In Struggle: SNCC and the Black Awakening of the 1960s* (1981); Forman, James, *The Making of Black Revolutionaries: A Personal Account* (1972); Sitkoff, Harvard, *The Struggle for Black Equality, 1954–1980* (1981); Zinn, Howard, *SNCC: The New Abolitionists* (1964).

Students for a Democratic Society

Centered on college campuses, Students for a Democratic Society (SDS) challenged conservatives and liberals alike in raising questions about injustices in the American political and economic system, including the Vietnam War. SDS developed a revolutionary consciousness seldom seen in the United States. *Life* magazine went so far as to proclaim: "Never in the history of this country has a small group, standing outside the pale of conventional power, made such an impact or created such havoc."

SDS emerged in 1960 from the League for Industrial Democracy, an old liberal organization that, in the 1930s, had done battle on behalf of labor unions. Led by Al Haber, a student at the University of Michigan (UM), younger activists within the League formed SDS as part of a resurgent college Left. Nationally, the burgeoning student population provided a recruiting base for SDS, and the civil rights movement stirred social consciousness. The oppression faced by blacks and their white supporters convinced many liberal students that American society did not meet the patriotic images they had learned in elementary and high school. To them, oppression seemed real.

Into 1962, the organization remained small and largely a two-person operation run by Haber (its first president) and Tom Hayden, editor of the student newspaper at UM. At this point, SDS decided to more forcefully support the civil rights drive in the South. This gained the organization recognition on college campuses, and as its members saw liberals such as President John Kennedy vacillate on a black voting rights drive, they came to distrust authority. Liberals, they believed, differed little from conservatives in protecting a corrupt system, a cold-war state with an unfailing devotion to the status quo. Hayden called liberalism bankrupt and criticized it as little more than a smile on the face of conservatism.

With this, in June 1962, SDS held its national meeting at Port Huron, near Detroit. The delegates produced the Port Huron Statement, a wordy, cumbersome document that took society to task for its moral impoverishment and oppression. The Port Huron Statement called for greater individual rights and a participatory democracy that would diminish the power of the corporate elite and government bureaucrats and place more power in local communities. The document committed SDS to building a base not among labor unions but among college students. Although read by few outside SDS, the Port Huron Statement expressed a political awakening among college students.

In 1964, SDS, under increasing criticism for inaction and wanting to attack social injustice, launched the Economic Research and Action Project (ERAP). Through it, SDSers worked in the ghettos to help the poor, including forming committees to lobby police and landlords.

In 1965, SDS participated in protests against the Vietnam War. The group sponsored a march on Washington that, in April, attracted 25,000 people—the largest peace demonstration in American history up to that time. As a result, SDS gained additional prominence on campuses—with more than 50 chapters and several hundred members—and moved toward a policy of confrontation under the belief that power must be met with power.

Despite its growth, SDS failed to build a strong, cohesive national structure, partly because it wanted to remain open to diverse ideologies and partly because it let local chapters take the lead in choosing which issues to pursue. This loose organization remained a constant handicap.

At the same time, foes of the antiwar movement targeted SDS. Senator John Stennis of Mississippi asserted that the government had to destroy SDS and "grind it to bits." Despite these problems, by the end of 1965 SDS had 124 chapters and over 4,000 members.

When, in 1965, President Lyndon Johnson announced his plan to end draft exemptions for college students, SDSers felt more compelled to act. They believed there existed a real chance to create a generation of committed radicals. In 1966, SDS organized no fewer than six sizable protests on campuses, aimed at the military and Dow Chemical.

SDS supported draft resistance, and its members led in sponsoring a mass draft card burning held in New York City on 15 April 1967. As the organization's membership reached 30,000, some SDSers talked about the need for sweeping changes in American institutions. Indeed, many SDS leaders saw themselves as the vanguard of revolution. But not all within the organization agreed, and an already-weak structure came under greater pressure.

An SDS chapter helped lead a student protest at Columbia University in spring 1968, one in which 1,000 students occupied five buildings. This produced a surge in student protests, some even at normally quiescent colleges, such as Stanford University, the University of Miami, and Northwestern University. That year, Bernardine Dohrn won election as SDS interorganizational national secretary and proclaimed herself a "revolutionary communist."

Then came the notorious demonstrations at the 1968 Democratic National Convention in Chicago. SDS initially opposed the protest and never officially endorsed it. Further, it wanted to continue pursuing diversification beyond the war issue; as its vice-president had said a few months earlier: "We must deal with questions of power rather than act out our generational alienation." (Farber 1988, 81) Nevertheless, several SDSers and former SDSers participated in the protest. Overall, the crowd varied in action and makeup, at times young and unruly, pelting police officers with rocks and bottles; at other times, older and restrained. Irrespective of the crowd's nature, the police resorted to bashing heads in a bloody confrontation. As a result, SDS membership boomed to well over 100,000—many young people had looked at Chicago and concluded that those in power, the establishment, were at war with them.

College protests increased in 1969 and sometimes turned violent, as in the bombings and arson directed at Reserve Officer Training Corps (ROTC) buildings. (Many campuses had such structures used by the ROTC, a military program.) Yet SDS membership declined as factions within it fought for control and many members balked at radicalism gone too far.

A faction within SDS organized that summer and called itself Weatherman. Led by Dohrn, it sought to advance communism through violent revolution, and called on America's youth to escalate their struggle at home to show unity with third-world liberation movements. SDS, now hardly more than a skeletal organization, officially rejected Dohrn and her followers, but the formation of Weatherman, along with the infiltration and harassment by government agents, so shattered SDS that in 1970 it collapsed, passing from the scene as the decade to which it had linked its hopes ended. SDS reappeared in the 1990s, linked to a leftist environmental movement.

See also Democratic National Convention of 1968; Dohrn, Bernardine; Gitlin, Todd; Hayden, Tom; New Left; Participatory Democracy; Port Huron Statement; Rudd, Mark; Weather Underground.

References Adelson, Alan, *SDS* (1972); Farber, David, *Chicago '68* (1988); Gitlin, Todd, *The Sixties: Years of Hope, Days of Rage* (1987) and *The Whole World Is Watching: Mass Media in the Making and Unmaking of the New Left* (1980); Heath, G. Louis, ed., *Vandals in the Bomb Factory: The History and Literature of the Students for a Democratic Society* (1976); Kelman, Steven, *Push Comes to Shove: The Escalation of Student Protest* (1970); Miller, James, *Democracy Is in the Streets: From Port Huron to the Siege of Chicago* (1987); Myers, R. David, ed., *Toward a History of the New Left: Essays from within the Movement* (1989); Sale, Kirkpatrick, *SDS* (1973); Unger, Irwin, *The Movement: A History of the American New Left, 1959–1972* (1974).

Summer of Love

In the summer of 1967, the nation exploded as riots swept several urban ghettos: Boston, Tampa, Buffalo, and most intensely, Newark, New Jersey, and Detroit, Michigan. In Newark, National Guard troops fired 13,000 rounds of ammunition, wounded 1,200 blacks, and killed 25. At the same time, the Vietnam War intensified—more troops, more deaths. Amid this, the Summer of Love took place—a "holy pilgrimage" said hippies in San Francisco's Haight-Ashbury district, "to affirm and celebrate a new spiritual dawn." (Anderson 1995, 172) For the Haight, though, dawn never came.

For three years prior to the Summer of Love, hippies had been trying to build an alternative society in Haight-Ashbury, one dedicated to living life as a spiritual and psychedelic exploration, where straight society's greed and materialism would be left behind. The hippie population expanded, and with it, numerous hip businesses, such as the Psychedelic Shop and the *San Francisco Oracle* newspaper. In the spring of 1967, hippie leaders in the Haight called for young people from around the nation to journey to San Francisco and experience the good vibrations, the spiritual enlightenment.

The announcement, however, caused problems before the young even arrived: many hippies criticized it as a tactic developed by the hip businesses to make money, and they feared that the Haight, already beset with tourists who jammed its streets and sidewalks, would never be able to handle the expected crowds. Still, the official hippie Council for a Summer of Love reported:

> This city is not a wasteland; our children will not discover drought and famine here. . . . Already individuals and groups who have seen deeply into the situation are making preparations. Kitchens are being made ready. Food is being gathered. Hotels and houses are being prepared to supply free lodging. . . . It is the will of God that His children will be met with Love. It is His will that Love will grow and flourish in this country, in America, so its great power will finally turn to the right path—that is, the path of life. (Cohen 1991, 235)

All summer long youth invaded—youngsters hitchhiked or arrived in vans bedecked with psychedelic Day-Glo images, and they arrived by the tens of thousands. Many only in their teens, they had no commitment to developing an alternative society, and sought only adventure or escape from problems at home or in school: "My mother was . . . really troublesome about hair," said one refugee. "And she didn't like boots. It was really weird. . . . If I didn't finish ironing my shirts for the week, I couldn't go out for the weekend. Wow." (Didion 1967, 27)

The invaders donned beads and took drugs, LSD and the more dangerous speed, and other concoctions contaminated by rip-off artists; they crowded the streets, panhandled, and promoted a disease epidemic that severely strained Haight's free clinic. Rape emerged as an ever-present danger and the crime rate skyrocketed. In one instance, the police discovered a black drug dealer dead from multiple stabbings and a gunshot wound and arrested a suspect after finding him with the victim's severed arm wrapped in a blood-soaked cloth.

The Summer of Love crashed. Many hippies fled the Haight, and as an alternative society, the district never recovered. "We were seeing something important," said journalist Joan Didion about that historic summer. "We were seeing the desperate attempt of a handful of pathetically unequipped children to create a community in a social vacuum." (Didion 1968, 94)

See also Haight-Ashbury; Hippies; Psychedelic Shop; *San Francisco Oracle.*

References Anderson, Terry H., *The Movement and the Sixties* (1995); Cohen, Allen, *The San Francisco Oracle, Facsimile Edition: The Psychedelic Newspaper of the Haight Ashbury, 1966–1968* (1991); Didion, Joan, "Slouching toward Bethlehem," *Saturday Evening Post*, 23 September 1967, 25–31+; Didion, Joan, *Slouching toward Bethlehem* (1968).

Surfing

Although as a sport surfing predated the sixties, it did not emerge as a popular social phenomenon until that tumultuous decade, when it developed a split personality: opposed to mainstream society, it merged into commercialism.

Surfing first appeared in North America when a Hawaiian surfer, George Freeth, brought it to southern California in 1907. The sport spread slowly at first, but this changed in the 1950s, when Bob Simmons, an avid surfer, pioneered new surfing locations by riding the waves in areas previously ignored or considered unsuitable. Even more importantly, he designed boards constructed from balsa wood and fiberglass, lighter and more maneuverable than those used earlier. Although he died in a surfing accident in 1954, his efforts attracted more people to the sport.

Surfing developed behavior patterns that distinguished it from mainstream society and attracted those who desired an alternative to suburban conformity. Surfers had their own jargon, spent long hours at the beach, and treated their sport as more than that—it entailed a different mentality. Tom Wolfe says about surfers in *The Pump House Gang:* "They have this life all their own; it's like a glass-bottom boat, and it floats over the 'real' world, or the square world or whatever one wants to call it . . . they float right through the real world, but it can't touch them." (Wolfe 1968, 29–30)

In the sixties, thousands of young people took up surfing. One commented:

> When I went to school damn near everything was organized. Little league baseball, stoop-tag, the three major sports . . . everything was concocted around the buddy system. They never left you alone. But with surfing I could go to the beach and not have to depend on anybody. I could take a wave and forget about it. (Irwin 1977, 132)

With this popularity, though, surfing commercialized: surf shops, surfboard brand names, swim wear—all on an unprecedented scale. But more than that: surf movies, surf magazines, and the ubiquitous surf rock 'n' roll, most prominent with the Beach Boys and Jan and Dean. Many pseudosurfers joined the scene, those who could not surf but who liked to hang out at the beach, color their hair to resemble the sun-bleached surfer look, and copy the surfer clothes (such as the oversized swim trunks called "baggies") and surfer language.

See also The Beach Boys.

References Irwin, John, *Scenes* (1977); Wolfe, Tom, *The Pump House Gang* (1968).

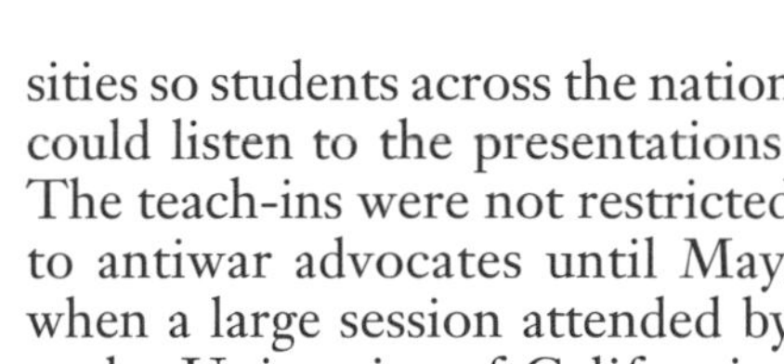

Tamalpais, Mount

Hippies gathered often at Mount Tamalpais near San Francisco, in Marin County, because they considered this beautiful spot, with its pine trees and grassy ridges, golden in appearance, to be spiritually uplifting and infused with magical qualities. But commercialized countercultural events occurred there, too. In June 1967, a rock radio station sponsored a musical festival, called the Magic Mountain Fantasy Fair, featuring a geodesic dome with a light show inside, a nine-foot-high statue of the Buddha, and rock bands, including Jefferson Airplane, the Doors, and Country Joe and the Fish.

A similar gathering a few weeks later, the Festival of Growing Things, presented all the major San Francisco bands, including the Grateful Dead.

Teach-In

An innovative format emerged at the University of Michigan in March 1965: a teach-in. Shortly after the first massive American bombing of North Vietnam, professors used this tactic to educate students about the conflict in Southeast Asia. The first teach-in involved an all-night symposium taught by the professors, who generally opposed the war, and various guests, among them representatives from the State Department, who supported the war and participated in a debate. Over 3,500 students attended the session, held in four auditoriums, which lasted until dawn the following morning. There followed teach-ins at Columbia University, the University of Wisconsin, New York University, Rutgers, the University of Oregon, and at least one junior college.

This led to an all-day National Teach-In held in Washington, D.C., on 15 May, with telephone hookups to various universities so students across the nation could listen to the presentations. The teach-ins were not restricted to antiwar advocates until May, when a large session attended by 12,000 at the University of California–Berkeley heard only from those who opposed the war.

Teeny-Bopper

The word *teeny-bopper* emerged in the mid-1960s in reference to youngsters in their early teens who adopted the latest trendy clothes and listened to simplistic rock music, often created with them in mind. Bands such as the 1910 Fruit Gum Company and Ohio Express aimed their songs at teeny-boppers. Such titles as "Yummy, Yummy, Yummy, I've Got Love in My Tummy" and "Indian Giver" revealed their appeal. Older, more serious countercultural youths rejected this juvenile music as exploitive rubbish.

Television

The post–World War II technological marvel, television, inadvertently helped create the counterculture, first by presenting in the 1950s stories of innocence and then in the 1960s reports of domestic protest and wartime brutality. The medium and the message thus combined to raise idealistic expectations and later shatter them.

Imagine yourself a young girl or boy watching television in the 1950s. Much as your parents, you would likely have marveled at this device that captured moving images from thin air, a process that in itself confirmed America's greatness and the new medium's power. You would most likely have watched westerns and situation comedies, the two predominant types of programs. *Gunsmoke*, *The Life and Legend of Wyatt Earp*, *Have Gun Will Travel*, and

Wagon Train typified the TV western, along with *Hopalong Cassidy* and *Roy Rogers* for the youngest kids. These programs presented simple plots in which a clear line separated the good guys from the bad, and in which the good guys always won. They bespoke definite moral rules not yet under widespread assault. And they stressed community either through family or family-like relationships. For example, *Gunsmoke's* hero Matt Dillon, marshal of Dodge City, although single, still enjoyed a close, loving relationship with the other characters who appeared each week.

Situation comedies made definite moral proclamations, too, and laid out distinct gender roles within a white, suburban setting. *Father Knows Best* typified this. The Anderson family had a comfortable home surrounded by a picket fence. Everyone in the family dressed neatly, with dad almost always wearing a jacket, and mom a dress. Few family squabbles erupted, nor did any crisis that could not be solved within 30 minutes. No African Americans or Hispanics appeared, nor anyone else who might disturb white homogeneity. And the show's title bespoke the proper family arrangement: father did know best and should be the head and the authority.

The moral certainty found in these shows reflected World War II and the cold war, events that said good and evil could be easily recognized, and the latter defeated. The cold war made Americans feel that moral certainty must be embraced in order to preserve democracy.

With this said, it should be noted that television's entertainment shows did criticize society in a minor way, what Todd Gitlin, writing in *The Sixties*, calls an "opening wedge" in the assault on conformity. For example, comedians Steve Allen, Sid Caesar, and Ernie Kovacs satirized mainstream attitudes, and rock 'n' roll performers appeared, playing music that expressed teenage rebelliousness—although Ed Sullivan and Dick Clark tried hard on their programs to sanitize the message.

Further, television showed its own moral inconsistencies when scandal raked its popular quiz shows. Evidence that producers and contestants had engaged in rigging the shows contradicted TV's effort to present only positive moral messages, and shook those who believed in society's innate goodness or that somehow the new technology would be uncorrupted.

By and large, though, the conformist fortress held firm, and a young person leaving the fifties behind and entering a new decade felt secure in mainstream society's goodness. Television had presented it that way.

But 1960 revealed another side. That year, African American college students staged a sit-in at a lunch counter in Greensboro, North Carolina, and television carried the story, vivid pictures, across the nation. Brave blacks, hateful whites, and a segregationist society could be seen in stark contrast to *Father Knows Best*. Television's power to shape images and consciences worked this time in protest against mainstream practices. Thousands of black students who watched the coverage of Greensboro joined the cause, staging sit-ins in communities across the nation. White students, too, felt compelled to help, displaying a peculiar cross-influence from their experience with television in the fifties: their attachment to democratic ideals as TV had portrayed them, but their shock and dismay that those ideals were not already in force, a reality TV had kept hidden.

With this exposure at Greensboro, television inadvertently contributed to the birth of the counterculture, to attacks on the very mainstream it championed. Soon came the Freedom Rides and the voting rights march at Selma, Alabama, and numerous other civil rights protests that further assaulted fifties illusions and motivated college students. Suddenly America appeared not just but unjust; not humane but cruel; not compassionate but cold.

Then came Vietnam. When television first began covering the war, it presented, overall, a positive picture. News reporters called the enemy "Reds" and accepted the cold-war rationale for sending American troops into combat. Editorial comments depicted the Vietcong and the National Liberation Front (NLF) as untrustworthy.

This portrayal began to change in 1967 when some critical reports of the war appeared, and even more so after the Tet Offensive. Launched by the NLF early in 1968, Tet showed that, contrary to the assurances of America's political leaders, victory remained elusive. Although in the sixties only 3 percent of the news reports from Vietnam showed heavy fighting, the few graphic images that did appear left an indelible impression on the American conscience: a GI using a pocket cigarette lighter to set fire to a fragile-looking Vietnamese house made of wood and thatched straw; a general in South Vietnam's army walking up to a prisoner who had already been bound, hands behind his back, and shooting him point blank through the head; the Tet Offensive itself, chaotic and bloody.

The coverage often contradicted government assertions and revealed shortcomings in military strategy. Writing in David Farber's book *The Sixties*, Chester J. Pach, Jr. says that "Television presented a war that was puzzling and incoherent. . . . Night after night, television slowly exposed the illogic of attrition." (Farber 1994, 112) Witnessing what they considered to be another display of American injustice, one that complemented racial segregation, young people felt compelled, in ever greater numbers, to protest. Many other Americans came to oppose the war, too, although less stridently.

Thus, television unintentionally undermined the very values—conformity and obedience to authority—it had promoted in the fifties (and was still promoting with most of its programming). In fact, while some young people, appalled by the war, engaged in antiwar protests, others looked at the scenes on television and found proof that society had grown so corrupt and twisted that the only hope was to drop out and pursue an alternative. Consequently, the hippie movement arose and rejected political protest as irrelevant and useless.

Civil rights workers, antiwar activists, hippies—father no longer knew best. In fact, the counterculture said he knew least, whether it be father at home, father as president, father as Uncle Sam. Don't trust authority.

As the counterculture and turmoil expanded, television helped to divide the nation into warring cultural and political camps. The radicals learned how to use TV. Jerry Rubin, Abbie Hoffman, and other Yippies, for example, staged media events to expose straight society's absurdities. Yet straight society used TV, too, spreading hatred against the counterculture, as when President Richard Nixon sent Vice-President Spiro Agnew on speaking tours to excoriate protesters and college students with vituperative language, among the harshest ever used by a national leader.

Television showed the violent protest in 1968 by radical students at Columbia University, the bloody confrontations between protesters and the authorities at the Democratic National Convention, and, in 1970, the tragic shooting at Kent State University. For many young people (certainly not all), the televised scenes proved mainstream society's barbarity; for the mainstream, they proved young America's anarchistic insanity.

Television still provided diversionary balm, entertainment shows in the 1960s to which middle America could escape in order to relive the previous decade's moral certainties: *The Andy Griffith Show*, *Green Acres*, and *Gomer Pyle*. But the new society intervened even in this category: *Laugh-In*, with its countercultural-like fast pace and bright colors; *The Smothers Brothers Comedy Hour*, with its controversial antiwar sentiments; *Julia*, with its African American star. These led to *All in the Family* in the early 1970s, a situation comedy that broke new ground with its topical humor and whose main story line involved a generational conflict between a liberal, long-haired young man and his blue-collar, reactionary father-in-law.

There are no statistics that measure television's overall influence in the 1950s and the 1960s, but there can be little doubt that this technology helped shape people's values and views. A young person raised on *Hopalong Cassidy* and *Gunsmoke* one decade, and exposed to racism and Vietnam the next, encountered enormous dissonance. From this the counterculture obtained its vitality.

See also Columbia University; Hippies; Kent State; *Laugh-In;* New Left; Vietnam War.

References Farber, David, ed., *The Sixties: From Memory to History* (1994); Gitlin, Todd, *The Sixties: Years of Hope, Days of Rage* (1987).

Third World Strike

Late in 1968, protests and demonstrations escalated in America and ushered in a year when tempers flared, violence erupted, and the gulf between extremists and mainstream society widened. Nowhere did this appear more evident than at San Francisco State College, where black students and their supporters clashed with a conservative administration.

San Francisco State had been, at least since the 1950s, a school that attracted bohemians and artists, or what Leonard Wolf in *Voices from the Love Generation* calls "an ever-increasing number of misfit exiles from staider institutions." (xix) Diversity and leniency toward dissent prevailed.

In 1967, tension began to build at San Francisco State, whose enrollment had reached 18,000, after several blacks physically attacked the white editor of the campus newspaper for having printed an article denigrating boxer Muhammed Ali. At the same time, the Black Student Union (BSU), numbering about 100, announced its support of a third-world revolution in which all nonwhites would rebel and establish power in their own communities separate from white influence. This ideology reflected the close relationship among the BSU, the Black Panthers, and Students for a Democratic Society. The latter two moved toward a formal alliance based on a shared view that blacks and ethnic groups constituted a third-world colony within the United States and had much in common with people in underdeveloped nations who suffered from American imperialism.

In 1968, the BSU demanded a black studies program, the hiring of 12 black professors to teach in it, open admission for students of color (only 700 African Americans attended the college), and the waiving of tuition for them. The administration agreed to the black studies program, although on a more limited basis, and promised to lower admission standards but stopped short of establishing an open-door policy. These measures did not satisfy the BSU, and the situation worsened after a BSU leader advised black students to begin carrying guns on campus to defend themselves against racist administrators.

When the BSU called a student strike in November, the college board of trustees reacted by making S. I. Hayakawa president. A professor with no previous administrative experience, Hayakawa nevertheless had impeccable conservative credentials and immediately announced he would defy the strikers and keep the college operating at all costs. By this time, few students were attending classes and many teachers supported the strike. Outsiders had appeared, too, including SDS activist Todd Gitlin, who lent support to the students.

Hayakawa imposed stern measures, and in January 1969 prohibited campus demonstrations. When protesters rallied anyhow, mass arrests ensued—the police jailed 450 students and several professors. Hayakawa followed this by suspending all students arrested on campus since the strike began. The strike continued, though, as did hundreds of police on patrol and violence that included 12 firebombings.

As January came to an end, exhaustion overcame both sides in the dispute, and they decided to negotiate. The administration agreed to expand its plans for a black studies program; waive admission requirements for "third world students," primarily blacks and Hispanics; and appoint a black financial administrator. On the other hand, the college refused to drop charges against 700 students arrested during the strike, and it fired 24 professors.

The strike thus ended, after 134 days, but left deep wounds both on campus and in society at large as activists called Hayakawa's actions excessive, and middle America hailed him as a hero. The strike had another effect in that it stirred minority militancy at other colleges in behalf of blacks, Asian Americans, Indians, and Chicanos.

See also Black Panthers; New Left; Students for a Democratic Society.

References Karagueuzian, Dikran, *Blow It Up! The Black Student Revolt at San Francisco State College and the Emergence of Dr. Hayakawa* (1971); McGill, William J., *The Year of the Monkey: Revolt on Campus, 1968–69* (1982); Wolf, Leonard, ed., *Voices from the Love Generation* (1968).

Thompson, Hunter S. (1939–)

Hunter S. Thompson invented "gonzo" journalism, a countercultural writing style that castigated mainstream politics, rationality, and social convention by throwing out objectivity and using subjective analysis filled with humor, satire, perceptive observation, and participation by the reporter in the event reported.

Born on 18 July 1939 in Louisville, Kentucky, Thompson displayed his penchant for rebelliousness and writing while still a child. In 1947, he and several friends published a short-lived mimeographed newspaper. As a student at Male High School, he read extensively and exhibited a quick intelligence, but got into numerous scrapes with the law, including an episode in 1955 that kept him from graduating and sent him to a children's home, followed by the military.

Thompson arrived at Kelly Air Force Base in San Antonio so drunk that he vomited during roll call. His demeanor in the military expressed resentment—a theme that appeared time and again in his writing. After his initial training, he was forced into a school for electronics technicians at Eglin Air Force Base near Pensacola, Florida. Thompson hated this assignment and soon managed to obtain a position as sports editor of the base's newspaper, the *Command Courier*. His continuing rebelliousness led him to violate policy and publish an article about an athlete who received a special discharge so he could play pro football. Considering Thompson too much trouble, the air force granted him his own discharge in 1957, an honorable one, asserting: "This airman, although talented, will not be guided by policy or personal advice." (Thompson 1979, 14)

Thompson then went to Puerto Rico, where he accepted a job with a sports publication, *Sportivo*, only to find himself stuck with reporting the local bowling scores. At the same time, he wrote a few articles for his hometown newspaper, the *Louisville Courier-Journal*, in which he mixed fact with fiction. Thus began a journalistic style he developed over the years, one that blurred the distinction between objectivity and subjectivity and treated truth as revelatory through imaginative contrivances.

After a short stay in California, Thompson returned to Louisville in 1961. One year later, he landed a writing assignment for *The Observer*, a new weekly published by Dow Jones. He journeyed to South America and wrote stories about politics and smuggling, including "A Footloose American in a Smuggler's Den," filled with dubious references that caused his editors to question whether the town he wrote about—Puerto Estrella, a settlement given exclusively to illicit activities—even existed. Thompson moved back to California in 1964 and lived at Haight-Ashbury in San Francisco. He soon split with *The Observer*, worked on a novel, and, to survive, found odd jobs. He had married Sandy Dawn the previous year, and until their divorce in the late 1970s, they had a sometimes close but often tumultuous relationship.

Then the renegade writer scored big—he wrote an article about the Hell's Angels for *The Nation* that led to publishers calling him for a book contract. Thompson signed with Random House, and in 1966 there appeared *Hell's Angels: A Strange and Terrible Saga*. He had done something unique: rather than rely on police reports to get his facts, he rode with the Angels for nearly a year, an episode that turned ugly when several of them demanded money from him and, soon after he refused, brutally stomped him. Thompson's style reflected a new journalism then emerging in the works of Tom Wolfe, Gay Talese, Terry Southern, and others: extensive detail gathered through hands-on investigation, even immersion in the activity being reported, and crafting nonfiction to read like a novel or short story.

Hell's Angels obtained critical acclaim; United Press International, for example, noted that its "violent episodes . . . have an impact reminiscent of the old master, Hemingway." (Perry 1992, 121) At this time, Thompson fled the commercialism overtaking Haight-Ashbury and moved to Woody Creek, near Aspen, Colorado, where he continued his immersion in the counterculture drug scene. As his biographer Paul Perry observes in *Fear and Loathing*, at Woody Creek Thompson "could chew mescaline and turn up the stereo to one hundred decibels without pissing off the neighbors or having a billy club rapped on his door." (128)

In great demand, Thompson continued to write articles. Then he attended the 1968 Democratic National Convention in Chicago, which erupted into a bloody melee between protesters and police. The "police riot," as some people called it, stirred Thompson's political interest and a desire to advance reform at the local level. "I went to the Democratic Convention as a journalist," he later observed, "and returned a raving beast." (131)

In Aspen, he formed the Freak Power Party to challenge the traditional political establishment—the liberals, who believed the system could work and, more pointedly, the conservatives, who wanted to develop the town into a tourist jungle. The Freak Power Party organized the long-hair dropouts who usually rejected all politics, and promoted an unusual platform. As Thompson recalled: "We had run the whole campaign from a long oaken table in the Jerome Tavern on Main Street. . . . Our program, basically, was to drive the real estate goons completely out of the valley; to prevent the State Highway Department from bringing a four-lane highway into the town, and in fact to ban all auto traffic from every downtown street. Turn them all into grassy malls where everybody, even freaks, could do whatever's right." (Thompson 1979, 160) The party's mayoral candidate lost by only six votes.

Shortly after this, Thompson ran, in 1970, as the freak candidate for sheriff—calling for disarming the cops, making drug deals legal, and changing the name Aspen to Fat City, so as to make the town less attractive to exploiters. He ran a strong race but lost.

Meanwhile, Thompson covered the Kentucky Derby for *Scanlon's Magazine*, but when it came time to write the article, he suffered writer's block. Frustrated and desperate, he resorted to tearing pages from his notebook and sending them to his editor as the story. He felt sure he would be reprimanded for submitting gibberish, but to his surprise, *Scanlon's* gushed over the apparently innovative writing technique. Thus emerged what Thompson later called gonzo journalism.

His article, "The Kentucky Derby Is Decadent and Depraved," fit roughly into the new journalism, with dialogue and descriptive scenes and the reporter's adventure—in this case Thompson's—part of the story. But for Thompson, journalism involved contriving some scenes to communicate the overall truth, as he did with this article. In many ways, his work complemented the countercultural underground press—its innovative technique, its attacks on the establishment, and its raw language, drugginess, and irreverence.

Soon *Rolling Stone* magazine, wanting to diversify beyond its coverage of rock music, hired Thompson. He wrote an article for them about the freak power scene in Aspen and then traveled to Las Vegas in 1970 with a Los Angeles lawyer, Oscar Zeta Acosta, to write a story for *Sports Illustrated* about a motorcycle race. After the magazine rejected his account, which had more to do with his and Acosta's adventures with drugs than with the race, he returned to Vegas with Acosta, covered the National District Attorney Association's Third Annual Institute on Narcotics and Dangerous Drugs, and submitted the story to *Rolling Stone*.

In book form his account, *Fear and Loathing in Las Vegas*, received tremendous reviews, with one critic calling it "the most brilliant piece of writing about the dope subculture since Tom Wolfe's *Electric Kool-Aid Acid Test*," and a hilarious, searing critique of straight America. In the novel, Thompson's drug excesses seem to represent the dissolution of the counterculture, and Vegas itself the corruption of the American dream. The book's lunacy was highlighted by Ralph Steadman's bizarre artwork.

Thompson relished his association with *Rolling Stone*. One of the publication's editors later observed: "He was too much a nonconformist and a misfit for any magazine besides us." (169)

In 1972, *Rolling Stone* assigned Thompson to cover the presidential campaign. He arrived in Washington, admitting he knew nothing about national politics, and moved into a decrepit house in what he called a two-Doberman neighborhood. Thompson made contacts quickly, and his gonzo approach led to several successful articles and a book, *Fear and Loathing on the Campaign Trail '72*, whose analysis received wide praise; one political pro called it "the least accurate yet most truthful" campaign reportage.

Perhaps so, but also controversial: Thompson portrayed presidential candidate Edmund Muskie as addicted to the drug Ibogiane. As a furor arose, Thompson said he never reported that Muskie actually used the drug, only the rumor of such—one he concocted.

After this, Thompson's writing grew moribund—as if wedded to the counterculture's demise, the sheer exhaustion that swept America in the early seventies. Perhaps substance abuse took its toll, particularly his infatuation with cocaine. Or maybe it was the gonzo typecast—the constant pressure to be crazier and the insistence by his readers that he be nothing less. Except for *The Curse of Lono*, published in 1983, Thompson's articles and books fell flat. He remained popular on the college speaking circuit, although again controversial, as when he appeared at Duke University drunk, insulted the president, and threw a whiskey bottle at the stage curtain. Garry Trudeau soon caricatured Thompson in his comic strip *Doonesbury* as Uncle Duke, and he was also portrayed, in this instance badly and one-dimensionally, in the movie *Where the Buffalo Roam*.

Back home at Woody Creek, the county sheriff arrested Thompson in 1990 on drug possession charges but did not have the evidence to make them stick. In 1994, Thompson, while still writing articles for *Rolling Stone*, wrote a book about the 1992 presidential campaign, *Better than Sex: Confessions of a Political Junkie*, and two years later readied another one about the 1996 campaign.

"True Gonzo reporting needs the talents of a master journalist, the eye of an artist/photographer, and the heavy balls of an actor," Thompson once asserted, "because the writer must be the participant in the scene." (160) But stripped from its countercultural surroundings, gonzo journalism, some analysts claim, may have deteriorated into a mere parody of itself.

See also *The Electric Kool-Aid Acid Test;* New Journalism.

References Perry, Paul, *Fear and Loathing: The Strange and Terrible Saga of Hunter S. Thompson* (1992); Thompson, Hunter S., *Fear and Loathing in Las Vegas: A Savage Journey to the Heart of the American Dream* (1972), *Fear and Loathing on the Campaign Trail '72* (1973), *The Great Shark Hunt: Strange Tales from a Strange Time* (1979), *Hell's Angels: A Strange and Terrible Saga* (1966), and *The Proud Highway: Saga of a Desperate Southern Gentleman: The Fear and Loathing Letters, Volume 1, 1955–1967* (1997).

Thoreau, Henry David (1817–1862)

How much influence could the renowned nineteenth-century American writer Henry David Thoreau possibly have had on the counterculture? As it turned out, plenty. Thoreau's ideas affected both political activists and hippies.

Thoreau is remembered mainly as the Harvard-educated native of Concord, Massachusetts, who built a cabin on Walden Pond, where, from 1845 to 1847, he lived simply and communed with nature, later recalling his experience in the book *Walden*, today considered a literary masterpiece. Thoreau wrote another classic in American literature, an 1849 essay known as "Civil Disobedience" (originally titled "Resistance to Civil Government"), in which he says: "The state never intentionally confronts a man's sense, intellectual or moral, but only his body, his senses. It is not armed with superior wit or honesty, but with superior physical strength. I was not born to be forced. I will breathe after my own fashion." (Stern 1970, 469)

"Civil Disobedience" affected counterculture activists, for it discussed nonviolent resistance and the moral justification for protesting societal oppression. Numerous civil rights leaders in the 1950s and 1960s studied Thoreau's essay. So, too, did leaders in the New Left. In *On Our Own* historian Douglas T. Miller claims that, similar to Thoreau, political activists in the counterculture "acted as moral witnesses against what they perceived to be an unjust society." (342) A New Left leader, Todd Gitlin, recounts in his book *The Sixties* how the counterculture acted in agreement with "Civil Disobedience," and how he had kept on his desk a sign bearing a quotation from Thoreau: "The memory of my country spoils my walk." (249)

Thoreau influenced hippies, too, with his belief that to change life first required changing consciousness. Further, ideas from *Walden* filtered through the underground press and later affected the back-to-the-earth movement, attesting to the influence of Thoreau's simplicity, his closeness to nature, his land ethic.

Similarly, *Walden*, and Thoreau's ideas in general, influenced the environmental movement, whose leaders recalled his insistence that wilderness preserves be created. They agreed with Thoreau's statement: "What is the use of a house if you haven't got a tolerable planet to live on?"

References Gitlin, Todd, *The Sixties: Years of Hope, Days of Rage* (1987); Miller, Douglas T., *On Our Own: Americans in the Sixties* (1996); Thoreau, Henry David, *Walden* (1985).

Tibetan Book of the Dead

The counterculture used the *Tibetan Book of the Dead*, an ancient Eastern spiritual tract, as a guidebook for persons taking LSD.

To hippies, the acid experience seemed similar to the book's story about a dead man facing the Clear Light of the Void, staring into the maw of an egoless existence. Aldous Huxley first drew the comparison in his *Doors of Perception*, where he recounts his experience with mescaline. "One couldn't face [the Clear Light] by oneself," he writes. "That's the point, I suppose, of the Tibetan Ritual—somebody sitting there all the time and telling you what's what." (54–58)

Influenced by this, LSD guru Timothy Leary promoted the *Book of the Dead* as a guide for the journey into the mind, with revisions added by him. Thus, the book served as a psychedelic manual to enable a person to deal with the Clear Light. Yet Leary's approach stirred controversy in the counterculture as some claimed that by reading his revised work a person poisoned the mystical waters with interpretations, even obligations, as to what should be experienced—a pressure that produced feelings of inadequacy whenever the Clear Light was not encountered.

See also Hippies; Huxley, Aldous; Leary, Timothy; LSD.

Reference Huxley, Aldous, *The Doors of Perception* (1954).

Tie-Dye

Young people created tie-dye shirts at home during the sixties by taking fabric, knotting it to prevent color from spreading into certain areas, and then dyeing it. They used vivid dyes, and the splash-color effect replicated psychedelic images. This clothing presented an alternative to traditional styles and store-bought designs. As with many other countercultural developments, though, when the shirts grew popular, corporations stepped in and made a profit. They began mass-producing them, and tie-dye clothes then appeared in department stores, the rebelliousness coopted by materialism.

Tiny Tim (1930–1996)

Born Herbert Khaury in New York City on 12 April 1930, Tiny Tim intrigued audiences in the sixties—from rock scenes such as the Fillmore in San Francisco to the Johnny Carson Show on television—with his rendition of old-time songs, or modern songs presented in an old-time style.

After dropping out of high school in the late 1940s, Tiny Tim worked for years on the Greenwich Village circuit, performing songs from the 1920s and singing duets with himself, imitating stars such as Sonny and Cher, during which he typically alternated from a falsetto voice to a baritone one and strummed the ukulele. With his scraggly shoulder-length hair, long nose, and pearly skin, many considered him odd, if not freakish. Most listeners gawked and paid little attention to his music.

This changed in 1965 when he appeared at The Scene, a leading New York nightclub, and developed a cult following. Peter Yarrow of the folk trio Peter, Paul, and Mary brought Tiny Tim to the attention of a producer, and Reprise Records released his first album in 1968, *God Bless Tiny Tim*. That year, he achieved his only hit single, "Tip Toe through the Tulips," characterized by his trademark falsetto and strumming ukulele. His fame spread, too, through his appearances on TV's top comedy show, *Laugh-In*, where he sang an unusual duet with actor Carol Channing: she as Nelson Eddy, he as Jeannette MacDonald.

Tiny Tim gained his most notoriety, though, when, in December 1969, he married a fan, Victoria May Budinger (Miss Vicky, he called her), on Johnny Carson's show. After that, his fame quickly faded, and he and his wife divorced in 1977. (A second marriage also ended in divorce, and he married a third time.) In the 1980s and 1990s, he continued to perform at small venues, record occasional singles and albums, and appeared on an MTV game show. His LP *Girl* included a cha-cha version of the Beatles' song "Hey Jude."

Although many people wondered how much of Tiny Tim was act and how much authentic, his infatuation with old music, his effeminate style, and his strange mannerisms predated his show business career. *Rolling Stone* magazine said what many countercultural youths believed: "Tiny Tim is real . . . he is, in a sense, a peculiar butterfly . . . like nothing you've ever experienced before, quite odd, but above all, gentle and beautiful." (Hopkins 1968, 17) Tiny Tim died from a heart attack on 30 November 1996 in Minneapolis, Minnesota. He had collapsed on stage immediately after completing "Tip Toe through the Tulips."

Reference Hopkins, Jerry, "Tiny Tim," *Rolling Stone*, 6 July 1968, 15–17.

Tocsin

Named after the alarm bell used during the French Revolution, in 1960 Tocsin emerged as a peace group based at Harvard University and Radcliffe College in Massachusetts and sounded its own notice that college students had arrived to challenge political lethargy.

Tocsin attracted bright, motivated students—liberals and a few radical leftists who sympathized with communism. Members of the group read extensively to learn about different political ideologies and the workings of the cold war. Although they debated many specific points, they agreed that the arms buildup then under way in the United States and Soviet Union threatened world peace and the very survival of the human race.

Largely under the leadership of Todd Gitlin, a Harvard student, Tocsin used a variety of tactics to push for an end to American nuclear weapons tests and a reduction in military spending. In December 1960, a Tocsin-sponsored walk for peace at Harvard attracted over a thousand students. At the same time, three Tocsin leaders flew to Washington to present Congress with a proposed test-ban treaty for the American and Soviet governments to consider. Tocsin circulated petitions, too, urging support for its position.

When, in 1961, President John Kennedy, whom the students admired, rejected Tocsin's overtures, discontentment spread within the group. Many considered Kennedy a sellout and believed the American political system had been captured by a military-industrial complex.

That same year, Tocsin established a speakers' bureau, and several of the group's members began planning for a march on Washington. The demonstration, sponsored by Tocsin and other organizations, occurred in February 1962. A snowstorm erupted during the two-day protest, but despite this, over 8,000 students turned out from several colleges. When Kennedy and Congress again proved unreceptive, students learned they would have to intensify their activism, and some decided they would have to push for bold political changes. The Cuban missile crisis later that year reinforced the view of an impending catastrophe should reforms not be undertaken.

Although Tocsin faded in the succeeding years of protest, it had helped to politicize normally dormant college campuses and provided an education for activists, some of whom joined Students for a Democratic Society, the most prominent New Left group in the counterculture.

See also Gitlin, Todd; Harvard University; Students for a Democratic Society.

Reference Gitlin, Todd, *The Sixties: Years of Hope, Days of Rage* (1987).

Toke

Toke meant to take a puff or hit of marijuana; "toking" meant several hits. Hence, "She took a toke," "They were toking on that joint," "She toked a joint and then left for the peace march."

J. R. R. Tolkien, 1973

Tolkien, J. R. R. (1892–1973)

Hobbits dwell in Middle Earth—small, peace-loving, hairy-footed beings. That's how J. R. R. Tolkien portrayed them in his books that counterculture youths read avidly.

John Ronald Reuel Tolkien was born on 3 January 1892 in Bloemfontein, South Africa, to Arthur Reuel Tolkien and Mabel Suffield Tolkien of Birmingham, England. His father managed a bank, and his mother worked as a missionary. After young Tolkien's father died in 1896, his mother took him to Sarehole, a small English village near Birmingham. She, however, lived only until 1904, after which time guardians raised the boy and his brother.

After completing preparatory school, Tolkien attended Exeter College at Oxford, from which he graduated in 1915. By then, World War I had begun, and he served in the British army. Some observers believe Tolkien's war experience influenced his writing, particularly his fairy tales, by deepening his desire for escapism and his cherishing of camaraderie.

Philology, the study of language, worked its influence, too—it had intrigued him at an early age, and after the war he obtained his master's degree from Oxford and for two years worked as an assistant on the *Oxford English Dictionary*. In 1920, he began teaching English language at the University of Leeds, but five years later he returned to Oxford as a professor. Tolkien's *A Middle English Vocabulary*, published in 1922, earned him an international reputation in English philology. In the 1930s, he wrote a scholarly study dealing with *Beowulf* and edited a text on medieval practices.

Then came *The Hobbit*, first published in 1938. Tolkien developed the story while reading a boring student exam paper. Although many reviewers labeled *The Hobbit* a children's tale, Tolkien denied he created it in that style, and in any event, it appealed to adults equally as much.

In Tolkien's story, to which he contributed drawings, the Hobbits inhabit an imaginary Middle Earth, where they enjoy six meals a day and live in tree hollows and other unusual habitats. These beings stand about a yard tall and dress in bright colors. The story follows Bilbo Baggins, a Hobbit who joins some dwarfs on an expedition to recover a treasure stolen by Smaug, a dangerous dragon. On his journey, Baggins discovers a magic ring, so powerful it can corrupt its owner.

Tolkien continued the fantasy surrounding the ring in *The Lord of the Rings*, a trilogy comprising *The Fellowship of the Rings*, *The Two Towers*, and *The Return of the King*, all first published in the 1950s and all more serious in style than *The Hobbit*. His trilogy includes glossaries, maps, genealogical charts, and documentary items used to fully develop the fantasy world.

Not even Tolkien's publisher anticipated how popular *The Hobbit* and *The Lord of the Rings* would become in the 1960s. To this day, no one quite understands how these works spread from a limited audience to a large one, but young people, especially college students, flocked to them. Perhaps Tolkien's appeal rested on escapism—that America's youth turned to reading about Hobbits as an alternative to a society burdened by war and impersonal relationships. Tolkien himself once said he saw nothing wrong with escaping from a world filled with factories, machine guns, and bombs. Or perhaps the simplistic conflict between good and evil in Tolkien's stories served as an antidote to modern complexity. Maybe, for some, Tolkien's fantasies replicated or enhanced the fantastical experiences derived from hallucinogenic drugs. Whatever the case, Tolkien clubs appeared on campuses, as well as a journal dedicated to his fairy tales, and by 1967 worldwide sales of Tolkien's books had exceeded 3 million copies.

An unassuming man, Tolkien continued as a professor at Oxford until his retirement in 1959. He died in England on 2 September 1973. A writer in the countercultural magazine *Rolling Stone* noted that Tolkien had "cast a spell over tens of thousands of Americans in the Sixties." ("J. R. R. Tolkien" 1973, 8)

References Carpenter, Humphrey, *J. R. R. Tolkien: A Biography* (1977); "J. R. R. Tolkien: Lord of the Middle Earth," *Rolling Stone*, 11 October 1973, 8–9; Tolkien, J. R. R., *The Hobbit* (1938) and *The Lord of the Rings* (1954–1956).

Topless Bathing Suit

Time magazine said in June 1964: "Rudi Gernreich was bored to tears with necklines." So what did the fashion designer do? He ended them altogether, at least with his latest innovation for women: the topless bathing suit. Gernreich called it "a prediction of things to come." The suit only covered the body from the thighs to a high waist, where two thin straps crossed between the breasts and over the back.

Few women wore the topless bathing suit (and for many countercultural youths skinny dipping seemed to better Gernreich's idea), but it exemplified a decade that challenged society's conventions about dress and sexuality. Gernreich said: "What I do is watch what kids are putting together for themselves." And the kids showed more skin, inspiring Gernreich's design.

Travel

Wanderlust struck young people in the 1960s. They traveled by the hundreds of thousands throughout America, to Europe, and to exotic locations such as Nepal. Cash-short, and rejecting materialism anyway, they journeyed cheaply: hitchhiking, riding busses, staying at hostels. If they traveled overseas, they may have looked for escape from oppression, as represented by the Vietnam War and numerous police crackdowns on longhairs, as well as contact with the international counterculture, for the movement was not simply an American one. Or they may have searched for an elusive brotherhood and sisterhood, a community tied to rejecting mainstream values and smoking dope, finding Zen, and living in the mountains. In the late 1960s, 800,000 young Americans were traveling in Europe and well over a million within the United States. The International Harvester school bus, VW van, and backpack came to symbolize the counterculture in its quest for alternatives.

See also Hitchhiking; Volkswagen Minivan.

Trip

Trip had more than one meaning. Sometimes, it referred to taking drugs, especially psychedelic ones; at other times, it meant a fantastic experience, as in "That concert last night was a real trip" or "She's a trip."

Trips Festival

Stewart Brand, a photographer, developed the idea for the Trips Festival as an "electronic circus" that would combine all the developments linked to psychedelia then unfolding in San Francisco's Haight-Ashbury—music, lights, sounds, and theatre. He portrayed the festival as an LSD experience without drugs.

To bring his idea to fruition, Brand asked Bill Graham, manager of the San Francisco Mime Troupe, to stage the event. Graham agreed and booked Longshoreman's Hall, located on Beach Street near the Haight-Ashbury district. Posters advertised the festival, as did the mainstream press, and Ken Kesey and the Merry Pranksters who drove their notorious Day-Glo bus to Union Square and, dressed in garish outfits, unloosed balloons and talked to reporters. Kesey considered the festival part of a "Neon Renaissance," which he defined as "a need to find a new way to look at the world, an attempt to locate a better reality, now that the old reality is riddled with radioactive poison."

The festival, which began on Friday night, 21 January 1966, transformed Longshoreman's Hall into a swirling psychedelic bacchanal. Five movie projectors cast fulgurous images on the walls, light machines flashed colors, strobes pulsated . . . Day-Glo paint, black lights, loud speakers, amplifiers, rock bands . . . all jumbled together at the same time. And packed in: a huge crowd—straights wearing jackets and ties; hippies in serapes, beads, and Indian headbands, jumping and dancing, while others jammed into the balcony and gawked.

On this first night, a message flashed red: "Anybody Who Knows He Is God Go Up on Stage," and actors presented a show, but only briefly. The crowd wanted rock music and that's what it got. While bands played, someone passed around a bag loaded with acid tablets. Despite Brand's portrayal, this would be a true LSD experience.

Ken Kesey and the Merry the Pranksters arrived and enraged Bill Graham by opening the exit door and letting Hell's Angels in for free. Graham knew he could do nothing, and the show went on—Big Brother and the Holding Company, Jefferson Airplane, Allen Ginsberg, Marshall McLuhan, more Big Brother (the

Dead showed up but, according to its leader Jerry Garcia, the band never played—by then, everyone was too drugged out), and acrobats jumping from the balcony onto a huge trampoline.

After three jubilant, exhausting nights, the festival, which attracted thousands, left its impact. Bill Graham made a small profit (shared with the Pranksters) and went on to sponsor rock concerts at the nearby Fillmore Auditorium. A more important outcome was that the underground psychedelic movement paraded more publicly than ever—its influence stronger, its distinctive rock, art, and lights soon commercialized.

See also Awareness Festival; *The Electric Kool-Aid Acid Test;* Graham, Bill; LSD.

References Anthony, Gene, *The Summer of Love: Haight-Ashbury at Its Highest* (1980); Perry, Charles, *The Haight-Ashbury: A History* (1984); Wolfe, Tom, *The Electric Kool-Aid Acid Test* (1968).

Trout Fishing in America

Criticizing mainstream America for its corruption and praising nature for its redemptive qualities, *Trout Fishing in America*, an offbeat novel by Richard Brautigan, reached the best-seller list and made such an impression with young people that several communes adopted the book's title for their name.

Brautigan, born in Spokane, Washington, in 1935 but a resident Californian, wrote in a style akin to the 1950s beats. He expressed, however, countercultural themes, particularly the loss of the American Dream and the belief that people cannot find personal fulfillment without connection to an uncontaminated, natural environment. In this sense, *Trout Fishing*, written in 1967, is a hip reincarnation of nineteenth-century writer Henry David Thoreau, another counterculture favorite.

Brautigan's themes appear when he describes a great house built by a movie actor:

> The mansion was on a promontory, high over the Pacific. Money could see farther in the 1920s, and one could look out and see whales and the Hawaiian Islands and the Kuomintang in China.
>
> The mansion burned down years ago.
> The actor died.
> His mules were made into soap.
> His mistresses became birds nests of wrinkles.
> Now only the fireplace remains as a sort of Carthaginian homage to Hollywood. (103)

At another point, he writes amusingly, but also sadly, about finding a used trout stream for sale in a junkyard at $6.50 per foot:

> O, I had never in my life seen anything like that trout stream. It was stacked in piles of various lengths: ten, fifteen, twenty feet, etc. There was one pile of hundred-foot lengths. There was also a box of scraps. The scraps were in odd sizes ranging from six inches to a couple of feet. (106–107)

If finding an unpolluted trout stream meant salvation, this writer, whose career received an early boost from author Kurt Vonnegut, did not find his, not even with his literary success. After the countercultural era, Brautigan's audience dwindled. He committed suicide in September 1984.

Reference Brautigan, Richard, *Trout Fishing in America, The Pill versus the Springhill Mine Disaster, and In Watermelon Sugar* (1989).

Turn On

"Turn on" meant to be introduced to a drug, such as marijuana or LSD. The phrase could also mean an intense experience, as in "That movie was a real turn on" or "He really turned me on."

Twiggy (1949–)

"H'its not really wot you'd call a figger," Twiggy said, "but with me funny face, me funny skirts and me funny accent somehow it all combined to work just lovely." Or, as fashion expert Mary Quant said about Twiggy: "[She's] the knockout beauty of our time." Thin as a rail, with large, wide eyes, Twiggy emerged as the leading fashion model in the counterculture era, capturing the penchant for innovative clothes and appearances.

Twiggy, the strikingly thin teenage model, arrives at JFK International Airport on 20 March 1967.

Twiggy was born Leslie Hornby on 19 September 1949 in Neasden, a working-class suburb of London. She quit school at age 15, about the time she began dating Nigel Davies, a 25-year-old hairdresser and antiques dealer. Davies adopted the name Justin de Villeneuve and decided to promote his girlfriend as a model, using her nickname, Twiggy. Shrewd and ambitious, he convinced the London *Daily Express* to declare her "the face of 1966." Twiggy gained attention throughout Europe when she appeared on the cover of *Elle*, the continent's leading fashion magazine. She wore mod clothes: unusual, bright color combinations and miniskirts.

De Villeneuve quickly turned Twiggy into a business, establishing a company, Twiggy Enterprises, that manufactured clothes under her name. They sold well in London department stores, making him, Twiggy, and her parents (directors in the company) wealthy.

Twiggy made her first U.S. appearance in March 1967, when she was featured in several leading magazines, namely *Mademoiselle*, *Look*, *Ladies' Home Journal*, *Saturday Evening Post*, and *McCall's*. Then she posed for Richard Avedon, the nation's leading fashion photographer, and her public recognition intensified after she appeared later that year in a three-part television special that covered her career.

As they had in Britain, Twiggy and de Villeneuve marketed her clothes in America, and they signed licensing agreements that resulted in everything from Twiggy false eyelashes to a Twiggy doll manufactured by Mattel toys. From the latter alone, she received well over $1 million. As the decade came to an end she adopted other styles but remained most famous as the 1960s mod girl.

See also Miniskirt; Mod.

Reference Twiggy, *Twiggy: An Autobiography* (1975).

U

Underground Newspapers

With their vivid colors, oddly shaped layouts, and stories markedly original and frequently provocative, underground newspapers offered a striking alternative to traditional journalism.

The *Village Voice* may have been the leading precursor to the underground newspapers. This New York weekly first appeared in 1955 and presented a personal and informal writing style, coupled with pointed political views and coverage of the bohemian beat culture in Greenwich Village, a scene usually ignored by the standard city papers.

Nearly a decade later, in 1964, the *Los Angeles Free Press (Freep)* hit the newsstands. Although it emulated the *Village Voice*'s style, it stressed leftist politics and radical change. This slant, added to its clearly bohemian appeal, made *Freep* the first underground newspaper. Like other such publications, it relied on offset printing, a new technology that lowered printing costs and gave rise to independent papers.

Two years later, the *San Francisco Oracle* appeared in a hippie countercultural style. The *Oracle* ventured occasionally into politics, but its stories stressed culture, particularly the psychedelic LSD scene.

The underground press belittled mainstream journalism's self-proclaimed objectivity, showing how the objective actually reflected bias. Underground reporting thus admitted its subjectivity. These newspapers often abandoned standard columns for a free-flowing style that corresponded with their attempt to break linear thought patterns, and in their artwork they sometimes used vivid colors combined with psychedelic imagery. Their language reflected a nonchalant attitude toward proper grammar (perhaps in itself a form of protest), so extensively that one mainstream observer called them "stylistic disaster areas."

The newspapers spoke the issues and vocabulary central to counterculture youth. For example, in 1969 the *Miami Free Press/Daily Planet* commented on a marijuana drought: "The problem just isn't here in Miami. It's everywhere. Seems like the world's gone dry. For weeks people been scurrying around, whispering to each other, 'Can you lay a joint on me?' The answer is always the same: 'No, I hoped you had some.'" ("In Search of . . ." 1969)

The paper criticized a recent finding issued by local authorities that called pot dangerous: "Now, I'm not going to come right out and say BULLSHIT, but I've been doing my homework and something's wrong somewhere. . . . Of this I'm certain, there is nothing in any major and a few minor magazines, journals, and otherwise, that in the last three years even hints at this possibility." And one of its writers said in a record review: "I'm pretty stoned, but it sounds to me like Crosby, Stills, and Nash have an album at least as strong as any ever done by the Byrds or Buffalo Springfield."("An Open Letter . . ." 1969, 27)

Underground newspapers sprang up in big cities, such as Chicago, Detroit, and Denver, and in smaller areas, such as Austin, Texas. They circulated on university and even high school campuses. Indeed, a close connection evolved with colleges: many students read the underground publications, and those who worked as reporters for student newspapers sometimes showed their discontent with policies that censored the campus press by writing underground. A national survey in 1967 discovered some 30 underground papers, a few making money, most struggling to break even. At their peak, both the *Oracle* and *Freep* distributed over 100,000 copies weekly, and nationwide, underground readership may have reached into the millions, clearly showing widespread discontent with traditional reportage.

The underground newspapers were not uniform, and they experienced an ongoing internal battle between "politicos" and "culturalists." The former developed their papers along New Left lines, attacking government policies, including the Vietnam War. The latter expressed hippie values and frequently criticized protest as useless against an unbending, authoritarian political structure. As a whole, the underground press reshaped newspaper reporting and raised serious questions about middle-class practices while showing a distinct countercultural mentality.

See also *East Village Other;* Liberation News Service; *Los Angeles Free Press; Rat; Rolling Stone; San Francisco Oracle; Screw; Seed;* Underground Press Syndicate; *Village Voice.*

References Hopkins, Jerry, ed., *The Hippie Papers: Notes from the Underground Press* (1968); "In Search of the Miami Scene," *Miami Free Press/Daily Planet*, 18 July 1969; Leamer, Laurence, *The Paper Revolutionaries: The Rise of the Underground Press*, (1972); "An Open Letter to the Dade County Youth Grand Jury," *Miami Free Press/Daily Planet*, 2 July 1969, 27; Peck, Abe, *Uncovering the Sixties: The Life and Times of the Underground Press* (1985); Wachsberger, Ken, ed., *Voices from the Underground: Insider Histories of the Vietnam Era Underground Press* (1993).

Underground Press Syndicate

In the spring of 1967, 30 editors and writers from several underground newspapers met at Stinson Beach, California, where they took a leaderless group, the Underground Press Syndicate (UPS), and organized it into a network for exchanging stories and sharing subscription lists.

John Wilcock, editor of New York City's leading underground newspaper, the *East Village Other*, developed the idea for UPS. The group developed a loose arrangement whereby any newspaper could join simply by agreeing to let member publications reprint its articles. Later in 1967, UPS established a national office in New York City and charged a small onetime membership fee. The office staff coordinated national advertising for UPS newspapers and issued a weekly newsletter, the *Free Ranger Intertribal News Service*.

But conflict between hippie newspapers and political ones divided UPS, and the latter broke away and organized the Liberation News Service. UPS continued in existence into the early 1970s, when the underground press began collapsing due to its inflexible radical message and to repressive measures by the federal government.

See also East *Village Other;* Liberation News Service; *San Francisco Oracle; Seed;* Underground Newspapers.

Reference Peck, Abe, *Uncovering the Sixties: The Life and Times of the Underground Press* (1985).

Unisex

First evident among the hippies, and then spreading throughout the young generation, unisex styling produced an androgynous look. At unisex boutiques customers purchased pants, shirts, and jewelry. Long-haired men donned brightly colored garments and sometimes carried bags; women rejected makeup and wore denims and boots, causing many observers to remark, "You can't tell the boys from the girls."

University of California–Berkeley

Upheaval at the University of California–Berkeley signaled that a counterculture would challenge middle-class society and polarize the nation, for here emerged youthful protest at a level not seen in America's normally quiescent colleges.

In 1964, few people expected Berkeley to erupt. The university had some 27,000 students and 12,000 teachers, administrators, and support personnel, and its low tuition made higher education affordable to many—the route to success in corporate America. Quality predominated: students came from the top 10 percent of their high school classes and faculty from the finest graduate programs. Further, the university had earned renown in several disciplines.

Yet trouble brewed. The large campus bureaucracy contributed to a sense among students of depersonalization, as did the classes held in enormous lecture halls and the computer cards that governed registration. Everything indicated an uncaring technocratic setting, one that symbolized society at large. In addition to this, Berkeley, tied to California's big business interests and through the Board of Regents dominated by them, restricted political speech. Those who wanted to organize civil rights rallies or social protests could not—and this meant much at a university whose students had, in substantial numbers, participated in the civil rights movement in the South and returned to campus determined to eradicate social injustice.

Within this atmosphere, Berkeley in the 1960s served as both a microcosm for the tension in society at large and a stimulant to confrontation and change. In 1964, Berkeley displayed the agenda of the early political counterculture when the Free Speech Movement demanded freedom of speech and assembly. These demands reverberated throughout the nation, affecting other colleges, community colleges, even high schools.

Two years later, Berkeley displayed the hardening political side of the counterculture and the crosscurrent between the New Left and hippies. Cries for student rights had changed to ones for student power, and when protesters staged sit-ins they sang such emblematic hippie songs as "Yellow Submarine."

By this time, the Berkeley protesters had lost the optimism they once had to change America. Everywhere, from Berkeley to Vietnam, the established political powers proved duplicitous and unwilling to go beyond token reforms. On the other hand, mainstream society reacted with a determination to maintain order and restrict dissent at Berkeley. This appeared evident in Ronald Reagan's election as governor of California in 1966 and his demand that protesting students either restrict themselves to the classroom or leave the college. Two cultures in conflict at Berkeley stood in conflict across the nation.

See also Free Speech Movement; Savio, Mario.

References Draper, Hal, *Berkeley: The New Student Revolt* (1965); Wolin, Sheldon, and John H. Schar, *The Berkeley Rebellion and Beyond: Essays on Politics and Education in the Technological Society* (1970).

University of Michigan

Protests erupted with such frequency and intensity at the University of Michigan (UM) that it gained a reputation as a radical campus.

As with most colleges, UM, located in Ann Arbor, experienced tremendous growth in student enrollment between 1958 and 1970, from 17,000 to 34,000. This youthful population grew disenchanted with what it called an impersonal, cruel, undemocratic nation. Thus, in 1960, a student, Al Haber, dropped out of the university and decided to organize Students for a Democratic Society (SDS) that within a short time emerged as the leading New Left group in America. He recruited UM students to help build it. Activist Todd Gitlin affirmed UM's attraction when he enrolled in graduate school there, not so much, he said, to study political science, his declared major, as to pursue radical reform.

Another momentous development occurred at UM when, in 1965, several professors staged the nation's first teach-in. There later followed numerous protests against the Vietnam War, including picketing at the Ann Arbor draft board, peace vigils, and violent demonstrations in 1970 against President Nixon's decision to send U.S. troops into Cambodia, protests so intense they prompted the governor to declare UM and other Michigan college campuses in a state of emergency.

See also Students for a Democratic Society; Teach-In.

University of Wisconsin–Madison

Demonstrations and a huge explosion rocked the University of Wisconsin (UW) in the sixties.

Located in Madison, UW experienced substantial growth from 1958 to 1970: enrollment surged from 14,000 at the beginning of the period to 35,000 at its end. In this youthful environment, the first large demonstration erupted at UW in 1967 when students picketed recruiters for Dow Chemical. The protesters considered Dow a criminal corporation for its manufacturing of napalm used by the American military in Vietnam. After the police arrested three of the protesters, more students appeared, about 800 in all, and staged a sit-in.

A second demonstration against Dow later that year turned bloody after police dispersed 300 protesters by using billy clubs. This prompted the faculty to issue a statement condemning the police action, while the state legislature demanded that student "radicals" be expelled. The UW administration decided to suspend the Dow Chemical job interviews.

Yet another violent incident erupted in 1970 after the decision by President Nixon to send troops into Cambodia, and after the National Guard shot several students at Kent State University in Ohio. In fact, the Cambodian invasion galvanized college students across the nation, and more than ever before they considered themselves radicals and Nixon the enemy. At UW, several hundred students invaded the streets of Madison and smashed storefront windows.

Then on 24 August 1970, four militants, who called themselves the New Year's Gang, loaded a stolen van with explosives and parked it on campus outside the Army Mathematics Research Center (AMRC). After they lit a fuse and escaped in a getaway car, an enormous blast devastated the six-story building, injuring three people and killing Robert Fassnacht, a young, postdoctoral physicist. The explosion damaged 26 other campus buildings and could be heard for miles around. In a printed statement the New Year's Gang said:

> The AMRC, a think-tank of Amerikan militarism, was a fitting target for such revolutionary violence. As the major U.S. Army center for solving military mathematical problems, it bears full responsibility for Amerikan military genocide throughout the world. While hiding behind the facade of academic "neutrality," the AMRC plays a vital role in doing the research necessary for the development of heavy artillery, conventional and nuclear bombs and missiles, guns and mobile weapons, biological weapons, chemical weapons, and much more. (Bates 1992, photo insert)

The explosion, though, repulsed many Americans, and the antiwar movement repudiated it.

Reference Bates, Tom, *Rads: The 1970 Bombing of the Army Math Research Center at the University of Wisconsin and Its Aftermath* (1992).

V

Velvet Underground

Closely connected with Andy Warhol and the pop art movement, the rock band Velvet Underground answered optimistic hippies with gritty songs born from alienation—songs about sexual deviance, drug addiction, violence, and despair. Although never producing a hit record, the band's music rippled through the counterculture and influenced numerous musicians in the sixties and for years later.

In 1964, John Cale, a classical violinist, met Lou Reed in New York City. Reed, who had grown up in Freeport, Long Island, and wrote poetry, had classical training in playing the piano. (He eventually had several poems published and won literary prizes, including the French Order of Arts and Letters.) The two joined Sterling Morrison and Angus MacLise to form a band that went through several names, among them the Warlocks and the Primitives. They specialized in playing at art galleries and poetry readings in New York.

The next year, after MacLise, who played drums, left the band and was replaced by Maureen Tucker, the group adopted the name Velvet Underground. In 1966, Andy Warhol, the eccentric pop artist, invited them to perform at his film shows. While the band members played their music, he projected movies onto their bodies. He added Nico, a singer and actor, to the group; however, she recorded only a few songs with them. Warhol also provided the artwork, an illustration of a banana, for the band's first album cover.

In 1967, however, the Velvet Underground had a falling out with Warhol, and Cale quit amid disputes with Reed. Doug Yule replaced Cale, but the change in personnel changed the sound, and Velvet Underground lost many fans. In 1970, Reed left the band, and although it continued to perform for three more years, few people noticed.

Velvet Underground reunited for a performance in 1988 and another in 1991, but internal disagreements again caused a split. With its brief existence, Velvet Underground achieved only a limited following in the sixties, but it reshaped rock through its influence in the 1970s on David Bowie and punk bands, and ten years later, on alternative bands such as R.E.M. and Sonic Youth.

See also Rock Music.

Reference Bockris, Victor, *Transformer: The Lou Reed Story* (1995).

Vermont

To communards and those in the back-to-the-earth movement Vermont had tremendous appeal: the most rural state in the Northeast, reasonably priced land, beautiful scenery, and a tolerant attitude. Further, a notable commune had succeeded there: Quarry Hill in Rochester, founded in the 1940s (and still in existence today). Although no one knows for sure how many communes developed in Vermont in the 1960s, enough appeared to form Free Vermont, an affiliation of them that sought political reform. Free Vermont established a school and a people's bank and helped found two institutions important in Burlington: the Community Health Center and the Onion River Food Co-op.

Some today claim that the communes and nature freaks attached to the back-to-the-earth movement reshaped Vermont in ways still felt: an ethic of nonviolence, ecological awareness, and respect for freedom of thought. One longtime Vermonter believes "the thing that came from these [1960s] cultures is prevailing and spread out all over." (Pollak 1995, D1)

See also Back-to-the-Earth Movement; Commune.
Reference Pollak, Sally, "When Communes Were Common," *Burlington Free Press*, 13 August 1995, D1.

Vibes (Vibrations)

As slang, the word *vibes* or *vibrations* referred to the feelings, sensations, or atmosphere communicated in a situation or during a psychedelic experience. Vibes could be positive or negative, thus in a popular rock song the Beach Boys sing about "good vibrations," while in a particular setting someone might remark: "I get bad vibes from this scene."

Vietnam Day Committee

The Vietnam Day Committee formed in Berkeley, California, in 1965 and organized that year's teach-in to educate students at the University of California about the Vietnam War. The Committee, which at one point had Jerry Rubin as its leader, also organized several protest marches against the army base in nearby Oakland in an attempt to stop troop trains.
See also Rubin, Jerry; Teach-In.

Vietnam Veterans against the War

They gathered at the steps of the Capitol in April 1969, angry and defiant—800 men who had fought in Vietnam, who had won medals. One by one they stepped forward and threw their bronze stars, their silver stars, their purple hearts, or what one called his "merit badges for murder" onto the steps. The protest, sponsored by the Vietnam Veterans against the War, displayed deep revulsion toward the war.

Formed late in the 1960s, the Vietnam Veterans against the War held several protests that gained national attention and embarrassed the U.S. government. The April 1969 demonstration included a march by 1,000 veterans, some on crutches or in wheelchairs, to Arlington National Cemetery, where authorities refused them entry, and it included an encampment at the Mall, from which the protesters marched to the Pentagon and visited congressmen.

In 1970, the organization conducted what it called "war crime hearings" in Washington, where over 100 veterans testified about atrocities, including brutal rapes and murders of civilian women and children, committed by American troops in Vietnam:

> They didn't believe our body counts. So we had to cut off the right ear of everybody we killed to prove our body count. . . . I saw one case where a woman was shot by a sniper, one of our snipers. When we got up to her she was asking for water. And the lieutenant said to kill her. So he ripped off her clothes, they stabbed her in both breasts . . . spread an E tool up her vagina, an entrenching tool, and she was still asking for water . . . and they used a tree limb and then she was shot. . . . When you shot someone you didn't think you were shooting at a human. They were a gook or a Commie and it was okay. (Anderson 1995, 372)

The Nixon administration portrayed the Vietnam Veterans against the War as unpatriotic cowards. Yet they had served bravely in the military and decided that, whatever the risk, they had to speak out.
See also Vietnam War.
Reference Anderson, Terry H., *The Movement and the Sixties* (1995).

Vietnam War

As late as 1967, *Ramparts* magazine wondered how National Liberation Front troops could time and again raid U.S. installations in South Vietnam and escape undetected "without a single neighborhood village sounding the alarm." The magazine declared: "Few American officials in Saigon believe the war is going anything other than badly." The picture had not changed, and indeed may have worsened, since two years earlier when *New York Times* reporter David Halberstam called the Vietnam War "the making of a quagmire." This seemingly endless conflict—more and more lives lost for objectives never clear in a land hostile and alien—stimulated the counterculture, causing young Americans to condemn

Antiwar demonstrators march from the Lincoln Memorial to the Pentagon on 21 October 1967.

mainstream society and pursue alternatives, be they rejecting all politics or embracing political radicalism.

Even before American combat troops arrived in Vietnam, a few college students protested the sending there of military advisors, numbering in the thousands, by President John Kennedy. Nevertheless, most students, raised in a cold-war environment that taught them to fear communism and to consider national leaders truthful and expert, accepted government explanations.

This mentality and its accompanying complacency began to change markedly in 1965 when President Lyndon Johnson escalated Kennedy's Vietnam policy and committed American ground forces to engage the enemy, the National Liberation Front (NLF). At the same time, Johnson began massive air attacks on North Vietnam in an attempt to force its Communist leaders to withdraw the NLF from South Vietnam.

As the carnage expanded and Americans died in increasing numbers, protests against the war spread, centered first on college campuses and then moving beyond to the general population. In 1965, an antiwar rally in Washington signaled that more than a few people opposed the war, although Americans still overwhelmingly supported Johnson's policy.

By 1966, America's combat role had intensified with attacks against Vietnam's neighboring nation, Cambodia, while B-52 aircraft dropped bombs on the North Vietnamese capital of Hanoi. At year's end, the United States had 385,300 troops stationed in South Vietnam and another 60,000 offshore—this despite protesters warning Americans about a senseless, hopeless conflict.

To many young people, the war by this point had reinforced their view that corruption and cruelty dominated mainstream society. But a large question loomed: how to react to this situation? Some youths turned their backs on the old society, or in the language of the time, they "dropped out," lived as hippies, and tuned in to the psychedelic-inspired message emanating from San Francisco's Haight-Ashbury district: peace, love, and harmony. Others joined the New Left and pursued radical politics, working to get America out of Vietnam, but more than that, considering the war symptomatic of larger evils in society that necessitated revolutionary changes in the political system.

Yet the differences between hippies and New Leftists blurred, and some young people participated in both, or involved themselves only partially in them, such as joining in the New Left antiwar effort but not its larger, often ill-defined agenda to radically alter the political system. Whatever the individual decisions, antiwar activists staged a huge march on the Pentagon in October 1967 that drew enormous publicity for their cause. Still, for many more Americans, young and old, the correct course meant supporting President Johnson. He had, after all, reassured everyone that victory neared.

The Tet Offensive shattered this view. A massive effort in January 1968 by the NLF to capture facilities across South Vietnam, Tet failed in that American troops beat back the attackers, but it succeeded in showing that even after years of tremendous sacrifice in money and lives, the United States had come no closer to victory, no closer to peace. The enemy could still mobilize at will. Clearly, Johnson had been fooled or had lied.

Tet unleashed bigger antiwar demonstrations and convinced many in the mainstream, including many journalists, that the United States had to withdraw from Vietnam. This sentiment so intensified that, a few weeks after Tet, Johnson suffered a devastating setback in the New Hampshire Democratic presidential primary, receiving fewer delegates than Eugene McCarthy, an avowed peace candidate. As a result, the president withdrew from the race and in May began peace negotiations with Hanoi.

Soon after Richard Nixon assumed the presidency in January 1969, American troops began coming home under his policy to turn the fighting over to the South Vietnamese army, what he called Vietnamization. This did not immediately end the antiwar protests, however. Many criticized his approach as too slow, guaranteed to prolong the fighting and deaths for years to come. Then, in November, newspapers reported a massacre the previous year by U.S. troops at My Lai in South Vietnam. They had killed hundreds of civilians. For many Americans, the tragedy confirmed the war's barbarity and reinforced the belief withdrawal should come immediately.

The revelation that early in 1969 Nixon had launched secret air attacks on Cambodia propelled a massive antiwar demonstration in Washington that turned violent. By this time, many Americans held hardened views about the war—Nixon among them. He considered the demonstrators nothing less than anti-American filth. Nevertheless, his Vietnamization policy defused the antiwar movement.

That is, until April 1970, when he sent American troops into Cambodia to attack NLF bases there (a mission that largely failed). College campuses erupted in massive protests, the most famous one at Kent Sate University in Ohio where the National Guard opened fire and killed four students.

In the fall, calm returned to the campuses and for the most part to the nation as a whole. After the sobering experience at Kent State, and with fewer and fewer American troops in Vietnam, the antiwar movement declined, although not without additional, small-scale demonstrations until 1973, when the United States signed a peace pact with Hanoi and the last American troops left South Vietnam.

Before this, though, the *New York Times* published the Pentagon papers, a previously top-secret account of the war written by government analysts. The papers revealed that presidential administrations from Harry Truman through Richard Nixon had violated international agreements and repeatedly lied to the public in their Vietnam policy. Thus, the antiwar protesters had been accurate in portraying the government as deceitful.

They had been accurate, too, in asserting that the government in South Vietnam had little popular support, that once American troops left the area, it would quickly fall to the North. Despite massive American economic and military aid to South Vietnam, that government collapsed in April 1975, and North Vietnam emerged victorious. The war had taken an enormous toll: over 211,000 casualties, including more than 47,000 deaths among American forces alone. In its attempt to win, the United States had used free-fire zones, killing enemy soldiers, women, and children indiscriminately; defoliated large areas with chemicals; unleashed skin-burning napalm from jet aircraft; and pounded North Vietnam, a small agricultural country, with more bombs than had been dropped by all the nations involved in World War II.

To this day, historians debate the effectiveness of the antiwar movement. Did it hasten American withdrawal? Or did it prolong the American presence by stiffening Nixon's resolve? The answer may never be known for sure, but the protests raised moral questions the nation had to confront, forced into the open society's injustices, and stimulated a counterculture whose own impact remains hotly debated.

See also Democratic National Convention of 1968; Ellsberg, Daniel; Fonda, Jane; Gitlin, Todd; Hayden, Tom; Kent State; March on the Pentagon, 1967; National Mobilization Committee To End the War in Vietnam.

References Halberstam, David, *The Making of a Quagmire: America and Vietnam during the Kennedy Era* (1988); Kolko, Gabriel, *Anatomy of a War: Vietnam, the United States, and the Modern Historical Experience* (1985); Sheehan, Neil, *A Bright Shining Lie: John Paul Vann and America in Vietnam* (1988).

Village Voice

In 1955, Ed Fancher, Dan Wolf, and Norman Mailer began the *Village Voice* to cover New York City's Greenwich Village scene—its beat writers, abstract artists, actors, and others in the avant-garde. In doing so, the *Voice* acted as a precursor to the counterculture's underground newspapers.

Fancher, Wolf, and Mailer desired a paper that would not hew to any party line, one that would help protect Greenwich Village as a distinct community. They wanted the *Voice* to be independent in thought, and toward this end they rejected any reliance on one or two financial sources and instead obtained advertising dollars from many different supporters. They started the *Voice* in a cramped, two-room apartment at 22 Greenwich Avenue and relied on three or four battered typewriters and a well-used mimeograph machine to crank out copies.

The *Voice* exhibited features that later characterized the underground press: attacks on conservatives, traditional liberals, and Marxists; attention to bohemian cultural events; personal and informal writing; and trust in unproved writers. The newspaper gained support from young artists—Mailer helped shape the early editions with his editorial advice and stories—and gained a readership well beyond Greenwich Village.

In 1970, Fancher, Wolf, and Mailer sold the paper, although Wolf stayed on as editor and Fancher as publisher until 1974. Under this new ownership, and particularly after Wolf and Fancher departed, the *Voice* took a standardized New Left position on almost all issues. Before then, however, it had shown the possibilities of creative journalism outside the mainstream, and when the founders of the prominent underground newspaper the *Los Angeles Free Press* looked for a publication to emulate, they chose the *Village Voice*.

See also *Los Angeles Free Press;* Mailer, Norman; Underground Newspapers.

Reference McAuliffe, Kevin Michael, *The Great American Newspaper: The Rise and Fall of the Village Voice* (1975).

Volkswagen Microbus

Cheap to purchase and operate, the VW, or Volkswagen, microbus captivated hippies and other countercultural youths and remains, today, a symbol of that era—the oval-shaped, German-made vehicle adorned with psychedelic colors, twirling designs, astrological and Oriental religious symbols. The VW microbus was great for picking up hitchhikers and roomy enough for sex or group pot smoking, and owning one snubbed the big American car corporations.

Vonnegut, Kurt, Jr. (1922–)

> Newt remained curled in the chair. He held out his painty hands as though a cat's cradle were strung between them. "No wonder kids grow up crazy. A cat's cradle is nothing but a bunch of X's between somebody's hands, and little kids look and look and look at all those X's . . ."
>
> "And?"
>
> "*No damn cat, and no damn cradle.*"
>
> (Vonnegut 1963, 114)

With his novel *Cat's Cradle*, Kurt Vonnegut, Jr. not only vaulted to enormous popularity but also emerged as the literary representative for the counterculture generation. His simple style, condemnatory attitude toward war and inhumanity, impatience with political hypocrisy, irreverence and concern with life's absurdities all complemented what many counterculture youths thought and felt.

Vonnegut was born on 11 November 1922 in Indianapolis, Indiana, to Kurt Vonnegut, Sr., an architect, and Edith Sophia Lieber Vonnegut. From his father, he developed an interest in technology, and from both parents a politically progressive worldview accompanied by a distrust of authority. After completing his secondary education at Shortridge High School, where he edited the student newspaper *Echo*, he enrolled at Cornell University. There, Vonnegut studied biochemistry for two years before transferring to the Carnegie Institute of Technology. World War II interrupted his studies, however, and, inducted into the army, he fought in Europe until captured by the Germans in the Battle of the Bulge. His experience as a prisoner of war in Dresden, Germany, later formed the basis for one of his novels.

After the war, Vonnegut enrolled at the University of Chicago but did not complete his degree. Instead, he worked in public relations for the General Electric Company in Schenectady, New York. In 1950, he began working as a full-time freelance writer, and his short fiction appeared in numerous popular magazines. At the same time, he wrote his first novel, *Player Piano*, based on his observations at General Electric. The book, a satire published in 1952, tells of engineers who impose an oppressive automation on American society, and how one engineer leads a revolution against the system. Vonnegut's second novel, *The Sirens of Titan*, published in 1959, presents extraterrestrial forces who rearrange the course of human history in order to obtain a spare part for a spacecraft.

Then came *Cat's Cradle*, about a scientist whose pursuit of truth without moral concern leads him to develop ice-nine, a molecular-locking catalyst that can freeze all the earth's liquids. After being accidentally released, the ice-nine destroys civilization. Among its characters, the story includes a religious prophet who preaches "Bokononist" scripture that teaches the unpredictability of life and the seemingly unrelated interrelationships that determine people's actions.

Cat's Cradle jabs at religion, technology, customs, war, and politics. Early in the story, Vonnegut's main character says: "Anyone unable to understand how a useful religion can be founded on lies will not understand this book." (14) And later:

> I remembered *The Fourteenth Book of Bokonon*, which I had read in its entirety the night before. *The Fourteenth Book* is entitled, "What Can a Thoughtful Man Hope for Mankind on Earth, Given the Experience of the Past Million Years?"
>
> It doesn't take long to read *The Fourteenth Book*. It consists of one word and a period.
>
> This is it:
>
> "Nothing." (164)

Vonnegut followed *Cat's Cradle* with *God Bless You, Mr. Rosewater*, and then his most critically acclaimed novel, *Slaughterhouse-Five, or the Children's Crusade*. In telling about the allied bombing of Dresden during World War II, this story twists chronology around, moving back and forth in a time warp where past, present, and future happen all at once. Vonnegut portrays the bombing as an atrocity—the city had no military or industrial importance, and the bombs dropped there killed more people than did the atomic attacks on Japan—but he goes beyond this and sees human beings as trapped into repeating barbaric acts because they are numb to life's cruelties.

Taken together, *Cat's Cradle* and *Slaughterhouse-Five* corresponded with the countercultural challenge to existing institutions—its discontentment with traditional religion and an impersonal technological society that seemed to forswear compassion. Vonnegut's antiwar theme and satirical undressing of political charlatans found a wide audience among young people disgusted with the Vietnam War and the government lies behind it.

Yet Vonnegut, who continued writing novels into the 1990s, said something that counterculture political activists often overlooked, a point presented strongly in his 1961 book *Mother Night*: all social and political affiliations are absurd.

References Vonnegut, Kurt, Jr., *Cat's Cradle* (1963), *God Bless You, Mr. Rosewater* (1965), *Mother Night* (1961), *Player Piano* (1952), *The Sirens of Titan* (1959), and *Slaughterhouse-Five, or the Children's Crusade* (1969).

W

Warhol, Andy (1928–1987)
Perhaps the most influential painter and mixed-media artist of the 1960s, Andy Warhol promoted commercialized pop art while the decade swirled around him, a great life storm he watched, participated in, and used. Writer Kurt Loder later said Warhol "helped invent the Sixties." (Loder 1987, 32) There is no doubt that Warhol personified the modern influences on the counterculture, most tellingly expressed in his statement: "A whole day of life is like a whole day of television." (31)

An eccentric, Warhol hid behind a mythological wall, spinning various tales about his origins or letting people conclude whatever they desired. Thus, speculation continues as to his childhood. Warhol was born Andrew Warhola most likely on 6 August 1928 (although some sources argue for 28 September 1930) somewhere in Pennsylvania. He grew up in McKeesport, where his father, a Czech immigrant, worked in a steel factory. Warhol lived in poverty after his father died, and as a child suffered nervous bouts caused by a viral infection that gave him blotchy skin.

Through odd jobs, such as working at a local department store, he saved enough money to attend the Carnegie Institute of Technology in Pittsburgh, from which he graduated in 1949 with a bachelor's degree in pictorial design. From there, he settled in New York City and shortened his last name to Warhol. Ambitious, Warhol sought money, fame, and social recognition. He got his first break illustrating shoes for *Glamour* magazine, but his big step toward achieving his goal came in 1955 when the I. Miller shoe store paid him $50,000 a year to do its weekly ads in the Sunday *New York Times*. He quickly prospered as a commercial artist—a field serious painters disdained—and after living in a roach-infested tenement, purchased a town house on Lexington Avenue. In *Holy Terror*, Bob Colacello, formerly a Warhol associate, describes his colleague's style:

> He'd do a pencil sketch of the subject, displaying the same quick, facile talent that he had shown as a child. Then he'd trace the drawing on a piece of blotting paper, or even toilet tissue, in ink. And then, while the ink was still wet, he'd press the drawing onto a third piece of paper, sometimes over and over on a single sheet to achieve a wallpaper look, sometimes on sheet after sheet, producing fainter and fainter multiples of the original drawing—which he threw away. It was fast, easy, cheap, different, and modern—all the things Andy liked his work to be. (22)

Warhol did freelance work for books and record albums and developed an unusual appearance by dying his hair silver. Wanting to expand beyond commercial art, he began trying different styles and in 1956 participated in his first group exhibition with other painters.

Warhol's efforts corresponded with the experimental fervor that characterized the sixties, such as when he decided to challenge abstract expressionism with pop art. Abstract expressionism had dominated American painting in the late 1940s and 1950s, characterized by emotionalism and distorted images. For abstract expressionists, painting was largely an uncontrolled irrational act whereby the process of painting superseded in importance the painting itself. Hence, Jackson Pollock's work, sometimes referred to as action painting, in which he dragged, dripped, and splattered materials on canvas attached not to an easel but stretched outward on the ground.

Warhol's pop art (a form he did not invent but that originated in Europe) aimed to present its subjects realistically. In this sense, it resembled art called realism. But

Andy Warhol poses with two companions in front of his "cow" wallpaper and self portraits in New York, 29 April 1971.

it used subjects that differed markedly from the older style, as evident when Warhol painted the expendable, commercialized forms that had come to dominate affluent, suburban society. Thus, in 1962, he exhibited his work *Campbell Soup Cans*, first at a gallery in Los Angeles where few people took notice, and then, a few months later, at one in New York City. *Campbell Soup Cans* comprised 32 canvases representing each of the available soup mixes, from *Cream of Asparagus* to *Tomato*. This work, along with his *Gold Marilyn* and *Red Elvis*, also displayed at the gallery, obtained critical notice and acclaim.

As objective as Warhol may have intended his pop art to be, its emotionless, cold, sometimes repetitious appearance made some wonder if it contained a hidden commentary on modern society as impersonal. Whether it did or not, it had the immediate effect of democratizing art through its subject: middle-class consumer items. As Warhol said: "The Pop Artists did images that anyone . . . could recognize in a split second." (32)

In 1964, Warhol moved to a loft at 231 East 47th Street, soon known as the Factory partly because the building used to house such an enterprise, but more so because it was here that he and art student Gerard Malanga applied Warhol's mass-production technique, using silk-screening to produce prints with an "assembly-line effect." "I tried doing them by hand, but I find it easier to use a screen," Warhol said about his artwork. "This way, I don't have to work on my objects at all. One of my assistants or anyone else, for that matter, can reproduce the designs as well as I could." (91)

Strange characters from the counterculture's depths began hanging out at the Factory, and Warhol used them in movies he started producing. These films recorded everyday events in an attempt to portray life's mundane aspects, and they minimized barriers between art and real life by using no actors and little direction. His movie *Sleep*, for example, simply showed a man sleeping for eight hours. After *Soap Opera*, released in 1964, made one of its participants a star, Warhol responded with his memorable remark: "In the future, everyone will be world famous for fifteen minutes."

In 1966, Warhol brought the Velvet Underground, a rock band, to the Factory. He teamed them up with Nico, a German actress-model, and had them appear in his underground theatre where he projected movies on their bodies while they performed, a technique that replicated the San Francisco rock scene and took it in new, multimedia directions. Warhol produced the Velvet Underground's first album and designed its cover: a painting of a banana. The following year, he pushed his mass reproduction into a new realm when he convinced Allen Midgette to spray his hair silver and pass himself off as Warhol. Midgette made several public appearances this way and the ruse fooled nearly everyone.

Warhol moved the Factory in 1968 to plush quarters at 33 Union Square West, and the scene got wilder. That June, Valerie Solanas, a disturbed member of an extreme feminist group, shot and nearly killed him. The incident left Warhol psychologically shaken, and he subsequently limited entry to the Factory and did little work for several months.

In 1969, he launched a gossip magazine, *Interview*, that carried mainly fashion news and appealed to the jet set. At the same time, he backed Paul Morrissey, who directed movies such as *Trash* that continued Warhol's emphasis on real-life portraits. A political right-winger, Morrisey disparaged democracy and the masses. As to cinematic style, he commented: "What could be more ridiculous than the pompous, pseudointellectual notion that the director is the most important person on a movie. Everyone knows that the most important person on a movie is the *star!*" (34)

In the 1970s, Warhol, now the best-known artist in the world, socialized mainly with jet-set figures: Elizabeth Taylor, Bianca Jagger, Michael Jackson, and so on. While he partied frequently, he kept his distance, usually returning home early in the evening.

The following decade, Warhol painted portraits commissioned by wealthy persons, began his own cable television show, did a brief series on MTV, and appeared in rock videos. On 21 February 1987, he entered a hospital for gallbladder surgery. The operation appeared to be successful, but the following morning he suffered a heart attack and died.

Despite his eccentricity, Warhol rejected drugs, practiced Catholicism devoutly, and had a reputation for treating people fairly and honestly. His most ardent fans in the 1960s came from the young counterculture crowd. Without a doubt, Warhol had revolutionized popular culture, as he intended to, and set into motion an ongoing debate: did pop art destroy art or resurrect it? Warhol thought that somehow he might have done both.

See also Psychedelic Art; Velvet Underground.

References Bockris, Victor, *The Life and Death of Andy Warhol* (1989); Colacello, Bob, *Holy Terror: Andy Warhol Close Up* (1990); Guiles, Fred Lawrence, *Loner at the Ball: The Life of Andy Warhol* (1989); Loder, Kurt, "Andy Warhol, 1928–1987," *Rolling Stone*, 9 April 1987, 31–33, 35–36.

Wasted

To get wasted meant to get excessively high on drugs.

Watts

The riot in 1965 that swept through Watts, a black ghetto in Los Angeles, after similar upheavals a year earlier in Harlem and other northern cities stunned white Americans. They wondered, "After so much progress in civil rights, how could this be happening?" They could not understand what journalist Kenneth B. Clark observed, that civil rights legislation "was more relevant to the predicament of the Southern Negro than to Negroes in Northern ghettos." The ghetto African American, Clark said, "sees no positive changes in his day-to-day life . . . [and] is suffering from a pervasive, intensive and at times self-righteous form of American racism that does not understand the depth of his need." (Meier, Rudwick, and Bracey 1991, 111–112)

A traffic violation sparked the rioting. On 11 August 1965, a white police officer stopped a young black and arrested him for drunken driving. Soon, an argument erupted, a crowd assembled, and the officer called for reinforcements. Then blacks began pelting the police with rocks and bottles, and a mob took to the streets, attacking white drivers and setting fire to cars. Watts community leaders called for calm, but during the next night violence spread as more than 5,000 blacks smashed windows, set fire to buildings, looted stores, and attacked white passersby. When police and firemen entered the ghetto, some rioters fired at them from rooftops. At that point, the authorities called in the National Guard.

Still, the turmoil continued, with the neighborhood aflame and rioters exchanging gunfire with police and troops. It took six days to quell the uprising—after $35 million in property damage, 4,000 arrests, 1,000 injuries, and 34 deaths, the latter all African Americans. The rage that had swept Watts ignited riots later that summer in Chicago and in Springfield, Massachusetts. All three riots, in turn, produced a backlash, an adamant belief among many whites that blacks did not appreciate the accomplishments made in civil rights, that they had gone too far, and that their lawlessness—which many felt innate to blacks—amounted to a race war, a desire to annihilate whites.

Some analytical whites, however, saw the situation differently and realized that Watts and other ghettos had for years suffered intense poverty and unemployment, and had been exploited by white store owners who charged high prices for groceries and the items that symbolized material comfort: televisions and appliances. Blacks could no longer tolerate these conditions that separated them from middle-class comfort. Nor could they tolerate the police, portrayed in legend as guardians of the law, taking bribes and, as an all-white force, treating blacks cruelly. Kenneth Clark insisted: "The wonder is that there have been so few riots, that Negroes generally are law-abiding in a world where the law itself has seemed the enemy." (107)

Other riots did erupt, though, worse than those in 1965, most notably two years later in Detroit, where President Lyndon Johnson had to use army troops to bring order. With increasing frequency, as each new year approached, Americans talked about the prospects of "another long, hot summer."

A special commission formed by Johnson and led by Otto Kerner, governor of Illinois, studied the riots and concluded they had erupted spontaneously, and that rioters aimed their wrath at white-owned property. The Kerner report blamed the riots on poverty, unemployment, and antagonistic police practices, all supported by racism. The report said: "Our nation is moving toward two societies, one black, one white—separate and unequal." (Miller 1996, 138–139)

References Meier, August, Elliot Rudwick, and John Bracey, Jr., eds., *Black Protest in the Sixties* (1991); Miller, Douglas T., *On Our Own: Americans in the Sixties* (1996); Murphy, William S., *Burn, Baby, Burn! The Los Angeles Race Riot, August 1965* (1966).

Watts, Alan (1915–1973)

When *Rolling Stone* wrote an obituary about Alan Watts, it emphasized his radio program on KPFA-FM in Berkeley, California. The show, after all, epitomized the public Watts: glib, erudite, with an ability to communicate complex religious philosophy, particularly Eastern beliefs, to the layman. This talent, even more evident in his writings, made Watts an influential proponent of Zen Buddhism among, first, beatniks, and later, hippies. In *The Making of a Counterculture*, Theodore Roszak calls him "America's foremost popularizer of Zen." (132)

Born to Emily Mary Buchan Watts and Laurence Wilson Watts at Chislehurst in

Kent, England, on 6 January 1915, Watts developed an interest in Eastern books and art in his early teens, and declared his conversion to Buddhism. He later described his experience with meditation: "Instantly my weight vanished. I owned nothing. All hang-ups disappeared. I walked on air." (Furlong 1986, 41) In 1932, he completed his secondary education at King's School in Canterbury, England (to which he had won a scholarship).

That year, he began attending a Buddhist lodge founded by Christmas Humphreys, with whom he established a lasting friendship. Humphreys later recounted that Watts "didn't just talk *about* Zen, he *talked* Zen." (44)

Watts wrote several philosophical articles, followed in 1937 by his first book, *The Legacy of Asia and Western Man*. He edited a Buddhist journal, *The Middle Way*, in London from 1934 to 1938 and coedited a book series, *Wisdom of the East*, from 1937 to 1941.

While still working on this assignment in 1938, Watts, recently married into a wealthy family and wanting to avoid being drafted into the British military, immigrated to the United States. Three years later, he decided to make Episcopal Christianity a part of his life and began studying at Seabury-Western Theological Seminary in Evanston, Illinois. (No one is quite sure why he chose the Episcopal Church—some speculate he had a sincere attachment to the religion, others that, amid a world war, he wanted to make sure he would not be a combatant in the military.) Watts obtained a Master of Sacred Theology degree in 1948, but even before this, beginning in 1944, he served as Episcopal chaplain at Northwestern University. In the latter year, Watts left the Episcopal Church after expressing dissatisfaction with what he considered excessive preaching. Another factor in the break may have been the personal turmoil produced by the collapse of his marriage.

Watts then taught comparative psychology and philosophy at the American Academy of Asian Studies, which he helped found in 1951 with the intent to revolutionize human consciousness. The school attracted artists, poets, and other bohemian types. Watts continued teaching there until 1957—two years before the school folded—and also served a three-year stint as dean. He left the academy to concentrate on his writing.

Indeed, Watts had never ceased his prolific output, with the *Meaning of Happiness* in 1940, *Behold the Spirit* in 1947, and in the 1950s, *The Supreme Identity; Easter: Its Story and Meaning; Wisdom and Security; Myth and Ritual in Christianity; The Way of Zen;* and *Nature, Man, and Woman*.

Two important influences shaped Watts's writing: Christmas Humphreys—from Watts's days in England—and LSD, a psychedelic drug Watts tried in 1958, at that time legal and actually part of a drug experimentation program he participated in at the University of California–Los Angeles. LSD convinced Watts that he had reached a cosmic oneness. Since he had many friends in the San Francisco bohemian community, his positive experience with acid helped spread its use there.

Watts's greatest impact, however, came from his attachment to Zen Buddhism and his promotion of it; this "gave him a strong influence on the hippie culture" and even made him a "revered figure." (174–175) He promoted a Zen deeply rooted in the ancient Chinese T'ang dynasty, and thus strongly attached to Taoism. This Zen, he believed, liberated people from their egos and conventional thought, heavily mired in scientific rationality.

In *The Way of Zen*, Watts embraces Taoism as a means to understand life directly rather than through linear constructs. He writes positively about the *I Ching*, a book of divination, an oracle actually, that communicates the spontaneity and intuition underlying Taoism. Watts describes Zen Buddhism as resisting description, as promoting understanding through nonsymbolic action. Hence, an answer is an action as it stands, not by what it represents.

The Way of Zen and Watts's later books, *Psychotherapy, East and West* and *The Joyous Cosmology: Adventures in the Chemistry of*

Consciousness, particularly affected the counterculture. Many hippies found in these works an adventure into religions, drugs, and thoughts that provided a mysticism and spiritual fulfillment they could not find in Christianity. Watts himself insisted that Western civilization could learn from the East "methods for changing human consciousness," thus enabling the individual to "*feel* his identity." In the 1960s, Watts took his message to college campuses, where he appeared frequently as a lecturer, and on the airwaves, where he presented a series for public television. According to Monica Furlong in *Zen Effects*, Watts dropped his shyness and emerged a "full-scale flower child, as committed to the colorful, the experimental, the provisional, and the original as any campus dropout or high school runaway." (179)

But his fame, the reverence and adulation many offered him as their guru, took its toll, and by 1969 fatigue had settled in. He began drinking heavily, and nothing seemed able to change his self-destruction, not even his work on a new book, *Tao: The Watercourse Way*. He could not, as it turned out, live his philosophy.

Watts died of heart failure on 16 November 1973 at his home in Mill Valley, California. He had called himself a "spiritual entertainer," on a mission to "enliven religion," and his influence continued in the 1990s among adherents to New Age beliefs. (Marine 1973, 10)

See also Zen Buddhism.

References Furlong, Monica, *Zen Effects: The Life of Alan Watts* (1986); Marine, Gene, "Alan Watts, 1915–1973," *Rolling Stone*, 20 December, 1973 20-21; Roszak, Theodore, *The Making of a Counterculture: Reflections on the Technocratic Society and Its Youthful Opposition* (1968); Watts, Alan, *Beat Zen, Square Zen, and Zen* (1959), *Behold the Spirit: A Study in the Necessity of Mystical Religion* (1947), *The Book: On the Taboo against Knowing Who You Are* (1966), *Does It Matter? Essays on Man's Relation to Materiality* (1970), *In My Own Way: An Autobiography* (1972), *The Joyous Cosmology: Adventures in the Chemistry of Consciousness* (1962), *The Meaning of Happiness: The Quest for Freedom of the Spirit in Modern Psychology and the Wisdom of the East* (1979), *Myth and Ritual in Christianity* (1960), *Nature, Man, and Woman* (1958); *Psychotherapy, East and West* (1961), *Tao: The Watercourse Way* (1975), *This Is It, and Other Essays on Zen and Spiritual Experience* (1960), *The Way of Zen* (1957), and *Zen Buddhism: A New Outline and Introduction* (1947).

Weather Underground

Amid the assassinations of Martin Luther King, Jr. and Robert Kennedy, the violence at the Democratic National Convention in Chicago, and the smoldering ruins from ghetto fires, some leaders within the leftist Students for a Democratic Society (SDS) believed revolution neared, and in 1969 they formed a militant group to hasten it: Weatherman.

Weatherman evolved from the Third World Marxists, a faction within SDS led by James Mellen, Bernardine Dohrn, and Mark Rudd. This group advocated street fighting to weaken U.S. imperialism—a rear guard action that would coincide with the revolutions then under way in third-world nations. With this position, Third World Marxists conflicted with another faction, Progressive Labor (PL), that believed street fights would only create a reactionary backlash among industrial workers, a group needed in any socialist revolt. At the SDS national convention in June 1969, the Third World Marxists presented a position paper, titled "You Don't Need a Weatherman To Know Which Way the Wind Blows"—lyrics from a song by Bob Dylan. The paper gave the group their name and expressed their desire for violent revolutionary tactics.

SDS split apart at the convention, with Weatherman evicting PL. Although Weatherman produced tedious and pedantic doctrinal pamphlets, the organization developed an intense militancy. To foster unity, Weatherman began collectives intended to eliminate individualism and destroy male dominance by ending monogamous relationships; couples, for example, could be broken up by a decision of the collective—men ordered to sleep with men, women with women, men with a variety of women, and so on.

In the summer of 1969, Weatherman launched an offensive. In one action, it tried to recruit at community colleges and high schools—sometimes marching into classrooms, tying up and gagging teachers, and presenting revolutionary speeches. At the Harvard Institute for International Affairs (suspect for its conservatism), they smashed windows, tore out phones, and beat up professors.

In September, several women from Weatherman marched through a hippie neighborhood in Pittsburgh, carrying the flag of North Vietnam's National Liberation Front, and chanting "Ho Lives!" (in reference to Ho Chi Minh). They then converged on South Hills High School, where they distributed leaflets and fought with police. These actions failed to gain recruits.

Still bent on fomenting violent revolution, Weatherman invaded Chicago on 8 October to begin what it called National Action but what newspapers called the Days of Rage—a direct assault on the police, or in Weatherman's parlance, the pigs. Weatherman declared: "The pigs are the capitalist state, and as such define the limits of all political struggles." (Jacobs 1970, 84) The group expected several thousand supporters to appear, but only a few hundred turned out, and during three days of street fighting the police bloodied and arrested many of them.

Undaunted, Weatherman participated that November in the Moratorium, an anti–Vietnam War protest in Washington, which attracted at least 250,000 demonstrators. Although fewer than 3,000 followed Weatherman, the radicals attacked the South Vietnamese Embassy and assaulted the Justice Department with rocks, bottles, and smoke bombs. This violence only helped President Richard Nixon, though, who used it to reinforce his position that the antiwar movement was dangerous and un-American.

The Moratorium was the last major organized appearance by Weatherman. Disappointed by their failure to gain greater support, the core members, about 100 in all, decided at their national War Council in December 1969 to go underground, hence the name Weather Underground. In the process, they turned inward, convinced they needed neither the proletariat nor college students to make a revolution. Instead, they intended to weaken the government through terrorist acts. Rudd, Dohrn, and others disappeared from view.

Then, on 6 March 1970, a town house in New York City collapsed in a huge explosion after Weathermen living there accidentally detonated a bomb. The blast killed three of the radicals while two others escaped. After this, Weatherman continued its violent tactics with several bombings, including one at the New York City police headquarters on Centre Street, and it issued threatening communiqués, such as in July 1970 when it declared: "The time is now. Political power grows out of a gun, a Molotov, a riot, a commune . . . and from the soul of the people." (512)

Isolated from even fellow radicals who disliked Weatherman's tactics and Marxist ideology, the group accomplished little with its extremism. In the mid-1970s, Weatherman shattered into two quarreling factions. Some Weathermen drifted back into society, but in 1981 several former members, reorganized as the May 19th Coalition, allied with the Black Liberation Army and raided a Brink's armored car near New York City, killing a guard and two policemen. With the perpetrators imprisoned in 1984, the revolutionary energy from Weatherman had dissipated.

See also Boudin, Kathy; Days of Rage; Dohrn, Bernardine; Mellen, James; Moratorium; Rudd, Mark; Students for a Democratic Society.

References Jacobs, Harold, ed., *Weatherman* (1970); Sale, Kirkpatrick, *SDS* (1973); Stern, Susan, *With the Weathermen: The Personal Journal of a Revolutionary Woman* (1975); Viorst, Milton, *Fire in the Streets: America in the 1960s* (1979).

Weatherman

See Weather Underground.

Weed

Weed referred to marijuana, sometimes called the "noble weed."

White Panther Party

The White Panther Party emerged in the late sixties from a hippie commune, The Trans-Love Energies Unlimited, led by John and Leni Sinclair. Based in Ann Arbor, Michigan, the White Panthers promoted cultural and political revolution through whatever means necessary . . . rock 'n' roll, dope, and sex, to name a few. Cultural revolution, the White Panthers believed, would destroy the capitalist state.

See also Sinclair Incident.

The Who

"The result, of course, was magnificent, one of the best concerts I have been at and one which points . . . to utilization of music and theater in new sounds way past *Hair* and such really old-fashioned concepts," said one reviewer in 1970 about the band the Who after it had presented its new rock opera, *Tommy.* (Gleason 1970, 8)

Before they emerged as a dominant counterculture band, the Who struggled mightily to gain in the United States the recognition they had obtained in Britain. In the early 1960s, guitarist and art college student Pete Townshend; vocalist, guitarist, and sheet-metal worker Roger Daltrey; bass guitarist and government bureaucrat John Entwistle; and drummer Doug Sanden formed a band in the working-class neighborhood of West London, where they had grown up. Called the Detours, they played mainly rhythm and blues, along with a few Beatles tunes. In 1963, their new manager convinced them to replace Sanden, whom he considered too old. The group invited Keith Moon, and he added to their loudness with the incredible power and energy that characterized his drumming. Renamed the Who, the band recorded six singles that, in 1965 and 1966, reached the British top ten. But these, including "My Generation," did not do nearly as well in the United States.

This changed in 1967 with the Who's appearance at the Monterey Pop Festival in California, an event that boosted the reputation of nearly everyone who performed there. That same year, the Who had an American top-ten hit, "I Can See for Miles." But they faded and seemed to be sinking into obscurity until their notable set in August 1969 at Woodstock. Townshend, known for smashing his guitar on stage, did so at the festival, and the group's energy excited the crowd; more important, the Who presented songs from their rock opera *Tommy*. "Pinball Wizard" had already entered the top ten, and the album *Tommy*, released in April, moved steadily up the charts, eventually reaching number four.

The Who continued to record and perform in concert through the 1970s. They released *Who's Next* in 1971, considered one of their stronger albums, *Quadrophenia* two years later, and, in 1975, *The Who by Numbers*. By this time, though, their work had deteriorated. In 1978, Keith Moon died from a drug overdose, and the band hired Kenney Jones to replace him. The Who performed sporadically into the 1990s, when *Tommy*, previously made into a movie, became a hit play on Broadway.

See also Rock Music.

References Gleason, Ralph, "Theater Dead, Tommy Lives," *Rolling Stone*, 23 July 1970, 8; Tremlett, George, *The Who* (1975).

The Whole Earth Catalog

Young people read *The Whole Earth Catalog*, first published in 1968, for its advertisements and for its advice on how to farm and build communes and how to live a simpler existence. In its introduction, *Whole Earth* declares:

> We are as god and might as well get good at it. So far remotely done power and glory—as via government, big business, formal education, church—has succeeded to point where defects obscure actual gains. In response to this dilemma and to these gains a realm of intimate, personal power is developing—power of the individual to conduct his own education, find his own inspiration, shape his own environment, and share his adventure with whoever is interested. Tools that aid this process are sought and promoted by *The Whole Earth Catalog*. (Brand 1971, 1)

Stewart Brand, a San Francisco hippie who had helped organize the Trips Festival, put together *Whole Earth*—claiming the insights of inventor-philosopher Buckminster Fuller had initiated it. From 1968 to 1970, *Whole Earth* sold 2 million copies, and after Random House published it in 1971, it won the National Book Award.

Whole Earth displayed woodstoves, earth shoes, wind generators, organic foods, and many similar items that could be ordered; it offered practical-advice books: *How To Have a Green Thumb without an Aching Back*, *The Encyclopedia of Organic Gardening*, *The Oxford Book of Food Plants*, *The Maple Sugar Book*, *The Cultivator's Handbook of Marijuana;* and it provided guidance on how to mediate, get by without money, file as a nonprofit tax-exempt corporation, use the *I Ching*—"To consult the oracle, the wisdom of chance (or synchronicity, no matter) is to step out of the cycle of no change and address a specific story on the nature of change" (433)—make a teepee, prepare foods—"peaches can be peeled easily if they are dipped in boiling water, then in cold water" (197)—and the following:

> By processing methane gas from rotted chicken manure and feeding it into the engine through a device he invented, [Harold] Bate says he has managed to drive his 1953 Hillman at speeds up to 75 m.p.h. without the use of gasoline. (52)

One observer called *Whole Earth* "the Sears catalog for the New Age." But its black-and-white layout, quaint pictures, and long narratives made *Whole Earth* resemble more the Sears catalog of a hundred years earlier—a simpler, agricultural time.

See also Back-to-the-Earth Movement; Commune; Fuller, R. Buckminster.

Reference Brand, Stewart, ed., *The Whole Earth Catalog* (1971).

Women's Movement

In 1968, *Time* magazine used the phrase "women's liberation" in reference to a demonstration at that year's Miss America Pageant in Atlantic City, New Jersey. About 100 women had gathered along the city's famous boardwalk to protest male oppression and racism, which they considered blatant in the way the pageant treated women as objects and discouraged nonwhite contestants. They threw away bras and girdles, tore up an issue of *Playboy* magazine, and shouted "Liberation Now!," thus providing the main word in the phrase used by *Time*.

The protest heralded a women's movement in an era when movements abounded—black, Chicano, gay, antiwar, environmental . . . seemingly ad infinitum. No one knew how to precisely describe the women's movement—it meant more than rights; it meant an existential freedom, a desire to break through society's confines. Above all, women wanted to be heard.

At the time of the Atlantic City protest, women faced massive discrimination. For example, the federal government hired few women as professionals, and only 1 percent of those females who worked in the bureaucracy held the more lucrative rank of GS-13 or higher; universities remained male bastions as women occupied only 10 percent of all faculty positions; in public schools, women made up about 80 percent of the faculty but only 10 percent of the principals and 3 percent of the superintendents; nationwide, over a third of all wives worked for wages but earned only 58 cents for every dollar men earned; and several states prohibited women from buying stocks or bonds, starting a business, or getting a loan without a man's cosignature.

These conditions stimulated the women's movement, as did earlier protests. Civil rights and New Left activism had raised most everyone's political consciousness, and, in particular, many women had joined these causes. The countercultural criticism of liberalism also affected women—the belief within the New Left, for example, that liberals had sold out and that effective change could be accomplished only through radical reform, perhaps even revolution.

As a result, in the late 1960s and early 1970s, the women's movement gained a wider following and expanded its protests. Indeed, some historians believe that after 1969 the women's movement kept radicalism alive and showed that the spirit and activism of the sixties did not end with the decade.

Like so many other countercultural movements, the women's movement displayed ideological differences, a split between moderates and radicals. The moderates, represented most prominently by the National Organization of Women (NOW), sought equal rights and wanted to integrate women into mainstream establishment power positions; the radicals, represented most prominently by the group Redstockings, unequivocally condemned men and wanted separatism and liberation through a revolutionary movement—peaceful or otherwise. Technically speaking, NOW supporters fit within the "feminist" category, while Redstockings supporters fit within the "women's liberationists" category, sometimes referred to as "radical feminists."

Robin Morgan, a radical, clarified the difference when she said that "NOW is essentially an organization that wants reforms [in the] second-class citizenship of women—and this is where it differs drastically from the rest of the Women's Liberation Movement." (Echols 1989, 157) The difference, however, did not always appear distinct, as when both feminists and liberationists supported (at least for a time) an equal rights amendment, along with abortion rights.

Liberationists believed that women's secondary place in the public area resulted from their subordination to a patriarchal system within the family—thus, patriarchy must be destroyed. They wanted also to destroy capitalism, which they believed exploited women. "Sexism has no chance of being eliminated under capitalism," declared one radical. "Should some of us think that we have 'made it,' whatever that means, the rest of us will still be used to supply cheap, free, and reserve labor, to consume, to scab on each other." (Goodman, Mitchell 1970, 47) Radicals insisted as well that women must gain control over their own bodies, such as in determining whether to bear children. And they considered class division secondary to other ones—in this case gender; consequently, they sought to unite women irrespective of their economic, racial, and ethnic differences. Overall, they wanted to raise the consciousness of women, to create a group identity, and to make women everywhere aware of sexism.

In this spirit, there appeared works such as "Lilith's Manifesto" in 1970 that argued against false dichotomies between the sexes. The manifesto declared: "If assertiveness . . . is a virtue in a man, it is a virtue also in a woman; if forbearance is a virtue in a woman, it is likewise a virtue in a man." (Tanner 1970, 115) The Congress To Unite Women, held in late November 1969 in New York City, demanded nationwide, free child-care centers; an end to tracking systems in school that directed women into home economics; the establishment of women's studies sections in all public libraries and women's programs at colleges; the representation of women in all political bodies proportionate to their numbers in society; the addition of an equal rights amendment to the Constitution; and the end to all legal restrictions on abortions.

In "The Myth of the Vaginal Orgasm," written in 1970, radical Ann Koedt asserts that women do not have vaginal orgasms, and that when Freud criticized clitoral orgasms as inferior to vaginal ones, he did so not from an accurate anatomical perspective but from a belief in women's inferiority to men. Koedt states that the vagina has several purposes: for menstruation, to receive the penis, to hold semen, and to serve as a birth passage. The clitoris, however, has one function: sexual pleasure. Thus, she says, "We must discard the 'normal' concepts of sex and create new guidelines which take into account mutual sexual enjoyment." (159) She insists that women should not define sex solely according to

Secretary Shelly Drake shyly displays the brassiere she took off during the "Anti Bra Day" in San Francisco on 1 August 1968.

what pleases men, and sexual positions not conducive to mutual enjoyment should no longer be defined as standard.

In short, some radicals said, oppression in sexual intercourse and in the public world existed together. "The personal is the political," liberationists declared, and to oppress one is to oppress the other; conversely, for a woman to change her life is a political act.

Another radical, Dana Densmore, said that women should not be criticized for celibacy—it can be rewarding, she insisted, and in any event, the craving for sex often comes from a consumer economy that uses it to sell goods. Although she did not advocate celibacy, she called it an honorable alternative, declaring: "It is only when we accept the idea of celibacy completely that we will ever be able to liberate ourselves."

In 1970, feminists, radical and otherwise, confronted men in several high-profile actions: a sit-in at the *Ladies' Home Journal* to demand a free day-care center and the end to exploitive advertisements; protests and suits by female workers at *Newsweek* and *Time;* and a demonstration against radio station WBCN in Boston for running an employment ad with the statement, "If you're a chick, we need typists."

These and other protests caused a backlash among conservative men and women, especially after NOW and radical groups pushed for an equal rights amendment to the Constitution. Nevertheless, the assault against male domination continued through demonstrations, boycotts, and lawsuits, and many oppressive practices came to an end. For example, corporations and colleges hired more women as professionals and revised their procedures for promotions, states changed their abortion laws, and more women ran for public office. To radicals, the gains—mainly illusory, they said—paled in comparison to the continuing exploitive, bourgeois system; to feminists, the gains—while incomplete—had been notable.

See also Friedan, Betty; Morgan, Robin; Redstockings; SCUM; Steinem, Gloria.

References Brown, Elaine, *A Taste of Power: A Black Woman's Story* (1992); Echols, Alice, *Daring To Be Bad: Radical Feminism in America, 1967–1975* (1989); Evans, Sara, *Personal Politics: The Roots of Women's Liberation in the Civil Rights Movement and the New Left* (1980); Farber, David, ed., *The Sixties: From Memory to History* (1994); Goodman, Mitchell, ed., *The Movement toward a New America: The Beginnings of a Long Revolution* (1970); Morgan, Robin, *Going Too Far: The Personal Chronicle of a Feminist* (1977); Tanner, Leslie B., ed., *Voices from Women's Liberation* (1970).

Women's Strike for Equality

Proclaiming "Don't Iron While the Strike Is Hot," the National Organization of Women (NOW) sponsored a nationwide Women's Strike for Equality that intended to build support in Congress for an equal rights amendment to the Constitution, spotlight discriminatory practices against women in the workplace, and promote equal educational opportunities, day-care centers, and abortion rights.

NOW targeted 26 August 1970 for the strike (a notable anniversary date in the successful fight for women's suffrage) and urged women to leave their jobs that day, give up their household chores, and demonstrate. Protesters appeared in nearly every major city and many smaller ones, often in substantial numbers. Thousands marched in Boston, San Francisco, Los Angeles, Washington, and Chicago. The largest demonstration occurred in New York City, when 40,000 joined activist Betty Friedan in a march down Fifth Avenue and heard another leader declare: "Today is the beginning of a new movement." (Anderson 1995, 359)

Although the strike caused conservatives to criticize the demonstrators as extremists who threatened family values—much as they labeled everything else emanating from the counterculture—women felt solidarity, Congress began considering an equal rights amendment (never ratified by the states), businesses and government agencies started rethinking their discriminatory practices, and NOW and other organizations, encouraged and strengthened, filed lawsuits against corporations that had been violating the 1963 Equal Pay Act.

See also Friedan, Betty; Morgan, Robin; Steinem, Gloria; Women's Movement.

Reference Anderson, Terry H., *The Movement and the Sixties* (1995).

Woodstock

"An Aquarian Exposition in Wallkill, New York," proclaimed an ad in an underground newspaper, the *Miami Daily Planet*, in its 4 August 1969 edition (17). "Three Days of Peace and Music" at "The Woodstock Music and Art Fair." The ad promised appearances by over 20 performers, among them Joan Baez, Arlo Guthrie, Canned Heat, Jefferson Airplane, the Who, the Grateful Dead, and Jimi Hendrix. And it promised an art show ("paintings and sculpture on trees, on grass, surrounded by the beautiful Hudson Valley"), a crafts bazaar ("You'll see imaginative leather, ceramic, bead and silver creations, as well as Zodiac Charts, camp clothes, and worn out shoes"), work shops ("if you like playing with beads, or improvising on a guitar, or writing poetry, or molding clay, stop by . . . and see what you can give and take"), food ("there will be cokes and hot dogs and dozens of curious . . . combinations"), and "hundreds of acres to roam on."

Woodstock went down in history as more than a rock and art festival—it personified counterculture ideals, an idyllic interlude that the *New York Times* called "a phenomenon of innocence." (Ward, Stokes, and Tucker 1986, 431)

Woodstock followed large pop festivals in Monterey, California; Atlanta, Georgia; Seattle, Washington; and Atlantic City, New Jersey. When the promoters started putting Woodstock together, they expected to attract about 100,000 people over three days and make money, a considerable amount, by selling tickets at $18 each and by filming the event for release as a motion picture. Originally scheduled for Wallkill, opposition from the townspeople there forced the festival's relocation to

Two people take a nap on the back of a car as thousands of people descend upon Bethel, New York, the site of the Woodstock Festival in 1969.

nearby Bethel. For $50,000, the promoters leased 600 acres of land owned by a local farmer, Max Yasgur.

Woodstock quickly exceeded everyone's expectations. On 14 August, the day before the festival began, cars jammed the New York Thruway, immobilizing everyone. Young people left their Day-Glo VW vans and walked miles to the site, long hair flowing over their shoulders, guitar and tambourine music arising from instruments they carried. So many people arrived that the promoters had to let everyone in.

The music paled in importance to the crowd. Little security existed, practically no police, and the masses overwhelmed Bethel, where, for the most part, residents graciously provided food and water. As the crowd reached 500,000, mainstream newspapers predicted a catastrophe, with violence and deaths worse than could be found in the cities. Violence, though, never erupted—not even a fistfight—despite food shortages, an overwhelmed medical staff, and inadequate toilet facilities. Young people frolicked naked in the woods and in a lake, consumed drugs, listened to the music, and when thunderstorms struck and turned the area into a muddy mess, they huddled together. "For many participants," says historian Terry H. Anderson in *The Movement and the Sixties*, "the growing sense of community turned this rock festival into an unforgettable countercultural experience." (278) Or, as one young man observed: "It was like balling for the first time." (277)

Of course, a few serious problems marred Woodstock: bad drug trips, dehydration, injuries, and even three deaths—two related to drugs, one to a tractor accident. On the other hand, there occurred three births and who knows how many conceptions, and when the marijuana haze had cleared and the concert ended, the fact remained that 500,000 people had come together peacefully. Perhaps, some dreamt, a counterculture could supersede the old, violence-torn society. Then, the Manson murders and, a few weeks later, the disastrous concert at Altamont, California, ended the dream.

See also Altamont; Manson, Charles.

References Anderson, Terry H., *The Movement and the Sixties* (1995); Curry, Jack, *Woodstock: The Summer of Our Lives* (1989); Makower, Joel, *Woodstock: The Oral History* (1989); Santelli, Robert, *Aquarius Rising: The Rock Festival Years* (1980); Spitz, Bob, *Barefoot in Babylon: The Creation of the Woodstock Music Festival, 1969* (1979); Ward, Ed, Geoffrey Stokes, and Ken Tucker, *Rock of Ages: The Rolling Stone History of Rock & Roll* (1986); Young, Jean, and Michael Lang, *Woodstock Festival Remembered* (1979).

Work

The counterculture rebelled against traditional attitudes toward work. Many youths objected to the regimentation in the corporate jobs that dominated the nation's economy: the eight-to-five routine; the uniform white shirt, jacket, and tie (for men, of course, since so few women were allowed to hold these jobs); the impersonal atmosphere.

In reaction, some young people who held corporate jobs initiated a mild rebellion: flexible work hours, weakened dress regulations, more input from lower-level workers. Others took a more extreme tact, a truly countercultural one, and rejected mainstream work routines altogether; they lived as hippies and emphasized pursuing the meaning of life over making money, cultivating gardens in their heads and souls rather than mowing lawns around a suburban house. Although hippies never constituted more than a minority, they represented a new mentality, as evident in opinion surveys at colleges that showed a widespread disdain for material pursuit.

Some hippies shunned work completely, but most labored—they farmed, pursued crafts, or opened shops and other alternative businesses. New work habits appeared in communes, collectives, and the back-to-the-earth movement. Writing in *The Making of a Counterculture*, Theodore Roszak summarizes the driving force behind the countercultural attitude when he says that to its followers "building the good society is not primarily social, but a psychic task. What makes the youthful disaffiliation of our time a cultural phenomenon . . . is the fact that it strikes beyond ideology to the level of consciousness, seeking to transform our deepest sense of the self, the other, the environment." (49)

See also Back-to-the Earth Movement; Commune; Hippies.

Reference Roszak, Theodore, *The Making of a Counterculture: Reflections on the Technocratic Society and Its Youthful Opposition* (1968).

Work Shirt

New Left political activists often wore plain-looking blue work shirts to show their unity with the working class and with poor farmers. The shirts were especially popular among whites who joined the Student Nonviolent Coordinating Committee in its civil rights efforts. Work shirts were worn with denim jackets, jeans, or bib overalls.

Yippies

The Yippies began as a joke and ended up using street theatre techniques to expose straight society's absurdities and stimulate radical reform.

The idea for the Yippies emerged on New Year's Eve 1967 when Abbie Hoffman and his wife Anita, Jerry Rubin, Nancy Kurshan, and Paul Krassner gathered at Hoffman's apartment in New York City to smoke pot and have a good time. They started talking about putting together an event, some sort of protest, to be held at the Democratic National Convention in Chicago that coming August. Hoffman believed the under-30 generation needed something to watch and participate in that would transcend politics and speeches. He began talking about a Festival of Life juxtaposed with what he called the Convention of Death. When Krassner reacted to this idea by pointing out how, in making a peace sign to form a V, the arm extended beneath really made it a Y, others in the group started shouting "Eye! Eye!," then "Pee! Pee!," and finally "Yippie!"—inadvertently concocting the new group's name.

In order to satisfy the mainstream press as to what Yippie meant, Anita Hoffman, or perhaps Paul Krassner—the stories contradict—contrived an officious-sounding title: Youth International Party. In January 1968, the Yippies began promoting their Chicago protest, releasing a call through the Liberation News Service: "Come all you rebels, youth spirits, rock minstrels, truth seekers, peacock freaks, poets, barricade jumpers, dancers, lovers, artisans." (Farber 1988, 17) Hoffman cranked out flyers, posters, and 50,000 buttons bearing the word "Yippie!" in pink psychedelic letters against a purple background. Rubin explained the reason for the festival/protest: since it was hard to reach people with words, the Yippies would do it with emotion. Writing in *Revolution for the Hell of It*, Hoffman claims the Yippies had four main objectives:

> 1. The blending of pot and politics into a political grass leaves movement—a cross-fertilization of the hippie and New Left philosophies
> 2. A connecting link that would tie together as much of the underground as was willing into some gigantic national get-together
> 3. The development of a model for an alternative society
> 4. The need to make some statement, especially in action-theater terms, about LBJ [President Johnson], the Democratic Party, electoral politics, and the state of the nation. (Albert and Albert 1984, 421)

By March 1968, small Yippie groups had appeared in Washington, Philadelphia, Boston, Berkeley, San Francisco, Los Angeles, and Chicago. The New York City Yippies opened their meetings to anyone who wanted to come, and they held them at their office, at nearby Free University, and outdoors at Union Square. As they planned for Chicago, friction developed between Hoffman, who wanted only outrageous acts and fun, and Rubin, who wanted political content. Nevertheless, the planning continued, and the Yippies decided that in order to get needed recognition and to show their true colors, they would hold several pre-Chicago events.

So in March, the Yippies announced a Yip-in at Grand Central Station—a party and celebration with minimal planning. More than 5,000 people turned out, but police, unprovoked, attacked the revelers with clubs, sending Hoffman and several others to the hospital with bloodied heads.

As Chicago approached and it appeared the authorities would use force to prevent any demonstrations, the Yippies encountered opposition from New Left organizations that took their politics seriously.

Two Yippies celebrate the Yip-out, a gathering dedicated to the "resurrection of the free," which drew close to 20,000 people to Central Park's Sheep Meadow on 14 April 1968.

Students for a Democratic Society called the Yippies irresponsible, and stated that the group's "intention to bring thousands of young people to Chicago during the DNC [Democratic National Convention] to groove on rock bands and smoke grass and then put them up against bayonets—viewing that as a radicalizing experience—seems manipulative at best." (Farber 1988, 33) The National Mobilization Committee To End the War in Vietnam, or MOBE, the largest organization behind the political protests at Chicago, objected to the Yippies' plan, fearing it would detract from any antiwar message.

With all the disagreements and, added to them, the assassinations of Martin Luther King, Jr. and Robert Kennedy, Hoffman considered canceling the Festival of Life. In *Revolution for the Hell of It*, Hoffman writes that "Yippie . . . hovered close to death somewhere between the 50/50 state of Andy Warhol and the 0/0 state of Bobby Kennedy." (Albert and Albert 1984, 424)

After deciding to continue, the Yippies tweaked the media and Chicago's hard-nosed mayor, Richard Daley, by announcing plans to drop LSD in the city's water supply; have Yippies dress up like Vietcong, hijack the Chicago office of Nabisco, and distribute free cookies; and rally young people to run naked through the streets. Perhaps the highlight for the Yippies occurred on 23 August, the Friday before the Convention opened. Marching in front of the Chicago Civic Center, Jerry Rubin introduced the Yippie presidential nominee: Pigasus, a 200-pound pig they had bought from a farmer. Rubin declared: "They nominate a president and he eats the people. We nominate a president and the people eat him." (Anderson 1995, 221) The police had other ideas, however, and they confiscated Pigasus and arrested Rubin. (The Yippies could only laugh at "pigs" corralling a pig!)

As for the Festival of Life, violence swallowed it whole. After the Yippies tried to stage a rock concert at Lincoln Park on Sunday night, only to find the police opposing them and strictly enforcing an 11:00 P.M. curfew, a melee broke out. Other violent episodes erupted during the succeeding nights as militant radicals battled angry cops.

Early in 1969, the federal government indicted Hoffman, Rubin, and six others, including officials with MOBE, for conspiring to riot. Known as the Chicago Eight, they were found guilty of rioting (although not of engaging in conspiracy), but a higher court overturned their convictions.

See also Chicago Eight; Democratic National Convention of 1968; Hoffman, Abbie; Krassner, Paul; National Mobilization Committee To End the War in Vietnam; Rubin, Jerry.

References Albert, Judith Clavir, and Stewart Edward Albert, eds., *The Sixties Papers: Documents of a Rebellious Decade* (1984); Anderson, Terry H., *The Movement and the Sixties* (1995); Farber, David, *Chicago '68* (1988); Hoffman, Abbie, *Revolution for the Hell of It* (1968); Rubin, Jerry, *Do It! Scenarios of the Revolution* (1970).

Young, Neil (1945–)

As a solo performer and with the groups Buffalo Springfield and Crosby, Stills, Nash, and Young, Neil Young helped define rock in the counterculture, reflecting the era's concern with social issues and introspection, which he presented in a style infused with haunting, poetical lyrics. As a result he ranked, and remains ranked, among the most influential musicians in rock music history.

Born on 12 November 1945 in Toronto, Canada, Young grew up in Winnipeg. As a teenager, he listened on the radio to Bill Haley and Elvis Presley and played the ukulele before getting an acoustic guitar. As with many young people in the early 1960s, folk music attracted him, and he started performing at coffeehouses in Winnipeg and Toronto. Soon, he organized a folk-rock band called the Squires.

Young moved to Los Angeles in 1966, hoping to pursue a solo career, but ran into his Canadian friend Stephen Stills, another aspiring musician, who persuaded him to join a new group, Buffalo Springfield. Known for its country-rock sound, over its two-year existence the band recorded some of Young's greatest songs—"On the Way Home," "Broken Arrow," "Expecting To Fly," "Mr. Soul," "I Am a Child"—along with "For What Its Worth" that chronicled the confrontations then under way between hippies and police in Los Angeles along Sunset Strip.

Young did not like the constraints that came from playing with a group, however, and later said this caused Buffalo Springfield's demise. "I'd do what they wanted with their stuff," he said, "but I needed more space with my own. And that was a constant problem in my head. So that's why I had to quit. . . . I just wasn't mature enough to deal with it. Everything was going much too fast." (Crow 1979, 41)

Young again went solo, but at the same time joined Stills, along with David Crosby and Graham Nash, in forming Crosby, Stills, Nash, and Young (CSN&Y). In mid-1969, Young released two albums, *Neil Young* and *Everybody Knows This Is Nowhere*. For the latter, he used as backup Crazy Horse, a band whose members he had met during his first six months in Los Angeles. Over the years, they collaborated with him on his most successful records. Young's third solo album, *After the Gold Rush*, released in 1970, earned widespread acclaim and included "Only Love Can Break Your Heart," "Southern Man," and "I Believe in You." In these, he attracted listeners through his evocative imagery. That same year, he collaborated on a highly successful CSN&Y album, *Deja Vu*.

Young recorded another album with CSN&Y in 1971, *Four Way Street*, and it went gold. A year later, another solo album, *Harvest*, included "Old Man," "War Song," and "Heart of Gold"—a number one single and since that time a rock classic.

As the counterculture faded, Young's music took many different turns. In 1973, he released *Zuma*, an intense, brooding work, while his 1978 album, *Comes a Time*, exhibited folk and country arrangements.

For a time in the 1980s, he used a computerized vocal recorder that distorted his voice, but this experimentation disappointed his fans. In 1989, *Freedom*, his comeback album, sold well. *Harvest Moon* in 1992 proved even more successful and represented a return to acoustic work. In 1995, Young teamed with the grunge band Pearl Jam and recorded *Mirror Ball;* the following year, he rejoined Crazy Horse for *Broken Arrow*.

Many new rock musicians idolized Young in the mid-1990s as the progenitor of grunge and other alternative music—they learned from the feedback style he used on guitar with its rough, ragged edge and from his lyrics. In 1996, Young and Crazy Horse staged a national tour.

See also Buffalo Springfield; Rock Music.

Reference Crow, Cameron, "Neil Young: The Last American Hero," *Rolling Stone*, 8 February 1979, 41–46.

Z

Zappa, Frank (1940–1993)

An innovative rock musician with a keen business sense, Frank Zappa produced music that some critics labeled as nothing more than a cacophonous put-on and that others hailed as cutting-edge material.

Born on 21 December 1940 in Baltimore, Maryland, Zappa grew up in California, living in small towns near Los Angeles. At Antelope High School in Lancaster, from which he graduated in 1958, he played guitar and put together his first band, the Black Outs. In 1960, he played music in cocktail lounges and made an appearance on the Steve Allen television show, where he performed what he called a "bicycle concerto," plucking spokes and blowing through handlebars.

After that, his music got, if at all possible, more curious. In 1964, he formed the Mothers of Invention, a band that represented the emerging counterculture's freak artistic fringe. In many ways, the Mothers' experiments echoed avant-garde developments then under way in the theatre, such as with the San Francisco Mime Troupe, and the arts, such as with fluxus. When the Mothers appeared on stage they mixed music with performance; for example, mutilating dolls, or leaving the audience to wonder about long intervals of silence and inaction while the band members stood on stage and stared at them. The music itself rejected standard formulas and can best be described as jazz mixed with rock and free-form noises, for example, feedback through amplifiers (a reason, perhaps, that the Mothers never had a hit single).

The Mothers attracted large audiences and produced several albums in the late 1960s that contained satirical songs slamming society's conformist commercialism. As the decade ended, the Mothers disbanded, but Zappa founded his own record company that released works by other alternative musicians, and in 1972 a nine-disk set, *The Story of the Mothers.*

Zappa continued to experiment in the late 1970s, trying to merge rock with classical music, reviving the Mothers for several more albums, and producing a movie, *200 Motels.* The following decade found him producing more music for himself, his daughter, and various groups, and earning national attention for his stand against legislation to require labels on record albums warning about offensive lyrics. Zappa died on 4 December 1993 in Los Angeles from prostate cancer, his bizarre satire remembered as another manifestation of counterculture desires to challenge conventional standards.

See also Rock Music.

Zen Buddhism

Largely Taoist in content, Zen Buddhism developed in ancient China and later Japan from a combination of Mahayana Buddhism and Taoism. Zen emphasizes obtaining a state where the mind breaks free of conventional beliefs, sees the self as part of an undifferentiated whole merged with the universe, and has no grasping thoughts. Such freedom comes from contemplation and immediate insights, as opposed to gradual practice.

With its mysticism and its emphasis on the spontaneous and intuitive rather than the objective and rational, Zen had a strong following among hippies and others in the counterculture—it seemed to offer an alternative to a mainstream society immersed in war and materialism and to a Christianity that had lost its spirituality. Zen's main proponent, Alan Watts, called it "a way and a view of life" and claimed it defied any classification.

See also I Ching; Watts, Alan.

Zinn, Howard (1922–)

A leftist historian, Howard Zinn influenced political activists in the counterculture with his writings and his work in the civil rights and antiwar movements.

Zinn was born on 24 August 1922 in New York City, the son of Edward Zinn and Jenny Rabinowitz Zinn. He obtained his doctorate in history from Columbia University in 1958, shortly after he had begun teaching at Spelman College, a black school, in Atlanta, Georgia. As a civil rights activist, he joined the Student Nonviolent Coordinating Committee (SNCC) in the 1960s, an organization committed to direct action and one that attracted many African American college students who considered the more mainstream civil rights groups too moderate.

Zinn participated in SNCC's program to register black voters in the South and in 1964 wrote *SNCC: The New Abolitionists*. In this book Zinn hails SNCC as dedicated to change without any "pretense of martyrdom." SNCC, he believes, exhibits an existential character, an "emotional approach to life, aiming, beyond politics and economics, simply to remove the barriers that prevent human beings from making contact with one another." (Gitlin 1987, 165)

This romantic image appealed to the emerging counterculture that sought not only social justice but also a society freed from the technological coldness that had gripped it. Zinn's book influenced young whites to join SNCC, at least until the organization decided to restrict its leadership positions only to blacks.

The antiwar movement attracted Zinn, too, and he made his most notable contribution in this area when, in 1968, he and Daniel Berrigan traveled to North Vietnam to assist in getting three American prisoners of war released. Shortly before, he had stated his antiwar argument in *Vietnam: The Logic of Withdrawal* and had moved to Massachusetts, where he taught in the political science department at Boston University.

In the late 1970s, Zinn wrote his influential *A People's History of the United States* that recast America's past by presenting a sweeping picture from the standpoint of society's underclass—Indians, blacks, women, the poor, immigrants, and laborers. Zinn revised the book for a second edition, published in 1995.

See also Berrigan, Daniel; Student Nonviolent Coordinating Committee.

References Gitlin, Todd, *The Sixties: Years of Hope, Days of Rage* (1987); Zinn, Howard, *SNCC: The New Abolitionists* (1964) and *Vietnam: The Logic of Withdrawal* (1967).

Chronology

1960 **(January)** John F. Kennedy, Democratic senator from Massachusetts, announces his candidacy for the presidency.

Under Al Haber's guidance, Students for a Democratic Society organizes as a New Left group.

(February) Black college students in Greensboro, North Carolina, stage a sit-in to desegregate a Woolworth's lunch counter, thus intensifying direct action in the civil rights movement and providing an important stimulant to the counterculture.

(May) The recently organized Student Nonviolent Coordinating Committee (SNCC) opens an office in Atlanta, beginning its formal entry into the civil rights movement.

President Eisenhower signs the Civil Rights Act of 1960 into law.

Federal Drug Administration approves the first birth-control pill, Envoid, as safe for use, thus contributing to the development of the sexual revolution.

(July) John F. Kennedy is nominated for president at the Democratic National Convention.

Vice-President Richard M. Nixon is nominated for president at the Republican National Convention.

(August) Harvard psychologist Timothy Leary tries a psilocybin mushroom in Mexico.

(September) Presidential campaign debate between Kennedy and Nixon is the first to be televised.

(November) Kennedy is elected president, defeating Nixon by a narrow margin.

1961 **(January)** Kennedy is inaugurated as president.

Bob Dylan plays at the Cafe Wha?, a coffeehouse in Greenwich Village.

(March) President Kennedy issues an executive order creating the Peace Corps.

(April) Soviet cosmonaut Yuri Gagarin becomes the first man to orbit earth.

The United States launches an abortive invasion of Communist Cuba by Cuban exiles who are supplied and directed by American officials.

(May) Freedom Riders board buses and challenge segregation laws in the South.

(August) East Germany closes its border at Berlin and begins building a wall to partition the city.

1961 *cont.* **(October)** Joseph Heller's *Catch-22* is published.

1962 **(February)** Ken Kesey's *One Flew over the Cuckoo's Nest* is published.

John Glenn becomes the first American to orbit earth.

(March) Bob Dylan's first record album, self-titled, appears.

(April) Cesar Chavez begins organizing the Farm Workers Association in California to unite migrant farmworkers.

(June) The Beatles sign with Parlophone Records—their first recording contract.

Students for a Democratic Society (SDS) holds its first national convention at Port Huron, Michigan, and writes the Port Huron Statement.

(November) Andy Warhol holds his first major show of paintings in New York City.

(December) Over 11,000 U.S. military personnel in South Vietnam.

1963 **(February)** Betty Friedan's *The Feminine Mystique* is published.

(April) Martin Luther King, Jr. leads a campaign against segregation in Birmingham, Alabama, that results in Sheriff Bull Connor setting police dogs on the demonstrators.

(June) Civil rights worker Medgar Evers is murdered in Mississippi.

Timothy Leary and Richard Alpert are fired by Harvard in a controversy over their LSD experiments involving students; Leary begins his LSD sessions at Millbrook, New York.

(August) A massive civil rights march on Washington includes Martin Luther King, Jr.'s "I Have a Dream" speech.

(November) President Kennedy is assassinated in Dallas, Texas; Lyndon Johnson assumes office.

Kennedy's alleged assassin, Lee Harvey Oswald, is shot and killed by Jack Ruby.

Aldous Huxley, author and a pioneer in mescaline and LSD exploration, dies.

1964 **(January)** President Johnson announces his war on poverty.

(February) The Beatles make their first appearance in the United States with a performance on the *Ed Sullivan Show*; their song "I Want To Hold Your Hand" reaches number one on the charts.

(April) A march on Washington against the war in Vietnam attracts thousands of young people.

(July) President Johnson signs the 1964 Civil Rights Act into law.

(August) The Gulf of Tonkin resolution, which gives President Johnson a "blank check" to fight the war in Vietnam, passes the Senate.

The Mississippi Freedom Democratic Party is denied seating at the Democratic National Convention; Lyndon Johnson is chosen by the delegates as their party's nominee for president.

Bodies of three civil rights workers are found in Philadelphia, Mississippi.

(October) The Free Speech Movement erupts at the University of California-Berkeley, igniting protests at other campuses and beginning a national student movement.

(November) Lyndon Johnson defeats Republican Barry Goldwater in a landslide to win the presidency.

1965 **(February)** President Johnson orders bombing raids on North Vietnam.

(**March**) Civil rights worker Viola Liuzzo is murdered in Lowndes County, Alabama.

The first teach-in to protest the Vietnam War is held at the University of Michigan and followed within days by others at colleges across the nation.

(**June**) The Red Dog Saloon opens and brings psychedelia to Virginia City, Nevada.

(**July**) The Rolling Stones song "Satisfaction" reaches number one on the charts.

Bob Dylan appears on stage with an electric guitar at the Newport Folk Festival.

(**August**) Riots sweep through Watts, a ghetto in Los Angeles, and start a white backlash.

Ken Kesey has the Hell's Angels take LSD at his home in La Honda, California.

(**November**) Bill Graham stages his first benefit to raise money for the San Francisco Mime Troupe.

1966 (**January**) Young people flock to the acid-laced three-day Trips Festival in San Francisco.

The Psychedelic Shop opens in Haight-Ashbury.

(**February**) Bill Graham begins staging rock dance concerts at the Fillmore in San Francisco.

Chet Helms begins staging rock shows at San Francisco's Avalon Ballroom.

(**June**) Civil rights worker James Meredith is wounded by a sniper on a march near Hernando, Mississippi.

Stokely Carmichael demands "black power."

(**July**) Blacks riot in Chicago, Brooklyn, and Cleveland.

(**September**) The *San Francisco Oracle* makes its first appearance under that name.

(**October**) U.S. troops in Vietnam now exceed 320,000.

Hippies in Haight-Ashbury stage the Love Pageant.

The Black Panthers are founded in Oakland, California, where they proclaim a militant ten-point program.

1967 (**January**) The Human Be-In is held in San Francisco.

David Harris organizes The Resistance to protest the draft and the Vietnam War.

(**March**) The *Berkeley Barb* prints a rumor about how smoking banana peels can make a person high.

(**June**) The Summer of Love begins in San Francisco's Haight-Ashbury district.

Sgt. Pepper's Lonely Hearts Club Band is released, a Beatles album that revolutionizes rock 'n' roll.

Jimi Hendrix makes his American debut at the Monterey Pop Festival.

(**August**) Stokely Carmichael appears at a conference in Havana, Cuba, and calls for a black revolution.

The Om Festival in San Francisco attracts thousands.

Bonnie and Clyde, directed by Arthur Penn, appears in theatres.

(**September**) American level in Vietnam reaches 464,000.

(**October**) *Rolling Stone* magazine appears as a commercialized offshoot of the underground press.

The March on the Pentagon, coordinated by MOBE, attracts 100,000 protesters.

1967 *cont.* **(December)** *The Graduate*, directed by Mike Nichols and starring Dustin Hoffman, is released.

The Yippies organize and decide to demonstrate at the Democratic National Convention.

1968 **(January)** The Vietcong's Tet Offensive makes it clear that the United States is far from victory in Vietnam.

(March) Peace candidate Eugene McCarthy comes in second to Lyndon Johnson in the New Hampshire Democratic presidential primary but gets most of the delegates, thus stunning the political establishment; as a result, President Johnson announces he will not seek reelection.

(April) Martin Luther King, Jr. is assassinated in Memphis, Tennessee, and, in reaction, riots break out in several ghettos, the worst in Washington, D.C.

Student protesters take over several buildings at Columbia University.

Hair opens on Broadway.

(May) Norman Mailer's *Armies of the Night* is published.

Daniel and Philip Berrigan destroy files at the Selective Service office in Cantonsville, Maryland.

(June) Andy Warhol is shot by radical feminist Valerie Solanas.

Robert Kennedy is assassinated in Los Angeles after winning the California Democratic presidential primary.

(August) Richard Nixon obtains the Republican presidential nomination.

Riots erupt at the Democratic National Convention in Chicago as police assault demonstrators and passersby; Hubert Humphrey is nominated for the presidency.

(September) The women's liberation movement emerges with a protest outside the Miss America Pageant in Atlantic City, New Jersey.

(November) Richard Nixon defeats Hubert Humphrey to win the presidency in a close election.

The Third World Strike at San Francisco State College pits student militants against a hard-nosed conservative president.

1969 **(January)** U.S. troop strength in Vietnam peaks at 542,000.

(March) Kurt Vonnegut's *Slaughter-house Five* is published.

(April) Jack Kerouac dies at his mother's home in St. Petersburg, Florida.

(May) The fight for People's Park begins in Berkeley, California.

John Lennon and Yoko Ono begin their "bed-in" for peace in Montreal.

(July) Rolling Stone Brian Jones drowns in his swimming pool in a drug-related death.

President Nixon announces the first American troop withdrawals from Vietnam.

Neil Armstrong and Buzz Aldrin become the first human beings to walk on the moon.

Easy Rider, starring Dennis Hopper, Peter Fonda, and Jack Nicholson, premieres.

(August) Charles Manson and his gang commit the Tate-LaBianca murders in Los Angeles.

The Woodstock rock festival is held near Bethel, New York, attracting over 500,000 young people.

(September) The Chicago Eight conspiracy trial begins.

(October) Weatherman launches its revolutionary Days of Rage in Chicago.

Hundreds of thousands of Americans participate in Vietnam Moratorium Day.

(November) Indian protesters occupy Alcatraz Island in San Francisco Bay.

Lieutenant William Calley is charged with the multiple murders of civilians at a village in South Vietnam.

(December) The Altamont rock concert near San Francisco turns violent when the Hell's Angels go berserk.

Chicago police kill Black Panther leader Freddie Hampton.

1970 **(February)** A jury acquits seven of the Chicago Eight of conspiracy charges but finds five of the defendants guilty of individual acts of incitement to riot.

Protesters attack and burn a branch of the Bank of America in Isla Vista, California.

(March) Four Weathermen are killed when they accidentally detonate a bomb in their New York City town house.

(April) The first Earth Day is held as the environmental movement gains widespread support.

The Beatles officially announce their breakup.

(May) President Nixon announces that he has sent American troops into Cambodia.

National Guardsmen fire at and kill unarmed student protesters at Kent State University in Ohio; as protests escalate, National Guard troops are stationed on 21 college campuses in 16 states.

Police kill two students and wound several others at Jackson State University, a black college in Mississippi.

(August) Radicals detonate a bomb at the University of Wisconsin, injuring three people and killing one.

(September) U.S. troop strength in Vietnam falls below 400,000.

Timothy Leary escapes from prison.

Jimi Hendrix dies of a drug overdose in London.

(October) Janis Joplin dies of a drug overdose in Hollywood, California.

1971 **(January)** Charles Manson and three of his followers are found guilty of murder in the Tate-LaBianca slayings.

(March) In a court-martial, Lieutenant Calley is found guilty of the murder of at least 20 Vietnamese civilians.

(April) About 200,000 veterans march in Washington, D.C., against the Vietnam War.

(May) Mass arrests of antiwar demonstrators in Washington, D.C., reach 12,000 in a three-day period.

(June) The *New York Times* publishes the classified Pentagon Papers, which reveal the government's deceit in the Vietnam War.

(July) Jim Morrison, lead singer of the Doors, dies of heart failure in Paris, France.

1972 **(February)** President Nixon visits communist China.

(April) The federal government fails to get a conviction of Reverend Philip F. Berrigan on a charge of plotting to kidnap Secretary of State Henry Kissinger.

(May) George Wallace is shot and wounded while campaigning at a rally in Maryland during his quest for the presidency.

1972 *cont.* **(June)** Angela Davis is acquitted by an all-white jury of murder, kidnapping, and criminal conspiracy.

Burglars break into the Democratic National Headquarters at the Watergate complex in Washington.

(November) Richard Nixon is reelected president in a landslide, defeating Democratic candidate George McGovern.

1973 **(February)** The U.S. Senate establishes a select committee to investigate the Watergate break-in.

A confrontation occurs between the American Indian Movement and the federal government at Wounded Knee in South Dakota.

(March) The last U.S. combat troops are withdrawn from Vietnam.

Bibliography

Articles

"An Audience with Charles Manson, aka Jesus Christ." *Rolling Stone*, 25 June 1970, 35+.

Buckley, Tom. "Young Rebels Set Up Own Community in Jersey." *New York Times*, 26 August 1968, 41.

Burks, John. "An Appreciation." *Rolling Stone*, 15 October 1970, 8.

_____. "In the County of Dade." *Rolling Stone*, 5 April 1969, 1, 6.

Campbell, Elizabeth. "Easy Rider." *Rolling Stone*, 6 September 1969, 18–20.

Carney, Leigh. "Hair Rock." *Rolling Stone*, 7 December 1968, 21.

Cott, Jonathan. "Van Morrison." *Rolling Stone*, 30 November 1978, 50–54.

Crow, Cameron. "Neil Young: The Last American Hero." *Rolling Stone*, 8 February 1979, 41–46.

Didion, Joan. "Slouching toward Bethlehem." *Saturday Evening Post*, 23 September 1967, 25–31+.

Donahue, Tommy. "Easy Rider." *Miami Daily Planet*, 24 October 1969.

Ebert, Roger. "Easy Rider." *Cinemania 1996*, Microsoft Corporation, 1995.

Findley, Tim. "Tom Hayden Rolling Stone Interview Part 1." *Rolling Stone*, 26 October 1972, 36–50.

_____. "Tom Hayden Rolling Stone Interview Part 2." *Rolling Stone*, 9 November 1972, 28–34.

Gates, Henry Louis, Jr. "After the Revolution." *New Yorker*, 29 April/6 May 1996, 59–61.

Gilmore, Mikhail. "Jerry Garcia." *Rolling Stone*, 21 September 1995, 44+.

Gitlin, Todd. "1968: The Two Popular Cultures." *Spectator*, Spring 1988, 8–17.

Gleason, Ralph. "Theater Dead, Tommy Lives." *Rolling Stone*, 23 July 1970, 8.

Grissim, John, Jr. "Joan Baez." *Rolling Stone*, 7 December 1968, 12–14.

Handelman, David. "Abbie Hoffman." *Rolling Stone*, 1 June 1989, 49.

Hopkins, Jerry. "Tiny Tim." *Rolling Stone*, 6 July 1968, 15–17.

"In Search of the Miami Scene." *Miami Free Press/Daily Planet*, 18 July 1969.

"J. R. R. Tolkien: Lord of the Middle Earth." *Rolling Stone*, 11 October 1973, 8–9.

"Jimi." *Rolling Stone*, 15 October 1970, 1, 6–8.

Kael, Pauline. "Bonnie and Clyde." *Cinemania 1996*, Microsoft Corporation, 1995.

_____. "Midnight Cowboy." *Cinemania 1996*, Microsoft Corporation, 1995.

Kemp, Dan. "I Ching." *Rolling Stone*, 9 July 1970, 17.

Loder, Kurt. "Andy Warhol, 1928–1987." *Rolling Stone*, 9 April 1987, 31–33, 35–36.

Marine, Gene. "Alan Watts, 1915–1973." *Rolling Stone*, 20 December 1973, 20–21.

Masters, R. E. L. "Sex, Ecstasy, and the Psychdelic Drugs." November 1967. Available from Internet: http://www.hyperreal.com/psychedelics/. (Cited 15 March 1997).

Mehren, Elizabeth. "Radicals of '60s Preserve the Spirit." *Eugene (Oregon) Register-Guard*, 6 August 1995, 1, 4.

"1960s Highlights—Colorful Television." *Time Almanac of the 20th Century*. Softkey International, 1995.

"1960s Highlights—Fashion." *Time Almanac of the 20th Century*. Softkey International, 1995.

"1960s Highlights—Folk and Rock Music." *Time Almanac of the 20th Century*. Softkey International, 1995.

"Om United Nude Brigade." *Rolling Stone*, 23 July 1970, 8.

"An Open Letter to the Dade County Youth Grand Jury." *Miami Free Press/Daily Planet*, 2 July 1969, 27.

Pace, Eric. "Mario Savio, Protest Leader Who Set a Style, Dies at 53." *New York Times*, 8 November 1996, C21.

Pollak, Sally. "When Communes Were Common." *Burlington Free Press*, 13 August 1995, D1.

Sager, Mike. "Joan Baez." *Rolling Stone*, 5 November–10 December 1987, 163–164.

"The Sexual Revolution." *Time Almanac of the 2oth Century*. Softkey International, 1995.

Smith, Giles. "The Beatles' Straight Man." *New Yorker*, 20 November 1995, 84–90.

"The South: Death in Two Cities." *Time*, 25 May 1970, 22–23.

Stern, Michael. "Teen-Age Revolt: Is It Deeper Today?" *New York Times*, 7 October 1968, 49, 67.

Books

Ackroyd, Peter. *Blake*. New York: Knopf, 1995.

Acuna, Rodolfo. *Occupied America: A History of Chicanos*. New York: Harper and Row, 1981.

Adam, Barry D. *The Rise of a Gay and Lesbian Movement.* Boston: Twayne, 1987.

Adams, Laura. *Existential Battles: The Growth of Norman Mailer*. Athens: Ohio University Press, 1976.

Adelson, Alan. *SDS*. New York: Scribner's, 1972.

Albert, Judith Clavir, and Stewart Edward Albert, eds. *The Sixties Papers: Documents of a Rebellious Decade*. New York: Praeger, 1984.

Alexander, Paul. *Boulevard of Broken Dreams: The Life, Times, and Legend of James Dean*. New York: Viking, 1994.

Alinsky, Saul D. *Rules for Radicals: A Practical Primer for Realistic Radicals.* New York: Random House, 1971.

Allyn, Douglas. *Motown Underground*. New York: St. Martin's, 1993.

Alpert, Richard, and Sidney Cohen. *LSD*. New York: New American Library, 1966.

Amburn, Ellis. *Pearls: The Obsessions and Passions of Janis Joplin: A Biography*. New York: Warner, 1992.

Anderson, Terry H. *The Movement and the Sixties.* New York: Oxford, 1995.

Andrews, Robert. *Death in a Promised Land.* New York: Pocket Books, 1993.

Anthony, Gene. *The Summer of Love: Haight-Ashbury at Its Highest*. Millbrae, CA: Celestial Arts, 1980.

Atcheson, Richard. *The Bearded Lady: Going on the Commune Trip and Beyond*. New York: John Day, 1971.

Bacciocca, Edward, Jr. *The New Left in America: Reform to Revolution: 1956 to 1970.* Stanford, CA: Hoover Institution, 1974.

Baez, Joan. *And a Voice To Sing With: A Memoir*. New York: Summit, 1987.

Baldwin, James. *Another Country*. New York: Dial, 1962.

———. *The Fire Next Time*. New York: The Dial Press, 1963.

_____. *Giovanni's Room*. New York: Dell, 1956.

_____. *Go Tell It on the Mountain*. New York: Grosset and Dunlap, 1953.

_____. *Going To Meet the Man*. New York: Dial, 1965.

_____. *Nobody Knows My Name*. New York: Dial, 1961.

_____. *Tell Me How Long the Train's Been Gone*. New York: Dell, 1968.

Banes, Sally. *Greenwich Village 1963*. Durham, NC: Duke University Press, 1993.

Bates, Tom. *Rads: The 1970 Bombing of the Army Math Research Center at the University of Wisconsin and Its Aftermath*. New York: HarperCollins, 1992.

Beauvoir, Simone de. *The Second Sex*. New York: Knopf, 1953.

Bedford, Sybil. *Aldous Huxley: A Biography*. New York: Knopf, 1974.

Belin, David. *Final Disclosure: The Full Truth about the Assassination of President Kennedy*. Garden City, NY: Doubleday, 1988.

Benjaminson, Peter. *The Story of Motown*. New York: Grove, 1979.

Benton, Mike. *The Comic Book in America: An Illustrated History*. Dallas, TX: Taylor, 1989.

Berrigan, Daniel. *Absurd Convictions, Modest Hopes: Conversations after Prison*. New York: Vintage, 1973.

_____. *Consequences: Truth and . . . .* New York: Macmillan, 1967.

_____. *The Dark Night of Resistance*. Garden City, NY: Doubleday, 1971.

_____. *False Gods, Real Men: New Poems*. New York: Macmillan, 1969.

_____. *Night Flight to Hanoi*. New York: Macmillan, 1968.

_____. *No Bars to Manhood*. Garden City, NY: Doubleday, 1970.

_____. *Time without Number*. New York: Macmillan, 1957.

_____. *The Trial of the Cantonsville Nine*. Boston: Beacon, 1970.

Berrigan, Philip. *No More Strangers*. New York: Macmillan, 1965.

_____. *Prison Journals of a Priest Revolutionary*. Compiled and edited by Vincent McGhee. New York: Holt, 1970.

_____. *A Punishment for Peace*. New York: Macmillan, 1969.

Bloom, Lynn Z. *Doctor Spock: Biography of a Conservative Radical*. Indianapolis, IN: Bobbs-Merrill, 1972.

Blum, John Morton. *Years of Discord: American Politics and Society, 1961–1974*. New York: W. W. Norton, 1991.

Bockris, Victor. *The Life and Death of Andy Warhol*. New York: Bantam, 1989.

_____. *Transformer: The Lou Reed Story*. New York: Simon and Schuster, 1995.

Booth, Stanley. *Dance with the Devil: The Rolling Stones and Their Times*. New York: Random House, 1984.

Braden, William. *The Age of Aquarius: Technology and the Cultural Revolution*. Chicago: Quadrangle, 1970.

Branch, Taylor. *Parting the Waters: America in the King Years, 1954–63*. New York: Simon and Schuster, 1988.

Brand, Stewart, ed. *The Whole Earth Catalog*. New York: Random House, 1971.

Brautigan, Richard. *Trout Fishing in America, The Pill versus the Springhill Mine Disaster, and In Watermelon Sugar*. Boston: Houghton Mifflin, 1989.

Breines, Wini. *Community and Organization in the New Left, 1962–1968: The Great Refusal*. New Brunswick, NJ: Rutgers University Press, 1989.

Brown, Elaine. *A Taste of Power: A Black Woman's Story*. New York: Pantheon, 1992.

Brown, Helen Gurley. *Sex and the Single Girl*. New York: Pocket Books, 1962.

Brown, Norman O. *Life against Death: The Psychoanalytical Meaning of History*.

Middletown, CT: Weslyan University Press, 1959.

Brown, Peter, and Steven Gaines. *The Love You Make: An Insider's Story of the Beatles*. New York: McGraw-Hill, 1983.

Bufithis, Philip H. *Norman Mailer*. New York: Ungar, 1978.

Bugliosi, Vincent, and Curt Gentry. *Helter Skelter: The True Story of the Manson Murders*. New York: W. W. Norton, 1974.

Burner, Eric. *And Gently He Shall Lead Them: Robert Parris Moses and Civil Rights in Mississippi*. New York: New York University Press, 1994.

Burns, Stewart. *Social Movements of the 1960s: Searching for Democracy*. Boston: Twayne, 1990.

Burroughs, William S. *Cities of the Red Night*. New York: Holt, 1981.

_____. *The Exterminator*. San Francisco: Auerhahn, 1960.

_____. *Junkie: Confessions of an Unredeemed Drug Addict*. New York: Ace, 1953.

_____. *Naked Lunch*. Paris: Olympia, 1959.

_____. *Nova Express*. New York: Grove, 1964.

_____. *The Soft Machine*. Paris: Olympia, 1961.

_____. *The Ticket That Exploded*. Paris: Olympia, 1962.

_____. *The Wild Boys: A Book of the Dead*. New York: Grove, 1971.

Cackett, Alan. *The Harmony Illustrated Encyclopedia of Country Music*. New York: Crown Trade, 1994.

Campbell, James. *Talking at the Gates: A Life of James Baldwin*. New York: Viking, 1991.

Cantwell, Robert. *When We Were Good: The Folk Revival*. Cambridge, MA: Harvard University Press, 1996.

Capote, Truman. *In Cold Blood*. New York: Random House, 1965.

Carey, Gary. *Lenny, Janis, and Jimi*. New York: Pocket Books, 1975.

Carmichael, Stokely. *Stokely Speaks: Black Power to Pan-Africanism*. New York: Random House, 1971. *See also* Ture, Kwame.

Carpenter, Humphrey. *J. R. R. Tolkien: A Biography*. London: Allen & Unwin, 1977.

Carson, Clayborne. *In Struggle: SNCC and the Black Awakening of the 1960s*. Cambridge, MA: Harvard University Press, 1981.

Carson, Rachel. *Silent Spring*. Boston: Houghton Mifflin, 1962.

Cash, June Carter. *From the Heart*. New York: Prentice Hall, 1987.

Cassady, Carolyn. *Off the Road: My Years with Cassady, Kerouac, and Ginsberg*. New York: Morrow, 1990.

Castaneda, Carlos. *Journey to Ixtlan: The Lessons of Don Juan*. New York: Simon and Schuster, 1972.

_____. *A Separate Reality: Further Conversations with Don Juan*. New York: Simon and Schuster, 1971.

_____. *The Teachings of Don Juan: A Yaqui Way of Knowledge*. Berkeley: University of California Press, 1968.

Castellucci, John. *The Big Dance: The Untold Story of Kathy Boudin and the Terrorist Family That Committed the Brink's Robbery Murders*. New York: Dodd, Mead, 1986.

Castro, Tony. *Chicano Power: The Emergence of Mexican America*. New York: Dutton, 1974.

Cattier, Michel. *The Life and Work of Wilhelm Reich*. Translated by Ghislaine Boulanger. New York: Horizon, 1971.

Caute, David. *The Year of the Barricades: A Journey through 1968*. New York: Harper and Row, 1988.

Chafe, William. *The Unfinished Journey: America since World War II*. New York: Oxford, 1995.

Challis, Chris. *Quest for Kerouac*. London: Faber and Faber, 1984.

Charters, Ann. *Kerouac: A Biography*. San Francisco: Straight Arrow, 1973.

_____, ed. *The Portable Kerouac*. New York: Penguin, 1995.

Cherkovski, Neeli. *Ferlinghetti: A Biography*. Garden City, NY: Doubleday, 1979.

Churchill, Ward, and Jim Vander Wall. *Agents of Repression: The FBI's Secret Wars against the Black Panther Party and the*

American Indian Movement. Boston: South End, 1988.

Clark, Ronald W. *Bertrand Russell and His World*. London: Thames and Hudson, 1981.

_____. *The Huxleys*. London: Heinemann, 1968.

Clark, Tom. *Jack Kerouac*. San Diego, CA: Harcourt Brace Jovanovich, 1984.

Cleaver, Eldridge. *Soul on Fire*. Waco, TX: World, 1978.

_____. *Soul on Ice*. New York: McGraw-Hill, 1968.

Cohen, Allen. *The San Francisco Oracle, Facsimile Edition: The Psychedelic Newspaper of the Haight Ashbury, 1966–1968*. Berkeley, CA: Regent, 1991.

Colacello, Bob. *Holy Terror: Andy Warhol Close Up*. New York: HarperCollins, 1990.

Cole, Richard. *Stairway to Heaven: Led Zeppelin Uncensored*. New York: HarperCollins, 1992.

Collier, Peter, ed. *Crisis: A Contemporary Reader*. New York: Harcourt Brace and World, 1969.

Cott, Jonathan. *Dylan*. Garden City, NY: Doubleday, 1984.

Cronkie, Kathy. *On the Edge of the Spotlight: Celebrities' Children Speak Out about Their Success and Struggles*. New York: Morrow, 1981.

Crumb, R. *R. Crumb's Head Comix*. New York: Simon and Schuster, 1988.

Curry, Jack. *Woodstock: The Summer of Our Lives*. New York: Widenfeld and Nicolson, 1989.

Curtis, Richard. *The Berrigan Brothers: The Story of Daniel and Philip Berrigan*. New York: Hawthorn, 1974.

Dalton, David. *James Dean, The Mutant King: A Biography*. San Francisco: Straight Arrow, 1974.

_____. *Piece of My Heart: The Life, Times, and Legend of Janis Joplin*. New York: St. Martin's, 1985.

Daniels, Les. *Comix: A History of Comic Books in America*. New York: Outerbridge and Dienstfrey, 1971.

_____. *Marvel: Five Fabulous Decades of the World's Greatest Comics*. New York: Abrams, 1991.

Davidson, Bill. *Jane Fonda: An Intimate Biography*. New York: Dutton, 1990.

Davies, Dave. *Kink: An Autobiography*. New York: Hyperion, 1997.

Davies, Hunter. *The Beatles: The Only Authorized Biography*. London: Arrow, 1992.

Davies, Peter. *The Truth about Kent State: A Challenge to the American Conscience*. New York: Farrar, Straus, and Giroux, 1973.

Davis, Angela. *Angela Davis: An Autobiography*. New York: Random House, 1974.

DeBenedetti, Charles. *The Peace Reform in American History*. Bloomington: Indiana University Press, 1980.

Dellinger, David. *From Yale to Jail: The Life Story of a Moral Dissenter*. New York: Pantheon, 1993.

Deloria, Vine, Jr. *Custer Died for Your Sins: An Indian Manifesto*. New York: Macmillan, 1969.

Densmore, John. *Riders on the Storm: My Life with Jim Morrison and the Doors*. New York: Delacorte, 1990.

Dickstein, Morris. *Gates of Eden: American Culture in the Sixties*. New York: Basic, 1977.

Didion, Joan. *Slouching toward Bethlehem*. New York: Farrar, Straus and Giroux, 1968.

Donner, Frank J. *The Age of Surveillance: The Aims and Methods of America's Political Intelligence System*. New York: Knopf, 1980.

Dorson, Richard M. *America in Legend: Folklore from the Colonial Period to the Present*. New York: Pantheon, 1973.

Douglas, Alfred. *How To Consult the I Ching, The Oracle of Change*. New York: Putnam's, 1971.

Draper, Hal. *Berkeley: The New Student Revolt*. New York: Grove, 1965.

Draper, Robert. *Rolling Stone Magazine: The Uncensored History*. New York: Doubleday, 1990.

Duberman, Martin. *Stonewall*. New York: Dutton, 1993.

Dunaway, David King. *How Can I Keep from Singing: Pete Seeger*. New York: McGraw-Hill, 1981.

Dunne, John Gregory. *Delano: The Story of the California Grape Strike*. New York: Farrar, Strauss, and Giroux, 1967.

Dylan, Bob. *Bob Dylan in His Own Words*. New York: Omnibus, 1993.

Echols, Alice. *Daring To Be Bad: Radical Feminism in America, 1967–1975*. Minneapolis: University of Minnesota Press, 1989.

Ehrlich, Robert. *Norman Mailer: The Radical as Hipster*. Metuchen, NJ: Scarecrow, 1978.

Eisen, Jonathan, ed. *Altamont: The Death of Innocence in the Woodstock Nation*. New York: Avon, 1970.

Ellsberg, Daniel. *Papers on the War*. New York: Simon and Schuster, 1972.

Epstein, Edward Jay. *Inquest: The Warren Commission and the Establishment of Truth*. New York: Viking, 1966.

Estleman, Loren D. *Motown*. New York: Bantam, 1991.

Estren, Mark James. *A History of Underground Comics*. Berkeley, CA: Ronin, 1974.

Evans, Sara. *Born for Liberty: A History of Women in America*. New York: Free Press, 1989.

_____. *Personal Politics: The Roots of Women's Liberation in the Civil Rights Movement and the New Left*. New York: Vintage, 1980.

Fanon, Frantz. *Black Skin, White Masks*. Translated by Charles Markmann. New York: Grove, 1967.

_____. *The Wretched of the Earth*. Translated by Constance Farrington. New York: Ballantine, 1963.

Farber, David. *Chicago '68*. Chicago: University of Chicago Press, 1988.

———, ed. *The Sixties: From Memory to History*. Chapel Hill: University of North Carolina Press, 1994.

Feiffer, Jules. *Feiffer's Album*. New York: Random House, 1963.

Feiffer, Jules, with Steven Heller, ed. *Jules Feiffer's America: From Eisenhower to Reagan*. New York: Knopf, 1982.

Ferlinghetti, Lawrence. *A Coney Island of the Mind*. New York: New Directions, 1958.

_____. *Endless Life: Selected Poems*. New York: New Directions, 1981.

_____. *Her*. New York: New Directions, 1960.

_____. *Howl of the Censor*. San Carlos, CA: Nourse, 1961.

_____. *Open Eye, Open Heart*. New York: New Directions, 1973.

_____. *Starting from San Francisco*. Norfolk, CT: New Directions, 1961.

Finlayson, Iain. *Denim: An American Legend*. New York: Simon and Schuster, 1990.

Firestone, Shulamith. *The Dialectic of Sex: The Case for Feminist Revolution*. New York: Morrow, 1970.

Forman, James. *The Making of Black Revolutionaries: A Personal Account*. New York: Macmillan, 1972.

Frankfort, Ellen. *Kathy Boudin and the Dance of Death*. New York: Stein and Day, 1983.

French, Warren G. *Jack Kerouac*. Boston: Twayne, 1986.

Friedan, Betty. *The Feminine Mystique*. New York: Norton, 1963.

_____. *It Changed My Life: Writings on the Women's Movement*. New York: Norton, 1985.

_____. *The Second Stage*. New York: Summit, 1981.

Friedman, Myra. *Buried Alive: The Biography of Janis Joplin*. New York: Morrow, 1973.

Fuller, R. Buckminster. *Nine Chains to the Moon*. Carbondale: University of Southern Illinois Press, 1963.

_____. *Operating Manual for Spaceship Earth*. New York: Simon and Schuster, 1969.

Furlong, Monica. *Zen Effects: The Life of Alan Watts*. Boston: Houghton Mifflin, 1986.

Gans, David. *Conversations with the Dead: The Grateful Dead Interview Book*. New York: Citadel Underground, 1991.

Gans, David, and Peter Simon. *Playing in the Band: An Oral and Visual Portrait of the Grateful Dead*. New York: St. Martin's Griffin, 1996.

Gardener, Hugh. *The Children of Prosperity: Thirteen Modern American Communes*. New York: St. Martin's, 1978.

Gaskin, Stephen. *Haight-Ashbury Flashbacks*. Berkeley, CA: Ronin, 1990.

George, Nelson. *Where Did Our Love Go? The Rise and Fall of the Motown Sound*. New York: St. Martin's, 1985.

Gifford, Barry, and Lawrence Lee. *Jack's Book: An Oral Biography of Jack Kerouac*. New York: St. Martin's, 1978.

Ginsberg, Allen. *Howl and Other Poems*. San Francisco: City Lights, 1956.

Gitlin, Todd. *The Sixties: Years of Hope, Days of Rage*. New York: Bantam, 1987.

_____. *The Whole World Is Watching: Mass Media in the Making and Unmaking of the New Left*. Berkeley: University of California Press, 1980.

Gleason, Ralph J. *The Jefferson Airplane and the San Francisco Sound*. New York: Ballantine, 1969.

Glenday, Michael K. *Norman Mailer*. New York: St. Martin's, 1995.

Goldman, Albert. *Ladies and Gentlemen: It's Lenny Bruce!* New York: Random House, 1971.

Goode, Stephen. *Assassination! Kennedy, King, Kennedy*. New York: Watts, 1979.

Goodman, Michael B. *Contemporary Literary Censorship: The Case History of Burroughs' Naked Lunch*. Metuchen, NJ: Scarecrow, 1981.

Goodman, Mitchell. *The End of It*. Sagaponack, NY: Second Chance, 1980.

_____, ed. *The Movement toward a New America: The Beginnings of a Long Revolution*. New York: Knopf, 1970.

Goodman, Paul. *Compulsory Mis-education*. New York: Horizon, 1964.

_____. *Growing Up Absurd: Problems of Youth in the Organized System*. New York: Random House, 1960.

_____. *New Reformation: Notes of a Neolithic Conservative*. New York: Random House, 1970.

Goodman, Paul, and Percival Goodman. *Communitas: Means of Livelihood and Ways of Life*. New York: Vintage, 1947.

Gordon, William A. *Four Dead in Ohio: Was There a Conspiracy at Kent State?* Laguna Hills, CA: North Ridge, 1995.

_____. *The Fourth of May: Killings and Coverups at Kent State*. Buffalo, NY: Prometheus, 1990.

Gordy, Berry. *To Be Loved: The Music, the Magic, the Memories of Motown: An Autobiography*. New York: Warner, 1994.

Gottlieb, Annie. *Do You Believe in Magic? Bringing the Sixties Back Home*. New York: Simon and Schuster, 1987.

Graham, Bill, and Robert Greenfield. *Bill Graham Presents: My Life inside Rock and Out*. New York: Doubleday, 1992.

Greene, Herb. *Book of the Dead: Celebrating 25 Years with the Grateful Dead*. New York: Delacorte, 1990.

Griswold del Castillo, Richard, and Richard A. Garcia. *Cesar Chavez: A Triumph of Spirit*. Norman: University of Oklahoma Press, 1995.

Grogan, Emmett. *Ringolevio: A Life Played for Keeps*. Boston: Little, Brown, 1972.

Grossman, Mark. *The ABC-CLIO Companion to the Environmental Movement*. Santa Barbara, CA: ABC-CLIO, 1994.

Guiles, Fred Lawrence. *Loner at the Ball: The Life of Andy Warhol*. New York: Bantam, 1989.

Guthrie, Woody. *Bound for Glory*. New York: Dutton, 1943.

Halberstam, David. *The Making of a Quagmire: America and Vietnam during the Kennedy Era*. New York: Knopf, 1988.

Halper, Jon, ed. *Gary Snyder: Dimensions of a Life*. San Francisco: Sierra Club, 1991.

Halstead, Fred. *Out Now! A Participant's Account of the American Movement against the Vietnam War*. New York: Monad, 1978.

Harrington, Michael. *The Other America: Poverty in the United States*. New York: Macmillan, 1962.

Harris, David. *Dreams Die Hard: Three Men's Journey through the Sixties*. San Francisco: Mercury House, 1993.

Harrison, Hank. *The Dead Book: A Social History of the Grateful Dead*. New York: Links, 1973.

Haskins, James. *Profiles in Black Power*. New York: Doubleday, 1972.

Hatch, Alden. *Buckminster Fuller: At Home in the Universe*. New York: Crown, 1974.

Hayden, Tom. *The American Future: New Visions beyond Old Frontiers*. Boston: South End, 1980.

_____. *The Love of Possession Is a Disease with Them*. Chicago: Holt, 1972.

_____. *Reunion: A Memoir*. New York: Random House, 1988.

_____. *Trial*. New York: Holt, 1970.

Heath, G. Louis, ed. *Vandals in the Bomb Factory: The History and Literature of the Students for a Democratic Society*. Metuchen, NJ: Scarecrow, 1976.

Heilbrun, Carolyn G. *The Education of a Woman: The Life of Gloria Steinem*. New York: Dial, 1995.

Heineman, Kenneth J. *Campus Wars: The Peace Movement at American State Universities in the Vietnam Era*. New York: New York University Press, 1993.

Hesse, Hermann. *Siddhartha*. Translated by Hilda Rosner. New York: New Directions, 1951.

_____. *Steppenwolf*. Translated by Basil Creighton. New York: Modern Library, 1963.

Heylin, Clinton. *Bob Dylan: Behind the Shades*. New York: Summit, 1991.

Hilliard, David, and Lewis Cole. *This Side of Glory: The Autobiography of David Hilliard and the Story of the Black Panther Party*. Boston: Little, Brown, 1993.

Hodgson, Godfrey. *America in Our Time*. New York: Vintage, 1976.

Hoffman, Abbie. *Revolution for the Hell of It*. New York: Dial, 1968.

_____. *Soon To Be a Major Motion Picture*. New York: Putnam, 1980.

_____. *Steal This Book*. Worcester, MA: Jack Hoffman Presents, n.d.

_____. *Woodstock Nation: A Talk-Rock Album*. New York: Vintage, 1969.

Hofmann, Albert. *LSD: My Problem Child*. Translated by Jonathan Ott. New York: McGraw-Hill, 1980.

Hood, Phil, ed. *Artists of American Folk Music*. New York: Quill, 1986.

Hopkins, Jerry, ed. *The Hippie Papers: Notes from the Underground Press*. New York: Signet, 1968.

_____. *Hit and Run: The Jimi Hendrix Story*. New York: Perigee, 1983.

_____. *Yoko Ono*. New York: Macmillan, 1986.

Hopkins, Jerry, and Danny Sugerman. *No One Here Gets out Alive*. New York: Warner, 1980.

Howard, Gerald, ed. *The Sixties: Art, Politics and Media of Our Most Explosive Decade*. New York: Washington Square, 1982.

Humphries, Patrick. *Absolutely Dylan*. New York: Viking Studio, 1991.

Hurtado, Albert L., and Peter Iverson. *Major Problems in American Indian History*. Lexington, MA: Heath, 1994.

Huxley, Aldous. *Brave New World*. London: Chatto and Windus, 1966.

_____. *The Doors of Perception*. New York: Harper and Row, 1954.

_____. *The Doors of Perception and Heaven and Hell*. New York: Harper and Row, 1956.

Irwin, John. *Scenes*. Beverly Hills, CA: Sage, 1977.

Isserman, Maurice. *If I Had a Hammer: The Death of the Old Left and the Birth of the New Left*. New York: Basic, 1987.

Jackson, Blair. *Grateful Dead: The Music Never Stopped*. New York: Delilah, 1983.

Jacobs, Frank. *The Mad World of William Gaines*. New York: Lyle Stuart, 1972.

Jacobs, Harold, ed. *Weatherman*. Berkeley, CA: Ramparts, 1970.

Jefferson, William. *The Story of Maharishi*. New York: Pocket Books, 1976.

Jezer, Marty. *Abbie Hoffman: American Rebel*. New Brunswick, NJ: Rutgers University Press, 1992.

Joplin, Laura. *Love, Janis*. New York: Villard, 1992.

Joseph, Peter. *Good Times: An Oral History of America in the 1960s*. New York: Morrow, 1974.

Kahn, Roger. *The Battle for Morningside Heights: Why Students Rebel*. New York: Morrow, 1970.

Karagueuzian, Dikran. *Blow It Up! The Black Student Revolt at San Francisco State College and the Emergence of Dr. Hayakawa*. Boston: Gambit, 1971.

Katz, Jonathan. *Gay American History: Lesbians and Gay Men in the U.S.A.: A Documentary*. New York: Crowell, 1976.

Kelman, Steven. *Push Comes to Shove: The Escalation of Student Protest*. Boston: Houghton Mifflin, 1970.

Kelner, Joseph, and James Munves. *The Kent State Coverup*. New York: Harper and Row, 1980.

Kerouac, Jack. *Big Sur*. New York: Farrar, Straus Cudahy, 1962.

———. *Book of Dreams*. San Francisco: City Lights Books, 1961.

———. *The Dharma Bums*. New York: Viking, 1958.

———. *Doctor Sax*. New York: Grove, 1959.

———. *Maggie Cassidy*. New York: Avon, 1959.

———. *On the Road*. New York: Viking, 1957.

———. *Satori in Paris*. New York: Grove, 1966.

———. *The Subterraneans*. New York: Grove, 1958.

———. *The Town and the City*. New York: Harcourt, Brace, 1950.

———. *Tristessa*. New York: Avon, 1960.

———. *Vanity of Duluoz*. New York: Coward-McCann, 1968.

———. *Visions of Cody*. New York: New Directions, 1959.

Kesey, Ken. *Ken Kesey's Garage Sale*. New York: Viking, 1973.

_____. *One Flew over the Cuckoo's Nest*. New York: Viking, 1962.

_____. *Sometimes a Great Notion*. New York: Penguin, 1964.

Kirby, Michael. *Happenings*. New York: Dutton, 1965.

Klein, Joe. *Woody Guthrie: A Life*. New York: Knopf, 1980.

Kolko, Gabriel. *Anatomy of a War: Vietnam, the United States, and the Modern Historical Experience*. New York: Pantheon, 1985.

Krassner, Paul. *Confessions of a Raving, Unconfined Nut: Misadventures in the Counterculture*. New York: Simon and Schuster, 1993.

Kreiger, Susan. *Hip Capitalism*. Beverly Hills, CA: Sage, 1979.

Kunen, James Simon. *The Strawberry Statement: Notes of a College Revolutionary*. New York: Random House, 1968.

Laing, R. D. *The Divided Self: An Existential Study in Sanity and Madness*. London: Tavistock, 1960.

_____. *The Politics of Experience*. New York: Pantheon, 1967.

_____. *The Politics of the Family and Other Essays*. New York: Vintage, 1971.

_____. *The Self and Others*. London: Tavistock, 1961.

Leamer, Laurence. *The Paper Revolutionaries: The Rise of the Underground Press*. New York: Simon and Schuster, 1972.

Leary, Timothy. *Confessions of a Hope Fiend*. New York: Bantam, 1973.

_____. *Flashbacks: An Autobiography*. Los Angeles: Tarcher, 1983.

_____. *High Priest*. Cleveland: World, 1968.

_____. *Jail Notes*. New York: Douglas, 1970.

_____. *The Politics of Ecstasy*. London: Paladin, 1970.

_____. *Psychedelic Prayers*. Kerhonskon, NY: Poets, 1966.

Leary, Timothy, Ralph Metzner, and Richard Alpert. *The Psychedelic Experience*. Secaucus, NY: Citadel, 1970.

Lee, Martin A., and Bruce Shlain. *Acid Dreams: The CIA, LSD, and the Sixties Rebellion*. New York: Grove, 1985.

Leeds, Barry H. *Ken Kesey*. New York: Ungar, 1981.

Lincoln, C. Eric. *The Black Muslims in America*. Grand Rapids, MI: Africa World, 1994.

Lindesmith, Alfred R. *The Addict and the Law*. Bloomington: Indiana University Press, 1965.

Liungman, Carl G. *Dictionary of Symbols*. Santa Barbara, CA: ABC-CLIO, 1991.

Lottman, Herbert R. *Albert Camus: A Biography*. Garden City, NY: Doubleday, 1979.

Lynd, Staughton. *Anti-Federalism in Dutchess County, New York: A Study of Democracy and Class Conflict in the Revolutionary Era*. Chicago: Loyola University Press, 1962.

_____. *Intellectual Origins of American Radicalism*. New York: Pantheon, 1968.

_____ , ed. *Non-Violence in America: A Documentary History* . Indianapolis, IN: Bobbs-Merrill, 1966.

_____, ed. *Reconstruction*. New York: Harper and Row, 1967.

Lynd, Staughton, and Tom Hayden. *The Other Side*. New York: New American Library, 1966.

McAuliffe, Kevin Michael. *The Great American Newspaper: The Rise and Fall of the Village Voice*. New York: Scribner's, 1975.

McCarthy, Eugene. *The Year of the People*. Garden City, NY: Doubleday, 1969.

McGill, William J. *The Year of the Monkey: Revolt on Campus, 1968–69*. New York: McGraw-Hill, 1982.

McKuen, Rod. *Listen to the Warm*. New York: Random House, 1967.

_____. *Lonesome Cities*. New York: Random House, 1968.

_____. *Stanyan Street and Other Sorrows*. New York: Random House, 1966.

McLuhan, Marshall. *Counterblast*. Toronto: McLelland and Stewart, 1969.

_____. *Culture Is Our Business*. New York: McGraw-Hill, 1970.

_____. *The Gutenberg Galaxy: The Making of Typographic Man*. Toronto: University of Toronto Press, 1962.

_____. *The Mechanical Bride: Folklore of Industrial Man*. New York: Vanguard, 1951.

_____. *Understanding Media: The Extensions of Man*. New York: McGraw-Hill, 1964.

_____. *War and Peace in the Global Village: An Inventory of Some Current Spastic Situations That Could Be Eliminated by More Feedforward*. New York: McGraw-Hill, 1968.

McLuhan, Marshall, and Quentin Fiore. *The Medium Is the Message: An Inventory of Effects*. New York: Bantam, 1967.

McKissick, Floyd. *Three-Fifths of a Man*. New York: Macmillan, 1969.

McNally, Dennis. *Desolate Angel: Jack Kerouac, the Beat Generation, and America*. New York: Random House, 1979.

Maharishi Mahesh Yogi. *Meditations of Maharsihi Mahesh Yogi*. New York: Bantam, 1968.

_____. *Science of Being and Art of Living*. London: International SRM Publications, 1963.

Mailer, Norman. *Advertisements for Myself*. New York: Putnam's, 1959.

_____. *An American Dream*. New York: Dial, 1965.

_____. *The Armies of the Night: History as a Novel/The Novel as History*. New York: New American Library, 1968.

_____. *Barbary Shore*. New York: Holt, 1951.

_____. *Cannibals and Christians*. New York: Dial, 1966.

_____. *The Deer Park*. New York: Putnam's, 1955.

_____. *Miami and the Siege of Chicago*. New York: New American Library, 1968.

_____. *The Naked and the Dead*. New York: Holt, 1948.

_____. *Of a Fire on the Moon*. Boston: Little, Brown, 1970.

_____. *The Short Fiction of Norman Mailer*. New York: Dell, 1967.

_____. *The White Negro: Superficial Reflections on the Hipster*. San Francisco: City Light, 1957.

_____. *Why Are We in Vietnam?* New York: Putnam's, 1967.

Makower, Joel. *Woodstock: The Oral History*. New York: Doubleday, 1989.

Manso, Peter, ed. *Mailer: His Life and Times*. New York: Simon and Schuster, 1985.

Marchand, Philip. *Marshall McLuhan: The Medium and the Messenger*. Toronto: Random House, 1989.

Marcuse, Herbert. *One Dimensional Man: Studies in the Ideology of Advanced Industrial Society*. Boston: Beacon, 1964.

_____. *Reason and Revolution: Hegel and the Rise of Social Theory*. Boston: Beacon, 1964.

Marine, Gene. *Black Panthers*. New York: New American Library, 1969.

Matthiessen, Peter. *In the Spirit of Crazy Horse*. New York: Viking, 1991.

Matusow, Allen J. *The Unraveling of America: A History of Liberalism in the 1960s*. New York: Harper and Row, 1984.

Max, Peter. *The Peter Max Poster Book*. New York: Crown, 1970.

Meier, August, Elliot Rudwick, and John Bracey, Jr., eds. *Black Protest in the Sixties*. New York: Markus Wiener, 1991.

Melanson, Philip H. *The Martin Luther King Assassination: New Revelations of the Conspiracy and Cover-Up, 1968–1991*. New York: Shapolsky, 1991.

Melinkoff, Ellen. *What We Wore: An Offbeat Social History of Women's Clothing, 1950 to 1980*. New York: Quill, 1984.

Melville, Keith. *Communes in the Counterculture: Origins, Theories, Styles of Life*. New York: Morrow, 1972.

Mendelssohn, John. *The Kinks Kronikles*. New York: Quill, 1985.

Merrill, Robert. *Norman Mailer*. Boston: Twayne, 1978.

_____. *Norman Mailer Revisited*. New York: Twayne, 1992.

Michener, James A. *Kent State: What Happened and Why*. New York: Random House, 1971.

Miles, Barry. *Ginsberg: A Biography*. New York: Simon and Schuster, 1989.

Miller, Douglas T. *On Our Own: Americans in the Sixties*. Lexington, MA: Heath, 1996.

Miller, James. *Democracy Is in the Streets: From Port Huron to the Siege of Chicago*. New York: Simon and Schuster, 1987.

Miller, Terry. *Greenwich Village and How It Got That Way*. New York: Crown, 1990.

Miller, Timothy. *The Hippies and American Values*. Knoxville: University of Tennessee Press, 1991.

Mills, C. Wright. *The Power Elite*. New York: Oxford, 1956.

Mills, Hilary. *Mailer: A Biography*. New York: Empire, 1982.

Moldea, Dan E. *The Killing of Robert F. Kennedy: An Investigation of Motive, Means, and Opportunity*. New York: Norton, 1995.

Moore, Barrington, Jr. *Social Origins of Dictatorship and Democracy: Lord and Peasant in the Making of the Modern World*. New York: Oxford, 1966.

Morgan, Robert. *Conceptual Art: An American Perspective*. Jefferson, NC: McFarland, 1994.

Morgan, Robin. *The Anatomy of Freedom: Feminism, Physics, and Global Politics*. Garden City, NY: Doubleday, 1982.

_____. *Going Too Far: The Personal Chronicle of a Feminist*. New York: Random House, 1977.

_____, ed. *Sisterhood Is Global: The International Women's Movement Anthology*. Garden City, NY: Doubleday, 1984.

______, ed. *Sisterhood Is Powerful: An Anthology of Writings from the Women's Liberation Movement* . New York: Vintage, 1970.

Morgan, Ted. *The Life and Times of William S. Burroughs*. New York: Holt, 1988.

Morrow, Robert D. *Betrayal*. Chicago: Regnery, 1976.

Mungo, Ray. *Famous Long Ago: My Life and Hard Times with the Liberation News Service*. Boston: Beacon, 1970.

Munoz, Carlos, Jr. *Youth, Identity, Power: The Chicano Movement*. New York: Verso, 1989.

Murphy, William S. *Burn, Baby, Burn! The Los Angeles Race Riot, August 1965*. New York: Dutton, 1966.

Muste, Abraham John. *The Essays of A. J. Muste*. Edited by Nat Hentoff. Indianapolis, IN: Bobbs-Merrill, 1967.

Myers, R. David, ed. *Toward a History of the New Left: Essays from within the Movement*. Brooklyn, New York: Carlson, 1989.

Nader, Ralph. *Unsafe at Any Speed: The Designed-In Dangers of the American Automobile*. New York: Grossman, 1965.

Newton, Huey P. *Revolutionary Suicide*. New York: Harcourt Brace Jovanovich, 1973.

_____. *To Die for the People: The Writings of Huey P. Newton*. New York: Vintage, 1972.

Nicosia, Gerald. *Memory Babe: A Critical Biography of Jack Kerouac*. New York: Grove, 1983.

Norman, Philip. *Shout! The Beatles in Their Generation*. New York: Simon and Schuster, 1981.

_____. *Symphony for the Devil: The Rolling Stones Story*. New York: Linden/Simon and Schuster, 1984.

Norton, Mary Beth, ed. *Major Problems in American Women's History*. Lexington, MA: Heath, 1989.

Oates, Stephen B. *Let the Trumpet Sound: The Life of Martin Luther King, Jr.* New York: New American Library, 1982.

O'Neill, William L. *Coming Apart: An Informal History of America in the 1960s*. Chicago: Quadrangle, 1971.

O'Reilly, Kenneth. *"Racial Matters": The FBI's Secret File on Black America, 1960–1972*. New York: Free Press, 1989.

Pawley, Martin. *Buckminster Fuller*. London: Trefoil, 1990.

Pearson, Hugh. *The Shadow of the Black Panther: Huey Newton and the Price of Black Power in America*. Reading, MA: Addison-Wesley, 1994.

Peck, Abe. *Uncovering the Sixties: The Life and Times of the Underground Press*. New York: Pantheon, 1985.

Pepper, William. *Conspiracy: The Truth behind Martin Luther King Jr.'s Murder*. New York: HarperCollins, 1995.

Perry, Charles. *The Haight-Ashbury: A History*. New York: Vintage, 1984.

Perry, Helen Swick. *The Human Be-In*. New York: Basic, 1970.

Perry, Paul. *Fear and Loathing: The Strange Saga of Hunter S. Thompson*. New York: Thunder's Mouth, 1992.

Phillips, John. *Papa John: An Autobiogrpahy*. Garden City, NY: Doubleday, 1986.

Phillips, Michelle. *California Dreamin': The True Story of the Mamas and the Papas*. New York: Warner, 1986.

Plimpton, George. *Paper Lion*. New York: Harper and Row, 1965.

Plummer, William. *The Holy Goof: A Biography of Neal Cassady*. Englewood Cliffs, NJ: Prentice-Hall, 1981.

Poirier, Richard. *Norman Mailer*. New York: Viking, 1972.

Porter, M. Gilbert. *The Art of Grit: Ken Kesey's Fiction*. Columbia: University of Missouri Press, 1982.

_____. *One Flew over the Cuckoo's Nest: Rising to Heroism*. Boston: Twayne, 1989.

Preiss, Byron. *The Beach Boys*. New York: St. Martin's, 1983.

Ram Dass. *Be Here Now*. San Cristobal, NM: Lama Foundation, 1971.

Raskin, Jonah. *The Life and Times of Abbie Hoffman*. Berkeley: University of California Press, 1997.

Redstockings. *Feminist Revolution*. New Paltz, NY: Redstockings, n.d.

Reich, Charles A. *The Greening of America*. New York: Random House, 1970.

Reich, Ilse Ollendorff. *Wilhelm Reich: A Personal Biography*. London: Elek, 1969.

Reich, Wilhelm. *Passion of Youth: An Autobiography, 1897–1922*. Edited by Mary Boyd Higgins and Chester M. Raphael. Translated by Philip Schmitz and Jerri Tompkins. New York: Farrar, Straus and Giroux, 1988.

Reidelbach, Maria. *Completely Mad: A History of the Comic Book and Magazine*. Boston: Little, Brown, 1991.

Riley, Tim. *Hard Rain: A Dylan Commentary*. New York: Knopf, 1992.

Rimmer, Robert H. *The Harrad Experiment*. Los Angeles: Sherbourne, 1966.

Ritz, David. *Divided Soul: The Life of Marvin Gaye*. New York: McGraw-Hill, 1985.

Rodnitzky, Jerome L. *Minstrels of the Dawn: The Folk-Protest Singer as a Cultural Hero*. Chicago: Nelson-Hall, 1976.

Rodriguez, Consuelo. *Cesar Chavez*. New York: Chelsea House, 1991.

Rollyson, Carl E. *The Lives of Norman Mailer: A Biography*. New York: Paragon House, 1991.

Rorabaugh, W. J. *Berkeley at War: The 1960s*. New York: Oxford, 1989.

Rosenblatt, Roger. *Coming Apart: A Memoir of the Harvard Wars of 1969*. Boston: Little, Brown, 1997.

Roszak, Theodore. *The Making of a Counterculture: Reflections on the Technocratic Society and Its Youthful Opposition*. Berkeley: University of California Press, 1968.

Rout, Kathleen. *Eldridge Cleaver*. Boston: Twayne, 1991.

Roxon, Lillian. *Rock Encyclopedia*. New York: Grosset and Dunlap, 1969.

Rubin, Jerry. *Do It! Scenarios of the Revolution*. New York: Simon and Schuster, 1970.

_____. *Growing (Up) at Thirty-Seven*. New York: Evans, 1976.

Russell, Bertrand. *The Autobiography of Bertrand Russell*. 3 vols. Boston: Little, Brown, 1967–1969.

_____. *Marriage and Morals*. New York: Liveright, 1929.

_____. *What I Believe*. New York: Dutton, 1925.

Sale, Kirkpatrick. *SDS*. New York: Random House, 1973.

Salter, Kenneth W. *The Pentagon Papers Trial*. Berekely, CA: Editorial Justa, 1975.

Sanders, Ed. *The Family: The Story of Charles Manson's Dune Buggy Attack Battalion*. New York: Dutton, 1971.

Santelli, Robert. *Aquarius Rising: The Rock Festival Years*. New York: Dell, 1980.

Savage, Jon. *The Kinks: The Official Biography*. Boston: Faber and Faber, 1984.

Sawyers, June Skinner. *Chicago Sketches: Urban Tales, Stories and Legends from Chicago History*. Chicago: Loyola Press, 1995.

Scaduto, Anthony. *Bob Dylan*. New York: Grosset and Dunlap, 1971.

Scheim, David E. *Contract on America: The Mafia Murder of President John F. Kennedy*. Silver Spring, MD: Argyle, 1983.

Schumacher, Michael. *Dharma Lion: A Critical Biography of Allen Ginsberg*. New York: St. Martin's, 1992.

Scott, Nathan A., Jr. *Three American Moralists: Mailer, Bellow, Trilling*. Notre Dame, IN: University of Notre Dame Press, 1973.

Scott, Peter Dale, Paul L. Hoch, and Russell Stetler, eds. *The Assassinations: Dallas and Beyond: A Guide to Cover-Ups and Investigations*. New York: Random House, 1976.

Seale, Bobby. *A Lonely Rage: The Autobiography of Bobby Seale*. New York: Times, 1978.

_____. *Seize the Time: The Story of the Black Panther Party and Huey P. Newton*. New York: Random House, 1970.

Selvin, Joel. *Summer of Love: The Inside Story of LSD, Rock & Roll, Free Love and High Times in the Wild West*. New York: Plume, 1994.

Shapiro, Harry, and Caesar Glebbeek. *Jimi Hendrix: Electric Gypsy*. New York: St. Martin's, 1990.

Sheehan, Neil. *A Bright Shining Lie: John Paul Vann and America in Vietnam*. New York: Random House, 1988.

Shelton, Robert. *No Direction Home: The Life and Music of Bob Dylan*. New York: Morrow, 1986.

Sitkoff, Harvard. *The Struggle for Black Equality, 1954–1980*. New York: Hill and Wang, 1981.

Skerl, Jennie. *William Burroughs*. Boston: Twayne, 1985.

Small, Melvin. *Johnson, Nixon, and the Doves*. New Brunswick, NJ: Rutgers University Press, 1988.

Small, Melvin, and William D. Hoover, eds. *Give Peace a Chance: Exploring the Vietnam Antiwar Movement*. Syracuse, NY: Syracuse University Press, 1992.

Smith, Dennis. *Barrington Moore: Violence, Morality, and Political Change*. London: Macmillan, 1983.

Smith, Larry R. *Lawrence Ferlinghetti: Poet-at-Large*. Carbondale: Southern Illinois University Press, 1983.

Snyder, Gary. *The Back Country*. New York: New Directions, 1968.

_____. *Earth House Hold: Technical Notes and Queries to Fellow Dharma Revolutionaries*. New York: New Directions, 1969.

_____. *Myths and Texts*. New York: Totem, 1960.

_____. *Riprap*. San Francisco: Grey Fox, 1965.

_____. *Turtle Island*. New York: New Directions, 1974.

Solomon, David, ed. *LSD: The Consciousness-Expanding Drug*. Boston: Putnam's, 1966.

_____. *The Marihuana Papers*. New York: Mentor, 1966.

Southern, Terry. *Red-Dirt Marijuana and Other Tastes*. New York: New American Library, 1967.

Spitz, Bob. *Barefoot in Babylon: The Creation of the Woodstock Music Festival, 1969*. New York: Viking, 1979.

Spock, Benjamin. *Common Sense Book of Baby and Child Care*. New York: Meredith, 1968.

_____. *Dr. Spock on Vietnam*. New York: Dell, 1968.

Spofford, Tim. *Dylan: A Biography*. New York: McGraw-Hill, 1989.

_____. *Lynch Street: The May 1970 Slayings at Jackson State College*. Kent, OH: Kent State University Press, 1988.

Stambler, Irwin. *Encyclopedia of Pop, Rock, and Soul*. New York: St. Martin's, 1974.

Stern, Philip Van Doren. *The Annotated Walden*. New York: Potter, 1970.

Stern, Susan. *With the Weathermen: The Personal Journal of a Revolutionary Woman*. New York: Doubleday, 1975.

Stevens, Jay. *Storming Heaven: LSD and the American Dream*. New York: Harper and Row, 1987.

Stevenson, W. H. *William Blake: Selected Poetry*. New York: Penguin, 1988.

Stone, I. F. *The Hidden History of the Korean War*. New York: Monthly Review, 1952.

_____. *In a Time of Torment*. New York: Random House, 1967.

_____. *The Killings at Kent State: How Murder Went Unpunished*. New York: Vintage, 1971.

_____. *Polemics and Prophecies, 1967–1970*. New York: Random House, 1970.

_____. *The Truman Era*. New York: Random House, 1953.

Sullivan, Nancy, ed. *The Treasury of American Poetry*. New York: Barnes and Noble, 1978.

Talese, Gay. *The Overreachers*. New York: Harper and Row, 1965.

Tanner, Leslie B., ed. *Voices from Women's Liberation*. New York: New American Library, 1970.

Tanner, Stephen L. *Ken Kesey*. Boston: Twayne, 1983.

Taraborrelli, J. Randy. *Hot Wax, City Cool and Solid Gold*. Garden City, NY: Doubleday, 1986.

Tart, Charles T. *On Being Stoned*. Palo Alto, CA: Science and Behavior, 1971.

Thompson, Hunter S. *Fear and Loathing in Las Vegas: A Savage Journey to the Heart of the American Dream*. New York: Random House, 1972.

_____. *Fear and Loathing on the Campaign Trail '72*. San Francisco: Straight Arrow, 1973.

_____. *The Great Shark Hunt: Strange Tales from a Strange Time*. New York: Ballantine, 1979.

_____. *Hell's Angels: A Strange and Terrible Saga*. New York: Ballantine, 1966.

_____. *The Proud Highway: Saga of a Desperate Southern Gentleman: The Fear and Loathing Letters, Volume I, 1955–1967*. New York: Villard, 1997.

Thoreau, Henry David. *Walden*. New York: Library of America, 1985.

Tolkien, J. R. R. *The Hobbit*. New York: Ballantine, 1966.

_____. *The Lord of the Rings*. Boston: Houghton Mifflin, 1954–1956.

Tremlett, George. *The Who*. New York: Warner, 1975.

Troy, Sandy. *One More Saturday Night: Reflections with the Grateful Dead, Dead Family, and Deadheads*. New York: St. Martin's, 1991.

Ture, Kwame (formerly Stokely Carmichael), and Charles V. Hamilton. *Black Power: The Politics of Liberation in America*. New York: Vintage, 1992.

Turner, William W. *The Assassination of Robert F. Kennedy: A Searching Look at the Conspiracy and Cover-Up, 1968–1978*. New York: Random House, 1978.

Twiggy. *Twiggy: An Autobiography*. London: Hart-Davis, MacGibbon, 1975.

Ungar, Sanford J. *The Papers and the Papers: An Account of the Legal and Political Battle over the Pentagon Papers*. New York: Columbia University Press, 1989.

Unger, Irwin. *The Movement: A History of the American New Left, 1959–1972*. New York: Dodd, Mead, 1974.

Viorst, Milton. *Fire in the Streets: America in the 1960s*. New York: Simon and Schuster, 1979.

Von Hoffman, Nicholas. *We Are the People Our Parents Warned Us Against*. Chicago: Dee, 1968.

Vonnegut, Kurt, Jr. *Cat's Cradle*. New York: Holt, 1963.

_____. *God Bless You, Mr. Rosewater*. New York: Holt, 1965.

_____. *Mother Night*. New York: Harper and Row, 1961.

_____. *Player Piano*. New York: Scribner, 1952.

_____. *The Sirens of Titan*. Boston: Houghton Mifflin, 1959.

_____. *Slaughterhouse-Five, or the Children's Crusade*. New York: Delacorte, 1969.

Wachsberger, Ken, ed. *Voices from the Underground: Insider Histories of the Vietnam Era Underground Press*. Tempe, AZ: Mica's, 1993.

Walker, Brian Browne. *The I Ching or Book of Changes*. New York: St. Martin's Griffin, 1992.

Waller, Don. *The Motown Story*. New York: Scribner's, 1985.

Ward, Ed, Geoffrey Stokes, and Ken Tucker. *Rock of Ages: The Rolling Stone History of Rock & Roll*. Englewood Cliffs, NJ: Prentice-Hall, 1986.

Watts, Alan. *Beat Zen, Square Zen, and Zen*. San Francisco: City Light, 1959.

_______. *Behold the Spirit: A Study in the Necessity of Mystical Religion*. New York: Pantheon, 1947.

_______. *The Book: On the Taboo against Knowing Who You Are*. New York: Pantheon, 1966.

_____. *Does It Matter? Essays on Man's Relation to Materiality*. New York: Pantheon, 1970.

_____. *In My Own Way: An Autobiography*. New York: Pantheon, 1972.

_____. *The Joyous Cosmology: Adventures in the Chemistry of Consciousness*. New York: Pantheon, 1962.

_____. *The Meaning of Happiness: The Quest for Freedom of the Spirit in Modern Psychology and the Wisdom of the East*. New York: Harper and Row, 1979.

_____. *Myth and Ritual in Christianity*. New York: Grove, 1960.

_____. *Nature, Man, and Woman*. New York: Pantheon, 1958.

_____. *Psychotherapy, East and West*. New York: Pantheon, 1961.

_____. *Tao: The Watercourse Way*. New York: Pantheon, 1975.

_____. *This Is It, and Other Essays on Zen and Spiritual Experience*. New York: Pantheon, 1960.

_____. *The Way of Zen*. New York: Pantheon, 1957.

_____. *Zen Buddhism: A New Outline and Introduction*. London: Buddhist Society, 1947.

Weatherby, James. *Artist on Fire: A Portrait.* New York: Fine, 1989.

Weiss, Walter F. *America's Wandering Youth: A Sociological Study of Young Hitchhikers in the United States*. Jericho, NY: Exposition, 1974.

Wenke, Joseph. *Mailer's America*. Hanover, NH: University Press of New England, 1987.

Whyte, William H., Jr. *The Organization Man.* New York: Simon and Schuster, 1956.

Wilson, Brian. *Wouldn't It Be Nice: My Own Story*. New York: HarperCollins, 1991.

Wolf, Leonard, ed. *Voices from the Love Generation*. Boston: Little, Brown, 1968.

Wolfe, Burton. *The Hippies*. New York: Signet, 1968.

Wolfe, Tom. *The Electric Kool-Aid Acid Test*. New York: Bantam, 1968.

_____. *The New Journalism*. New York: Harper and Row, 1973.

_____ . *The Pump House Gang*. New York: Farrar, Straus and Giroux, 1968.

_____. *Radical Chic and Mau-Mauing the Flak Catchers*. New York: Farrar, Straus and Giroux, 1970.

Wolff, Miles. *How It All Began: The Greensboro Sit-Ins*. New York: Stein and Day, 1971.

Wolin, Sheldon, and James H. Schar. *The Berkeley Rebellion and Beyond: Essays on Politics and Education in the Technological Society*. New York: Random House, 1970.

X, Malcolm, with Alex Haley. *The Autobiography of Malcolm X*. New York: Grove, 1965.

Yablonsky, Lewis. *The Hippie Trip*. New York: Pegasus, 1968.

Yinger, J. Milton. *Countercultures: The Promise and Peril of a World Turned Upside Down*. New York: Free Press, 1982.

Young, Andrew. *The Civil Rights Movement and the Transformation of America*. New York: HarperCollins, 1996.

Young, Jean, and Michael Lang. *Woodstock Festival Remembered*. New York: Ballantine, 1979.

Zinn, Howard. *SNCC: The New Abolitionists*. Boston: Beacon, 1964.

_____. *Vietnam: The Logic of Withdrawal*. Boston: Beacon, 1967.

Websites

The Beatles:
http://kiwi.imgen.bcm.tmc.edu:8088/public/rmb.html

Burroughs, William S.:
http://www.hyperreal.com/wsb/

Castaneda, Carlos:
http://www.earth.com/castaneda/

Chavez, Cesar:
http://www.fiestanet.com/~www/8/chavez/index2.htm

Diggers:
http://www.webcom.com/~enoble/diggers/diggers.html

Drugs:
http://www. hyperreal.com/drugs/psychedelics/

The Family Dog:
http://www.familydog.com/

Ginsberg, Allen:
http://www.levity.com/corduroy/ginsberg.htm

The Grateful Dead:
http://www.rockument.com/haimg.html
ftp://gdead.berkeley.edu/pub/gdead/

Hippies:
http://www.rockument.com/links.html

Joplin, Janis:
http://www.rockument.com/haimg.html

Kerouac, Jack:
http://www.cmgww.com/historic/kerouac/kerouac.html

Leary, Timothy:
http://www.leary.com

Led Zepplin:
http://www-eleves.int-evry.fr/~noel/ledzep/ledzep.html

Merry Pranksters:
http://www.key-z.com/

National Organization for Women:
http://www.now.org/history/history.html

The Realist:
http://www.primenet.com/~lippard/realist.html

The Rolling Stones:
http://www.stones.com/

Students for a Democratic Society:
http://www.cpcug.org/user/kopp/bob/sds/

Illustration Credits

ii UPI/Corbis-Bettmann
8 UPI/Corbis-Bettmann
11 Corbis-Bettmann
23 UPI/Corbis-Bettmann
30 UPI/Corbis-Bettmann
33 UPI/Corbis-Bettmann
40 UPI/Corbis-Bettmann
46 Corbis-Bettmann
49 UPI/Corbis-Bettmann
50 UPI/Corbis-Bettmann
56 UPI/Corbis-Bettmann
59 UPI/Corbis-Bettmann
64 UPI/Corbis-Bettmann
72 UPI/Corbis-Bettmann
84 UPI/Corbis-Bettmann
89 UPI/Corbis-Bettmann
92 UPI/Corbis-Bettmann
105 MTI/Eastfoto
112 UPI/Corbis-Bettmann
119 UPI/Corbis-Bettmann
127 Corbis-Bettmann
131 Frank Driggs/Corbis-Bettmann
134 UPI/Corbis-Bettmann
141 UPI/Corbis-Bettmann
147 Amalie Rothschild/Corbis-Bettmann
149 UPI/Corbis-Bettmann
152 UPI/Corbis-Bettmann
160 Corbis-Bettmann
165 UPI/Corbis-Bettmann
168 UPI/Corbis-Bettmann
171 UPI/Corbis-Bettmann
180 UPI/Corbis-Bettmann
183 UPI/Corbis-Bettmann
191 UPI/Corbis-Bettmann
196 UPI/Corbis-Bettmann
203 UPI/Corbis-Bettmann
206 UPI/Corbis-Bettmann
219 UPI/Corbis-Bettmann
237 UPI/Bettmann
244 UPI/Corbis-Bettmann
257 UPI/Corbis-Bettmann
260 UPI/Corbis-Bettmann
270 UPI/Corbis-Bettmann
273 UPI/Corbis-Bettmann
284 UPI/Corbis-Bettmann
290 UPI/Corbis-Bettmann
306 UPI/Corbis Bettmann
310 UPI/Corbis-Bettmann
319 UPI/Corbis-Bettmann
326 UPI/Corbis-Bettmann
335 UPI/Corbis-Bettmann
337 UPI/Bettmann
340 Corbis/Bettmann

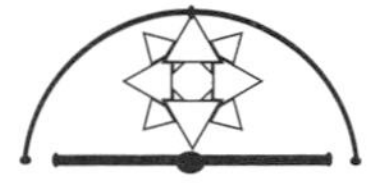

Index

Note: page numbers in **bold** refer to main entries.